REORGANIZING AMERICA'S DEFENSE

Leadership in War and Peace

Pergamon Titles of Related Interest

Bowman, Little & Sicilia THE ALL-VOLUNTEER FORCE AFTER
A DECADE
Hunt & Blair LEADERSHIP ON THE FUTURE BATTLEFIELD
Kronenberg PLANNING U.S. SECURITY
Record REVISING U.S. MILITARY STRATEGY
Rusi BRASSEY'S DEFENCE YEARBOOK 1984
Schelling & Halperin STRATEGY AND ARMS CONTROL
Segal & Sinaiko LIFE IN THE RANK AND FILE
Tsipis & Janeway REVIEW OF U.S. MILITARY RESEARCH AND
DEVELOPMENT 1984
Tyroler ALERTING AMERICA: THE PAPERS OF THE COMMITTEE
ON THE PRESENT DANGER

Related Journals*

DEFENSE ANALYSIS

*Free specimen copies available on request.

REORGANIZING AMERICA'S DEFENSE

Leadership in War and Peace

EDITED BY

Robert J. Art
Vincent Davis
Samuel P. Huntington

Published with the cooperation of the Ford Foundation

PERGAMON·BRASSEY'S
International Defense Publishers

Washington New York Oxford Toronto Sydney Frankfurt

Pergamon Press Offices:

U.S.A.	Pergamon-Brassey's International Defense Publishers, 1340 Old Chain Bridge Road, McLean, Virginia, 22101, USA
	Pergamon Press Inc., Maxwell House, Fairview Park, Elmsford, New York 10523, U.S.A.
U.K.	Pergamon Press Ltd., Headington Hill Hall, Oxford OX3 0BW, England
CANADA	Pergamon Press Canada Ltd., Suite 104, 150 Consumers Road, Willowdale, Ontario M2J 1P9, Canada
AUSTRALIA	Pergamon Press (Aust.) Pty. Ltd., P.O. Box 544, Potts Point, NSW 2011, Australia
FEDERAL REPUBLIC OF GERMANY	Pergamon Press GmbH, Hammerweg 6, D-6242 Kronberg-Taunus, Federal Republic of Germany

UA
23
- R446
1985

Library of Congress Cataloging in Publication Data
Main entry under title:

Reorganizing America's defenses.

    1. United States--Defenses--Addresses, essays,
lectures. 2. United States--Military policy--
Addresses, essays, lectures. I. Art, Robert J.
II. Davis, Vincent. III. Huntington, Samuel P.
UA23.R446   1985   355'.033073   85-9374
ISBN 0-08-031973-4
ISBN 0-08-031972-6 (pbk.)

Printed in the United States of America

Contents

PART II: DEFENSE REFORM IN THE UNITED STATES

List of Figures

List of Tables

Acknowledgements

The articles in this volume were presented at two conferences on Civilian-Military Management of the U. S. Defense Department. The first was held at the Center for International Affairs, Harvard University in November 1983; the second, at the Patterson School of Diplomacy and International Commerce, the University of Kentucky, in December 1983.

We should like to thank the Ford Foundation for funding the conferences and to express our appreciation to all the individuals who attended them and provided incisive comments to the authors.

The Editors

Introduction:
Pentagon Reform in Comparative and Historical Perspective

Robert J. Art

THE NEED FOR REFORM

Is the United States defense establishment today well run? To ask that question is to provoke a set of additional queries. For example, are resources allocated efficiently enough, in peacetime, to produce well trained and well equipped combat units? In wartime, will the command arrangements currently in force be sufficient to provide for the combined arms approach that modern battles require? Are the military properly organized so as to give timely and integrated advice to their civilian superiors? Have the civilians in the defense establishment usurped the traditional prerogatives of the military? Is there a process in place that produces a clear-cut, rational strategy to govern the use of force? Are decisions on programs and force structures clearly related to strategy? In its structure and operation, how does the American defense establishment compare to those of other nations? Is it better or more poorly managed? Are there lessons for improvement that can be derived from a study of how other nations manage their defense establishments? Finally, if some changes in structure and procedure are necessary, what are the alternatives, and the costs and benefits of each?

These are the range of subjects to which the authors in this volume address themselves. In treating these subjects, the authors provide us with three central conclusions. First, for a variety of reasons, the other nations analyzed in this volume—the Soviet Union, Israel, Great Britain, Canada, and the Federal Republic of Germany—have proceeded further in integrating their separate military services than has the United States. Each has forces more subject to central direction than does the United States, with an apparent increase in efficiency. Second, for political reasons, the United States after World War II created a defense organization that has a host of organizational inefficiencies built into it. Unification of the armed forces was purchased at the price of permitting duplication and overlap in function. Third, while the United States had a significant military superiority over the Soviet Union, these inefficiencies were more tolerable. Today they no longer are. The need for the U. S. to be more efficient in use of resources has become more pressing as the global capabilities of the Soviet Union continue to grow. The intention of this volume, then, is overtly reformist. The United States *must* improve the institutional arrangements that govern its defense establishment if it is to use its defense resources more effectively.

The authors of this volume accept the need for reform because, even if they do not accept every one of the recommendations, they largely concur with the criticisms of most experts and commissions that have studied the U. S. defense establishment over the last fifteen years. All such studies have concluded that the organizational arrangements in force in the United States since 1958 are not optimum. Witness the following:

> . . . . The President and the Secretary of Defense do not presently have the opportunity to consider all viable options as background for making major decisions, because differences of opinion are submerged or compromised at lower levels of the Department of Defense. . . . The present arrangement for staffing the military operations activities for the President and the Secretary of Defense through the Joint Chiefs of Staff and the Military Departments is awkward and unresponsive; it provides a forum for inter-Services conflicts to be injected into the decision-making process for military operations.[1]

> . . . the nature of the organization [the Joint Chiefs of Staff] virtually precludes effective addressal of those issues involving allocation of resources among the Services, such as budget levels, force structures, and procurement of new weapons systems—except to agree that they should be increased without consideration of resource constraints.[2]

> The JCS [Joint Chiefs of Staff] cannot carry out their statutory responsibilities. It is wrong to say there is nothing wrong with the JCS organization. The basic organizational concept is flawed. . . . The DoD [Department of Defense] focus is on programs, almost to the exclusion of systematic examinations of how resources should or would be used, an obvious concern of the JCS and the CINCs [Commanders in Chiefs of the unified and specified commands]. The result is a lack of effective planning, or more precisely a major mismatch between plans and resources. The JCS and the CINCs have very little corporate impact on shaping the Defense program.[3]

> The trend has accordingly been toward increased centralization [in the Office of the Secretary of Defense] and more layers of authority in an effort to impose some degree of order and coordination on the many and disparate groups in the national security community. But more often than not, the effort has led to the overburdening of a small number of senior officials with the details of foreign policy, defense planning, arms control, and crisis management. . . . This overloading has had a number of undesirable effects, among them . . . reaction to events rather than planning and initiatives; . . . the ability to handle only a

very small number of issues more or less simultaneously; the tendency of staffs to coordinate and compromise at the lowest common denominator rather than let issues escalate to their harried principals. . . . [4]

There has for some time been an imbalance in the degree of control that our civilian leadership exercises over operational and other defense matters. In operational matters, it is pervasive. . . . In other areas civilian influence is more often apparent than real. Defense Secretaries are given very little comprehensive advice on alternative strategies or systems. . . . That the Joint Chiefs of Staff, a committee beholden to the interests of the services, has not been able to provide such advice during its existence is amply documented in scores of studies over many years.[5]

If close students of the subject, officially commissioned studies, and many defense officials themselves have concluded that there are serious deficiencies in how America's defense establishment is run, why have these deficiencies been allowed to persist for so long? To understand this requires a brief look at the American experience with its defense establishment since 1947.

THE AMERICAN EXPERIENCE

Four characteristics capture the manner in which the United States has organized its defense establishment since 1947. First, the defense establishment remains a system of half measures, falling somewhere between a truly integrated, highly centralized system on the one hand and a loosely coordinated committee-run structure on the other. Second, the organizational changes that have been made since 1947 have been modest on the military side but radical on the civilian side. Third, through the three major reorganizations since 1945 (in 1947, 1949 and 1958), the services have managed to retain considerable autonomy to develop war plans and to allocate resources in a manner that each judges best suited to its own interests, without due regard for what the other services need or are doing, much less for what the overall national defense requires. Fourth, since the 1958 Defense Reorganization Act, when the Secretary of Defense was given considerable powers to assert real operating control over the entire defense establishment, a fundamental imbalance has persisted between the centralizing powers of the Office of the Secretary of Defense (OSD) and the coordinating powers of the Chairman of the Joint Chiefs of Staff.

With the expanded staff and authority given to him in 1958, the Secretary of Defense for the first time acquired the capability for central management. Beginning with Secretary of Defense Robert McNamara, and continuing in varying degrees with his successors, the secretary extended his purview more deeply into the services and more widely throughout the Pentagon than had previously been the case. On the other hand, the Chairman of the JCS was left with only the weak power to preside over, and attempt to coordinate, a committee that consisted of the Chiefs of Staff of each of the services and that, therefore, could reach agreement only by consensus, bargaining, or logrolling. As a consequence, since 1958, the Secretary of Defense has been the only force within the Pentagon with both the will *and* the authority to take a Pentagonwide perspective. The chairman of the JCS has sometimes had the will, but he has never had the authority. Because the military side of the defense establishment has lacked central governance, bureaucratic competition has reigned supreme there, and the ability of the military themselves to render collective advice on resource allocation and combat planning has remained extraordinarily poor. Finally, because the military are collectively unable to make difficult tradeoff decisions, the OSD has stepped in and done it for them.

Why has this structure persisted for nearly thirty years? There are at least two answers. First, until recently, there has been no compelling need to alter this state of affairs. Because the United States enjoyed high rates of economic growth and a perceived military superiority over the Soviet Union, it could afford to tolerate the inefficiencies inherent in the defense structure. The waste cost money, but, until recently, it was budgetarily affordable and not militarily dangerous. Second, the system suited the political interests of Congress. Congressmen have traditionally seen their ability to influence defense policy enhanced under a decentralized structure and have feared loss of influence under a more centralized one. If top defense officials did not have the ability to resolve disputes among competing factions within the Pentagon, then it would be Congress that did it for them. A powerful secretary and a powerful chairman would be able to settle disputes, close off the access of Congress to information, and thereby reduce its ability to influence policy. Therefore, not surprisingly, America's defense establishment has reflected the pluralistic and decentralized nature of America's national governmental system.

Because of its political interests, Congress has passed legislation for further Pentagon centralization only when the costs of retaining the decentralized structure appeared to have become prohibitive. Passage of such legislation has required an extraordinary external event and strong presidential backing. Both were present in 1957 in the forms of the Russian Sputnik and Dwight Eisenhower; both made possible the most recent major postwar alteration in defense organization. Sputnik caused Americans to wonder whether they were losing the technological race to the Russians and whether they could continue to afford the apparent organizational disarray in the Pentagon. Eisenhower had the military stature to overcome entrenched service and congressional opposition to further centralization. Short of such conditions, however, Congress has not acted.

Finally, what have been the costs and benefits of a structure that has provided for civilian centralization but preserved military decentralization?

With regard to benefits, there appear to be two. First, Congress has preserved its ability to influence defense policy by retaining a pluralistic and competitive military structure. Second, to the extent that pluralism among the services prevents them from resolving their differences, Pentagon civilian control over military decisions has been maintained.

These benefits are, however, more apparent than real. Congress has always been more effective in influencing the details rather than the general direction and broad contours of defense policy. A decentralized institution like Congress has difficulty initiating coherent policy. It is at its best when it oversees and reacts to presidential initiatives. Congressmen are best equipped to influence the broad direction of policy when they first require the President to set it for them. Congressional oversight of presidential initiatives remains the best way for Congress to influence policy. Incoherence in Pentagon decisions is not easily rectified by an institution like the Congress. Moreover, within the Pentagon, civilians may be making decisions that the military are unable to reach; but they are doing so without the benefit of a corporate and reasoned military position. The military do have an expertise that civilians lack. If the military is unable to apply its expertise effectively, others with less expertise must decide. Control for control's sake, whether it be of the congressional or Pentagon civilian variety, makes little sense if the substance of policy suffers.

The nature of these presumed benefits becomes even more dubious when one considers the costs of the present system. First, the OSD is overburdened. It is overextended and has proceeded too far into detailed management. Various Secretaries of Defense have tried to rectify this by reserving key policy decisions to the OSD and by delegating implementation of those decisions to the services. The present Pentagon team is no exception. Its management philosophy was described by former Deputy Secretary of Defense, Frank Carlucci, as follows.

> We will achieve better defense management by working toward a system of centralized control of executive policy direction and more decentralized policy execution. Working with the Service Secretaries, the Chairman of the Joint Chiefs of Staff, and OSD staff, the Secretary and I will concentrate on major policy decisions, definition of planning goals and the allocation of resources necessary to strengthen the horizontal integration of our four Services into a balanced Armed Forces Team to meet our national military strategy. . . . We will hold each of the Service Secretaries responsible for the development and execution of the necessary programs and the day-to-day management of the resources under their control. Through this controlled decentralization, subordinate line executives will be held accountable for the execution of our approved programs and policy decisions. . . . OSD staffs . . . will concentrate more on major DOD policy, planning and program issues, primarily those that cut across Service lines and programs and those that are of priority Presidential and Secretary of Defense interest.[6]

The difficulties in this approach have traditionally been the following: If the OSD has delegated management to the services, it has seen its major policy decisions too often diluted because the services retain considerable autonomy over spending; if the OSD has tried to implement those decisions through its own detailed management efforts, it has become overburdened, with the consequent necessity for selective attention and partial loss of control. Further, to the extent that any OSD team has tried to initiate programs that cut across services lines, it has had to use up considerable resources to define, defend, and implement them. No OSD team has so far been successful in striking the proper balance between centralized control of major policy decisions, on the one hand, and decentralized implementation and management of them, on the other. It is not for want of trying, as the most recent initiative illustrates. Rather, the fault lies with attempting to impose decentralized management on a military structure that is resistant to implementation of the choices made by top civilian officials.[7] Simply put, the OSD needs help from a more centralized military entity, for both advice in making decisions and assistance in executing them.

A second cost of the present system is the disconnection between the ultimate users of defense resources—the Commanders in Chiefs of the unified and specified commands—and the providers of them—the services. Those charged with the responsibility of command in wartime, the CINCs have little say over how resources are utilized in peacetime, because the services have retained considerable control over their own resource allocation. Therefore, what is supplied to the commands by the services is not necessarily what is sought from them. The 1958 Defense Reorganization Act was to have rectified this state of affairs by relegating the services to recruiting, training, and equipping the forces. The unified and specified commanders were to command and operate the forces. But because the services have retained considerable autonomy to spend as they see fit, they have emphasized their priorities—procurement of major and costly weapons systems—with the result of fewer systems being purchased and of the more mundane elements of readiness and sustainability being slighted.

The CINCs are unable to affect service spending priorities significantly because the unified and specified commands are, one way or another, dominated by the services.[8] The three specified commands (the Strategic Air Command, the Military Airlift Command, and the Aerospace Defense Command) are simply Air Force preserves. One of the unified commands, the Atlantic Command, is mainly a Navy preserve and has never had Army and Air Force units continuously assigned to it. All the other unified commands—the Readiness, Central, Pacific, Southern, and European Commands—contain two or more component commands, each of which is comprised of the forces of a given service. The commander of the component command is subordinate to the CINC on operational matters but reports directly to his service chief in Washington "for purposes other than operational direction"; "this . . . embraces the preparation of military forces and their administration and support."[9] Through this mechanism, the service component commanders and hence the services have retained control over the personnel and monies that are supposedly allocated to the CINC of the unified command. Finally, even for operational matters, JCS guidance has specified that operational control of the unified commands must be exercised through the service component commanders.[10] Thus, by these devices, the services have retained control over what the combatant commands will look like when they have to fight. Control over resource allocation in peacetime is, in effect, control over combat strategy in wartime.

A third cost of the present system is an overweening preoccupation with annual budgeting and resource allocation that slights strategy, operational planning, and long-term thinking. Because the services have been able to set their own spending priorities, too often they duplicate each other's efforts, fail to integrate them, and rarely provide the capabilities for missions that are needed but in which they have little interest. The inability of the Joint Chiefs to give collective advice on fiscally constrained resource tradeoffs and alternatives has stymied them in their efforts to provide truly integrated operational plans. Instead, they have been consumed in jockeying with each other to protect the budgetary allocations for their respective services. Unable to obtain collective military advice on alternatives, the OSD has become overburdened in its efforts to fight the annual resource allocation battles with the services. The result for all is continual competition in resource wars rather than meaningful planning for real wars. Budgeteering has displaced strategymaking and long-term planning.[11] Former Chairman of the Joint Chiefs of Staff, General David Jones, described the matter thus: "The Soviets talk of strategy and the big issues; we talk about weapons systems. Our time is consumed in the budgeting and programming cycle."[12]

An OSD that is overburdened, a JCS that is ineffective, and a slighting of intelligent addressal of the big issues—these are the costs of the present system. Ultimately, they are significantly, though not solely, products of the weaknesses in how the United States has chosen to organize its military command system. Good organization cannot remedy bad ideas, but bad organization can certainly foul up the implementation of good ideas. Can we do better? What can we learn by looking at what other countries have done?

THE EXPERIENCE OF OTHER NATIONS

Some nations have chosen a different path. Although their circumstances differ greatly, all five countries analyzed in this volume have a military establishment that in one way or another is more centralized than America's.

The country most similar to the United States in terms of size, diversity, and the tasks of its armed forces is, of course, the Soviet Union. As Edward Warner shows, there are two central characteristics that distinguish the Soviet Union's military establishment from that of the United States. First, the Soviet Ministry of Defense is almost entirely manned by senior military personnel and the most senior positions are staffed by professional military officers with long years of service in rank. Within the Defense Ministry, at least, the military dominate decisionmaking in a way unheard of in America's Pentagon.

The second distinguishing characteristic of the Soviet Union's military establishment is the existence and function of the Soviet General Staff. In America, the initiative for operational planning is left to the theater commanders. In theory, the JCS is to review and integrate these plans and to make certain that two or more CINC are not calling for use of the same resources in the event of a war that spans more than one theater. In fact, theater planning is given only cursory review in Washington, and, therefore, integrated contingency planning is not optimally done. In the Soviet case, the General Staff is heavily engaged in operational planning. It is, as Edward Warner says, "the central, directing force of the Soviet Armed Forces . . . and controls virtually all military activities. . . ." Elements of the General Staff prepare contingency operational plans for theater and intercontinental warfare, collect and assess intelligence, and draft the annual and long-term economic defense plans. The precise command relations between the General Staff and other elements of the military are not completely known, but it does have the mandate to ensure "the coordinated actions" of the services. Finally, the General Staff is manned by a cadre of officers who make their careers there. Some move on to key command and staff assignments with forces in the field. Therefore, the Soviet General staff has a continuity and corporate expertise unlike the American Joint Staff, where such staff assignments are not sought and are severely circumscribed by law in their allowed length.

Israel's military forces are not as centralized in form as the Soviet Union's, but they probably are in fact. As Major General Aharon Yariv details, there is a clear bifurcation within Israel's defense establishment between the civilian component, which is called the Ministry of Defense and is headed by the Director General of the Ministry, and the military component, which is called the Israel Defense Force (the IDF) and is headed by the Chief of the General Staff. The civilian component deals solely with support matters, such as research and development, procurement, construction, finance, and defense exports. It plays a supporting or logistical role for the military. The IDF is a command organization focused almost entirely upon training and operations. The IDF's General Staff focuses on short- and long-range planning at both the tactical and strategic levels. The Air Force, the Navy, the three territorial commands, and the logistical centers are all directly subordinated to it. The Chief of the General Staff is the nation's senior officer and is the only military official who carries the rank of Lieutenant General. Finally, in Israel's case, the General Staff serves both as the headquarters of the ground forces and as the operational directorate for the forces of the Air Force and Navy. The latter retain their separate staffs, but, as Yariv explains, due to the small size of its armed forces and the physical proximity of the three staffs, Israel has "integration in dynamics" even if it lacks a formal and fully integrated general staff structure.

Canada and the United Kingdom are two nations that have experienced a postwar organizational evolution similar to America's, except that both have gone further down the road of centralization than the United States has. As Harriet Critchley shows, Canada's defense establishment is probably as unified and centralized as is the Soviet Union's. In 1946, a single Minister of National Defense and Chairman of the Chiefs of Staff Committee were appointed; but until 1963, there were still three separate armed forces, with three separate headquarters in Ottawa. Coordination among the services and between them and the civilians was attempted through approximately 200 interservice committees. In 1964, functional divisions across the services were created; and a Chief of the Defense Staff was appointed to direct the armed forces and control their common elements. In 1968, Canada took the extreme step of abolishing its Army, Navy, and Air Force. They were replaced with the Canadian Forces, in which all military personnel wear the same uniform. Instead of three separate services, there were now land, air, and maritime "elements" of the Armed Forces.

Although the 1968 abolition of the services was the change most noted outside of Canada, the really revolutionary change came in 1972, when Canada integrated its military and civilian headquarters in Ottawa. Instead of maintaining separate military and civilian divisions for various functional tasks, Canada consolidated its defense headquarters into five groups — policy, personnel, finance, material and military plans, and doctrine and operations. Each of these is staffed by civilian and service personnel who before manned their respective counterpart divisions separately. Only the Soviet Defense Ministry, by virtue of being manned almost exclusively by military personnel, may be as integrated as is Canada's central defense establishment.

Britain, as Michael Hobkirk demonstrates, has proceeded further than the United States, but not as far as Canada, in centralization. Following a path roughly similar to Canada's, Britain has gone through three successive stages in centralization, from what Hobkirk terms defense by committee, to defense by bargaining, to defense by discussion. Defense by committee was characterized by interdepartmental committees that coordinated among three separate service departments. That system ended in 1946 when England, along with Canada and the United States, created a separate

Ministry of Defense, with a Minister to oversee the three services. The ministers for each of the services, however, still retained Cabinet rank and presented their own budgets to Parliament. During this period, which lasted until 1957, the defense budget was divided up by the three services through the striking of bargains among themselves, rather than by receiving directives from the Minister of Defense. Defense Minister Duncan Sandys ended that practice in 1957 and began the third phase, defense by discussion. This, together with the command reforms instituted subsequently by Lord Mountbatten, enhanced the powers of the central defense organization. By 1964, there was central ministerial allocation of service budgets, the service ministers lost independent status and Cabinet rank, and the Chief of the Defense Staff (CDS) strengthened somewhat his ability to produce independent solutions to problems, rather than simply continuing to accept compromises among the positions taken by the separate services.

This system has remained largely intact until the present, but with two notable changes. First, in 1981, the position of the CDS became what it was always supposed to be—the head of a defense staff able to propose solutions without regard for service interests. Previous to 1981, the CDS, although attempting to give independent advice, was charged with tendering the agreed collective advice of the Chiefs of Staff. From 1981 onward, the function of the CDS was to give independent military advice to the Secretary of State for Defense and to the government. The service chiefs still retain their access to the Minister of Defense and the Prime Minister, but the senior military authority in Britain is no longer a committee but an individual. Consonant with this change, the central defense policy staff now reports to the CDS, not to the Chiefs of Staff Committee. Although the central policy staff reports directly to the CDS, it is not a general staff. Britain makes no great efforts to indoctrinate its central defense staff the way the Soviet Union does, nor is there long staff tenure. For its effective functioning, a strong CDS is required.

Second, in 1984, Defense Minister Michael Heseltine took steps to strengthen the authority of the CDS. Heseltine ended the direct access that the service chiefs had to the defense minister. Now they must report to the minister through the CDS. And he abolished the policy sections of each of the separate service staffs. All policy matters, including military operations and budgeting, are to be handled by the Unified Defense Staff, which combines the former central policy staff with its civilian counterpart and which reports directly to the CDS. Both changes have significantly enhanced the formal authority of the CDS.

By all accounts, the Falklands campaign, demonstrated the utility of the 1981 changes—of making the CDS the senior military advisor. The chain of command ran from the Prime Minister to the CDS, and then directly to Admiral Fieldhouse, the Commander in Chief of the Falklands operation. This shortened chain of command enhanced the rapid implementation of decisions when speed was vital.

The British experience in the Falklands in 1982 stands in marked contrast to the American experience at the Beirut airport in 1983. In the former case, a shortened operational chain of command provided for quick action. In the latter case, a long and cumbersome chain of command was partially responsible for the failure to ensure the security of the American forces in the deteriorating situation in Lebanon. In the words of the Long Commission Report:

> The Commission concludes that the "presence" mission was not interpreted the same by all levels of the chain of command and that perceptual differences regarding that mission, including the responsibility of the USMNF [United States Multinational Forces] for the security of Beirut International Airport, should have been recognized and corrected by the chain of command.[13]

Responsibility for the Beirut operation ultimately fell on the United States Commander in Chief, Europe (USCINCEUR). Even though the entire chain of command was heavily involved in the planning and support of the American force, one must infer that the distance of USCINCEUR from the scene, together with the length of the chain of command, contributed to what the commission found to be a "a lack of effective command supervision of the United States Multinational Force (USMNF) security posture."

The last nation examined in this volume, the Federal Republic of Germany (FRG), possesses the least centralized defense establishment of the foreign nations analyzed. But the case of the FRG is also least relevant for insights on how to alter America's defense arrangements. As Catherine Kelleher explains: "No freestanding German command structure exists above the corps level; in operational terms, it is a command pyramid without a top element." German forces are fully integrated into North Atlantic Treaty Organization (NATO) forces. In short, Germany has no military force independent of NATO.

In the FRG, overall powers of command rest with the civilian Minister of Defense. He enjoys considerable autonomy within the general guidelines set by the Chancellor. The principal military figure who acts as a centralizing force in the German defense forces is the General-Inspector (GI), who is the principal military advisor to the minister and the government. He is enjoined to "consult" with the service chiefs, but also exercises "executive authority" over them in planning and in implementing an "overall concept of military defense." Each service chief reports directly to the Minister of Defense in his command function and has primary responsibility for the combat readiness of his forces. The GI does not have direct powers of command, but because the position carries with it the right of independent inspection of all military forces, the GI potentially can exert significant influence. First among equals with the service chiefs, yet principal military advisor to the minister, the GI derives his powers from both the position's planning and inspection functions and from the confidence the Minister of Defense has in him.

Finally, although Germany today has no general staff, it does have an Armed Forces Staff. It has seven functional divisions and has recently been given an enhanced role in coordination and oversight of the services, Although appointed by their respective services, all officers who serve on the Armed Forces Staff are graduates of the *Fuehrungsakademie*, which is the equivalent of a general staff academy, and which creates a shared experience. All who serve on the staff have had extensive line experience in their respective service. But unlike the Soviet case, all officers on the staff remain dependent on their respective services for additional professional advancement even though, when on the staff, they report to the GI. In terms of centralization, then, Germany's present organization is the closest to America's. Even here, however, one military officer, the GI, has been designated the principal military advisor. Even the Chairman of the JCS has not yet been given that role in this country.

I have highlighted the comparisons and contrasts among these five nations, and between them and the United States, only with regard to one factor — the degree of centralization of the military side of their defense establishments. In Part I, each author analyzes this issue and a host of others in greater detail. Topics covered include the state of civilian-military relations, the roles and missions of the services, and the various mechanisms for resource allocation used by civilians. Still, the single greatest point of contrast between all five nations and the United States remains what I stated at the outset; all have provided for more central planning and resource allocation by the military than the United States has. Israel, the Soviet Union, and Canada are at one end of the continuum. The United States is at the other. England and Germany remain in the middle, with England closer to the former group and Germany closer to the United States. By virtue of a near monopoly on staffing, the military are probably the most dominant in operational planning in the Soviet Union and Israel. But all five nations have achieved some military centralization, either by creating general staffs or their equivalents, or by giving a single military officer the authority to render advice independent of the services.

CONCLUSION – WHAT IS TO BE DONE?

In Part II of this volume, fourteen authors deal in some detail, not only with reforms to the Joint Chiefs of Staff system, but also with improvements in strategymaking, the quality of OSD oversight, resource allocation, the planning and budgeting system, weapons acquisition, and the relations between Congress and the Pentagon. Each piece assesses the current state of affairs in its area, details the advantages and disadvantages of the present system, and puts forth suggestions for improvement. All the authors agree that if the operation of America's defense establishment in peace and war is to be improved, then change in the JCS structure is the place to begin. But it is not the place to end. Getting the military to function better as a corporate entity will have significant affects on how other parts of the Pentagon operate. How these other parts should change and how other procedures outside the chain of command can be strengthened, along with reform of the JCS system, are the subjects of Part II.

NOTES

1. *Report to the President and the Secretary of Defense on the Department of Defense by the Blue Ribbon Defense Panel, 1 July 1970* (Washington, D. C.: U. S. Government Printing Office, 1970), p. 1. (Known as the Fitzhugh Report.)
2. *Report to the Secretary of Defense on the National Military Command Structure, July 1978* (Washington, D. C.: U. S. Government Printing Office, 1978), p. 52. (Known as the Steadman Report.)
3. *Report for the Chairman, Joint Chiefs of Staff by the Chairman's Special Study Group—the Reorganization and Functions of the JCS, April 1982* (Arlington, Virginia: Systems Research and Applications Corporation, 1982), p. 28. (Known as the Brehm Report.)
4. Kaufmann, William W., "Defense Policy," in Pechman, Joseph A., (Editor) *Setting National Priorities: Agenda for the 1980s* (Washington, D. C.: Brookings Institution, 1980), p. 285.
5. Jones, General David C., "What's Wrong with Our Defense Establishment," *The New York Times Sunday Magazine*, November 7, 1982, p. 76.
6. Carlucci, Frank, Deputy Secretary of Defense, "Memorandum on the Management of the DOD Planning, Programming and Budgeting System," March 27, 1981.
7. For a good analysis of how this proposition applies to the weapons acquisition area, see Lynn, Jr., Laurance E., and Smith, Richard I., "Can the Secretary of Defense Make a Difference?" *International Security*, Summer 1982, pp. 45–69.
8. For this discussion of the combatant commands, I have relied heavily on Cushman, John. H., *Command and Control of Theater Forces: Adequacy* (Program on Information Resources Policy, Harvard University, 1983), especially Chapter 3.
9. The language is from the Unified Action Armed Forces (UNAAF), which is the JCS guidance for the command structure of all U. S. combatant commands. See *ibid.*, pp. 3–50 and 3–51.
10. The UNAAF language reads as follows: ". . . Operational command by the unified commander will be exercised through the Service component commanders. . . . In exercising operational command, the unified commander shall take cognizance of the prerogatives and responsibilities of his Service component commanders. . . ." See *ibid.*, p. 3–55.
11. The current administration has tried to make the planning phase of the PPBS system more meaningful and to apply resource constraints to defense guidance. See Carlucci, Frank, Deputy Secretary of Defense, "Memorandum on the Planning Phase of the DoD PPB System," June 12, 1981; and Bellinger, John B.,

"Strategic Planning and Decision Making in the Defense Department," unpublished manuscript, June 1983.
12. Remarks at the first conference on "Civilian–Military Management of the U. S. Defense Department," Harvard University, November 17, 1983.
13. *Report of the DOD Commission on Beirut International Airport Terrorist Act, October 23, 1983*; 20 December 1983, p. 122.

REORGANIZING AMERICA'S DEFENSE

Leadership in War and Peace

PART I

DEFENSE ORGANIZATION
AT HOME AND ABROAD

Chapter 1

Defense Policymaking in the Soviet Union

Edward L. Warner III

INTRODUCTION

Given the closed nature of Soviet politics, it is extremely difficult to develop a detailed portrayal of the participants and processes involved in policy formulation, decision, and execution within the USSR. While this is the case across the full range of domestic and foreign policy issues, it is particularly true with regard to defense matters. The Soviets consider national security issues so sensitive that they have often hidden the very existence of key top-level decisional bodies active in this area, and have never discussed, in any detail, the nature of contemporary defense policymaking processes.

This is not to say, however, that we are unable to identify the individuals and institutions that play key roles in Soviet defense policymaking or to provide general descriptions of the manner in which they apparently interact. One can draw upon a wealth of Soviet books and journal articles, including those describing contemporary Soviet organizations and administrative practices, as well as a large number of biographical accounts and personal memoirs of leading military, defense industrial and even political figures who were deeply involved in defense matters in the past, and thus piece together a plausible description of contemporary Soviet defense policymaking. Such descriptions, of course, depend critically on the assumption that many of the organizational arrangements and procedural patterns prevalent in the late 1930s, 1940s, and 1950s remain generally valid today. Investigations by Western students of Soviet politics, occasional comments by Soviet officials, and the testimony of Soviet and Eastern European emigres with more recent experience in foreign policy and defense areas suggest that this is, in fact, the case.

This chapter draws upon a wide variety of primary and secondary sources to sketch the basic contours of Soviet defense policymaking. First, it describes the key organizations and individuals in the Communist Party and the Soviet government that appear to play significant roles in the defense area. Next, it briefly discusses the likely relationships among these bodies in addressing specific aspects of Soviet security policy, in particular the patterns of administrative and operational subordination among the elements of the Ministry of Defense, the development and acquisition of new weapons systems, and the formulation of Soviet military doctrine.

KEY SOVIET DEFENSE POLICYMAKING INSTITUTIONS

The Politburo

The nineteen-man Politburo of the Central Committee of the Communist Party is the most important political organ in the Soviet Union. Sitting at the pinnacle of the party and exercising control over its vast full-time professional apparatus, the members of the Politburo are called upon to make the decisions that establish the general guidelines for Soviet domestic and foreign policy, and to resolve specific policy questions. Defense matters are certain to be a frequent topic on the agenda of the Politburo's weekly meetings.

This small, senior party body has been the focus of top-level decision-making since Stalin's death in 1953.[1] Today the Politburo is likely to make the final decisions on a host of recurring defense matters, including the magnitude and composition of the annual and five-year economic plans for defense, the development and acquisition of major weapons systems, the overall character of Soviet military doctrine, the organization and peace-time deployments of the Soviet Armed Forces, and the employment of Soviet military forces. Given its control over all Communist Party and Soviet government institutions, Politburo decisions on these matters may take the form of the laws, decrees, directives, orders, or resolutions formally issued by a variety of party and state institutions.[2]

While the Politburo is almost certainly called upon to make the final decisions on these matters, it probably does so in response to specific policy alternatives prepared in advance of its deliberations. Moreover, once its decisions are made, it is not the Politburo, but other organs of the party and the Soviet government that are called upon to implement them. It is possible to identify a network of specialized party and state organizations that appear to fulfill these development and policy implementation roles with regard to Soviet military policy.

The Defense Council

The most important of these organizations is the USSR Defense Council (*Sovet Oborony*). This body, described by Soviet sources as the successor to the Council of Workers' and Peasants' Defense formed during the civil war

(1918–1920) and the State Defense Committee formed during World War II (1941–1945), is the latest in a long line of high-level councils or "soviets" which have overseen Soviet defense matters since the Bolsheviks came to power.

While a recent Soviet publication confirms that the Defense Council has existed since at least 1964,[3] the Soviets did not acknowledge its existence until, in 1976, they matter-of-factly noted that Leonid Brezhnev was its chairman.[4] More frequent references to the Defense Council, and occasional descriptions of its functions, have appeared following that disclosure. Nevertheless, Soviet sources have done no more, to date, than to reveal its existence, its chairmen (initially Brezhnev and more recently Yuri Andropov),[5] and its general responsibilities. With regard to the latter, Soviet sources assert that the Defense Council is called upon to coordinate the activities of those organs of the Soviet state that are active in the defense area, to examine and decide all fundamental questions relating to the security of the country, to establish the basic direction for the development of the Soviet Armed Forces, to approve plans for military development, and to establish the basic organization for the defense of the USSR.[6]

Many Western observers have speculated about the composition of the Defense Council and its likely mode of operations. Most agree that, although the Defense Council is formally linked to the Soviet government through Article 121 of the 1977 Constitution which empowers the Presidium of the Supreme Soviet to form it and approve its composition, and although Soviet writers have described it as an organ of "state administration,"[7] it functions, for all practical purposes, as the subgroup for defense matters of the party's Politburo.[8] Some believe that the Defense Council includes not only selected Politburo members, but also a few senior military leaders, such as the Chief of the General Staff and possibly the commanders in chief of the five services of the Soviet Armed Forces, although these officers are not members of the Politburo.[9]

The members of the Politburo most likely to be members of the Defense Council are those who occupy the most senior party–state positions — the General Secretary of the Party, Chairmen of the Presidia of the Supreme Soviet and of the Council of Ministers, the second- and third-ranking secretaries of the Central Committee, and those with special responsibilities for defense-related matters, such as the Minister of Defense, the Central Committee secretary supervising defense production, and possibly the Chairman of the Committee for State Security (KGB) and the Minister of Foreign Affairs.[10] According to this definition, the Politburo members serving on the Defense Council, as of the fall of 1983, would include Yu. V. Andropov (Party General Secretary and Chairman of the Presidium of the Supreme Soviet), N. A. Tikhonov (Chairman of the Presidium of the Council of Ministers), K. U. Chernenko (Second-Ranking Central Committee Secretary), D. F. Ustinov (Minister of Defense), G. V. Romanov (Central

Committee Secretary apparently supervising defense production), and possibly A. A. Gromyko (Minister of Foreign Affairs).

Whatever its precise configuration (and it may well have changed over the past 19 years, perhaps since the Andropov succession in November 1982[11]), Western observers agree that the Defense Council is likely to operate as the high-level body in which the full range of defense-related matters are regularly examined and policy alternatives are developed prior to submission to the full Politburo. Since the most influential Politburo members are apparently also members of the Defense Council, and since its deliberations are chaired by the General Secretary, it is very likely that recommendations hammered out in this forum will be approved by the Politburo. Whether senior military figures, such as the Chief of the General Staff, Marshal N. V. Ogarkov, or the commanders in chief of the services are formally members of the Defense Council or not, they, along with key figures in the weapons design and defense production areas, are virtually certain to be called upon to attend its meetings when critical issues in which they have relevant expertise and responsibilities are being discussed.

In the event of war, the Defense Council would almost certainly become the key "higher agency of leadership of the country and the Armed Forces" that has been discussed in Soviet military literature.[12] As such, it would serve as the new State Defense Committee, that is, a wartime cabinet that would coordinate the full range of economic, political, and military activities in concert with the Politburo. In my view, the apparent creation of the Defense Council at the outset of the Brezhnev period reflects both the commitment of the senior party oligarchs to supervise the defense effort more collectively following the fall of Khrushchev, and their desire to put in place in advance an important element of the command arrangements needed to manage a modern war with its anticipated rapid pace of operations.

With regard to the question of the wartime direction of military operations: during World War II the Soviets created a Supreme High Command (*verkhovnoe glavnokomandovanie* — VGK), which provided highly centralized strategic leadership for the planning and execution of military operations. Directly subordinate to the State Defense Committee, the VGK included a supreme commander in chief (Stalin), a deputy supreme commander in chief (Marshal Zhukov), the General Headquarters (*Stavka*) of the VGK (Stalin and Molotov plus some 7–10 senior military leaders), and various representatives of the *Stavka* of the VGK (Marshals Zhukov, Vasilevskiy, Voronov, Novikov, and others) who were periodically sent to the field to personally coordinate multifront operations. The critical staff support for the VGK was provided by its "working organ," the General Staff, and other elements of the Defense Commissariat.[13]

Most of these organs have been identified by the Soviets as wartime bodies, and many are reported to have been abolished at the end of the war.[14] There are indications, however, that various elements of the Supreme High Command may have been resurrected.[15] Both Khrushchev and Brezhnev, in their time, were publicly identified as being the supreme commander in chief, and Andropov very likely occupied that position as well. The Collegium of the Ministry of Defense, discussed below, which is composed of the fourteen top leaders of the ministry, could readily be called upon to function as the *Stavka*. The General Staff, with its several key staff elements and communications capabilities, appears well prepared to resume its vital support role. Finally, repeated recent Soviet statements regarding the importance of controlling military operations at the level of a theatre of military operations (TVD),[16] suggest that extensive preparations have been made to establish "high commands" (*glavnokomandovaniya*) in various regional TVDs along the periphery of the Soviet Union, which would operate directly as intermediate command entities between the Moscow-based Supreme High Command and the various fronts in the field.[17] All in all, the Soviets appear to be operating today with a peacetime command structure that could rapidly be put on a wartime footing as a full-fledged Supreme High Command.

Returning to the question of the contemporary Defense Council, it is not known whether the Defense Council has a permanent staff to support its deliberations and assist in translating its decisions into action. Soviet administrative practice suggests that some organization is charged with the crucial functions of setting the agenda, coordinating the preparation of relevant materials for the Council's deliberations, and drafting the necessary instructions to implement its decisions. This function may be performed by an element of the apparatus of the Central Committee, whose General Department provides such administrative support to the Politburo. It is more likely, however, that it is accomplished by the Ministry of Defense's General Staff.[18] If the latter is the case, and the general secrecy and compartmentalization that surrounds Soviet defense matters would be consistent with such a practice, the hand of the professional military, in general, and the Chief of the General Staff, in particular, in shaping defense issues would be substantially strengthened.

Personal Involvement of Senior Party Leaders

While collective direction of defense matters exercised by the Politburo and the Defense Council or Higher Military Council has been evident since the death of Stalin, over the years the ranking party leader has also consistently played a substantial role in this area. Iosif Stalin completely dominated Soviet defense matters, as was the case in all major policy areas after he had eliminated his potential rivals in the purges of the late 1930s. During World War II, Stalin assumed all of the top political–military leadership posts, becoming the Supreme Commander in Chief of the Armed Forces, Chairman of the State Defense Committee, Chairman of the Council of People's Commissars, People's Commissar of Defense, and Chairman of the General Headquarters (*Stavka*) of the Supreme High Command, while remaining the General Secretary of the Party. From this powerful position, Stalin vigorously directed the entire war effort. After the war, he surrendered many of these titles, but continued to monopolize political power. He remained the dominant force in defense matters, continuing to shuffle the key military commanders among various postings, to intervene in weapons developments, and to influence strongly the development of military doctrine.

Both Khrushchev and Brezhnev were also very active in defense matters. Although he relied upon the support of the professional military to help gain and retain his leading position in the mid-1950s, Nikita Khrushchev eventually alienated the military leadership (including most of his previous supporters from the "southern group" of senior commanders who were his comrades in arms when he was a leading political commissar during World War II).[19] He did so by persistently seeking to reduce defense expenditures and personally intervening to fundamentally reshape Soviet military doctrine, as well as the organizational structure and force posture of the Soviet Armed Forces.[20] Leonid Brezhnev's more businesslike style and undying support for steadily expanding defense budgets were undoubtedly appreciated by the Soviet military. Nevertheless, he too apparently played a prominent role in determining military policy, albeit one that appears to have been quite congenial to the marshals. Brezhnev's pride regarding his past and his continuing military contributions was reflected in his assumption of the rank of Marshal of the Soviet Union, the publicity regarding his role as the Chairman of the Defense Council and the Supreme Commander in Chief of the Armed Forces, and the publication of a spate of books and articles recalling his heroic exploits as a political commissar during World War II.[21]

Given his short tenure in office, we may never know the nature of Yuri Andropov's approach to defense matters. Many believe that the Minister of Defense, Marshal Ustinov, and the professional military played an important role in his accession to the post of General Secretary.[22] Andropov's long tenure as KGB Chief undoubtedly provided him with considerable exposure to national security issues. During his first year in power he was publicly identified as the Chairman of the Defense Council, and repeatedly stated his commitment to continue to strengthen Soviet defense capabilities. Presumably, Andropov, like Stalin, Khrushchev, and Brezhnev before him, came to know well the top weapons designers, defense industrialists, and military commanders whose collective labors sustain the military might that is so vital to Soviet fortunes on the world scene.

Given the active participation of these senior leaders and a few other Politburo members in defense matters, the question arises as to whether they have acquired independent sources of advice beyond that provided by the Ministry of Defense and the defense industrial producers later discussed, either from within their personal staffs or from other organizations, to assist them in addressing these issues. There is no sign that either has occurred. While Stalin, Khrushchev, and Brezhnev all had small personal staffs (Brezhnev's being somewhat larger than those of his predecessors), it does not appear that any of their assistants specialized in defense issues.[23]

With regard to other possible sources of staff support, the activities of certain figures associated with G. A. Arbatov's Institute for the Study of the USA and Canada (IUSAC) and the somewhat less well known Institute of World Economies and International Relations (IMEMO) have raised the possibility that specialists on defense issues from these organizations may be providing relevant advice to the senior party leadership. Some members of these institutes have encouraged such speculations.

There are, in fact, several civilian researchers and retired military officers with substantial expertise on Western military policy working within IUSAC and IMEMO.[24] These people regularly serve as spokesmen to the West about the peaceful character of the Soviet Union's "defensive" military doctrine.[25] Moreover, it appears that they have, on occasion, been called upon to prepare staff studies on defense-related matters for the apparatus of the Central Committee and, thus, presumably, for possible use by senior party leaders. These studies, however, are not likely to deal with the examination of Soviet military policy options both because these "institutniks" are not called upon to address such matters and because most of them are not given access to classified information.[26] Rather, they almost certainly contain analyses of Western purposes and policies, thus fulfilling a critical mission of these institutes, to wit, the provision of expert advice to top party policymakers regarding key developments in the international arena.

Nevertheless, one must recognize that extensive study of Western concepts and capabilities for the conduct of military operations, such as various nuclear warfighting scenarios, can yield a considerable degree of expertise on this question, which could, quite readily, be applied to the examination of Soviet policy choices. There are no signs, however, that this has yet occurred. And the professional Soviet military, which currently controls the relevant Soviet data and monopolizes the application of such expertise to Soviet defense issues, is presumably determined to continue to prevent it.

Rather, it appears that the senior party leaders have relied on a combination of their personal background in these matters, the specialized expertise of their Politburo colleagues with full-time defense responsibilities (including the party secretary overseeing defense production, discussed later), and the regular staffing mechanisms that currently support Defense Council deliberations. The last of these, I would speculate, are likely to consist of background materials prepared by a special section of the general staff, on the basis of submissions from the various organizations involved in a particular issue under consideration.

Party Secretariat. Day-to-day oversight of defense matters by the Communist Party cannot be performed by such high-level bodies as the Politburo or the Defense Council. An important aspect of this function has traditionally been assigned to one of the secretaries of the Central Committee who has been responsible for overseeing weapons development and defense production matters. This important post has generally been filled by a secretary who is also a Politburo member. Since the end of the Second World War, its occupants have included N. A. Bulganin (during Stalin's last years 1947–1953), L. I. Brezhnev (during much of the Khrushchev period),[27] D. F. Ustinov (1965–1976), Ya. P. Ryabov (1976–1979) during Brezhnev's rule. The position apparently remained unfilled from the time Ryabov left the Party Secretariat to become a first deputy chairman of the State Planning Committee (Gosplan) from early 1979 until June 1983. During much of this period the oversight function may have been performed by Brezhnev himself or, more likely, once again by D. F. Ustinov, in this case while he was simultaneously serving as Minister of Defense.

Some Western observers speculate that G. V. Romanov may have taken over this important position in June 1983 when he moved into the Secretariat from his previous post as leader of the Leningrad party organization.[28] If so, this would provide the basis for Romanov to become a member of the Defense Council, as noted above, and thus to gain valuable experience working closely with the professional military and the defense industrialists at the national level.

The party secretary with these defense production oversight responsibilities apparently supervises the work of the departments of the Central Committee within the Moscow-based central party apparatus which operate in the defense area. These include the Defense Industries Department, which helps monitor the weapons acquisition process, the Administrative Organs Department, which oversees fulfillment of party directives in the military and the secret police, and possibly the Main Political Administration. The latter is composed of the vast network of political officers who assist the commanders in matters of troop morale and discipline, supervise political indoctrination, and oversee the operation of Communist Party and Komsomol organizations within the Ministry of Defense,[29] which, although it is an element of the Ministry of Defense, also operates with "the rights of a department of the Central Committee."

With regard to party oversight, in most policy areas the party apparatus includes organs at the central and regional levels that duplicate and closely monitor the activities of the various governmental ministries. There is no department or section in the party apparatus, however, that directly monitors such critical Soviet defense questions as the development of Soviet military science, contingency planning for potential conflicts, or the operational training and deployment of the Armed Forces. It is unlikely that the party secretary overseeing defense production gets deeply involved in these matters. Rather, it is the professional military in the Ministry of Defense that has the unparalleled responsibility and unique expertise to address these key issues.

Ministry of Defense

The Ministry of Defense is, of course, a key institution in Soviet defense policy. While operating within the broad policy parameters and budgetary limits established by the senior party leadership, the various elements of the Ministry of Defense play major roles in virtually all aspects of the formulation and implementation of Soviet military policy. The most important organizations within the ministry are the General Staff, the five services of the Soviet Armed Forces — the Strategic Rocket Forces, Air Defense Forces, the Air Forces, the Navy, and the Ground Forces — the Main Political Administration, and a series of central directorates and technical agencies, including Rear Services, Civil Defense, the Main Inspectorate, Armaments, Construction and Billeting, and Personnel.[30]

The Ministry of Defense is run by its minister, Marshal D. F. Ustinov, with the assistance of three first deputy ministers and ten deputy ministers. The first deputies are Marshal N. V. Ogarkov, the Chief of the General Staff; Marshal V. G. Kulikov, the Commander in Chief of the Warsaw Pact; and Marshal S. L. Sokolov, who apparently supervises day-to-day administrative matters. General of the Army, A. A. Yepishev, who heads the Main Political Administration, is, for all practical purposes, a fourth first deputy minister.[31] As shown in Figure 1.1, the deputy ministers include the service commanders in chief and heads of key central directorates.

This group of sixteen make up the Collegium of the Ministry of Defense. According to the *Soviet Military Encyclopedia*, the Collegium is a consultative organ responsible for working out "solutions relating to the development of the Armed Forces, their combat and mobilization readiness, combat and political training, the selection, assignment and indoctrination of military personnel and other important issues," whose decisions are implemented in the form of orders of its chairman, the Minister of Defense.[32] It is likely to be convened by Marshal Ustinov on at least a weekly basis and to serve as a forum for reaching policy decisions on a wide range of matters. As noted previously, in wartime, the Collegium would almost certainly be converted into the *Stavka* (General Headquarters) of the Supreme High Command.

There is considerable confusion among Western students of Soviet

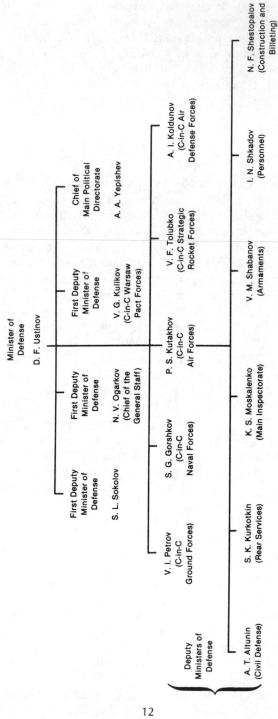

Minister of
Defense

D. F. Ustinov

First Deputy
Minister of
Defense

S. L. Sokolov

First Deputy
Minister of
Defense

N. V. Ogarkov
(Chief of the
General Staff)

First Deputy
Minister of
Defense

V. G. Kulikov
(C-in-C Warsaw
Pact Forces)

Chief of
Main Political
Directorate

A. A. Yepishev

S. G. Gorshkov
(C-in-C
Naval Forces)

P. S. Kutakhov
(C-in-C
Air Forces)

V. F. Tolubko
(C-in-C Strategic
Rocket Forces)

A. I. Koldunov
(C-in-C Air
Defense Forces)

V. I. Petrov
(C-in-C
Ground Forces)

S. K. Kurkotkin
(Rear Services)

K. S. Moskalenko
(Main Inspectorate)

V. M. Shabanov
(Armaments)

I. N. Shkadov
(Personnel)

N. F. Shestopalov
(Construction and
Billeting)

Deputy
Ministers of
Defense

A. T. Altunin
(Civil Defense)

FIGURE 1.1. The Collegium of the Ministry of Defense (as of 1983)

12

military affairs regarding the status of another high-level body, the Main Military Soviet (*Glavnyi Voennyi Sovet*), which continues to be mentioned occasionally in Soviet publications.[33] Collective organs with this title have had major roles in the defense area in the past.[34] Some Western observers believe that the Collegium of the Ministry of Defense is also known today as the Main Military Soviet.[35] Others, including myself, believe that the Main Military Soviet is, instead, a very large, purely consultative body, which is convened in Moscow at infrequent intervals to review topical defense matters. According to this view, its membership is likely to include not only the Defense Minister and his deputies, who serve on the Collegium of the Ministry of Defense but also the deputy commanders and senior political officers from the five services, the chiefs of the Ministry's various central administrative and technical directorates, and the commanders, chiefs of staff and top political officers from the sixteen military districts within the USSR and the four groups of Soviet forces deployed in Eastern Europe.[36]

Such a body would be similar to the large, eighty-man consultative Military Soviet (*Voennyi Sovet*) that existed in the mid-1930s. General Secretary Brezhnev's well publicized address to a large gathering of senior military leaders in October 1982 may well have occurred at a session of the Main Military Soviet.[37]

The Soviet Ministry of Defense is largely manned by uniformed military personnel. The senior leadership posts in the ministry are filled almost exclusively by professional military officers who have served for some thirty to fifty years. Important exceptions in this regard are the Minister of Defense himself, Marshal D. F. Ustinov, the Deputy Minister of Defense for Armaments, General of the Army V. M. Shabanov, and the Chief of the Main Political Administration (MPA), General of the Army A. A. Yepishev.

Ustinov's career was largely spent in the supervision of defense production, first in the defense industrial sector of the economy and then in the Central Committee Secretariat, prior to his becoming Defense Minister in April 1976. His selection as Defense Minister was consistent with a long tradition of placing trusted senior party figures in this sensitive post.[38] Given his extensive background in and presumed support[38] for arms production, Ustinov's selection is likely to have been generally welcomed by the marshals, although they would certainly prefer that the job were held by a true military professional, as was the case from 1956 to 1976.[39]

Shabanov, although serving initially as a junior officer in the Air Forces, spent many years as a test pilot, then as a weapons designer, and eventually rose to become Deputy Minister for Radio Industry before assuming his current post in July 1978.[40] The careers of Ustinov and Shabanov, who had already been awarded high military rank in recognition of their roles as key defense industrial managers prior to their movement into top Defense Ministry positions, serve to underscore the close relationship between the military customer and its defense producers in the Soviet "military industrial complex."

Yepishev's is a different story. Although his varied career had included work as a wartime political commissar, as a regional party secretary, as an executive with the secret police, and as a foreign ambassador, he was apparently handpicked by Khrushchev to become Chief of the Main Political Administration when Khrushchev found himself at odds with most of the High Command in the early 1960s. Yepishev steered an independent course while Khrushchev was in power[41] and has long outlasted his erstwhile patron, having now served as MPA Chief for over twenty years.

There are substantial numbers of full-fledged civilians working within the Ministry of Defense as well. They are, for the most part, working in the nonprofessional, less skilled positions. Thus, one finds civilian agricultural workers on military farms, civilian employees within the military trade and supply organizations, and civilian instructors in the ministry's higher schools and academies, particularly in fields like foreign language and literature.[42] However, there is no layer of civilian defense intellectuals in the central organs of the Ministry of Defense, addressing issues of Soviet military doctrine, weapons development, or other defense policy matters.

General Staff

Within the Soviet military establishment itself, the General Staff is unquestionably the most important staff organ. As the central, directing force of the Soviet Armed Forces, it has come to play the role envisioned for it by two of its creators, Defense Commissar Mikhail Frunze and Marshal Boris Shaposhnikov, both of whom called for the creation of a Soviet General Staff that would serve as "the brain of the army.[43]

The Soviet General Staff directs and controls virtually all the military activities of the Soviet Armed Forces. Its most important elements are the Main Operations, Main Intelligence, Main Organization and Mobilization, Main Foreign Military Assistance, and Military Science Directorates. These organizations play the dominant role in such diverse undertakings as the drafting of operational plans for theater and intercontinental warfare, the collection and assessment of military intelligence, the refinement of Soviet military organization, the development of nationwide mobilization plans, the preparation of the annual and long-term economic plans for defense, the management of foreign military assistance arrangements, the formulation of doctrinal concepts, as well as the peacetime training and, if need be, the wartime operational direction of the Soviet Armed Forces.

The General Staff also contains a Treaty and Legal Department, which participates actively in international arms negotiations. This department is headed today by Colonel General N. Chervov, who has been a leading public spokesman regarding Soviet views on the Intermediate Nuclear Forces negotiations.[44] Officers assigned to this department, or its predecessor, have been participants in U. S.–Soviet arms control talks since the late 1950s.[45] This activity continues a tradition of General Staff support for international negotiations with substantial military content, which was evident on the eve of and during World War II.[46]

The General Staff is manned by both a cadre of career staff officers, a number of whom spend decades working in the General Staff's specialized directorates, and some of the most promising line officers drawn from the different services. Members of the latter group move on from postings in the General Staff to key command and staff assignments with the forces in the field, the central directorates of the services in Moscow, and other elements of the Ministry of Defense.

Most of the leading figures in the General Staff and, for that matter, throughout the higher echelons of the Soviet Armed Forces, are graduates of the two-year course offered by the prestigious Voroshilov Academy of the General Staff in Moscow, which operates under its direct supervision. This course is attended by specially selected lieutenant colonels, colonels, and major generals or its equivalent, from all of the services. In most cases, these officers have already completed a higher academy, such as the Frunze Military Academy. All graduates of the Voroshilov Academy may, in some sense, be considered and consider themselves *genshtabisty*, that is, an elite element of general staffers, who have been carefully selected and specially trained in the planning and conduct of combined-arms operations at the operational and strategic levels.[47]

It is noteworthy that this core of *genshtabisty*, all of whom wear the distinctive diamond-shaped *znachok* (badge) awarded to graduates of the Voroshilov Academy on their uniform, includes both senior commanders and chiefs of staff. The fact is that the majority of senior officers serving as deputy ministers of defense and commanding the military districts and groups of forces are graduates of the Voroshilov Academy of the General Staff.[48] It is likely that this common experience forms the basis for various networks of professional friendships and a shared intellectual background that has significant impact on such matters as personnel assignments and the informal resolution of policy issues within the Ministry of Defense.

The precise relationships between the General Staff and other elements of the Ministry of Defense in Moscow and in the field are not altogether known. The Chief of the General Staff is the ranking first deputy minister and is reported to be the only individual with the right to issue orders in the name of the Minister of Defense.[49] Moreover, the General Staff has the comprehensive mandate to ensure "the coordinated actions" of the main staffs of the services, the staffs of Rear Services, Civil Defense, the main and central administrations of the Ministry of Defense, and the staffs of the military districts, groups of forces, air defense districts and fleets.[50] In addition, it would appear that the commanders of the forces in the field, that is, the commanders of the sixteen military districts,[51] the four groups of forces deployed in Eastern Europe[52] and the four fleets,[53] while directly subordinate to the Minister of Defense, function, as a practical matter, under the direction of the General Staff for all organizational, mobilization, and operational matters, as shown in Figure 1.2.

During the Second World War, representatives of the General Staff were sent out to man the operational groups that accompanied the representatives of the *Stavka*, who coordindated large-scale multifront operations. Another group of officers, who became known as the "officer corps-representatives of the general staff," were sent out to monitor the activities of the staffs of the fronts and armies in the field and to maintain close contact with the Main Operations Directorate of the General Staff in Moscow. This corps was disbanded at the end of the war.[54] Today the General Staff is probably prepared to send some of its cadre to fill out the intermediate high commands that are likely to be activated to conduct multifront combined-arms operations in the various continental theaters of military operations around the periphery of the Soviet Union.

THE MILITARY SERVICES AND PATTERNS
OF OPERATIONAL SUBORDINATION

The five services are all responsible for the development of service-specific operational art and for the peacetime training and equipping of their various subelements. These activities are overseen by the service commanders in chief, who are assisted by their military councils, whose members include their several deputy commanders, chief of staff, and the member of the military council who heads the service political administration, as well as the service main staffs.

The operational command responsibilities of the various services are not altogether known. In peacetime, the headquarters of the Navy, the Strategic Rocket Forces, and possibly the Air Defense Forces appear to exercise operational control over their respective forces in the field — the fleets, the strategic missile armies, and the air defense interceptors, surface-to-air missile units and radar tracking and control facilities, respectively. The case of the Air Defense Forces has been muddied by a recent reorganization, which has apparently eliminated several of the ten air defense districts in the USSR and resulted in a resubordination of their air defense assets to the local military district commander, while retaining other air defense districts in their previous form.[55]

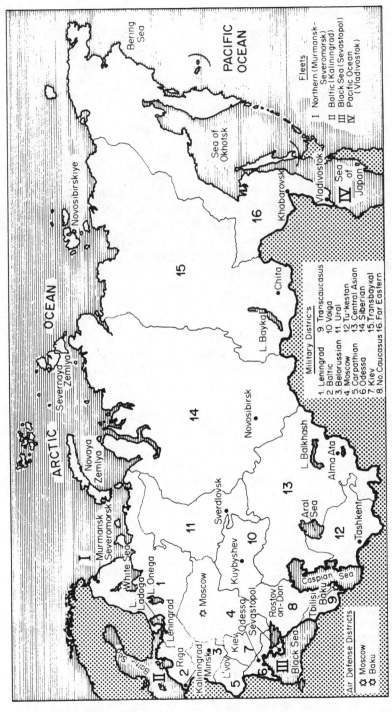

FIGURE 1.2. Map of sixteen military districts, four fleets, and the Moscow Air Defense District. (Note: Reprinted with permission from *Air Force* magazine, March 1975, © Air Force Association.)

Whatever the precise organizational arrangements at the district level, surveillance information collected by the network of warning and tracking radar located throughout the USSR and in Eastern Europe, and information on the status of Soviet and allied air defense assets is almost certainly passed routinely to a central command post in or near Moscow operated by the Air Defense Forces. In times of war, this command center, operating under the general direction of a national command center run by the General Staff, would presumably help manage the homeland air defense effort.

The central headquarters of the Air Forces and Ground Forces do not appear to have very substantial operational roles in peacetime. Frontal Aviation's fighters and fighter-bombers are either operationally subordinated to the military district commander through his deputy commander for air forces or fall within four of the five recently created Air Armies of the Soviet Union. The strategic bombers of Long-Range Aviation appear to fall under the control of the fifth new air army, which may, in turn, be directly subordinated to the Minister of Defense. Finally, the transport aircraft of Military Transport Aviation are likely to be the only element operating under the direction of Air Forces Headquarters.

The approximately 184 tank and motorized rifle divisions of the Ground Forces fall under the operational control of the commanders of the military districts and groups of forces in which they are located. The seven airborne divisions may fall under the local military district commander or, alternatively, may be assigned to the Commander of Airborne Forces, Colonel General D. S. Sukhorukov, in Moscow, who, in turn, is directly subordinated to the Minister of Defense.

In times of war, the commanders in chief of the Air Forces and the Ground Forces would probably be called upon to assist in the overall direction of combat operations as members of the *Stavka* of the VGK. Their main staffs would be involved in providing operational support to their commanders in chief, acting in their *Stavka* roles, and in continuing to direct service training and equipping activities that support the war effort. Members of these staffs might also be tapped for duty with the General Staff, as it is expanded to play its many wartime roles.

In wartime, most Soviet forces would be controlled by a series of geographically organized commands. The medium-, intermediate-, and intercontinental-range ballistic missiles of the Strategic Rocket Forces, while deployed in several missile armies scattered throughout the USSR, would almost certainly be directed from higher headquarters in Moscow.[56] The strike planning for these missile systems is likely to be done by a section of the General Staff's Main Operations Directorate. The authorization to employ these nuclear-armed forces, at least for their initial strikes, most certainly lies with the highest political authority, that is, the Politburo and, presumably, the reconstituted State Defense Committee. The responsibility for passing the strike execution order to the units in the field is almost certainly assigned to the General Staff, which could rely upon its own specialized communication channels or, alternatively, on those maintained by the central apparatus of the Strategic Rocket Forces.

Some of the fighter-bombers associated with Frontal Aviation and the strategic bombers of the Air Forces' Long-Range Aviation have recently been reorganized into five Air Armies of the Soviet Union. Four of these air armies contain fighters, fighter-bombers, and medium-range bombers for coordinated attacks in theaters along the borders of the USSR. Three of these four are apparently postured to support conventional or nuclear strikes in Western Europe, while a fourth is located in and oriented toward the Far East. The fifth, headquartered in Moscow, apparently controls heavy bombers for possible attack on naval task forces on the open oceans and against the United States.[57] Planning for these air operations is likely to rest with the Operations Directorate of the General Staff, and possibly with the high command staffs responsible for the key theaters of military operations in Western Europe and the Far East.

The missile-carrying strategic submarines, which make up the final component of the Soviet strategic *troika*, are assigned to the Northern and Pacific Fleets. Planning for their employment and the decisional authority for initial use will rest, as in the case of the land-based missiles, with the General Staff and the highest political authority, respectively. The Navy is likely to have special responsibility for assuring that strike execution messages can be successfully transmitted to submarines at sea.

It is difficult even to speculate about the current arrangements for operational control of the Air Defense Forces in the wake of the recent reorganization noted earlier. Not only is the situation regarding the status of the air defense districts and their relationship to the military districts confused, but also unclear is the relationship between the air defense interceptors and other fighter-interceptors belonging to Frontal Aviation and deployed in the military districts. Moreover, the Air Defense Forces have apparently absorbed the Troop Air Defense (*PVO voisk*) branch, which was formerly included in the Ground Forces, thus taking over training and equipping responsibilities for all surface-to-air antiaircraft missile and artillery units. Nevertheless, in my view, the Soviets almost certainly continue to defend the homeland with a vast integrated network of radar troops, surface-to-air missiles and fighter-interceptor units, operating within an arrangement of districts and smaller air defense zones (two to five per district),[58] all under the overall direction of a central command organ manned by the Air Defense Forces in Moscow.

In the event of war, those motorized rifle and tank divisions at full combat strength,[59] located in the groups of forces and frontier military districts facing active theaters of military operations, are likely to be integrated into several multidivisional fronts.[60] These fronts, supported by the Air Forces' Frontal Aviation and recently reconstituted Army Aviation, will be called upon, in most cases, to launch combined-arms offensive operations beyond Soviet-controlled territory. These fronts would operate either directly under the control of the Moscow-based *Stavka* of the VGK and its working organ, the General Staff, or, alternatively, under the control of the commander in chief of one of the high commands, operating in a theater of military operations (TVD).

The military districts are designed to perform several different functions in both peacetime and wartime. Their primary purpose is to serve as a geographic command map, in which the actions of the majority of military units and installations within a given area can be coordinated by a single military district commander and his staff. Operational units of the Strategic Rocket Forces, military transport aviation, possibly the airborne forces, naval shore units and headquarters, the Air Armies of the Soviet Union and, in some cases, the Air Defense Forces, although located in the military districts, do not fall under the district commander's control.[61] While the military district commander is directly subordinate to the Minister of Defense, much of the centralized direction provided to the military district apparently comes from the General Staff. In peacetime the General Staff works closely with the military district commander and the commander's staff, to assure that his forces are properly trained and combat-ready, to assure that mobilization preparations are well organized, and to develop specific operational plans for various contingencies in the event of war.

Within each military district there are several activities that require substantial coordination between the military chain of command and the local civilian party, government, and economic organizations. To facilitate this coordination, the senior regional party secretaries are automatically included as members of the military councils which advise the military district commanders. Senior military officers, in turn, serve in regional and local party organizations and government bodies.[62]

Among the important areas where close civil–military coordination is required is in the operation of the network of military commissariats (*voenkomats*) within each military district, which are responsible for registering and inducting new conscripts twice each year, and for maintaining the necessary arrangements to mobilize the vast pool of reservists. In time of war this network would be used to fill out understrength Ground Forces formations and to create new ones. Members of the military district staff also coordinate civil defense preparations with local party and government officials and provide peacetime assistance to the military–patriotic education campaigns and preinduction military training. These efforts, conducted in the schools and in the workplace, often through the aid of the Voluntary Society for the Support of the Armed Forces (DOSAAF), are designed to teach basic military skills and to reinforce patriotism among Soviet youth.

Finally, the surface fleet and attack submarines of the increasingly active Soviet Navy are divided among four widely separated fleets, the Northern, Baltic, Black Sea, and Pacific fleets, with headquarters in Severomorsk, Kaliningrad, Sevastopol, and Vladivostok, respectively. The planning and execution of their wartime missions is likely to be in the hands of the Main Staff of the Navy which has traditionally enjoyed a considerable degree of autonomy vis-a-vis the General Staff. The only area where the General Staff would be likely to call the shots would be in amphibious or fire support operations, closely coordinated with land operations.

The Central Directorates of the Ministry of Defense

Each of the central directorates of the Defense Ministry is responsible for a particular defense function in both peace and war. The Armaments Directorate, headed by General of the Army V. M. Shabanov, for example, plays an important role in the management of weapons research, development, and production. The Rear Services Directorate, led by Marshal S. K. Kurkotkin, Chief of the Rear, coordinates logistic support activities among the rear services organization in the services, the fleets, the military districts, and the groups of forces. The Civil Defense Directorate, led by General of the Army A. T. Altunin, directs the extensive national civil defense program. Soviet civil defense efforts involve not only a substantial cadre of regular troops assigned to civil defense duties at their Moscow headquarters and throughout the USSR, but also a vast regional network that combines the efforts of local party and government organizations, economic enterprises, and educational institutions. Each of these deputy ministers is empowered to direct work within his area of competence that takes place in the various military districts, groups of forces and fleets.[63]

WEAPONS DEVELOPMENT AND ACQUISITION

Although the Ministry of Defense dominates the policy preparation and implementation stages in most defense-related matters, several civilian, state, and party organizations outside the Ministry of Defense play important roles in the areas of weapons design, development, and production. The largest of these organizations are the several industrial ministries engaged in defense research, development, and production. This group includes the nine defense production ministries, whose primary products are military equipment, and several other ministries that provide important support to the armaments effort.[64] Each of these industrial ministries contains a central management structure, design bureaus, production plants, and, in some cases, research institutes, all of which are deeply involved in the weapons acquisition process. Basic research in defense-related technologies is largely conducted within the research establishments of the Academy of Sciences, although some is also carried out in research institutes attached to the defense production ministries and the Ministry of Defense.

The weapons design bureaus within the defense–industrial ministries have come to play a particularly prominent role in the Soviet weapons acquisition process. These bureaus, which are called upon to develop new designs, produce initial prototypes and monitor the series production of their creations, apparently influence all weapons areas, from strategic ballistic missiles to small arms. The more successful chief designers have been richly rewarded, gaining material benefits, prestige within the Soviet system, and even international fame.[65]

Soviet memoirs and biographical literature indicates that some of these designers have enjoyed regular access to the highest party leadership, which they have used, on occasion, to push vigorously for support of their latest ideas.[66] In combination with the veteran managers of the defense industrial enterprises, the designers represent an entrepreneurial element that provides a strong impetus for the continuous introduction of new weaponry into the Soviet Armed Forces.

This is not to say, of course, that this activity occurs independently from or contrary to the wishes of the party leadership or the military customers. Rather, it is an important aspect of a cooperative relationship that benefits all concerned. The party leaders clearly value Soviet military strength. They have often become deeply involved in supervising weapons development and have proven themselves willing to expend enormous resources on the nearly continuous procurement of new weapons for more than fifty years. The marshals, too, are more than pleased to acquire successive generations of increasingly capable weapons systems. They depend upon the defense industrial sector to produce the large numbers and diverse types of weapons needed to underwrite Soviet doctrinal concepts for various potential warfare scenarios. Furthermore, the weapons designers and producers are certainly well aware of the military's requirements. Given the comprehensive character of contemporary Soviet military doctrine, with its fundamental imperative that the Soviet Armed Forces be prepared to fight and defeat resourceful foes, in either conventional or nuclear conflict, and in several different theaters, the designers and weapons manufacturers have the opportunity to create and gain support for a wide variety of new weapons systems that can be readily justified in doctrinal terms.

The arrangements within the Ministry of Defense for developing the technical specifications for new weapons, coordinating their development and production with the institutes of the Academy of Sciences and the industrial ministries, and managing their acceptance into active inventory have varied over time. The General Staff has long been responsible for developing the overall doctrinal framework that establishes the basic military requirements. Over the past several decades, the task of coordinating weapons development and acquisition on a ministry-wide basis has apparently shifted back and forth between one, and sometimes two, deputy ministers of defense for armaments and a deputy chief of the General Staff. During some periods both of these posts have existed.[67] Since 1970, when the post of deputy minister of defense for armaments was reinstated, this responsibility has apparently rested primarily with its occupant, initially Colonel General Alekseev and now General of the Army Shabanov and his staff. It is not clear whether the General Staff has a deputy chief for armaments, a scientific technical committee, or a department or administration active in the weapons area at this time.

The work of developing detailed system specifications and maintaining day-to-day contact with the weapons designers and producers appears to lie primarily with a series of armaments directorates organized along broad product lines. Each service is almost certainly supported by at least one such directorate.[68] These directorates most likely operate under a form of dual subordination, working for both the Deputy Minister of Defense for Armaments, General of the Army Shabanov, and the commanders in chief of the five services.

These armament directorates contain one of the most important links between the weapons design organizations and defense production plants and their military customers: the so-called military representatives (*voenpredi*); officers serving within the armaments directorates who are posted at the various design bureaus and production plants. These specially trained officers work closely with designers and managers in relaying military requirements to the defense industrialists, in identifying and promoting new designs, in approving modifications for systems under development and in production, and in assuring that the weapons produced meet the stringent military quality-control standards.[69] The independent checking function is particularly important, since it distinguishes the defense sector from other Soviet industrial production, where the customer, be it another enterprise or the Soviet consumer, has no effective voice in enforcing high-quality production.

Relations between the Ministry of Defense and the defense–industrial ministries also appear to be the business of the Military Industrial Commission (VPK, according to its Russian acronym) and the Secretary of the Central Committee supervising defense production. We know very little about the structure or activities of the VPK, which has been headed since 1963 by L. V. Smirnov, a veteran defense industrial manager, who is also a deputy chairman of the Council of Ministers. Smirnov's familiarity with strategic weapons issues was apparent when he emerged to play a critical role in the negotiations with Henry Kissinger on the SALT I agreements during the Nixon–Brezhnev summit meeting, in Moscow, in May of 1962;[70] and again during SALT II when he participated in negotiations with the American delegation led by Secretary of State Vance, in Moscow, in March of 1977.

Western observers have generally described the VPK as an agency that manages the weapons research, development and production efforts among the defense–industrial ministries and coordinates the relationships between those defense producers and the Ministry of Defense. As such, it is likely to operate as a collegial working group, whose members include high-level representatives from the Ministry of Defense, the defense production ministries, the State Planning Commission (Gosplan), and the party secretariat, supported by a full-time staff under Smirnov that assembles the necessary materials for its meetings and monitors implementation of its decisions. It is very likely that the staff of the VPK works closely with the Defense Industries Department of the Central Committee and under the close scrutiny of the Central Committee secretary in charge of defense production.[71]

In summary, there is a large and active party–military–industrial complex in the Soviet Union, which relentlessly grinds out generation after generation of new weaponry at the behest of the senior political leadership. The process of Soviet weapons acquisition within this complex is marked by a combination of "demand–pull" in which the design and production organizations of the defense–industrial ministries produce weapons in response to the requirements and specifications laid down by the military, and "design–push" in which armaments are produced as a result of the initiative of weapon designers and defense executives who "sell" their latest models of the military and the political leadership.[72] All of this occurs with the active support and substantial personal involvement of the top party leadership.

MILITARY STRATEGY AND DOCTRINE

The Soviets devote an extraordinary effort to the study of how wars should be prepared for and fought. Much of this work is done by specially trained military officers holding advanced degrees in military or philosophical science, who work within the staffs and academies of the Ministry of Defense. Yet, Soviet military writings repeatedly emphasize that it is not the military but the leadership of the Communist Party and Soviet state that ultimately "elaborates and defines" a unified series of views called "military doctrine."[73] This doctrine is said to set forth Soviet war aims, the probable methods of waging armed combat, the tasks to be performed by the Armed Forces, and the measures required for the all-round social, economic, and military-technical preparation of the country as a whole for war.[74]

In the Soviet view, military doctrine has both a political and a military dimension. The political side is concerned with the probable causes, the broad political–economic character of, and the consequences of war. Officers specially trained in Marxist–Leninist philosophy, who are often affiliated with the Main Political Administration and its Lenin Military Political Academy, are frequent writers on these matters. Soviet civilian commentators also appear to have some license to articulate views on these questions, albeit within the context of the general line approved by the party leadership.

The technical aspect of Soviet military doctrine refers to the study of military operational matters. This activity appears to fall strictly within the purview of the Ministry of Defense. While perfectly prepared to accord the party leadership the right to make the final decisions on the nation's military doctrine, the professional military clearly believes that this doctrine should be firmly based upon their expert views on operational matters. This sentiment is vividly captured in the judgment that "military doctrine becomes more scientifically sound and, therefore, more vital, the greater its relevance on the objective evaluations and conclusions of military science."[75]

The Soviets have developed a complex taxonomy of military science, the components of which include a general theory of military science, military art, military history, military pedagogy, military administration, military geography, military economics, and military–technical sciences.[76] Groups of uniformed specialists actively research and write in all of these areas. Among these disciplines, Soviet work on military art, with its three sub-categories (strategy, operational art, and tactics), has the most significant impact on the day-to-day business of the Ministry of Defense.

The elaboration of Soviet military strategy, which investigates the preparation for and waging of campaigns and war as a whole, is largely done in the General Staff's Military Science Administration and the Voroshilov Academy of the General Staff. Its guiding tenets — the need to prepare for multitheater, global, and coalition war; the call for the development of capabilities to wage war of short or protracted duration with both nuclear and conventional means; the primacy of the offensive; the emphasis on combined-arms warfare involving the coordinated efforts of all services as the prerequisite for final victory; and so forth — are reflected, not only in the operational plans developed by the General Staff's Main Operations Directorate, but also in the adjustments in the organizational structure of the Armed Forces, in peacetime training and exercises, and in the logistic planning that the General Staff oversees.

Operational art, which the Soviets define as that portion of military art concerned with the preparation and conduct of operations at the front and army levels, is developed by both the General Staff and the individual services. The General Staff's Military Science Administration and the Voroshilov Academy of the General Staff address this level when it involves coordinated multiservice, combined-arms operations. The operations departments of the services' main staffs and their specialized higher academies work out matters of operational art related to planning, operational control, and logistics support, with regard to their unique spheres of action. Thus, commanders, staff officers, and academic researchers in the Air Forces are involved, for example, in continuous study of the conduct of independent theater air operations, which combine fighter, fighter-bomber, and bomber elements, to inflict massive conventional or nuclear strikes on key targets in the enemy's rear. Similarly, staff officers and military theorists in the Navy are likely to be continuously refining concepts for mounting operations against U. S. carrier task forces and strategic submarines, while their Ground Forces' compatriots seek to perfect the manner in which they can introduce follow-on maneuver units into the battle, to exploit the anticipated breakthrough in the enemy's forward defenses.

Finally, tactics, which deals with the preparation and conduct of operations at the division level and below, also has both a combined and an individual service dimension. Work on the former is done in the Voroshilov Academy of the General Staff and probably the Frunze Military Academy as well, while the latter is clearly the business of each of the services and their constituent branches of troops.

Over the years, the Soviet military has worked hard to apply the latest scientific techniques to military problems. Military philosophers and military scientists have been true to the scientific aspirations of their Marxist–Leninist ideology, as they have diligently sought to discover the Marxist–Leninist laws of war.[77] On a more practical level, military officers have developed several analytical modeling techniques designed, for example, to assist in calculating the correlation of military forces, to illuminate cost and effectiveness tradeoffs in weapons acquisition, to investigate and improve processes of military command and control, to develop optimum tactics for various engagements and to establish "norms" regarding optimum rates of advance, firepower support requirements, and general logistic support. Work of this type is apparently conducted in the research bodies attached to the major military academies, the service staffs and the General Staff.[78] These efforts have produced an enormous body of specialized, highly technical literature, which has not yet been well mined by Western students of Soviet military affairs.[79] Those Soviet analytical efforts that are viewed as particularly useful are likely to find their way to the operating forces, in the form of new norms for staffs and commanders to employ in planning and conducting combat operations, computational devices, including computers with programs to rapidly solve equations that can assist in performing key command or staff functions, and new tactics for accomplishing a given mission.

There is little doubt that military doctrine and its cornerstone, military art, largely influence the shaping of Soviet military policy. They establish the broad direction of this policy and identify specific operational capabilities to which the Soviet political and military leaders aspire. As such, military doctrine provides the context in which the General Staff oversees adjustments in military organization, the drafting of war plans and mobilization plans and the training of troops, and establishes the requirements for the development and procurement of new weapons.

From all indications, the Soviet doctrinal mandate is an exceptionally broad one. While displaying certain distinctive characteristics — reliance on mass, maneuver, the offensive, and echelonment in depth, a proclivity toward preemptive attack, et cetera — Soviet doctrine is so inclusive, calling for the ability to support such a wide range of operations in all conceivable environments, as to provide little assistance in identifying the most critical capabilities to be sought or a particular type of weapon system to develop and procure. Rather, it provides a supporting rationale for an across-the-board expansion of Soviet military capabilities. It is, as the Soviets are fond of saying, probably not accidental that this ambitious omnibus, military doctrine, provides very ample justification for each of the services to maintain and improve a wide range of capabilities. By all indications, this is precisely what has occurred.

Finally, the manner in which military science and doctrine is developed in the Soviet Union greatly strengthens the position for the professional military vis-a-vis the civilian party leadership and other groups that might seek to influence Soviet military policy. From all indications the military monopolizes the expertise and, to a considerable degree, the relevant information in this area. While the party leadership undoubtedly sets the broad policy directives, has the option of approving or rejecting major weapons procurements, and regulates the available budgetary resources, the Soviet military would appear to have a significant hand in shaping this overall guidance, as well as having considerable leeway in developing the military capabilities that are requested.

CONCLUSION

The persistent pursuit of enhanced military capabilities has been a hallmark of the Soviet system over the past fifty years. This massive, high-priority effort has been undertaken by a series of party, military, and defense–industrial organizations within a basic institutional framework that had largely emerged in its present form by the late 1930s. From all indications, the senior leadership of the Soviet Communist Party fully appreciates the fact that the Soviet Union's superpower status is largely a reflection of its military strength. Moreover, they are bound to see both challenges and opportunities on the international scene that incline them to continue to augment that strength. Consequently, we can anticipate that, despite serious difficulties with the economy as a whole, Soviet political leaders, with the enthusiastic support of the marshals and their defense–industrial partners, will implement policies to maintain and improve the military capabilities of the Soviet state, albeit at a somewhat slower pace than in the past.

NOTES

1. This body, called the Politburo from 1918 until 1952, was retitled the Presidium of the Central Committee between 1952 and 1966 before being redesignated the Politburo, which it has remained up to the present.
2. Leading institutions of the Soviet government, including the national legislature, the Supreme Soviet, its standing executive committee, the Presidium of the Supreme Soviet, and the Council of Ministers, are formally empowered to pass laws, issue decrees, and adopt resolutions concerning defense matters in such areas as the declaration of war, martial law and mobilization, the determination of defense expenditures, and the organization of the leadership of the Armed Forces. These actions, however, simply represent the formal promulgation of policies already decided upon by the Politburo of the Communist Party. For an excellent and exhaustive survey of Soviet sources regarding the organization and formal duties of the leading bodies of the Communist Party and Soviet government concerned with defense matters, see Jones, Ellen, *The Soviet Ministry of Defense and Military Management*, Defense Intelligence Report, DDB-2610-22-79 (Washington, D.C.: Defense Intelligence Agency, December 1979), pp. 5–8.
3. This date was revealed in the short biographical sketch on "Brezhnev, Leonid Il'ich," *Voennyi entsiklopedicheskii slovar'* (Military Encyclopedia Dictionary) Moscow: Voenizdat, 1983), p. 100.
4. *Pravda*, April 7, 1976.
5. Ibid., May 9, 1983.
6. Romanov, Col. P. I., and Belyavskii, Col. V. G., *Konstitutsiia SSSR i zashchita otchestva* (The Constitution of the USSR, and the Defense of the Fatherland) (Moscow: Voenizdat, 1983), p. 100.
7. Cf. General of the Army Shkadov, I., "Sacred Duty," in *Kommunist vooruzhennykh sil* (Communist of the Armed Forces), No. 23, December 1977, p. 16, and *Sovetskoe administrativnoe pravo* (Soviet Administrative Law) (Moscow: Yuridicheskaya literatura, 1981), p. 37,
8. Cf. Sadykiewicz, Michael, "Soviet Military Politics," *Survey*, Vol. 26, No. 1, Winter 1982, pp. 180–90; Odom, William E., "Choice and Change in Soviet Politics," *Problems of Communism*, May–June 1983, pp. 3–4; Scott, Harriet Fast and William F., *The Soviet Control Structure: Capabilities for Wartime Survival* (New York: Crane Russak, 1983), pp. 47–8; Garthoff, Raymond L., "SALT and the Soviet Military," *Problems of Communism*, Jan–Feb 1975, p. 29; and Warner, Edward L., *The Military in Contemporary Soviet Politics* (New York: Praeger, 1977), pp. 46–7.
9. Cf. Wolfe, Thomas W., *The SALT Experience* (Cambridge, Mass.: Ballinger Publishing Co., 1979), pp. 57–8; Jones, Ellen, *The Soviet Ministry of Defense and Military Management,* pp. 3–4; Donnelly, Christopher, who would also include the chief of the Committee on State Security and the Minister of Internal Affairs, "The Organization of Soviet Forces," in Menaul, S., (ed.), *Russian Military Power* (London: Salamander Book, 1982), p. 28.

10. Harriet Fast Scott's excellent analysis of Politburo signatures on the obituaries of defense-related figures between 1960 and 1982 provides strong evidence that neither Yu. V. Andropov, head of the KGB, nor A. A. Gromyko, the Minister of Foreign Affairs, appeared to have become members of the Defense Council in 1973 when both, along with the Defense Minister Marshal A. A. Grechko, were brought into the Politburo. This methodology does indicate that Andropov joined the Defense Council in the spring of 1982, after he succeeded M. A. Suslov as one of the ranking Secretaries of the Central Committee. "Possible Members of the Council of Defense Derived from Obituaries," unpublished paper, April 1983. Other observers such as William Odom and Michael Sadykiewicz, in the works cited in note 8, are convinced that Andropov became a member of the Defense Council in 1973 due to the obvious defense responsibilities of the KGB he headed.

11. The most recent Soviet "tip" on Defense Council composition comes from retired Major General M. A. Mil'shteyn, a former general staff officer, now working at the Institute for the Study of the USA and Canada (IUSAC). Mil'shteyn told Raymond Garthoff, visiting in Moscow in September 1983, that the Defense Council included Andropov, other selected Politburo members, Marshal Ogarkov, the Chief of the General Staff, and the five deputy ministers of defense who are the commanders in chief of the services. Personal conversation with author, October 19, 1983.

12. Sokolovskiy, Marshal V. D. (ed.), *Soviet Military Strategy*, 3rd ed., with analysis and commentary by Harriet Fast Scott (New York: Crane Russak and Co., Inc., 1975), p. 361.

13. The best Soviet descriptions of the manner in which Stalin worked with the military in directing the Soviet war effort are found in the memoirs of Marshals Zhukov and Vasilevskiy and General of the Army Shtemenko, all of whom played key roles in the *Stavka* or the General Staff. See Zhukov, Marshal G. K., *The Memoirs of Marshal Zhukov* (New York: Delacroix Press, 1971), pp. 234–68, 279–89; Vasilevskiy, Marshal A. M., *Delo vsei zhizni* (Cause of a Lifetime) (Moscow: Voenizdat, 1975), pp. 115–602; and General of the Army Shtemenko, S. M., *General'nyi shtab v gody voiny* (The General Staff in the War Years), Books 1 and 2, (Moscow: Voenizdat, 1968 and 1973), passim. An excellent secondary analysis of this process is found in Whitton, Tommy L., "Soviet Strategic Wartime Leadership," conference paper, September 26, 1980.

14. Such was the case for the State Defense Committee and *Stavka*, abolished on September 4, 1945. Zakharov, Marshal M. V., (ed.), *50 let vooruzhennykh sil SSSR* (50 years of the Armed Forces of the USSR) (Moscow: Voenizdat, 1968), p. 477. Stalin, however, appears to have remained Supreme Commander in Chief until his death. Duevel, Christian, "Brezhnev Named Supreme Commander-in-Chief of the Soviet Armed Forces," Radio Liberty Research, RL260/77, November, 11, 1977, p. 2.

15. For example, Colonel N. P. Skirdo, writing in 1970, stated, "Direct leadership of the Armed Forces *both in peacetime* and in war is exercised by the *Supreme High Command*, the General Staff, and the appropriate military leadership" (emphasis added). Skirdo, Colonel N. P., *The People, the Army, the Commander* (Moscow: Voenizdat, 1970), translated and published under the auspices of the U.S. Air Force, p. 109. Similarly, the discussion of the supreme high command in the *Soviet Military Encyclopedia* notes that this organ can "sometimes exist in peacetime." "Supreme High Command," *Sovetskaia voennaia entsiklopediia* (Soviet Military Encyclopedia) (hereafter cited as *SME*) (Moscow: Voenizdat, 1976), Vol. 2, p. 113.

16. Cf. Ogarkov, Marshal N. V., "For Our Soviet Motherland: Guarding Peaceful Labor," *Kommunist*, No. 10, 1981, p. 86.

17. For the best discussions of the Soviet past and present uses of high commands and theaters of military operations, see Baird, Gregory C., *Soviet Intermediary Strategic C² Entities — The Historical Experience* (McLean, Va.: BDM Corporation, April 30, 1979), and Petersen, Phillip A., *The Soviet Conceptual Framework for the Development and Application of Military Power*, Defense Intelligence Report, DDB-2610-36-81 (Washington, D.C.: Defense Intelligence Agency, June 1981).

18. There is precedent for such an arrangement, in that General Shtemenko writes that while Chief of the General Staff in the late 1940s, he was the secretary of the Higher (Supreme) Military Soviet, the precursor of the Defense Council, Shtemenko, *The General Staff in the Years of the War, Book 2*, p. 500. See also Erickson, John, "The General Staff: Theory and Practice from the Tsarist to the Soviet Regime," *Soviet Military Digest*, Defence Studies, University of Edinburgh, October 1983, pp. 137–8. Ellen Jones reports that recent research in Eastern European sources indicate that sections of the general staffs in Czechoslovakia, East Germany, and Hungary act as the secretariats for their respective Supreme Defense Councils, which were established in the 1960s. Conversation with author, October 28, 1983.

19. The best discussions of Khrushchev's apparent patronage links with these wartime associates are found in Hough, Jerry, F., *Soviet Leadership in Transition* (Washington, D.C.: The Brookings Institution, 1980), pp. 93–7, and Garthoff, Raymond L., *Soviet Military Policy* (New York: Praeger, 1966), pp. 46–56.

20. For accounts of this extended conflict, see Wolfe, Thomas W., *Soviet Strategy at the Crossroads* (Cambridge, Mass: Harvard University Press, 1965), passim, and Warner, Edward L., *The Military in Contemporary Soviet Politics*, pp. 137–46.

21. Brezhnev too appeared to have developed a series of allies in the military on the basis of their common wartime experience that included the man he promoted to Minister of Defense, Marshal A. A. Grechko. Hough, *Soviet Leadership in Transition*, pp. 97–9.

22. Cf. Brown, Archie, "Andropov: Discipline and Reform?" *Problems of Communism*, Jan–Feb 1983, p. 24; Rush, Myron, "Succeeding Brezhnev," *Problems of Communism*, Jan–Feb 1983, pp. 4–5; and Bilinskiy, Yaroslav, "Shcherbitsky, Ukraine, and Kremlin Politics," *Problems of Communism*, Jul–Aug 1983, p. 15.

23. Hough, Jerry F., and Fainsod, Merle, *How the Soviet Union Is Governed* (Cambridge, Mass.: Harvard University Press, 1979), pp. 418–19.

24. The most prominent of these have been retired military officers, such as generals N. A. Lomov, M. A. Mil'shteyn, and colonels L. S. Semeyko, D. M. Proektor, V. M. Kulish, and V. V. Larionov (who, after some four years at IUSAC, returned to active duty in the mid-1970s to serve in the Ministry of Defense's Institute of Military History, and was subsequently promoted to the rank of major general), and several civilians, including G. A. Trofimenko, O. Bykov, R. A. Bogdanov, Yu. Kostko, and A. G. Arbatov, son of the director of IUSAC. For discussions of the role of these institutes in foreign policy and defense matters, see Scott, William F. and Scott, Harriet, Fast, "The Social Science Institutes of the Soviet Academy of Sciences," *Air Force Magazine*, March 1980, pp. 60–5, and Dash, Barbara, "A Defector Reports: The Institute of the USA and Canada," report by Delphic Associates, Inc., Washington, D.C., 1982.

25. IUSAC staffers told Western visitors in the fall of 1981 that they were the anonymous authors of the pamphlet, *The Threat to Europe* (Moscow: Progress

Publishers, 1981), a tract stressing the peaceful character of Soviet foreign and defense policy, which was published in direct response to the Reagan Administration's booklet on the Soviet military threat, *Soviet Military Power* (Washington, D. C., GPO, 1981), which had appeared earlier that year.

26. Simes, Dmitri, "National Security under Andropov," *Problems of Communism*, Jan–Feb 1983, p. 37.

27. For a flattering account of Brezhnev's involvement in the Soviet strategic missile programs from this position during the late 1950s, see the biography of Marshal M. I. Nedelin, a deputy minister of defense for armaments during the 1950s and first commander in chief of the Strategic Rocket Forces, written by the current head of the rocket forces, Marshal V. F. Tolubko. Tolubko, V. F., *Nedelin: Pervyi glavkom strategicheskikh* (Nedelin: First Commander in Chief of the Strategic Rocket Forces) (Moscow: Molodaia Gvardiia, 1979), p. 183.

28. Hough, Jerry F., "Soviet Politics Under Andropov," *Current History*, October 1983, p. 331.

29. The best account of the history and roles of the Main Political Administration is found in Timothy Colton's outstanding work, *Commissars, Commanders and Civilian Authority: The Structure of Soviet Military Politics* (Cambridge, Mass.: Harvard University Press, 1979).

30. In addition to these elements of the Ministry of Defense, the Soviet Armed Forces also include the Border Troops of the Committee of State Security and the Internal Troops of the Ministry of Internal Affairs. "Armed Forces," *SME*, p. 346. For a detailed discussion of the history, organization, and responsibilities of these troops, see Reitz, James T., "The Soviet Security Troops—The Kremlin's Other Armies," in Jones, David R., (ed.), *Soviet Armed Forces Review Annual*, Vol. 6, 1982 (Gulf Breeze, Fla.: Academic International Press, 1982), pp. 279–27.

31. Although he does not carry the title of first deputy minister of defense, the current chief of the MPA, General Yepishev, is always listed fourth in protocol ranking among the military leadership, falling behind Marshals Ustinov, Ogarkov, and Kulikov, but in front of Marshal Sokolov.

32. "Collegium of the Ministry of Defense of the USSR," *SME*, Vol. 4, pp. 235–6.

33. Zheltov, General A. S., (ed.), *V. I. Lenin i sovetskie vooruzhennie sily* (V. I. Lenin and the Soviet Armed Forces) (Moscow: Voenizdat, 1980), p. 184.

34. The main military soviets that existed between 1938 and 1941 in both the People's Commissariat of Defense and the People's Commissariat of the Navy were small, predominantly military bodies with a single additional Politburo member (Stalin for the first body, Zhdanov for the second) which played extremely active roles as forums in which policies were adopted regarding Soviet military organization, weapons acquisition, and the lessons to be drawn from the opening campaigns of World War II. Both bodies were replaced when the *Stavka* and other organs of the VGK were formed, following the Nazi invasion in June 1941. Main military soviets reappeared after the war, but since 1946 their functions have been difficult to ascertain, since they have coexisted with, first, the Higher (Supreme) Military Soviet (*vyshhiy voennyi sovet*) and then the Defense Council.

35. Scott and Scott, *The Soviet Control Structure: Capabilities for Wartime Survival*, pp. 48–53.

36. Sadykiewicz, Michael, "Soviet Military Politics," pp. 200–2; Erickson, John, *Soviet Military Power* (London: Royal United Services Institute for Defense Studies, 1971), p. 14.

37. *Pravda*, October 2, 1982. A similar meeting involving Soviet military leaders

from the Ministry of Defense and the forces in the field, which corresponds to this description of the Main Military Council, was reported by Radio Moscow as being held on April 24–5, 1972.

38. Previous examples include Leon Trotsky (1918–1925), K. E. Voroshilov (1925–1940), I. V. Stalin himself (1941–1946), and N. A. Bulganin (1947–1949 and 1953–1956). Voroshilov held a number of military posts during his career but he was, as John Erickson has noted, a military ignoramus, who owed his position to his loyal political support of Stalin, with whom he had worked closely during the civil war.

39. Marshals G. K. Zhukov (1956–1957), R. Ya. Malinovskiy (1957–1967), and A. A. Grechko (1967–1976). In addition, military professionals Marshal Vasilevskiy (1949–1953) and Marshal Timoshenko (1940–1941) also served in this position.

40. "Shabanov, Vitalii Mikhailovich," *SME*, Vol. 8, p. 488.

41. Yepishev, for example, wrote an article in *Voprosy istorii KPSS*, in February 1963, publicly supporting the continuing need for a mass army in the nuclear age, thus contradicting a key point that Khrushchev was making at the time, as he sought to cut back drastically on the size of the Ground Forces.

42. Jones, Ellen, "Soviet Civil–Military Relations: A Focus on the Military District," in Hansen, L., and Minckler, R. D., (eds.), *The Soviet Military District in Peace and War: Manpower, Manning and Mobilization* (Washington, D.C.: General Electric Co., Tempo Center for Advanced Studies, 1979), p. F–15.

43. In 1924 Frunze spoke of the staff of the Red Army as the "brain," not only of the army, but serving "the entire Soviet state." Frunze, M. V., *Izbrannye proizvedeniia* (Selected Works) (Moscow: Voenizdat, 1965), p. 155. Shaposhnikov used this term in the title of his three-volume classic, *Mozg armii* (The Brain of the Army), published in 1927–1929. This historical treatise on the role of the Austro-Hungarian General Staff prior to and during World War I makes the case for a powerful general staff as a key element of a nation's military power.

44. Colonel General Chervov claimed this responsibility in a discussion with Raymond Garthoff in Moscow in September 1983. Conversation with Garthoff, October 19, 1983. In addition to General Chervov, Marshals Ogarkov and Akhromeyev, the Chief and First Deputy Chief of the General Staff, have served as spokesmen to the Western press and to visiting U.S. congressional delegations regarding the Strategic Arms Reduction and the INF talks.

45. For a description of this involvement, see the Edward L. Warner's *The Military in Contemporary Soviet Politics*, pp. 224–44.

46. The Chief of the General Staff and officers of Main Operations Directorate played important roles in negotiations on possible military cooperation with the British and French in August 1939 and in support of Stalin's participation in the Big Three summit conferences during the latter stages of the war. See Zakhonov, Marshal M. V., *Uchenyi i voin* (Scholar and Soldier) (Moscow: Voenizdat, 2nd ed, 1978), p. 82. Shtemenko, *The General Staff in the War Years, Book 1*, pp. 189–98, 358–9.

47. For an illuminating discussion of the emergence of a similar elite group of specially educated *genshtabisty* within the Russian Imperial Army in the latter half of the nineteenth century, see Erickson, John, *The Russian Imperial/Soviet General Staff*, College Station Papers, No. 3 (College Station, Tx.: Texas A & M University, April 1981), pp. 14–50.

48. All three first deputy ministers, and five of the nine deputy ministers, graduated from the Voroshilov Academy. In addition, Marshal Petrov, Commander in Chief of the Ground Forces, is reported to have completed command courses at

Voroshilov, while Admiral Gorshkov, Commander in Chief of the Navy, attended the Frunze Academy in the early 1930s when it was doubling as a higher academy for combined-arms training, prior to the opening of the General Staff Academy in 1936. Information on attendance at the Academy of the General Staff is gathered from Kulikov, Marshal V. G., (ed.), *Akademiia general'nogo shtaba* (The Academy of the General Staff) (Moscow: Voenizdat, 1976), and biographical essays on occupants of top Ministry of Defense positions found in the *Soviet Military Encyclopedia.*

49. Interview with Michael Sadykiewicz, a former Polish colonel, who completed the two-year course at the Voroshilov Academy of the General Staff in 1957 and held several senior staff and command positions in the Polish Army. October 18, 1982.

50. "General Staff," *SME*, Vol. 2, p. 513.

51. These, listed in alphabetical order, are the Baltic, Byelorussian, Carpathian, Central Asian, Far Eastern Kiev, Leningrad, Moscow, North Caucasus, Odessa, Siberian, Transbaikal, Transcaucasus, Turkestan, Ural, and Volga military districts.

52. These groups are the Group of Soviet Forces Germany (GSFG) in East Germany, the Northern Group in Poland, the Central Group in Czechoslovakia, and the Southern Group in Hungary.

53. These are the Northern, Baltic, Black Sea, and Pacific fleets, with headquarters in Severomorsk, Kaliningrad, Sevastopol, and Vladivostok, respectively.

54. For discussions of this corps, see Shtemenko, *The General Staff in the War Years*, Book 1, pp. 139–41, and Golubovich, Col. V., and Kulikov, I., "About the Corps of Officers—Representatives of the General Staff," *Voenno-istoricheskii zhurnal* (Military History Journal), No. 12, 1975, pp. 67–71.

55. See Isby, David C., "Soviet Air Forces Recast; Air Units in Poland and Hungary Are Disbanded," *Defense Week*, July 25, 1983, pp. 4–5; Jones, David R., "Air Defense Forces," in Jones, David R., (ed.) *Soviet Armed Forces Review Annual*, Vol. 5, 1981 (Gulf Breeze, Fla.: Academic International Press, 1981), pp. 83–5; Jones, David R., "Air Defense Forces," in Jones, David R., (ed.), *Soviet Armed Forces Review Annual*, Vol. 6, 1982, pp. 138–40, 175–7; and Wolff, Richard, "Soviet Air Force Command Changes and Restructuring of Air Assets: Part III — The Soviet Air Defense Troops Command," Rapid Report No. 6 (Part III), Center of Strategic Technology (College Station, Tx.: Texas A & M University, September 1982).

56. For the most thorough treatment of the organization, deployment, missions and capabilities of the Strategic Rocket Forces, see Berman, Robert P., and Baker, John C., *Soviet Strategic Forces* (Washington, D.C.: The Brookings Institution, 1982).

57. See Isby, "Soviet Air Forces Recast," pp. 4–5, and Urban, Mark, "Major Reorganization of the Soviet Air Forces," *International Defense Review*, No. 6, 1983, p. 756.

58. Isby, "Soviet Air Forces Recast," p. 4.

59. Soviet divisions have three degrees of combat-readiness: Category I with at least 75 percent of their authorized manpower strength and full equipment; Category II, 50 to 75 percent manned with a full complement of fighting vehicles; and Category III, below 50 percent manned, presently fully equipped with fighting vehicles, but older models. *Military Balance, 1983–1984* (London: International Institute of Strategic Studies, September 1983), p. 16.

60. There is no standard organizational form for a Soviet wartime front. It is likely to include the forces of some three to five combined arms or tank armies, each

of which, could in turn consist of four to five motorized rifle or tank divisions. In addition, the front will have a major air component and a host of additional missile, artillery, engineering, and other support assets.

61. Scott and Scott, *The Soviet Command Structure*, pp. 70–1.
62. Timothy Colton marshals historical evidence to argue that in order to discourage the formation of alliances between military commanders and regional party bosses the leadership of the Communist Party has traditionally sought to minimize the Soviet contacts between the party organizations of the military forces in the field and the local party organizations. Colton, *Commissars, Commanders and Civilian Authority*, pp. 254–5, 284. Ellen Jones and Richard Woff have reached an opposite conclusion in recent studies of the role of Soviet military districts. They cite repeated exhortations calling for the military to improve its ties to the populace and frequent contacts between the military leadership and local party and government officials reported in the Soviet press to argue that the military district commander and his subordinates tend to develop close working relationships with the local party and state officials. Cf. Woff, Richard, "The Military District: A Study of the Relationship Between the Military, Party and Civil Authorities" and Jones, Ellen, "Soviet Civil-Military Relations: A Focus on the Military District," in Hansen and Minckler (eds.), *The Soviet Military District in Peace and War*, pp. E–1 to E–15 and F–1 to F–40.
63. Interview with M. Sadykiewicz, October 18, 1982.
64. The nine defense production ministries and their primary products are: the Ministry of Defense Industries, conventional weapons; the Ministry of Aviation Industry, aircraft and cruise missiles; the Ministry of Shipbuilding Industry, ships and submarines; the Ministry of Electronics Industry, electronic components; the Ministry of Radio Industry, electronic products; the Ministry of Medium Machine Building, ballistic missiles; the Ministry of Machine Building, ammunition; and the Ministry of the Means of Communication, telecommunication equipment.
65. This has been particularly true for leading aircraft designers, such as A. N. Tupolev, A. S. Yakovlev, and the A. I. Mikoyan and M. Gurevich team, whose initials "Tu," "Yak," and "MiG" have been included in the designations of several military and civilian aircraft they have designed (e.g., the Tu-16 bomber, Yak-25 fighter, and MiG-15, -17, -19, etc. fighters).
66. Khrushchev's memoirs contain several recollections about his recurrent encounters with leading missile and aircraft designers who often behaved, in his words, "like businessmen dealing with a good customer," as they sought his support for their latest projects. Khruschev, Nikita, *Khrushchev Remembers: The Last Testament* (Boston: Little, Brown, 1974), pp. 41–4, 46, 50, 59, and 68. Numerous Soviet memoirs describe Stalin's dealings with weapons designers as well.
67. For descriptions of this rather confusing pattern, see McDonnell, John A., "The Soviet Weapons Acquisition System," in Jones, David R., (ed.), *Soviet Armed Forces Review Annual*, Vol. 3, 1979, pp. 177–8; Alexander, Arthur J., *Decision-Making in Soviet Weapons Procurement*, Adelphi Papers, Nos. 147 and 148 (London: International Institute of Strategic Studies, 1978), p. 18, and Hough, Jerry F., "The Historical Legacy in Soviet Weapons Development," in Valenta, Jiri, and Potter, William (eds.), *Soviet Decisionmaking for National Security* (London: Allen & Unwin, 1984), pp. 107–8.
68. These directorates apparently include the Main Missile and Artillery Directorate, the Main Armor Directorate, the Armaments Directorate of the Air Defense

Troops, the Directorate for Shipbuilding, the Directorate for Naval Armaments, and the Aviation Engineering Directorate. No such directorate has yet been identified in the Strategic Rocket Forces, although the biography of Marshal Nedelin makes clear that Nedelin headed such an organization when he presided over the development of the first generations of Soviet strategic missiles as Deputy Minister of Defense for Armaments in the 1950s. Tolubko, V., *Nedelin: First Commander-in-Chief of the Strategic Rocket Forces*, pp. 152–86.

69. On the role of the military representative, see Alexander, *Decision-Making in Soviet Weapons Procurement*, p. 19; Agursky, Mikhail, *The Soviet Military Industrial Complex* (Jerusalem: Hebrew University, The Magnes Press, 1980), p. 10, and Holloway, David, "Innovation in the Defense Sector," in Amann, Ronald, and Cooper, Julian, *Industrial Innovation in the Soviet Union* (New Haven: Yale University Press, 1982), pp. 324–5.

70. Newhouse, John, *Cold Dawn: The Story of SALT* (New York: Holt, Rinehart and Winston, 1973), pp. 251–2.

71. Jerry Hough argues that the VPK, headed by a non-Politburo member, is not likely to have sufficient clout to serve as a mediator between the research institutes, the Ministry of Defense, and the defense–industrial ministries. Rather, he believes, it is likely to serve primarily as an agency coordinating supply procurement and the preparation of technical documentation within the defense–industrial sector. Hough, "The Historical Legacy in Soviet Weapons Development," p. 106.

72. V. G. Grabin, a prominent artillery designer, wrote explicitly of the mix between designer initiative and the assignment of tasks by the military when he described the operation of his design bureau in the 1930s and 1940s. "As a rule, our plant received its tactical–technical specifications for the development of new guns from the Main Artillery Directorate. But several guns were developed on our own initiative." Grabin, V. G., "Contribution to Victory," *Tekhnika i vooruzhenie*, No. 5, May 1970, p. 7.

73. Kozlov, Major General S. N., (ed.), *The Officer's Handbook* (Moscow: Voenizdat, 1971), translated and published under the auspices of the U.S. Air Force, p. 62; "Military Doctrine," *SME*, Vol. 3, p. 229.

74. "Military Doctrine," *SME*, Vol. 3, p. 225; Sokolovskiy (ed.), *Soviet Military Strategy*, p. 38.

75. Kozlov (ed.), *The Officer's Handbook*, p. 64.

76. Ibid., pp. 50–61, "Military Science," *SME*, Vol. 2, p. 184.

77. Cf. Savkin, Colonel V. Ye. *The Basic Principles of Operational Art and Tactics* (Moscow: Voenizdat, 1972), translated and published under the auspices of the U.S. Air Force, passim.

78. Holloway, David, *Technology, Management and the Military Establishment*, Adelphi Papers, No. 76 (London: International Institute of Strategic Studies, 1971), pp. 6–9. Major General Petro G. Grigorenko, reports that he initiated work on cybernetics in the Scientific Research Branch of the Frunze Military Academy in the mid-1950s and created a faculty for military cybernetics in 1959. Grigorenko, Petro G., *Memoirs* (New York: W. W. Norton & Co., 1982), p. 229. For a lengthy description of the extensive military scientific research activities undertaken at the Voroshilov Academy of the General Staff, which are ranked on a par with its teaching activities, see Kulikov, *The Academy of the General Staff*, pp. 178–225.

79. Some good efforts, however, have been made, including Holloway, *Technology, Management and the Soviet Military Establishment*; Rehm, Allen S., *An Assess-*

ment of Military Operations Research in the USSR, Professional Paper No. 116 (Arlington, Va.: Center of Naval Analyses, September 1963); Erickson, John, "Soviet Military Operational Research: Objectives and Methods," *Strategic Review*, Vol. V, No. 2, Spring 1977, pp. 63–73; Hemsley, John, *Soviet Troop Control* (New York: Brassey's Publishers Ltd., 1982), passim; and Meyer, Stephen M., *Soviet Theater Nuclear Forces*, Parts 1 and 2, Adelphi Papers, Nos. 187, 188 (London: International Institute of Strategic Studies, 1983–84).

Chapter 2

Civilian and Military Influence in Managing the Arms Race in the U.S.S.R.

Stephen M. Meyer

Who controls whom in Moscow?[1] Western interest in Soviet civil–military relations ultimately reduces to some variant on this question. However, this simple query is far from a mere academic exercise. The balance of decisionmaking power between the Soviet civilian political leadership and the Soviet professional military leadership is of considerable importance to American national security policy. Unless one prefers U.S. foreign and defense policies that are totally reactive, some anticipation is necessary in the conduct of diplomacy, in the development and maintenance of American military capabilities, the pursuit of arms control, and the management of crises and conflicts. In each of these areas anticipation involves a great deal of second guessing Soviet actions and reactions. This requires some understanding of the identities of the various individual actors and the elite groups that constitute the Soviet defense decisionmaking process, and of their roles and relative influence.

In Western literature one encounters a variety of interpretations about the nature and dynamics of Soviet civil–military relations.[2] Some writers envision a recurring challenge to Soviet civilian governing authority by the "man on horseback." The Communist Party of the USSR may indeed run the country, it is argued, but it is haunted by the ever-present specter of Bonepartism. From this perspective, even if the Soviet military has no overt designs on the reigns of government, it acts as a high-powered pressure group whose interests and preferences are readily acknowledged, sometimes resisted, and other times accommodated by the civilian political leadership.

Others take a different position and argue that shared goals, perspectives, and perceptions between the civilian political leadership and the military leadership far outweigh any differences. Policy disagreements that may

37

emerge are seen as tactical in nature, not as true issues of high politics. Continuous indoctrination with Marxist–Leninist ideology and the experiences of World War II are posited to have homogenized views within the leadership of both groups on issues of national security. Aside from the political aspirations of individual military officers, it is argued, the Soviet military does not pose a serious threat to civilian governing authority, nor need it act as a pressure group, for the two are largely indistinguishable.

As one might suspect, the empirical evidence suggests that both these opposing views accurately describe some aspects of Soviet civil–military relations in the postwar period. There is no doubt that the civilian political leadership firmly holds the reigns of decisionmaking authority in the Soviet Union; ultimately, the Soviet military takes marching orders from it. Recall the relative ease with which Khrushchev removed Marshal Zhukov from the Politburo. Similarly, Khrushchev's decisions to place offensive missiles in Cuba and to abolish the independent command of the Ground Forces were implemented over the strong objections of the military leadership.[3] Brezhnev publically declared a policy of no first-use of nuclear weapons, despite what appeared to be strong misgivings among the professional military. Furthermore, even as his political power seemed to be waning in October 1982, Brezhnev told an assembly of the top military leaders that, contrary to their wishes, no new resources would be allocated for defense.[4]

Yet, we know that the professional military has played a significant role in decisions relating to contemporary Soviet defense policy, arms control policy, and its use of force. For example, general-grade officers have figured prominently in Soviet SALT and MBFR negotiating teams, and have appeared to orchestrate major bargaining efforts. Indeed, Marshal Ogarkov was ultimately rewarded for his leading role in the SALT negotiations with a promotion to Deputy Minister of Defense, and subsequently to Chief of the General Staff. As portrayed by Ogarkov and other Soviet spokesmen, the shooting down of the South Korean airliner over the Sakhalin Islands in the fall of 1983 was a military decision, taken without civilian consultation.

It is also true that the independent political weight of the military leadership has been sought and felt, in what were wholly civilian political affairs—most notably in political leadership transitions. Khrushchev played towards military interests in his struggle with Malenkov in the mid-1950s, and again in 1957 in his struggle with the anti-party group. The Brezhnev–Kosygin–Podgorny troika apparently consulted with the military leadership before moving to depose Khrushchev. Also, it is alleged that military support was instrumental in Andropov's rise to power, following Brezhnev's death.[5]

At first glance, the historical record presents a rather confused picture. Considerable clarity, however, is introduced if we realize that there are two independent dynamics at work. The first is cyclical, and is driven by transitions in political leadership. Periods of transition in leadership appear to open windows for direct, though temporary, military participation in Soviet leadership transitions. The ebb and flow of military officers into party ranks, the rise and fall of professional military officers to the post of Minister of Defense and to positions on the Politburo, and the expansion and contraction of authority of the military commanders relative to the military commissar (officers of the Main Political Administration) chart the rhythms of this aspect of Soviet civil–military relations.[6]

I believe, however, that what is evolving is a more fundamental and enduring trend of enhanced military influence in Soviet national security decisionmaking.[7] In contrast to the transient effects of the cyclical dynamic associated with Soviet leadership politics, the second trend could mean a major and long-term shift towards greater defense decisionmaking influence by the professional military leadership. It is this second, underlying, dynamic, together with its effect on peacetime Soviet defense decisionmaking, that are the subject of this paper.

DECISION AUTHORITY vs. DECISION INFLUENCE

Much of the ambiguity over who controls whom in Moscow results from an overemphasis on the actual act of decisionmaking; on who gives the orders. But orders are only the final step in the decisionmaking process. Before decisions are made, issues must be identified and options outlined. The eventual decision is a function of both the definition of the problem and the perception of available options. Therefore, it is useful to distinguish between two aspects of decisionmaking power: *decision influence* and *decision authority*.

Decision influence connotes the degree to which the collection and processing of decision-relevant data, the analysis of the data, and the preparation and structuring of options and alternatives are controlled or manipulated by a given party. *Decision authority* is the role of selecting the option for implementation; of having the final word on the content of the decision. For omnipotent and completely rational decisionmakers this distinction is not relevant, but in the real world it is. The perceptions, images, expectations, and assessments of those with decision authority can be greatly influenced by those who are well placed to structure, if not to manipulate, the flow of information. In this way those without formal decision authority may, nonetheless, ensure that those subsets of choices that they prefer appear as the most logical and obvious solutions to those with the authority to decide.

The significance of this distinction is reinforced by what we know of the structure of defense decisionmaking in the Soviet Union. As Edward Warner's (Chapter 1) excellent presentation shows, historically the Soviet professional military has had little or no direct decision authority in areas of high policy—including national security policy.[8] Yet, it is also true that the structure of defense decisionmaking is such that the professional military has faced little effective institutional competition for decision influence in areas of national security policy, such as military force planning, weapons acquisition, and arms control. Thus, while the Soviet military may not be able to make defense policy, it is certainly in a strong position to influence it.

DETERMINANTS OF LONG-TERM CHANGE

Since the late 1950s, a slowly evolving long-term dynamic has been at work that threatens to shift the balance of decision influence further in favor of the professional military over the next decade. This trend is driven by four readily identifiable factors, all of which are mutually reinforcing

. The increasing technological content of defense and arms control policy.
. The continuing monopoly on military analytic capabilities held by the Soviet professional military elite.
. The lack of relevant politico–military experience among the new generation of Soviet political leaders.
. The increasing divergence in structure and orientation between the Soviet civilian and military economies.

Technology: The Facts Gap

Since the end of World War II the fundamental problems of defense and arms control have increasingly revolved around issues of technology. Defense decisionmaking, therefore, has come to depend heavily on technical arguments, scientific judgments, and engineering evaluations. The Soviet professional military, among all the institutions and groups that may have access and expertise in science and technology, is emerging as the single most concentrated source of competence in the USSR on issues that involve the application of science and technology to national security affairs.

The effects of this growing concentration of expertise within the Soviet professional military are compounded by the fact that many of the alternative sources of technical data—for example, civilian scientists and engineers—are part of the military–industrial sector. Both the nature of the relationship between the professional military and the Soviet defense science community and the structure of Soviet defense decisionmaking, are likely to impede substantially the flow of alternative information.

Soviet Military Doctrine

Soviet military doctrine — party sanctioned views on the correct assumptions for peacetime Soviet defense planning — is divided into two dimensions: the social-political aspect and the military-technical aspect.[9] As the labels imply, the social-political dimension of Soviet military doctrine is primarily concerned with the sources and scenarios of future conflicts, the definition of the likely adversary, the specification of the political goals to be pursued in war, and the delineation of alliance relationships. This is the obvious domain of the political leadership.

The military-technical dimension is mainly concerned with the peacetime development of the defense capacity of the Soviet state, the enhancement of the combat power of the Soviet armed forces (i.e., running the Soviet side of the arms race) and, by extension, the use of forces and weapons in war. Historically, both the Soviet political and military elites have played significant roles in developing the military-technical dimension of doctrine, although the military leadership has tended to assume a subordinate position.[10] Since the ouster of Khrushchev in 1964, however, the professional military has gradually ascended to a position where, today, it appears to assume primary responsibility for establishing and elaborating the military-technical content of Soviet military doctrine. Far from being a sinister effort to usurp power, this change is, in fact, a natural, evolutionary consequence of the scientific-technical revolution in military affairs. It means that an ever growing number of the national security policy options and alternatives confronting Soviet political leaders revolve around scientific and technical considerations that are beyond their experience and competence and that of their advisors and staffs.[11]

Even within the Soviet military leadership, one may be able to detect the first traces of this effect as reflected in the rise of technologically competent officers such as Marshal Ogarkov, Chief of the General Staff, and what may be the declining upward mobility of operational commanders, such as Marshal Kulikov, Chief of the Warsaw Pact Forces. Naturally, during extended periods of peace, the criteria for assessing and evaluating military officers gradually shifts away from command experience and prowess in battle to measures of peacetime defense management. The demands and requirements of the scientific-technical revolution in military affairs seem to have provided a concrete foundation for such measures.[12]

With the achievement of rough numerical parity in nuclear weapons, the nuclear arms race has moved to qualitative competition. The high costs of modern weapons technologies, coupled with the quickening pace of the military-technical competition between the United States and the USSR have heightened the pressures for "correct" technical decisions. It is clear to all Soviet leaders that they must stay in the arms race, the question is: What, specifically, should be bought, and how much of it? Thus, the driving dimension of Soviet military doctrine has been gradually shifting away from the social–political towards the military–technical aspect. The decision influence of those with military–technical and military–economic competence — specifically, the professional military — can be expected to rise accordingly.

Who Knows What?

There are four kinds of technological data that are particularly relevant to the military–technical dimension of Soviet military doctrine

. Microtechnical data on Soviet and foreign military technologies.
. Broad systems data on Soviet and foreign weaponry.
. Cost data on Soviet and foreign weaponry.
. Force balance data and "threat forecasts."

A number of groups in the Soviet Union have partial access to portions of this information and the competence to evaluate it: the professional military; the KGB; the scientists, engineers, designers, and managers of the military industries; the Military Department of Gosplan; the Department of the Defense Industries of the Central Committee; and select members of the Academy of Sciences (most of whom are also members of one of the other groups). Yet, only one group has both access to all the data and the know-how necessary to use it: The professional military.

In trumpeting the importance of technological expertise, one finds the Soviet military press increasingly exhalting what it terms the "technical culture" of the armed forces; its intimate familiarity with military technology.

> . . . Military technical culture is a broad notion. It includes the degree of education and the general intellectual development of the troops, the level of their military technical knowledge, knowledge in related natural and technical sciences, and also know-how in the practical use of military technology in modern combat and for solving the tasks of military preparedness. . . . Thus military technical culture presumes of soldiers, sergeants, and officers, on the one hand, deep theoretical knowledge in areas of military technology and weaponry, and on the other hand, sound practical training in the combat use of available technology and arms.[13]

The Soviet military's hold over the technology of military systems is partly the result of the excessive compulsion for secrecy in the USSR. In both Soviet open source and restricted access military journals, discussions of new weapons and technologies are framed in terms of foreign weapons, not in terms of Soviet systems. So pervasive is the secrecy surrounding the state of Soviet military technology that many lower-level Soviet military officers may never see, let alone be trained on, the current weapons they would be expected to use in wartime. Rather, they work with older, outdated models.[14] Further, there is the well known story of the ignorance of the leading civilian negotiators on the Soviet SALT delegation over the most basic characteristics of their own strategic weapons, as well as the effort by the Soviet military's SALT representative to prevent the U.S. delegation from divulging this information to the Soviet civilian negotiators.[15]

The KGB and the GRU (the military intelligence service) compete in the collection of foreign military intelligence and, in particular, of data on foreign military technologies, weapons programs (including costs), and force deployments. Most, if not all, of the military data collected by the KGB eventually ends up in the hands of the Ministry of Defense for use in threat studies and weapons development projects. Although Soviet defense industry scientists and engineers can request information on foreign technologies (from the KGB department attached to their laboratories), they have limited access to information on Soviet technologies outside their own narrow areas of specialty.[16] In fact, through access to western trade publications and professional journals, Soviet industry specialists can acquire a more complete picture of technological developments outside their country than inside it.

In any case, this knowledge is very microtechnical in nature. Soviet scientists working on ABM radar, for example, may be given specific data on the characteristics of U.S. reentry vehicles and penetration aids. They may also get technical data on corresponding U.S. ABM radar research. However, they will not have anything approaching a comprehensive systems view, either of U.S. ABM efforts or of the U.S. strategic threat.[17]

The same observations hold true about the costs of weapons programs. Individual program managers in the defense industries know precisely what their projects are expected to cost, but only a few industrial ministers are in a position to have a sense of overall levels of investment in broad program areas (e.g., fighter aircraft or ICBMs). Outside the Ministry of Defense, the Military Department of Gosplan and the Military–Industrial Commission are likely to be the best informed group on the overall magnitude of defense procurement and production.

As one might expect, there is a close working relationship between the armaments staffs of the Soviet armed forces and the civilian scientists, engineers, and managers in the corresponding military industries. In many ways, the latter are supplicants to the military, because the armaments staffs select designers and producers of new weaponry on the basis of proposals submitted by the various defense industry enterprises.[18] (This is in direct contrast to the past, when many senior designers and scientists had considerable independence and prestige as a result of their wartime credentials.) Moreover, specialization within the command Soviet economy has led to direct and enduring associations between particular groups of design bureaus and production enterprises and particular armed service armaments staffs. Defense industry civilians do not have a free market economy that permits them to move to other jobs; and the special nature of their work effectively prevents easy mobility even within the defense sector. For these reasons, one could expect defense industry civilians to be especially careful about *articulating* opinions significantly different from those of their professional military sponsors.[19]

If there are independent-minded scientists willing to provide contrary testimony, their potential influence on defense decisions is likely to be effectively moderated by the fact that the staff of the highest defense decision-making organ in the Soviet Union—the Defense Council—is none other than the General Staff of the Ministry of Defense.[20] Thus, even if the Defense Council does have some form of extended consulting apparatus of civilian scientists and designers, their views are likely to be orchestrated and filtered by judicious use of staff power on the part of the General Staff. (This is not an unfamiliar phenomenon to those who study U.S. Congressional committee politics.)

There are no independent civilian defense specialists in Soviet universities or research institutes who move in and out of the military establishment, as is done in the West. There is no rotation of civilian defense managers into positions of authority within the Ministry of Defense, with the exception of the Defense Minister.

In the one area where civilian researchers are allowed access—military history—the data are tightly controlled by the Ministry of Defense. Moreover, all the notable civilians working on Soviet military history are teachers or researchers at one of the many military academies. Researchers at Academy of Sciences Institutes, such as the Institute for the Study of the USA and Canada, are allowed to study only foreign military histories, and, when contemporary issues are to be examined, only after receiving special clearance from the KGB.

None of this implies that the Soviet civilian political leadership will soon become captives of the professional military. The political leadership can request information from sources other than the military. However, the new generation of Soviet civilian leaders will be in an ever weakening position as far as knowing what questions to ask. Moreover, there are no civilian staff defense specialists to aid them, such as those that assist U.S. congressmen and senators. As a consequence, the decision influence of the Soviet professional military is likely to grow.

Military Science: The Analysis Gap

Defense decisionmaking requires more than access to, or knowledge of, facts. Information must be compiled in an organized fashion and marshalled to address the issues at hand. In short, defense decisionmaking requires analysis. This is where the Soviet professional military truly stands alone. They have no institutional competitors. As the formulation of Soviet defense and arms control policies requires the use of more sophisticated and esoteric forms of defense analysis, one should expect a corresponding increase in the decision influence of the professional military.

To be sure, civilian scientists, engineers, and designers from the various defense industries and from the Academy of Sciences have at their disposal knowledge relevant to examining specific aspects of military tactical–technical issues. They are quite capable of carrying out analyses within the bounds of their own particular fields of specialization. For example, the chief designer of Soviet antitank guided missiles could provide testimony on the effectiveness of a specific antitank missile system against the latest U.S. tanks. Or, a chief designer of Soviet submarines could provide a cost-benefit comparison between a new submarine design and an older production model. But simple technical evaluations are only one, quite small component of the analytic requirements for defense decisionmaking.

Defense analysis incorporates a broad range of concepts and skills to support decisionmaking. In the Soviet Union, this broad analytic task falls under military science, which is defined as

> . . . a system of developing theoretical knowledge concerning the laws of war and armed struggle, the nature and military–technical characteristics of modern wars, and ways of waging such wars in the interests of defending the socialist Motherland. It formulates the principles governing military skill and determines theoretical and practical recommendations on questions relating to the building and all-round preparation of the Armed Forces for war . . . military science studies ways to improve old means of armed struggle and create new ones, making use of the other sciences, particularly the natural sciences.[21]

Although a number of institutions and groups may share access to military–technical data relevant to defense decisionmaking, over the last two decades the Soviet professional military has acquired a virtual monopoly on the conceptual, qualitative, and quantitative skills used in contemporary force posture planning, force balance studies, threat analyses, and in the construction of decision options, They are the only ones who devise and develop such skills. Apparently, the KGB does not have the charter (or ability) to analyze much of the data it collects on foreign military capabilities. Only the professional military, for example, is prepared to undertake assessments of the NATO–Warsaw Pact conventional balance, conduct analyses on the vulnerability of Soviet strategic forces to a first strike attack, or for that matter, assess the vulnerability of U.S. strategic forces to a Soviet first strike.

There are no Soviet civilian defense analysts analogous to those found in American universities, think tanks, or government agencies, who can undertake independent studies and challenge with authority the studies and analyses produced by the Soviet professional military. As mentioned earlier, the arms control specialists residing in Academy of Sciences institutes, such as the Institute for the Study of the USA and Canada, are students of the *Western* arms control literature. They are allowed to have access to *The New York Times, Foreign Affairs, International Security,* and the *Bulletin of the Atomic Scientists.*[22] They have neither the authority, the access to informed people or written information, the training, nor the experience to undertake independent military analyses. Most importantly, they are not privy to Soviet defense deliberations. Therefore, when the Defense Council (or the full Politburo) gathered to deliberate over President Reagan's zero option plan for intermediate range nuclear forces, assessments of its military merits and risks were forthcoming only from the professional military.

Even in military–economic and defense budget analysis, the professional military are well placed for having influence. The Military Department of Gosplan is populated with professional military officers who help to synchronize the annual and five-year defense plans with the annual and five-year economic plans for the country. For many years the head of this department (who was also a first deputy minister of Gosplan) was a general-grade officer. Within the military department, the major subbranches may be headed by general-grade officers who rotate through on assignment.[23]

An enhancement of the decision influence of the professional military, resulting from its monopoly on the analytic skills of military science, is likely to be particularly telling in the areas of modern warfare, that is, in strategic and theater nuclear weapons capabilities. However, here there is no experience to call upon. Military policy is guided only by theory, intuition, and judgment — military science — dressed up in the form of analysis. Thus, the increasing technological content of defense and arms control policy enhances the decision influence of the professional military's analytic monopoly.

Strategic threat forecasting, studies of alternative strategic force postures, and program options for defense budgeting, all depend heavily on the tools of military science. Tactical–technical data on Soviet strategic weapons systems and forces must be combined to give a coherent picture of the state of the Soviet force posture. Similar force posture studies must be done for likely adversaries. These analyses provide the basis for understanding the static balance. Assessments and evaluations of alternative employment strategies and tactics are then undertaken to develop and to determine the ways in which military forces and means are likely to be used. Dynamic balance analyses are conducted in the context of likely contingencies. The results provide the foundation for the military–technical aspect of Soviet military doctrine.

Since the mid-1960s, military systems analysis and combat modeling through mathematical analysis have rapidly become important components of the military decisionmaking process in the Soviet Union, perhaps much more than is true in the United States. In the areas of both nuclear force planning and general purpose force planning, the Soviet military has undertaken broad and extensive efforts to develop analytic combat models to guide military–technical and military–economic decisionmaking, and, thereby, make military policy more "rational."[24] One could imagine that because Marxist–Leninist theory places such a high premium on "objective decisionmaking," and because political and military leaders wish to insulate themselves from future allegations of "subjectivism," military studies that utilize advanced mathematical techniques and sophisticated computer models are likely to have a substantial edge in military policy and arms control policy deliberations.[25]

Thus, when it comes to questions of how to think about issues in military affairs and how to perceive the defense environment of the USSR, the Soviet professional military is likely to be in a good position to influence the tone and direction of discussions within the Defense Council and the Politburo to a degree not previously achieved.

The New Generation of Political Leaders

Since the end of World War II, movement by individuals up through the ranks of the Communist Party and the state bureaucracy has proceeded at a glacial pace. Brezhnev practically institutionalized generational stagnation in his effort to bring stability to the cadres. Hence, generational change in the Soviet political leadership has been a slowly evolving process over the last four decades.

Nonetheless, there have been some noticeable generational changes in the profile of the leading decisionmaking organ of the Soviet Union, the Politburo. In particular, there is a clear trend of decreasing politico–military experience with each new generation of political leaders in the USSR. (See Appendix at the end of this chapter) This, in turn, suggests that the civilian political leadership may become less and less capable of devising and evaluating defense and arms control issues outside of the framework presented in studies and analyses supplied by the professional military. By implication, the decision influence of the professional military should increase.

There are several components of politico–military experience that are particularly relevant to considerations of the balance of decision influence. The first is direct high-level experience in the direction of state wartime activities, such as that acquired by the founders of the Soviet state, and later by Khrushchev, Brezhnev, Ustinov, and others during World War II. Their political maturation took place in a militarized, wartime environment. They acquired authoritative status by virtue of their participation in top party and state organs directing the war effort.

Indeed, one is struck by the ways in which the old guard has used appeals to this authority, often based on inflated or total false reconstructions of history, to bolster its domestic political stature. Both Brezhnev and Ustinov eventually acquired the military rank of Marshal of the Soviet Union to enhance their military credentials. There can be no doubt that Soviet political leaders have found their wartime credentials, either real or imagined, to be invaluable in managing Soviet civil–military relations, and in constraining the decision influence of the professional military over the last four decades. Obviously, the new generation of Soviet civilian political leaders will not be able to make such appeals to authority.

Another related component is a leader's network of associations. Mostly as a result of wartime experience, enduring personal networks of political and military leaders have figured prominently in Soviet civil–military relations since the founding of the USSR.[26] Such personal associations have greatly affected the career patterns of both elite groups since 1945 and, consequently, have significantly influenced the relationship between the political and military leaders in the defense decisionmaking process.

More powerful political leaders, such as Khrushchev and Brezhnev, were able to fill key military posts with officers from within their respective personal networks. Not only did this put trusted friends in important positions, but it also ensured that back-channel military advice could be obtained outside the formal structure of Soviet civil–military relations. Although less powerful political leaders could not always place their military comrades in the most important slots, they could, nonetheless, benefit from private advice and consultations with professional military colleagues. One should not underestimate the importance of personal networks in the socio–political environment that surrounds the Soviet political leadership, in general, and its importance in Soviet party–military relations, in particular.

Today, few peacetime civilian occupations offer the opportunity for the development of civil–military associational networks comparable to those that all past generations of Soviet political and military leaders have had. With each successive Politburo, the diversity and strength of these networks have decreased. The coming generation of Soviet political leaders is likely to have neither direct nor indirect experience in politico–military affairs. They will lack the authoritative status associated with wartime service. And they will lack a network of buddies in the professional military to whom they might turn for candid advice, or whom they could appoint to key military command positions.

On the one hand, this suggests that the off the record and unofficial (but reliable) views of the higher military leadership may be less available to the civilian political leaders than at any time in the past. On the other hand, it also means that the military will not have a ready back-channel to the political leadership, which one might suppose could lessen the military's decision influence. In either case, it is likely that the net effect will be to lessen the variety and diversity of viewpoints reaching the political leadership, thereby strengthening the military leadership's influence over defense decisionmaking.

Another component of the new leadership involves the managerial experience of Soviet political leaders in relevant areas of the defense industries. After the war ended, many of the old guard political leaders played major roles in the development of new weapons technologies and military industries. Brezhnev, for example, is reported to have overseen the Soviet missile development programs of the late 1950s. Ustinov headed the Soviet military industries from 1942 to 1976. Since this area is not tied to wartime experience, it is quite possible that the political leadership could maintain some strength through this form of politico–military experience. For example, Romanov has been acquiring such experience as a result of his appointment as the Central Committee Secretary overseeing the defense industries.

The strength of this trend away from politico–military experience within the Soviet political leadership is shown in Table 2.1. There, the memberships of the Politburos (full and candidate members) of 1953, 1957, 1966, 1978, and 1983 are compared in terms of five components of experience related to national security.

. Military-administrative (MA) experience.
. Military-industrial (MI) experience.
. Military-technical (MT) experience.
. Foreign affairs/intelligence (FA/IN) experience.
. Senior military officer (MO) experience.

(Definitions and the full data can be found in the appendix.)

Table 2.1. Changes in the Distribution of Politburo Members
with National Security Related Experience

YEAR	NUMBER OF INDIVIDUALS WITH RELEVANT EXPERIENCE*					
	MA	MI	MT	FA/IN	MO	TOTAL
1953	11	1	1	2	0	14
1957	9	0	0	0	1	23
1966	5	2	1	0	1	19
1978	5	1	2	4	0	21
1984	2	1	4	4	0	20

*Individuals with several areas of experience are represented in each category as appropriate.

Key: Experience categories
  MA = military administrative/military political work
  MI = military industrial work
  MT = military technical work
  FA/IN = foreign affairs/intelligence
  MO = senior military officer (professional)
  TOTAL = total Politburo membership

Table 2.2. Changes in Number of Politburo Members
with Politburo Politico–Military Experience*

YEAR	NUMBER OF INDIVIDUALS**	FRACTION OF POLITBURO
1953	11	79%
1957	9	39%
1966	6	32%
1978	6	28%
1984	5	25%

*Defined as any individual with experience in any category other
than foreign affairs/intelligence.
**Individuals who fall in more than one category are counted
only once.

If one considers relevant politico–military experience as any category
except foreign affairs/intelligence (FA/IN) experience, then a steady trend
of *decreasing* politico–military experience is apparent. Table 2.2 shows that
the fraction of the Politburo membership with any type of politico–military
experience dropped from 79% in 1953 to 25% as of January 1984.

More generally, as shown in Table 2.1, between the time of the first post-
Stalin Politburo and the January 1984 Andropov Politburo, there was an
evolving shift from a strong concentration of military–administrative experience to a general diffusion of experience, and then to a dominant concentration of foreign affairs/intelligence experience. There is no doubt that
the center of gravity of Politburo national security experience has been
moving incrementally, but continuously, from military–related experience
towards foreign affairs/intelligence experience. The increase in representation on the Politburo of those with intelligence experience may moderate to
some extent the professional military's decision influence in areas related to
foreign affairs and the use of Soviet military forces.

This trend of decreasing politico–military experience among the Politburo membership must be considered in the context of the other factors
previously described. The trends in technology and defense analysis suggest
a need for increased politico–military experience among the Soviet political
leadership in order to stabilize the balance of decision influence with the
professional military. But the fact is that the reverse is happening. This can
only reinforce the long-term trend towards greater decision influence by the
professional military.

The Civilian Economy and the Military Economy

Yet another contributing factor influencing the balance of decisionmaking influence is the growing tension between the civilian sector and the
military sector of the Soviet industrial economy. The Soviets distinguish

between the civilian economy and the military economy. Military economics is, in fact, a separate field of study in the USSR. This distinction is neither academic nor semantic. The civilian and military economies of the Soviet Union are structurally two separate economic and industrial systems, although they are tied together by an interlocking web of dependencies. As defined in the new Soviet *Voennyy Entsiklopedicheskiy Slovar'*, the military economy is

> . . . a special part of the national economy that provides for the military requirements of the state. It is also a system of theoretical-scientific knowledge of principles of its maintenance. As part of the national economy it includes the material-technical basis, labor resources, and military finance marked for economic satisfaction of military requirements. In the planning structure, the military economy refers to the military (defense) branches of industry; the basic branches of industry which provide military (defense) branches with means of production. . .[27]

The special treatment enjoyed by the Soviet military economy (often to the detriment of the civilian economy) is well documented.[28] First, the best scientists, engineers, and managers are attracted by the higher salaries, special bonuses, and side benefits of working within the military economy. Second, the military economy receives preferential treatment in the allocation of materials, supplies, instrumentation, and equipment. This also serves to draw the best personnel into the military economy. Third, higher enforced standards of quality control result in a technological level in military plants and products that is, on the average, higher than that found in civilian industries.[29] Lastly, the military industries can request special covert efforts to acquire western technology. These illegal transfers of technology, coordinated between the Soviet and the Eastern European intelligence services, are the basis for Soviet prototyping (copying) of designs, or for supplying designs that are directly used for Soviet equipment. This illegal use of western technology also has the effect of raising the technological level of some sectors of the military economy (for example, electronics) above that encountered in the civilian economy.

Perhaps the most signficant difference between the two economies is their respective orientations. The Soviet civilian economy is inward looking — that is, it is centrally administered and noncompetitive. Its behavior borders on autism, in the sense that product diversity, characteristics, quality, and quantities, are simply set, without reference to consumer requirements or demand. There is little or no impetus for product innovation, because consumer preference is not a significant factor in civilian economic planning. Despite the adoption of partial reforms, there are no incentives to maintain or to improve product quality, something that is frequently sacrificed to meet artificially imposed production quotas.

In contrast, the Soviet military economy is outward looking. It is centrally administered, but it is in direct competition with western defense industrial capabilities. For the USSR to remain in the arms race, its military economy must be responsive to this external competition. Therefore, the Soviet military economy, unlike its civilian economy, cannot be tied to artificial requirements derived arbitrarily from internal planning factors. Instead, it is driven by the need to mount a credible challenge to the defense industries of the West.

When the Soviet national economic product, of which the civilian sector comprises about 85 percent, could support the military economy at the "necessary" level, the differences between the two economies were of little immediate importance. By the mid-1970s, however, serious strains developed. Under the Brezhnev regime, the structural problems of the Soviet national economy went uncorrected, and the differences between the civil and the military sectors grew appreciably larger. Moreover, this happened at a time when the scientific–technical competition in armaments between the USSR and the United States began to intensify.

This appears to be creating doubts about the long-term ability of the Soviet economy to maintain the defense capacity of the state, vis-a-vis the West.[30] As the qualitative (scientific–technical) aspects of the arms race begin to dominate the quantitative (military–industrial production) aspect, the old procurement formula of substituting quantity for quality is no longer practical. The new technologies of electronics, microprocessors, automated systems, sophisticated sensor packages, and exotic construction materials have been mastered in Soviet laboratories, but cannot be readily introduced into Soviet production enterprises on a mass scale. The existing means of production, so useful in the past when new weapons were largely incremental improvements over previous designs, are not flexible enough to adapt to contemporary requirements. In contrast with the past, production within the Soviet civilian industries is not easily diverted to assist in defense production. Despite the assistance of the Eastern European defense industries, the Soviet military economy is developing significant bottlenecks in the production and supply of key weapons subsystems, thereby slowing production and significantly raising the unit cost of new weapons.

Professional military concern is amply reflected in the growing number of speeches and articles containing themes on military economics (and national economics) authored by senior military officers and instructors at the higher military academies. Some of the themes follow the line of thought established by Andropov; the need for greater worker discipline to increase productivity and the need to apply the latest developments in modern science and technology to the means of production. Other themes are distinctly military in origin, for example, enhancing the mobilization base of the national economy and preparing it for rapid transformation to wartime support.

Despite hints of past and present disputes among the Soviet leadership over "guns vs. butter," a core value of both the civilian and the military elites is the maintenance of the defense capacity of the state. The issue has never been whether to stay in the arms race, but, rather, how to use most effectively Soviet military–economic resources in the competition with the West. Therefore, unless some fundamental change occurs soon, then the coming years will see

. An increased need to make military–technical and military–economic tradeoffs in weapons procurement, leading to a more visible contest between quality and quantity in Soviet weapons production.

. Greater pressures for weapons effectiveness analyses and "paper" competitions between alternative designs, in order to reduce development costs and minimize the nonproductive use of R & D resources.

. An extension of the military production mobilization base (i.e., slack production in peacetime) to include a larger number of civilian industrial facilities.

. A reduction in the proportion of civilian goods produced within the military economy.

Some of these effects have already begun to appear in intelligence data.[31]

On the one hand, the first two effects listed will significantly enhance the impact of the military's virtual monopoly on the analytic tools of military science on Soviet military policy. This is particularly true of its expertise in military–technical and military–economic analysis. Defense decisionmaking on military doctrine will be pushed further towards military–technical and military–economic issues, and away from social–political issues. On the other hand, the second two effects listed will raise the salience of military considerations in Soviet economic–industrial planning. Specifically, a more rigorous effort to develop the civilian economy as a mobilization base will require increased military participation in economic planning. In many respects, this is a throwback to the situation that prevailed in the late 1930s. In the 1930s, however, the party held the expertise in military economics. Thus, military decision influence could spill over into areas of general economic–industrial policy.

CONCLUSIONS

The civil–military relationship in Soviet defense decisionmaking appears to be in transition. As has been described, the long-term trend towards increased decision influence by the professional military is the product of many factors. In particular, technology seems to have accomplished what sixty-five years of Soviet party–military relations have attempted to prevent, the movement of the professional military into the heart of the defense decisionmaking structure. This is especially true with respect to Soviet military economics and the making of the Soviet defense budget.

The trend was accelerated by the cronyism of the Brezhnev era. Upward mobility among the cadres of the party and the state bureaucracy ground to a halt under Brezhnev. Meanwhile, the military officer corps remained a path for rapid promotion to positions of leadership for relatively young men (in Soviet terms). This may have created a situation where "the stooge and the worst" came to occupy important middle level party and state positions, while "the best and the brightest" filled equivalent military slots.

Is there any evidence of increased decision influence by the professional military? Consider, for example, Soviet decisions for armed intervention in other countries. Who conducted on site inspections prior to the decision to intervene? Table 2.3 looks at five significant cases of intervention. Until recently it was the Politburo members who visited the prospective target country before final decisions were made. Yet, in the most recent cases of Afghanistan and Poland (aborted), senior military officers were sent to assess the situation and report back to the Politburo. (Based on the testimony of a KGB defector, the Politburo accepted the military view that Afghanistan could be successfully invaded and pacified, rejecting KGB advice that such a move was too risky to chance.)

There is nothing deterministic about the trends discussed in this paper. There are a number of actions that the Soviet political leadership could take to halt, or even to reverse, them. The most obvious step would be the creation of a dedicated staff for the Defense Council manned by civilians. Since the Defense Council is a state organ, staff specialists could be drawn from civilians in Gosplan's military department, from the Military Industrial Commission (VPK), the Academy of Sciences, and from the various defense production ministries, research institutes, and laboratories. Party staffers from the Central Committee's Department of Defense Industries could be transferred to the new staff. This might help to close the facts gap. Indeed, there were rumors at the time of the June 1983 Plenum of the Central Committee that Andropov was considering creating a civilian staff for the Defense Council. Nothing, however, appears to have been done along these lines and, with Andropov's death, the whole idea may have been shelved.

Another possibility would be the creation of a new Central Committee Department to oversee planning in the Ministry of Defense. While the Main

Table 2.3. Soviet High Level Missions
Preceding the Use of the Soviet Armed Force

EVENT	SOVIET MISSION
Poland 1956	Khrushchev, Molotov, Kaganovich, Mikoyan
Hungary 1956	Suslov, Mikoyan
Czechoslovakia 1968	Brezhnev, Kosygin
Afghanistan 1979	General Pavlovskiy
Poland 1981	Marshall Kulikov

Political Administration may have been intended to assume such a role, today it focuses solely on political indoctrination, morale, and other aspects of service life. Thus, the Ministry of Defense is the only major government ministry without a corresponding Central Committee department to oversee operations and administration. These new department staffers could be drawn from the ranks of the younger generation of scientists and engineers and given military–technical training at one of the many higher military academies. Eventually, they would mature to become a body of civilian defense specialists, thereby closing the analysis gap. Unfortunately, no matter how great a priority might be given to such an effort, it would take at least a decade to produce a significant number of competent civilian defense experts who were well schooled in military science.

In elevating individuals to candidate and member status to the Politburo, explicit consideration could be given to prior military–industrial and military–technical experience. This might prove to be more satisfactory and effective than ex post facto on the job training, as in the case of Romanov. An explicit rule could be introduced that no military officer could assume the position of Minister of Defense. Moreover, positions such as the Deputy Defense Minister for Armaments and the Deputy Defense Minister of General Affairs could be made civilian posts. These changes might ameliorate some of the problems likely to be encountered by the new generation of Soviet political leaders who lack politico–military experience.

Yet, the current trend on the Politburo seems to be towards those with foreign affairs/intelligence experience. And given how slowly generational change occurs on the Politburo, no major shift could be expected over the next decade. Contrary to popular impressions, however, this does suggest that the formulation of Soviet foreign policy will become less sensitive to the decision influence of the professional military. Ironically, this could lead either to a decrease or an increase in the use of force in the conduct of Soviet foreign policy.

In the area of weapons procurement, the demand for weapons of significantly higher quality, but in fewer numbers, will accentuate the divergences between the Soviet military and civilian economies. If one assumes that the technological level of the Soviet military and civilian economics are roughly equal in terms of performance, then the higher rejection rate (for quality control) of the former, means that the military economy is less efficient than the civilian economy. Acceptable products in the military economy must cost more. Additionally, if one assumes that the technological level of the military economy is truly higher, then its products must still be more costly. Consequently, until the strain between the two economies is reduced, the military economy's need to produce weaponry on par with the technology of the West means that the Soviet military burden must grow, irrespective of any decision to raise military spending.

Ultimately, the Soviet military economy depends on the civilian economy.

In order to remain an effective competitor in the arms race over the long term, both Soviet economies will have to function effectively. Thus, the need to slow down, and to eventually reverse, the divergent courses of the civil and military economies is necessary both for security and for economic reasons. Certainly, the Brezhnev policies of detente, technology imports from the West (which fed both sectors), and strategic arms control were a partial attempt to do this. In place of this, the types of fundamental economic reforms required for an internal cure are not likely to be forthcoming over the next few years.

In summary, it is likely that the general trend in Soviet defense decision-making towards increased influence of the professional military will continue and will probably accelerate. There is nothing that the West can do to alter this trend significantly. Thus, we need to consider how it is likely to affect our dealings with the Soviet Union both in conflict and in cooperation.

NOTES

1. Taken from the title of a provocative article by William Odom. Odom, William, "Who Controls Whom in Moscow?" *Foreign Policy*, No. 19 (Winter, 1975), pp. 195–210.
2. For a review of the relevant literature, see Meyer, Stephen M. "Soviet Defense Decisionmaking: What Do We Know and What do We Understand?" *ACIS Working Paper No. 33* (Los Angeles Center for International and Strategic Affairs, UCLA, 1982).
3. Tatu, Michael, *Power in the Kremlin* (New York: Viking Press, 1969), pp. 230–244.
4. Strode, Dan L., and Rebecca V. Strode, "Diplomacy and Defense in Soviet National Security Policy," *International Security*, Vol. 8, No. 2 (1983), pp. 91–116; Meyer, Stephen M., *The Soviet Economy and the Demands of Military Preparedness* (Cambridge, MA.: paper delivered at a conference on the Soviet Military Burden, Russian Research Center, Harvard University, May, 1983).
5. Most readers will be familiar with Khrushchev's use of the professional military to bolster his political position, and the military's subsequent role in his ouster. See Kolkowicz, Roman, *The Soviet Military and the Communist Party* (Princeton: Princeton University Press, 1967). Many Kremlin watchers saw military influence in the selection of Andropov as General Secretary over Brezhnev's presumed hand-picked successor, Chernenko. It is unclear, however, whether the military has any real influence in political leadership succession, whether it has enough influence to pick the winner, or whether it has only enough influence to veto unacceptable choices.
6. See Kolkowicz, *Soviet Military and Communist Party*, 1967; Deane, Michael, *Political Control of the Soviet Armed Forces* (New York: Crane, Russak, and Co., 1977); Colton, Timothy, *Commissars, Commanders, and Civilian Authority* (Cambridge, MA.: Harvard University Press, 1979).
7. Here I am speaking about the influence of the military institution on Soviet decisionmaking, not the influence of military factors.
8. Currently, the Soviet Minister of Defense sits on the Politburo and the Defense Council, but despite his rank of Marshal of the Soviet Union, Ustinov is not a professional military officer.

9. Ogarkov, N. V., *Vsegda v qotovnosti k zashchite otechestva* (Moscow: Voenizdat, 1982), pp. 53–54.
10. See Garthoff, Raymond, *Soviet Military Policy* (New York: Praeger, 1966); Tyushkevich, S. A., *Sovetskaya vooruzhennyye sily* (Moscow: Voenizdat, 1978).
11. This is certainly true in the West as well.
12. Again, this is also true in the West.
13. Kirchenko, N. V., *Tekhnicheskaya kul'tura sovetskogo voina* (Moscow: Voenizdat, 1971), pp. 25–26.
14. Suvorov, Victor, *The Liberators* (London: Hamish Hamilton, 1981); Suvorov, Victor, *Inside the Red Army* (New York: MacMillan Publishing Co., 1982).
15. Newhouse, John, *Cold Dawn* (New York: Holt, Rinehart and Winston, 1973), p. 56.
16. Fedoseev, A., "A Designer's Experiences," seminar lecture at the Russian Research Center, Harvard University, 1983.
17. Past exceptions were a few chief designers.
18. Meyer, Stephen M., *The Soviet Weapons Selection Process* (Cambridge, MA.: Center for International Studies, MIT, report prepared for the Defense Advanced Research Projects Agency, 1983).
19. Consider the example of Sakharov, now exiled in Gorky.
20. Blacker, Coit, "Military Forces," in Byrnes, Robert F. (ed) *After Brezhnev: Sources of Soviet Conduct in the 1980s* (Bloomington: Indiana University Press, 1983) p. 141.
21. Kulikov, V. G. "Sovetskiye vooruzhennye sily i voennaya nauka," *Kommunist*, No. 3, p. 79. 1973.
22. Here again, special security clearance is required.
23. It is well known that the head of the military department of Gosplan from 1961 to 1974 was General-Colonel Ryabikov. A recent Soviet emigre who worked on economic analysis noted in an interview that the head of a naval armaments section of the military department was an admiral.
24. This work is done by senior officers and specialists at the military academies. Many hold doctorates in military science, economics, engineering, or mathematics. See Parkomenko, A. "Analysis of Armament Systems," *Military Thought*, No. 1, 33–7, 1968; Tarakanov, K. V. *Matematika i vooruzhennaya bor'ba*, (Moscow: Voenizdat, 1974); Makeev, B. "Hekotorye vzglyady na teoriyu vooruzheniya VMF," *Morskoi Sbornik*, No. 4., p. 27–31; Anureev, I. I. *Primenenie matematicheskikh metodov v voennom dele*, (Moscow: Voenizdat, 1967).
25. This does not mean that ideology guides military policy, but rather, that it is used post hoc to legitimize and lend authority to arguments and decisions.
26. See Kolkowicz, *Soviet Military and Communist Party*, 1967; Deane, *Political Control*, 1977.
27. Ogarkov, N. V., (ed) "Ekonomika Voennaya," *Voennyy Entsiklopedicheskiy Slovar'* (Moscow: Voenizdat, 1983).
28. Ofer, Gur, *The Opportunity Cost of the Nonmonetary Advantages of the Soviet Military R&D Effort* (Santa Monica: Rand Corp., R-1241-DDRE, 1975); Alexander, Arthur, "Decisionmaking in Soviet Weapons Procurement," *Adelphi Papers*, Nos. 147–8 (London: International Institute for Strategic Studies, 1978).
29. Holloway, David, "Innovation in the Defense Sector," in Ammann, Ronald, and Cooper, Julian (eds), *Industrial Innovation in the Soviet Union* (New Haven: Yale University Press, 1982), 368–410.
30. See Gurov, A., "Effektivnost' material'nogo obespecheniya," *Krasnaya Zvezda*, (9 December 1982), p. 2; Kozlov, M. "Vydayushchiycya voennyy deyatel' i

teoretik," *Krasnaya Zvezda*, 2 October, p. 2, 1982.

31. Joint Economic Committee *Soviet Defense Trends*, staff study prepared for the Subcommittee on International Trade, Finance, and Security Economics, September, 1983.

APPENDIX
MEMBERS OF THE POLITBURO

Explanation of Tables and Categories

The purpose of the tables presented here is to outline the backgrounds of key Politburo members from 1953 to the present, highlighting those features that relate to military affairs. An "x" in a category indicates that the person has had at least seven years of relevant experience or served in that category during World War II; an "o" indicates that the person's connection is one of less than seven years, or is in a field that touches, but may not be directly related to, defense matters (e.g., heavy machine building), or that there is some ambiguity in the biographical material.

Military–administrative work (MA) includes membership on the GKO during the war, or service on a front-level military council. Military–industrial work (MI) includes those involved in managing or coordinating defense industries at a managerial and/or a ministerial level. Military–technical work (MT) consists of experience as a designer or "technolog" in defense industries. Foreign affairs and intelligence experience (FA/IN) includes work in the Cheka/NKVD/MVD/KGB systems, the Ministry of Foreign Affairs, or the Department of Foreign Relations. It does not include ambassadorial postings (as these seem to come at the end of one's career). Members of the Politburo whose principal career has been in the military and who have achieved a senior rank are noted in the militiary officer (MO) column. An asterisk (*) before a name indicates that the person's background was in none of these areas.

Biographical information is drawn primarily from Levytsky, Boris, *The Soviet Political Elite*, (Stanford, Calif: Hoover Institute Press, 1970), and the annual volumes of the *Yearbook* to the *Great Soviet Encyclopedia*.

Table 2A. Members of the Politburo with Military,
Foreign Affairs, or Intelligence Backgrounds

	MA	MI	MT	FA/IN	MO
1953					
Full					
Malenkov	x	o			
Beria	x	o		x	
Molotov	x				

	MA	MI	MT	FA/IN	MO
Voroshilov[1]	x				
Khrushchev	x				
Bulganin[2]	x	'			
Kaganovich	x				
Mikoian	x	o			
Saburov	x	x	x		
Pervukhin		o		o	
Candidates					
*Shvernik					
Ponomarenko	x				
Melnikov				x	
Bagirov	x				
1957					
Full					
Khrushchev	x				
*Aristov					
Brezhnev[3]	x				
*Furtseva					
Ignatov					
Kirichenko[4]	x				
*Kuusinen					
*Mukhitdinov					
Suslov	x				
*Shvernik					
*Beliaev					
Voroshilov[1]	x				
Bulganin[2]	x				
Mikoian	x	o			
Kozlov		o			
Candidates					
*Pospelov					
*Kalnberzin					
Kirilenko	x	o	o		
*Mazurov					
Mzhavanadze	x				x
*Kosygin					
Pervukhin		o		o	
*Korotchenko					
1966					
Full					
Brezhnev[3]	x				
Kirilenko	x	o	o		
*Shelepin					
Suslov	x				
*Pelshe					
Shelest		x			
*Kosygin					
*Podgorny					
*Mazurov					
*Polyansky					
*Voronov					

	MA	MI	MT	FA/IN	MO
Candidates					
*Demichev					
Ustinov	x	x	x		
*Kunaev					
*Masherov					
Mzhavanadze	x				x
*Rashidov					
Grishin		o			
Shcherbitsky					o
1978					
Full					
Brezhnev[3]	x				
Andropov				x	
Grishin		o			
Gromyko				x	
Kirilenko	x	o	o		
*Kosygin					
*Kulakov					
*Kunaev					
*Mazurov					
*Pelshe					
Romanov			x		
Suslov	x				
Ustinov	x	x	x		
Candidates					
Aliev				x	
*Chernenko					
*Demichev					
Kuznetsov	x				
*Masherov					
Ponomarev				x	
*Rashidov					
Solmentsev		o			
1983–84[5]					
Full					
Aliev				x	
Andropov				x	
*Chernenko					
*Gorbachev					
Grishin		o			
Gromyko				x	
*Kunaev					
Romanov			x		
Solomentsev[6]		o			
Shcherbitsky					o
*Tikhonov					
Ustinov	x	x	x		
*Vorotnikov[6]			x		

	MA	MI	MT	FA/IN	MO
Candidates					
*Demichev					
Dolgikh		o			
Kuznetsov	x				
Ponomarev				x	
*Rashidov					
*Shevardnadze					
Chebrikov			x		

[1] Voroshilov became a MSU in 1940
[2] Bulganin became a MSU in 1947
[3] Brezhnev became a major general in 1943
[4] Kirichenko became a major general at some point in WW2.
[5] Includes all members on the Politburo from late 1983 and early 1984.
[6] Solomentsev and Vorotnikov became full members and Chebrikov a candidate in December, 1983

Chapter 3

Central Defense Organization in the United Kingdom

Michael Hobkirk

DEFENSE BY COMMITTEE

"During the first half of this century Britain was defended by Inter-Departmental Committees."[1] Michael Howard's description of defense before 1939 stresses that coordination, not control of the services, was the objective, and that decisions on strategy and on the allocation of resources were left to the service department concerned, subject, of course, to the overriding authority of the government of the day.

It is true that when the Chiefs of Staff Committee was formed in 1924, it was given collective responsibility for advising on defense policy as a whole. However, if, as President Truman pointed out in 1947, "strategy, programs and budgets are all aspects of the same basic decisions,"[2] then the Chiefs' of Staff advice on strategy should have carried with it a commitment to accept any reallocation of available defense resources needed to carry out the proposed strategy. There is little evidence that the Chiefs of Staff ever considered, save in the most general way, the resource constraints on what they proposed; and the literature is full of examples of the services fighting tooth and nail for the requirements of their own service. The prime task of a central defense organization is first to devise a viable strategy, and then to suballocate available resources for the services to spend in conformity with that strategy. Successive reorganizations of the U.K.'s defense will be judged by their ability to perform this task. Plainly, by this criterion, Britain did not have an effective central defense organization before World War II.

Even during World War II, when Mr. Churchill, the Prime Minister, became Minister of Defense (but did not create a Defense Ministry), the coordination of defense needs and the allocation of scarce resources, such as manpower, shipping, food, industrial capacity, and so on, was either done, or recommended to the War Cabinet, by interdepartmental committees on which the three services were likely to be separately represented. There was, in fact, no central defense organization responsible for deciding priorities among the services and presenting a coherent defense view on the best use of available resources. As a final resort, decisions on these matters would be made by the cabinet or by the relevant cabinet committee.

DEFENSE BY BARGAINING

Those concerned with defense organizations in 1946 evidently thought that the wartime arrangements had worked well enough. Therefore, the creation of a separate Ministry of Defense, with a senior government minister in charge of it, did not make as much difference as might have been expected. The Government White Paper on the subject seemed to go out of its way to stress continuity, rather than change. The Defense Committee of the Cabinet, presided over by the Prime Minister, with the Chiefs of Staff in attendance, was to be responsible for all defense matters. The Minister of Defense was, of course, a member of the committee but so were the government ministers in charge of the three service departments. Moreover, these ministers, although they were not in the cabinet, were made separately responsible to Parliament for their own service budgets, and soon acquired much the same public prestige as their prewar counterparts. They were generally regarded as, and soon became the advocates for and defenders of, the service for which they were responsible. By contrast, the Minister of Defense was a much more remote figure in the eyes of the public at large.

If, as has already been suggested, the essential attribute of any central defense organization is the power to allocate and, if necessary, reallocate scarce resources among the competing demands of the services, then the 1946 reorganization did not represent a great advance on the prewar position. It is true that for the first time the need to consider all defense requirements as part of one package, paid for from one purse, was recognized and emphasized in the Defense White Paper. Moreover, the Minister of Defense was made responsible for suballocating available resources between the three services, but was not given the power to do this job effectively. In defense budgeting, knowledge is power, and the service departments alone had the knowledge to adjust their budgets so as to make cuts when economy was the watchword or to undertake additional tasks within the same budget when, as usual, the unexpected occurred.

Under these conditions, Ministers of Defense found it difficult, if not impossible, to cut or restrain expenditures on weapons projects that the service concerned considered vital for its future. Whatever the overall defense policy, the service departments would normally find room within their own budgets for those weapons projects required for their most cherished roles and missions. A sad illustration of this is the fact that, by 1967, thirty-two major weapons projects had been cancelled at a cost of 500 million pounds, not for technical reasons, but mainly because they proved too expensive for available defense resources.[3]

The years between 1946 and 1957 saw the emergence of what Laurence Martin has called "defense by bargaining" under which the defense budget was shared out between the services as the result of bargains between them, rather than as the result of directives from the Minister of Defense. This can have serious implications for defense policy. "To set a crude financial ceiling and leave the selection of strategy and design of forces wholly to bargaining among the services is," to quote Laurence Martin again, "frequently regarded as an invitation to aimlessness."[4] The essential feature of this method of resource allocation is the ability of the service departments to decide on the spending priorities for their own share of the defense budget without any overriding direction from the central defense organization (save on such major public issues as compulsory military service or the creation of a nuclear deterrent). If defense by bargaining prevails, as it did between 1946 and 1957, then defense strategy is likely to be a compromise between the competing demands of the three services. The same description could also be applied to the period from 1958 to 1964, when the next reorganization of the defense departments took place; but first came Mr. Duncan Sandys.

Some of the unsatisfactory results of defense by bargaining were becoming apparent by 1957, when a former Minister of Defense, Mr. MacMillan, became Prime Minister. The new Minister of Defense, Mr. Sandys, was, therefore, given "authority to give decisions on all matters of policy affecting the size, shape, or organization and disposition of the Armed Forces, their equipment and supply (including defense research and development) and their pay and conditions of service." He was also to be allowed to decide on any matters of service administration or appointments that he considered to be important.[5]

This was a decisive break with the past, and Mr. Sandys used his enlarged authority to produce, in 1957, a new defense policy which, he claimed, entailed the most far reaching changes ever effected in peacetime. The policy was explicitly based on the nuclear deterrent and envisaged the disappearance of manned combat aircraft, the end of conscription, and a largely reduced role for the Navy. Such a radical reallocation of resources between the services involved long discussions between Mr. Sandys and the Chiefs of Staff. The new policy was not wholly accepted by the services when it was announced in April of 1957. Many of the main planks of the Sandys defense policy platform have since been discarded, but the efforts involved in achieving it had significant consequences for defense organization.

Mr. Sandys himself made some changes in the Ministry of Defense structure in 1958, but these were not very significant. The position of the Chairman of the Chiefs of Staff, which had been created in 1955, was renamed the Chief of Defense Staff (CDS), and a defense board of government ministers, senior service officers, and officials was created to advise the minister on policy. The change of title added little to the powers of the CDS and the defense board was not generally used. The most important development during these years was the start of the annual costings of defense plans for five (and later ten) years ahead. In due course, this became an essential tool for defense planners who were now able to plan weapons systems for the future with some assurance that the cash to pay for them would be available at the right time.

THE MOUNTBATTEN REFORMS

Mr. Sandys left the Ministry of Defense in 1959, a few months after the appointment of Lord Mountbatten as CDS. The next few years saw intense efforts by the services to reverse or drastically change many of the Sandys decisions on defense. At the same time, largely thanks to the efforts of Lord Mountbatten, the power of the central defense organization was increased. These apparently contradictory tendencies of policy revision and centralization of power were, in fact, complementary.

The most important move made by the incoming CDS to strengthen his position was directed at the Joint Planning Staff. At the time this consisted of a hierarchy of three planning committees with representatives of the three service departments at the Brigadier, Colonel, and Lieutenant Colonel levels. These committees were responsible for advising the Chiefs of Staff on all aspects of strategy, including, if relevant, resource allocation. The Directors of Plans had sat as the Joint Planning Committee since 1927. The Joint Intelligence Committee, consisting of the three Service Directors of Intelligence and a Foreign Office representative had been created in 1939. These two committees (and their subcommittees) had been the only two organizations working directly for the Chiefs of Staff during and since World War II. This had important consequences. The Directors of Plans were tasked directly by the Chiefs of Staff, and came to see themselves as ambassadors of their own service in a joint service forum; they certainly did not regard themselves as a central or general staff, divorced from their parent service department. They felt bound to take a single service view, rather than a Defense view of any problem. This is not to suggest that they could not compromise. The directors would try to resolve differences and submit agreed papers to the Chiefs of Staff if only to avoid the extra work and risks involved in presenting "split" papers. These agreements, however, were likely to be the extent of their compromises; solutions that the three services collectively found least damaging to their own interests. Obviously, this is not the way to find the best solution to strategic problems.

Lord Mountbatten's method of introducing a defense dimension into the Joint Planning Staff was to add a fourth director, the Director of Defense Plans, at the Brigadier level. The Director of Defense Plans chaired the Directors' meetings and was responsible for producing a coherent defense solution to strategic problems, rather than accepting a compromise among single service positions. The CDSs' own briefing staff were also increased in size, with the welcome result that the civilian staff in the ministry now had military colleagues in the center who were able to take a defense view of problems, rather than being required (or feeling that they were required) to act solely as advocates for the solutions that best suited their own service. This creation of a defense staff in the center was the beginning of the transition from defense by bargaining to defense by discussion.

It is doubtful whether the service departments would have accepted these changes if they had not been so concerned about making major shifts in the Sandys defense policy. Any major realignment of this policy had to be both rational and defendable in public debate. The service departments evidently saw some advantages in accepting changes to strengthen the position of the CDS, since this would add force and credibility to their proposed revisions of defense policy. It was clearly opportune that Lord Mountbatten should begin his appointment as CDS during this period of the "Appeal against Sandys,"[6] when the service bureaucracies were prepared to accept some organizational change and some reduction of their own powers in order to further the radical policy changes that they considered essential for the future of their own services.

Discussion about defense reorganization continued, both inside and outside the government, throughout the late 1950s and early 1960s. Lord Mountbatten first concentrated on reforming the command structure overseas, in an effort to show that unified command could work in peacetime as it had in war. Hitherto, Britain's overseas commands (outside NATO) had in peacetime been run by Commanders' in Chief Committees (sometimes with a Foreign Office chairman) consisting of two or three coequal Commanders in Chief, each with his own staff and each having links back to his Service department in London. These arrangements were replaced, not by the installation of Supreme Commanders and Staffs (on the lines of Supreme Allied Commander, Europe [SACEUR] in NATO), but the Unified Commanders; for the Middle East at Aden in 1962, then for the Near East in Cyprus, and finally for the Far East at Singapore. The Unified Commander had authority over all British forces in his command and was responsible to the minister through the Chiefs of Staff Committee for the planning and execution of defense policy in his area. The Unified Commander had a small personal staff for planning and coordination, but mainly used the planning and administrative staffs of his subordinate Fleet, Army, and Air Commanders where appropriate. The Unified Commander also used these subordinate commanders and their staffs for the execution of operations. This method of indirect operational control distinguishes the concept of unified command from that of supreme command (such as in NATO or in Lord Mountbatten's former wartime command in Southeast Asia), where the commander has a complete range of operational, administrative, and personnel staffs in command headquarters. Although operational control rested, as before, with the Chiefs of Staff Committee in London, operational orders were sent out in the name of the CDS, and, as time passed, the Unified Commanders came to rely on the CDS to fight their battles in Whitehall's corridors of power. This creation of unified commands was an important step on the road to a unified defense department, and the new arrangements were reckoned to have proved themselves in subsequent military operations in Borneo and Aden. The Near East Command in Cyprus was disbanded after a relatively short existence, partly because of the limited forces under command, but also because, after the Central Treaty Organization declined in importance, it was hard to combine the Near East Command neatly with the existing NATO commands in the same general area. The Middle East and the Far East Commands remained for as long as there were significant British forces there.

A number of those who originally opposed unified commands were, in time, converted by the improvement in planning and operational control that resulted from this change. In marked contrast to subsequent events in Whitehall, where frequent attempts were made after the 1964 reorganization to turn back the clock, no serious moves were made to unscramble either the Middle East or the Far East Commands. Cynics may suggest that since the withdrawal of British forces and the disbandment of these commands was decided some years in advance, opponents had little need to strive to destroy what would soon disappear anyway. However, most if not all, military operations that the U.K. has conducted overseas since the 1960s have been made the responsibility of one commander. Few senior officers would now contest the advisability of such a step. Overseas garrisons, such as Hong Kong, have also been made the responsibility of one joint commander.

The Falklands operation in 1982 provides a good example of U.K. practice. Responsibility for conduct of these operations was delegated to Admiral Fieldhouse, Commander in Chief Fleet, at Northwood, England, and he was given Land and Air Deputy Commanders to assist him. The Commander of the British Naval Task Force subsequently said: "It is the single most important lesson of this whole operation that large scale joint operations do need a single joint force commander in a joint force headquarters."[7] It has been noted that when speedy decisions were vital, the chain of command tended to be from the Cabinet to the CDS, and then directly to Admiral Fieldhouse. This emphasizes the importance of the reforms discussed later, under which the CDS, rather than the Chiefs of Staff Committee, became the source of defense advice to the government and the channel by which operational decisions were conveyed to the forces. Although commentaries on the Falklands campaign have been somewhat critical of certain aspects of command and control, no responsible critics have questioned the concept of a single task force commander. By contrast, it is plain that interservice rivalry and divided command caused grave problems for the Argentine forces. In comparison, Britain's command and control problems were negligible.[8]

Before returning from command and control in 1982 to 1962 and organization for defense resource allocation, one unfortunate consequence of Britain's reduced military role must be mentioned. The withdrawal of most British forces from the Far East and the Middle East and the very few opportunities for joint command by British officers in NATO has concentrated the attention of senior officers on the problems of their major single service commands. At earlier states in their careers, the Chiefs of Staff will probably have had experience with these commands and will be able to get advice from the present commanders when major issues confront their service; but Defense Ministers and the CDS have virtually no officers with experience of joint command at a senior level to whom they can turn for advice in similar circumstances. This must be a handicap when the roles and missions of the services have to be critically examined.

By 1962, Lord Mountbatten felt able, with the support of Mr. Thorneycroft, Minister of Defense, to set out his detailed proposals for a unified Ministry of Defense. These were approved by both the Minister of Defense and the Prime Minister, but it was wisely decided to put the problem of defense organization to two independent experts, Lord Ismay and Lt. General Sir Ian Jacob, both of whom had been concerned with higher defense organization during and just after World War II. Their report, in 1963, made recommendations very much along the lines favored by Lord Mountbatten.[9] As a result, the government decided to impose a unified Ministry of Defense upon the service departments, which would take effect on April 1, 1964.

THE 1964 REORGANIZATION

The 1963 White Paper, which followed and largely implemented the Ismay–Jacob report, made some trenchant criticisms of the existing defense organization. It pointed to the separation of the planning staffs in the Ministry of Defense from the administrative staffs in the service departments as being a major defect. The solution was simple and drastic. The Ministry of Defense absorbed the three service departments, which lost all independent status and were no longer able to present separate Navy,

Army, and Air estimates to Parliament for approval. In the future, one combined defense estimate was to be presented by the Government each year, although it was recognized that the service departments within the new ministry would be responsible for preparing their own sections of the defense estimate and for administering the expenditure when it had been approved. The supremacy of the Secretary of State for Defense, as the Minister of Defense was to be called in the future, was emphasized, and the government ministers in charge of the new service departments within the ministry were reduced in rank so that they lost the status of cabinet rank.

It is a tribute to the Mountbatten reforms of the late 1950s that little change was made in the position of the CDS, the Chiefs of Staff, and the joint planning staffs (to be renamed the Defense Policy Staff in 1968). In due course they were supported by a number of integrated organizations, such as the Defense Operations Executive, the Defense Signals Staff, the Defense Intelligence Staff, and the Defense Operational Requirements Staff. The Defense Operations Executive was needed to ensure that the CDS could control current military operations when issuing orders on behalf of the Chiefs of Staff. The Defense Intelligence and Defense Signals Staff provided better advice and support for the Secretary of State and the CDS than the three single service organizations from whom they took over (although in both areas the relevant single service organizations had worked closely together in the past). However, two other considerations probably played a large part in the decisions to set up these staffs. First, it was believed that integration in these and similar areas would make the ministry as a whole more defense minded, by removing the possibility of single service prejudice or myopia in the conduct of business. Second, it was expected that integrating these single service organizations into one would save resources by cutting out duplication of staff and equipment. As time went on, a number of supporting functions, such as accounting for funds and contracts, auditing of accounts, administration of defense owned land, postal services, and so on were integrated. This latter consideration became paramount. Opponents of integration were quick to point out that the new integrated organizations often required more staff than the three separate single service organizations that it had replaced. Supporters of integration were curiously reluctant to reply that extra staff should not be the prime consideration if the new organization could save capital expenditure costing many times as much. Be that as it may, integration of supporting functions, though important, does not have a direct effect on major decisions about resource allocation among the services.

Two further reforms not greatly emphasized at the time were eventually to have far reaching effects upon defense budgeting. The senior civil servant in the ministry, the Permanent Under Secretary, who was responsible for the defense budget, was given authority over all civil servants in the enlarged ministry, whether they worked in the center or for one of the services. Similarly, the Chief Scientific Adviser could call for advice and assistance from all defense scientists, wherever they worked. In consequence, all three parties to the discussion on defense resource allocation, the central military planners concerned with strategy, the civil servants with budget responsibilities, and the scientists concerned with weapon development and the theoretical analysis of tactics, were relieved to some extent of their single service loyalties and could debate matters in the more neutral forum of the enlarged Ministry of Defense. Therefore, there was a better chance that coherent decisions on resource allocation would be made by rational discussion, instead of by horse-trading among the services. If defense of bargaining describes the method of resource allocation practiced between 1945 and 1963, then defense by discussion is an apt name for what succeeded it.

DEFENSE BY DISCUSSION

The main features of the U.K. central defense organization have remained essentially unchanged since 1964. The addition in 1972 of the Procurement Executive (a mixed service and civilian organization responsible for the research, development, and procurement of weapons and stores for all three services) has not encouraged centralized decisionmaking as much as might have been expected. This is mainly because the executive is now organized into Sea, Land and Air Weapons divisions, and each division has tended to identify itself with the service that is the main user of its equipment, rather than with the central defense authority. Therefore, the Procurement Executive is often neutral in any debate between the center and one or more of the services.[10]

Two strands can, however, be followed through the various changes in organization and procedure since 1964. First, there have been successive moves to reduce the authority and independence of the service departments, which, because of their control of administration, have remained strong, despite unification. An obvious way to do this is to reduce the status of the government minister in charge of each service department. These ministers were subordinate to the Secretary of State, but tended to identify themselves with the service for which they were responsible. Twice since 1964, a Service Minister has resigned and spoken publicly in the House of Commons against government defense policy that penalized "his" service by denying it funds and, therefore, in his view, endangering national security. The decision to resign is not taken lightly, since it usually means the end of any hope of higher political office; but the resulting debate about defense priorities is very unwelcome to the government. After each of these two resignations, changes took place that might be defended as steps to economize in the number of political appointments, but which could also be seen as removing a focus for continuing discontent in the service department affected. On the first occasion when the Minister of State in charge of the Navy Department resigned in 1966, he was not replaced. His two colleagues were relieved of their single service responsibilities and given across-the-board duties, one covering administration and the other procurement. Three politicians with the more junior rank of Parliamentary Under Secretary were put in charge of the three service departments. When some years later, in 1981, Mr. Keith Speed, the Parliamentary Under Secretary for the Navy, resigned in protest against planned cuts in the surface fleet, he was not replaced, and the two remaining Parliamentary Under Secretaries were given other responsibilities, one for administration and the other for procurement, reporting to their immediate superiors, the Ministers of State for Defense. Thus, after 1981 no government minister in defense had responsibility for any individual service department, and a potential focus for future discontent had been removed.

The other trend to note is the progressive enhancement of the position of the Chief of the Defense Staff. The last and most notable example of this was the decision in 1981 that he should become what the title had always implied, the head of a defense staff able to propose the best strategy without regard for single service interests. The previous responsibility of tendering the agreed collective advice of the Chiefs of Staff was amended, so that in the future the Chief of the Defense Staff would be required to tender independent military advice to the Secretary of State and the government of the day. The single Service Chiefs of Staff still have access to the Secretary of State and the Prime Minister, but can no longer assume that the CDS will be prepared to modify his advice to reflect their views. With this amendment, the Senior Central Military Authority was no longer the Chiefs of Staff Committee. Instead, it would now be one person, the CDS. These changes, instituted before the Falklands Campaign, were surely inspired by the experience of the 1981 defense review, which was particularly hard fought and which involved, as has been mentioned, the resignation of the government minister responsible for the Royal Navy.

Some may doubt whether the CDS's extensive new powers would actually be used to deal with difficult resource allocation problems. The radical reorganization of the defense policy staff, now reporting only to the CDS, and not to the Chiefs of Staff Committee, should reassure the doubters. Previously, defense policy (i.e., planning) and defense operations were handled by separate two-star Assistant Chiefs of the Defense Staff (ACDS) reporting to the CDS, who had no three-star deputy to coordinate these and other activites. Now there is one three-star Deputy Chief of the Defense Staff to coordinate operational requirements, policy, operations and signal communications. At the two-star level there are the

1. ACDS (programs) responsible for overall strategy, operational requirements, programs, and resource allocation.
2. ACDS (commitments) responsible for coordinating policy, operational and training matters that arise from the U.K.'s world-wide defense commitments.
3. ACDS (command central, communications and information systems) responsible for planning, implementing, and coordinating such systems.

The former defense policy staff has been much altered. In the past there had been a triservice planning team for each major theater in which the U.K. expected to be involved in the event of war. The terms of reference and organization of the teams appeared to pay little attention to across-the-board and interservice problems. Today, over half the former policy staff works for the ACDS (commitments) on theatre planning and problems. The staff remaining with ACDS (programs) have the key responsibilities for overall defense policy and strategy, resource allocation, and other interservice matters. The new organization is very well placed to look across service or theater boundaries, and it has been explicitly accepted that it must form a defense view, particularly on those matters that cut across single service interests.[11]

So far the new arrangements appear to be working well. According to reports, the Chiefs of Staff are happy to be relieved of their secondary and corporate roles as defense advisors (as part of the Chiefs of Staff Committee). They are now free to concentrate on their roles as Heads of Service, and can advise the government from a single service viewpoint. As a result, they do not need to water down the options that they put forward to solve defense problems in order to secure their colleagues' agreement. Debate among the services can be sharper, and better defense solutions may evolve. However, the real test of the new organizations will be the next major defense review, when a shortage of resources forces the abandonment of one or more service roles or missions. If the new organization is to work, it must enable the CDS to offer clear advice that is not an uneasy compromise among competing claimants for resources. Moreover, if that advice is accepted, the central defense organization must be able to implement unpalatable decisions in such a way that they are not delayed or sabotaged by the aggrieved service. It is certain that the causes of interservice rivalry will not disappear, for no reorganization can, of itself, produce enough funds for the needs of all three services. It is, nevertheless, a real step forward to bring strategy programs and budgets together in terms of reference of the military staff responsible for strategy, and to make one service officer, rather than a committee, responsible for advising the government on defense resource allocation.

THE PRESENT POSITION

A description of the U.K.'s central defense organization would not be complete without an attempt to place it in the context of the Ministry of Defense as a whole. The Appendix to this chapter shows the position, in early 1982, before the Defense Staff had been reorganized to meet the increased responsibility of the CDS. The following section, which describes defense policymaking through the medium of the annual budget process, gives a good example of the interdependence of the Center and the service departments. The structure of the department that dictates this close relationship is shaped by two requirements.

1. The ministry is concerned, not only with policy formulation, but is also an operational headquarters and management authority for the Armed Forces and many supporting establishments for research, arms manufacture, etc.
2. The Secretary of State must have complete control of policy and administration, with the proviso that the services must preserve their separate identities.

Therefore, the work of the department is arranged along two axes, and, inevitably, a large number of senior staff have dual loyalties.

On the horizontal axis of the chart there are the three service departments. These are run on a day-to-day basis by service boards, which are committees of senior officers and civil servants normally presided over by the Minister of State for Defense (Armed Forces) (referred to as Minister AF in Figure 3A). With the exception of the Minister and one senior civil servant, the members of the service boards will have a functional responsibility (e.g., operations, logistics, personnel, or finance) within their service. The boards consider themselves to be the final authority on all matters affecting their service. If changes are accepted by a service board, they are likely to be accepted by the service as a whole.

On the vertical axis, there are functional officers, such as the Chief of the Defense Staff, the Permanent Under Secretary of State, the Chief Scientific Adviser, and others, either giving across-the-board advice or managing functions across-the-board, or both. It is from them and from the senior officers on the service boards (who are also in the vertical, functional axis) that the Secretary of State must obtain across-the-board defense advice. Orders to implement the Secretary's decisions may run down the vertical axis and then along the horizontal axis to the services.

It is important to recognize the conflicting pressures on those at or near the top. When the ministry is engaged in what is arguably its most important task, that of administering the services (whether this involves the development and support of the Falklands campaign or a revision of service pay scales), the management units mainly concerned are the three service departments within the ministry. Only they can assess and cost what is required. The same is true if the minister has to ask for budget cuts, When, however, it is necessary to make long-term plans and revise existing defense policy and weapons programs, many senior staff, both service and civilian, are required to put on their second hat and respond to problems as a member of a defense, rather than a single service, organization. This means that they must view the whole problem without being too concerned for that part for which they are administratively responsible. This is not an easy transition to make, in defense or in any other organization.

It is not surprising that no one has yet found a satisfactory method of showing these diverse responsibilities on a neat two-dimensional diagram. The conventional type of a family tree organization chart becomes a jungle when it is realized that some officials at two-star level have responsibilities to no less than four senior officers. Figure 3A would seem to be the best available method of illustrating the current organization, using a grid pattern to show interlocking responsibilities of permanent staff at the three-star level, all of whom work both in a management unit (service department or central policy) and in a functional grouping (dealing, for example, with operations and strategy or personnel and logistics, or budget, etc.). If defense by discussion is to succeed, in the long run, it will owe much to the ability of senior staff to work "under two flags."

DEFENSE POLICYMAKING TODAY

The British method of making defense policy depends almost as much on certain budgetary procedures adopted within the Ministry of Defense as on the way in which the ministry itself is organized. These procedures are known as the "long term costings." Each year, the ministry and all other government departments are required to produce costings of their plans and policies for five (and, in less detail, ten) years ahead. These costings constitute, in effect, a claim on the forecasted resources of the nation for future defense requirements. They are considered in that light by the government of the day, which publishes its decisions each autumn on future levels of defense and other government expenditures in a document called the *Public Expenditure Survey*.

The costings are prepared each winter on the basis of assumptions agreed upon within the ministry. These assumptions are derived from the government's decisions in the latest *Public Expenditure Survey*, and include specific financial targets for each service department. Often they go further, and set down, in addition to future force levels, some assumptions about the weapons systems with which they will be armed. During the winter and spring, the service departments cost and tailor their plans to fit within their targets and submit them to the Secretary of State, who will approve them or perhaps modify them to take account of the problems of other services. During the summer the plans will be submitted to the treasury. When the totals have secured cabinet approval, they will then be published in the autumn as part of the *Public Expenditure Survey*, which advances the budget targets by one year so that the whole process can begin again.

This is an idealized picture concealing the confusion, changes of plan, and uncertainty surrounding any projections of this sort. Moreover, defense planners are not so naive as to believe that what is forecast for the years five through ten is nearly as dependable as the plan forecast, for example, for year two of the costings. Nevertheless, the ability to plan for the short and medium term in the reasonable assurance that funds will be available is very important to defense by discussion. If it is necessary to rob Peter for Paul's weapons, then the aggrieved Peter may be sufficiently mollified if the long-term costings give him a reasonably firm promise of jam tomorrow.

However effective, long-term planning cannot, of itself, ensure that the crucial choices about weapons for Peter and Paul are made correctly. This is the task of two central committees, the Operational Requirements Committee (ORC), chaired by the Deputy Chief of Defense Staff, and the Defense Equipment Policy Committee (DEPC), chaired by the Chief Scientific Adviser. No major weapons project can proceed without the agreement of both committees. The former must approve, in broad terms, the function and desired performances of the new weapon, and ensure that these are consistent with strategic policy, harmonized with other service and allied weapons, and soundly based from a technical and financial point of view. Once the ORC hurdle is crossed, the DEPC must satisfy itself that the project can be fitted within the available budget, manpower, and industrial resources. Both committees will continue to monitor projects at various stages, but normally the first jumps over these two hurdles are regarded as the worst.

Although these are high-level central committees, well aware of defense policy and of budget limitations, they both contain senior representatives of all three service departments, who will be anxious to scrutinize closely any proposal from another service that could jeopardize their own projects, because of cost or other reasons. Discussion, of course, takes place in these committees well before the weapons project requires a significant share of the defense budget and, therefore, need not be conducted against tight budget deadlines. All these factors clearly aid rational discussion but, in the end, a defense solution, as opposed to a single service compromise, will only be achieved if the Secretary of State and his or her senior staff are determined to do so.

CONCLUSIONS

Defense policymaking in Britain has evolved over the last forty years from defense by bargaining to defense by discussion. This has entailed greater centralization of decisionmaking and, as the cost of weapon development has increased, a greater involvement of civilian staff in strategy–program–budget discussions. At the same time, service officers have had to take an increased interest in the defense budget. Forty years ago the Chiefs of Staff rarely concerned themselves directly with resource allocation problems; now they recognize it as one of their most important tasks. In this context, it is hard to decide whether the balance of power has shifted towards civilians or towards the military. In the past, civilians, including politicians, settled budget totals, and the military staff sought to settle strategy without much reference to resources. Now all these decisions are, to some extent, shared.

There is no easy proof that the 1964 reorganization (and successive refinements) have improved defense decisions. One cause for satisfaction is that there has been no repetition of the string of canceled weapons projects that aroused so much criticism in the late 1950s. This is partly because there are better methods of controlling the costs of advanced weapons projects. Also, better central control of budgeting has made it more difficult for the service departments to include doubtful weapons projects in their long-term budgets in the expectation that, even if they were canceled before large-scale production began, the service affected would retain control of the long-term allocation of funds for the canceled project, which could then be used for other weapons systems. This method of padding future defense budgets is now rare, and some credit for this should go to the central defense organization.

Perhaps the best evidence of a change for the better comes, not unexpectedly, from the major defense reviews when one service (as it happens it was the Navy in both these reviews) had to accept cuts in projected weapons (or, in these cases, ships) that it considered vital for its future role. In the first, in 1965–66, the Secretary of Staff for Defense rejected the case for replacing the existing aircraft carriers (and the high performance aircraft on them), on the basis that the projected purchase of U.S. F-111 aircraft for the Royal Air Force (RAF) could carry out the tasks, mainly in the Indian Ocean, for which the carriers were previously thought essential.

This appeared to be the end of organic fixed-wing aircraft for the Navy. It is ironic that the F-111 purchase was cancelled, and with the introduction of through-deck cruisers, VSTOL aircraft, such as Harriers, again became part of the fleet. Perhaps time will also upset the decisions of the 1981 defense review that foreshadowed significant cuts in the future surface fleet. This decision was bitterly resisted by the Navy, which was later able to point out that the recapture of the Falkland Islands would not have been possible if the Argentine invasion had been delayed until after the cuts in the fleet had been implemented. Whatever the merits or demerits of these decisions in the light of subsequent events, they can still be seen as determined attempts to search for economies, not by allocating proportionately equal cuts to each service, but by examining all service roles and missions to see which could be discarded with the least damage to national security. The decisions arising from these two reviews were the result of defense by discussion, not of defense by bargaining.

There is a fairly general assumption that the ministry's contingency planning has improved since the 1964 organization, with the Suez operation of 1956 being cited, rightly or wrongly, as a previous example of poor planning. Perhaps the best recent example of integrated operational planning by the ministry and subordinate commands is the 1982 Falklands campaign, for which, it has been admitted, no contingency plans existed. If hurried planning by all concerned can be as generally successful as it was then, one may dare to hope that contingency planning undertaken for known commitments (e.g., in NATO) may be at least as successful. This planning will have been unhurried and subject to amendments in the light of major exercises, such as the very successful 1981 reinforcement exercise, which doubled the strength of the British Army of the Rhine by the transport of reservists from the U.K.

Despite this progress towards better decisionmaking, there are two areas at least in which there has been little or no appreciable change for the better. First, there has been no attempt to create a recognizable cadre of officers from all three services for defense staff duties in the center. Since the 1982 reforms, the CDS deals with promotions at three- and four-star levels, but no specific defense training or education is given to more junior officers on joining the defense staff. Their selection and subsequent employment is left in the hands of the relevant service department.[12] The second cause for concern is the apparent failure to use some potentially useful work done by the Defense Operational Analysis Establishment (DOAE). Some time ago, this establishment "developed an impressive array of models which are representative of land–air warfare in the Central Region of Allied Command Europe and of a range of maritime operations."[13] There is no evidence that such studies have been used to illuminate any of the difficult choices between land and air, or between sea and air weapons systems. Since these are some of the most difficult questions faced in strategy–program–budget discussions, the failure to involve the DOAE is all the more disappointing.

Nevertheless, the U.K. would seem to have some useful experience to offer other countries that have unified their departments of defense and are seeking to improve defense decisionmaking still further. The most obvious step after unification of the departments would seem to be that taken belatedly by the U.K. in 1982, namely, the creation of a single point for military advice to the government, whether on operations or policy, particularly when these affect more than one service. Only when the Chief of Defense Staff is really one, rather than Chairman of a Chiefs of Staff Committee, can the political head of defense get the military advice that he is entitled to expect when deciding the allocation of resources to the three services. Almost as important is a system of long-term financial planning, underwritten by the government with a permanent cadre of senior civil servants to administer it. This increases control of costly weapons projects, first by limiting the number that can be developed, and then by ensuring that cost overruns are borne on the long-term budget of the service responsible. Long-term costings, to use U.K. nomenclature, also enable the services to negotiate among themselves over the timing of major weapons projects. This avoids bunching of projects and the consequent peaking of costs. It also means that when budget cuts have to be made, a service will more readily accept postponement of a weapons program if the long-term costing, which has been agreed upon by the other two services, allows for the postponed project to start in two or three years time. Sensible planning entails long-term budgeting, and this can make for easier budgeting. Moreover, when the unexpected happens, the sharing of past decisions about the budget can make revisions easier and less divisive.

Despite these changes the service departments still play a crucial part in defense decisionmaking. Each service sees a vital role for itself in any conventional war in Europe and the North Atlantic, and tends to concentrate its resources on these tasks. This essential inner vision of each service has survived both the withdrawal of Britain from her policing role east of Suez and the transfer of responsibility for the nuclear deterrent from the Air Force to the Navy. In consequence, their adherence to traditional roles is strong, and loyalty to service is focused on each service department within the ministry. Necessary as these feelings are for the morale of the fighting services, they can be hostile to any dispassionate decisions on strategy and resource allocation. Defense by discussion tries to secure a coherent defense policy without destroying these loyalties.

NOTES

1. Howard, Michael, *The Central Organization for Defense* (London: London Royal United Services Institution, 1970), p. 5.
2. "Public Papers of Presidents of the U.S.A. — Harry Truman 1945" (Washington, D.C.: Government Printing Office, 1961), p. 551
3. This point is discussed more fully in the chapter's conclusions. See Howard, Michael, op. cit., p. II, for a further description of this period.
4. See Martin, L. W., "The Market for Strategic Ideas in Britain: the 'Sandys' era." *American Political Science Review 56*, March 1962, p. 23–6.
5. House of Commons Official Report, 24 January 1957, Column 396.
6. Martin, L. W., op. cit., p. 31.

7. Woodward, Rear Admiral Sir John, "The Falklands Experience," *RUSI Journal*, March 1983, p. 27.
8. See Hastings, Max, and Jenkins, Simon, *The Battle for the Falklands* (London: Michael Joseph, 1983), Chapter 17.
9. Howard, M., op. cit., p. 15.
10. Smith, R. Hastie, "The Tin Wedding" in the *Seaford House Papers* (London, 1974), p. 35 et seq.
11. Johnston, Lieutenant General Sir Maurice, "MOD Reorganization," *RUSI Journal*, March 1983, p. 9.
12. The creation of a National Defense College in 1971 to train officers in mid-career for defense staff duties could be seen as an important step towards creating a cadre of defense staff officers. However, subsequent decisions to shorten the course and change the syllabus have meant that, by 1983, the college has reverted to its pre-1971 role as a center for joint staff training. It cannot, in its present form, be seen as providing a true defense staff course.
13. Gibson, J. W., "Systems Analysis in British Policymaking," in *The Management of Defense*. Martin, L., (ed) (London, Macmillan Press, 1976), p. 97.

FIGURE 3A.[4] MOD Higher Organization (Spring 1982)[3]

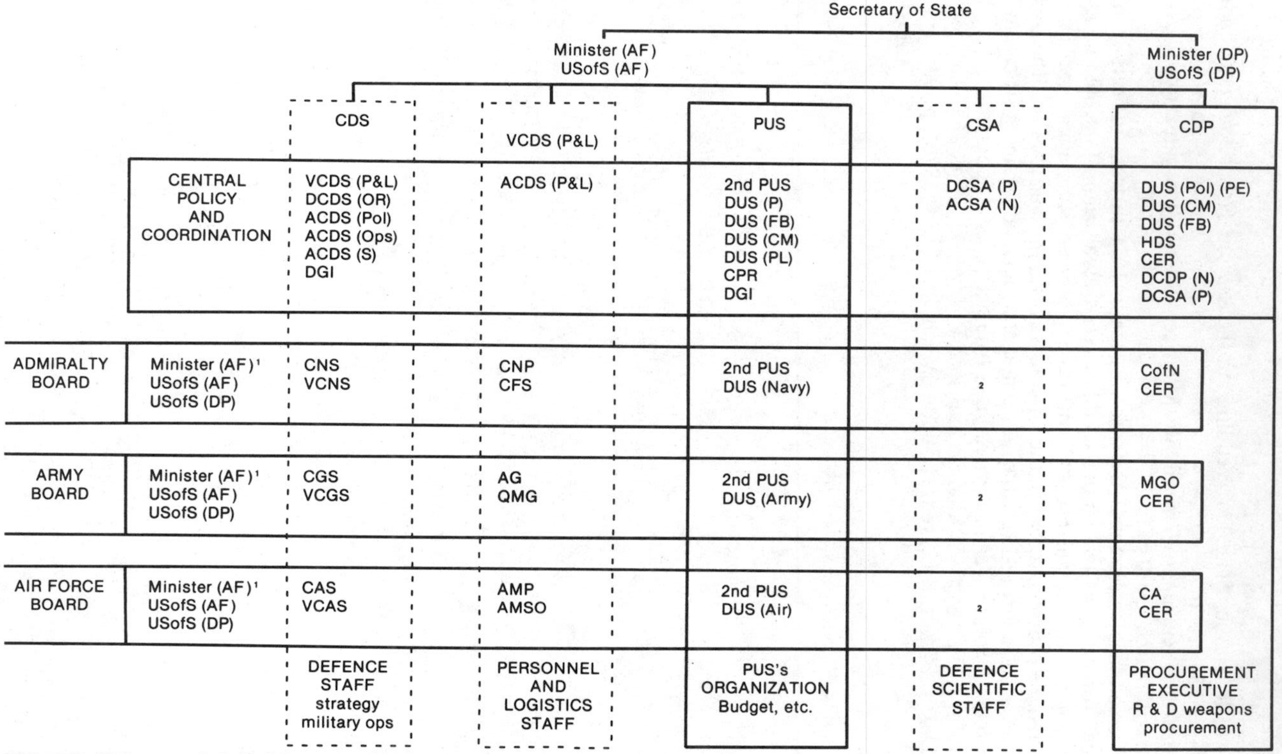

Secretary of State

| | Minister (AF) / USofS (AF) | | | Minister (DP) / USofS (DP) |
	CDS	VCDS (P&L)	PUS	CSA	CDP
CENTRAL POLICY AND COORDINATION	VCDS (P&L) DCDS (OR) ACDS (Pol) ACDS (Ops) ACDS (S) DGI	ACDS (P&L)	2nd PUS DUS (P) DUS (FB) DUS (CM) DUS (PL) CPR DGI	DCSA (P) ACSA (N)	DUS (Pol) (PE) DUS (CM) DUS (FB) HDS CER DCDP (N) DCSA (P)
ADMIRALTY BOARD Minister (AF)[1] USofS (AF) USofS (DP)	CNS VCNS	CNP CFS	2nd PUS DUS (Navy)	2	CofN CER
ARMY BOARD Minister (AF)[1] USofS (AF) USofS (DP)	CGS VCGS	AG QMG	2nd PUS DUS (Army)	2	MGO CER
AIR FORCE BOARD Minister (AF)[1] USofS (AF) USofS (DP)	CAS VCAS	AMP AMSO	2nd PUS DUS (Air)	2	CA CER
	DEFENCE STAFF strategy military ops	PERSONNEL AND LOGISTICS STAFF	PUS's ORGANIZATION Budget, etc.	DEFENCE SCIENTIFIC STAFF	PROCUREMENT EXECUTIVE R & D weapons procurement

[1] Normally Chairman on behalf of Secretary of State.
[2] Scientific advice to the Admiralty, Army and Air Force Boards is provided by CER.
[3] The only posts shown are those at and above three-star level (that is Lieutenant General and its equivalent service and civilian ranks).
[4] For key to acronyms, see separate list, following.

Acronyms used in Figure 3A.

ACDS (Ops)	Assistant Chief of the Defense Staff (Operations)
ACDS (Pol)	Assistant Chief of the Defense Staff (Policy)
ACDS (Sigs)	Assistant Chief of the Defense Staff (Signals)
ACSA	Assistant Chief Scientific Adviser
AG	Adjutant General
AMP	Air Member for Personnel
AMSO	Air Member for Supply and Organization
CA	Controller, Aircraft
CAS	Chief of the Air Staff
CDP	Chief of Defense Procurement
CDS	Chief of the Defense Staff
CER	Controller of Research and Development—Establishments and Research
CFS	Chief of Fleet Support
CGS	Chief of the General Staff
CNP	Chief of Naval Personnel
CNS	Chief of the Naval Staff
C of N	Controller of the Navy
CPR	Chief of Public Relations
DCDP (P)	Deputy Chief of Defense Procurement (Policy)
DCDS (OR)	Deputy Chief of the Defense Staff (Operational Requirements)
DCSA (P)	Deputy Chief Scientific Adviser (Policy)
DGI	Director General of Intelligence
DUS	Deputy Under Secretary
DUS (FB)	Deputy Under Secretary (Finance–Budget)
DUS (CM)	Deputy Under Secretary (Civilian Management)
DUS (P)	Deputy Under Secretary (Policy)
DUS (PL)	Deputy Under Secretary (Personnel and Logistics)
DUS (POL PE)	Deputy Under Secretary (Policy) (Procurement Executive)
HDS	Head of Defense Sales
MGO	Master-General of the Ordnance
PUS	Permanent Under Secretary of State
QMG	Quartermaster General
US of S (AF)	Parliamentary Under Secretary of State for Defense (Armed Forces)
US of S (P)	Parliamentary Under Secretary of State for Defense (Procurement)
VCAS	Vice Chief of the Air Staff
VCDS (PL)	Vice Chief of the Defense Staff (Personnel and Logistics)
VCDS	Vice Chief of the Defense Staff
VCNS	Vice Chief of the Naval Staff

Chapter 4

Defense Organization in Germany: A Twice Told Tale

Catherine McArdle Kelleher

INTRODUCTION

Of all the major industrialized states, the Federal Republic of Germany may have the least to offer in terms of lessons that can be generalized for the organization of a central defense establishment. Its system is not only quite new, it is also specifically organized to exercise neither broad operational control nor independent planning for standing national forces. Times of testing and change have come as a result of bureaucratic mismanagement and economic stringency, not through war experience or grand political design. Fundamentally, it is a system still in slow evolution, and is circumscribed by both domestic questioning and international controls.

Nonetheless, the German postwar experience is of clear significance for Americans interested in defense change and reform. In many ways, the German system represents a natural experiment, a self-conscious attempt to combine the best of American practices with both the continental administrative tradition and the dictates of parliamentary democracy. It constitutes a clear break with past patterns of military organization rooted in preconstitutional allegiance to the sovereign state and reflective of the social and political prominence of distinct military class. Its vulnerability to constant political oversight means that the points of change are sharply defined. And the integration of German forces into the NATO structure makes joint and combined operations the normal framework of national action.

The sources for this paper include a number of interviews with political and military leaders in Bonn and Washington in 1983 and 1984. Helpful criticisms and suggestions, not always taken, also came from J. Baldauf, H. Buch, W. Domke, R. Eichenberg, H. Linnenkamp, G. Mattox, and P. Schmitz.

Finally, the evolving German pattern may be of greater significance to America in terms of future choices than for present proposals. Until now, the German central defense organization has functioned most often as an "unstructured structure," dependent more on the harmonization of personalities and political styles than on formal rules for ultimate decisions. Hard economic times, together with new political pressures at home and within the alliance, will almost certainly force choices about future force structure and organization, and shifts in present patterns of influence, both civilian and military. These will provide new lessons, as well as critical new inputs for the American central defense organization, particularly that concerned with central front security.

THE CONTEXT OF CENTRAL DEFENSE ORGANIZATION IN THE FEDERAL REPUBLIC

Germany's central defense organization reflects the unique political–military context in which the Federal Republic has built and now maintains its defense. A critical alliance partner for more than twenty-five years, Germany is still the enemy of the past; the prod to three European civil wars in the last hundred years. The postwar solution of the "German question" through division was acceptable to ally and opponent alike. As the strongest of the continental European states, the Federal Republic has earned more than equity of treatment in its political and economic relations with the East, as with the West. German military programs, however, remain an area of constraint and suspicion where informal allied control, both politically and militarily, is still the norm.

Nowhere is this more obvious than in the structure of Bonn's standing forces, the Bundeswehr. Almost all German regular forces are assigned to Supreme Allied Commander, Europe (SACEUR) in peacetime, rather than simply allocated as are other NATO states. Moreover, at a specified level of NATO alert, all will come under the operational control of NATO commanders. In each of the seven relevant NATO commands, German forces constitute the major, but never the dominant, force element. Only two of these commands are always held by a German general officer. No freestanding German command structure exists above the corps level. In operational terms, it is a command pyramid without a top element. There is no German command reporting to the minister that controls a contiguously deployed total force, or which parallels the status of the headquarters of the U. S. Seventh Army, let alone a field or theater headquarters. Moreover, all powers of overall command (*Befehls-und Kommandogewalt*, not *Oberbefehl* as earlier) rests in peacetime with a political Minister of Defense. Only in conditions of war or grave emergency do these powers pass to the Chancellor.[1]

Apprehensions About German Military Autonomy

Several critical concerns dating from the early days of German rearmament sustain this structure as appropriate for a German military role. Many of Germany's closest allies are determined to learn from their mistakes of the 1920's and from the insufficiently-controlled German rearmament after World War I. The preferred solution in the immediate post World War II era was a complete break with all dysfunctional aspects of Germany's past (i.e., to set the clock at zero, at *Stunde Null*) and a rebuilding of German society from the bottom up. There were far-reaching prohibitions against all things military — ceremonies, writings, uniforms. Although discussed within three years of Germany's unconditional surrender, rearmament was envisaged only within an integrating, subsuming structure. This would continue the military controls of the occupation days and put direct restraints on Bonn's capacity for independent military action.

These restraints were, and in many ways still are, France's paramount concerns. They are to be pursued by a mixture of carrot-and-stick tactics of both French military prowess (especially nuclear), and cooperative Franco–German alliance. The most dramatic French attempt to capture German rearmament was the abortive European Defense Community (EDC) plan of 1950 to 1954. Rene Pleven's original conception allowed for autonomous German units only at the battalion level, and even these were to be embedded in a commonly-controlled support structure.[2] France's defeat of the EDC in 1954 led to direct German membership in NATO, but again, only after it was hedged by a formal system of control, the Western European Union (WEU) and its control protocols. Parallelling proposed EDC stipulations, these protocols established a new organization to monitor the maximum set for German manpower and the production and possession limits placed on German armament.

All of the restrictions are now lifted, save for those in Germany's direct political advantage (such as the ceilings on some offensive weapons systems and on atomic, biological, or chemical armaments). Today NATO is far more concerned with ensuring minimum troop strengths and in encouraging national investments in capital equipment and hardware. Moreover, the rapid creation of a national military command authority on a home battlefield is always possible and, some observers have remarked, not terribly difficult in an advanced industrial society. Yet, a German move to establish an autonomous national command would not only be impolitic at home, but would also stimulate political criticism in France, Britain, and Holland, not to mention in Eastern Europe and in the Soviet Union.[3]

It is also hard to see the net political gain to the Federal Republic of such actions, short, of course, of a major change in alliance patterns in Europe. The achievement of full normalization in its Eastern European relations has always seemed to Bonn to hinge on its full military integration into the West. The integration of NATO also provides Bonn with allied forces stationed on its territory that are responsive to its security requirements and susceptable to its political influence. Past struggles for equity and present plans for full modernization are posited on full force interchange, particularly with American forces, which constitute the second largest national contingent in the central front.[4] Most important of all, integration and interdependence mean continuing influence over the implementation of the American security guarantee, which most Germans still regard as the primary guarantee of their national security.

Germany's Tortured History of Civil–Military Relations

A related concern, significant for both international perceptions and domestic political calculations, is the tortured history of German civil-military relations. Establishment of a formal German military high command structure would presuppose a long-postponed sorting out of the strands of this complex relationship. The Federal Republic is the first German state structure to precede the creation of a national military establishment; it has, as yet, faced only minor tests of the new democratic political control over the Bundeswehr.

Most present critics, inside and outside Germany, see the major challenge to be renewed military dominance in central decisionmaking on security issues. The specter invoked is that of the German General Staff, often embellished by a historically inaccurate emphasis on the staff's antidemocratic role in the Weimar Republic and its assumed subordination during the Hitler period. But the debates basically turn on the role that the German military, especially the officer class, played in the defeat of democracy and constitutionalism before 1945.[5]

In simple terms, critics view the German military elite of the nineteenth and early twentieth centuries as both the foundation of and the beneficiary of the autocratic expansionist empire. The achievements of this elite were remarkable, not only in the Prussian past, but especially in the three quick, brilliantly executed wars of the period from 1860 through 1870. Yet, the cost was considerable. The army was a closed institution, with a constitutional life of its own, responsible only to the Kaiser and accorded virtually coequal status with the civilian government in foreign and defense policy. Its privilege was maintained only through the constant sacrifice of democratic values and the rights (and eventually the lives) of others. The result was a state rushing toward confrontation, a state bound largely to military ambition and the dictates of blind pursuit of imperial order and honor.

The mainspring of this institution, it is argued, was the General Staff, which nurtured and perpetuated militarism, not only in Germany but among its continental and American imitators as well. Its greatest achievement lay in the separation of military policy, and especially military planning, from political control and political requirements, whether domestic or international. At stake was the development of the highest standards of individual professional competence in service to the sovereign state, and a code of military ethics defined as superior to that of any other profession or political class. The staff's intellectual legacy came from its undisputed geniuses, from Clausewitz to Moltke. But its political heritage was the fine art of confrontation and compromise in defense of a military which formed a state within a state.

Under the empire, particularly under the Great Moltke, the General Staff seemingly exercised decisive influence over the selection of both ministers and foreign policy goals, and resisted all efforts to insure even a weak system of parliamentary accountability in defense matters. The end of World War I saw the imposed end of the General Staff—at least formally. Yet the system lived on—with a general military leadership aloof and separated from the political hurley-burley, subordinated only to the *Reichspraesident*, and able, through allies and their own devices, to overcome the *Diktat* of Versailles. Allegedly they were passive, if not unwilling, in the defense of the Republic against its many internal enemies, and a number supported Hitler to regain privilege and order, whatever the democratic costs.

Clearly, this argument holds true for a number of individuals (the notorious Ludendorff, for example) or for the role of the General Staff "red stripers" in earlier periods (particularly 1906–1914). But sweeping assertions about the unrelenting military drive for power and autonomy seem neither commensurate with all the historical evidence nor without major dispute in German historiography.[6] By the time of Bismarck's era, the position and influence of the German military was not unlike that of its continental counterparts, particularly the French. The arrogant authoritarianism, the repressive system of total obedience and class loyalty, the closed professionalism, the antidemocratic and antisocialist tendencies of the officer corps—all were at least as true for the French military from 1860 to 1914 (as the Dreyfus affair and General MacMahon well show, to mention only two examples) as for the German. The military itself was undergoing major changes and internal contradictions. As its social basis shifted, its primary technology changed, and its responsibilities, in Europe and outside of it, grew. The external image of a purposeful, aggressive, monolithic army, paralleling those of the empire and its political leadership, was, in many respects a mask. Inertia carried the past forward within a structure increasingly unable to escape criticism and constraint. New decisions were difficult; plans to catch the political future were neither possible nor conceivable.

The mystique of the General Staff was politically attractive, largely because it stood simultaneously for the best of the past and the hopes of the future. The General Staff's forte lay in systematic planning and the careful collection and exploitation of information prior to conflict, not in superior leadership or political–military acumen, or even policy direction which transcended Army operations. They represented an attempt, in T. N. Dupuy's formulation, to institutionalize excellence in a society undergoing rapid political, economic, and social change.[7] They drew largely from the landed aristocracy, but also from a growing number of nonaristocratic officers, often better trained and educated than the fabled *Junker* officers. Their protected position came through a series of able chiefs (especially after Bismarck's fall), from their social prestige, and from their generally self-conscious attempt to act in a studiously nonpolitical manner.[8]

The high point of General Staff influence came just before World War I; their proclaimed "abandonment by the State" during that war became their frustrated, embittered theme throughout much of Weimar, and hampered both their integration and their effectiveness in the Republic. No less important was what many saw as their military failure—their inability to adapt to new technological constraints, their rigid adherence to plans overtaken by events, and their mistakes in coordination and organization after the initial phases of the war. As David Schoenbaum has argued, the Schlieffen Plan can be viewed as the Staff's ultimate product: "continuing strategic vision, historical extrapolation, technical virtuosity, and disasterous political naivete."[9] Others might have conceived similar plans and even carried them through but "without the consistency and astigmatism that made German general [and the staff] both better and worse than their foreign colleagues."

Close examination of the military's relationsnip to Hitler also reveals somewhat contradictory tendencies. The armed forces, and especially the Army, might well have done more to oppose Hitler's coming to power. It is however questionable whether the army leadership would have found the necessary republican allies or legitimation in what was, after all, a democratic process for direct military action to bar the events of 1933 and 1934. Once Hitler assumed dictatorial powers, he moved to co-opt and change the military itself—the ultimate exercise of civilian control, however illegitimate.[10] The Nazis sought to destroy the military elite, both as a whole and as individuals. Their aim was to subvert professional ties and standards, to prevent the further evolution of a separate military professionalism, and to popularize the officer classes with rapid promotion of Hitler's favorites and the creation of People's Generals (like Rommel, from nonaristocratic backgrounds). The vast majority of officers soldiered on, remaining, however unhappily, bound within their primary responsibilities to their professional ethic and their sworn oath to defend the state in the person of Hitler. There were efforts by some military at *Putsch*, the most serious being those in Munich during 1938 and the series of attempts leading to the July 20 plot in 1944. But in the view of a number of critics, German and non-German, these are interpretable as plans to restore the old order based on military expertise and authority, as well as designs to overthrow a governmental system gone mad.

In objective terms, the distinction between political irresponsibility and conspiracy, even if in support of somewhat reactionary goals, seems a choice between equal evils. In the specific case of Hitler's Germany, given a knowledge of the outcomes involved, the lesser evil is clear. Those who created the new Bundeswehr acted on this assessment: the military and civil servants who planned the Bundeswehr from 1950 to 1954 in *Amt Blank* and those parliamentarians (as the CSU Richard Jaeger) involved in day-to-day oversight of that planning.[11] Their aim was not simply to overturn the elite General Staff tradition or to change the excessive disciplinary practices or social isolation practiced on and by the lower ranks. Rather, it was to establish and foster the system of *Innere Fuehrung*, of reliance on individual conscience and protection of the rights of the soldier as citizen. Perhaps most famous were the words attributed to the founding father, Wolf Graf Baudissin — those which spoke of the "citizen in uniform." From this perspective the soldier is recognized first as a citizen and is expected to accept military discipline and individual constraint only within the limits set by his individual conscience.

For the bulk of the present German population, both sets of apprehensions reflect a largely inarticulate sense that the limits of the military role in the Bonn Republic are somehow not yet fixed. The social status of officers is now higher than at the low points in the 1950s; it is now an acceptable, if no longer a socially desirable, profession for one's son.[12] The potential for stronger discipline is welcomed by the older generation on what they see as soft, self-indulgent younger citizens who have forgotten the old values and past achievements. But most see the pursuit of peace as the nation's highest priority, and agree that defense spending is more or less right, if not a little too high, and that nuclear war, now perceived as more imminent than before, would mean Armageddon.[13] Neither the military nor the politicians, at home or among allies, are to be supported if their acts mean that war in Europe becomes more probable. The majority believe that the military can and should be part of the society which they are to defend, if only because the threat of nuclear war places maximum importance on the maintenance of deterrence and a defensive national security posture.

Security as an Ambiguous National Political Symbol

Indeed, the third core element structuring the context of German defense decisionmaking is the wide-spread ambivalence among both elites and the general public towards the political symbols of national security.

Throughout most of the Federal Republic's existence, defense policy has been the aspect of state activity most visibly consigned to the experts. However large its claim on the federal budget, defense was generally immune from prolonged, continuous debate about medium-term goals or the effectiveness of overall policy. The broad questions of NATO membership and nuclear defense seemingly had been settled in the wracking debates of the 1950s, and broad policy was now largely the province of alliance political and military leaders. For most Germans, and most parliamentarians, the further details were of little direct consequence, except in cases of obvious mismanagement of weapons procurement or direct bureaucratic challenge within the ministry. In these instances, the focus was partisan politics or the avoidance of military dominance, in general terms.

In many respects, these attitudes flowed directly from Konrad Adenauer's approach, both to defense issues and to the problems of domestic political stability. The first Chancellor was, in the words of one observer, "the compleat civilian," throughout his career the political foe of Prussian militarism and military ascendancy. He pursued rearmament at a very early point because of its utility for the full political rehabilitation of Germany and its firm integration into the postwar West, away from the temptations of the East. The domestic costs were clear: the intensity of popular opposition, the competition with the requirements of postwar economic reconstruction, and the need for an early confrontation with the unburied past, both Nazi and military. The existence of German forces would only emphasize Germany's political vulnerability to both allies and opponents. This would reveal its dependence for basic security upon NATO and establish continuing good, if not real, grounds for charges of renewed German interest in military adventure.

Therefore, Adenauer's approach was to focus attention only on the central decisions — the joining of NATO, full participation in the alliance on as equal a basis as possible, and a minimization of imposed control. The details could then be left to the experts, civilian and military, for consideration out of the public eye and with as little parliamentary or public attention as possible. So far as possible, the Defense Ministry was to pursue a low public profile, as should the Bundeswehr in both national and international forums. Moreover, if there would, indeed, ever be an appropriate time for prolonged debate on defense or reconsideration of the basic decisions of the 1950s, it would come only after economic prosperity and political stability in the new democracy had been fully assured.

The consignment of defense matters to the experts was also in tune with the initial decade of raising the Bundeswehr. The learning requirements were fairly steep; the civilian and military leadership had much to learn in terms of possible technological options, the channels of increasing NATO influence, and the difficulties of raising a fully equipped armed force of nearly a half-million within ten years. Adenauer's approach seemed even more appropriate during the time of NATO's *Harmel Report*, which set forth the strategy of seeking both defense and detente during the period of greatest East-West detente in the early 1970s.[14]

In continuing cycles, however, both the substance and the process of defense decisionmaking broke to the forefront of public discussion. In part, this was a consequence of the strong political leaders attracted to and selected for the post of Defense Minister. At least half of the Defense Ministers have been potential candidates for the Chancellorship; at least that number — Strauss, Schröder, Schmidt, and Wörner — have had both strong personalities and independent ideas about strategy, defense organization, and the political-military requirements of alliance membership. Moreover, all German Defense Ministers have faced at least one major public controversy during their tenure — over their attempts to move towards new, more demanding programs or force structures or simply to control perhaps the most unwieldy of Bonn's bureaucracies.

Indeed, the struggle to overcome a decade of noninvolvement in things military led to a series of ill-informed or simply mistaken decisions about weapons and procedures. In the first phase of rearmament, Strauss's attempts to ensure a technological "great leap forward" created a string of parliamentary investigations and public scandals about weapons procurement. So too did implicit pressures from various allies for the purchase of particular weapons or support systems. In addition, the policy of a clean break with the military past often faltered in choosing which elements of that tradition could and should be maintained. Even now, the limits are not certain, either in ceremonial honors to past heroes or in the tradeoffs between efficiency and the new systems of discipline and authority. The implementation of a thoroughgoing system of Innere Fuehrung has meant constant debate, challenge, and reconsideration — even from those who are among its most enthusiastic supporters.

Most critical of all was the realization, often to be discovered anew by each new political generation, of the implications of Germany's fate as the most likely site of European conflict, however improbable such conflict increasingly appeared. The specific ebb and flow of political debate had much to do with the particular concerns or changes in American military strategy, particularly in terms of nuclear use. The discussions were often muted, dominated by expert debates and the unwillingness, even among political elites, to focus on the requirements of actual defense, rather than those of a deterrence posture. But since the late 1970s, the implications of strategic nuclear parity, and the West's basic dependence on nuclear weapons, both for deterrence and for direct defense in Europe, have led to widespread political mobilization. There is new availability of detailed information on defense, and some evidence that this debate phase will become routinized within German schools and churches.[15] This particular cycle may now be in the downturn phase. In all probability, it will surface again, especially as

Bonn faces the hard economic and political choices inherent in its relations, both with the Soviet Union and with its NATO allies in the 1980s and the 1990s.

THE PRESENT GERMAN CENTRAL DEFENSE ORGANIZATION

The central defense organization which has emerged from this political–military context is a relatively unique mixture of organic and adapted elements, largely new, but with traces of the past. Its major players and decisionmaking procedures parallel those in other parliamentary democracies. But a number reflect the requirements imposed by alliance membership, the continuing national and international distrust of past military tendencies, and the ambiguity surrounding the politics of national security in the Federal Republic.

The Defense Executive: Political Control

The hub of all German defense decisionmaking is the Defense Minister. Under the German Cabinet system, the Defense Minister enjoys a significant degree of ministerial autonomy within the general policy guidelines established by the Chancellor. Most Ministers have also had an independent political constituency and have held their post at their own behest. Only two of eight have been explicitly forced from office, the unlucky Theodor Blank charged with initial planning and implementation, and Franz Josef Strauss, dismissed for his abuse of ministerial power in the *Spiegel* affair of 1962.[16]

According to the formal definition given in the 1979 White Paper, the Minister "commands, controls, and manages the Bundeswehr, develops long-term political-military goals, and defines and delineates the limits and objectives of Bundeswehr planning." All instructions and directives are issued either by or on behalf of the minister, a symbol of the primacy of civilian political control, even over day-to-day Bundeswehr operations. Moreover, in sharpest contrast to the patterns of the past the minister is "the supreme authority over all servicemen, exercising both administrative control and disciplinary power."[17]

The defense executive also includes the supporting state secretaries, now four in number and roughly equivalent in rank to an American under secretary. The political deputy is the Parliamentary State Secretary, senior officials drawn from within the ministry or the higher federal civil service act as State Secretary for Armament, for Policy, and for Administration, respectively. All four may act in the name of the minister and, since the Apel Reforms, exercise independent, although accountable, powers in their functional areas of responsibility. The specific division of labor has been subject to frequent change as the result of individual ministerial styles, formal reforms, and the meshing of particular politicians and senior civil servants.

Below the defense executive is a system of mixed functional and service departments, involving military and civilian employees (Figure 4.1). At present this comprises five military departments (the Armed Forces Staff, the Army, Air Force, and Navy Staff, and the Directorate of Medical and Health Services) and six major ministerial divisions (Budget, Personnel, Administrative and Legal Affairs, Armament, Quartering and Facilities, and Social Services). There are numerous points of overlap and redundancy, often involving several chains of authority. Each of the military service chiefs, and the General Inspector, the head of the joint Armed Forces Staff, is also subordinate to the minister as a department head. There are also important functional offices directly responsible and responsive to the minister: the Information and Press Office, the Organization Staff, and the Planning Staff.

A final formal structure is a set of ministerial conferences that provide both a channel and a vehicle for authoritative decisions and allocations within the ministry. The most frequently convened is the Heads of Division Conference (ALK), chaired by the minister, and which meets at regular intervals. Formerly under Hans Apel, and now under the present Minister, Manfred Wörner, there is usually a weekly meeting. Other meetings are specially convened, as was the Armaments Conference during the budgetary crisis of 1980 and 1981 for matters of particular importance. Wörner has largely carried out his intention to call a quarterly planning conference, modelled on industrial practices.[18] He has attended at least two of these meetings, which stressed the continuing interrelationship between the present budget and armament profiles, and planning for both the short- and long-term.

There has been a basic division in the way in which the eight Defense Ministers have defined and implemented their command and control functions. The clearest differences emerged in the styles of the three "activist" Defense Ministers—Strauss, Schmidt, and Wörner. Each entered with recognized expertise, with ideas for policy actions, and with a political legacy to be overcome. Strauss was the man of action after the somewhat hapless Blank—ambitious, combative, and vocal, both in domestic and alliance forums. Schmidt came to power as the first Socialist Defense Minister since Weimar, after a series of procurement scandals and explosive military resignations under von Hassel and Schröder. Wörner has had a double challenge: (1) to reinstitute calm after the ministry upheavals caused by the Tornado financing difficulties; and (2) to reshape Bundeswehr planning and budgeting for economic austerity and the coming drop in available manpower for conscription. One challenge, however, remained constant: to

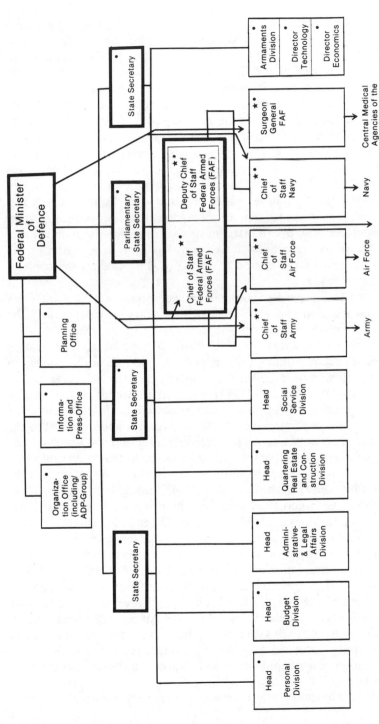

* *Member of the Permanent Conference of the Heads of Divisions (ALK)*
★ *Member of the Federal Armed Forces Defense Council*

FIGURE 4.1. System of Mixed Functional and Service Departments

bring the ministry under a control which both satisfied parliamentary (and increasingly public) critics, and quieted international questioning.

The tools they used reflected not only the direction of criticism but also the evolutionary phases of the Bundeswehr itself. Strauss unsuccessfully sought a new organizational basis for ministerial policy direction. His efforts to develop an expert analytic group (*Leitungsstab*) responsive to the minister laid the foundations for what emerged under Schmidt as the Planning Staff (*Plannungsstab*). As it has evolved under successive ministers, the staff is at its best in direct ministerial support, made up of "the best and the brightest," balanced in the direction of the minister's politics, but not his partisans, and selected from military and civilian officials. It has been used variously, to generate both broad statements and special studies, to act as a fire brigade to compensate for temporary organizational weakness, or to insure a Minister's control over a difficult or sensitive issue. Its function as a link, particularly to the military leadership, has been a reflection of the minister's style and of the degree of difficulty surrounding the contemporary defense agenda.

Schmidt also emphasized organizational tools, but for a very different goal: the consolidation and revision of fifteen years' experience with the Bundeswehr. By his own authority, he issued several fundamental decrees, notably the *Blankeneser Erlass* of March 1970, the first formal specification of the interacting responsibilities of the political and military leadership in ministerial and governmental affairs.[19] Similarly, he directed formalization of new procurement procedures (1971) and specification of clearer lines of disciplinary authority (1970). Each was preceded by intensive internal discussions and negotiations; each received informal approval within the Cabinet's Federal Security Council (*Bundesverteidungsrat*) and was discussed with parliamentary leaders. These edicts, and those that have followed, however, are seen as being within the "household" autonomy of the minister, and his role as peacetime head of the Bundeswehr.

Towards his external constituencies, Schmidt made good use of two other instruments. The first was the White Paper on Defense, an expansion on an earlier Schröder initiative. Coordinated through and largely prepared by the Planning Staff, this is a major statement on the national security agenda, on actions already taken, plans for the future, and questions still outstanding. As clear signals, if not always comprehensive explanations, of contemporary German defense policy, these White Papers are best compared with the Report to Congress prepared annually by the American Secretary of Defense. Continued by Schmidt's successors, they have ranked far above those prepared by most European governments and, somewhat paradoxically, have often enjoyed a wider public audience outside of the Federal Republic than within it.

A final, somewhat more controversial management tool was Schmidt's use of outside experts. This might involve a single individual — such as the calling in of Ernst Wolf Mommsen, a leader in private industry, in 1970, to help avoid further procurement scandals. A more extensive effort was the convening of an independent expert group, the *Wehrstruktur* or Force Structure Commission, charged with examining alternative models for future German force posture.[20] Reporting directly to the minister, the group involved military and civilian officials, many of whom came into the ministry for the duration of the study, from positions of outside expertise. The conclusions, in essence, foresaw only incremental change. But the report, as subsequently published, represented the most searching, vigorous, and public examination of both the costs and future options for the organization of German defense.

In each approach, Schmidt sought several aims. He wanted to: (1) seize hold and dampen discussion within the ministry and government; (2) define the policy agenda in his terms; and (3) create a framework within which to elicit and/or insure public acceptance. On the whole he was successful, and he ended his unexpectedly brief term as minister having won general recognition for his fairness and renewed respect from his military subordinates. Perhaps more significantly, parliamentary criticisms returned to a relatively low level with little public attention or interest.

The difficulties in these approaches to the problems of a maturing Bundeswehr were perhaps more evident under Schmidt's successors. Hans Apel, faced with mounting difficulties surrounding Tornado procurement, turned to another set of industrial consultants, Manfred Ehmcke and the McKinsey Company, for proposals regarding better procurement control.[21] He also suggested the creation of the post of controller, under the minister, to ensure direct continuous financial oversight. Furthermore, he convoked a mixed commission — civilian and military, public and private sector — on the requirements of long-term planning for the Bundeswehr of the 1990s. Chaired by General Inspector Juergen Brandt, this group was to review and suggest changes in all planning aspects — personnel, materiel, organization, infrastructure and financing.[22]

The relative lack of success each of these efforts enjoyed was a combination of many factors — the personalities involved, unforeseen events, and the narrowing room for policy maneuver within an increasingly divided coalition government. Of particular impact, however, were three aspects, all related to the growing signficance of structure as the Bundeswehr has matured. The first was the observable *lack of general consensus* among the ministry's military and civilian leadership, especially the division between the minister and the service chiefs over procurement issues, and managerial responsibilities, and lines of authority. The second was the *prior involvement* of public and parliamentary groups with stakes in change, and few incentives for compromise. The third was the *nature* of the Bundeswehr's problems, once its twentieth year had passed. Expenditures for force modernization or third-generation procurement were far less defensible than those associated with the earlier rearmament dynamic or those presented as special investments required by Alliance obligations in the 1950s and 1960s.

Moreover, the involvement of special expert groups from outside the ministry and the use of mixed commissions were less and less useful. A more confident military and civilian group within the ministry resented the assumption of competence accorded to outsiders. Without an insider–outsider coalition, such expert assessments were simply unacceptable. Parliamentarians, many with increasing interest and expertise in defense issues, believed they were thus shut out, or inadequately briefed about problems they should decide. The outsiders proved both less interested and less supportive of objectives formulated by ideal evolutions in the long-term future. At issue was not the overcoming of the past but decisions at the moment and ways in which choices would be implemented in the future. Furthermore, the choices for the future were no longer an adequate defense of present turbulence and policy and managerial shortfalls.

Military Leadership: Control and Some Command

The Bundeswehr's military leadership structure has been subject to continuing controversy and change since inception. The strains are familiar ones—the tensions between services, between the service chiefs and the joint General Inspector (GI), and between the minister and all or most of the military leadership. The difficulties have been magnified, however, by the painful evolution of the Bundeswehr structure and the strong political sanctions against any evocation of the military past. In a very direct sense, every effort has been made to avoid any hint of a General Staff, of an autonomous, self-steering military. Indeed, over the past ten years or so, there are signs of what seems to be overcompensation—the drawing into politics of the top military leadership. Critics—inside as well as outside the military establishment—argue that not only is their tenure politically determined; not only do they act as political–military advisors to minister and government; they themselves have become political players—in outlook, in behavior, and, ultimately, in their acceptance of responsibility.

The General Inspector. At the head is the General Inspector (GI), who is designated as the principal military advisor to the minister and to the federal government.[23] The General Inspector sits in his own right as a nonvoting member of the Cabinet's Federal Security Council and can be called on by that body or by the Chancellor to answer questions or provide, formally or informally, an expert or advisory opinion. The GI's term is not fixed and is affected by, but not coterminous with, the normal cycle of governmental elections (four years). Formally, at least, the GI may be drawn from any command. Appointment by the Chancellor has, in practice, been a function of both personal ability and acceptability to the party in power. The pool from which the GI and the service chiefs are drawn is fairly well defined: those officers who have completed the advanced course at the *Fuehrungsakademie*, who have major command experience, and who have had major exposure in NATO, at least at the staff level. The most favored service has been the Army, hardly surprising, given its numerical and historical predominance. The present General Inspector is Wolfgang Altenburg, the ninth since 1955 and the first GI without World War II experience (see Appendix at the end of this chapter).

The relation of the GI to the other service chiefs is still evolving and has more than once involved fundamental conflicts over authority and policy direction. The major formal basis is still Schmidt's decree of 1970, and a few authoritative clarifications by Apel and Wörner. The parliamentary Tornado inquiry, for example, led to Apel's strong reaffirmation of the GI's pilot responsibility for overall Bundeswehr planning—including for procurement and financing, broadly defined, and for the distribution of resources among broad service and functional categories. The GI is enjoined to consult with the service chiefs but exercises "executive authority" over them in planning and in the implementation of an "overall concept of military defense." Wörner has indeed defined the GI's role as one of *primacy* in planning, and in ensuring that the individual service financial plans stay within the guidelines hammered out with the Finance Ministry. He has also expanded the range of the GI's responsibilities still further— especially towards the harmonizing and coordinating of service views on how to meet the economic, demographic, and social constraints that will shape the Bundeswehr in the 1990s.[24]

The planning instrument is probably the most powerful means available to the GI and the Deputy GI, who has day-to-day responsibility. Involved is the work of the Armed Forces Staff (Fu S) carried out in cooperation with the service staffs, the Procurement Division and the Budget Office. Prior to 1968, the services put forward their own plans and budgets. In the 1970s, the products were the Bundeswehr Five-Year Program (medium-term) and the Force Plan (long-term). These are now coordinated in an overall Armed Forces Plan (*Bundeswehrplan*), which not only provides the basis for annual budgetary estimates but also allows fifteen-year budgetary projections for closer monitoring of costs and, hopefully, cross-project comparisons.

The *Fuehrungsstab* itself is probably the most consistently significant *structural* element in German military policymaking, but it evokes few shades of the earlier General Staff tradition. Its members are officers appointed for specific terms by each of the services. All are graduates of the advanced course of the *Fuehrungsakademie* and, therefore, are entitled to use the "GS" in their military rank designation. Almost all, however, have also had extensive line and service responsibilities, and are dependent on service judgments alone for further professional advancement. The staff has seven interrelated divisions, each headed by a general or an admiral (Figure 4.2). In the past, Division I (Personnel), responsible always for at least 40% of the budget, and Division III (Military Policy) with broad political–military tasks, have been preeminent. Under Wörner and Altenburg, Division VI (Planning) has been given new responsibilities and greater scope for coordination and oversight.

In his military–political functions, the GI seems to rely most heavily on Division III, headed at present by a Major General with a Brigadier General as deputy. It is further divided into nine offices (*Referate*), each a group of seven to ten lieutenant colonels under a full colonel. These officers not only assume responsibility for their issues (e.g., military relations with NATO and WEU, military operations, arms control), but also, since the 1970s, coordinate directly both with the Minister's Planning Staff and with the corresponding groups in the Foreign Office, and the Chancellor's Office.

Thus, the GI's role is clearly a mixture of political tasks, as well as military responsibilities. The GI's direct operational responsibilities are to the minister. It is within this framework that the GI acts as an advisor to the cabinet, as a nonvoting member of the Federal Security Council and as the representative to the NATO Military Committee. Disagreement outside of the ministry is neither welcome nor common.

There is an inevitable tension between the GI's role as *primus inter pares* with the service chiefs and his position of principal military advisor. Any attempt to impose a joint or overall perspective on a heated service issue brings criticism. One example of this was the Air Force's objections to GI Harald Wust's efforts to centralize support functions. Another example involved service opposition in 1981 to GI Juergen Brandt's failure to mount a sufficiently energetic defense (particularly for the Air Force regarding the Roland program) against Apel's search for budget-balancing reductions.[25] A third example was the critique of two service chiefs against Apel himself (and therefore against Brandt), which leaked during Weinberger's first visit and which reflected a struggle within the ministry over managerial and planning responsibilities.[26] The weapons in the hands of the service chiefs are familiar to American observers: the control over the present quality and the professional future of officers assigned to the joint staff; the ability to develop coalitions or a united front against the GI; the tactical skills to delay or ignore coordination efforts; and the invocation of service identity and loyalty. The GI must fundamentally rely on his or her relationship with the minister. Without this, the GI has no alternative but to resign. However, in all but the most extreme cases, the GI has usually attempted to lead by persuasion or by consensus.

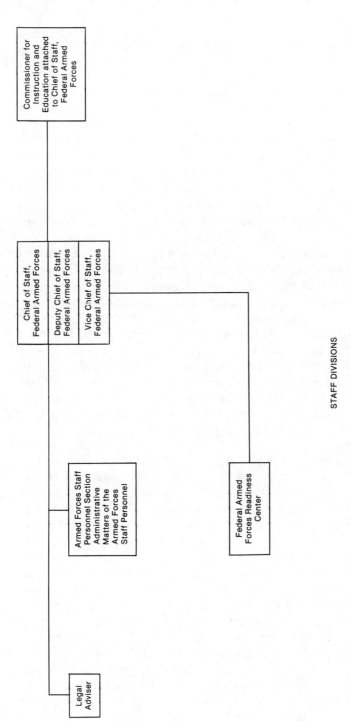

FIGURE 4.2. Armed Forces Staff

Yet, the GI's relationship with the minister has often been less than easy. The past twenty-five years have seen some marked disagreements, such as GI Trettner with von Hassel over excessive "civilianization" and "unionization" of the Bundeswehr, and Wust with Apel on a cluster of questions arising out of ministerial operations. Most have been the result of personal and political disagreements, overlaid by great differences in style and expectations of change. Some ministers, such as Leber, have sought to preserve their access to the service chiefs. Sharp disputes have eventually led to resignations (Trettner, Wust) or early retirements among other service chiefs. A number of lesser difficulties among other officials have been at least partially submerged in daily practice, or after political intervention. As one former GI remarked in a recent interview, "It's a job guaranteed to satisfy no one — neither the Minister, not the service peers, not even yourself."

To be effective, the primary prerequisite is a strong degree of mutual respect and broad agreement between minister and GI. Several former officials cited, as a most dramatic case, the breakdown of the relationship between Apel and Wust in 1978.[27] Indeed, in his official resignation Wust, not altogether disingenuously, stated his primary reason for resignation as the failure of the minister to rely on him for primary military advice. Wust charged Apel with going directly to the Joint Staff on issues without prior consultation, with ignoring established planning procedures, and with relegating Wust's direct reporting function only to the level of State Secretary. Alleged to be in sharp contrast is at least the initial relationship between Wörner and Altenburg, the latter of whom has repeatedly been recognized as being in charge of military coordination.

The Service Chiefs. The GI's informal relation to the service chiefs is greatly affected by the state of their respective relations with the minister. Each service chief reports directly to the minister in his command functions, as well as to a division head through the General Inspector. The service chief is recognized as having primary responsibility in all questions relating to the combat readiness (*Einsatzbereitschaft*), and disciplinary power (*Diziplinargewalt*) through the service role (*truppendienstliche Unterstellung*).[28] This guaranteed access was established in 1970, after nearly a decade of dispute over the interference of ministry civil servants in military affairs, even down to the battalion level. Implicit, too, was the perceived interference of the GI, who does not have any powers of direct command over forces but who does have the right of independent inspection of all military forces and installations, which allows broad scope for comment and questioning.

Under the present structure, the service chiefs sit with the Inspector General, his deputy, and the Surgeon General, as the Federal Armed Forces Defense Council (*Militaerische Fuehrungsrat*). Their formal charge is to "arrive at unity of purpose" on issues of general concern to the military forces. As with its American counterpart, much of the council's work represents the validation of outcomes previously bargained out. Plans and joint declarations receive thorough review on the service staff level before full council submission. Members of the Armed Forces Staff report to the GI but are primarily subject to their services for promotion and subsequent assignment. From 1969 to 1982, most resource allocations for procurement were done on a relatively rigid service share basis—with the ratios 50:30:20 for Army, Air Force, and Navy, respectively, reflecting relative size and equipment unit costs.

The services derive some measure of control, as well, from their direct integration into all ministry functions. In the past, this often constituted a negative veto in the often confusing, intertwined channels of civilian and military reporting authority. One example, highlighted in the Tornado inquiry and the subject by one of Apel's 1981 reforms, was the complex role of System Manager (SM) for a major weapons project. The Tornado SM was responsible to the Air Force Inspector for military affairs, and to the Armament Division for technical, economic, and contractual matters, Until 1981, there was no clear priority in responsibility, especially in terms of cost control. This was complicated by the residual oversight powers of the Budget Division, reporting to a second state secretary regarding the preparation of budget estimates and acting with sole responsibility for actual expenditures. Under the Apel reforms, the Tornado SM is now firmly established with the Air Force staff, with continuing secondary accountability to a clearly responsible Head of Armament.[29]

Centralized Functions. The period of 1970 to 1983 witnessed several attempts to expand centralization and rationalization of defense operations and control. Perhaps the most far reaching were the attempts towards centralization of those military functions under national control that were made by General Inspector Wust, first under Defense Minister Leber and then under Apel. Wust's mandate was broad ministerial support and the recommendations of the Force Structure Commission under the Model III guidelines: to streamline and reorganize ministry operations against costly redundancy and inefficient rigidity. A further basis was the explicit recognition, in the 1960s, that Germany's forward defense required the "joint, common" operations of all three services. A final, less obvious, factor, was the recognition of the need to establish clear lines of responsibility, to allow, in the words of one interviewee "the accountable, efficient administration of the deficits that were surely to come."

A number of these centralizing initiatives were reflected in the 1975/1976 *White Paper*, issued by Defense Minister Leber.[30] Explicitly contrasted were two models. Model A was the "pilot service approach," in which one service is assigned a common *functional* responsibility for all—as an Army mandate for the development of all wheeled vehicles for the total Bundeswehr. The preferred approach was Model B, the rationalization of common functions under the General Inspector. This consolidation, envisaged as a "first step toward a functional reorganization of the armed forces into a combat and a support component," included the centralization of five functions:

- Long lines communication support
- Electronic reconnaissance
- Intelligence support
- Medical support
- Logistic support

The primary area of interest, particularly for Wust, was the last item, a common centralized logistical command. The overarching framework was to be a central support organization (the Armed Forces Support Command), operating for both the regular Bundeswehr and the Territorial Reserves (TV) under national command. It was to be placed immediately under the Armed Forces Staff and divided into several mission-specific agencies. After several years, when commonality had been established, there was to be a general review of the overall Bundeswehr command structure.

The centralization struggle was extremely intense and continued into Apel's first year as Defense Minister. The opposition, within but also outside the ministry, succeeded in blunting most of the initiatives. Apel was not particularly interested; the troubled Wust–Apel relationship was a factor and there were few political incentives. No service chief was willing to totally surrender any function, each arguing about his inability to insure combat readiness. The 1979 *White Paper* reflected the final results: (1) the reorganization of intelligence, medical, and to a lesser degree, communications support; and (2) the assignment of all other common functions, either to pilot services or to territorial commands. The basic assessment was:

> The possible increase in effectiveness [of a central support organization] would not be in acceptable proportion to the additional cost, major structural and procedural changes, and the personal hardship involved for servicemen and their families.

A provision was made that "there will be no separate operations of any individual service."[31]

None of the present changes under Manfred Wörner suggest a rebirth of interest in formal centralization efforts. He has reinforced the existing powers of the General Inspector, and insured rationalization of existing functional overlaps through more rigorous application of the pilot service approach. His explicit order for the new "1990s" study indicates the need for competitive assessment among planned projects, and tightened monitoring of the procurement and budgetary implications of present programs. Several interviews in Bonn, in 1983 and 1984, emphasized that: (1) present service budget requests had overshot the five-year estimated levels by at least one-third; and (2) Altenburg had been empowered to "crack heads" to bring expenditures within bounds. Furthermore, Wöener had also decided not to go ahead with the centralization of the civilian staff planned by Apel.[32] There will not be a new post of controller and the audit agency will be subsumed under existing divisions.

FUTURE PROSPECTS: A POSTSCRIPT

The prospects for the future evolution of the German central defense organization are somewhat uncertain. At the outset of the Kohl government, the turbulence and debate which has been the hallmark of the past seem stilled. There had been a significant clarification of the lines of administrative and military responsibility in favor of the General Inspector. Wörner seemed both able and interested in assuming direct managerial responsibility within the ministry.

Much of that calm and rationalizing momentum seems to have been sacrificed late in 1983, in the turmoil surrounding the forced retirement and then the reinstatement of General Kiesling. Whatever the root causes, Wörner's control of his ministry was severely tested and, in the opinion of his critics, found wanting. The response of the retired military, the *ad hominem* character of the parliamentary inquiry, the resignation and transfer of senior ministry officials — all suggested points of political and administrative vulnerability.

Calm has again been restored but, to many, its continuation for any indefinite period appears doubtful. The principal source of conflict will not be any particular personality but, rather, the adjustments that must be made in future expenditures. There seems almost no chance that the ministry will receive additional resources in the years ahead, and considerable likelihood that their share of real resources will fall. At a time in which each service has already embarked on a major weapons system acquisition, as well as an overall modernization, hard choices and continuing turmoil appear virtually certain.

A further complication, a major demographic shrinkage in the pool of available conscripts, has long been foreseen, but not yet been offset. Short of continued high unemployment, the cost of personnel will almost surely rise, and the need for force reorganization will dominate the ministry's political agenda. A Bundeswehr of 430,000 or less by 1995 seems to many as almost inevitable without major restructuring. Parliament and public will be attentive from the first, given the limiting effects of the present law on conscientious objection, and present resistance to changes in draft terms or reserve obligation beyond those now foreseen. Proposals for the inclusion of women, which go beyond the projected 15,000 level, or for the induction of foreign workers and their children, merely increase the level of attention and the number of political tasks, both domestic and international, involved.

Should these not prove sufficient stimuli for change, there is the emerging German debate on NATO strategy. The focus of attention is the set of conventionalization options current in the American and Alliance discussions — ranging from no-first-use and direct conventional substitution to the various plans advanced under the air-land battle rubric. The most vocal opponents of INF seek reconsideration in favor of a conventional option. Others, most notably the Social Democratic Party (SPD) center, are searching for a new defense concept around which to regroup. The civilian and military leadership of the ministry cannot escape the debate, even if they adopt merely a reactive stance.

These challenges will, in all probability, force yet another reconsideration of the fundamental questions posed at the outset of this essay. What will be the limits of independent analysis and independent decision within the ministry itself, and in discussion with its domestic critics and alliance partners? What role can now be ceded to military leadership and expertise? What levels of confidence and trust can be ensured among a population appropriately fearful of war, conventional or nuclear, on its own territory? What assurance can be given about the changing nature of deterrence and defense?

New balances will have to be struck; new rules set in a more formal style. But the basic points of tension and direct constraint will almost certainly remain, as will the domestic and international political consensus which support them.

NOTES

1. The Federal Minister of Defense, *White Paper: The Security of the Federal Republic of Germany and the Development of the Federal Armed Forces*, (Bonn: English ed, 1979) p. 140 (Hereafter WP 79).
2. Fursdon, Edward, *The European Defense Community: A History* (New York: St. Martins Press, 1980), Chapter 3.
3. Should there be any doubt, the lifting of the last WEU restrictions on German production in June of 1984 provides a contemporary example. Although the remaining restrictions had been largely symbolic — as on the production of long-range bombers — there was an immediate protest by the Soviet Union and wide publicity in the Eastern European press.
4. Kelleher, Catherine M., *Germany and the Politics of Nuclear Weapons* (New York: Columbia University Press, 1975).
5. The continuing debate about this role is reflected in such books as Craig, Gordon, *The Politics of the Prussian Army* (New York: Oxford University Press, 1964); Dupuy, T. N., *A Genius for War* (Englewood Cliffs, N.J.: Prentice-Hall,

1977); Goerlitz, Walter, *History of the German General Staff* (Westport, Conn.: Greenwood Press, 1975); Kitchen, Martin, *A Military History of Germany, from the Eighteenth Century to the Present Day* (Bloomington, Ind.: Indiana University Press, 1974); O'Neil, Robert J., *The German Army and the Nazi Party 1933-1939* (New York: James Heineman, 1966); and Ritter, Gerhard, *The Sword and the Scepter: The Problem of Militarism in Germany* (Coral Gables, Fla.: University of Miami Press, 1969). The military reform movement in the United States — and particularly the writings of Steven Canby, T. N. Dupuy, and William Lind — have generated even greater interest in applying the lessons of the German past to current dilemmas.

6. Of particular importance in this context is David Schoenbaum's insightful examination of a specific test of these larger civil-military issues: *Zabern 1913: Consensus Politics in Imperial Germany* (London: George Allen and Unwin, 1982).

7. Dupuy, T. N., *op. cit.*, Ch. III.

8. Compare Huntington, Samuel P., *The Soldier and the State*, (Cambridge: Harvard University Press, 1957) and Speier, Hans, "German Rearmanent and the Old Military Elite," *World Politics*, January 1954.

9. Schoenbaum, *op. cit.*, p. 52.

10. See here Schoenbaum, David, *Hitler's Social Revolution* (London: Oxford University Press, 1966).

11. Wettig, Gerhard, *Entmilitarisierung und Wiederbewaffnung in Deutschland 1943-1955* (Munich: Oldenbourg, 1967).

12. Waldman, Eric, *The Goose Step is Verboten* (New York: Free Press, 1964), especially Chapter 9.

13. Eichenberg, Richard, "Germany" in Capitanchik, David, and Eichenberg, Richard, *Public Opinion and Defence* (London: Chatham House 1983).

14. Kelleher, Catherine M., "The Defense Policy of the Federal Republic of Germany" in Murray, Douglas J., and Viotti, Paul R., eds, *The Defense Policies of Nations* (Baltimore: Johns Hopkins Press. 1982). See also White Paper 1975-1976: *The Security of the Federal Republic of Germany and the Development of the Federal Armed Forces* (Bonn: The Federal Minister of Defence, 1976), especially Chapters 1 and 2, (Hereafter WP 75/76).

15. Sigal, Lee, *Nuclear Forces in Europe: Enduring Dilemmas, Present Prospects* (Washington: The Brookings Institution, forthcoming).

16. On the latter case, see Schoenbaum, David, *The Spiegel Affair* (New York: Doubleday, 1968) See Table 4.B which lists the postwar officeholders and their governmental coalitions. One might add a third — George Leber, who was essentially forced out of office because of irregularities in the office of military counter-intelligence (MAD), but who was allowed to leave with dignity.

17. Until the Apel reforms, the minister was assisted by one chief deputy and two lesser deputies with broad, overlapping responsibilities. They acted in what one interviewee described as "ministerial conference with all the resulting confusion." WP 79, p. 140.

18. *Rheinischer Merkur*, 25 February 1983.

19. The decree takes its name from the Hamburg site of the Bundeswehr's *Fuehrungsakademie* where the agreement on the appropriate division of responsibility was finally reached.

20. See *The Report of the Force Structure Commission* (Bonn: The Federal Minister of Defense, 1972).

21. *Financial Times*, 18 March 1981. *Der Spiegel*, 13 September 1982.

22. *The Times* (London) 12 March 1981. *Die Zeit* (North American ed) 16 July 1982.
23. WP79, pp. 141–2. Perhaps the best insights into the role played by the GI in the past is General Ulrich de Maiziere's *Fuehren im Frieden* (Munich: Bernard & Graefe, 1974).
24. *Die Zeit* (NA), 29 July 1983. In part, Wörner has built on a *Plannungserlass* prepared but not announced under Apel in his last year. See also the forthcoming RAND report by John Van Oudenaren "Nuclear Policy in the Federal Republic of Germany." now listed as WD-2163-AF, 1984.
25. *The Times* (London) 12 March 1981.
26. *International Herald Tribune* 6 April 1981.
27. One helpful summary is Gina Cowen's unpublished study "MRCA Tornado: A Circle Squared or a Lesson Learned?" Arms Control Program, University of Lancaster 1982.
28. WP79, p. 142.
29. Cowen, *op. cit.*
30. WP75/76, pp. 115–18.
31. WP79, pp. 147–62.
32. *Frankfurter Algemeine Zeitung*, 10 February 1983; ibid., 28 March 1983.

APPENDIX

Table 4A. Military Leadership: 1957–1983

GENERAL INSPECTOR
Gen. A. Heusinger, 1957–1961
Gen. F. Foertsch, 1961–1963
Gen. H. Trettner, 1964–1966
Gen. U. deMaiziere, 1966–1972
Adm. A. Zimmerman, 1972–1976
Gen. H. Wust, 1976–1978
Gen. J. Brandt, 1978–1983
Gen. W. Altenburg, 1983–present

Table 4B. Principals in West German Defense Policymaking, 1955–1983

PARLIAMENT	COALITION PARTIES	CHANCELLOR	FOREIGN MINISTER	DEFENSE MINISTER
1st (1949–53)	CDU/CSU, FDP, and others	Konrad Adenauer, CDU	Adenauer	
2nd (1953–57)	CDU/CSU, FDP	Adenauer, CDU	Adenauer (–1955)	Theodore Blank, CDU (1955–56)
			Heinrich von Brentano CDU (1955–)	Franz Josef Strauss, CSU (1956–)
3rd (1957–61)	CDU/CSU	Adenauer, CDU	von Brentano, CDU	Strauss, CSU
4th (1961–65)	CDU/CSU, FDP	Adenauer, CDU (–1963)	Gerhard Schröder, CDU	Strauss, CSU (–1962)
		Ludwig Erhard, CDU (1963–)		Kai-Uwe von Hassel, CDU (1963–)
5th (1965–69)	CDU/CSU, FDP	Erhard, CDU (–1966)	Schröder, CDU (–1966)	von Hassel, CDU (–1966)
	CDU/CSU, SPD (Grand Coalition)	Kurt George Kiesinger, CDU (1966–)	Willy Brandt, SPD (1966–)	Schröder, CDU (1966–)
6th (1969–72)	SPD, FDP	Brandt, SPD	Walter Scheel, FDP	Helmut Schmidt, SPD (–1972)
				Georg Leber, SPD (1972–)
7th (1972–76)	SPD, FDP	Brandt, SPD (–1974)	Scheel, FDP (–1974) Hans Dietrich	Leber, SPD
		Schmidt, SPD (1974–)	Genscher, FDP (1974–)	
8th (1976–80)	SPD, FDP	Schmidt, SPD	Genscher, FDP	Leber, SPD (–1978)
				Hans Apel, SPD (1978–80)
9th (1980–82)	SPD, FDP	Schmidt, SPD	Genscher, FDP	Apel, SPD (–1982)
/82–3/83	CDU/CSU, FDP	Kohl, CDU	Genscher, FDP	Wörner, CDU
10th (1983)	CDU/CSU, FDP	Kohl, CDU	Genscher, FDP	Wörner, CDU

Chapter 5

Military Organizations and Policymaking in Israel

Aharon Yariv

CIVIL-MILITARY RELATIONS IN ISRAEL

Military organization and policymaking in Israel have been heavily influenced by the following four factors.

1. The historical background; that is, the prestate socio–political development of the Jewish community in Palestine, as well as the politically controlled growth of its major military arm in the underground, the *Haganah.*
2. The centrality of defense to national existence, due to Israel's peculiar geopolitical situation and the traditional secrecy surrounding defense matters.
3. The heavy and lasting imprint of Ben-Gurion, the chief architect of the State and of Zahal, Israel's defense forces (IDF).
4. Israel's continuous need to maintain a capability for total mobilization as a nation in arms.

These factors have generally ensured civil control, although of a particular nature, over the military during the state's thirty-five years of turbulent existence. These years included six wars and many more years of tension and violence.

I agree with Welch and Smith who say, "No nation's armed forces remain apart from politics."[1] But this does not suffice to explain the nature of civil control as devised by Ben-Gurion, who stated:

Zahal has been established and is being activated in a popular state, which is based on freedom of thought, human liberty and the right of every citizen to join any economic, cultural or political organization existing legitimately in the state. It is none of the commanders' business to check the opinions of those who are under their command and the army has no authority over its members' outlook and ideas. A soldier has freedom of thought, like any other citizen in the state, and he is allowed to join any legitimate organization and party in the state . . . The army is not to determine policy, regime, laws and government procedures in the state. The army is not to determine by itself even its own structure, procedure and policies, and it does not, of course, decide about peace and war. The army is only an executive arm for defense and security, of the Israeli government.[2]

On the other hand, Ben-Gurion was deeply concerned about the possible pernicious influence of the polity's partisan political factors on defense. Therefore, he strove to make defense[3] an autonomous neutral sphere based on national consensus, so that it would not suffer from "the basic defeats and obstructions in our national life: the many cleavages and divisions . . . (party, ideological and political rifts), and in particular another cleavage, flowing from social, cultural and ethnic divisions."[4]

These two main elements in Ben-Gurion's policy—the upholding of the democratic principle of the military's subservience to the legitimate political authorities, and the effort to prevent partisan political encroachment on the military—have determined the particular nature of civil control in Israel, especially in view of Ben-Gurion's broad interpretation of it. What characterizes Israel's type of civil control is the considerable degree of autonomy that the military enjoys. The military is subject primarily to the authority of the minister of defense and the prime minister (Ben-Gurion combined the two), to the cabinet, to a much lesser extent, and to the Knesset (Parliament), to a quite limited degree. But this autonomy has another aspect: it means considerable involvement of the military in defense policymaking at the political level (government), albeit in a nonpartisan fashion. As a result, the degree of civil control depends to a decisive extent on the personality of the minister of defense. Therefore, it was strongest under the leadership of Ben-Gurion, but has varied under his successors.

Nevertheless, it must be stressed, as Peri put it, "that the Israeli pattern of military–political relations is based on the instrumentalist principle that the army should be subordinate to the civil authority and should serve as the professional instrument of the state's political institutions."[5]

As to the organization of Israel's defense establishment, it has been marked from the beginning by a clear-cut division between two parallel components, both of which are under the control of the minister of defense: the military component, called the Israel Defense Force, headed by the Chief of the General Staff and the civil component, called the Ministry of Defense, headed by the director general of the ministry. Taken together, these two constitute the defense establishment (*Ma'arechet Habitachon*), which is headed by the defense minister. Depending on personal preference, the defense minister sometimes has a deputy (if the person occupying the post is a Knesset member) or an assistant (if the person is not a member of the Knesset). If there is a deputy or an assistant, difficulties may arise, as they have in the past, over the distribution of functions between him and the director general. Some military personnel serve in the civil component and quite a large number of civil employees serve in the military one.

In addition, because the state does not have a constitution, its laws, statutes and procedures have evolved over time, and been stamped by tradition from pre- and early-state days. Israel does have a series of basic laws that cover certain constitutional aspects. There is, therefore, no law defining any person as commander in chief of the IDF. In the wake of the Yom Kippur War and the Agranat Committee Report,[6] a ministerial committee worked out a proposal for a basic law (called Basic Law — Army), which was subsequently approved by the Knesset in 1976 and spelled out the following:

> The Army is subject to the authority of the government. The minister in charge of the Army on behalf of the Government is the minister of defense.
> The chief of the General Staff is subject to the authority of the Government and subordinate to the minister of defense. The chief of the General Staff shall be appointed by the Government upon the recommendation of the minister of defense.[7]

This basic law clearly establishes the principle of civil control, but it failed to clarify certain ambiguities that existed beforehand, such as who is the commander in chief. It is certainly not the Chief of the General Staff, although this post is defined in the same law as the "highest military command echelon." Is it the prime minister, the minister of defense, or the government (cabinet) as a whole? Under the prevailing circumstances, the latter seems to me to be the appropriate answer, as the government (cabinet) carries, according to law, collective responsibility for its members' activities. In this context a heated exchange did take place between Prime Minister Begin and Defense Minister Weizman in May 1979, with Weizman maintaining that he and the Chief of the General Staff were responsible for defense, while Begin retorted that the cabinet was responsible and that Weizman did not understand the constitution.

Another ambiguity is to whom the Chief of the General Staff is subordinate. Although subordinate to the minister of defense, the chief is also "subject to the authority of the government." It is accepted that the Chief of the General Staff is subordinate to the minister in day-to-day life. There is no ambiguity about his status as chief military advisor to the government. It must be noted that the government (cabinet) delegated wide prerogatives to the prime minister and the minister of defense, most of them not defined by law or by statute. These prerogatives have evolved with experience and have varied according to specific situations and personalities, but have always been strongly influenced by the Ben-Gurion tradition. It is probably due to this that the above ambiguities have not created major problems between the military and civil authorities.

It seems to me justified to say that under the circumstances described, the various governments (prime ministers, defense ministers and cabinets) have shown care and respect in handling the military on one hand and apprehension about "rocking the boat" over defense issues on the other hand. The military have guarded their autonomy jealously, with the help of the prime ministers and the defense ministers and have generally accepted without question the democratic principle of civilian political supremacy.

The dividing line between the military and the civil component of the defense establishment, which has been maintained without great change for over thirty years, can be defined as follows. The military component deals with all matters relating to military operations (at all levels—from the strategic to the tactical), as well as with those directly connected with them (for example, intelligence, personnel, and logistics). It employs the resources put at its disposal by the Defense Ministry. The civil component deals with all matters pertaining to the support of the military. For this purpose, the civil component draws on resources put at the disposal of the defense establishment by the government. This organization stems from Ben-Gurion's concept of civil control and from his effort to minimize contact between the military, on the one hand, and other government agencies and nongovernmental actors, on the other. Thus, the military component should be freed from activities that do not directly contribute to the primary mission of military operations and that would have a negative influence on the component's members. Thus, procurement and production of materiel, construction, real estate, rehabilitation (of personnel released from service, bereaved families and widows), finance, and the like are handled by the civil component, the Ministry of Defense. The military component presents its requirements for resources within the limits of the approved programs and the budget (if necessary, with special approval from the minister) to the relevant bureaus in the civil component, the Ministry of Defense. It is up to the latter to do their best to satisfy these requirements.

The Military Component—The IDF

The continuing Arab–Israeli conflict and the constraints of Israel's geostrategic situation have shaped Israeli military organization, but it has undergone few significant changes since 1949. It is characterized by

. A capability for total mobilization (of personnel and relevant materiel).
. A heavy reliance on a sophisticated, well-exercised and trained reserve system (similar to the Swiss one).
. A standing force comprising the national service contingent of men and women (three years service for men and two years for women), a relatively small body of career officers and noncommissioned officers (NCOs), and a number of civilian employees.

- A strong emphasis on intelligence for early warning.
- A high priority for the Air Force as the overall shield and a swift sword of reaction, which, therefore, is less dependent on mobilization of reserves than the other services.
- A territorial defense, based on border settlements.

The main missions of the IDF's standing force are:

- To be the producer of the Order of Battle in both the quantitative and the qualitative sense. Quantitatively — the trained contingents "feed" the reserve Order of Battle upon completion of national service. Qualitatively — the standing force sets the standards to be maintained in combat by the whole Order of Battle.
- To serve as a first line of defense in case of surprise attack.
- To fulfill all current security duties, for example, securing the border, maintaining security in the administered territories, carrying out across-the-border operations, and guarding military installations. For this purpose, the standing force is reinforced by reserve units to a varying degree that depends on circumstances.

The Chief of the General Staff is the most senior echelon of command in Zahal and is the only officer carrying the rank of lieutenant general. The chief is assisted by the General Staff, which consists of the coordinating staff (personnel, intelligence, planning, operations, etc.) and the special staff (chief of infantry and paratrooper corps, chief of armored corps, chief of artillery corps, chief of signal corps, chief of medical corps, chief of ordnance corps, etc.).

The General Staff combines three functions.

1. It constitutes what the famous Soviet World War II Chief of Staff General Shaposhnikoff called the "Brain of the Army" and deals with short and long range overall concepts at the strategic and higher tactical levels.
2. It functions as a theater headquarters for all military operations and directs the land–air battle through the headquarters of the three territorial commands (see Figure 5.1). The air and sea battles are directed by the Air Force and Navy headquarters, respectively, under the overall guidance of, and with approval by, the Chief of the General Staff.
3. It serves as the headquarters of the ground forces.

A headquarters for the combat arms (infantry and paratroop, armor, artillery, engineer, signals and combat intelligence) has recently been established in order to assist the General Staff in carrying out the third function, especially as far as doctrine, training, and research and development are concerned. The Air Force, Navy, territorial commands, functional commands (Gadna, Nahal), and logistical centers are directly subordinated to the Chief of the General Staff (see Figure 5.1).

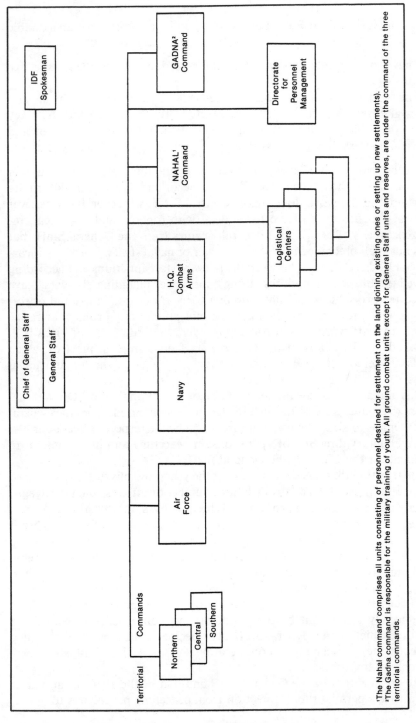

FIGURE 5.1. Organization of the Israel Defense Forces (the military component).

¹The Nahal command comprises all units consisting of personnel destined for settlement on the land (joining existing ones or setting up new settlements).
²The Gadna command is responsible for the military training of youth. All ground combat units, except for General Staff units and reserves, are under the command of the three territorial commands.

113

The chiefs of the Air Force and the Navy and their staffs serve in a double role.

1. They serve commanders and staff in the headquarters of their respective forces.
2. They serve as an integral part of the General Staff as far as the air and naval aspects are concerned. The chiefs of the Air Force and the Navy are the principal advisors to the Chief of the General Staff on air and naval matters. They are assisted in this role by their respective staffs.

In other words, the General Staff is not a fully integrated one, as it is in Canada. But in their "general staff" role, the air and naval staffs contribute their input to the work done by the General Staff, wherever and whenever necessary, befitting the issue to be dealt with (operational, logistical, intelligence, etc.). The initiative generally comes from the General Staff, but does not at all preclude initiatives by the air or naval staffs. The work is carried out by direct contact between the relevant staff functions and according to well-established procedures. Long experience, including six wars, have honed the procedures, so that planning for war and for individual operations (a retaliatory raid or the like) does not present any problem as far as integrated staff work is concerned. The overall coordination of plans is in the hands of the heads of the General Staff departments, most of which heads are senior in rank to that of their colleagues in the air and naval staffs.

This also applies to the implementation of operational plans. Operational orders to ground units go through the territorial commands from the General Staff. Orders to air and naval units are issued by the respective headquarters. Overall military direction of operations, in peacetime and in wartime, is in the hands of the Chief of the General Staff.

The tradition that has developed over the years, the physical proximity of the three staffs, and the relatively limited number of officers who are engaged directly in the integration process — all three enable smooth staff work to be carried out. These factors, as well as the small size of the country, permit close contact between the main components of the military: the General Staff, the Air Force, the Navy, and the territorial commands. Thereby, good mutual communications are maintained, which are conducive both to integrated staff work and to smooth policymaking at the military level.

Difficulties that arise in integrating staff work at the General Staff level are generally ironed out by the senior officers concerned, but sometimes reach the Chief of the General Staff, who decides as he sees fit. When they do occur, they are usually in nonoperational cases, such as budgeting, personnel, and logistics.

The organization of the General Staff and that of the air force and navy headquarters permits rapid transition from peacetime procedures to operations on a full wartime basis. The procedures mentioned extend to the minister of defense and beyond. In most cases, the initiative for individual operations comes from the military.

The IDF does not have a General Staff corps. Officers serving on the General Staff, as well as on the staffs of the Air Force and Navy headquarters, are chosen for their capability and know-how. Suitable command and staff experience is a requisite. Only outstanding officers are chosen for the focal and sensitive spots. Service in these slots means that the officer is destined for higher command. As a rule, officers posted to the more important posts on the three staffs have completed the regular Command and General Staff College course. This is a combined-services college for officers with the rank of major and lieutenant colonel and there is no other command and/or staff college. In this fashion, unity of command and staff concepts and procedures among the three services are ensured. The regular course consists of parts common to students from the three services and parts distinctly destined for students from each service.

In the light of what has been said so far, the question of command in combined-arms operations does not present special difficulties. At the General Staff level, the command structure for such operations is, as described, permanently in place and functions through integrated staff work. For command in the field, the person in command of the operation will usually be the commander of the ground component, and he will have the necessary air and naval elements on his staff. Combined arms operations can be controlled either by the General Staff or by a territorial command, as required by circumstances.

In the Israeli case, we do not, therefore, have an integrated staff structure. What we *do* have is integration in dynamics, that is, in the staff work at the highest military level, with the General Staff playing a somewhat senior role to the staffs in air force and navy headquarters. The fact that the chief of the General Staff is formally and actually the topmost military person (the only one carrying the rank of lieutenant general), in addition to other reasons mentioned before, makes the concept of integrated dynamics into an effective working proposition, with unity of command at the top. In principle, this arrangement has not changed since it was instituted in 1950. What has evolved and developed over time are the procedures and the techniques commensurate with experience and changes in warfare and technology. As to service missions, there have been very few changes since they were determined at the beginning of the 1950s.

As described, unity of command is achieved in the military component and is accompanied by integrated staff work. However, it still grants a status to the Air Force and the Navy that enables adequate development of these two services. This has also helped in producing a military force that is well-balanced in its main components—ground, air, and naval—in consonance with prevailing strategic requirements. The structure was achieved as a result of a quite serious struggle within the senior military in 1949, with Ben-Gurion deciding against the establishment of three separate services, each having its own chief of staff. The structure is not without problems, but these are far outweighed by its merits, as experience has clearly shown.

The Civil Component

The civil component is headed by the Defense Ministry's director general. The main functions of the civilian component are as follows: budgeting; financing; procurement; research, development and production; directing specific major projects of development and production (e.g., the Kfir, the Merkava); construction; rehabilitation; defense export; and administration of the civil component.

The director general does not deal with strategy, so that, in effect, the civil component plays only a logistical role. Therefore, the relations between it and the military component bear a mainly coordinative–cooperative stamp, and the supervising role reverts to the Minister of Defense, personally. This is a direct result of Ben-Gurion's concept, as described earlier.

The organs subordinated to the director general (see Figure 5.2) are: (1) the various departments; (2) the various affiliated units and enterprises. The heads of two departments operate in a double role.

1. The head of the budget department also serves as financial adviser to the Chief of the General Staff.
2. The head of the research and development department also serves the Chief of the General Staff.

This arrangement was designed to ensure as smooth a cooperation and coordination as possible between the military and the civilian components in these two vital areas. For research and development, the arrangement enables that department to meet budgeted requirements from the military component in concert with the general R & D policy, as approved by the minister of defense, without undue difficulty and friction. Nevertheless, the twin arrangement does create a situation that impinges on the personal control by the minister over two important areas (budget and R & D). By definition, both components must be considered parties with vested interests. The minister of defense has no directly subordinate staff to him with which to independently evaluate programs presented for approval by the military. This also refers to plans and programs presented by the civil component. In addition, the military component is always better equipped with data because of its strong staff structure. Therefore, it is difficult for the minister to form an independent opinion, and the influence of the military component in these areas is far reaching.

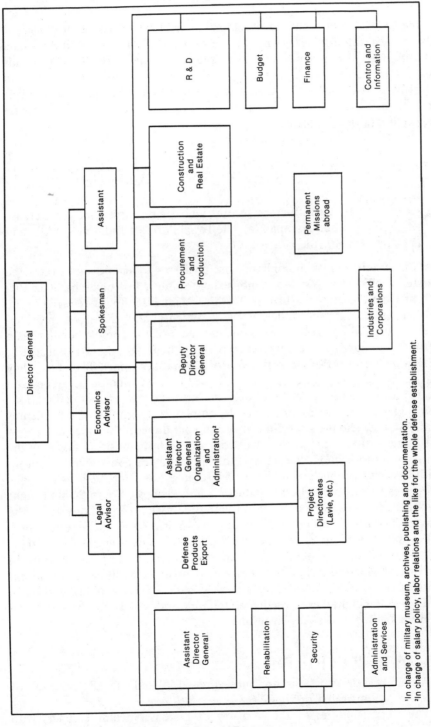

FIGURE 5.2. Organization of the Ministry of Defense (the civil component).

[1] In charge of military museum, archives, publishing and documentation.
[2] In charge of salary policy, labor relations and the like for the whole defense establishment.

The chief of research and development, in his civil component role, is also responsible for developing the necessary technological and personnel base to meet the approved and budgeted requirements for R & D. In this respect the chief can rely heavily on the defense establishment's own resources. Notwithstanding that, a consistent and increasingly successful effort is being made to bring nongovernmental enterprise into defense research and development.

The Defense Ministry's own resources are of two kinds.

1. Bodies affiliated with the ministry. For example, (a) Israel Military Industries (IMI); and (b) The Authority for Development of Combat Means.
2. Corporations constitute the second kind of resource that the Defense Ministry has. For example, (a) The Israel Aircraft Industries (IAI); and (b) The *Shekem* (the Israeli PX).

This description of the military and civil components demonstrates the existence of a strong military–industrial complex, but of a character different from the one to which the late President Eisenhower referred in the U.S. In Israel, it is preponderantly governmental and, therefore, in principle, under civil control. Each of the elements of the complex comprises a rather large number of employees (especially the Israel Aircraft Industries), with a high proportion of qualified professional personnel. Therefore, they have considerable political potential, which they can and do use. They can exert pressure on the minister of defense and the cabinet to act in directions suiting their interests by, for example, emphasizing the risk of sizeable unemployment, should a certain project be abandoned. This does not necessarily mean that their pressure will coincide with the position taken by the military component. If it does not, the latter may be constrained to put up with a decision contrary to its perceived interests. For instance, various pressures from Israel Aircraft Industries and groups close to them brought about the final decision to go ahead with the Lavie project. Conversely, the existence of this complex facilities contacts and smoothes the necessary procedures between consumer and supplier and, thereby, increases flexibility. In recent years, the number of nongovernmental enterprises dealing in defense production has grown, and they contribute significantly to the export of defense products. Over a period of time, this may bring about a change in the character of the Israeli military–industrial complex and make it more similar to the American one.

The Minister of Defense

A number of functions are subordinated directly to the minister of defense, as illustrated in Figure 5.3.

The responsibilities of the Ministry of Defense include contacts with

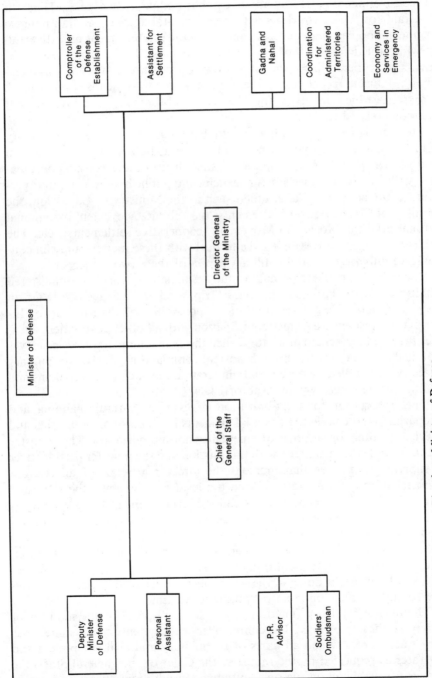

FIGURE 5.3. Positions that Report Directly to Minister of Defense.

other government agencies and have public and political aspects. Thus, the assistant for settlement deals with governmental agencies and all nongovernmental bodies in all matters concerning the establishment of settlements in which the defense establishment has an interest. In the past, these settlements were determined almost entirely by defense considerations. This changed during recent years, due to the Likud government's Greater Israel Program, which involved the defense establishment in activities only remotely related to defense.

The department for Gadna (youth battalions, ie., preservice military training) and Nahal (pioneering combat youth, i.e., national service men and women volunteering to settle on land) ensures the necessary coordination with all relevant government agencies and public bodies on matters pertaining to Gadna and Nahal units, such as the Ministry of Education, the Ministerial Committee on Settlements, the Kibbutz Movement (communal settlements), the Moshavim Movement (cooperative settlements), etc. The military component does not have to deal with these matters and can concentrate fully on the purely military aspect of these two subjects.

The Ministry of Defense has overall responsibility for the administered territories (West Bank and the Gaza Strip; after the passage of the Golan Law, the Golan Heights became the responsibility of the Ministry of Interior). It must ensure proper coordination with all other government agencies that are represented in what is called the civil administration. Security is handled by the military, through normal command channels. Nonmilitary matters are handled by the civil administration in which Israeli civilians and military serve together with Arab officials.

The concept of total mobilization necessitates careful planning and preparations to enable the essential elements of the economy and the vital services to function in times of emergency and mobilization. The Ministry of Defense has been charged with this mission and the minister presides over a supreme committee that includes the director generals of all relevant ministries, and representatives from the local governments, the IDF, and the police. The minister appoints a senior official of the Defense Ministry as his permanent representative to preside over continuous planning, preparations and war games. Among the areas covered by the Supreme Committee for Economy and Services in Emergency are health and hospitalization, education, personnel, agriculture, and energy. There are similar committees at lower levels, right down to the local sphere. This arrangement facilitates the country's transition from peacetime to wartime.

The only supervisory function at the direct disposal of the minister of defense is the comptroller. The comptroller of the defense establishment has direct access to any and all parts of the military and civil component and operates as requested by the minister, the Chief of the General Staff, the director general, or on his own initiative. In addition, there are internal comptrollers in all ministry departments. But there are none in the military component because, according to IDF doctrine, comptrolling is an inherent command and staff function. However, the civil and the military components are closely and continuously scrutinized by the state comptroller, who is appointed by the president of the state, upon recommendation of the Knesset committee for state comptrolling matters.

Except for the comptroller and, to a limited degree, the finance and budget departments, civil control at the defense establishment is exercised personally by the defense minister. As mentioned before, the defense minister has no staff that can analyze programs presented to him by the military component, or the civil one for that matter, which, of course, affects his capability for control. The minister of defense can rely on the economics advisor (who is subordinate to the director general) for information on the economic implications of the defense establishment's major activities. This is important in itself, but it does not constitute an important means of supervision or control.

Last, but not least, is strategy. For this highly important subject, the minister of defense has to rely on the planning and intelligence departments of the General Staff. Naturally, the minister also has his own views, which stem from the political platform of the party he represents.

Policymaking

The special nature of civil control designed by Ben-Gurion, which Peri calls "nominal control"[8] (the cabinet and the Knesset would theoretically serve as supreme authority, as in all other fields, but, in fact, their role would be restricted), has naturally shaped not only organization, but policymaking as well. Basically, the pattern has not changed over thirty-five years, but certain inroads have made civil control slightly less unusual than before. That is to say, there is a greater degree of civil control, but there is still considerable involvement of the military in all policymaking aspects of defense, although generally not in party politics concerning defense. This involvement is due to the fact that the military component of the defense establishment is much better equipped to deal with the policy aspects of defense than are other relevant government agencies. Should officers (generally senior ones, who have achieved public notice) desire to become really effective in partisan politics, they have to leave the army and join a party. Quite a number of them have done so and have been sought by parties anxious to exploit their public appeal. But this had not impinged on the basic pattern of civil control of the military, as designed by Ben-Gurion. I accept Perlmutter's statement: "Thus the rapid turnover of officers, the absorptive capacity of the economy, the economic and social integration of Zahal veterans, the nation's dependence upon the reserve system, the identity of political goals and the army's professionalism, preclude Zahal's active intervention in politics. In addition, the institutional legitimacy of the independent political structures furnish an effective guarantee of civilian control."[9]

These are indeed strong and enduring factors, but they do not exclude military influence over the policymaking aspects of defense. How is this influence expressed in policymaking, while civil control, Ben-Gurion style, is maintained?

Cabinet and Knesset Roles. Before going into specifics, I must touch on the Israeli political system. Two factors must be emphasized: the character of the executive branch of government, the cabinet, and the weight of the legislative branch.

Due to the Israeli electoral system (countrywide, proportionate, by party list), no single party, or even bloc of parties, has yet been able to achieve a majority in the Knesset and, thereby, set up a single party or party bloc cabinet. A majority in the Knesset, enabling the government to govern, has, to date, been achieved only by a coalition of parties, and has necessitated a coalition cabinet. The offices of prime minister and minister of defense have always been in the hands of the strongest party—Labour in the present and Herut under Begin. Usually, the cabinet forms a ministerial committee on defense to deal with defense problems. Often, however, depending on the nature of the problem, the situation and the personalities, defense problems are discussed in the cabinet plenum.

Since defense is regarded as the most important national issue in Israel, all party representatives forming the cabinet want to participate in the defense committee and have a say in defense issues. Consequently, the ministerial defense committee is a cumbersome body that encourages the prime minister and the minister of defense to treat as many issues as possible between them. They are sometimes joined by the foreign minister and/or the finance minister.

Except for actual legislation, the Knesset has limited influence on executive activities. Whatever influence it has is also motivated by party considerations, with the members of the coalition doing their best to support the government. According to Article 14 of the "Government and Law Procedure Order," the government is defined as the "executive authority of the State," not as the implementing institution of the Knesset, except in those cases in which the decisions of the Knesset and its committees are anchored in a specific law binding the government legally. Otherwise, a decision by the Knesset or one of its committees cannot impose obligations on the cabinet to act and is considered only as advice. Most defense issues in the Knesset are dealt with by the Knesset Committee for Foreign and Defense Affairs.

The committee is informed about current and important defense and security matters on a routine basis. The committee can invite members of the defense establishment to attend meetings only through the minister of defense and with his approval. The extent of information brought before the committee has increased since the Yom Kippur War and especially since 1978, when, under the chairmanship of Professor M. Arens, subcommittees covering the most important defense issues were formed. Briefing in the subcommittees is more detailed and discussion-oriented. Discussions in the plenum of the committee, which are often heated, tend to follow party lines. In any case, information presented by the military in the committee (plenum or subcommittee) is within the limits of what has been cleared by the minister or the Chief of the General Staff.

Of course, the committee also deals with matters of specific legislation, the implementation of which is the responsibility of the minister of defense. These include about thirty statutes and laws, a number of which empower the minister to pass regulations that must be extended from time to time. The committee has no professional staff to help it (this applies to all Knesset committees), which weakens it in exercising civil control over the defense establishment.

There are almost no laws or statutes governing military policy and very few written procedures concerning policymaking beyond the Ministry of Defense. Matters of military policy are brought up for discussion outside the defense establishment by request (prime minister, cabinet member, Knesset committee) or on the initiative of the minister of defense.

How Military Policy is Made. In view of what has been said so far, how is military policy made?

We have to distinguish between the following four levels:

1. The military level
2. The ministerial (defense) level
3. The prime ministerial level
4. The cabinet level

All policy on military organization (except for major changes), training, combat doctrine, combat intelligence, and hardware requirements (except for capital items) is made on the military level, by the Chief of the General Staff. In addition to the General Staff departments, the chief is assisted in policymaking by the General Staff Forum. It meets weekly and includes the Chief of the General Staff, the heads of the General Staff departments, the chiefs of the Air Force, Navy, three territorial commands and the Combat Arms command, the Defense Ministry's director general, its head of the research and development department, and the head of the budget department (who serves as the financial advisor).

There are no laws governing the decisionmaking process for military operations. All military operations in peacetime are dealt with at the ministerial level, most also at the prime ministerial level, and, on many decisions, the cabinet–ministerial committee level is included. Any military operation involving the crossing of borderlines or firing across the borderline (ground, air, and naval fire) requires approval at least by the prime minister. If it is an operation of more than minimal size and impact, it will have to be approved by the ministerial committee or by the cabinet. Operational policy in peacetime is usually dealt with first at the ministerial, and then often at the prime ministerial level, and at the ministerial committee level as well. An issue of peace and war can be dealt with only by the cabinet. At certain times, under varying security circumstances and depending on the government in power, there may be standard operating procedures approved by the cabinet that grant limited authority to the Chief of the General Staff, the minister of defense and the prime minister. Such was the case, for example, during the war of attrition, from 1968 to 1970, when, for the first time, what was called the constitution (actual authority), was worked out.

An interesting case in point was the agreement reached between Prime Minister Eshkol and Defense Minister Dayan, when the latter took over the portfolio from the former in June of 1967, on the eve of the Six Day War:

The minister of defense will not act without the approval of the
A. Prime minister in all matters relating
   1. To the commencement of ground hostilities of war against any country;
   2. To military action in wartime deviating from the principal fixed guidelines;
   3. To commencement of military action against any country, which has not taken part, up to that moment, in hostile actions;
   4. To bombing of central towns in enemy territory if this was preceded by bombing of Israeli towns by that enemy;
   5. To retaliatory action in the defense sphere in response to incidents.
B. The prime minister can with the knowledge of the minister of defense invite the chief of staff, the director of Intelligence, the director general of the Ministry of Defense, the assistant minister of defense, to give information.[10]

The military component participates in all these discussions and is usually represented by the Chief of the General Staff, the director of Military Intelligence and sometimes by other senior officers, such as the commander of the Air Force. Prior to participating in these discussions, the issue will be discussed at the military level, where the Chief of the General Staff will formulate his position. The chief will then present it at the defense minister's level, where the relevant members of the military and the civil components will participate in the discussions. In the meetings at the prime ministerial or the cabinet level, the minister of defense and the Chief of the General Staff might present differing positions, although this is the exception, rather than the rule.

The Budgetary Process. Both the military and the civil components work according to an overall multiannual and an annual program. These programs are based on general directives from the minister of defense. The preparation and approval of the programs are governed by a well-established and detailed procedure.

The key to all the programs is, naturally, the budget, for the establishment of which there are, again, detailed procedures. The battle of the budget is waged within the military component and within the civil component by the various contenders, between the military and civil components for the apportionment of the overall budget of the defense establishment, between the officials of the Ministry of Defense and the officials of the Ministry of Finance, and then between the ministers themselves, involving the prime minister, and, finally, in the cabinet. There were years in which the defense minister and the finance minister came to an agreement without further ado. But in the majority of cases, and especially in the last decade, the subject usually reached the cabinet.

In the initial discussions at the minister of defense level, with a view to establishing primary directives, the military and the civil component present their requirements. Already, at this stage, the military have an advantage in claim staking; first, because they present and describe the threats, usually in a bona fide way without exaggerations, and second, because they represent the sharp edge that must cope with the threat. Add to that what has been mentioned earlier about the strength of the General Staff, and its relative advantage in producing the mass of necessary data on one hand, and the absence of any proper staff at the defense minister's level for the analysis of these data on the other. This is the situation in the following stages of the budgetary process. There are permanent representatives of the Finance Ministry in the Defense Ministry, who monitor all budgetary matters and can equip their minister with important data and advice; but for the reasons mentioned, they are in an inferior position when confronting the defense establishment.

In the years prior to the Six Day War, the development of the defense budget was conditioned more by national economic capability considerations than by defense requirements. After the Six Day War, however, the emphasis shifted to defense requirements, which grew exponentially. At present, due to the difficult economic situation, the emphasis is shifting back towards the national economic capability, from what is required to what is feasible. The struggle between requirement and feasibility inevitably pushes the issue of the defense budget upward to the cabinet level, where the ultimate responsibility lies and where the minister of defense and the Chief of the General Staff can present the risk taken if this or the other requirement is not to be met. Because the cabinet carries ultimate and collective responsibility for all decisions, it is not always ready to accept what is economically feasible as being what is required by the defense establishment. On the other hand, in view of past experience, especially the Yom Kippur War and, in its wake, the *Agranat Report*, the defense establishment feels it must emphasize its requirements so as not to be later accused of neglect. In this context, the position taken by the Chief of the General Staff is of particular importance. The cabinet will feel very uncomfortable in rejecting a strong plea by the chief to meet those requirements for which he sees a great need. Over the years, only one minister of defense and one Chief of the General Staff have resigned because of the defense budget. It must also be noted that the cabinet is bereft of any staff unit that could provide it with an analysis independent of the defense establishment and the Finance Ministry.

The main burden for the annual battle of the budget rests on the shoulders of the minister of defense and, as such, it does not interfere with the primary duties of the Chief of the General Staff. Even so, however, the Chief of the General Staff still has to work out the budget within the military component, and his is the recommendation that goes to the minister. Nevertheless, there have been cases in which the chiefs of the Air Force and Navy have dissented and brought their case before the minister of defense. The Chief of the General Staff is assisted in the budgetary process by a financial advisor, whose other role, as mentioned before, is as head of the Defense Ministry's budget department. That can put him into a delicate position, especially if he happens to be a military person.

Once the budget has been approved by the cabinet, it is then submitted to the joint Knesset committees (defense and finance). Quite detailed discussions are then held, in which partisan politics play a role. Under these circumstances, it is sometimes possible for the defense establishment to reduce cuts that have been decided upon by the cabinet. After approval by the joint Knesset committee, the defense budget is finally voted upon in the Knesset plenary within the framework of the overall annual budget law.

Weapons Procurement. As to policy on procurement of major weaponry items (aircraft, armor, artillery), the Chief of the General Staff presents the requirements and the recommendations of the military component to the minister of defense. There they are discussed with the director general and other relevant officials from the Ministry, and with senior military personnel. Because capital items must be procured from outside of Israel, there are also weighty political and economic considerations involved. As a result, policy is actually set at the prime ministerial level. However, important details may be decided upon by the minister of defense, after coordination with the ministers for finance and foreign affairs.

Decisions regarding procurement of capital items that can be produced locally (e.g., the Kfir and the Merkava tank) are made by the minister of defense once the original project has been approved by the prime minister, the ministerial committee for defense, or the cabinet. The defense minister, of course, takes into account military requirements, budgetary possibilities, and local industrial interests, such as the export of defense products.

The chief of the research and development department, who serves both the Chief of the General Staff and the director general of the Defense Ministry, proposes policy after coordination with his two superiors. There is input from both components. But it is clearly the minister of defense who decides on policy, although the Chief of the General Staff and other senior officers can exert considerable influence over the important details of R & D programs.

Policy on the export of defense products is decided by the minister of defense. In cases that may be politically sensitive, the decision will be made by the prime minister after deliberation with the ministers of foreign affairs and defense. Decisions that exceed a certain quantity, or that involve sensitive items, must be made at the cabinet level, where political considerations play a role.

Personnel. As far as military personnel is concerned, many policy aspects are decided at the military level. Policies that have implications beyond the military, for example, regarding salaries, pensions, and so on, are decided by the minister and dealt with by the civil component. Sometimes policy concerning military personnel requires additional budgeting, which, in turn, might necessitate approval by the Knesset finance committee. But these are exceptional cases.

The number of general officers is not defined by law and changes from time to time as the military require. The necessary ministerial approval does not usually present a serious obstacle. Promotion of officers to the rank of colonel and above must have the minister's approval. The chief of staff's recommendations are of decisive influence and only rarely does the minister reject them. Postings of general officers and, in certain cases, of colonels, is dealt with in an identical manner. In the promotion and posting of senior officers, especially generals, political considerations *do* play a role, although definitely not an overwhelming one. It would be justified to say that such promotions are less subject to politics in this sphere than in all other government bodies.

Overall Strategy. There is a most conspicuous weakness in the Israeli governmental system, with regard to the development of overall strategy. In the past, of all the four policymaking levels mentioned, only the military possessed the staff requisite for strategy development. All of the ministers, including the minister of defense, have had to rely on the military. Therefore,

the military viewpoint has inevitably been influential. The military viewpoint has had the additional advantage of not being influenced by partisan
politics; whereas at the ministerial level, especially at the prime ministerial
and cabinet levels, politics have played a legitimately important role.

Defense Minister Weizman saw fit to correct this situation and established
an advisor on national security (a major general), who had a small subordinate staff. Most of the personnel were military. Defense Minister Sharon
enlarged this staff and turned it into what was called the unit for national
security. The adviser and the unit (again mostly military) played an important role in strategic matters. Defense Minister Arens disbanded the unit
and has relied instead on the military (the General Staff's planning and intelligence departments). In the summer of 1983, Minister Arens publicly
proposed the establishment of a national security council at the prime
minister's level, where there is not and never has been a staff unit to deal
with strategic problems. Nor does the Foreign Ministry have any proper
policy planning unit.

The result is that the prime minister and the cabinet have nobody (except
the military and the intelligence services) to rely upon. The problem with
this is not that the military and the intelligence services are narrowminded.
However, by definition, they represent a certain sector and are an interested
party. They cannot represent an overall point of view objectively, which is
of primary importance at the prime ministerial and cabinet levels. It would
be the same for a staff unit at the defense minister's level. What is called for
is what has already been proposed by Minister Arens. I have no doubt that
if a national security unit had existed in the prime minister's office, the
whole Lebanon problem would have evolved differently. But in spite of bit-
ter experience and several proposals, no such unit has been created. It seems
as if "God has shut their eyes so that they cannot see, and closed their minds
from understanding."[11]

Conclusion

The following seems to me to be an appropriate summary of the main
characteristics of my subject.

1. In Israel, the military organization is focused on its mission operations
   (combat).
2. Unity of command in the Israeli military organization, assisted by the integrated staff work process, lessens the detrimental effects of interservice
   struggles and contributes to operational efficiency and flexibility.
3. The top echelon of the government's structure for defense, from the
   prime minister and the cabinet, down to and including the Chief of the
   General Staff, lacks legal definition and clarity (where such definition
   exists) over the distribution of duties and authority.

4. Stable and generally firm civil control of the military, although of a particular nature, is exercised by the executive branch of government, but there is only limited control by the legislative branch. This type of control actually produces considerable influence by the military in defense policymaking. Nevertheless, examples, such as the conduct and the execution of the evacuation of settlers from the Rafiah area in April 1982 (in concert with the Camp David agreement), constitute concrete evidence of the complete acceptance by the military of the principle of civilian supremacy.

NOTES

1. Welch, Claude, Jr, and Smith, Arthur, K., *Military Role and Rule* (Duxbury, MA: Duxbury Press, 1974).
2. Author's translation from: Ben-Gurion, David, "Army and Defense." A lecture delivered on "The Army's Structure and Way" on October 27, 1949. (Tel-Aviv, Ma'arachot, October 1955), p. 141.
3. I use the term defense to cover two Hebrew terms: a) *Haganah*—defense; b) *Bitachon*—security. The Ministry of Defense is called the Ministry of Security.
4. Ben-Gurion, David, "Army and Defense," p. 60. Author's translation.
5. Peri, Y., *Between Battles and Ballots* (Cambridge: Cambridge University Press, 1983), p. 25.
6. The Agranat committee was appointed by the Israeli Cabinet in November 1973 with the mission to inquire into: (1) events preceding the Yom Kippur War as they refer to information about the enemys' moves and intentions as well as information about the preparations made and decisions taken by the relevant military and civil authorities in view of the former. (2) The IDF preparedness for war in general, their preparedness on the eve of the Yom Kippur War in particular and their operations up to the time the enemy's advance was stopped. The committee submitted its report to the cabinet and the Knesset Committee for Foreign Affairs and Defense. Only a part of the report was released for publication. The report included a significant number of recommendations. Some of them referred to personalities. Thus, the committee recommended to "release from their posts" the Chief of the General Staff, the director of Military Intelligence, the commander of southern command, and three senior officers from the military intelligence. Other recommendations referred to organizational subjects, such as the appointment of an advisor to the Prime Minister, on intelligence matters, and the establishment of bodies for the production of intelligence estimates in the *Mossad* and the Foreign Ministry, in addition to the one existing in the military intelligence. There was also a long list of recommendations pertaining to purely military subjects.
7. Laws of the State of Israel, Vol 30 (Jerusalem, Published by the Government Printer, 1975–1976), pp. 150, 151.
8. Peri, Y., *Between Battles and Ballots* (Cambridge: Cambridge Univ. Press, 1983).
9. Perlmutter, Amos, *Military and Politics* (London: Frank Cass & Co., Ltd., 1969), p. 126.
10. Dayan, M., *Milestones*, pp. 422–3.
11. Isaiah, Ch. 44.

Chapter 6

The Dynamics of Israeli National Security Decisionmaking

Amos Perlmutter

INTRODUCTION

The process of policymaking in military organizations is a technical activity, but also a political one. As General Yariv correctly points out, the Israeli military and the Ministry of Defense comprise a two-headed structure, and an unbalanced one. He notes that the Israeli Defense Force (IDF) is the stronger portion of the organization and the Ministry of Defense (MOD) the weaker one. The most telling fact is that the administrative staff of the IDF has no equivalent in the Defense Ministry, with the possible exception of the national security unit that was attached to Defense Ministers Weizmann and Sharon, but which has since been abolished.

Since the time of Prime Minister Ben Gurion, there has emerged an informal but institutionalized security executive represented in the ministerial committee on security, which is an ad hoc group of key ministers to advise the Prime Minister. In Ben Gurion's time, the committee did not exist. As Yariv correctly argues, Ben Gurion was the founding father of the IDF. His patrimonial relationship with the IDF, combined with his vast experience in diplomacy and security, made an institutionalized procedure for security decisionmaking superfluous. The present security committee, virtually an ad hoc war cabinet, is under the authority of the prime minister and is supervised by the Knesset committee on foreign affairs and security. Only since the Likud Party came into power in 1977, however, has the committee become something more than the rubber stamp it was under previous Labor governments.

General Yariv's analysis is highly detailed and presents a nearly complete portrait of the formal organization of the IDF, the parliamentary committee on defense and security, and the special departments of the Defense Ministry and the IDF. The analysis is, however, formal, static, and almost entirely apolitical. What is required is an examination of the political dynamics of Israel's security doctrine and its relation to real life. Political and historical factors are left unexamined, including such issues as the processes involved in the appointment, selection and promotion of the two key IDF officers, the chief of staff and the chief of intelligence, not to mention the political issues involved in appointing the defense ministers. Nor is any of this put in a historical context, so that we learn little of the political dynamics under the various prime ministers and defense ministers from 1948 through 1983. Yariv gives us the constitutional formalities of the hierarchical, functional relationships between the IDF and the Defense Ministry, but what is needed is a comprehensive analysis of the evolution of Israel's security policy over the last four decades.

DECISIONMAKING DURING CRISES

I have no intention of giving an overview of civil–military relations and the IDF–Defense Ministry relationships. What I think is necessary is to emphasize what can be drawn in this vein from General Yariv's paper. The best way to do that is to focus on periods of crisis. For there is no better situation under which to decipher complexities, weaknesses, deformities and imperfections than when officials are under extreme duress and strain.

A number of enduring lessons and a more complete picture of the IDF emerges from a study of these crises. Most significant is a portrait of the IDF as the most enduring, resilient and influential professional military organization in modern times, with the possible exception of the Soviet military. The heart of the matter is that the IDF is the institution that formulates Israel's grand strategy and makes its tactical decisions, although not necessarily the decision to go to war. As Yariv correctly points out, the IDF has at its disposal the most sophisticated, complex, and efficient staff system in Israel, far outdistancing the staffs of the prime minister, the foreign minister, the Defense Ministry, or the Knesset. Again, with the exception of the Soviet military, the IDF can be said to be the only military organization in the world that wields almost complete power over strategic and tactical questions.

The intelligence, planning and operational branches of the IDF, as well as the chief of staff, mold Israel's security doctrines. Rarely do civilian leaders make inroads into that decisionmaking process, even when they are as ideological as a Menachem Begin. Ariel Sharon, and to some extent Ezer Weizman, performed what was, in effect, an end run around the IDF when they created the national security unit. Headed by General Avraham Tamir, this was a twenty-five officer unit that acted as a buffer between civilian authorities and the IDF itself, and that also played a key role in the Egyptian and Lebanese negotiations. Only Ariel Sharon, using Begin's political prestige and power and his own devious methods, managed to slightly dent the IDF's wall of power and expertise.

The supreme decision, however, is the decision for a nation to go to war. It behooves us to examine the dynamics of that type of decision and to see how the results affect the behavior of the entire security structure.

The 1956 War

Ben Gurion, the authoritative founding father of Israel, decided to go to war without consulting his cabinet or party executives. He kept the preparation for war a secret from the cabinet and was aided only by two officers, Chief of Staff Moshe Dayan and Director General of the MOD, Shimon Peres. The IDF had little or no influence on the decision. In fact, the IDF prepared a war against Jordan when Ben Gurion was actually planning a war against Egypt in the Sinai.

The 1967 War

Prior to 1967, David Ben Gurion seemed to have a secure grip on the military, the MOD, and the government. Until 1963, the General Staff and the high command served as Ben Gurion's military advisors. With the departure of Ben Gurion and with the elevation of the more dependent Levi Eshkol to prime minister, those boundaries became irrevocably blurred, even as the administration of the Ministry of Defense became streamlined.

The crisis of 1967, precipitated by both Nasser and the withdrawal of UN troops from the Sinai, saw the IDF move to the forefront of strategic and tactical decisionmaking. Eshkol, who had little or no experience in IDF matters, even though he was the first director general of the Ministry of Defense from 1947 to 1949, became dependent on the General Staff for military, strategic and tactical advice, so much so that Chief of Staff General Yitzhak Rabin acted almost as a surrogate minister of defense. Thus, the decision to go to war lay almost entirely within the purview of the IDF in the absence of an alternative strategic conception by the prime minister, the cabinet, or the government.

This dependency was slightly corrected by the pressure of public opinion and resulted in the appointment of the charismatic Moshe Dayan as defense minister. In the public eye, at least, Dayan represented an institutional authority of sufficient stature and power to either accept or to counter the IDF's policies. In my view, Dayan may have boosted the government's prestige by his charismatic presence, but he had little influence on the actual operational aspects of the war. In fact, he was overruled on his decisions not to go all the way to the Suez Canal and not to occupy the Golan Heights. As defense minister, Dayan had little influence over the IDF's tactical thinking and operations.

The 1973 Yom Kippur War

The 1973 Yom Kippur War is a perfect example of what happens when the IDF becomes the sole author and arbiter of Israel's security policy. What happened was a disaster. Defense Minister Dayan, who was even less staff-conscious than Ben Gurion, depended almost entirely on the IDF for his information and planning, and depended quite heavily as well on the chief of intelligence. Dayan had no staff of his own to examine the validity of the intelligence he was receiving. The result was the machdal (misdeed) in which Israel came dangerously close to being overwhelmed in a surprise attack.

In the aftermath of the war, the Agranat Commission was created to investigate the causes of the initial military and intelligence setback. It took a deep look at the IDF and the intelligence organization. The commission recommended certain reforms that could have clarified the institutional arrangements for intelligence analysis by delineating the institutional boundaries of authority among the IDF, the prime minister, the Defense Ministry, and the government. It recommended the nomination both of an intelligence advisor to the prime minister and a special research staff to the ministries of defense and foreign affairs. The IDF resisted the reforms and won the drawn-out bureaucratic struggles.

The 1982 War in Lebanon

The 1982 War in Lebanon was characterized by Sharon's flagrant attempt to wrest strategical and tactical security authority from the IDF and to dominate the decision to go to war. Sharon managed to succeed, partly because of the coalitional nature of Begin's second government and partly because of the lack of military experience in the Begin cabinet. In the end, Sharon failed, not because of the discovery of his deception, but because of his total lack of statesmanship and diplomacy. What is essential to note, however, is that Sharon was able to collude with a small, but highly placed, segment of the IDF, in order to develop the contingency war plans for the Lebanon campaign entirely without consulting the prime minister or cabinet.

CONCLUSION

There are several important lessons to be learned by viewing the IDF in its three most recent major crises. First, it is obvious that lacking the presence of a militarily experienced, charismatic, or strong figure in the government, such as Ben Gurion, there are no groups, organizations or institutions in the Israeli parliamentary multiparty and coalitional system that can compete with the IDF. The IDF is an autonomous, efficient, experienced, imaginative, and highly zealous military organization. In Israel, where war is almost a way of life, the IDF is the best organized, most cohesive, enduring, and central organization within the state. As of yet, the IDF has not developed a separate national ideology of its own; but it *does* chart the direction of Israel's security policies, because there is no other structure that can equal it. It is a singularly restrained organization. It chooses to lobby the government, but it is jealous of its professional, insitutional, and organizational structure and of its decisionmaking perogatives in security matters.

Over the years, the IDF has demonstrated a remarkable resiliency and has survived ideologically-oriented cabinets of the right and the left, to remain the central security institution in Israel. The IDF is at the heart of Israel's society, politics and culture, and, to a great degree, in spite of the chilling and controversial experience in Lebanon, it remains so.

Second, in spite of the unchallenged and unchanging position of the IDF as arbiter of Israel's security policies, the nation itself steadfastly remains a democratic political culture. This is so, not in spite of the IDF, but, often, because of the IDF. Often, as was the case with Sharon and his ambitions, the IDF has served as a buffer between the nation and the undemocratic practices of individuals. The IDF, as a unit, is imbued with an inclination and a duty to defend Israel's democratic institutions, even though there might be a tiny minority of individuals within the IDF who may view democracy with either dislike or skepticism. The IDF also remains probably the only national institution still heavily imbued with the values of early Zionism, which makes its struggles against the Palestinian nationalist guerrillas a doubly painful chore.

Third, on a more technical level, what can be gleaned from studying Israel's armed forces is that there appears to be a necessity for organizational and technological reform. Only in Israel does the chief of staff always also hold the position of the chief of the army. The Air Force and Navy both have their separate organizational staffs. General Israel Tal has become the chief spokesman of the need to reform the structures of the IDF and the MOD, with an eye toward creating a separate chief for the Army and a specialized staff attached to the minister of defense for research and development.

Recent Chiefs of Staff Gur and Eitan were opposed to any reform and fearful of the loss of their control over the IDF. The likelihood of reform in the near future is low, because the IDF is as jealous of its prerogatives and as conservative as the old German general staff.

As in the case of other armies, the Israeli Army seems to be lagging technologically when compared to the Air Force and Navy. The Air Force and the small, but efficient, Navy are vigorously pursuing a research and development policy because they rely so heavily on technological innovation.

Fourth, the IDF is an army of commanders, not administrators. The IDF chief of staff is not only the senior military strategist but also its senior *field* commander. In war, the IDF chief of staff is directly in charge of all military commanders and continuously intervenes in major decisions made by the field and staff officers on both strategic and tactical levels. The IDF chief is a fighting officer and *all* chiefs have had considerable experience as field commanders.

The IDF chief of staff considers all the wars of Israel as a single theater. Thus, no extensive bureaucratic networks are needed to coordinate all the three fronts (north, central, south), which are actually a single war theater.

Fifth, the IDF's role as coordinator of the occupied territories, the West Bank, Gaza, Northern Lebanon (to 1981, also Sinai), extends its functions to military administration. Here, the danger of politicization (as was the case with the IDF administrator under Defense Minister Sharon, the minister responsible for occupied or administered territories) is one of great concern to liberal Israelis. Here again the IDF, while carrying out governmental orders, is constrained by the volatile environment of the occupied territories. What is significant for the IDF's morale and for its professional integrity, is that it does not execute government policy with the zealotry it did under the leadership of Defense Minister Sharon and the zealot Chief of Staff Rafael (Raful) Eitan. Both were exceptions to the rule, inspired by a militant government. What effects sustained occupation will have on IDF morale, we are yet to witness. Once again, much depends on who the civilian leaders of the nation are and their political *Weltanschauung*.

In conclusion, the basic rules of democratic and pluralistic behavior are today being observed in Israel, in spite of the long shadow cast by the IDF. Strangely enough, although Israel appears to be a highly militaristic society, Israel has never suffered from militarism, as such. The mechanism for correction and pressure—public opinion, a free and free-wheeling media— remain in place and function, much in the same manner that they do in the American and British models. What is readily apparent is that the IDF, even though it is often the sole arbiter of security policies, is also in the position of being the defender of democratic and Zionist values. If one looks at the political history of Israel, one notes that it has been a few civilian leaders who have shown autocratic and militaristic tendencies, not the military.

The nature of the IDF is that it is at once separate but loyal, autonomous but a servant, nonideological but protective of the government. Israeli governments have tended to recognize this and have not attempted to instill the IDF with a particular ideology.

The IDF will remain the guarantor of Israeli democracy, as long as it remains independent and does not become servile to the whims of the likes of a Sharon. Its very strengths and autonomy also are its virtues as the protector of political democracy.

Here General Yariv's contribution is of tremendous significance.

Chapter 7

Changes in Canada's Organization for Defense: 1963–1983

W. Harriet Critchley

Canada, more than any other nation in the West, has experienced a number of major changes in its organization and management of defense in the postwar years. In every instance, these changes were made in order to provide for greater coordination of policy, greater integration of common functions and greater efficiency in the use of both human and financial resources.

Many contemporary observers, both foreign and domestic, tend to focus exclusively on one change that occurred in 1968, when Canada's three-armed services were unified into a single armed force. Such a focus seriously distorts the analysis of Canada's management of defense in at least two ways: it ignores the continuous, though not necessarily consciously planned, evolution of organizational structure for the central purposes just mentioned; and it leaves the false impression that the organizational structures and procedures instituted since 1968 are only possible with a unified armed force. This chapter attempts to sketch the evolution of Canada's management of defense in the postwar years. Because of the confusion concerning unification and its effects on the organizational structure, particular emphasis will be placed on changes that have taken place over the last two decades.

Canada had emerged from World War II with three separate defense ministries—one each for the Army, Navy and Air Force. Each had its own minister, deputy minister, chief of service and staff of officers and civil servants. The Chief of the General Staff also held the position of chairman of the chiefs of staff committee, but this position and the committee had little formal authority. The small degree of coordination in the management of defense that did occur, took place largely within the cabinet. In 1946, in an attempt to enforce greater coordination and reduce costs, a single minister of national defense and a single deputy minister were appointed, the chairman of the chiefs of staff committee was charged with interservice coordination and a series of interservice committees were created. In 1950, parliament passed the National Defence Act, which consolidated the statutes of the three separate ministries, codified the changes mentioned previously, and attempted to provide for further coordination by creating the new position of chairman of the chiefs of staff committee, which was to be filled by a senior officer who was not a service chief. This committee was provided with a rather large joint staff, and had the responsibility of coordinating defense activities and integrating certain common functions among the three separate services. The chiefs of staff committee was to advise the minister on such military matters as defense policy, plans, operations and training, while the deputy minister had the civilian administrative and financial responsibilities for the ministry and for the ministry's dealings with other departments and agencies of the government. Although the division of responsibilities into military and civilian looked clear on paper, in reality, the management of defense required the committee to interact with the deputy minister (and vice versa) on the whole range of responsibilities for the purposes of preparing the annual defense budget and overseeing the expenditure of budgeted funds.

For the twelve years following 1950, there was little significant change in either the management structure or the responsibilities that had been set out in the National Defence Act. By 1963, Canada still had three separate armed forces—the Canadian Army, the Royal Canadian Navy and the Royal Canadian Air Force—with three separate headquarters in Ottawa. Each headquarters was responsible for military plans and their consequent operational requirements for personnel, training, equipment, supply and general welfare of the military. As shown in Figure 7.1, coordination of military activities was to be achieved through the chiefs of staff committee headed by the chairman. In addition to these armed forces organizations, there was a departmental organization headed by the deputy minister of defense. The latter organization was staffed predominantly by civil servants and had administrative, legal, financial, procurement, construction and civilian personnel responsibilities.

Although the three service headquarters and the departmental organization were virtually four separate structures with information flows occurring vertically up and down within each structure, coordination was attempted by the creation of some 200 interservice committees and by meetings of the defense council. The defense council included the minister of defense, parliamentary secretary, deputy minister, associate deputy minister and the members of the chiefs of staff committee. Depending on the issues being discussed, civil servants from other departments of the federal government and the cabinet secretariat would attend both defense council

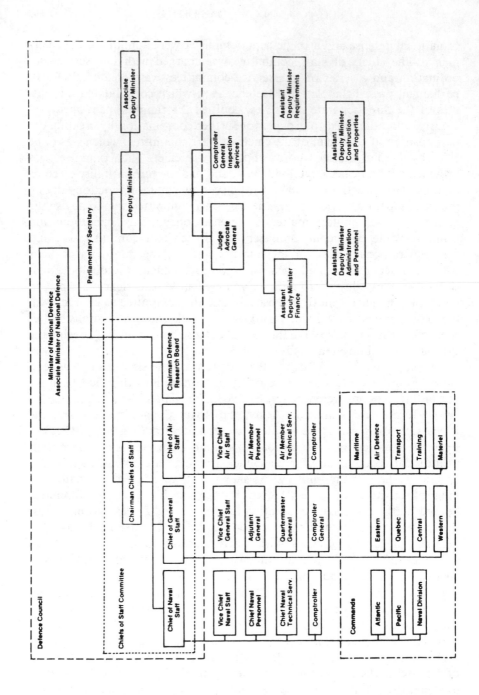

FIGURE 7.1. Department of National Defense Organization, 1963 (Source: *Task Force on Review of Unification of the Canadian Forces: Final Report, 15 March 1980*, Annex D, p. 101.)

and chiefs of staff committee meetings — indeed, they attended meetings of interservice committees as well.

The structure just described reflected a priority accorded to defense and an organizational evolution based on Canada's military requirements, experiences, and activities during World War II and the Korean War. However, by 1961, governmental decisions on defense were beset by quite a different constellation of concerns: Other domestic political priorities were competing for governmental attention and expenditure; new strategic concepts and developments in military technology were being discussed in the Western alliance; the armed forces had suffered a series of embarrassing and expensive weapons procurement fiascoes; and personnel and administrative costs within the armed forces were rising dramatically, to the point where it was predicted that, without significant budget increases, there would be no money for capital equipment acquisition by 1969.

In 1961 the federal government appointed the royal commission on government organization, known as the Glassco Commission, to examine the whole of the government service, to eliminate duplication and uneconomical operations, and to recommend improvements in decentralization and in more efficient management practices. Defense was a major focus of that commission's inquiry.

The Glassco Commission made a series of recommendations regarding the department of national defense in order to promote more efficient management and eliminate uneconomic operations. The most important of these were: the replacement of the chairman of the chiefs of staff committee by an appointed chief of the Canadian defense staffs, to direct the armed forces and control their common elements; the assertion of civilian control by giving the deputy minister of defense greater responsibilities for review of the department's organization and administration on behalf of the minister; the requirement to review civilian and military personnel needs in each of the three services and their headquarters. Although these and other recommendations addressed the need for better coordination of activities common to the three services and for more effective application of personnel, they also focused on the need to promote efficiency in combat operations. In short, the commission's recommendations were designed to promote better coordination among the separate services and between the armed forces' headquarters and the department. By promoting such coordination and further integration of support functions (including greater utilization of civilian personnel), the commission felt that the true tasks of providing national defense could be achieved more efficiently than had been previously predicted.

It should be noted that although integration and even unification of the armed forces are mentioned in passing, the whole tenor of the commission's report clearly assumed the continued existence of three separate services. In other words, the commission was concerned with improvements in the management of the *existing* defense organization and armed services, not in their complete reorganization.

The Glassco Commission's report was published in 1963. The analysis and recommendations it contained eventually exerted considerable influence on the management of defense in Canada. Before those recommendations could be implemented, however, a separate series of events intervened and changed the whole context for seeking better coordination and efficiency.

In 1963, a new government took office and, among other things, decided to conduct a wide-ranging review of defense policy and organization. The result was the publication of the White Paper on Defence in March, 1964 and, shortly thereafter, the introduction of legislation to reorganize the headquarters of the department of national defense and the field command structure. The legislation—Bill C-90—is commonly seen as the one that integrated Canada's three armed services. The purpose of the reorganization was to allow Canada's armed forces to meet the objectives of Canadian defense policy, as enunciated in the White Paper on Defence, more efficiently and effectively. However, the continued lack of intradepartmental coordination (despite the existence of all of the interservice committees), the slow progress being made in integrating common services and functions, and the escalating costs of providing for defense under the existing structure—all were equally important considerations in drawing up the legislation.

As shown in Figure 7.2, coordination of military activities at headquarters was to be achieved by appointing a single chief of the defense staff and creating a headquarters organized along functional lines. Whereas in the past there were functional subdivisions within headquarters—personnel, comptroller, and technical services, for example—each of these was separated according to service. That is, as shown very clearly in Figure 7.1, there were three different subdivisions for each function. To take the example of the comptroller function, there was a comptroller subdivision in Naval headquarters, another in Army headquarters and a third in Air Force headquarters. The same was true for the personnel and technical services functions. In addition, the service chief of staff was the commander for both the service headquarters and the operational units in the field.

The reorganization of 1964 changed this structure. Functional divisions across the services were created, and each service contributed personnel to each of the divisions. The chief of defense staff commanded all the new functional divisions, as well as all the operational units in the field.

Prior to the 1964 reorganization, the defense council had consisted of four senior military officers (the chiefs of staff committee) and five civilians, including the minister. Depending on the issue, other military officers

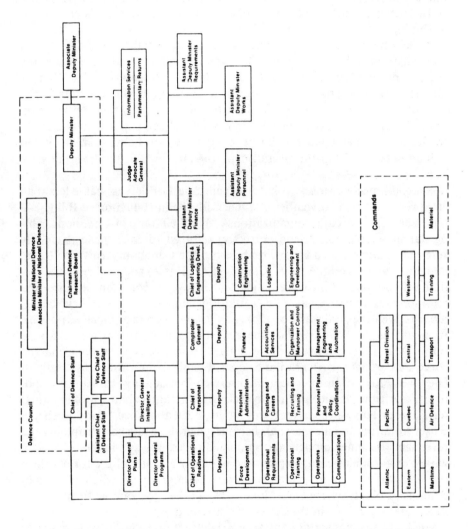

FIGURE 7.2. Department of National Defense Organization, 1964 (Source: *Task Force on Review of Unification of the Canadian Forces: Final Report, 15 March 1980*, Annex E, p. 102.)

and civil servants attended. After the 1964 reorganization, the defense council consisted of two senior military officers (the chief and the vice chief of the defense staff) and three civilians, including the minister. Again, depending on the issue, other military officers and civil servants attended. Although the new defense council was somewhat smaller, and there was a determination to make this the forum where final decisions were made, the relative proportion of military to civilian representation had hardly changed. By comparison to the organizational revolution occurring in the chief of defense staff's part of the department, the deputy minister's role remained unchanged. Thus, the reorganization of 1964 had a dramatic effect on the services headquarters, but it left the division between military and civilian aspects within the overall departmental organization virtually intact.

A second major revolution in the organization of defense came less than three years later, in November of 1966, with the introduction of Bill C-243 (The Canadian Forces Reorganization Act) in the House of Commons. This legislation is commonly, and correctly, referred to as the one that truly unified Canada's armed forces. It abolished the Canadian Army, the Royal Canadian Navy, and the Royal Canadian Air Force, and in their place created the Canadian Forces — a single service with a common uniform and common rank designations. This legislation came into effect on February 1, 1968. In 1964 the goal was, to put it simply, to integrate as much as possible as rapidly as possible. In 1968, the goal was, simply, to unify everything.

For the military personnel at headquarters, as elsewhere in the Canadian Forces, a personal reorientation of considerable proportions was required. They were now all in the one armed service, but some were with the land, air, or maritime "environments" or "elements," rather than with the Army, Air Force or Navy — the latter terms having been abolished from speech and prose. Admirals and air marshals became generals, while naval captains and lieutenants became colonels and majors. Procedures and modes of organization or administration, as practised in one or another of the former three services, were chosen to be applied across-the-board in the whole of the new Canadian Forces, without time having been taken to examine the potential effects on operations in the different "environments."

Much of the commentary and scholarly attention to unification has been focused on these issues. It may therefore be surprising to stand back from such issues and see the degree to which such a revolution in military organization was *not* reflected in the basic organization of the headquarters. As Figure 7.3 indicates, many of the major divisions within headquarters and the lines of authority remained the same as those that had been instituted by the 1964 reorganization. The basic division within headquarters remained the predominantly military organization, which, including the operational units in the field, was commanded by the chief of the defense staff and the

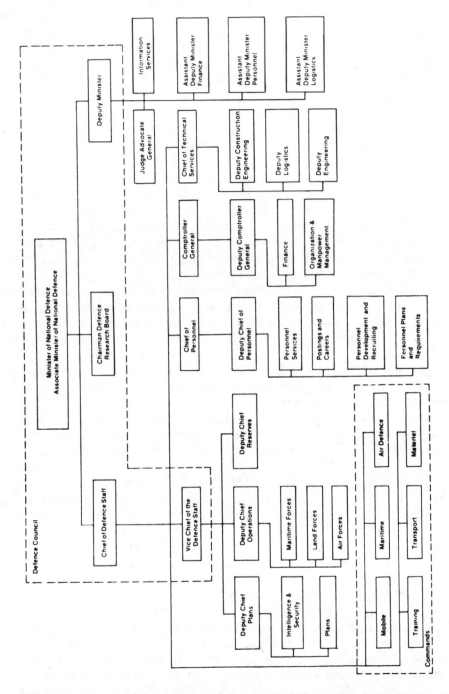

FIGURE 7.3. Department of National Defense Organization, 1968 (Source: *Task Force on Review of Unification of the Canadian Forces: Final Report, 15 March 1980*, Annex F, p. 103.)

143

predominantly civilian organization headed by the deputy minister. The membership of the defense council remained unchanged, as did the basic organization of the whole headquarters along functional lines.

Within the military part of headquarters, the only change of any significance was the restriction of the vice chief of defense staff's responsibilities to supervising the plans, operations and reserves divisions, and the consequent "promotion" of the chiefs of personnel, technical services and comptroller general to the level of vice chief in the organization. Each of the four officers now reported directly to the chief of the defense staff. Other changes occurred within the divisions supervised by the vice chief.

To summarize, the institution of unification did produce a revolution, both within the structure of the armed forces and personally, for many military officers and other ranks, including those serving in headquarters. However, unification did *not* produce changes on anything approximating the same scope or scale in the basic organization of headquarters. That particular revolution came four years later.

In spite of consolidation into one department in 1946, creation of a chairman, chiefs of staff in 1953, integration of the armed services under the command of a chief of defense staff and reorganization of headquarters along function lines in 1964, and reorganization of the armed forces into a single service in 1968, there were still problems in the management of the department of national defense. The needs still not being fulfilled were better coordination of planning and budgeting, better accountability and control of capital acquisition, elimination of costly duplication of effort and expense, and more effective relationships with those other government departments that had an input into defense decisionmaking. The persistence of these basic problems led to the appointment of the Management Review Group (MRG) in 1971.

The MRG study was commissioned by all of the major components of the Ministry of Defense: the offices of the minister and the deputy minister, the defense research board and the Canadian Armed Forces.[1] The study was to examine such continuing problems as duplication of function and activities among several of the major components of the ministry, lack of a coherent view of the purpose and overall functions of departmental and Canadian Forces, imperfect management, if not mismanagement, of weapons procurement for the Canadian Forces, and lack of progress in implementing the recommendations of the Glassco Commission.

The MRG study appears to have been the most comprehensive analysis of defense management in Canada conducted to date. It reviewed strategic studies, planning and policy development, the command and control system, military support services, research, engineering, logistics, finance, and personnel. The MRG study made a large number of specific recommendations. These were based on three guiding principles which would resolve the ministry's central management problems: to restructure national defense headquarters into a single entity; to provide for a greater focus on the operational activities of the Canadian Forces; and, to provide for more delegation of authority within the ministry.

The MRG submitted its report to the minister of national defense in July of 1972. The subsequent implementation of its recommendations amounted, in effect, to a reorganization of the one area of departmental organization that had remained unchanged in the post World War II era: the separation of the military and civilian parts of the headquarters organization. That reorganization can best be characterized as the *integration* of these two parts to form a single organization.

As shown in Figure 7.4, the implementation of the MRG's recommendations resulted in a comprehensive restructuring of the entire organization, and particularly of the senior management structure. In the past, plans and projects could, and often did, filter up through the military organization, and, in the process, become fully elaborated and approved within that part of headquarters, only to be rejected by the civilian side, that is, by the deputy minister. That, in turn, required a complete reprocessing, by the military part of the organization, to reach an amended plan or project. This was a laborious, time consuming and wasteful procedure, which carried no guarantee that the result of another military review would succeed in gaining the approval of the deputy minister. The basic flaw was that headquarters was structured in such a way that it operated with little meaningful interaction between the civilian and military parts of the organization, except at the very top. Total integration of the two parts into a single organization was seen as the optimal solution to the problem. It would mandate close interaction at the outset of any plan or project and, thereby, allow for difficulties or problems to be seen and resolved at the early or middle stages of development. It would also provide for real coordination within the *whole* headquarters organization. As a consequence of the 1972 reorganization the functional divisions created in the 1964 reorganization and retained in the 1968 reorganization were not simply retained, but reinforced.

A comparison of Figures 7.3 and 7.4 shows how the integration of headquarters was accomplished. What had been the military organization for personnel, for example, headed by a chief of personnel, was amalgamated with the civilian organization for personnel, headed by an assistant deputy minister, assisted by an associate deputy minister. If the assistant deputy minister was a civilian, the associate deputy minister would be a military officer, and vice versa. Civil servants and military officers who had worked separately in each division were now amalgamated and worked together. This same integration occurred for finance/comptroller general, which became finance, and for technical services/logistics, which became materiel.

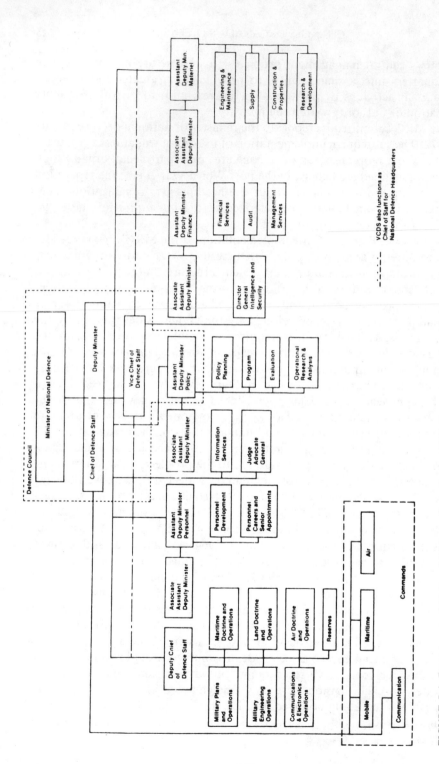

FIGURE 7.4. Department of National Defence Organization 1979 (Source: *Task Force on Review of Unification of the Canadian Forces: Final Report, 15 March 1980,* Annex G, p. 104.)

Information and the judge advocate general's (JAG) divisions remained distinct units, while intelligence and security was removed from the plans division, to become a separate division. The remainder of the old plans division was divided and elaborated. One series of divisions, headed by an assistant deputy minister, was responsible for overall planning and program control, along with independent operational research and evaluation of plans and programs. Another series of divisions, headed by the deputy chief of defense staff (a new position), was responsible for military planning, tactical doctrine development, military operations and reserve forces.

The integrated organization, now consists of five major groups or divisions—policy, personnel, finance, materiel and military plans, doctrine and operations—with each group headed by a group principal. The group principals are at the assistant deputy minister or three-star rank. They can be either civil servants or military officers. In addition to the five major groups, there are the three independent divisions (information, JAG, intelligence and security). The vice chief of defense staff acts as the general manager of the entire headquarters organization and is second in command to the chief of the defense staff in the Canadian Forces. The chief of the defense staff and the deputy minister are seen as coequals, who, though having distinct tasks, share responsibility for the effective and efficient functioning of the integrated headquarters structure. In turn, they are responsible to the minister of national defense.

The evolution of unification did not end with the 1972 reorganization of national defense headquarters. Many problems remained, and they continued to create a variety of difficulties. Of the changes instituted since 1972, the most significant was the formation of the air command in 1975, by drawing together the former air transport and air defense commands and those tactical air units deployed in Europe or attached to mobile and maritime commands. Again, it was the need to cut costs and improve coordination in planning and operations that prompted change. Although this change had virtually no impact on the organization of the national defense headquarters at the time, it did mark the re-emergence of an Air Force (air command), a Navy (maritime command), and an Army (mobile command). Use of the terms Army, Navy, and Air Force received official public sanction when they appeared in the report of the Task Force on Review of Unification in 1980, although the formal titles of the commands still remain as they were in 1975.

Integration of the military and civilian parts of headquarters did not result in an influx of civil servants into the organization. It merely brought the two sets of people, who had been working largely separately from each other in their two hierarchies, together throughout the organization.

The aim of integration and the organization of headquarters along functional lines was to provide for better coordination and management of defense in Canada. In the process, by virtue of an increased membership on each of a larger number of senior committees, the military now has *more* influence over a broader range of issues and at a higher level than in the past. This phenomenon is now a source of concern for some knowledgeable Canadian analysts. Other difficulties remain as a focus for future attention.

In my opinion, however, the current national defense headquarters organization and the management system for defense in Canada reflect substantial progress towards achieving the central objections of greater efficiency, coordination and control. In this sense, the Canadian experience over the past twenty years should be instructive for those analysts in the United States who are concerned with the management of U.S. defense. Although Canada seems to have traveled much further along the road of a functional, as opposed to a service-oriented, approach to the problems of defense management, and although there are significant differences in size of military forces, scale of defense commitments, and governmental systems, political culture and history, nevertheless, the basic outlines of Canada's postwar evolution in the organization and management of defense should be applicable to defense management in other Western countries.

NOTE

1. Much of the information on the MRG in this and following paragraphs is based on a paper by C. R. Nixon, entitled "Management of Canadian Defence," which was presented at the Conference on Civilian–Military Management of the Pentagon, Harvard University, November 1983. I am indebted to the sponsors of the conference for their kind permission to include these data.

Chapter 8

The Evolution of Central U.S. Defense Management

Vincent Davis

INTRODUCTION

Major efforts to reorganize the U.S. military establishment have recurred throughout American history, especially since the late nineteenth century. Several circumstances have brought about these endeavors. First, the gradually expanding international role of the United States required a concomitantly growing and evolving military establishment, which, in turn, called for new organizational formats. Second, the accelerating pace of scientific and technological advances dictated new strategies, tactics, and doctrine, all of which necessitated new organizational modes if the new capabilities were to be fully realized. Third, the military establishment was frequently a target of the more general governmental reform movements that arose from time to time and that were driven by typically American desires for more efficiency in government, for the elimination of waste and duplication, and for appeals for greater fairness.

Beyond these broad circumstances, specific catalysts for reform have been required to propel it. These have ordinarily been of two types. First, anxieties about perceived military unreadiness for growing external threats have created one occasion for military reorganization. Almost all American military involvements have taken the United States largely by surprise, leading to rapid military expansion and a perception that the existing peacetime organizational modes would be inadequate for prospective wartime needs. Second, once a war ended, postwar reviews have typically determined that wartime organizational improvisations were an imperfect match for anticipated postwar demands. Therefore, most large-scale American military reorganizations have occurred in response to anxieties and criticisms generated shortly before and soon after American wars. The movement for organizational reform of the military establishment during 1982 and 1983 was probably derived, in large part, from both these impulses — the long-delayed response to whatever organizational lessons might have been learned from the Vietnam War, but also a response to perceptions of rapidly evolving and ominous threats ahead.

Regardless of the circumstances that have led to change, America's military reorganizations have achieved considerably less than their reformers had hoped for. Large-scale reorganizations in any setting are inherently controversial and acrimonious, with apprehensive conservatives arguing the continuing advantages of the status quo and easily outnumbering the reformers promising dramatic new benefits. These debates have been exacerbated because most of the parties have had hidden agendas, especially the uniformed leaders who have sought special gains for their separate armed services. In these bureaucratic and political struggles, the Army, and later the Air Force, have been loosely joined on one side, while the Navy and the Marines have been arrayed on the other. The Army and the Air Force have been far more receptive to reorganization proposals than the Navy and Marines — a generalization once again supported in the alignments emerging in the wake of the reform movement of early 1982.

To characterize these debates as bureaucratic and political, however, is not to say that they are trivial. To the contrary, important stakes are on the table, even, potentially, the survival of the United States. But the history of American military reorganization suggests that not much is likely to happen unless a newly elected or re-elected president is determined to invest a considerable amount of political capital in these efforts during the typical honeymoon period following inauguration.

In light of the foregoing generalizations, the remainder of this chapter will review the main events in the history of American military organization and reorganization and conclude with observations on the problems and prospects for future organizational reforms.

A REVIEW OF ORGANIZATIONAL CHANGE

Centralization has been the inexorable trend in virtually all large formal organizations in this century. For our purposes, it can be defined as the creation of a new layer of authority at a level in the organizational pyramid that reduces the autonomy of the levels below it. This has been the dominant trend in all reorganizations of the U.S. military establishment, a trend always supported by reformers, and always resisted by those whose roles it threatened.

In the twentieth century, the first concrete steps were taken in the immediate aftermath of the Spanish–American War, which, though short and successful, nevertheless revealed numerous organizational shortcomings. The zeal for correcting the deficiencies was reinforced, both by the more general reform movement within American government and by the perception that the United States was on the eve of a substantial and continuing international involvement. Thus, to achieve greater cohesion and coordination within the two armed services, the general board was created in the Navy in 1900, and the general staff system was created in the Army in 1903. Then, to achieve greater coordination between these two services, the joint Army–Navy board was also created in 1903 and served as the forerunner to the Joint Chiefs of Staff system, which emerged forty years later. These new entities were committees that lacked true command authority and were imperfect, both in precept and in practice. Nevertheless, they represented dramatic steps when compared to the previous fragmentation within and between the war department and the Navy.

The period of World War I was the next occasion for reform. In 1915 the Congress established, by law, the office of the chief of naval operations (CNO) and, thus, brought the Navy's structure more into line with the Army's general staff system. More important, in 1916 President Wilson experimented with an entity called the council of national defense. This was akin to a cabinet level committee, and represented the first effort in this century to achieve some centralization on military matters at the highest civilian levels. When the United States finally became an active participant in World War I, Wilson did what so many other presidents have done, both before and since: he turned the war effort over to the uniformed leaders (in this case, General Pershing). Nevertheless, Wilson's council of national defense could be regarded as the forerunner to the National Security Council created after World War II.

In 1938, as the events abroad turned more ominous, President Roosevelt created the first mixed civilian–military group assigned to undertake military planning at the highest levels of government. Called the Standing Liaison Committee, it did not achieve a great deal before Roosevelt turned over most military planning and direction to the uniformed personnel who reported directly to him, as Wilson had twenty-two years earlier. These uniformed leaders subsequently constituted the Joint Chiefs of Staff. In 1944, as planning for the postwar period became increasingly important, Roosevelt experimented with a second variation of a high-level mixed civilian–military group, called the State–War–Navy Coordinating Committee (SWNCC). The rush of events overwhelmed SWNCC as World War II drew to a close, and it, too, accomplished relatively little, except to set the stage for the outbreak of acrimonious new debates over the ideal way to reorganize governmental/military machinery for the postwar era.

The search for the ideal U.S. military establishment in the immediate aftermath of World War II was inevitably a tortured process. In the first place, there was little if any consensus on the basic "friends and enemies" question. What new challenges, threats and opportunities lay ahead? With old enemies vanquished, were there new adversaries on the horizon? Were there stalwart friends to join the United States in whatever needed to be done? Could public opinion be generated to support new international efforts, just at the time when most Americans wanted nothing so much as a return to peacetime normalcy? Beyond these considerations lay the awesome task of figuring out the implications of new technologies, most particularly of nuclear weapons, but also radar, jet aviation, and, soon, missiles.

First, however, an older technology, military aviation, heated up the organizational debate even more than the newer ones. The invention of the airplane around 1900 had erased the utility of what Laurence J. Legere called the "coastline principle," according to which all military organizations had traditionally been grouped either into armies or navies. The best way for the United States government to organize both the civilian and military uses of airplanes was a large controversy between World Wars I and II. As for the military uses, the issue was resolved by gradually converting the U.S. Army Air Corps into a virtually autonomous service separate from the U.S. Army, although aviation units remained organic within the Navy. Key issues still to be resolved after 1945 were whether to incorporate Navy and Marine aviation units within any such separate aviation service and whether to embrace all changes within an overall new organizational format for the entire military establishment.

Many other issues surfaced within the post-1945 debate over the needs and uses of the armed services, for example, regarding the question of whether to retain conscription and perhaps even to expand it into something called universal military training. But the most acrimonious issues revolved primarily around the question of whether to reorganize the separate services under some type of new centralizing umbrella structure, and reduce service autonomy in the process.

This debate opened rather quietly within the Pentagon in 1943, but it erupted in full public fury in late 1945 under the rubric "unification of the armed forces." The eventual result was the National Security Act of 1947 (NSA) and—as is typical when resolving controversies in a democracy—it was a compromise. It was and still remains the most significant piece of American legislation on the organization of the government for military and foreign policy purposes. The Air Force was a major winner because it achieved its most cherished goal as a statutorily separate service. The Army, Navy, and the Marines retained equivalent degrees of autonomy, and both the Navy and Marines kept their aviation components. But the four other main provisions of the NSA were major steps toward more centralization. The NSA created the office of the secretary of defense and accorded statutory permanence to the Joint Chiefs of Staff. Beyond the Pentagon, the NSA created the National Security Council and the Central Intelligence Agency.

Even after the passage of the National Security Act of 1947, the struggle continued over questions of military organization, because white-hot controversies are rarely resolved in a final manner in democracies as long as key parties remain alive and kicking. However, thereafter, the conflict proceeded along two roads that were not always clearly connected. On what might be called the high road—because it was almost always visible as an ongoing formal and official process—the NSA and its 1949, 1953, and 1958 amendments were the major landmarks. These changes were aimed primarily at strengthening the centralized entities on the civilian side of the Pentagon, starting with the creation of the department of defense (DOD) itself in the 1949 amendments, the provisions for an expanding bureaucracy within the office of the secretary of defense (OSD) to support the secretary (SECDEF), and a set of substantially greater authorities entrusted to the SECDEF in the 1958 amendments. Secretary Gates, the first to serve under the provisions of the 1958 amendments, identified twenty-five new types of clout that the SECDEF could exercise, and Gates began to exercise them. His immediate successor, Secretary McNamara, took office and quickly began to exploit fully all the powers inherent in his office, in addition to utilizing a number of imaginative, although less formal, techniques for imposing his personal control over the DOD.[1]

Whereas this chain of events on the high road of military reorganization from the late 1940s into the early 1960s steadily strengthened the top civilian officials of the Pentagon, it gave the appearance of downgrading the separate services and of adding very little new clout to the relatively weak Joint Chiefs of Staff (JCS) mechanisms. The service secretaries were demoted from cabinet status and, by the mid-1960s, appeared to be little more than administrative flunkies in the outer court surrounding the defense secretary.

To summarize, then, an observer would have received the following impressions about three key sets of Pentagon actors if he could see only the evidence provided along the high road of military reorganization from the late 1940s into the middle 1960s:

- First, the entire civilian hierarchy or "secretariat" generally embraced by the OSD concept, and most particularly the SECDEF, were vastly strengthened as the dominant actors.
- Second, the overall JCS apparatus was only very modestly strengthened, primarily via evolutionary new increments of authority for the JCS chairman.
- Third, the separate services, including their civilian secretariats, were diminished as autonomous actors.

But appearances can be deceiving. There was no question that the OSD civilian hierarchy gained new bureaucratic strength, and it is largely correct that the overall JCS apparatus, in comparison to the growing clout on the civilian side within the OSD, remained generally weak and ineffective. But it would have been a serious mistake to believe that the services were somehow withering on the vine. On the contrary, they accommodated, but never surrendered to, McNamara, even during his heyday. They began to exhibit a resurgence toward the end of McNamara's era as he lost credibility because of Vietnam. Laird, McNamara's successor in the Nixon Administration, explicitly reversed McNamara's denigration of professional military influence, although knowledgeable observers have contended that Laird's publicized decentralization back toward stronger roles for the uniformed leaders was considerably less than advertised. Even so, the steadily louder, if not clearer, voices of the professional military were a continuing phenomenon from the later 1960s until it reached a new zenith in Secretary Weinberger's tenure in the Reagan Administration. The professional officers sometimes used the JCS mechanism as their chosen instrument in asserting their positions, creating the mistaken impression that the JCS itself was gaining a stronger voice. In fact, it was ordinarily the separate services speaking through the JCS microphone.[2]

The "high road" of military organization reform gradually came to an end in the mid-1960s. Prior to 1982, the Jackson preparedness subcomittee's hearings and studies of the late 1950s represented the last time that Congress attempted to delve deeply into military organizaton issues; and the 1958 amendments were the last time that the National Security Act was legislatively modified. Of course, there were many further study groups and reports. The Legere studies at the Institute for Defense Analyses (IDA, 1968), the Fitzhugh Blue Ribbon Panel report (1970), the Ignatius report (1978), the Steadman report (1978), the Rice report (1979), the Odeen report (1979), and the Brehm report (1982) were the informal names given to several key efforts. But the only results were sporadic, quite modest, and incremental changes. As for formal, high-level, comprehensive change, it was the familiar case of *plus ca change, plus c'est la meme chose.*

The paucity of significant and substantial changes in the JCS arena was well summarized in the opening sentences of a document entitled, "The Evolving Role of the Joint Chiefs of Staff in the National Security Structure" (produced and distributed by the Historical Division, Joint Secretariat, Joints Chiefs of Staff, July 1977).

> The institution of the Joint Chiefs of Staff was born of necessity in World War II, shortly after the United States became a belligerent. The years since then have seen fundamental changes in national defense organization, notably the creation of the Secretary of Defense and the National Security Council, the establishment of a separate Air Force, and a marked decline in the relative importance of the Service Departments and their Secretaries. By comparison, the Joint Chiefs of Staff have undergone relatively little change in their status and functions.

The high road of military organizational reform within the Pentagon ended in the mid-1960s. But at an even higher level, that is, the White House, a variety of developments occurred that had significant implications for the department of defense. Almost all of these included a greater degree of direct presidential involvement in making policy and strategy, and, sometimes, even in tactical operational decisions. The foremost development was the larger and larger role played by the president's national security advisor.

The greater involvement of the White House in military matters reduced the incentives to rectify the pervasive problems in the Pentagon. Congressional, media, and public attention focused on the White House as the source, not only of overall policy guidance, but the day-to-day management of policy. What they neglected to notice, however, were three other developments. First, the White House, even with its own burgeoning bureaucracy, was ill-equipped to handle these newly assumed responsibilities, and thus contributed to the frequency and magnitude of breakdowns, both in the making and in the implementing of national security policy. Second, the severity of the breakdowns exacerbated what, by the mid-1960s, was already becoming the growing struggle between the White House and Congress for control over security policy, with Congress attacking the White House, rather than the Pentagon, except when it used the Pentagon as a device to whip the commander in chief. Third, with attention diverted toward the high-level strife along Pennsylvania Avenue, officials and officers across the river at the Pentagon were free to play their bureaucratic games against each other; games that the flawed centralization schemes imposed on the military establishment, from the National Security Act of 1947 until about the time of Secretary McNamara's departure some twenty years later, never cured.

Simply put, the armed forces were never truly unified. The low road trend, starting with the battles over unification of the armed forces, was a major contributing cause for the Pentagon's nickname: *Malfunction Junction*. (Other nicknames with similar connotations include the *Puzzle Palace*, the *Concrete Carousel*, and *Disneyland East*.) These low road developments were far less publicized than the high road landmarks. These decisions, often made by the Secretary of Defense, had the effect of establishing turf boundaries, in the manner of treaties after great bureaucratic wars had erupted and re-erupted. These "agreements" (and there was ordinarily very little actual agreement) were critically important in organizational terms, because they staked out the ground to be occupied and defended by the most important of the large visible components of the department of defense — the separate services. Holding the organizational high ground was fundamental to each of the services, because it saw its very survival to be dependent on winning these struggles, which were rather like border wars between none too friendly tribes.

Probably the most important of the roles and missions treaties are those known as the Key West and Newport agreements. These were hammered out by Defense Secretary Forrestal after he had taken the JCS away to those cities in March and August 1948 on the assumption that it would be easier to hold these negotiations away from the Pentagon, where each of the armed services had its political support groups fully deployed for battle. The main fight was between the Air Force and the Navy over the question of which service would be allowed the prime role in developing and using atomic bombs. This was critical to the Air Force, because it saw strategic bombing as its primary *raison d'etre*. It was critical to the Navy because, given that Congress was increasingly enamored with this idea as an all-purpose military capability for the United States, the Navy could justify and expand its carrier task groups. "Deterrence" was then the new strategic concept. It promised "warless warfare" in which no adversary would ever dare lift a finger against this country.

The Air Force won the important 1948 skirmishes at Key West and Newport, although the Navy salvaged a consolation prize that allowed it to continue modest efforts to build super-carriers for delivering nuclear ordnance. The Navy made a major effort to expand on its consolation award, which merely set the stage for the next skirmish, known as the "B-36 bombers vs. super-carriers controversy of 1949." Ultimately, what saved the Navy's case—essentially an argument that carriers of all types remained quite useful for delivering many kinds of ordnance in various sorts of conflicts—was the Korean War of 1950, when carriers indeed proved useful. Nevertheless, the Air Force won the appropriations contest throughout the 1950s as the United States steadily built up its strategic deterrence capabilities while downgrading conventional elements. Looking at the total budget for all three of the main armed services during the 1950s, the Air Force routinely received an average of about 50% of it, leaving the Army (about 23%) and the Navy (about 27%) to struggle over the other half. It could be added that, over the next twenty-five years, starting around 1961 when newly inaugurated President Kennedy first attempted a rebuilding of conventional forces, the Air Force percentage gradually declined, as the original heavy investments in strategic nuclear deterrent forces were completed, while the Navy percentage gradually rose in view of the Navy's dual capabilities for both nuclear and conventional warfare.

Nevertheless, the United States is a high-tech country and, thus, will always inherently prefer the high-tech armed services, the Air Force and Navy. This means that the Army, still widely perceived as a low-tech infantry organization, experienced continuing troubles in raising its percentage of the total defense budget. The Reagan Administration's 1984 budget proposals have continued this historic trend; the Air Force at 37.9%, but the Navy closing fast at 35.4%, while the Army lagged at 26.7%. The Administration's projections for 1989 show the Navy finally ahead at 38.0%, with the Air Force slightly behind at 34.9%, and the Army still back at 27.0%.[3]

These disparities in percentages have fanned the fires of interservice competition as each service struggled to increase its share of the pie. These low road organizational battles, however, became more muted and submerged from public view from about the mid-1950s onward—for at least two reasons. First, presidents grew weary of highly-publicized interservice squabbles, since these tended to create the appearance of administrative disarray, and took steps to suppress them. Second, by the end of the Eisenhower Administration, each of the services had won enough rounds to at least assure its survival in an acceptable form.

On the other hand, mere institutional survival has never been the sole goal of each service, and, therefore, interservice rivalries continued in a variety of ways. Numerous knowledgeable observers, for example, have said that the Air Force and the Navy flew many missions in both the Korean and Vietnam Wars more to score bureaucratic points against each other than to inflict significant damage on foreign adversaries. These quarrels gained some new publicity in the late 1970s and early 1980s, over the question of which service (in this case the Army and the Marines, as contrasted to the usual contest between the Air Force and the Navy) would dominate the rapid deployment force—later renamed the new central command. Further, it was only a matter of time until the public's attention would be drawn to a significant new struggle between the Air Force and the Navy over preeminence in the military use of space. The point is that the services have never competed merely for larger budgets and more personnel—behavior typical of virtually all government agencies. They have also sought to dominate those roles and missions that each service has believed belongs to it. Each service has been less concerned about budgets and personnel as long as it felt that it had a secure clamp on its preferred roles and missions. But the logic behind many of the interservice disputes has also meant that many important roles and missions that happen to have no traditional appeal for any of the services, such as logistical support capabilities for the Air Force and Navy, and mine warfare within the Navy, have chronically endured grievous neglect.

One final illustration of the fact that the armed services have remained basically separate and contentious bureaucratic rivals, notwithstanding the entire set of attempts and actions since about 1900 to bring them more harmoniously together, can be found in the history of the joint unified and specified command system. An authoritative article by John L. Frisbee, entitled "Command Lines for Combat Forces," in the August 1983 issue of

Defense/81 magazine, summarized the formality well understood by senior military officers but not by many others: ". . . neither the Chiefs of Staff of the Army and the Air Force, the Chief of Naval Operations, nor the Commandant of the Marine Corps exercise operational command over any of their combat units." The article continued, "That has been true either in practice or by law since 1942," thus dating the origins of the joint unified and specified command system. Under the title "Unified Action Armed Forces," JCS Pub 2 spelled out other formalities when it said that a unified command is "a command with a broad continuing mission, under a single commander and composed of significant assigned components [component commands] of two or more Services, and which is established by the President, through the Secretary of Defense, with the advice and assistance of the Joint Chiefs of Staff, or when so authorized by the Joint Chiefs of Staff, by a commander or an existing command established by the President."

All the formal niceties about the joint unified and specified command system amount to a polite fiction. In practice, each and every one of the commands has been a wholly owned subsidiary of one or another of the traditional and separate armed services. It is well understood that each will always be headed by a commander in chief (CINC) from the service dominating it. Rather than exercising actual command or management authority over these formally joint fighting forces, the JCS has mainly served as the arena in which deals over CINC management are negotiated among the separate armed services. According to the logic of the joint system, the services were residual appendages relegated to the inglorious roles of recruiting, training, and providing force components for the joint commands. The joint system has always been a bastardized political compromise, and the separate services have proven highly competent in refusing to be smothered under this improvisation. The separate services always resisted this arrangement, largely because the choice jobs for three- and four-star officers are provided by the joint commands. The failure of the system was illustrated when the "MACV" concept was invented to fight the Vietnam War, whereas the logic of the system would have required that Commander in Chief Pacific (CINCPAC) be in charge.

THE POLITICAL CONSTRAINTS ON ORGANIZATIONAL CHANGE

This brief review of developments since 1900 shows that efforts on how best to organize the American military establishment have produced two opposite trends. On the one hand, a steady centralization of power was imposed on the civilian side of the American military establishment. On the other hand, there was no comparable centralization on the professional military side of the American armed forces. The anomaly, therefore, was the steady centralization in the higher civilian hierarchies, both within the military establishment, as represented now by the term "the Pentagon," and at even higher levels, as signified by the term "the White House," while the separate armed services remained significantly decentralized. & fractious

This disjuncture raises a question that begs for an answer. Why were the separate services left decentralized under a mass of centralized civilian layers? The same question could be put another way: Why were the JCS mechanisms—which constituted the obvious effort toward centralization on the professional military side in the Pentagon—never truly effective? One way to answer this question is to indicate at least three sets of actors who never actually wanted the military to be centralized.

The first and perhaps the most important group resisting effective JCS mechanisms consisted of the separate services themselves. In the absence of a consensus on an ideal way to organize armed forces, the senior leaders of the American services did the expected: they took a conservative position and consistently argued the allegedly proven advantages of retaining considerable autonomy among the separate services. However, the heart of their opposition was distrust among the uniformed leaders toward each other—a distrust born of decades of intense competition and of even more decades of existence in their separate tribal cultures largely isolated from one other. To expect Air Force generals and Navy admirals fully to trust one another is akin to expecting a large number of Greeks and Turks fully to trust each other. It was one thing for the senior officers to accommodate to the ever-shifting centralized civilian authorities at the top. But it would have been something entirely different for an admiral, for example, to have operated under a general as a boss, because a military person knows the meaning of taking an order from another military person, which is not the same as taking a directive from a politically appointed civilian boss. A truly effective set of JCS mechanisms would have clearly required that senior officers receive and obey orders from other senior officers not of their own service. This was close to intolerable given the longstanding distrust already noted.

The second set of people never truly desirous of genuinely effective JCS mechanisms was the Congress. Thus, the Congress was the most effective political ally of the separate services in their determination to retain their maximum degree of autonomy. The most effective precondition for maximizing congressional impact on national security policy—and, not incidentally, for obtaining politically useful decisions on matters such as defense contracts—is to keep the military establishment decentralized. It is a bureaucratic version of ancient divide and conquer tactics. If the JCS mechanisms had ever constituted a firm link in a chain of command, from the president to the secretary of defense to the JCS to the services, this would have seriously undermined the potential for congressional influence on a wide range of military decisions. Thus, Congress legislated the centralized veneer at the top civilian levels, but collaborated with the separate services in maintaining substantial decentralization at the level of the services.

The third set of people never truly desirous of genuinely effective JCS mechanisms consisted of those serving in high positions within the top civilian hierarchy in the Pentagon — the OSD secretariat. Those individuals, sometimes supported by academicians, lawyers and others who worried about maintaining the constitutional principle of civilian supremacy over the military, tended to agonize that an effectively centralized set of JCS mechanisms on top of the military side of the Pentagon could pose a threat to the centralized OSD civilian side, and thus pose a challenge to civilian supremacy. A parallel to this existed prior to World War I, when Navy Secretary Josephus Daniels opposed the creation of the office of the chief of naval operations. When this legislation was nonetheless enacted, it turned out that the navy secretary and the CNO were natural allies, rather than adversaries, because they were the only two people with Navy-wide perspectives, in contrast to the sectarian factions within this service. A similar kind of alliance would probably emerge between OSD and a truly effective JCS, but the fact remains that incumbent defense secretaries and their OSD staffs have, ironically, tacitly sided with the Congress and the separate services in squeezing the JCS mechanisms into bureaucratic inconsequentiality (even though neither the Congress nor the senior service personnel have ever been overly fond of the OSD secretariat as an institution). It was noteworthy during the period of 1982 to 1983, when General David Jones became the only incumbent JCS Chairman openly to advocate JCS reforms, that recently retired Defense Secretary Harold Brown became the only individual in this category to join the appeals for a strengthened JCS. No incumbent or recently retired defense secretary had ever taken this position before.

In short, significant political forces have actively opposed (or never supported) a genuinely effective JCS as a centralized command and management structure. But there have been two other explanations for the incomplete nature of military reform. First, there never has been any guiding philosophy or theory of organization to suggest precisely what tasks and functions should most appropriately be performed (either on the civilian or the military side of the defense department), or how those separate inputs should be harmonized into a single integrated perspective. In the 1930s and during World War II, the Navy agonized a great deal over such issues, developing something called a "dual and parallel tracks concept," wherein certain functions deemed to be essentially civilian in nature (such as contracting, procurement, and also political tasks) were reserved for the Navy's civilian secretariat, and other functions deemed to be essentially military in nature (such as the design of ships and weapons, operational planning, and command) were reserved for the admirals. Some of these functions were loosely shared at certain points up the chain of authority on both tracks but, for the most part, the tracks were not bent together until close to the very top. The Navy Department tried to sell this same general approach in its Eberstadt Plan, which became the primary basis for the National Security Act of 1947. But it was not a successful selling job and, thereafter, one could have looked in vain in all of the high road and low road reorganizational struggles for any sense of a guiding philosophy or theory of organization.[4]

Ideally, there would have emerged some consensus on the leadership and management tasks for which the politically appointed civilians in the OSD secretariat were better qualified, and a parallel set of tasks for which the career admirals and generals were better qualified. Ideally, the OSD civilian secretariat would never have dominated and suppressed the admirals and generals but, also ideally, the admirals and generals would always have been well-prepared with uniquely professional military consensus judgments to offer. The top OSD civilians often had little or no prior experience in military matters, and then served for an average of only about two years — scarcely long enough to learn the basic ropes. However, even though the admirals and generals typically claimed to have uniquely valuable professional judgments, their determined failure to come together in a genuinely effective JCS context, authentically integrating, rather than logrolling, their views into a true national strategy, often discredited their voices, particularly within the OSD secretariat, and further contributed to the OSD disinclination to urge a major role for a stronger JCS. Finally, the fact that at least some of the top civilian appointees had been previously militarized by virtue of extensive research and other specializations on military subjects, and the parallel fact that many of the admirals and generals had been civilianized by mastering budgets, systems analysis, and bureaucratic politics, meant that neither the OSD civilians nor the uniformed officers were willing to surrender exclusive functions to the other side. The old Navy concept, attempting to make clear distinctions between essentially civilian and essentially military tasks, was obsolete.

Second, the president and the White House assistant, who are among the most important players in the making of national security policy, have equivocal interests in Pentagon reform. Their perspectives have not often coincided with Pentagon perspectives. For one thing, a president is never likely to provide the kind of crisp, clear, policy guidance that the Pentagon wants, because the American political system is configured in such a way that the president must provide almost all of the needed political flexibility that any national political system requires. The only way a president can do this is to speak in broad policy generalities and, sometimes, to obfuscate underlying reasons with less important, but plausible, superficialities, all the time trying to avoid appearing inconsistent or confused. Presidents must maintain political maneuvering room if the government is not to become even more crippled by bureaucratic rigidities, but maneuvering room can be reduced almost to zero if presidents always make crisp, clear, policy statements. Maneuvering room is also gained by avoiding a tightly structured hierarchy in executive agencies, including the Pentagon. A president needs to play off one group or school of thought in the Pentagon against another group or school of thought at the Department of State or elsewhere. Americans, particularly military officers, have a low tolerance for ambiguity and uncertainty, but presidents have a vested interest in both. Presidents are not likely to surrender these merely to accommodate the pleas of Pentagon reformers.

If there is any lesson to be learned from this review of the limits on the possible achievements of military reorganizations, it might be that the reformers should be far more sweeping and comprehensive in their proposals, but far more modest in their expectations. Specifically, these lessons and guidelines for reform can be adduced.

- Most reform efforts have been piecemeal attempts, and these have not worked. Any truly successful attempts at improving the efficiency and the quality of policies and capabilities pertaining to the American military establishment would need to go well beyond the Pentagon and embrace the other governmental actors in this activity, most particularly the Congress.

- The history of military reorganizations after World War II reveals an almost exclusive emphasis on centralization, at or near the top on the civilian side of the Pentagon, that failed significantly to touch the autonomous bureaucratic capabilities remaining very strong within the separate services under their uniformed leaders.

- Indeed, the continuing strength of the separate services in pursuing their separate interests remains the basic starting point and the main problem identified by almost all of the studies and proposals for reorganizing the Joint Chiefs of Staff mechanisms, but these documents have mistakenly thought that the problem could be fixed by tinkering with the JCS itself in the absence of due consideration for the enormous importance of the overall political–social environment surrounding the JCS.

- Organizations can ordinarily be made more rational by strengthening and clarifying chains of command, reporting, and accountability, making authority commensurate with responsibility, and removing anomalies and anachronisms. These are textbook platitudes, but much could be accomplished along these lines in the Pentagon. Most of the reform proposals emerging during the period of 1982 to 1984 were aimed in these directions.

- Given that further centralizations in policy formulation could well occur, the evidence suggests that important efficiencies could be gained by some decentralization in policy implementation. Some of this was attempted during the early years of the Reagan Administration, although it needs to be emphasized that any decentralization in implementation should be accompanied by careful monitoring of performance by the centralized decisionmakers.

• Although large formal organizations are not readily convertible from one mode to another, certain configurations are better than other types for particular purposes. For example, it is fairly clear in the social science literature that a flat pyramid, with relatively easy access to top decisionmakers and easy communication among peers, is ideal if an organization perceives itself to have strong needs for creative new thinking, innovations, and personal initiatives. On the other hand, a tall pyramid is more appropriate if the main need is rapidly to implement and manage decisions already made, without time to consider any significant range of further proposals. These and other descriptive configurations can be considered when striving to optimize an organizational structure with appropriate balance and compromise among a mixed range of goals and purposes.

In summary, if ambitious proposals but modest expectations ought to be the order of the day among military reformers, a final advisory opinion might be to work toward long-range improvements in addition to the typically short-range quick-fix ideas submitted by reform advocates. The concluding part of this chapter will review several final thoughts, preliminary to proposing a concept so ambitious as to fall into the category of the radical.

FINAL THOUGHTS, AND A RADICAL PROPOSAL

The history of American military reform and its results in the twentieth century raise three fundamental questions. First, is the need for reform more urgent today than before? Second, can new forms of centralization achieve the results desired by the reformers without excessive damage to the separate services? Third, are strengthened JCS mechanisms both the necessary and sufficient conditions to deal with the excessive autonomy of the services?

The answer to the first question is an unequivocal "yes." The situation is more urgent today because of the massive gap between the threats posed and the resources available. Applications of military force must become far more sophisticated, surgically precise, more flexible, and timely. The Brehm report (April 1982, p. 14) summarized the urgent need for change by saying:

... now the limitations are more serious than before because of the great need for careful and flexible planning, maximum efficiency in the use of defense resources, faster response capability, and greater emphasis on Joint operations.

The question as to whether new centralization reforms would excessively damage the services implies that there is something uniquely valuable in their separateness. Indeed, it is well understood in the literature on organizational behavior that morale is a highly valued asset. Professional military leaders have argued that morale, motivation, and performance of personnel — particularly in combat — have always been a function partly of the sentiments attached to a tradition and heritage and to the elusive mystique embodied in loyalty to a military organization. Furthermore, it has been contended that more good than harm has come from interservice rivalries because a competitive environment, in military as well as in business organizations, can be a healthy stimulus toward progress. On these points, however, I have reached two conclusions.

- First, the balance between the constructive and the destructive consequences of interservice rivalries has gradually been tipped toward the latter.
- Second, the need to protect the traditions, heritage and mystique inherent in the separate services, although still important, is probably exaggerated, because these have proven to be remarkably resilient against erosion for decades.

The third question, then, is whether reformed JCS mechanisms constitute both the necessary and sufficient conditions for solving the problems that stem from excessive service autonomy. The answer here is, necessary, "yes"; sufficient, "no." More centralization, whether on the civilian OSD side, the uniformed JCS side, or both, would represent another dose of the old medicine, which has not been adequate.

The main difficulty with any kind of centralization is that, by definition, it occurs only at the top of organizations, with a built-in assumption that some kind of trickle-down effects will bring things together at all lower levels. But this has been demonstrably untrue in the American military establishment, where the main agencies at the bottom of the pyramid, that is, the separate services, have been powerfully resistant — along with their allies in places, such as Capitol Hill — to consolidations.

The fundamental problem, then, is not so much a matter of new organizational formats emphasizing more centralization at the top, but, rather, a question of basic attitudes and orientations throughout the ranks of the separate services. An officer will typically serve, for at least the first fifteen years of his or her military career, exclusively within the isolated and sheltered confines of his or her separate service before getting a "purple suit" assignment within the joint arena. The scientific literature makes it very clear that the early period of an individual's life is the formative time when values become firmly set. Yet, for the American military officer, this period is spent totally within the officer's own service, deeply immersed in its tribal rites and customs. At the end of that period, it is a bit too much to expect that the officer will suddenly develop a genuinely multiservice perspective, and instantly escape the dominant influence of his or her earlier years of parochial confinement.

What really needs changing over the long run, therefore, is not simply the organizational structure but, also, the deep-seated organizational *cultures.* Therefore, the radical concept here is to endorse the general thrusts of the proposals from the JCS reformers emerging during 1982 through 1984, but also to devise ways to give virtually all military officers a substantial exposure to broad multiservice perspectives from their very first days in uniform. This would not aim at drastic reductions in service autonomy, and it would certainly not call for a replication of the flawed Canadian experiment with a single uniform. The goal would be to give American officers more opportunities at critical early stages in their careers to work with each other and to develop both an enhanced respect for each other and a deeper loyalty to the nation's overriding national security needs.

A part of the solution would be to convert all service academy and Reserve Officers' Training Corps (ROTC) programs to five-year curricula, with the first and fifth years in multiservice environments. This could include the awarding of an M. A. degree, alongside the B. A. degree, following patterns well-established in respected civilian institutions. Beyond this, more "purple splashes" should be applied at frequent intervals in the multiservice contexts throughout officers' early careers. At this point in career development, the Brehm report suggests attendance at a "purple suit" command and staff school to establish eligibility for joint staff or similar non-service specific assignments. Further, of course, would be the necessity, as carefully stipulated in the Brehm report, to make those assignments important for career enhancement, in contrast to the present situation, wherein to be assigned, for very long, away from your service flagpole can be the career kiss of death.

These ideas are likely to be rejected by senior officers for many reasons, given the strong resistance to any form of tampering with the service cultures — most particularly a service academy, which can be likened to a service's mother church. However, it is precisely this kind of resistance that illustrates both the magnitude of the problem and the need for radical change. It is considerably more than a trifle when national security could well be at stake, and when only the sternest orders from a secretary of defense can generate even a bare modicum of true interservice cooperation. Robert J. Murray, former Under Secretary of the Navy, caught the essential needs when he said:

[We must] talk instead about [each service's] contribution to national strategy. . . . Otherwise, we will continue to have . . . debilitating debates about [such matters as] whether the country should rely upon a maritime strategy . . . or a continental strategy, when either one would be a false choice. A strategy that counts on winning at sea while losing on land is no strategy. A strategy that attempts to win on land without also winning at sea is untenable.[5]

Major business corporations have discovered some of these same facts in their own operations. They have learned that corporate cultures can be either a major asset or a major liability in pursuit of corporate strategies. While they have also learned that changing an entrenched culture is a formidable, risky, and, in some cases, perhaps impossible task, many have decided that they cannot shrink from the challenge.[6] This same challenge confronts the American military establishment. Reforms in JCS mechanisms, practices, and procedures are doubtless required. However, these could once again prove to be merely cosmetic innovations in the absence of long-range programs designed to make fundamental shifts toward a stronger "purple-suit" mentality in the officer corps of each of the services. If service officers truly believe that national survival could be at stake, they might eventually appreciate that national survival is more urgent than service survival in the old traditional forms, and, therefore, come to endorse the necessity for proposals such as those suggested here.

NOTES

1. For one of the best scholarly analyses of the early stages of the "McNamara Revolution," and how this man managed to dominate the DOD more thoroughly and aggressively than any of his predecessors and most of his successors, see Art, Robert J., *The TFX Decision: McNamara and the Military* (Boston: Little, Brown, 1968).
2. This story was ably traced in papers written by Lawrence J. Korb in the early 1970s, later printed as chapters in his book, *The Joint Chiefs of Staff: The First Twenty-five Years* (Bloomington: Indiana University Press, 1976), although his conclusions were more firmly stated in the original papers than in the book. Also see his later work, *The Fall and Rise of the Pentagon: American Defense Policies in the 1970s* (Westport: Greenwood Publisher, 1979).
3. These percentages were calculated from a chart labeled "Defense Department Budget Proposals," derived from Department of Defense sources, as printed on page 15 of the National Edition of the *New York Times*, on October 20, 1983.

   On the earlier history of interservice disputes over the years following World War II, many books and articles have been published on this subject. One good book summarizing the prewar events of the 1930s and then the post-war period to about 1958, was written by Millis, Walter; Mansfield, Harvery C.; and Stein, Harold, *Arms and the State: Civil-Military Elements in National Policy* (New York: Columbia University Press, 1958). Paul Y. Hammond's definitive case study, "Super Carriers and B-36 Bombers: Appropriations, Strategy and Politics," was printed by Stein, Harold, editor, *American Civil-Military Decisions: A Book of Case Studies* (Alabama: University of Alabama Press, 1963). Another useful source is Caraley, Demetrios, *The Politics of Military Unification: A Study of Conflict and the Policy Process* (New York: Columbia University Press, 1966). Other references include two books by this author, Davis, Vincent, *Postwar Defense Policy and the U.S. Navy, 1943-1946*, and *The Admirals Lobby* (Chapel Hill, NC: University of North Carolina Press, 1962 and 1967). However, the classic work on those earlier struggles (from which all other authors cited here borrowed significantly) remains Laurence J. Legere's doctoral dissertation, *Unification of the Armed Forces* (Harvard, 1950).

4. One of the best (but often neglected) sources of information on all issues pertaining to U.S. defense policy from 1945 to 1966 was a series published by the Library of Congress (written by Senior Specialist in National Defense, Charles H. Donnelly) at the request of Congressman Melvin Price, U.S. House of Representatives. The initial paper was *United States Defense Policies Since World War II*, House Document No. 100, 85th Congress, 1st Session, dated November 1956 but appearing in 1957. The series continued on an annual basis starting with *United States Defense Policies in 1957*, through . . . in 1965.

5. For Murray's remarks, see the *U.S. Naval Institute Proceedings*, October 1983, p. 70.

6. For one report on the efforts to change entrenched cultural patterns in many large business corporations, see the long special article, "The Corporate Culture Vultures," *Fortune* Magazine, October 17, 1983, starting on page 66. Also see Deal, Terrence E., *Corporate Cultures: The Rites and Rituals of Corporate Life* (New York: 1982).

Chapter 9

The Wars Within: The Joint Military Structure and Its Critics

William J. Lynn

[S]eparate ground, sea and air warfare is gone forever. If ever again we should be involved in war, we will fight it in all elements, with all Services, as one single concentrated effort. Peacetime preparation and organizational activity must conform to this fact.[1]

Dwight D. Eisenhower

Accumulating evidence of problems in strategic planning, force development, and military operations has raised questions about the adequacy of the organization of the U.S. defense establishment in general, and the joint military structure, in particular. Indeed, the last three years have witnessed the most serious and extended debate over the structure of the Pentagon since 1958, when Congress enacted the last significant amendments to the National Security Act. A parade of former national security advisers, defense secretaries, and other senior defense officials have testified before Congress and in the media about serious inadequacies in the performance of the joint military apparatus.[2] But the most forceful criticism has come from the military itself. High level commissions, led by retired senior officers, have pointed to organizational deficiencies as important causes of both the failure of the 1980 mission to rescue the hostages at the embassy in Iran and the vulnerability to terrorist attack of the Marine peace-keeping force at the Beirut airport in 1983.[3]

Even more significant in igniting the current controversy was the public criticism of the joint military apparatus in 1982 by two then-incumbent members of the Joint Chiefs of Staff (JCS), General David C. Jones, Chairman of the Joint Chiefs, and General Edward C. Meyer, Chief of Staff of the Army.[4] General Jones and General Meyer have put forward different prescriptions for reform, but they have agreed on the diagnosis: the joint military structure has not performed effectively in its role as the primary military agent of integration in the defense establishment. At the source of this problem is the centralization–decentralization dilemma, which has plagued all efforts to build an effective joint structure since World War II. This dilemma derives from the inherent tension between the recognized requirement for centralized planning and direction of the armed forces, and the natural desire of the military services organized separately for land, sea, and air warfare to retain their historic autonomy. The history of postwar reform of the joint military structure consists of a series of efforts to reconcile these conflicting forces of service autonomy and centralized direction.

Since World War II, attempts to construct an effective joint military framework have sought to ensure that it could provide a national military perspective that integrated the views of the four military services. The joint structure is intended to perform three primary functions. First, it should supply civilian leaders with military advice that rises above individual service interests. Military advice from a national perspective is crucial to effective civilian leadership in all defense activities from the general formulation of national military strategy to specific decisions on the use of armed force in individual instances. Second, the joint military structure should do strategic planning, linking military means with political ends. Without this link between military capabilities and strategic objectives, U.S. national security priorities will not be reflected adequately in service force development plans. Third, the joint military structure is responsible for planning and conducting military operations. The nature of modern warfare requires combined-arms operations in which land, sea, and air forces are effectively integrated under a unified command.

None of these objectives has been controversial in principle. Senior officers of all the military services, together with civilian leaders in both the executive and legislative branches, have consistently endorsed the importance of achieving effective integration of our armed forces. The debate has not been over the importance of integration, but over which organizational arrangements will best achieve it. The crucial issue has been the extent to which effective performance of joint military functions requires more powerful, centralized military structures and reduced service autonomy. In short, the question is how much centralization is necessary to produce the requisite integration of military advice, planning, and operations.

Different judgments on the degree of centralization necessary underlie the different proposals for reform of the joint military structure. These proposals can be clustered into four general models of the joint military structure, each with a greater degree of centralization. At one extreme is the existing joint structure, which follows a *service-dominant model*, in which the highest source of joint military advice, planning, and direction is a committee of the senior officers in each service—the Joint Chiefs of Staff. A middle position, the *strong chairman model*, concurs that the JCS should be retained, but calls for the chairman supported by the joint staff to direct the joint structure and provide an independent perspective. The *national military advisers model* calls for elimination of the dual-hat system, by which each service chief serves both as a JCS member and as the senior military executive in his service. In this model, the senior military planning and advisory body would consist of officers without service responsibilities. Finally, at the other extreme, are proposals to establish an *armed forces general staff*, in which a single chief of staff would preside over a multiservice general staff of officers on permanent assignment.

The service-dominant model has prevailed since World War II. The other three models, however, have had significant proponents. The general staff model was strongly advocated by the Army after World War II, but has not received much support since. The national military advisers (NMA) model was first proposed at the start of the Kennedy Administration and has recently been revived by General Meyer. The most prominent alternative to the service-dominant model, both historically and in the current debate, has been the strong chairman model. In the 1940s and 1950s, the Truman and Eisenhower Administrations pressed hard for a joint system led by a strong chairman. The merit of the strong chairman model, compared to the existing system, is the focus of the current debate over what type of joint military structure the nation needs. After tracing the evolution of the present joint military structure since World War II, this chapter will examine these three alternative models in light of current proposals for reform. The chapter then will conclude with some observations about the politics of defense reform.

EVOLUTION OF THE JOINT MILITARY STRUCTURE

Origins

The joint military structure that came into existence during World War II was the consequence of the immediate and pressing need for alliance cooperation and interservice coordination. It was implemented without detailed study or thought about what would be the most effective form of military organization for war. Indeed, the structure was not the result of a single decision, but, rather, evolved over the course of World War II. At the outbreak of the war, President Franklin D. Roosevelt established the first element of the joint structure, the Joint Chiefs of Staff, to facilitate U.S.–British military cooperation and coordination. In order to represent the United States on the U.S.–British Combined Chiefs of Staff, Roosevelt formed the American equivalents to the British Chiefs of Staff Committee into the Joint Chiefs of Staff. The JCS initially consisted of the chief of naval operations, the chief of staff of the army, and the commanding general of the army air force. In mid-1942, Admiral William D. Leahy, the military chief of staff to the President, became the de facto chairman of the JCS, but his responsibilities were limited primarily to serving as a liaison between the JCS and the president. Over the course of the war, the JCS expanded their authority, assuming primary responsibility for setting military strategy and directing military operations. The responsibilities of the civilian secretaries of the war and Navy departments were limited largely to matters of administration, mobilization, and procurement. In all their roles, the JCS acted solely under presidential authority, without statutory recognition.[5]

In 1942, the second element of the joint military structure, a supporting organization for the Joint Chiefs of Staff came into existence. The support structure evolved during the war, more in response to immediate needs than in fulfillment of any conscious design. The structure that arose was not an independent, multiservice staff responsible directly to the JCS, but, rather, an interlocking series of over a dozen joint committees, boards, and agencies, which consisted of service representatives who were temporarily detailed from the service staffs.

The final element of the existing joint military structure, the system of unified operational commands, was also initiated during World War II. In the context of dividing areas of operating responsibility with the British, the United States established a series of operational commands. In the Pacific, two commands were created: the Southwest Pacific Command, under General Douglas A. MacArthur, and the Pacific Ocean Command, under Admiral Chester W. Nimitz. In preparation for D-Day, all allied forces in Europe were placed under the command of General Dwight D. Eisenhower. Toward the latter stages of the war, the heavy bomber forces operating in Europe and the Pacific were constituted as separate operational commands independent of the theater commanders. By the end of the war, the United States had thus established five operational commands, each of which was identified with a particular service: the European and Southwest Pacific commands with the Army; the Pacific Ocean command with the Navy; and the two bomber commands with the Army Air Force. The sponsoring service provided the commander and the bulk of the operating forces. It also acted as an executive agent for the command, and transmitted the directives of the Joint Chiefs of Staff. The World War II command arrangements resulted in a system in which each of the commands was, in effect, an operating arm of one of the services.

At the end of the war, there was a broad consensus among both civilian and uniformed leaders that the ad hoc reorganization of the defense establishment conducted during the war needed to be carefully reviewed to ensure its adequacy in meeting the expanded U.S. responsibilities of the postwar era. By demonstrating the importance of integrated processes for strategic planning, force development, and military operations, the war precluded a return to the prewar autonomy of the military services. There was, however, much disagreement as to the nature and extent of the changes necessary for defense integration. The central issue was whether the U.S. should unify the military departments into a single department of defense. The Army, supported by President Harry S. Truman and by the Air Force as well, argued strongly for unification. The Navy, supported by significant segments of Congress, contended that defense was a government-wide function that should not be restricted to a single department. The Navy proposed retaining the military department structure and creating a series of interdepartmental boards to integrate overall defense policies. The 1947 National Security Act reflected an initial compromise of the unification controversy, establishing a secretary of defense to preside over three independent, cabinet-level military departments. Amendments to the act, in 1949, established a greater degree of unification by strengthening the authority of the secretary and incorporating the military departments into the newly-created department of defense. With reforms in 1953 and 1958, President Dwight D. Eisenhower assured that the secretary of defense had a substantial staff and full authority over all defense activities.[6]

Within this unification debate, the Army and the Navy also took strongly opposing positions on reform of the joint military structure. Senior Army leaders, both military and civilian, judged the ad hoc wartime joint military arrangements to be inadequate. Army Chief of Staff General George C. Marshall observed that "the lack of real unity has handicapped the successful conduct of the war." In his view, the JCS organization "was a cumbersome and inefficient method of directing the efforts of the Armed Forces" that resulted in repeated compromises and delays.[7] Similarly, Secretary of War Henry L. Stimson declared the Joint Chiefs of Staff to be an "imperfect instrument of top-level decision" because "it remained incapable of enforcing a decision against the will of any one of its members."[8] Accordingly, the Army supported strengthening the authority of the joint military structure over the services. In a series of proposals culminating in the 1945 plan put forward by General J. Lawton Collins, the Army proposed a single chief of staff of the armed forces who would have direct authority over both the services and all operational commands and who would act as the principal military adviser to the president and secretary of defense.[9] This new armed forces chief of staff would also sit with the chiefs of staff of the Army and Air Force and the chief of naval operations as the United States chiefs of staff to advise the president on military policy, strategy, and budget requirements.

The Navy, in a report that Ferdinand Eberstadt drafted, rejected the concept of a single chief of staff for the armed forces.[10] Although conceding that the slowness of JCS decisionmaking had been a problem, the Eberstadt Report concluded that the Joint Chiefs of Staff system had performed satisfactorily during the war. Accordingly, the report called for retention of the wartime JCS structure with specific responsibilities for providing military advice to civilian leaders, preparing joint strategic and logistics plans, and providing strategic direction to the unified commands.

The Army–Navy disagreement over the joint military structure centered on the desirability of establishing a single armed forces chief of staff. The Army argued that the president and the secretary of defense should have the benefit of military advice and planning from a single senior officer with authority independent of the individual services. The Navy believed that the highest source of military advice and planning should be a committee of all services, in order to assure that the national leadership received all relevant perspectives. The Army also contended that to preserve unity of command, all orders should pass through a single military leader. The Navy rejoined that this would put too much authority in the hands of a single individual.

The National Security Act of 1947 settled the issue in favor of the Navy.[11] The act established a Joint Chiefs of Staff, consisting of the chiefs of staff of the Army and the Air Force and the chief of naval operations to serve as the principal military advisers to the president, secretary of defense, and the NSC. The JCS were assigned specific authority to prepare joint strategic and logistics plans, to assign logistics responsibilities, and to establish unified commands in strategic areas. To assist the JCS in carrying out these responsibilities, Congress established a joint staff of 100 officers. The JCS continued to function as a committee of service representatives, without a chairman and with only a small, service-dominated joint staff. The national Security Act of 1947 effectively codified the World War II joint military structure.

Prior to passage of the National Security Act of 1947, the Joint Chiefs of Staff had already decided to retain the system of operational overseas commands. In 1946, President Truman approved the first unified command plan, with six unified geographic commands (Europe, Atlantic, Caribbean, Alaska, Pacific, and the Far East) and one specified functional command (the strategic air command). To administer and direct these commands, the JCS also retained the World War II system whereby one of its members would act as the executive agent for each command.

The 1947 act did not end the debate over the character and functions of the joint military structure, as service dominance of the JCS quickly attracted heavy criticism. Most notably, Secretary of Defense James V. Forrestal, who had earlier opposed a more independent JCS, condemned their inability to offer integrated advice on any matter involving important service interests, particularly defense budget issues. Therefore, he recommended establishing a chairman of the Joint Chiefs of Staff.[12] He was supported in this recommendation by the 1948 Commission on Organization of the Executive Branch of the Government chaired by former President Hoover.[13] President Truman concurred, and proposed a chairman to head the Joint Chiefs of Staff and to act as the principal military adviser to the president and the secretary of defense.[14] Truman thus attempted to move from a service-dominated joint structure toward a system in which an independent chairman would assure that the joint structure produced military planning and advice that rose above individual service interests. He did not return, however, to the earlier Army proposals that called for an even stronger joint military leader — an armed forces chief of staff, who would both chair the JCS and command military operations. Indeed, the Truman Administration made no proposals to reduce service dominance of the operational commands.

The administration's reluctance to return to the Army's single chief of staff proposal was due in large part to strong opposition within Congress. In the 1949 amendments to the National Security Act,[15] Congress was emphatic in rejecting any suggestion that the establishment of a chairman meant acceptance of an armed forces chief of staff or an armed forces general staff system. Both were explicitly prohibited by amendments to the National Security Act's Declaration of Policy. In addition, Congress proscribed the new chairman from exercising command over either the JCS or the military services. Congress viewed even a moderately powerful chairman with distrust. The legislators preferred the model established by Admiral Leahy during World War II, in which the chair's authority was essentially limited to acting as the JCS's liasion with the civilian leadership. Accordingly, in enacting the 1949 amendments to the National Security Act, Congress limited the chairman to presiding over JCS meetings as a nonvoting member, providing their agenda, and reporting disagreements to the president and the secretary of defense. In short, the creation of the office of chairman did little to alter the fundamental character of the joint military structure. It remained largely incapable of producing military planning and advice that rose above individual service interests.

The Eisenhower Reforms

Having criticized the joint structure's performance severely during the campaign, President Eisenhower took office in 1953, intent on reforming it. Like Truman, Eisenhower sought to reduce service influence in the structure by strengthening its core actors — the chairman, the joint staff, and the unified and specified commanders. But Eisenhower proposed more comprehensive reforms than did his predecessor. With the 1953 Defense Reorganization Plan[16] and the Defense Reorganization Act of 1958,[17] Eisenhower attempted to address the four characteristics of the joint structure that inhibited its performance as an effective integrating force:

1. The chairman's lack of independent authority.
2. The dual-hatting of the service chiefs as members of the JCS and as military leaders of their services.
3. The dominance the individual services exercised over the Joint Staff.
4. The weakness of the unified and specified commanders.[18]

To strengthen the authority of the chairperson of the Joint Chiefs of Staff, Eisenhower's 1953 Reorganization Plan followed the recommendations of the Committee on Defense Organization chaired by Nelson Rockefeller.[19] The 1953 plan assigned the chairman authority to manage the joint staff and to approve JCS selection of officers to the joint staff. Additionally, JCS appointment of the director of the joint staff was made subject to the approval of the secretary of defense. The purpose of the 1953 reforms was to ensure that the chairman had sufficient authority to organize and direct the staff system and other subordinate structures that supported the Joint Chiefs of Staff, without detracting from the military advisory functions of the JCS as a group.

In 1958, Eisenhower sought two additional measures to enhance the authority of the JCS chairman. First, he proposed repeal of the provision that denied the chairman a vote in JCS proceedings. Eisenhower argued that although the JCS did not, in fact, function by vote, the provision suggested that the chairman was somehow inferior to the other JCS members. Second, Eisenhower sought to place the joint staff directly under the chairman's authority, by giving him authority both to assign duties to the joint staff and to select its director from the JCS.

Unlike the 1953 reorganization, which was accomplished under the provisions of a 1949 law that allowed the president to reorganize the executive branch subject to congressional veto, Eisenhower's 1958 proposals required affirmative congressional action. In enacting the Defense Reorganization Act of 1958, Congress substantially weakened Eisenhower's proposals. The act assigned the chairman greater responsibilities, but did not endow the position with the independent authority that the president had requested. Congress repealed the provision that denied the chairman a vote in JCS proceedings, but carefully circumscribed his authority over the joint staff. Instead of granting the chairman exclusive authority to assign duties to the joint staff, Congress retained a parallel authority for the JCS. Similarly, the chairman was given authority to select the director of the joint staff, but only in consultation with the JCS. Moreover, the chairman's previously unencumbered authority to manage the joint staff was qualified in the 1958 act by the phrase "on behalf of the Joint Chiefs of Staff."

The 1953 and 1958 defense reforms failed to enlarge the power of the chairman significantly. Because Congress rejected the Eisenhower Administration's efforts to give the chairman independent authority over the joint staff, the office emerged from the 1958 Defense Reorganization Act with somewhat greater management responsibilities but still without the authority to ensure that JCS products reflected a broad national perspective. Although he continued to have opportunities to provide civilian leaders with personal advice, the chairman lacked both the staff and the statutory mandate to be an effective independent participant in defense processes. His primary source of authority remained personal, not institutional. Some chairmen, such as Admiral Arthur Radford and General Maxwell Taylor, have wielded considerable influence because of their close relationship to the president. But no chairman, either before or after the 1958 act, has had the institutional leverage or the executive authority to provide the integrated advice, planning, and direction that the chiefs themselves cannot.

The second focus of Eisenhower's reform efforts was the conflict between the dual roles of the service chiefs as members of the JCS and as military leaders of their services. However, he rejected proposals that would have addressed this dual-hat dilemma by separating the service chiefs from the JCS.[20] Instead, he endorsed the conclusions of the Rockefeller committee, as well as those of outgoing Secretary of Defense Robert A. Lovett.[21] Both the committee and Secretary Lovett noted the tensions inherent in the dual roles of the service chiefs, but argued against proposals that would separate the two roles, such as an armed forces general staff or a single chief of staff. They concluded that the parochial nature of JCS deliberations could be alleviated by reducing the service workloads of the chiefs, which, in turn, would allow them to focus on their primary role of providing joint military planning and advice.

In his 1953 reorganization plan, Eisenhower tried to reduce the JCS workload in two ways. First, he encouraged the chiefs to reduce their administrative burdens by delegating some of their service responsibilities to their subordinates. Second, he revised the operational chain of command to exclude the JCS. The new chain ran from the president and secretary of defense to the military departments, and then to the operational commands. This second measure was more symbolic than substantive, in that the chiefs actually remained in the operational chain as representatives of their military departments. Eisenhower's objective was to emphasize that the primary role of the JCS was to act as a planning and advisory group, not as a command organization. In 1958, Eisenhower returned the JCS to the operational chain of command, but defined them as an operational staff to the secretary of defense, not as military commanders.

In 1958, Eisenhower reaffirmed his belief in the soundness of the dual-hat concept for the JCS, but took the objective of reducing the internal service demands on the chiefs one step further. He requested, and Congress granted, specific statutory authority for the service chiefs to assign many of their service duties to their vice chiefs. Eisenhower then envisioned that the secretary of defense could "require the chiefs to use their power of delegation to enable them to make their Joint Chiefs of Staff duties their principal duties."[22]

Eisenhower's objective of a nonparochial Joint Chiefs of Staff was never realized. The measures that allowed the service chiefs greater authority to delegate their service duties did not address the primary source of the chiefs' inability to put joint interests over service interests. It was not that a service chief lacked authority to divest himself of service duties, but rather that to do so would undermine the chief's principal source of authority within the service and principal source of power and stature outside of it. A service chief's authority over his service derives largely from how effectively he represents its interests in outside forums, such as the JCS. At the same time, the service chief's power and stature within the joint arena, the defense department, and before the Congress, derive primarily from the resources and personnel that he controls as the military leader of his service. Moreover, in formulating joint positions, a service chief relies on the staff that works exclusively and directly for him — the service staff, which itself has strong incentives to ensure that important service interests are not sacrificed in the joint forum. The service chief is as much a captive as a leader of his service staff. Given these organizational dynamics and the fact that a chief has spent most of his military career in service, not joint assignments, it is difficult for even the most well-intentioned service chief to abandon service positions in JCS deliberations. He would not only be inconsistent in opposing a position that he was instrumental in developing, but would also risk losing the loyalty and support of his service. Since the 1953 and 1958 reforms did nothing to alter these organizational realities, they had little affect on the character or content of JCS decisionmaking.

The third focus of the Eisenhower Administration's defense reforms was the structure and procedures of the joint staff. Criticizing the extent of service dominance of the joint staff, the president argued that it should operate as an independent and unified military staff, not a broker for service views. Although he did not suggest that joint staff products should be devoid of individual service views, Eisenhower believed that the joint decision procedures, which required each military department to review and approve each joint paper at multiple levels, subverted the development of integrated military positions. In a message to Congress on April 3, 1958, he stated:

> These laborious processes exist because each military department feels obliged to judge independently each work product of the Joint Staff. Had I allowed my interservice and interallied staff to be similarly organized . . . during World War II, the delays and resulting indecisiveness would have been unacceptable to my superiors.[23]

To abolish the implicit single service veto established by this practice, he instructed Secretary of Defense Neil H. McElroy to reform joint staff structures and procedures. In particular, the president called for the elimination of the joint staff committee system, by which representatives from the three military departments reviewed and approved all joint staff papers. To assist in this effort, he requested Congress to raise or eliminate the statutory limits on joint staff size. In response, the 1958 Defense Reorganization Act raised the statutory limit on the joint staff from 210 to 400 officers. At the same time, Congress reiterated its bar on the joint staff operating as an overall armed forces general staff.

These reforms of joint staff structures and procedures failed to transform it into an independent military staff with a unified national perspective. The joint staff committee system was abolished, but compliance was in form, not in substance. In four instances, the interservice committees continued to operate after being renamed "councils" or "groups." More importantly, even where the joint staff abandoned the committee system, it retained the single service veto through elaborate staffing procedures that continued to circulate papers to the military departments for approval at each level of preparation. Further, Eisenhower's reforms failed to address the issues created by service control of the selection and advancement of joint staff officers. Then, as now, the joint staff consisted of officers from all services who were selected by their service, who usually served only a single three-year tour, who looked to their service for promotions and future assignments, and who were judged on how effectively they represented their services' interests. Given this personnel structure, joint staff officers have little opportunity and even less incentive to oppose their services by attempting to inject joint considerations into the process. Thus, the 1958 reforms reorganized the joint staff, but they did not substantially change the procedures that prevented it from operating independently of the services. It continued to serve as an executive secretariat that coordinated, rather than integrated, service views.

The final area addressed in Eisenhower's reform efforts was the unified operational command structure. The president sought to reduce the uniformed services' grip on the combatant commands by establishing an operational command structure that would promote integrated operations. In 1953, he directed the secretary of defense to designate a military department, rather than a service chief, as the executive agent for each command. In this way, Eisenhower sought to assert greater civilian control over the operational chain of command.

In 1958, Eisenhower pursued more radical measures to assure unified operation control. One of his most important objectives in 1958 was to "organize our fighting forces into operational commands that are truly unified."[24] Toward that end, he proposed greater clarity in the division of labor between the military services and the operational commands. Under his scheme, the military services, organized along traditional distinctions between land, sea, and air warfare, would be responsible for the maintaining functions: recruiting, organizing, training, and equipping the forces. The unified commands, organized geographically, and the specified commands, organized functionally, would command and operate the forces. To establish this division between maintaining and operating functions, Congress, at Eisenhower's request, repealed the statutory authority that the service chiefs had to command forces. Congress also assigned authority for establishing unified and specified commands to the president, acting through the secretary of defense. Finally, the unified and specified commanders were assigned full operational control over their forces. The military services were to have only administrative authority, not operational responsibility, for deployed forces. With this in mind, a 1958 secretary of defense directive established two command lines: one for operational direction of the forces, the other for administration and support activities.[25] The operational chain runs by statute from the president to the secretary of defense, to the unified or specified commander. The directive, however, inserts the JCS into the operational chain of command to advise the secretary on military operations and to transmit orders to the commands. The administrative chain of command runs from the president to the secretary of defense to the service secretaries and, finally, to the service components of each operational command.

The necessity of unified operational command was the overriding objective of Eisenhower's 1958 reforms, but the reforms failed to remove the military services from operations. The statutory division of labor between operating and maintaining functions has not been followed in practice. The services have continued to dominate the operating functions in three ways. First, as members of the JCS, they are in the operational chain of command, albeit only to advise the secretary and transmit orders to the unified and specified commands. Nevertheless, as John Kester has observed, the distinction between one who commands and one who transmits the commands of another can be, and in this case is, blurry.[26] As the military interface between the secretary of defense and the unified and specified commands, the service chiefs, together with the chairman, have the dominant influence on operational planning and direction.

Second, the services have dominated the unified commands through their control of the administrative chain of command that runs through the service departments to the component commands. In each unified command, there is a component command corresponding to each military department from which forces have been drawn. Although the CINC exercises full operational authority over his forces, he does so only through these component commands. Moreover, on matters other than operations, such as logistics, procurement, maintenance, and training, the component commanders report directly to their respective military departments. As a result, the individual services effectively determine the composition, structure, and readiness of the forces for which the CINCs are operationally responsible. This fragmentation of authority has produced a system in which the CINCs' operational authority would make them preeminent during wartime, but the services' administrative authority assures them of the dominant influence in peacetime.

Finally, although Eisenhower's 1958 reforms abolished the system in which each operational command had a service department act as its executive agent, they did not eliminate the association of each command with an individual service. There remains an informal system by which there is a dominant service for each command. The three specified commands — the aerospace defense command, the military airlift command, and the strategic air command — are made up solely of Air Force units. With regard to the unified commands, the Navy effectively controls the Atlantic command and the Pacific command, and the Army exerts the dominant influence over the European command, the Southern command, and the readiness command. The newest unified command, the Central command, originated as the Marine-led rapid deployment force, but it, too, is now under Army command.

The Eisenhower Administration sought unsuccessfully to detach the JCS system from the grip of the individual services while retaining the system's dual-hatted architecture. The 1953 and 1958 reforms succeeded in strengthening some of the joint military actors and reducing service influence in the joint system. But they fell far short of achieving Eisenhower's objective of a more independent and integrated joint military structure, in which unburdened service chiefs, led by a strong chairman and supported by an independent joint staff, operated as a unified military planning and advisory body. The authority granted the service chiefs to delegate service responsibilities to their vice chiefs did not alter the fundamental character of the Joint Chiefs of Staff. They remained primarily a committee of special interest representatives who operated under the principles of partisan mutual adjustment. The 1953 and 1958 reforms *did* enhance the authority of the chairman, but not sufficiently to enable him to act as the primary integrating force in the joint structure. The failure of the joint staff reforms to establish it as an independent military staff further compromised the effectiveness of the chairman. Thus, the 1953 and 1958 reforms failed either to strengthen the chairman and the joint staff significantly or to shift the organizational incentives of the service chiefs away from service toward joint concerns. Similarly, Eisenhower did not succeed in fully establishing a division of labor in which the services performed the maintaining functions and the operational commands performed the employment functions. Although the creation of separate chains of command for operations and administration did enhance the authority of the unified and specified commands somewhat, the services still retained the dominant voice. In short, despite the concerted efforts of the Eisenhower Administration, the joint system continued to operate on the World War II model of a service-dominated, committee-coordinated structure.

The Current Joint System and Its Critics

The Defense Reorganization Act of 1958 culminated postwar reform of the joint military structure. The structure that emerged in 1958 is, with only minor changes, the one that remains today. Since the 1958 reorganization, there have been frequent, albeit unheeded, calls for further reform of the joint system. In particular, there have been three presidentially-initiated studies of defense organization: the 1960 Report of the Committee on the Defense Establishment for President John F. Kennedy (the Symington report);[27] the 1970 Blue Ribbon Defense Panel Report for President Richard M. Nixon (the Fitzhugh report);[28] and the 1978 Report on the National Military Command Structure for President Jimmy Carter (the Steadman report).[29] All three reports, as well as numerous individual commentaries from defense experts and senior military officers, have concluded that the ineffectiveness of the joint structure has severely inhibited the proper functioning of the U.S. defense establishment. The criticism has been directed at the joint system's performance in each of its three major functions: advice, planning, and operational direction.

With regard to the advisory function, the Steadman report noted that the Joint Chiefs of Staff have been consistently unable to provide military advice on issues involving important service interests or prerogatives. These issues include the most important on the JCS agenda: the formulation of national military strategy; the allocation of service roles and missions; the establishment of functional and geographic operational responsibilities; and, particularly, the allocation of scarce defense dollars. Even on issues that do not raise interservice passions, the Steadman report found that the JCS have been slow to develop formal advice, with the result that joint military recommendations are frequently unavailable when needed. Moreover, when the advice is finally rendered, it is often so diluted by joint staffing procedures that it is of little value to civilian officials. The Steadman report noted that although civilian leaders have indicated satisfaction with the quality of the advice they receive from military leaders individually, they are almost uniformly critical of JCS institutional products. These are criticized as being ponderous in presentation, predictably wedded to the status quo, and reactive, rather than innovative. Former Secretary of State Dean Acheson complained that military advice and guidance was often limited to "oracular utterances." He explained that "since [the JCS] is a committee and its views are the result of votes on formal papers prepared for it, it quite literally is like my favorite old lady who could not say what she thought until she heard what she said."[30] Dissatisfaction with formal JCS products is echoed by former Chairman of the Joint Chiefs of Staff David Jones.[31] He has argued that the corporate advice provided by the JCS is not crisp, timely, or very useful. Civilian leaders have understandably looked elsewhere for recommendations that properly should come from the JCS.

The Joint Chiefs of Staff organization participates in two separate, but related, types of planning: (1) strategic resource planning, that is, the connection of military means to political ends within established resource constraints; and (2) contingency planning, that is, the preparation of specific operational plans for possible contingencies in which the U.S. would employ armed force. The performance of the joint system in both types of planning has been heavily criticized. According to the Steadman report, the JCS contribution to strategic planning has been crippled by their inability to make realistic force structure recommendations within established resource constraints. The report concluded that the inherent conflict between the joint and service roles of the chiefs precludes effective JCS advice on resource allocation issues, except to agree that the forces should be increased without regard to resource constraints.

> A Chief's responsibility to manage and lead his Service conflicts directly with his agreement in the joint forum to recommendations which are inconsistent with programs desired by his own service. A Chief cannot, for example, be expected to argue for additional carriers, divisions, and air wings when constructing a Service budget and then agree in a joint forum that they should be deleted in favor of programs of other Services. In doing so he would not only be unreasonably inconsistent, but would risk losing leadership of his Service as well.[32]

As a consequence, civilian leaders must make force structure decisions without the benefit of joint military advice. Tradeoffs are made, priorities are set, and alternatives are developed in parallel dialogues between the individual services and the office of the secretary of defense.

The inability of the joint structure to tie planning to available resources is also the primary source of deficiencies in the contingency planning process. A review of the contingency plans made during the Carter Administration by Under Secretary of Defense Robert Komer suggested that contingency plans were not closely linked to available resources. According to Komer, execution of the plans frequently depended on resources that either did not exist or were committed to too many commands simultaneously.[33] Former Army Chief of Staff General Edward C. Meyer has testified that the links between contingency planning and resource allocation are not strong.[34] In other words, the CINCs, who draft the contingency plans in the first instance and who command the forces in wartime, have too little to say about what those forces will look like.

The final area of joint military responsibility is operational direction of the armed forces. Although the CINCs have full operational control of all forces assigned to them, the services control such vital related matters as logistics, personnel, training, procurement, and maintenance. The CINCs have little influence over the capabilities and readiness of the forces under their command. Both the Steadman report and the Blue Ribbon Defense Panel questioned whether, under this system, the CINCs have the requisite peacetime authority to carry out their wartime operational responsibilities. In particular, the reports suggested that the CINCs face fragmented logistics, have excessively layered headquarter staffs, lack uniform, command-wide readiness assessments, and often command several component forces, each of which may be designed to fight a different type of war. General Meyer has suggested that the system would have difficulty even managing the transition from the peacetime structure, in which the services have the dominant influence, to the wartime structure, in which the CINCs have a much greater role.

Confusion about the operational chain of command has compounded these problems further. According to the Blue Ribbon Defense Panel, the operational chain is awkward and unresponsive. The panel found that the presence of the JCS in the chain "provides a forum for inter-Service conflicts to be injected into the decision-making process for military operations; and it inhibits the flow of information to and from the combatant commands and the President and Secretary of Defense, often even in crisis situations."[35] Although not as forceful in its criticism of the command arrangements, the Steadman report also criticized the CINCs' lack of a single military superior in Washington. Similarly, the Symington report condemned the predominance of service influence in the planning and execution of military missions.

The dominant theme of these past studies is the imbalance between the role of the individual services and that of the joint military structure. There is substantial doubt of the premise underlying the current JCS system that joint advice, planning, and operational direction are best handled by a committee consisting of the senior officer from each service. Most critics have concluded that voluntary interservice cooperation cannot produce the integration necessary for useful military advice, coordinated planning, and unified combined-arms operations. The reforms put forward by these critics focus either on enhancing the authority of the current supraservice actors — the chairman, the joint staff, and the unified and specified commanders — or on creating new supraservice organizations, such as a council of national military advisers or an armed forces general staff. The next section will examine these proposals for more centralized joint military structures in detail.

ALTERNATIVE MODELS OF JOINT STRUCTURE

From World War II to the present, the overriding question in designing our joint military architecture has been how much centralization is required to produce effective military advice, planning, and operations. There are four aspects to the centralization issue.

- First is the issue of whether the senior military advisory body should consist of the chiefs of the military services or of officers without service responsibilities or functions.
- The second issue is how much authority should be granted to the senior military officer in the joint system.
- Another issue is whether the joint staff should be organized as a committee of service representatives, an independent military staff, or an armed forces general staff.
- Finally, there is the issue of how much authority the unified and specified commanders should be granted over the composition, equipping, training, and readiness of their forces.

These four issues have dominated postwar debates over the composition of the joint military structure. As Table 9.1 illustrates, and as was discussed earlier, positions on these issues have clustered to form three alternatives to the current service-dominant structure: (1) the strong-chairman model, (2) the national military advisers (NMA) model, and (3) the armed forces general staff model.

The present debate over the joint military structure has remained consistent with this historical typology. The service-dominant model of the joint military structure that has characterized the joint structure since World War II has been challenged by reform proposals that are extensions of the three more centralized models of the joint military structure. In this

Table 9.1. Model of Joint Structure

ISSUE	SERVICE DOMINANT	STRONG CHAIRMAN	NATIONAL MILITARY ADVISERS	GENERAL STAFF
Dual-hatting of Service Chiefs	Yes	Yes	No	No
Senior Military Officer	Weak Chairman	Strong Chairman	Strong Chairman	Single Armed Forces Chief of Staff
Joint Staff	Dominated by Services	Independently Organized	Independently Organized	Separate General Staff
Influence of CINCs	Weak	Moderate	Moderate	Moderate

context, it is useful to examine the current proposals in light of their historical precedents.

The Strong Chairman Model

This has been the most prominent alternative to the current system. It calls for retention of the existing joint framework, but with a strengthening of the three central actors. The model would balance service influence in the joint system by enhancing the power of the chairman, the joint staff, and the unified and specified commanders (CINCs). The most significant feature of this model is the independent authority granted to the chairman. Although the specific statutory authority varies with different versions of the model, all versions call for the chairman to play a strong leadership role in integrating service positions. The joint staff procedures would be revised so that the staff could act in support of the chairman, rather than as an executive secretariat to coordinate service views. Finally, the strong chairman model would remove the JCS from the operational chain of command and strengthen the authority of the CINCs to improve the cross-service planning and conduct of military operations.

The strong chairman model originated with the reforms in the joint structure proposed by the Truman and Eisenhower Administrations. The Truman Administration proposed that the chairman head the JCS and be the principal military adviser to the president and the secretary of defense. The Eisenhower Administration refrained from making the chairman the head of the JCS or the principal military adviser, but recommended that he be given full authority over the joint staff. Eisenhower also sought to eliminate the de facto service veto over joint staff products and to reduce service influence in operations by establishing separate chains of command for operations and administration.

Two more recent reform proposals picked up the threads of the Truman and Eisenhower efforts. The 1978 Steadman report and the current proposals of General David Jones both set forth versions of the strong chairman model.[36] They recommend specific measures to increase the authority of the three core actors in the joint structure: the chairman, the joint staff, and the CINCs.

With regard to the chairman, the Steadman report, the more modest of the two proposals, recommended granting the chair discrete authority to correct specific failures of the joint system. The report called for the secretary of defense to make the chairman responsible for providing military input on cross-service program and budget issues. It also recommended making the chairman a voting member of the Defense Systems Acquisition Review Council (DSARC), which selects new weapons for development and production. In contrast, General Jones recommended assigning more comprehensive authority to the chairman. Under the Jones proposal, the chairman would have a deputy with four-star rank and would replace the JCS as the principal military adviser to the president, secretary of defense, and the National Security Council. The chairman would still receive the counsel of the service chiefs, but the advice given to civilian leaders would ultimately be based on his own judgment of what was in the broad national interest. In order to assure that the chairman considered the chiefs' views seriously in formulating his advice, however, the Jones proposal would grant the service chiefs the right of dissent. Each chief would have authority to submit his views directly to the secretary of defense and the president whenever he thought it appropriate. Moreover, on issues of crucial national importance, such as arms control, the president and the secretary of defense would continue to seek the corporate advice of the Joint Chiefs of Staff.

To support the chairman, both the Steadman report and General Jones would grant him greater independent authority over the joint staff. Again, however, General Jones called for more far-reaching changes. Whereas the Steadman report recommended that the chairman receive "appropriate" joint staff support, General Jones proposed that the entire joint staff report directly to the chairman rather than the JCS. Both Steadman and Jones recommended that the JCS revise its internal procedures to make the joint staff alone responsible for authorship of JCS papers, thereby eliminating the implicit single service veto. They also recommended enhancing the career incentives for joint duty and giving the chairman a greater role in the selection and promotion of joint staff officers.

Finally, seeking a better balance between the services and the combat commands, both the Steadman report and General Jones sought a strengthened role for the unified and specified commanders. Under both proposals, the chairman would supervise the commands and represent their interests in resource allocation planning and decisions. To reinforce the chairman-CINC connection, both recommended revising the operational chain of command to the CINCs. It would run from the president to the secretary of defense through the chairman, rather than through the JCS. General Jones would have underscored this altered chain of command by amending the statute, whereas the Steadman report proposed simply revising the relevant department of defense directive. The Steadman report also recommended retaining the JCS as the military staff to the secretary of defense for operations. The recommendations of the Steadman report and those of General Jones differ in degree, but not in kind. Where the Steadman report would assign the chairman discrete authority to perform certain functions and somewhat greater control over the joint staff, General Jones would grant the chairman more comprehensive authority as principal military adviser and full control over the joint staff. Both sets of recommendations build on the reforms of Truman and, particularly, those of Eisenhower, seeking to promote development of an independent joint military perspective within the existing joint apparatus. Both see a chairman with greater independent authority, supported by the joint staff and acting in concert with the CINCs, as providing civilian leaders with military advice and planning integrated across service lines.

There are three fundamental criticisms of the strong chairman model in general, and the Jones proposals in particular. First, the strong chairman model is viewed as likely to limit the diversity of military advice available to civilian leaders.[37] It is argued that with a single officer providing the primary joint military input, expert minority opinions could be excluded. Instead of being exposed to a broad range of military opinions, political leaders would be isolated — exposed to only a single strategic perspective and philosophy of war. It is feared that the chairman, particularly if he were the principal military adviser, could be in a position to screen information and options not consistent with his perspective. It is argued, further, that the chairman, having significant experience in only one service, would lack expertise in the doctrine, capabilities, and readiness of all services and, therefore, could not provide comprehensive and balanced military advice. In other words, the full development of legitimate alternatives that derive from the experience and expertise of the senior officer in each service would be severely restricted under the strong chairman model.

This criticism implies that the current joint structure provides civilian leaders with multiple advice — that is, several options, each supported by one or more of the services. This, in fact, is rarely the case. Admiral Thomas H. Moorer has testified that during his tenure as chairman, the JCS made a single unanimous recommendation on 99 percent of the issues that came before it.[38] To achieve this high degree of consensus, the system suppresses or dilutes valid options, and, instead, presents homogenized products reflecting the lowest common denominator of service agreement. The Steadman report and General Jones both argue that the chairman, acting in an individual capacity, would be able to sharpen the alternatives for civilian leaders in a way that a committee cannot. Although these proposals would strengthen the chairman's independent authority, his links with the JCS would remain significant. In formulating his advice, the chairman would be required to solicit the views of the other JCS members, as well as those of the CINCs, and would have to rely on the multiservice joint staff for support. The joint staff itself would be more independent, but it would still consist of officers who had been selected from and who would return to the services. Moreover, the joint staff would continue to rely on the services for much necessary information. Accordingly, the influence of the individual services would remain significant even under the strong chairman model.

Even if the chairman were to be made the principal military adviser, as the Jones proposal recommends, he would still not be the sole source of military advice. Civilian leaders would retain direct access to service perspectives in four ways. First, service views on force programing and budgetary issues would continue to be represented in their annual program objective memoranda (POM). Second, the chief of staff of the Army, the chief of naval operations, and the chief of staff of the Air Force would continue to be responsible for advising the president and secretary of defense directly regarding land, sea, and air warfare, respectively. Third, the Jones proposals include a specific right of dissent for the service chiefs. Finally, the president and secretary of defense could request corporate JCS advice on issues where they believed it to be appropriate. In short, the objective of making the chairman the principal military adviser is, not to limit civilians to a single source of military advice, but to assure that the chairman has the requisite authority to develop national military advice, as a supplement to the views that civilians already receive from the individual services.

The second major criticism of the strong chairman model is that it would divorce the responsibility for formulating plans from the authority to execute them.[39] Winston Churchill put it more bluntly: "Any clever person can make plans for winning a war as long as he doesn't have to carry them out."[40] The most effective plans are drafted by those who must actually implement them. Separating planning from implementation reduces the accountability of both the planners and the implementors. Because the bedrock of sound military planning is knowledge about the capabilities and limitations of the forces, it is argued that the service chiefs are best qualified to do joint planning. In this view, only the service chiefs can inform the planning process with accurate assessments of the state and capabilities of the armed forces. The chiefs are the essential link between joint planning and the programs of the individual services.

This criticism confuses strategic and contingency planning. Strategic planning requires assessments of the threat, determination of a strategy to meet the threat, and allocation of resources to fulfill the strategy. Through the Joint Strategic Planning Document (JSPD), the JCS provides the primary joint military input to this process. After significant civilian review, the services execute the resulting plans in their POMs. In the sense that primary responsibility for drafting the JSPD would shift from the JCS to the chairman, the strong chairman model would separate responsibility for planning from authority for execution. But this separation exists under the current service-dominant model, because the JCS has already abdicated much of their joint planning responsibilities. The JCS has been unable to provide political leaders with force structure recommendations within existing resource constraints. The JSPD simply aggregates the unconstrained force structure requests of the individual services. It sets no priorities. The strong chairman model would not have the chairman supplant the JCS' current role in strategic planning. Rather, it would have the chairman perform the role that the JCS, as an institution, has proved incapable of performing: making cross-service military judgments on the tradeoffs in force planning made necessary by peacetime resource constraints.

Contingency planning, on the other hand, involves the preparation of operational plans that set forth how existing forces would be used to meet specific contingencies. The JCS has responsibility for coordinating this planning. But the unified and specified commands, not the military services, have the authority to prepare and execute those plans. Shifting responsibility for *coordinating* contingency plans from the JCS to the chairman would not separate responsibility for preparing the plans from authority for their execution. The CINCs would retain both functions. The real issue is whether the chairman, supported by the joint staff, or the JCS could better ensure that the contingency plans of the nine unified and specified commands are compatible with each other and consistent with national planning. Because the strong chairman model seeks generally to improve the links between the chairman and the CINCs, it seems likely that the chairman would be in a better position than the JCS, not only to coordinate contingency plans, but also to assure that resource planning takes the plans into account.

The final basis for criticism of the strong chairman model is the man-on-a-white-horse syndrome — the fear that the existence of a single, preeminent military commander would erode civilian control of the armed forces.[41] It is argued that by making the chairman the principal military adviser, assigning him full authority over the joint staff, and inserting him in the operational chain of command, the strong chairman model would make a single military leader too powerful. In this view, the model would undermine the system of checks and balances inherent in the current system of four relatively equal and competing services. It is implied that a single, powerful, military leader would threaten our democratic institutions and ideals.

Although this argument is often joined with the previous one about divorcing responsibility from authority, the two are contradictory. If the model, in fact, grants the chairman preeminent responsibility for planning but assigns authority for execution to the military services and the CINCs, it is disingenuous to claim that the chairman has the power to threaten civilian control over the armed forces. Either he combines responsibility and authority in the joint military structure, or he does not threaten civilian control. Both cannot be true simultaneously.

The implicit premise of the man-on-a-white-horse argument is that the chairman will gain authority and influence at the expense of civilian leaders, particularly the secretary of defense. The validity of this premise is doubtful. All of the specific powers granted to the chairman in the model are currently held by the JCS. It is the influence the individual services exercise on the joint system through the JCS, not the authority of the secretary, that the strong chairman model would reduce. Further, as John Kester has pointed out, the joint military apparatus has acquired many new rivals since the 1940s that work to neutralize its influence. Within the Department of Defense, there are the heavily staffed under and assistant secretaries of defense, as well as the defense agencies. Outside the department, there are the Arms Control and Disarmament Agency, the Bureau of Politico-Military Affairs in the State Department, and the National Security Council staff.[42] The independent authority granted the chairman would not allow him to dominate these civilian power centers. On the contrary, if the chairman is able to provide political leaders with military advice and planning from a broad, cross-service perspective, the strong chairman model would enhance civilian control of the military, in the practical sense that our leaders would better understand the implications of their decisions on defense matters.

In short, the three major criticism of the strong chairman model that are made by supporters of the existing service-dominant joint structure lack validity. The model would not establish the chairman as the sole source of military advice for civilian leaders, but, rather, would make him an additional source of advice, more independent of service perspectives. The problems inherent in divorcing responsibility for planning and advice from authority for execution are no more present in the strong chairman model than they are in the current structure. Most importantly, the strong chairman model poses no threat to democratic institutions or to civilian control of the military.

The most serious questions about the viability of the strong chairman model come, not from defenders of the current system, but from advocates of more radical reforms. Proponents of the national military advisers model and the general staff model contend that strengthening the authority of the chairman, the joint staff, and the CINCs, will not be sufficient to produce effective joint military advice, planning, and operational direction. They argue that such reforms fail to address the most important source of problems within the current joint structure: the dual hatting of service chiefs as JCS members and uniformed heads of their services. In this view, the dual-hatted character of the chiefs creates an insuperable conflict between their service and their joint responsibilities. It is argued that it is contradictory to ask a service chief to both represent the interests of his service and to provide military planning and advice from a national perspective. It is contended, further, that both positions — service chief and JCS member — are full-time responsibilities and cannot jointly be performed effectively by a single individual. Accordingly, both of the next two models begin from the premise that service administration must be separated from joint advice, planning, and operational direction.

The National Military Advisers Model

This model generally follows the lines of the strong chairman model, with the important difference being that it eliminates dual hatting. It would replace the Joint Chiefs of Staff with a national military advisory council of distinguished four-star officers who have no service responsibilities or functions. They would constitute the senior military advisory and planning body. Like the JCS, the council would be supported by a joint staff of officers selected from all four services. The service chiefs, their load lightened by removal of their joint duties, would concentrate on the internal management of their services. Finally, with regard to operations, this model would have the chairman of the national military advisory council transmit civilian orders to the unified and specified commands.

This proposal first surfaced during the Eisenhower Administration, when the first Chairman of the Joint Chiefs of Staff, General Omar Bradley, recommended replacing the JCS with a committee of superchiefs, freed of service ties.[43] But the model's full exposition came in the 1960 report of the Symington Committee. Commissioned by John F. Kennedy during the 1960 presidential campaign, the report asserted that a defense structure based on the World War II model had been rendered obsolete by the arrival of strategic nuclear weapons and the rise of Soviet power. Contending that the United States could no longer rely on a military structure whose organizing principle was whether a military man traveled by land, sea, or air, the Symington Committee recommended substantial reforms in the Joint Chiefs of Staff system, the unified command system, and the military department structure. The intent of the reforms was to reduce the influence of the individual services in defense planning and military operations.

The Symington Committee proposed abolishing the Joint Chiefs of Staff and making the chairman (redesignated the chairman of the joint staff) the principal military adviser to the president and the secretary of defense. Under this proposal, the chairman would direct an enlarged joint staff and preside over a military advisory council of senior officers from all services on their last tour of duty. These senior officers would have no service functions or responsibilities. The Symington Committee argued that this revamped joint military planning and advisory structure would be less constrained by the individual interests of the services and, thus, would be more capable of developing independent military judgments from a national perspective.

The Symington Committee also sought to reduce service influence in the operational chain of command. It proposed to simplify the unified command structure and emphasize combined-arms operations under unified command. The revised structure would consist of three functionally based unified commands: a strategic command, a tactical command, and a continental defense command. The commanders of each command would report directly to the chairman of the joint staff. Finally, the Symington Committee advocated abolishing the military departments. The military services would remain separate organic units under the direct control of the secretary of defense, but the civilian service secretariats would be eliminated. Their functions would be absorbed by two new under secretaries of defense, one for weapon acquisition and the other for administration.

The Kennedy Administration did not implement, or even seriously consider, the recommendations of the Symington Committee. Kennedy aid Theodore Sorenson suggested that the proposals were too controversial to be anything more than a stimulant to future planning.[44] Similarly, President Eisenhower advised Kennedy against undertaking any major defense reform initiatives early in his administration.[45] Most importantly, Secretary of Defense Robert S. McNamara opposed the committee's proposals, arguing persuasively for introduction of new management systems for DOD rather than further adjustments in the department's architecture.[46]

The NMA model was not raised again until 1978, in the Steadman report. The thrust of that report was to recommend reforms that would institute a version of the strong chairman model. But in a concluding section, the report stated that if strengthening the roles of the chairman, the joint staff, and the CINCs did not significantly improve joint military performance, reforms of a more fundamental nature would be necessary. They would have to separate joint advice, planning, and operations from service administration by replacing the JCS with a body of national military advisers who would be responsible for all joint functions. The NMA would be comprised of a senior officer from each service, one of whom would be chairman; and it would be supported by the joint staff. Unlike the Symington Committee, the Steadman report recommended that the NMA be the principal military advisers to the president, the secretary of defense, and the NSC. The Steadman report advocated adoption of the NMA model as a last resort, only if reforms along the lines of the strong chairman model failed to improve joint military effectiveness.

In 1982, General Edward C. Meyer, Chief of Staff of the Army, put forward his own version of the NMA model.[47] General Meyer's proposal tracks the Symington report quite closely. He advocates abolition of the JCS and replacement by a national military advisory council, consisting of a distinguished four-star officer from each of the military services and a chairman. These officers would have no service responsibilities or functions, and they would not return to their services at the end of their terms as council members. The chairman would preside over the council, direct its planning and operations, and direct a strengthened joint staff, which would support the council. The chairman would transmit orders from the president and the secretary of defense to the operational commanders. The senior member of the council would be designated the vice chairman. The council's primary responsibilities would be to develop military strategy and to translate policy guidance from civilian authorities into programming direction for the military departments. Once the secretary of defense had approved the strategic recommendations of the council, they would become binding on the services in shaping the general outlines of their programs. In General Meyer's view, this system would produce more coherent strategic planning and direction from the joint military structure. The individual service chiefs would have a reduced role in determining cross-service priorities, but they would have more time to devote to the internal management of their services.

The core of all versions of the NMA model is separation of the functions of joint military advice, planning, and operational direction from the administration of the military services. It is this separation that is also the source of most criticisms of the model. First, critics contend that to an even greater degree than with the strong chairman model, the NMA model would divorce responsibility for military planning from authority for its implementation.[48] It is argued that effective military planning cannot be done in a vacuum by a purely advisory group free of any responsibility to execute those plans. In this view, a national military advisory council would quickly take up residence in an ivory tower, and would lack current information on the doctrine, readiness, and capabilities of the forces. Accordingly, the NMA's advice, particularly on short-term budget and operational questions, would be of questionable relevance.

The issue of separation of responsibility from authority appears to have more validity in the case of the NMA model than it has with the strong chairman model. Unlike the chairman, the national military advisory council would lack any authority for either the conduct of military operations or the implementation of force planning decisions. Whereas the chairman would replace the JCS in the operational chain of command and supervise the CINCs, the NMA would be solely an advisory body. Although it might provide useful advice as a council of wise men, the NMA could not be held accountable for implementation of that advice.

Second, some critics of the NMA concept have suggested that splitting the dual-hatted functions of JCS members will reduce the military's overall voice in national security issues.[49] The NMA would split the national military influence now contained in the JCS into two power centers — the service chiefs and the NMA. The service chiefs, deprived of their statutory mandate as the senior national military planning and advisory body, would experience a reduction in their influence. Whether the NMA would be able to balance this loss of military influence is open to question. On the one hand, there are those who suggest that the NMA would be able to advise the secretary on cross-service priorities in the budget process — something that the

JCS has been unable to do—and, therefore, they might wield considerable influence. On the other hand, it is argued that, lacking authority over either the operational commands or the services, the NMA would quickly be reduced to a powerless panel. If the NMA is ineffective, it is suggested that greater power will devolve to the office of the secretary of defense (OSD). According to the Steadman report, many senior military officers believe that there has been a clear trend toward centralization of decisionmaking within the OSD, and that a major counterweight to this centralization is the dual role of the service chiefs as uniformed leaders of their services and as members of the JCS. In this view, the chiefs in their dual role have a voice in congressional and NSC decisions, which provides some offset to the OSD's influence. This balance between civilian and military influence could be lost under the NMA model.

By placing the emphasis on a shift of power from military to civilian hands, critics have somewhat misconstrued the potential problems of an ineffective NMA. Within the current system, the primary military influence derives from the individual services, not from the joint military structure. As members of the JCS, the service chiefs undoubtedly gain influence, but it is the service agendas, not the joint military agenda, that benefit. The primary objective of the NMA model is to enfranchise an independent joint military perspective. A necessary corollary is that service influence must be somewhat reduced. Accordingly, if the NMA were to prove an ineffective joint military body, the primary problem is not diminished service influence, but the continued absence of joint military advice and planning from a national perspective.

Finally, critics contend that the NMA model would lessen service cooperation in the joint arena.[50] By removing service chiefs from the senior military advisory body and, thus, denying them a direct say in joint decisions, the model could undermine service cooperation in the joint arena. The Steadman report cited fears that removal of service representatives from the joint forum would reverse the steady progress made since 1947 toward effective integration of the capabilities of the land, sea, and air forces. Even though the report was unable to assemble evidence, either to support or to refute this contention, it acknowledged that there was indeed such a risk in an NMA-type joint military structure.

The NMA model is the least studied of the three alternatives to the service-dominant model. It lacks both the historical experience of the general staff model and the considerable studies that have been done on the strong chairman model. There is no substantial body of literature examining the NMA model. The Symington Committee, under significant time pressure and chartered to review past studies, not to conduct a sweeping examination of their own, set forth the NMA framework, but offered little analysis of its impact. Similarly, the Steadman report considered the NMA model only in a short postscript and specifically advised that it be given more searching and detailed study before being adopted. Advocates of the NMA model, as well as its critics, are unable to speak with confidence about the impact that it would have on existing institutional relationships and power balances in the defense establishment.

The Armed Forces General Staff Model

By far the most controversial proposal for a revamped joint military structure is the armed forces general staff model. Two significant characteristics denote this model. First is the single uniformed military commander, a chief of staff, who presides over all activities of the armed forces with command authority over both the operational commands and the military services. Second, the chief of staff is supported by a multiservice staff organized along functional lines—operations, intelligence, logistics, etc. This staff usually has executive authority over its functional area, subject to the direction of the chief of staff. Officers are selected for general staff duty early in their careers. Although they return to their services for occasional tours, these officers form an entity that is independent of the services. They receive separate training, and the chief of staff, not the services, controls their promotions and assignments.

In the United States, the general staff model first came to light in the proposals of military study groups in the 1940s for a single armed forces chief of staff. The armed forces chief of staff concept was put forward twice in 1945, first by a special committee appointed by the JCS to study postwar defense organization and later by the Army in the Collins Plan.[51] Despite the Army's strong advocacy and the initial support of President Truman, Congress rejected the concept of a single armed forces chief of staff. Opposition to the general staff model was so firm that, in 1949, when Congress established a chairman of the Joint Chiefs of Staff and expanded the joint staff, it included a specific prohibition against establishment of either a single chief of staff or an armed forces general staff.

Since the 1940s, proposals for a general staff system have been put forward only infrequently, and have received little support in either the executive or legislative branches. In a 1952 letter to President Truman, in which he analyzed the strengths and weaknesses of the organization of the department of defense, outgoing Secretary of Defense Robert A. Lovett set forth a general staff proposal as one of two alternatives for reorganizing the JCS.[52] His proposal called for replacement of the JCS with a "combined staff" of senior officers from all services, who would be supported by a multiservice staff independent of the services. Although Lovett recommended that there be a rotating chairman instead of a single chief of staff, he acknowledged that institution of the system would violate the congressional prohibition against an armed forces general staff. Concluding that even his somewhat diluted version of a general staff system would be too abrupt a change from the current system, Lovett instead recommended strengthening the chairman and authorizing the service chiefs to delegate their service responsibilities to their vice chiefs.

In 1959, former Army Chief of Staff General Maxwell D. Taylor recommended adoption of a modified general staff system. In 1982, General Taylor, who in the interim served as chairman of the Joint Chiefs of Staff, revived his proposal in testimony before a congressional committee.[54] Under his plan, the JCS organization would be dissolved and two new entities would be established: a chief of staff to the national command authorities and a national military council. The chief of staff would be the senior officer of the armed forces, the immediate subordinate of the secretary of defense in the chain of command, and a statutory member of the National Security Council. In all these roles, he would be the principal military adviser on current military policy, strategy, and programs. Supporting the chief of staff would be two deputy chiefs of staff (from services other than his own), and a military staff organized along functional lines. Separate from the chief of staff office and its supporting organization would be the national military council. The council would consist of a chairman and about five senior or retired military officers with a very small staff. This body would provide the civilian authorities with mid- and long-term advice on overall national security policy and military strategy. General Taylor's proposal is essentially a hybrid of the NMA and general staff models. A general staff system would plan and direct military operations and provide military advice on short-term issues, while a national military council would provide military advice on longer-term issues and act as a counterweight to the general staff.

Former Secretary of Defense Harold Brown proposed replacing the JCS organization with a purer version of the general staff system.[55] His proposal calls for creation of a chief of military staff (with a deputy from the naval forces if he is an Army or Air Force officer, and vice versa) and a joint general staff drawn from all four services. Although there would be some movement between the general staff and the services, the general staff officers would have separate career paths from officers remaining within the services. The general staff would report to the chief of military staff alone, and would have principal authority for staff promotions. The chief of military staff, supported by the general staff, would have principal authority for planning and for executing military operations. The service chiefs would continue to have responsibility for structuring, equipping, and training the forces. They would make program and budget recommendations through their service secretaries, but they would no longer make recommendations in a separate chain under JCS auspices. Instead, the chief of military staff would recommend cross-service budget priorities to the secretary of defense. Brown argues that a general staff system would introduce a clearer and less parochial view on issues of military strategy and capabilities, and the relationship between the two.

Three arguments are most frequently raised against the general staff system. First, it is argued that whereas a general staff system is well suited for the conduct of military operations, it is poorly suited to be the senior national military planning and advisory body. In testimony before Congress, Marine Commandant General Robert H. Barrow alleged that a general staff organization would lead to only a single option being recommended to civilian leaders, instead of a range of all legitimate options. This assertion, however, contradicts General Barrow's earlier description of the functioning of a general staff system in which the staff would recommend a range of options in rank order. "The General Staff develops and evaluates alternative courses of action and provides them, in order of preference, to the commander."[56] Moreover, as noted in the discussion of the strong chairman model, the current joint system has the same tendency to forward single, consensus recommendations to civilian leaders, not the range of options General Barrow advocates. Nevertheless, there is a legitimate question as to whether a general staff system would cause military advice and planning to be slanted to reflect a particular strategic perspective. Although general staff officers would be selected from all services, once selected they would receive intensive training at a general staff school and would pursue a common career track separate from the services. This system might well produce a common mind set among general staff officers. Indeed, inculcation of a similar approach to problems in order to facilitate coordination is one of the objectives of a general staff system. Accordingly, over the long term, there is the possibility that the military advice and planning that civilians would receive from a general staff might reflect a particular strategic perspective, to the exclusion of other legitimate alternatives.

A second line of argument against the general staff system is that by creating an elite group, it will produce tensions between that group and the regular forces. Harold Brown acknowledges that strains between the general staff and the operational forces are a necessary cost of a general staff. He suggests, however, that the operational commanders—the CINCs —would probably prefer direction from an elite general staff to the current system in which they are subject to substantial, albeit informal, pressure from the service staffs.[57]

The final and most ominous argument leveled against a general staff system is that it would threaten our democratic institutions, generally, and civilian control of the military, particularly.[58] It is asserted that the inherent nature of a general staff system is to seek control of all national policies related to warmaking, notably foreign and economic policies. In this view, a general staff could ultimately come to dominate civilian leaders and institutions. The basis of this argument is historical analogy. Constant reference is made to the German General Staff system and to its role in two world wars. The analogy to the German experience, however, is fallacious for two reasons. First, the German General Staff was an army staff, not an all-arms institution, as has been proposed for the United States. The failure of the Germans to include the Navy, and later the Luftwaffe, inhibited their ability both to plan overall military strategy and to direct combined-arms operations.

Second, the record of the German General Staff with regard to civilian control is mixed. During World War I, it is true that as the political institutions disintegrated, the General Staff acquired authority way out of proportion to its military responsibilities. But, in World War II, the opposite phenomenon occurred. The General Staff was itself dominated by Hitler, who frequently intervened in the details of military operations. Thus, it seems likely that the character and strength of the political institutions, not the type of military organization, were the determining factors in the military's role in both world wars. In any event, the American military establishment has substantially different roots from those of the pre-World War II German army. Civilian control is deeply ingrained in the traditions and institutions of the American military establishment, and, unlike Wilhelmite Germany, military officers do not form a separate class with interests at odds with other groups in society.

It is significant that the specter of a general staff undermining civilian institutions is raised most frequently by military officers, not by political officials. More specifically, naval officers are the most dire in their predictions of the likely military tyranny resulting from institutionalization of a general staff system. But as James Schlesinger has suggested, the Navy's real concern is not that a general staff would dominate civilian institutions, but that it would dominate the Navy.

> You get a lot of utter tosh about the general staff. We do not want to allow a general staff to dominate civilians. I think that there is some element of disingenuousness in the worry about the civilians. The worry about the general staff is that it will dominate the Navy, not the civilians. Let the civilians fend for themselves.[59]

The Navy has historically been the most independent of the armed services. Even given today's increasing requirements for greater integration of land, sea, and air operations, the Navy remains far more self-sufficient than the other services. It possesses its own air force (naval aviation) and its own army (the Marine Corps), and its army has its own air force (marine aviation). Thus, the Navy possesses most of the resources it needs to perform its core mission of sea control. Given its self-sufficiency, the Navy's fear of a general staff—indeed of any central military authority—is twofold. First, it might have to sacrifice some control over its core mission because a stronger central military institution might require that more naval forces serve under commanders from other services, who, in the Navy's view, do not fully understand how to employ sea power. Second, a central military institution might recommend military budget priorities in which the Navy receives a smaller share of defense resources than under the current system, in which the Navy negotiates that share directly with civilian authorities.

Many Army officers have often supported a stronger central institution, such as a general staff, for the same reasons, that their Navy counterparts oppose them. The Army is the most dependent military service. It requires significant Navy and Air Force support to fulfill its primary mission of large-scale land warfare. The Army needs the Navy and the Air Force to transport it to the battlefields, and it needs the Air Force to provide close air support on the battlefield. The Army perceives that a stronger central military structure might well require its sister services to devote more resources to these support missions, which both now treat as secondary priorities. Moreover, Army officers also believe that their less glamorous requirements would fare better in the resource competition with the Navy and Air Force if a central military institution recommended budget priorities, than if the services continue to negotiate budgets individually.

In summary, the general staff model carries with it potential costs in terms of limiting the military perspectives to which civilians are exposed and in terms of producing the resentments inherent in the creation of any elite organization. But the claims that such an organization would endanger civilian control of military institutions and activities is a red herring, the product of threatened bureaucratic interests, not endangered democratic ideals.

CONCLUSION

In the current debate over the adequacy of the joint military structure, the strong chairman model has been the dominant alternative proposed to the existing joint system. Although both the NMA model and the armed forces general staff model have been proposed in the context of the current controversy, neither has attracted substantial support. Instead, most support for defense reform has coalesced around General David Jones' proposals for strengthening the chairman, the joint staff, and the operational commanders. Nevertheless, defenders of the present, service-dominant joint structure have tended to categorize all proposals for strengthening the central military structures as invitations to a general staff system. Even the most modest versions of the strong chairman model, in which the chairman is given authority to provide independent advice and given somewhat greater authority over the joint staff, are compared to the Prussian General Staff, thereby suggesting the specter of military threats to democratic institutions.

This line of argument fails on two counts. First, as previously explained, an American armed forces general staff system would pose little threat to civilian institutions and democratic ideals. Indeed, the general staff system has its potential dangers—creating intramilitary tensions between an elite staff and regular line officers and allowing civilian authorities to be exposed to only a single strategic perspective. But these dangers do not include undermining civilian control of the military establishment or the use of force.

Second, even if a general staff did somehow threaten civilian control, the strong chairman model of the joint structure would not constitute a general staff. A stronger chairman, even one with authority as principal military adviser, would have considerably less authority than a single armed forces chief of staff. A chief of staff would have command authority over the operational commands and the services. In contrast, a strong chairman would be an adviser, not a commander. He would have no authority over the individual services; and although he would supervise the operational commands and transmit orders to them from civilian authorities, all command authority would remain with the president and the secretary of defense. Similarly, a joint staff that operated as an independent military staff in support of the chairman is not equivalent to an armed forces general staff. Unlike general staff officers, members of the joint staff would return to their respective services after joint duty. Although some versions of a strong chairman model would give the joint system some say in the subsequent promotions of joint staff officers, the joint staff itself would not become a separate entity akin to a general staff in which the services would lose complete control of the officers' promotions, assignments, and training. Finally, unlike a general staff system, the strong chairman model would retain the Joint Chiefs of Staff, thus assuring the service chiefs a direct voice in joint matters. Although the individual service chiefs would no longer have a veto over JCS decisions, they would retain substantial influence in their formulation and direct access to civilian leaders for strong dissents from the joint position. In short, the strong chairman model assigns substantially less authority and independence to the central military institutions than would a true armed forces general staff system.

The emphasis of reformers on the strong chairman model is consistent with the historical development of the joint military structure. Postwar defense reform has involved a steadily increasing centralization of authority, but the process has been evolutionary, rather than revolutionary. Radical reforms have consistently been rejected. On the civilian side, greater centralization has not been achieved by abolishing the military departments, as was proposed at the end of World War II. Instead, a single department of defense was established that encompassed the military departments, and a strong central structure has been built around the secretary of defense to balance and integrate the interests and perspectives of the individual services. Similarly, the more radical measures of integrating the uniformed military establishment, such as establishing an armed forces general staff, were rejected after World War II and have received little support since. Instead, integration has been sought by creating a joint military structure around the chairman. Presidents Truman and Eisenhower attempted, with only partial success, to strengthen that joint structure. In effect, the current advocates of the strong chairman model, such as General Jones, are simply pursuing the unfulfilled legacy of the Truman–Eisenhower proposals.

NOTES

1. President Dwight D. Eisenhower's Message to Congress of April 3, 1958, in office of the secretary of defense, historical office, *The Department of Defense: Documents on Establishment and Organization, 1944–1978* (Washington: Government Printing Office, 1978), p. 149.
2. See, for example, U.S. Congress, House of Representatives, Committee on Armed Services, *Reorganization Proposals for the Joint Chiefs of Staff, Hearings before the Investigations Subcommittee.* 97th Congress, 2nd Session (1982). (Hereafter: *1982 HASC Hearings on JCS Reorganization.*)
3. The Holloway Report on the Iranian rescue mission concluded that the absence of a specific joint task force organization for counter-terrorist operations resulted in the use of ad hoc planning and organization that, ultimately, impaired the effectiveness of the rescue mission. United States, Joint Chiefs of Staff, special operations review group (Admiral James L. Holloway III, chairperson), *Rescue Mission Report* (Washington: Joint Chiefs of Staff, 1980). Following the Holloway Report's recommendation, the JCS have since established a joint task force for counter-terrorist operations.

    The Long Commission concluded that the operational chain of command of the U.S. European command did not effectively monitor and supervise the security measures and procedures of the Marine force at the Beirut International Airport. Admiral Robert L. J. Long, et al., *Report of the DOD Commission on Beirut International Airport Terrorist Act* (Mimeograph, December 20, 1983).
4. *1982 HASC Hearings on JCS Reorganization*, pp. 1–97.
5. On the World War II origins of the JCS, see Hammond, Paul Y., *Organizing for Defense: The American Military Establishment in the Twentieth Century* (Princeton: Princeton University Press, 1961), Korb, Lawrence, *The Joint Chiefs of Staff: The First Twenty-Five Years* (Bloomington: Indiana University Press, 1976), and The Historical Division of the Joint Secretariat, Joint Chiefs of Staff, *A Concise History of the Organization of the Joint Chiefs of Staff, 1942–1979* (Mimeograph, July 1980).
6. For more on the debates over military unification, see Caraley, Demetrios, *The Politics of Military Unification: A Study of Conflict and the Policy Process* (New York: Columbia University Press, 1966), and Legere, Laurence J., Jr., "Unification of the Armed Forces" (Ph. D. Thesis, Harvard University, 1951).
7. JCS Historical Division, *History of the JCS*, p. 13.
8. Ibid.
9. The Collins Plan is contained in U.S. Congress, Senate, Committee on Military Affairs, *Hearings on S. 84 and S. 1482: Department of the Armed Forces; Department of Military Security.* 79th Congress, 1st Session (1945).

10. The Eberstadt Report was printed as U.S. Congress, Senate, Committee on Naval Affairs, *Unification of the War and Navy Departments and Postwar Organization for National Security*, 79th Congress, 1st Session (1945).

11. *The National Security Act of 1947*, Public Law 253, 80th Congress (61 Stat. 495), reprinted in OSD Historical Division, *DOD Documents*, pp. 35–50. In fact, the Army conceded on the issue of a single armed forces chief of staff well before the passage of 1947 Act. See, May 31, 1946 Letter to the President from the Secretaries of War and the Navy, in OSD historical office, *DOD Documents*, pp. 22–6.

12. U.S. National Military Establishment, *First Report of the Secretary of Defense* (Washington: Government Printing Office, 1948).

13. The Hoover Commission established a Committee on National Security Organization, known after its chairman, Ferdinand Eberstadt, as the Eberstadt Task Force. This Task Force, clearly influencd by Secretary Forrestal, recommended that the secretary of defense be authorized to appoint a chairman of the JCS from among its members. United States, Commission on Organization of the Executive Branch of the Government, *Task Force Report on National Security Organization* (Appendix G), (Washington: Government Printing Office, 1949), portions reprinted in OSD historical office, *DOD Documents*, pp. 65–75.

    The Hoover Commission went somewhat further than its Eberstadt Task Force, recommending that the secretary of defense be empowered to appoint a chairperson as an additional member of the JCS. United States, The Commission on Organization of the Executive Branch of the Government, The National Security Organization (Washington: Government Printing Office, 1949), portions reprinted in OSD historical office, *DOD Documents*, pp. 75–7.

14. President Truman's proposals for amending the National Security Act of 1947 were contained in a message to the Congress dated March 5, 1949. Ibid., pp. 77–80.

15. *National Security Act Amendments of 1949*, Public Law 216, 81st Congress, (63 Stat. 578).

16. *Reorganization Plan No. 6 of 1953* is reprinted in OSD historical office, *DOD Documents*, pp. 157–8.

17. *The Department of Defense Reorganization Act of 1958*, Public Law 85-599 (72 Stat. 514).

18. On the reforms in the defense establishment initiated by President Eisenhower in 1953 and 1958, see Hammond, *Organizing for Defense*, and Ries, John C., *The Management of Defense* (Baltimore: Johns Hopkins University Press, 1964).

19. Redeeming his campaign promise to establish a commission to study the operations and functions of the department of defense, President Eisenhower had Secretary of Defense Charles E. Wilson appoint the Committee on Defense Organization under the chairmanship of Nelson Rockefeller. The report of the Rockefeller Committee on Department of Defense Reorganization is reprinted in OSD historical office, *DOD Documents*, pp. 126–49.

20. For example, General Omar N. Bradley, the first chairman of the JCS, proposed replacing the JCS with a committee of superchiefs freed from service responsibilities.

21. An analysis of the weaknesses and strengths of the organization of the department of defense was made by Secretary Lovett in a letter to President Truman dated November 18, 1952. OSD historical office, *DOD Documents,* pp. 115–26.

22. President Eisenhower's message to Congress of April 3, 1958, OSD historical office, *DOD Documents*, p. 181.

23. Ibid.

24. President Eisenhower's message to Congress of April 3, 1958, in OSD historical office, *DOD Documents*, p. 179.
25. Department of Defense Directive No. 5100.1, "Functions of the Department of Defense and its Major Components" (December 31, 1958), in OSD historical office, *DOD Documents*, pp. 316-24.
26. John G. Kester, "The Future of the Joint Chiefs of Staff," in *AEI Foreign and Defense Policy Review*, Vol. 2, No. 1 (1980), p. 5.
27. Committee on the Defense Establishment (Stuart Symington, chairperson), "Report on Reorganization of Department of Defense" (1960), reprinted in *1982 HASC Hearings on JCS Reorganization*, pp. 636-42. The Symington report was one of a series of reports on major issues that John F. Kennedy commissioned at the beginning of the 1960 presidential campaign.
28. Blue Ribbon Defense Panel, *Report to the President and the Secretary of Defense on the Department of Defense* (Washington: Government Printing Office, 1970). In fulfillment of a campaign promise, President Nixon established the Blue Ribbon Defense Panel under the chairmanship of Gilbert W. Fitzhugh to examine issues of defense organization.
29. Steadman, Richard C., *Report to the Secretary of Defense on the National Military Command Structure* (Washington: Government Printing Office, 1978). The Steadman report was one of several studies that the Carter administration commissioned to examine defense organization issues. Initially, the White House planned that the department of defense would integrate these individual reports into a final report for the president, recommending needed reforms. By the time the department had completed its internal review of the reports, however, White House attention had been diverted to more pressing concerns. As a result, the department of defense reorganization effort quickly receded and the intended final report for the president never materialized. For a good analysis of the Steadman report, as well as the other reports on defense organization done by the Carter administration, see Barrett, Archie D., *Reappraising Defense Organization: An Analysis Based on the Defense Organization Study of 1977-80* (Washington: National Defense University Press, 1983).
30. Acheson, Dean, *Present at the Creation: My Years at the State Department* (New York: W. W. Norton & Company, Inc., 1969), p. 243.
31. *1982 HASC Hearings on JCS Reorganization*, p. 54.
32. Steadman, *Report on the Military Command Structure*, p. 53.
33. *1982 HASC Hearings on JCS Reorganization*, p. 562-64.
34. Ibid., p. 41.
35. Blue Ribbon Defense Panel, *Report on the Department of Defense*, p. 27.
36. General Jones' proposals are contained in his 1982 congressional testimony. *1982 HASC Hearings on JCS Reorganization*, pp. 46-97.
37. See, for example, the testimony of Admiral Thomas H. Moorer, Ibid., pp. 155-75; and Holloway, James L., III, "The Quality of Military Advice," in *AEI Foreign Policy and Defense Review*, Vol. 2, No. 1 (1980), pp. 24-36.
38. *1982 HASC Hearings on JCS Reorganization*, p. 160.
39. See, for example, the testimony of General Robert H. Barrow, Ibid., pp. 195-211.
40. Ibid., p. 196.
41. *1984 SASC Hearings on DOD*.
42. Kester, John G., "The Future of the Joint Chiefs of Staff," pp. 20-1.
43. Ibid., p. 18.
44. Sorenson, Theodore C., *Kennedy* (New York: Harper & Row, 1965), p. 238.
45. Eisenhower, Dwight D., *The White House Years: Waging Peace, 1956-1961*

(New York: Doubleday, 1965), p. 713.

46. McNamara, Robert S., *The Essence of Security: Reflections in Office* (New York: Harper & Row, 1968), p. 88.

47. General Meyer's recommendations are contained in his testimony before the House Armed Services Committee. *1982 HASC Hearings on JCS Reorganization*, pp. 3–42.

48. See, for example, the testimony of General Lyman L. Lemnitzer, Ibid., pp. 153–4.

49. Steadman, *Report on the Military Command Structure*, p. 73.

50. Ibid., p. 74.

51. For both the report of the JCS special committee and the Collins Report, see U.S. Congress, Senate, Committee on Armed Services, *Hearings on S. 84 and S. 1482: Department of the Armed Forces; Department of Military Security*, 79th Congress, 1st Session (1945).

52. Letter from Secretary of Defense Robert Lovett to President Truman, November 18, 1952, OSD historical office, *DOD Documents*, pp. 115–26.

53. Taylor, Maxwell D., *The Uncertain Trumpet* (New York: Harper & Brothers, 1959).

54. *1982 HASC Hearings on JCS Reorganization*, pp. 801–17.

55. Brown, Harold, *Thinking about National Security: Defense and Foreign Policy in a Dangerous World* (Boulder, Colorado: Westview Press, 1983), pp. 209–14. See also, Kester, John G., "Designing a U.S. Defense General Staff," *Strategic Review*, Summer 1981, pp. 39–46.

56. *1982 HASC Hearings on JCS Reorganization*, pp. 210–11.

57. Brown, *National Security*, p. 211.

58. See, for example, Lemnitzer, Lyman L., et al., *A Report by the Committee on Civilian Military Relationships* (Indianapolis: Hudson Institute, 1984).

59. *1984 SASC Hearings on DOD Organization*, p. 205.

PART II

DEFENSE REFORM
IN THE UNITED STATES

Chapter 10

Strategymaking in the Pentagon

Robert W. Komer

This essay addresses two questions. How is U.S. defense strategy made in peacetime? How can we fix any parts of this decisionmaking process that do not work well enough? Having been a participant in the defense decision-making process, my approach is pragmatic, rather than theoretical.[1] My practical definition of strategymaking, especially in peacetime, is the art of making real life choices between missions and capabilities when resources are constrained. It is the linking of ends to means. This is hardly an elegant definition, but any student of past wars or veteran of Pentagon budget battles will know what I mean. This definition also fits the types of peacetime and wartime strategies that must be taken into account. Above all, it helps to illuminate the all-important link between strategy and the generation of capabilities to execute it.

Current U.S. strategy is a product of World War II and the time since then. For most of our history, strategy did not pose much of a problem. "In neglecting the subject, American thinkers were only following a traditional path. Grand strategy for a whole war . . . had never been an object of serious study in the United States. The geographical position of the nation and its relations to other countries seemed to make the development of a national strategy unnecessary."[2]

World War II had a revolutionary impact on U.S. strategic thinking. It marked our definitive entry into balance of power politics, further confirmed the value of overseas force projection, and was our first major multifront war. It also saw the birth of elaborate joint and combined planning mechanisms. Not until the 1903 creation of the Joint Army and Navy Board had peacetime joint planning even been addressed—and then only spasmodically.[3] Moreover, serious strategic differences between the services did not surface until World War II, when the Army and Navy quarrelled repeatedly over the allocation of resources to the European vs. the Pacific theaters. These differences were hashed out in the new Joint Chiefs of Staff (JCS) forum that was created in 1942 to facilitate development of U.S. positions vis-a-vis the British Chiefs of Staff (the model for the JCS). Joint Chiefs of Staff decisions were then thrashed out in a newly created U.S.-U.K. Combined Chiefs of Staff forum.

World War II also spurred a technological revolution—the advent of nuclear weapons and intercontinental delivery systems—with profound strategic implications. For the first time North America was no longer protected from the risk of devastasting attack. Up to this time, we had starved our armed forces in peacetime and then, while our allies held the ring, belatedly mobilized, after our peacetime unpreparedness had helped lead to war. Now our vulnerability compelled us to adopt a strategic aim of *deterrence*—backed up by large ready peacetime forces designed primarily to dissuade any foe from launching a major conflict in the first place.[4]

The advent of the perceived Soviet threat and the decline in allied capabilities to cope with it led to other radical U.S. strategy departures. America adopted a grand strategy of *containment*, which entailed yet other major changes. A major military aid program was begun in 1947, peacetime forces were semi-permanently deployed at numerous bases overseas, and we even reversed our longstanding aversion to peacetime alliances in favor of a globe-girdling network—NATO, then SEATO, ANZUS, and CENTO—designed to help contain Soviet expansionism in the so-called cold war.

The first formal U.S. national strategy was NSC 68 of 1950, in the drafting of which State's policy planning staff under Paul Nitze played the key role.[5] But our precipitate postwar demobilization and slashes in defense budgets led to declining conventional capabilities and forced heavy reliance on our nuclear monopoly for deterrence. The Korean War triggered a major U.S. rearmament program, and this impetus lasted through the Vietnam War, thus giving force to NSC 68's call to rectify the deterrent balance of power.

Its desire to hold down defense spending, together with continued U.S. nuclear superiority, led the Eisenhower Administration to shift after Korea to a massive retaliation strategy, which provided defense-on-the-cheap for us and defense-on-the-even-cheaper for our allies, who were sheltered under our extended nuclear umbrella. Conventional forces were reduced, especially ground forces. Even the Kennedy Administration's adoption of a flexible response strategy and some increase in conventional forces did not greatly alter our primary reliance on nuclear deterrence, especially since our allies were even less willing than we to increase spending on costly conventional capabilities. Nor did nuclear deterrence prevent costly limited wars, such as Korea and Vietnam. All in all, however, our nuclear deterrent and containment strategy worked. There has been no major conflict between the two superpowers for over 38 years. Nor have we lost any real estate that is vital to our interests.

The age of mass destruction weapons also led to a bifurcation of U.S.

strategic thinking. From 1945 on, the United States devoted considerable attention to nuclear strategy and posture. Continuing attempts at arms control agreements to stabilize the nuclear balance became an integral part of our security strategy, especially as we perceived the Soviets catching up. This perception also stimulated gradual adoption of more discriminating nuclear war fighting doctrines designed both to enhance deterrence and to facilitate escalation control if the nuclear firebreak were crossed. At least once in most administrations there is a top-level review of nuclear doctrine. Beginning in McNamara's time, the president and the secretary of defense have directed several evolutionary changes in nuclear strategy (for example, NSDM 242 of 1974, PD 59 of 1980, and most recently NSDD 13).

Despite the efforts of McNamara, Schlesinger, Brown, and Weinberger, however, *no comparable attention has been paid to nonnuclear strategy since 1945.* Partly as a result of this, no comparable efforts have been made to generate adequate conventional capabilities to meet growing security commitments, now including the defense of Persian Gulf oil. For a long time, our comfortable cushion of nuclear superiority reduced the need for innovations in nonnuclear strategic thinking. Moreover, primary reliance on nuclear weapons provided defense-on-the-cheap to successive U.S. administrations either reluctant or unable to get popular support for much more costly conventional capabilities (outlays on nuclear forces have averaged only 15% of U.S. defense budgets). But there are also many other reasons, some of them institutional, for this neglect of strategy. They are discussed below.

HOW MUCH DOES STRATEGY INFLUENCE POSTURE?

How large does peacetime strategymaking loom, especially in the all-important generation of capabilities? Logically, the strategymaking process should start with the definition of strategic interests, then the assessment of strategic alternatives for protecting these interests, and should only then proceed to the generation of capabilities sufficient to execute the strategy chosen at an acceptable level of risk. In theory, the U.S. process works in this manner. Grand strategy, or national strategy is supposed to be developed by an interagency process that culminates in a presidential decision. The National Security Council (NSC) was set up in 1947 for this purpose. However, this process usually results in no more than broad policy constructs, such as deterring nuclear war, containing Soviet expansionsm, or meeting our commitments. These are more like strategic goals than actual strategy. Therefore, the Department of Defense (DOD) is responsible for refining these presidential (NSC) guidelines into a coherent strategy, often after consulting other agencies, and sometimes after obtaining presidential approval. Then DOD prepares budgets and programs presumably aimed at generating capabilities to execute the strategy within likely resource constraints.[6]

In reality of course, the strategymaking process is far more complex and subject to many other influences besides preferred strategy. Indeed, preferred strategy seems to have had only limited influence on our conventional defense posture compared to many other factors that necessarily shape it. Even in the nuclear arena, it is hard to avoid the conclusion that our perceived nuclear capability, rather than our employment doctrine, is what has mostly deterred our enemies and reassured our allies.

In the conventional arena, strategy seems to have had even less definable impact. Instead of our force posture being geared to our strategic priorities, it is dictated more by political factors, economic constraints, technological imperatives, institutional inertia, and interservice competition for constrained resources. Naturally, the capabilities we have already generated determine what strategy we can realistically expect to support, especially in the short-term. The traditional reluctance of democracies to spend adequately on defense in peacetime is another powerful influence (as reflected frequently in congressional budget cuts). Commitments also affect our strategy, even though yesterday's commitments may no longer correspond with today's strategic interests (as in the case of Taiwan).[7] The sheer fact that a global superpower like the United States must posture against such a wide range of contingencies further complicates strategic planning. Another complication is that, in some cases, such as with NATO, we must adjust our own strategy to achieve consensus with our allies.

Technology also seems to drive strategy more than the reverse, particularly in the nuclear arena. In true American style, our services are eager to incorporate advancing technology into our forces, often without much thought about its strategic impact. For example, MIRVing of missile warheads probably proved destabilizing once the Soviets mastered the technique too. On the other hand, improvements in delivery system accuracy and command, control and communication (C^3) have facilitated adoption of a nuclear countervailing strategy and the current emphasis on escalation control. Similarly, the advent of new sensors and conventional munitions is permitting the emergence of a conventional deep strike option for targeting Warsaw Pact follow-on forces.

To a considerable extent, our neglect of strategy has been a cultural and societal matter too. Richard Betts argues that strategy will inevitably play only a limited role in a society like ours. He finds that "it is only realistic to recognize that domestic politics determine military options far more than expert strategic analysis does" and sees defense budget ceilings "determined by vague senses of threat and acceptable risk, not by strategy."[8] In analyzing U.S. Navy budgets, Abellera and Clark expound the thesis that "old habits of national security" are more likely to determine future Navy budgets than "the Navy's vision" of how it must develop to support national strategy.[9]

Political constraints inherent in our system make it difficult to achieve consensus on a coherent strategy. Betts argues that

> the problem lies in the juncture between the American political system and the ambiguity of conventional military requirements for a superpower in a world of both nuclear risks and changing commitments. Ambiguity fosters diverse notions of deterrence and defensive options while democratic politics make the dominance of any view ebb and flow. Only if U.S. administrations had the duration and consistency of the Soviet Politburo, or if Americans really saw their survival as being tenuous, could there be much more persistent congruence between U.S. strategy and force structure, and thus more room for subtle tuning of doctrine and tactics to strategic guidance.[10]

Despite the force of Betts's critique, I believe that some of the factors that have limited the role that strategy has played in U.S. policymaking are amenable to constructive change. Such a factor as the loss of our strategic nuclear superiority is already convincing many Americans that our survival has become more tenuous and has stimulated concern over the strategic alternatives open to us. The remainder of this chapter analyzes why there has been such limited and largely ineffectual nonnuclear U.S. strategymaking to date, and suggests remedial measures. As Sir James Cable reminds us, "those who refuse to consider alternative courses of action when they can—in times of peace—will be denied the chance when they want to" later, in a crisis.[11]

LINKAGE BETWEEN STRATEGY AND PROGRAM

The traditional way in which most administrations have sought to reconcile strategic needs with force structure since World War II has been *force-sizing exercises*, which attempt to relate the size of forces needed to strategic requirements. The driving factor in force sizing has been the NATO scenario, because it is the most demanding. An early force-sizing exercise done by the new Supreme Headquarters Allied Powers in Europe (SHAPE), led, in 1952, to the proposed "Lisbon Goals" of ninety-six active and reserve divisions for NATO. When our allies balked at such a massive requirement, this helped stimulate President Eisenhower to adopt instead his massive retaliation strategy, which sidetracked the U.S. conventional force buildup called for by NSC 68.[12]

When the Kennedy Administration shifted to a flexible response strategy, a 1962 joint staff study concluded that, in the event of a global war, U.S. ground and air forces would be needed simultaneously in *eleven* theaters. The resulting force requirements were so huge, and the likelihood of this scenario was so low, that the Pentagon cut them back to the so-called two-and-a-half war scenario—a simultaneous Warsaw Pact attack on NATO, a Chinese communist campaign in Korea or Southeast Asia, and a smaller contingency somewhere else.[13] Even this envisaged an ambitious U.S.

ground and air buildup, which was knocked into a cocked hat by the exigen-
cies of the Vietnam War.

The Nixon Administration's 1969 shift to a one-and-a-half war force-
sizing concept, after assessment of several alternative force postures, was a
shrewd adjustment to political realities as the Vietnam War wound down.
Carter, who began the long overdue rebuilding of U.S. defenses, also
started with an NSC force-sizing study pursuant to Presidential Review
Memorandum (PRM) 10. It did not lead to significant force structure
changes. On the contrary, what finally forced the Pentagon to rethink the
one-and-a-half war scenario was a looming new commitment in the Persian
Gulf.

The most innovative attempt to relate nonnuclear strategy, programs,
and resource requirements came in 1980, when Assistant Secretary of
Defense Russell Murray analyzed force balances in key theaters, developed
remedial programs, and then costed these programs over eight and fifteen
year time frames. His analysis even encompassed varying levels of allied effort and the effects of different defense budget levels on the U.S. economy.
Murray's purpose was to give the president and the secretary of defense an
understanding of what they could buy with various defense budgets. Regrettably, this comprehensive effort proved abortive because Carter lost the
1980 election.[14]

Even this cursory review suggests that force-sizing exercises have had only
limited impact on actual force size, largely because the requirements
generated by such exercises are so much in excess of the resources likely to
be made available. Of course, this has contributed to the mismatch between
our strategy and our resources, of which the JCS complain.

No Reagan Administration force-sizing exercise has apparently been attempted. Instead, by decentralizing authority back to the services, the administration seems to have relied mostly on the services' views on force
structure requirements. For example, a unilateral service estimate is the
source of the current requirement for at least a 600-ship Navy. Thus, the
Navy has been the chief beneficiary of increased Reagan defense budgets,
with over 600 ships built, being built or funded, whereas force structure increases for the other services have mostly been deferred to the outyears
(though they have received increased modernization funding).

The Role of the JCS

Let us turn now to the U.S. defense planning process. This takes place
primarily in the Pentagon and is steered by the secretary of defense.[15] The
logical source to which the White House, the NSC, and the secretary of
defense should look for strategic advice is, of course, the JCS. From World
War II until Kennedy, the joint chiefs exerted a powerful influence, using,

when necessary, their independent pipeline to the president, the NSC, and the State Department (the chairman regularly sits with the NSC, while JCS as well as Pentagon civilians usually attend interagency meetings), they did not hesitate to offer professional advice. They and the services played a greater role in strategic issues than the new office of the secretary of defense (OSD). The secretary also relied on them as his primary source of strategic and force planning advice, which he then tempered in the light of fiscal constraints.

The decline in JCS influence began with the advent of Robert McNamara. A powerful secretary of defense, he became the closest strategic advisor to Presidents Kennedy and Johnson. McNamara found the cumbersome JCS system incapable of producing the unified advice he needed in timely fashion or of advising him on strategic and program priorities. Therefore, influence flowed to the talented OSD staff that McNamara strengthened to fill the vacuum.[16] McNamara's managerial "reforms" enhanced their influence.

While JCS influence has waxed and waned since then, the trend has been toward a reduced role. In the Nixon and Ford Administrations, which had to conduct the long and painful disengagement from Vietnam and contend with sharply reduced defense budgets, Henry Kissinger and his staff played a dominant role in policy formulation, along with strong secretaries of defense like Laird, Schlesinger, and Rumsfeld. The erosion of JCS institutional influence continued under Harold Brown, another strong secretary, even though JCS Chairman David Jones was probably Brown's closest personal advisor.[17]

It is important to understand why the JCS have lost so much influence. It is not because they or the joint staff are incompetent. It is because the JCS, as an institution, is systemically incapable of dealing with the all-important issues of priorities on which any service may disagree. *Because of the way it operates, the JCS system is the prisoner of the services which comprise it.* The rule of unanimity that the JCS deliberately impose on themselves in order to achieve a unified view vis-a-vis the civilians, permits what amounts to a single service veto. This means, in turn, that JCS advice on any controversial issue almost invariably reflects the lowest common denominator of what the services can agree on.[18] In effect, although the JCS system deprives the nation's military of an adequate voice in defense decisionmaking, it must be regarded mostly as a self-inflicted wound.

The only member of the JCS no longer beholden to his own service is the chairman, but he has little independent authority. Even the joint staff does not work for him. Contrast the chairman's feeble institutional clout with the British system, where the chief of the defense staff is the statutory chief military advisor to the cabinet and has a large unified staff that reports directly to him.[19]

Another serious flaw in the JCS system is that, except for the chairman, the chiefs have a built-in conflict of interest. It is difficult for the same man to make decisions on a parochial service basis and then sit in judgment on these decisions. The JCS members naturally give most of their attention to their job as service chiefs. Since both are full-time jobs, it is not surprising that their JCS roles suffer from this dual responsibility. Few service JCS members have ever been able to give much time to their JCS roles, generally an hour or two three afternoons a week (though more in a crisis).

If the chiefs cannot spend enough time on JCS business in peacetime, the problem would be far worse in event of multifront war. General Meyer avers that then "joint strategic direction will totally consume the Chiefs' time," while the service chiefs will have equally full-time force generation needs to meet.[20] How can the same men do both? The present system would simply be unable to handle the far greater pressures on it in a major war.

Dominance of the Services

It is service dominance over the JCS which makes the latter unable to recommend a coherent unified military strategy properly relating military ends to available means. Instead, *we have what is basically four service strategies*, or, more accurately, strategic doctrines in some cases. The Navy institutionally focuses on command of the seas; the Marine Corps jealously fights for amphibious assault; the Air Force stresses victory through air power (independently if possible); and the Army (spread thinly over a variety of commitments and with a low priority for modernization) looks to mobilizing large forces for sustained overseas campaigns.

The inevitable result is a pyramiding of force requirements when the JCS cobble them together in the annual Joint Strategic Planning Document (JSPD), which contains all the service "wish lists" for global war. (This requirement exercise used to be called the Joint Strategic Objectives Plan, which looked five to eight years ahead.) Although the JCS rightly complain about the mismatch between strategy and resources, they feel compelled to duck the setting of priorities. Instead, they call for enough added resources to execute the same old multifront, mulitservice strategy, which, in effect, is a splicing together of individual service desires. Reportedly, the JSPD now calls for nine more carrier battlegroups, fourteen more tactical air wings, and nine more Army divisions to carry out the Reagan Administrations's expansive strategic guidance. This is why a DOD study that leaked concluded that a staggering $750 billion more than even Reagan's $1.6 trillion FY 1983–1987 FYDP would be needed to meet these requirements for a total of twenty-three carriers, fifty air wings, and thirty-three Army divisions.[21]

The huge size of these requirements is also driven by U.S. military propensities for *worst case* thinking, especially the view that any direct

US–Soviet regional clash would almost inevitably lead to worldwide non-nuclear (if not nuclear) war. This concept has been a feature of JCS thinking since the end of World War II. It should not be blamed on the Reagan Administration with its notions of horizontal escalation. For example, the 1962 joint staff study, which foresaw eleven separate theaters requiring U.S. force contributions, assumed that "all eleven theaters would come under attack more or less simultaneously."[22] Of course, we must hedge against simultaneous multifront war, but one major strategic issue that needs urgent review is how to forestall such a massive diffusion of scarce resources.

Service strategic thinking is driven more by competition over how to divide up the constrained defense pie than by clear-headed strategic analysis. Thus, bureaucratic politics (parochial service concerns) dominates the JCS process.[23] For example, what I regard as the chief nonnuclear strategic issue now before us—whether we are shifting by default toward a peripheral maritime strategy at the expense of our continental commitments—is driven largely by the competition for resources.[24] Another consequence is that crucial strategic needs, like airlift and sealift, regularly get underfunded because the Air Force and Navy prefer to buy resources for their own use, rather than to haul the Army overseas.

Sound strategy is also inhibited by the failure of our military educational system to focus systematically on it, for example, through strategic war games or the study of military history.[25] As Liddell Hart put it, "In all our military training . . . we invert the true order of thought—considering techniques first, tactics second, and strategy last."[26] Only recently have our senior military colleges been paying more attention to the latter. The Naval War College has been an exception, although it naturally focuses mostly on maritime strategy. Naval war games have been played since the early 1900s, and Admiral Nimitz is credited with saying that every move in World War II in the Pacific (even Pearl Harbor) had already been played out at one time or another at Newport.

Contingency Planning

The one strategic area in which JCS influence remains dominant is in the preparation of contingency plans (conplans) for what U.S. forces should actually do in various cases. These are mostly short-term capabilities plans, based on the use of currently available resources. The unified and specified commands are responsible for preparing them within overall JCS guidelines that are set out in the annual Joint Strategic Capabilities Plan (JSCP). When the JCS reports a new conplan or revision of an old one, or when the CINCs themselves propose this, the JCS also issues specific guidance and later review the CINC's plan before approving it. The more important war plans, like those for Europe, the Atlantic, the Pacific, and, now, the Persian Gulf, are supposed to be updated at least once each year, but this is usually only done with respect to the force requirements and other annexes.

Nuclear war planning deserves special mention because the civilian leadership naturally has taken great interest in nuclear war plans (as opposed to nonnuclear plans). It has long insisted on being regularly briefed on them and on related war games. Indeed, the civilians have taken the lead in providing strategic guidance for nuclear war planning. The first really integrated strategic nuclear war plan, the Single Integrated Operational Plan, or SIOP, was prepared pursuant to Secretary of Defense Gates's decision, in 1958, to make Commander in Chief, Strategic Air Command (CINCSAC) responsible for an integrated plan, and to assign an admiral as his deputy for the purpose. The latter heads a Joint Strategic Planning Staff, which prepares the SIOP. Presidents, as well as secretaries of defense, are regularly briefed on the SIOP. Once broad strategic guidance has been approved by the president, usually in the NSC, defense prepares, with JCS advice, a Nuclear Weapons Employment Plan (NUWEP) as more detailed guidance for preparation of the SIOP. Theater nuclear war plans are prepared by the CINCs, and must be "deconflicted" with those of the Strategic Air Command (SAC).

While acquiescing to civilian intrusion into nuclear war planning, the JCS and CINCs have jealously guarded the rest of their war planning role, partly on security grounds. They occasionally brief the secretary on specific conplans if he so requests, but this has generally been about the extent of it. One notable exception occurred briefly in 1980 when Secretary Brown promulgated the first Planning Guidance for Contingency Planning (PGCP), which was designed to provide broad policy guidelines and assumptions consonant with national policy and with the secretary's own defense guidance.[27] This directive also called for the under secretary for policy (USDP) to review any JCS directives ordering new or revised conplans before these were sent to the field, and then to review completed conplans for compliance with policy *after* the JCS approved them. This development could not have occurred without the shrewd realization of the chairman and chiefs of the time that this procedure would help educate the civilian leadership on what was feasible with the resources at hand. The experiment was short lived, however, because the next administration did not follow up by revalidating or revising the PGCP until 1982 — by which time a new chairman and director of joint staff persuaded the USDP to go back to the old procedure of the JCS briefing the secretary only upon request.

Having acquired more familiarity than most civilians with conplans, because I was the official briefly responsible for reviewing them, let me attempt to evaluate them. The wide variety of conplans (and their annexes) routinely prepared by the CINCs are indispensable for systematically addressing, in advance, force requirements, support and communications needs, and the like. But they are very thin on strategy, even recognizing that contingency plans can seldom anticipate the precise nature of an actual contingency that might occur. Moreover, the absence of civilian review makes them less realistic than might otherwise be the case. Furthermore, their force and deployment requirements often overlap each other. This factor forced the JCS to establish the Joint Deployment Agency (commanded by Commander in Chief, Readiness [CINCRED] wearing a second hat) in 1978, to advise the CINCs and the chiefs on what real life availabilities are likely to be.

Last but not least, the nonnuclear war planning process has become routinized, without much imaginative consideration at the CINC or the JCS level of strategic alternatives. All too few war plans over the last fifteen years or so have called for changing operational strategy in any significant respect. By and large, the strategy they call for remains the same, and the whole focus is on getting more resources to execute them.

POLICYMAKING IN DOD

Although the secretary of defense has eclipsed the JCS as the top defense planner, Collins notes how lacking most secretaries have been in relevant experiences or policymaking expertise, singling out Marshall as a notable exception.[28] At least Laird, Schlesinger, Rumsfeld, and Brown deserve to be considered exceptions. However, in reality, most secretaries have *focused primarily on policy and program, rather than on strategy*, except in the nuclear field. Hence it is essential to look at the DOD program process, because, since the McNamara days, this has been the chief method by which actual policy and strategymaking takes place.

In our democratic society *fiscal guidance*—the result of a bargaining process between the president, Office of Management and Budget (OMB), and DOD—has been more important than strategy in determining programs. In the 1950s, the secretary issued no formal annual policy guidance to the services and defense agencies, only fiscal guidance. McNamara's managerial reforms changed all this. The form he chose was the issue oriented draft presidential memorandum (DPM), which he often sent to the White House for presidential approval or to provide the president with information. The first DPM, in 1962, was on strategic nuclear forces on the occasion of the B-70 controversy. Later DPMs were expanded to cover the whole defense program. They were usually drafted by the new systems analysis office, created by McNamara and staffed largely with "whiz kids."[29]

Another McNamara reform was a rolling Five Year Defense Program (FYDP), started in 1961 to generate longer-range planning and programming. This was also prepared by his systems analysis staff. The FYDP was a force structure and program plan, containing only implicit fiscal guidance. To systematize Pentagon-wide procedures for translating policy into program and then into budget, McNamara introduced a Planning–Programming–Budgeting System (PPBS), which quickly became an indispensable tool of Pentagon management.

The OSD further assumed a major policy planning role, partly at the expense of the JCS, through a strengthened Office of International Security Affairs (ISA), led by talented assistant secretaries, like Paul Nitze and John McNaughton. Under them, the ISA had great influence on Vietnam, NATO, and nuclear policy and strategy, working directly with Secretay McNamara.[30]

McNamara's successor, Melvin Laird, redelegated much authority back to the services, instead of relying heavily on the systems analysis office and the ISA. He shifted the initiative for program formulation back to the service from the OSD, and issued *fiscal guidance* to which the service program memoranda were expected to adhere. In the mid-1970s, an annual defense guidance, mostly program oriented, also began to be issued by the secretary to provide the basis for the service Program Objectives Memoranda (POMs).

In 1977, Harold Brown instituted an annual consolidated guidance (CG), which combined all the policy, fiscal, and programming guidance for preparation of the next budget and the FYDP. He had it prepared largely by a strong systems analysis shop that he had reinvigorated. Another innovation was his creation in 1978 of a new undersecretary for policy (USDP), who was to be responsible for policy planning and politico–military affairs. When I was USDP, in the period of 1979 through 1981, I separated these two functions in an attempt to get greater OSD focus on policy–strategic planning. The USDP also prepared the first chapter of the CG now called defense policy guidance and included strategic guidelines. Brown formed a Defense Resources Board (DRB) in April of 1979 under his deputy secretary as chairman. It included most top OSD officials plus the chairman of the JCS. The board's job was to review the service POMs and to resolve as many program issues as possible before the secretary got into the act.[31]

Secretary Weinberger again decentralized much authority to the services. A strengthened DRB (expanded from seven members to sixteen, including the service secretaries) became the principal planning and programming forum in an attempt to put strategic requirements and resources in the same plan. No consolidated guidance for service POMs is issued, only a defense guidance now prepared by the USDP. Instead of the systems analysis shop, the under secretary for policy is now tasked with pulling the whole DRB process together. Thus, the DRB has become a more powerful instrument for defense planning and programming, usually the court of last resort, since only the secretary can reverse his deputy's decisions in the DRB.[32] With the service secretaries (and, informally, the service chiefs) in attendance, the

DRB is a much more collegial forum in which the services not only submit the programs, but sit in judgment on them. This procedure, in effect, puts the service secretaries back into the policy–strategy business, from which they had been debarred at least since McNamara. Moreover, by its very nature, it focuses primarily on program, rather than strategic issues, thus making program drive strategy even more.

There is another influential policy document, the annual defense posture statement used by secretaries of defense to explain to Congress and to the public, as well as to allies and adversaries what the Pentagon is seeking to do. Although its formal purpose is to introduce and explain each new budget and FYDP to the Congress, it also often serves as a vehicle for laying out major changes in policy direction.

EVALUATION OF U.S. POLICY/STRATEGYMAKING

As a former practitioner, my own evaluation of our nonnuclear strategy-making is harsh. There is all too little systematic strategymaking in the DOD, except in the strategic nuclear arena. Instead, the reality is best characterized as a piecemeal, irregular, highly informal process, largely driven by cumulative program decisions influenced more by budget constraints and consequent interservice competition than by notions of U.S. strategic priorities. Little long-term policy or strategic planning takes place, except for adaptation to new technology. There is little consideration of strategic alternatives.

In broad terms this last is properly grand strategy, the ultimate responsibility of the president and the NSC, who all too often fail to establish the necessary guidelines, at least in a manner that can effectively influence the program process. But the defense and the state departments, which should press the White House for such guidance, and make clear the costs and risks of alternative strategic choices, have usually failed to do so.[33] They rarely face up squarely to setting regional or functional priorities that are adjusted to resource constraints. Nor has the NSC staff generally shown much enthusiasm for informing the President on these issues and getting him to require the departments to perform adequately.

The DOD, which ought to play a key role in presenting the military aspects of grand strategy to the White House, in order to inform and discipline strategic choices and resource allocations, is poorly equipped to do so. The DRB is *not* the best vehicle to determine broad policy and strategy, if only because most issues are posed to it in programmatic terms. Its current large membership consists of officials who have little role in strategymaking. Nor can we get sound strategy from a committee, especially one in which the protagonists also sit as judges.

Because the current JCS system is institutionally incapable of deciding among service claims, it cannot provide realistically unified strategic advice. The fact of the matter is that the historical independence and political strength of the services is inconsistent with the goal of coherent unified strategy with clear priorities and better translation of those priorities into resource allocations. Because the JCS and the joint staff are service-dominated, at the expense of any joint perspective, bureaucratic politics has greater influence on JCS and service planning than does systematic strategic thinking.

Nor is the OSD properly set up to fill this gap, even if it could do an adequate job without military advice.[34] Nonetheless, the OSD has had to take over the task of adjudicating among the services. It does so primarily through the Planning, Programming, and Budgeting System (PPBS). But a major shortcoming of this process is the lack of sufficiently well-developed strategic guidance against which to generate issues and assess priorities. As was frequently said in McNamara's day, the first P in PPBS, which stands for planning, is silent. Such overall guidance as is provided tends to be too vague, generalized, and unprioritized (everything tends to be given priority) to be an adequate basis for programming. Moreover, such planning guidance as is given is often ignored by the programmers, whether in the services or in the OSD. Then, subsequent White House and congressional action on both overall budget levels and specific programs often signficantly change what the Pentagon proposes.

Thus programming tends to dictate strategy rather than the reverse. One good example of this is the way in which high spending on a carrier-heavy Navy at the expense of the programs of the other services seems to be driving us toward a primarily maritime strategy by default.[35]

The genesis of Persian Gulf strategy and the rapid deployment force (RDF) is an example of how civilians had to fill in for the military. What really put planning for the RDF into high gear was not the desultory staff work triggered in the Pentagon by the fall of the Shah in 1979. It was President Carter's pronouncement of the Carter doctrine in January of 1980. There was no agreed strategy, only an old U.S. European command conplan of dubious relevance. In 1979 to 1980 the JCS could not agree on a preferred strategy because the Army, Navy, Air Force, and Marines had sharply differing parochial views. Hence the initial proposals for sizing and equipping the RDF to meet a non-Soviet contingency and for later expanding it to meet a Soviet threat were primarily the product of the OSD systems analysts (working closely with the joint staff). They were laid out in the CGs of 1979 and 1980. As for the proposed Khuzistan strategy of defending well in front of the main oilfields, this emerged originally from a USDP memo to the secretary, which was later submitted to the NSC as part of a Persian Gulf policy framework.

Nor does the planning–programming process take adequately into account the needs created by our pursuit of a largely *coalition* policy and strategy that reflect the network of alliances and other commitments entered into after World War II. A NATO strategy is produced by the elaborate NATO hierarchy of commands and committees (Republic of Korea–U.S. strategy too is a combined affair, as is the defense of Japan). In practice, however, both we and our allies are guilty of what General Jones has called "the sin of unilateralism." We still plan and program on essentially a national, rather than a multinational basis. This is somewhat less true in NATO than elsewhere, but even in NATO, U.S. contingency plans until the seventies contemplated a withdrawal to the Rhine River line, whereas NATO had long since adopted a forward strategy of not yielding significant West German terrain. This is partly because of a lack of organizational focus within the United States or other governments on coalition issues. For example, until I became advisor to the secretary on NATO affairs in 1977, no single U.S. government official above the level of office director dealt exclusively with NATO matters, our largest single overseas commitment. This organizational innovation too disappeared when the next administration took over.

All this is not to say that policy and strategic thinking do not somehow influence programs and resource allocations, but only that they do so in a spasmodic, unstructured way. The Persian Gulf case just cited is a good example of strategy influencing program. Another is Harold Brown's abandonment of a mandatory swing strategy, whereby, in the event of war in Europe, large parts of our Pacific forces were to redeploy to the Atlantic. Brown's guidance that the number of carrier battle groups should be based on a concept of sequential operations (striking first in one place, then in another) rather than on simultaneous strikes in several widely separated areas, is yet another.[36] The rapid reinforcement program for NATO, particularly via prepositioning equipment, was designed to put muscle into NATO's forward strategy. But these examples are all too rare.

Secretary Weinberger and his staff started out with ambitious notions about changing strategy—toward protracted conventional and nuclear wars (which entailed major increases in sustainability), toward horizontal escalation, and the like. But the realities of resource constraints have led to considerable tempering of these notions, as has the Weinberger Pentagon's primary stress on costly force modernization at the expense of sustainability and readiness.[37]

Archie Barrett, in his searching critique based on the comprehensive defense organization study of 1977 through 1980, cogently summarizes the weaknesses most relevant to strategymaking:

1. The inability of the service-dominated joint organizations to provide adequate military advice from a national perspective.
2. The overwhelming influence of the services, wholly out of proportion to their formal responsibilities.

3. The "flawed management approach" of OSD, which slights the broad policy function by failing to define the linkages between national objectives and military planning, to evaluate alternative approaches to meeting military requirements, or to ensure that decisions are actually followed through.[38]

As a result, there is an enormous "disconnect" between U.S. strategy and posture. This, together with the perennial underfunding of what passes for U.S. strategy today, helps to explain the mismatch between our strategy and our resources.[39] In fact, one is tempted to ask whether under most postwar administrations, the United States has ever had much of a nonnuclear strategy beyond such broad constructs as deterring Soviet aggression, containing Soviet expansionism, honoring our commitments, or just staying flexible.

WHAT NEEDS CHANGING?

Unfortunately, our nation can no longer afford this hit-or-miss approach. More responsive defense policy and strategymaking, plus a better relationship between strategy–policy and resource allocation, is dictated by:

1. *The advent of nuclear stalemate*, which compels greater reliance on far more costly conventional forces, which, in turn, compounds the strategy-resource gap.
2. *The relative decline in U.S. economic power*, which dictates that we can no longer assume such a large share of the collective defense vis-a-vis our allies.
3. *The shift in the overall U.S.–USSR military balance*, particularly the big investment gap, which is largely a consequence of our enormous diversion of resources to the Vietnam War.
4. *The traditional reluctance of democracies to provide adequately for defense in peacetime*, in sharp contrast to the Soviet state.
5. *The expansion of U.S. strategic requirements*, now including defense of Persian Gulf oil and, to a lesser degree, Central America and the Caribbean (two new theaters, in effect).

These developments have widened the gap between our strategy and our resources, especially in the nonnuclear arena.[40]

The strategic implications of nuclear stalemate are particularly striking. To cite James Schlesinger, "in the past U.S. strategic superiority offset weaknesses . . . in our conventional force structure. . . . Our basic concern today is that our strategic forces can no longer compensate for deficiencies in our conventional forces."[41] Thus today we are in a *period of strategic transition* to greater reliance on nonnuclear means. This accentuates the dilemma for policy–strategy makers because of the higher cost of adequate conventional forces.

Nor is this just a U.S. dilemma. An America declining in relative power is more dependent than ever on its allies to help meet the needs of the common defense. Indeed, *our greatest single remaining strategic advantage over the USSR is that we have many rich allies, whereas it has only a handful of poor ones.* Is our current policymaking machinery adequate to manage this critical transition, including its coalition aspects? The answer is no.

Such grave problems make rethinking our strategy and posture a strategic imperative. True, these problems can hardly be solved by procedural or organizational changes alone. Since the disconnection between our present strategy and capabilities is due to many other factors besides the failure to address this issue systematically, institutional reform is no panacea. But the experience of the last thirty-five years also makes it clear that without organizational changes the rethinking process will continue to be severely inhibited. At the very least, we need:

1. *Better Focus on Strategic Choices.* Especially in the nonnuclear arena, we need more systematic interagency strategic review of grand strategy and of the relation of our interests to our capabilities. If the ends we seek are beyond the resources likely to be available, then the Pentagon is entitled to get from the president broad priority guidance as to which needs come first.

However, I am not persuaded that this requires new policymaking machinery, as opposed to making the existing machinery produce what is required. In the final analysis, this is a function of the top leadership asking the right questions and insisting upon adequate responses from the machinery that already exists—the NSC staff, State's policy planning staff, the OUSD/P and the JCS–joint staff. Perhaps the biggest problem is that the president, his assistant for national security, and the secretaries of state and defense have seldom posed the broad issues and insisted that they be addressed.

Whether he has been given adequate White House guidance on grand strategy, the secretary of defense must assume the responsibility for reviewing defense policy, strategy options, and contingency plans. He should submit them to higher authority if necessary, but, in any case, must lay down clear priority guidance for defense strategy and programs. Again, the OSD machinery is available if it is properly tasked and if staffs are not diverted to other functions.

2. *Better Linkage Between Policy–Strategy and Program–Forces.* Better strategic guidance will still prove ineffectual unless we can also improve the linkage between what it is we are trying to accomplish and the program process that generates the capabilities to do so. As my personal experience attests, strategy–policy considerations often have only an attenuated impact on what the Pentagon actually buys. In part this is a self-inflicted wound,

created by the way OSD and the JCS operate. Hence, it can be at least partially cured by their focusing much more on what strategy to pursue and
what priorities to lay down, and then instituting procedures that require
programs to follow these more closely.

To achieve such a focus, the present wholly inadequate process for linking strategy–policy to program needs to be overhauled. Probably the
secretary should insist on a stronger two-stage process. In the first stage,
once the previous budget has finally been put to bed, the USDP should
draft a revised policy–strategy guidance (in consultation with other relevant
parties), for formal review by the secretary no later than February. Relevant
issues, including alternative mission and program priorities, should be
clearly flagged by the USDP for discussion via brief issue papers. Then, the
resulting broad guidance, once approved by the secretary, should be the
basis for more detailed defense guidelines for development of the service
POMs.

A procedure is also needed whereby the USDP formally reviews each
POM for consistency with policy guidance (I tried to initiate this procedure,
but it proved very difficult, largely because so little time was available to
do so).

Lastly, a format is urgently needed for monitoring and evaluating
whether policies and programs are actually being carried out as intended.
As Archie Barrett points out, lack of such a follow-up procedure is a serious
current deficiency.[42] Half the time, even an activist secretary does not really
know how well guidance is being carried out. The OSD staff must perform
this function on the secretary's behalf, as part of its oversight role.

The JCS and joint staff should be *required* to actively participate in this
whole process, including providing formal advice on priorities when tradeoffs are required to stay within the budget. Both the joint staff and the
OUSD/P should be given strengthened analysis shops for the purpose, not
of replacing Program Analysis and Evaluation (PA&E), but of giving the
JCS and the USDP prompt staff work adequate to back up their views.
Then, the DRB could serve as a more useful forum for reconciling differing
views, including those of the services.

3. *Better and More Unified Military Advice.* Indispensable to better
strategy and policy is better quality and more unified military advice than
the present JCS system can provide. The often inexperienced Pentagon
civilian leadership badly needs professional military advice and a unified
military view on priorities. This is all the more necessary because senior
civilian officials tend to be "in-and-outers," which makes the military the
essential element of continuity. There is a desperate need for imaginative
strategic alternatives, instead of a continuing focus only on providing
capabilities to execute the same old strategy. Nor can we any longer afford
to have three or four distinct service strategies loosely cobbled together by

the JCS. The crying need is to institutionalize a joint perspective to offset service bias. How to reform the JCS system for this purpose is covered in the last section of this chapter.

4. *Greater Focus on Long-Range Policy–Strategic Planning.* Remedying this problem requires not just emphasis by top management but new formats as well. The USDP, who has this responsibility, should be required to strengthen his policy planning staff (which should be a mixture of civilian and military personnel), and tasked to produce long-range (five to fifteen year) analyses targeted on alternative ways to address emerging issues. Similarly, the JCS would do well to revive the Joint Strategic Survey Committee (JSSC) of senior three-star or even four-star officers (on terminal assignment), and charge them to produce independent strategic assessments with alternative courses of action.

5. *Better Trained Planners.* Institutional change alone will not suffice without overhaul of the military education and career planning systems to produce higher quality and better trained staff officers. A program to reorient the war colleges and their faculties to this end (beyond what is already under way) should be directed and monitored by both the OSD and the JCS. As for the joint staff, it needs to be upgraded, and its members given greater continuity and opportunity for career advancement.[43] Indeed, unified combined-arms thinking is so badly needed that the case for a unified defense general staff must be made.

6. *Better Focus on Coalition Matters.* The current system whereby the Pentagon develops plans and programs for unilateral American action also needs reform. Aside from the critical *lack of adequate alliance machinery* to efficiently generate and deploy collective forces, the Pentagon itself must develop a clearer focus on a coalition approach to strategy. On the principle that the squeaky wheel gets the grease, one solution is to set up vested interests in the Pentagon, with the job of representing the coalition approach.[44] For example, why not have a separate deputy director joint staff at the three-star level to handle coalition matters? The USDP needs a deputy undersecretary with much the same task, and the present deputy under secretary of defense for research and engineering (USD/RE) for international programs must be strengthened. Overlap and turf battles will inevitably result, but this adversarial process is precisely what is needed to make the system work, and it doesn't exist today.

JCS Reform

The patent need to provide better strategic advice to civilian decision makers and a unified military voice in the resource allocation process has revived the long-standing issue of JCS reform, recurrently debated since 1944. In 1982 the courage of two JCS members, Generals David Jones and

E. C. Meyer, in forcefully raising the issue has given it more impact. So too has the increased urgency of recasting this moribund institution at a time when the nation's looming security problems demand more effective military advice. Hence, both houses of Congress have now held hearings and various bills have been introduced, a welcome demonstration of congressional awareness that something needs fixing.

Two main types of reform have been proposed by the chief military protagonists, neither yet adequately reflected in the bills proposed. General Jones favors strengthening the chairman's role as chief military advisor to the secretary of defense and the president, along the lines of the British system. He wants the chairman to have a four-star deputy, and to have a strengthened joint staff work directly for the chairman as well as to support the chiefs.

Although General Meyer agrees with most of these changes, he would also solve the dual-hatting problem by decoupling the service chiefs from the JCS role, in effect, another step in the post-1947 trend toward making the services the providers of forces and resources. Users, like the secretary of defense and the chairman of the JCS would receive centralized military advice from a separate top level advisory body of four-star officers who have no remaining tie to their services, the latter having the right of dissent. This is the chief difference between the Jones and the Meyer proposals. In fact, reviving the JSSC (as suggested earlier) might fill the need for an independent, nonservice-affiliated, senior officer group to advise the chairman. These proposals would go a long way toward meeting the need for better and more unified military advice on policy–strategy matters.

However, neither would fully meet the need until the chairman and the chiefs are served by their own fully unified and carefully selected corps of "purple suit" staff officers; a corps with its own, at least partially separate, career ladder and promotion system, to insulate it from parochial service pressures. We will not get true "purple suiters" unless we train and protect them. This staff corps could man up to 9,000 key positions in not only the joint staff but in the staffs of all the unified commands, the interservice colleges, OSD offices, and the like.[45] Harold Brown has boldly advocated a defense general staff, and I would heartily endorse his view.[46] Lesser reforms would help some, but they are unlikely to meet the basic need. This may sound suspiciously like a German general staff system, but the oft-cited political risk of creating a military elite that could facilitate a military takeover is grossly exaggerated in a society like ours and has little historical validity.[47]

Two final cautions are in order. Although JCS reform is indispensable for overcoming the parochial service dominance that has so critically hampered sound strategymaking and resource allocation, it is no panacea. Better military inputs to defense decisionmaking will not solve the problem if such advice is ignored or unduly diluted by civilian leadership, or if wholly inadequate resources are provided. Nor will cosmetic reforms that do not really attack the basic problem of service dominance suffice to meet the need for realistic military advice on strategic and program priorities.

Lastly, we must bear in mind the powerful institutional forces arrayed against JCS–joint staff reform. Reorganization of the DOD or the JCS is "first and foremost a political process, involving the clash and adjustment of bureaucratic, legislative and private interests."[48] To this day, the Navy and Marine Corps, historically jealous of their autonomy, have vigorously opposed strengthening the JCS or centralizing more authority in the DOD.[49] But this is not the only reason why JCS reform and a more integrated defense establishment has been sidetracked so often. As Betts reminds us, Congress "normally prefers to constrain the executive by dividing it and to deal directly with the separate services. The putative fear of a man on horseback is more a rationale for maintaining legislative clout than for protecting the nation."[50]

NOTES

1. This essay also draws on my new book *Maritime Strategy or Coalition Defense?* (Cambridge, Mass: Abt Books, February 1984), which analyzes various non-nuclear strategic options open to the U.S.
2. Williams, T. Harry, *History of American Wars* (New York: Knopf, 1981), pp. 194–5.
3. Ibid., p. 736.
4. Weigley, Russell, *The American Way of War* (New York: Macmillan, 1973), pp. 365–7.
5. NSC 68 was revised as NSC 162 by President Eisenhower in 1953. Later iterations came to be called Basic National Security Policy. But the restatements became so complex and the subject of so much interagency nitpicking that the updating attempt was finally abandoned in the early Kennedy years (on the recommendation of the author, among others).
6. Collins, John M., *U.S. Defense Planning: A Critique* (Boulder, Colorado: Westview Press, 1982), lays out the details of this process.
7. While our commitments generally reflect our strategic interests, they do not always have as much direct impact on strategy and posture as such propagandistic justifications for greater defense spending as "meeting our treaty commitments to 40 nations" would imply. The North Atlantic Treaty and U.S.–Japan Security Treaty do greatly influence our strategy and posture, but much less so in the case of the Rio and ANZUS treaties, where we see far less of a threat. Moreover, some of our most strategically significant commitments, such as the defense of Persian Gulf oil access, rest on unilateral U.S. policy determinations, not on any treaty obligations.
8. Betts, R. K., "Conventional Strategy: New Critics, Old Choices," *International Security*, Spring 1983, pp. 148, 153.
9. Abellera, James, and Clark, Rolf, "Forces of Habit: Budgeting for Tomorrow's Fleets," *AEI Foreign Policy and Defense Review*, Vol. 3, Nos. 2 and 3, 1981, pp. 2–3.

10. Betts, op. cit., pp. 149–53.
11. Cable, op. cit., p. xv.
12. For the most incisive analysis of force-sizing exercises, see Kaufmann, W. W., *Planning Conventional Forces 1950–1980* (Brookings, 1982).
13. Ibid., pp. 4–11.
14. Murray II, Russell, "Policies, Prices and Presidents: The Need to Enlighten the Great Choices in National Security," *Armed Forces Journal*, June 1982, pp. 56–8.
15. Collins, op. cit., p. 39.
16. See Piller, Geoffrey, "DOD's Office of International Security Affairs: The Brief Ascendancy of An Advisory System," *Political Science Quarterly*, Spring 1983, pp. 59–78.
17. There is an important distinction between personal and institutional influence. As a close observer and participant in U.S. strategymaking 1977–1981, I would say that Jones probably had more personal impact than any Chairperson since Admiral Arthur Radford.
18. See Pustay, John, "The Problem is Systemic," *Armed Forces Journal*, February 1984, pp. xx.
19. See Johnston, Sir Maurice, "More Power to the Center: The MAD Reorganization," *RUSI Journal*, March 1983, pp. 7–10 for discussion of the latest strengthening of the CDS role. See also Sir Frank Cooper, "Perhaps Minister: Political and Military Relations Today and in the Future" in the same issue.
20. In *Understanding U.S. Strategy* (Washington, D.C.: National Defense University, 1983), p. 338.
21. Wilson, George, "U.S. Defense Paper Cites Gap Between Rhetoric, Intentions," *The Washington Post*, May 27, 1982, p. A-4.
22. Kaufmann, op. cit., pp. 5–6.
23. See Halperin, Morton and Halperin, David, "The Key West Key," *Foreign Policy*, No. 53, Winter, 1983–84, pp. 114–30 for a fascinating (though somewhat overdrawn) analysis of how the 1948 divvying-up of service roles and missions has hampered rational defense decisions.
24. Komer, "Maritime Strategy vs. Coalition Defense," *Foreign Affairs*, Summer 1982, pp. 1124–44.
25. Cable laments a similar lack of focus on strategy in British service schools, particularly the Royal Navy's (op. cit., pp. 6–7).
26. Hart, B. H. Liddell, *Thoughts on War* (London: Faber and Faber, 1944) p. 129.
27. The concept of a PGCP was the brainchild of Dr. William Brehm, former Assistant Secretary of Defense (ASD) for logistics and reserve affairs and then for congressional affairs. He discussed it extensively with the JCS and the services, and prepared a first draft. I revised it and checked it out informally with the JCS before submitting it to the secretary of defense.
28. Collins, op. cit., p. 56.
29. I am greatly indebted for this analysis to Russell Murray III, deputy head of the systems analysis shop under Alain Enthoven from 1961 to 1968, and then assistant secretary heading the office (renamed PA&E) in Harold Brown's Pentagon.
30. Piller, op. cit., pp. 62–70.
31. On the basis of a suggestion in Don Rice's 1978 study for DOD on defense resource management.
32. Collins appraises the current DRB as "superior to any predecessor" (op. cit., pp. 46–7).

33. When I was USDP I proposed setting clear regional and functional priorities in the FY82-86 Defense Policy Guidance. Loss of the 1980 election rendered this exercise moot.

34. My effort in late 1979 to upgrade the level of the OSD policy and strategic planning shop was reversed by the next administration. In September 1980, I also produced a paper on "Strategic Challenges of the 1980s," designed to lay out the key strategic issues which the next administration would have to address. It was discussed in the NSC, but only after Carter had lost the election. State's chief objection to the paper was its setting of regional priorities.

35. See Komer, "Maritime Strategy or Continental Defense," op. cit., Chapter 6.

36. Brown, Harold, op. cit., pp. 174, 178.

37. For a slashing critique see Record, Jeffrey, "Jousting with Unreality: Reagan's Military Strategy," *International Security*, Winter 1983–84.

38. Barrett, Archie D., *Reappraising Defense Organization* (Washington: National Defense University, 1983), 1983), pp. xix–xx.

39. Osgood contends that such a chronic gap between our expanding security interests and our ability to support them has been a persisting problem ever since World War II (Osgood, op. cit., pp. 5–7). However, it is much more acute today.

40. Osgood, Robert E., "American Grand Strategy," *Naval War College Review*, September–October 1983, p. 7, calls it the "interests-power gap."

41. *U.S. News and World Report*, January 10, 1983, p. 19.

42. Barrett, op. cit., pp. 234–38.

43. Statement of the special study group of the chairperson of the JCS before the investigations subcommittee, HASC (HASC No. 97-47) April–July 1982, pp. 707–69.

44. My own experience from 1977 to 1979 as advisor on NATO affairs reporting directly to the secretary of defense suggests what can be accomplished by this means.

45. According to the chairman's special study group, there are no less than 4,647 "joint" officer positions in the OSD, OJCS, unified commands, and NATO commands, plus 4,304 in other nonservice activities, such as defense agencies, etcetera (HASC 97-47, p. 745).

46. Ibid., p. 116. See also Brown, H., *Thinking About National Security* (Boulder, Colorado: Westview Press, 1983), pp. 210–12.

47. Ibid., pp. 118–19.

48. Barrett, op. cit., p. 7.

49. In this they are following the same path as the British Admiralty, which opposed creating a Ministry of Defense, a Chief of Defense Staff, a central staff, and any subsequent strengthening of their authority. Navies are different, after all.

50. Betts, op. cit., p. 155.

Chapter 11

Organization and Strategy*

Samuel P. Huntington

The U.S. department of defense is not as well organized as it should be to provide effective deterrence in peacetime or to achieve military success in wartime. That is the conclusion of almost all the participants—other than Navy admirals and Marine Corps generals—in the national debate on defense organization that occurred in 1982 and 1983. That debate was kicked off by critiques of the Joint Chiefs of Staff from two people who presumably could speak with authority: General David Jones, USAF, Chairman of the Joint Chiefs, and General Edward C. Meyer, USA, Chief of Staff of the Army. Their public criticism focused attention on defects in American defense organization about which officials, scholars, and study groups had expressed concern for years. The Jones–Meyer broadsides brought these concerns out in the open and stimulated the most wide-spread discussion of defense organization issues in over two decades. Hearings before House and Senate armed services committees led to the drafting in Congress of a bill mandating certain relatively modest changes in the structure of the joint chiefs. This bill met some of the criticisms, but its passage, if that occurs, clearly will end neither all the critical weaknesses in U.S. defense organization nor the debate over what should be done about them.

To some, this renewed attention to organizational issues seems like much ado about nothing. They argue that it is not the arrangement of boxes on a chart that counts, but rather the quality of the people in those boxes. Obviously, capable people are important, but it is also a mistake to downgrade the significance of formal organizational structure. Organizational structure both reflects and shapes an entity's priorities: It can facilitate or inhibit innovation; it helps define the issues that come to top decision makers; it is significant in determining who plays what roles in deciding what issues. It also shapes the nature of the decisions that are reached; decisions made by a

---

*This article appeared in *Public Interest*, Spring 1984. Reprinted with permission.

committee, for instance, will differ from those made by an individual. Good organization cannot guarantee wise policy or effective implementation, but bad organization can make both of these impossible.

Criticism has been directed at many aspects of Defense department organization, including, for instance, procedures for weapons procurement. Varied as the criticisms have been, however, they have tended to focus on the strategic side of the defense establishment—how decisions are made on overall policy, on the development of military forces, programs, and weapons, and on the use of military force. Those criticisms tend to articulate in a variety of ways a single underlying theme: that there is a gap between defense organization and strategic purpose. This gap is the result of the failure to achieve the purpose of organizational reforms instituted twenty-five years ago.

THE EISENHOWER AND McNAMARA REFORMS

The Department of Defense evolved through two major phases after World War II. The first phase, beginning with the end of the war and continuing until the early 1960s, saw the creation and gradual strengthening of the central defense organization. During this phase, the primary emphasis was on enhancing the authority and power of the secretary of defense. This was accomplished through a series of legislative enactments beginning with the National Security Act of 1947 and culminating in the Defense Reorganization Act of 1958. The latter bore the personal imprint of President Eisenhower and prescribed the basic legal structure of the department for the following quarter century. In the early 1960s, Secretary of Defense Robert McNamara exploited the formal authority of his office and introduced the so-called planning, programming, and budgeting system (PPBS).

The second phase in the evolution of the Defense department runs from the early 1960s to the early 1980s. During this phase, informed experts and official bodies often studied and frequently criticized defense organization, but virtually no significant change was made in the formal structure and processes by which the department conducted its business. The intense interservice controversy which had characterized the 1940s and 1950s subsided; and a high degree of consensus both among the services and, after the departure of McNamara, between civilian and military leaders seemed to prevail.

The reforms initiated by President Eisenhower and Secretary McNamara, concentrated on three areas, all related to ways in which the department went about constituting and planning to use military force: strategic planning, combat command, and resource allocation.

In transmitting his 1958 recommendations to Congress, Eisenhower stressed the "vital necessity of complete unity in our strategic planning and basic operational direction." The initiative for strategic planning should "rest not with the separate services but directly with the Secretary of Defense and his operational advisers, the Joint Chiefs of Staff. . . ." Eisenhower wanted to achieve unified strategic planning by making the Joint Chiefs of Staff and the joint staff serve as the military staff of the secretary of defense. Congress did not approve everything he wanted, but it did strengthen the overall authority of the secretary over the military services, increase the size of the joint staff, and authorize the service chiefs to delegate more of their service responsibilities to their vice chiefs, so that the chiefs themselves could give higher priority to their joint responsibilities as members of the JCS.

Eisenhower's second major goal, reflecting his experience as Supreme Allied Commander in Europe, was to ensure unity of command of the combat forces. "Separate ground, sea, and air warfare is gone forever," he said. "If ever again we should be involved in war, we will fight it in all elements, with all services, in one single concentrated effort." Hence combat forces must be "organized into combat commands." Congress implemented most of the changes Eisenhower wanted in this area. The president, acting through the secretary of defense, was authorized to "establish unified or specified combatant commands for the performance of military missions" and to determine what forces from the three military departments would be assigned to those commands. The chain of command for combat forces went from the president as commander in chief to the secretary of defense and then to the heads of these combat commands (known as commanders in chief, or CINCs). The CINCs had "full operational command" of the forces assigned to them from the services, but the services remained responsible for the "administration" of those forces. In due course, virtually all U.S. combat forces were assigned—at least in theory—to unified or specified commands.

The third major reform of this period was made legally possible by the increased authority given the secretary of defense in the 1958 reorganization act. It became a reality in 1961 and 1962 with McNamara's introduction of PPBS. Its purpose was to provide a more rational process for decisions on force structure, strategic programs, and weapons systems. It was to replace a system in which the secretary of defense set budget ceilings for the services, and the services then largely determined how they would spend that money. PPBS was an effort to tie together planning and budgeting, to look at programs "horizontally" across service lines, to determine in a comprehensive manner the true costs that might be associated with new programs, and to do all of this in terms of a rolling five-year planning cycle, instead of focusing simply upon next year's budget. McNamara moved quickly to introduce this system in 1961. Although congressional and bureaucratic resistance limited the extent of his success, he was, nonetheless, able to achieve a large part of what he wanted, and he created the framework within which resource allocation decisions were made within the department for twenty years thereafter.

The Eisenhower–McNamara reforms were thus designed to achieve the following: centralized and coherent strategic planning; the rational allocation of resources to forces, programs, and weapons; and unified command of combat forces. But during the following twenty years, none of these goals has been realized satisfactorily. The history of the Defense department has been a history of conflict between the intentions of Eisenhower and McNamara, on the one hand, and the interests of the services on the other. The outcome of that conflict was never in doubt. The services won, hands down. They successfully defeated the wishes of a five-star president and an awesomely vigorous secretary of defense, and made the legislative language and administrative procedures of those officials work to serve interests. Never have the American military services scored a more complete victory.

THE SERVICES AND "SERVICISM"

Under the Eisenhower–McNamara system, the individual services *per se* were not supposed to fight wars, to make strategy, or to determine overall force structure. In fact, they continued to exercise a prevailing influence in each of these areas. Instead of developing a system for coherent central strategic planning, the joint chiefs continued to give priority to their role as spokesmen for their services, and joint staff officers bargain among themselves, each trying to get the most for his service. Instead of rational choices of programs and weapons most needed to serve national purposes, such choices are still largely determined by service needs and service interests, resulting in duplication of some programs, misallocation of resources to others, and, most important, neglect of still others. Instead of the unified command of combat forces, command is often fragmented and the unified commanders (CINCs) almost always find their authority over their forces second to that of the services that supplied those forces.

The root cause of these problems stems from the fact that, except for the chairman of the joint chiefs, all military officers are *service* military officers. Their experiences, training, identification, personal associations, and, most important, their futures — all are wrapped up in their services. As a result, the only source of nonservice or transservice advice, apart from the chairman, to which a president or secretary of defense can turn, is civilians. The growth of civilian influence in strategy is directly attributable to the failure of the military to approach strategy freed from its service blinders. Not "militarism" but "servicism" is the central malady of the American military establishment.

How can it be limited and its most pernicious effects coped with? Servicism could, in theory, be abolished by abolishing the separate services. Such drastic action is not, however, desirable, possible, or necessary. The services are invaluable in the specialized expertise they develop, the training they provide, the historical traditions they embody, the loyalties they breed. Tank warfare, submarine operations, and air combat do require very different skills. The organization of the armed forces on the basis of the element in which they operate may not be most rational for some purposes, but it makes a great deal of sense in terms of producing tactical combat units capable of defeating comparable enemy units. One country, Canada, tried to eliminate its three services and merge them into a single entity. This was a dismal failure, and has, in effect, been reversed in practice. Attempting to abolish the U.S. services would be inefficient, wasteful, and counterproductive.

Elimination of the services would be the most extreme approach. The most modest one would be to rely primarily on exhortation to persuade military officers to think and act in nonservice terms. This has been tried — often. As has been mentioned, the 1958 reorganization act directed service chiefs to delegate more of their functions as service chiefs to their vice chiefs and to devote more time and energy to their joint responsibilities. Ideally this would have created a situation in which the vice chief would become the spokesman for the service point of view, while the chief of his service would think and act jointly with his colleagues on the joint chiefs. In fact, of course, the service chiefs could not act this way. They still wore their hats as service chiefs, their identifications were with, and their support came from, their services, and they continued to function primarily as service representatives. They also continued to give high priority to their duties as service chiefs, delegating to their deputies for operations a large portion of their joint responsibilities, thereby accomplishing just the reverse of what the reforms had attempted to promote.

Nor will exhortation through education suffice. Proposals have been advanced, for instance, for joint education for those selected for general or flag officer rank, or for one-year stints for all service academy cadets at the academy of another service. Such educational reforms may be desirable. They will not, however, deal with the problem of servicism. American military officers may learn the virtues of transcending service concerns at joint educational institutions, but when they leave those institutions they will respond to the incentives, rewards, and expectations of the environment in which they operate. Military officers want to serve their country ably and loyally, but the system is structured to make them want to serve their country by serving their service.

Neither elimination of the services nor exhortation to transcend service interests is an effective way of dealing with the evils of servicism. One is too much, the other too little. There are, however, three intermediate approaches that might offer some relief.

First, in some circumstances, incentives and rewards can be structured such that a service acting in its own self-interest will also be responding to national needs. Second, more military officers could be "divorced" from their services by offering them alternative careers in the central defense organization through a general staff corps or similar device, and by expanding the roles and strengthening the power of the JCS chairman. Third, an enhanced role in the formulation and execution of strategy could be assigned to nonservice oriented civilians; though to some extent, this has already occurred, civilians have not been adequately organized to make the most effective contribution to strategic planning and resource allocation. The application of one or more of these three approaches is essential in curbing the effects of servicism on the three most crucial functions of the military, as enumerated in the Eisenhower reform efforts—strategic planning, resource allocation, and combat command.

STRATEGIC PLANNING

The secretary of defense is responsible for developing a national military strategy which, when approved by the president and acquiesced in by Congress, should provide the basic guidelines and framework for decisions on force levels, programs, and weapons systems, and for the development of operational plans for the use of military force. The national military strategy should serve the nation's foreign policy goals and, at the same time, be compatible with the fiscal constraints that inevitably exist. Strategic planning thus involves first the assessment of threats and of needs, and then the determination of priorities among regions (e.g., Europe versus the Persian Gulf), types of forces (e.g., nuclear versus conventional, regular versus reserves), force dispositions (e.g., forward deployments versus enhanced mobility), timing requirements (e.g., modernization versus readiness), and weapons (e.g., smaller numbers of highly sophisticated weapons versus larger numbers of less capable weapons). It also involves a whole series of closely related issues as to the circumstances under which and how American forces would be used in combat: for example, offensively or defensively, in long wars or short wars, unilaterally or in conjunction with allies, in gradual increments or in a massive initial commitment. These more general and conceptual issues lead into more specific questions of how much of what specific types of force (ground divisions, aircraft carriers, fighter bombers) may be necessary to implement the strategic plans.

In many countries strategic planning is effectively dominated, if not totally monopolized, by the military acting through a central military staff. What is often lacking is an effective civilian counterweight to the strategic advice the military provides the government. In the United States, the situation is almost the reverse. Over the course of several decades, civilian agencies and groups have moved to shape strategy. The two principal offices in the Pentagon through which this has occurred are the office of program analysis and evaluation, created by McNamara to apply systems analysis to military issues, and the office of the undersecretary of defense for policy, which is an outgrowth of and has absorbed the earlier office of international security affairs.

Strategic planning, however, should not be dominated by civilian agencies. In the end, strategic plans have to be implemented by military officers commanding military units; and knowledgeable and responsible military officers ought to play a central role in the development of overall strategic plans. The agency through which the military engages in strategic planning is, of course, the Joint Chiefs of Staff. The most widely criticized deficiency in U.S. defense organization today is the failure of the JCS to play this role effectively.

The litany of criticism of the JCS is long and has been repeated consistently over the years. While some changes and improvements have been made in how it functions, the fundamental problems are still those that existed twenty-five years ago. They basically stem from the composition of the JCS as a committee (except for the chairman) of service representatives and of the joint staff as an organization of officers detailed from their services for brief periods of time and responsible to the JCS in its corporate capacity. Given this structure, the joint chiefs and its staff become the arena for the negotiation and resolution of an incredibly wide range of issues, trivial and important, that affect the services. This has several consequences for strategic planning.

First, strategic planning tends to be neglected. Attention is necessarily focused on issues affecting service interests, including resource allocation, personnel assignments, roles and missions, administrative and logistical practices (which service's procedures will be used if they are standardized), and similar types of issues. As a result, the JCS rarely if ever has taken the initiative in developing new strategic concepts or approaches. Over the years these have come from civilians, from individual services, and, at times, even from theater commands (e.g., SHAPE's "deep interdiction" concept); they have not come out of the joint military structure. As one informed observer wrote in 1976, "The JCS has become so bogged down in the cumbersome process which is so concerned with protecting each chief's own service interests that it has become addicted to the status quo and has never been a source of innovation in the national security policy-making process."[1] The neglect of strategy is reinforced by the demands of the annual budgetary authorization and appropriations process, which, to an extent unequalled in other countries, diverts the attention of top-ranking military officers from planning to fight next year's possible war to planning to fight next year's inevitable budget. The military services are, understandably, more concerned with the latter than the former.

Second, to the extent that the JCS does develop strategic plans, these plans often are unrealistic because each service wants them to be based on assumptions that reflect its own estimate of the threat and the forces it will need to counter that threat. Ideally, military strategy should provide for the use of available resources to deal with perceived threats. If strategy is based on the assumption that unavailable resources can be put to use, it is not of much help. But that tends to be the case. This does, however, serve two purposes for the services. First, it reduces conflict and facilitates agreement among them. Second, it enhances the ability of each service to develop the force capabilities it wants to develop. (If a service is told to develop capabilities that would require $50 billion in expenditures, but only gets $35 billion, the service will have the primary responsibility for deciding which capabilities to emphasize and which to eliminate.)

That strategic plans will often be unintegrated follows as a natural result of this system. The services may and often do plan to fight different wars. The interests of interservice harmony also dictate that almost all issues coming up within the JCS system be negotiated until a position is reached that all four services can accept. The result is language that is often vague, ambiguous, and of little use to those who must make the tough decisions on strategic issues.

Third, as a result of the need to produce four-service agreement, the JCS process usually operates very slowly. In times of crisis, of course, critical issues will be disposed of more expeditiously, but the snail's pace of JCS policy development has been a recurring theme for decades. In the early 1960s, according to Paul H. Nitze, "it would sometimes take them [the joint chiefs] three days to blow their nose." In 1970 the Blue Ribbon Defense Panel described JCS procedure as "ponderous and slow." In 1982, said the Air Force chief of staff, the planning process was "cumbersome" and took "too long."[2]

Fourth, the quality of the people assigned to the joint staff has left something to be desired. The services typically assign their best officers to their own staffs. Officers who have been assigned to the joint staff have not been promoted at the same rate as comparable officers who have remained with their services. Various directives requiring officers recommended for promotion to general or flag officer rank to have some joint service experience have not, so far, had much effect in countering this natural service tendency to keep their best for themselves.

Fifth, the functioning of the joint staff system creates obstacles to civil–military collaboration in strategic planning. The joint staff is a purely military organization, staffed by the services. The office of program analysis and evaluation is, at present, almost entirely civilian. The office of the undersecretary for policy is the only one of the three top offices in the Pentagon concerned with strategy that, as of 1982, had a reasonable balance of civilian and military talent among its top personnel (about a 60:40 ratio, civilian to military). Effective military planning, as Army Chief of Staff Edward C. Meyer said, requires "much greater interplay between the joint military and civilian leadership" than exists at present.[3] A major purpose of the joint staff system, however, is to generate position papers upon which all four services agree. To achieve this, civilians are excluded and the services meet *in camera* (or, more accurately, in "the tank," as the JCS meeting room is called) to thrash out their differences so that they then can provide united military advice to civilian decision makers.

NONSERVICE MILITARY INSTITUTIONS

How can those deficiencies in strategic planning be corrected? It is hard to conceive how service interests could be restructured so as to enable them to contribute positively to nonservice oriented strategic planning. Nor can failures in the military contribution to strategic planning be corrected by relying more on civilians. A responsible and powerful military role in strategic planning is essential. The conclusion is that curing the defects in U.S. strategic planning requires an increased role for *nonservice* military institutions, and virtually all proposals to deal with the defects of strategic planning attempt to provide for this.

These proposals, roughly speaking, embody two different approaches. The more radical approach would be to create a general staff corps of officers divorced from their services. This would constitute a "purple suit" entity to whom civilian officials could turn for nonservice oriented military advice. A full general staff system has five key characteristics. First, officers are selected to enter the general staff corps relatively early in their careers. Second, their entire subsequent military career is within that corps; they thus pursue a different career line from those officers who remain in the services. Third, upon selection for the general staff corps, officers undergo rigorous and prolonged training (two or three years) in a general staff academy. Fourth, their principal subsequent assignments are to the general staff, to other joint staffs, or to joint commands, with perhaps occasional rotation back to their services. Fifth, their assignments and promotions are made not by their services but by the head of the general staff. Not all general staff systems embody all these features to the same degree. Some minimum combination of them, however, is essential to constitute a general staff corps. Many countries, including the Federal Republic of Germany and the Soviet Union, have some variety of a general staff system.

The introduction of such a system in the United States would improve the effectiveness of military planning and the usefulness of military advice to civilian policymakers. Given the inherent pluralism in the American defense structure, the creation of this additional unit would not threaten civilian control or the legitimate interests of the services. Creation of such an organization, however, would mark a major innovation in American military structure and would only be accomplished, if at all, after prolonged debate and controversy. It would probably require a major military disaster to bring such a system into being.

Given this situation, the more modest alternative for improving strategic planning is to enhance the power and roles of the chairman of the Joint Chiefs of Staff. This could be done in a variety of ways. He could be given the authority to select officers for the joint staff and to have a decisive voice on their promotion while on that staff. He could be given authority in his own right, and not, as now, on behalf of the joint chiefs, to manage the joint staff. The chairperson could be designated, *vice* the joint chiefs, as the principal military advisor to Congress, the president, and the secretary of defense. This would not mean that the other chiefs would not also have direct access to these civilian officials, but it would place the initiative in making recommendations with the chairman, the other chiefs being able to file dissents from his views if they so desired. The chairman could also be given a deputy, who would preside over the chiefs in his absence and who could take the lead in resolving critical issues on behalf of the chairman. Several of these measures were incorporated in the bills on defense organization that Congress considered in 1982, 1983, and 1984. Measures such as these would not replace the Joint Chiefs of Staff system with a general staff system. They would, however, enable the military to play a more useful, timely, and positive role in strategic planning. In part, they embody changes that the British have already made in their joint staff system, and without which top British military and civilian officials say they could never have conducted the Falklands War as effectively as they did.

Any major organizational change has a variety of consequences. The anticipated and planned consequence of the changes discussed above would be more effective strategic planning. One additional probable consequence of these changes may appear less benign: If power is centralized to a greater degree in the chairman of the JCS, it is quite likely that the high level of consensus that has prevailed among the military chiefs will decline. At least some of the incentives to unanimity among the chiefs will be weakened. This does not necessarily mean a return to the age of contention that existed in the 1940s and 1950s. It does mean, however, that with the chairman exercising an independent role of his own, more incentives will exist for individual service chiefs to appeal to the secretary of defense. This is, indeed, what is necessary to impart greater precision and clearer choices to the strategic planning process. If major contentious issues are not swept under the rug, they will be fought over. Less harmony among the chiefs is the price of clearer choices, more coherent strategy, and more meaningful civilian direction.

RESOURCE ALLOCATION AND FORCE DEVELOPMENT

The second area where the Eisenhower–McNamara reforms did not achieve their objectives is the allocation of resources for force development. In various manifestations, PPBS has been followed in form, but it has not eliminated the irrationalities and imbalances in the assignment of resources to forces, programs, and weapons. Service priorities continue to prevail over strategic needs. The resulting deficiencies are many and important.

First, as with broader strategic issues, the tendency in the JCS process is for all services to approve the force goals and weapons programs of each. In the early 1980s, consequently, the joint chiefs approved requirements for twenty-three aircraft carriers (as against fourteen then existing), forty air wings (twenty-six existing) and thirty-three Army divisions (twenty-four existing). By endorsing each other's maximum goals, the chiefs created intramilitary consensus at the expense of extramilitary relevance. Even the Reagan Administration did not endorse such ambitious force levels.

Second, over the years there has been an occasional tendency to return to the practice whereby the secretary of defense would set the budget figures for the services and then allow the services to decide, within broad guidelines, how they would allocate their funds. This tendency has been most noticeable under Laird and Weinberger. Its reappearance flew in the face of the whole theory of PPBS, but it was also a natural political development. The secretary of defense has to be concerned about expenditure levels, and if the services will acquiesce in ceilings that he and the president find acceptable, it is not unreasonable to let them have the dominant voice in deciding how the money will be spent. The service, on the other hand, will accept lower spending levels in return for greater freedom to allocate resources to those programs that it considers essential to its central missions and identity. The result, however, is that service interests rather than strategic needs play the dominant role in shaping program decisions.

Third, the role of service interests in shaping forces and programs leads to imbalances in military capabilities. Those "orphan" functions that are not central to a service's own definition of its mission tend to be neglected. For example, given limited resources, the Air Force and the Navy are not going to give high priority to air and sea lift for the Army, as against bombers and carriers for themselves. Somewhat similarly, the Air Force has been slow to emphasize close air support for the Army, and has done so at times only in response to Army attempts to develop its own capability for close air support. In other cases, no service may wish to give high priority to developing the capabilities to meet a perceived strategic need. This has traditionally been the case with counterinsurgency capabilities, and it was very much the case with the rapid deployment force for intervention in areas such as the Persian Gulf. President Carter ordered the creation of such a force in August 1977, but no service had a major interest in espousing this mission.

Despite recurring prods from the White House, the concept languished in the Pentagon for over two years until the Iranian hostage seizure and the invasion of Afghanistan were able to produce a response that a presidential order had failed to generate. In general, extraordinarily active and sustained external prodding, as was the case with McNamara and airlift, is required to get services to develop capabilities that they do not see as central to their role.

Fourth, service dominance in determining programs tends to produce an overemphasis on procurement and investment, as against readiness. Lobbying for the latter has chiefly come only from the commanders in chief of the unified and specified commands. The CINCs' interest is to have forces that are well-equipped, supplied, trained, and exercised to fight effectively in the near term. The services, on the other hand, are in large part procurement agencies, and they tend to look toward the longer-term needs of investment and modernization. Since the services have more influence than the combat commands in the resource allocation and budgeting process, investment needs tend to be emphasized over readiness needs. This tendency is reinforced by the interests of defense contractors, congressmen, and their constitutents in promoting major weapons systems. It is at times even reinforced by the interests of comptrollers and fiscal officers in holding down immediate expenditure—at the cost of allowing larger new authorizations, the expenditures for which will not peak for three or four years. Clearly a better balance is needed between investment and readiness.

In the competition for resources, the emphasis is thus on service programs to meet service goals. This was the case in 1948 when the Air Force undertook a major compaign to get seventy wings; it remained true in 1981, when the Secretary of the Navy waged a major campaign to get 600 ships. The problem, of course, is that 600 ships may or may not meet the strategic needs of the country, although they certainly meet the service needs of the Navy. A large navy is properly the *instrument*, not the *goal*, of strategy. The United States has no interest in a 600-ship navy, as such. It does have an interest in having the right combination of ships to serve the strategic purposes of its foreign policy. Six hundred ships of one sort or another might or might not be necessary for those purposes, but that is something that is impossible for the Navy to determine rationally. As the process works, however, an instrumental, service goal supplants strategic goals.

The preeminence of service goals in the program development process stems from the failure of defense organization to reflect strategic purposes. At the broadest level, most strategists would agree that the United States has three major strategic purposes: strategic deterrence, that is, to deter nuclear attacks on the United States and its allies, and to limit the damage from such attacks should they occur; NATO defense, that is, to deter and, if necessary, to defeat an attack on European allies; and regional defense, that is, to be capable of projecting the forces necessary to defend vital U.S.

interests in East Asia, the Middle East and Persian Gulf, and the Western Hemisphere.

The most striking deficiency in U.S. defense organization today is the absence of any single official or office in the Pentagon with overall responsibility for any one of these strategic missions—and *only* for that mission. Individual officials and organizations are responsible for parts of each of these missions; other officials, such as the chairman of the JCS and the under secretary for policy, have a general responsibility for all these missions. The secretary of defense knows where to turn when he wants the individual officials responsible for the Air Force or the Marine Corps, for research and development or intelligence, for manpower or the budget. But where does he find an official with overall and exclusive responsibility for strategic deterrence? There is none. Nor is there any single official responsible for NATO defense or for force projection in the Third World. These are precisely the major strategic purposes of American defense policy, and they are virtually the only important interests in defense that are not represented in the defense organization.

How can this failure to represent strategic purpose in defense organization be remedied? There are three possible ways. One would be to restructure the services so as to make service interest coincide with strategic mission. In effect, this would involve a change in service roles and missions, as defined in the Key West Agreement of 1948, so as to define the competence of the services in terms of mission rather than in terms of element. Two proposals along these lines were advanced in 1983.[4] In general, they propose that the Air Force become the strategic deterrence force. It would lose its responsibilities for tactical air and airlift, but it would gain control of ballistic missile submarines and everything relating to ballistic missile defenses. The Army would be dedicated exclusively to land war and would gain control of everything necessary for the successful prosecution of land war, including tactical air, air lift, and sea lift. The Navy would lose its sea lift and ballistic missile submarines, but would keep everything else dedicated to the conduct of war at sea, including the Marine Corps, since amphibious operations cannot be separated from war at sea.

These changes, it is argued, would mean that the Air Force would no longer necessarily rule out basing MX missiles on small coastal submarines, since it would be assured that those submarines would be under its control rather than the Navy's. Similarly, the Army could greatly reduce its expensive and dubiously effective efforts to provide close air support by helicopters and instead purchase the cheaper and more effective fixed-wing planes which the Key West Agreement now bars it from procuring.

Undoubtedly, such a realignment of service roles and missions would produce program and weapon choices better suited to serve U.S. strategic purposes. There are, however, several problems with this proposal. The division of service responsibilities among strategic deterrence, ground war, and air war does not entirely relate services to missions. Indeed, it mixes purposive (strategic deterrence) and elemental (ground, sea) definitions of service responsibility. Undoubtedly the Army would be primarily oriented to European defense and the Navy to sea control and force projection. One key element of European defense, however, is the ability of the United States to mobilize and transport personnel and materiel to Europe in the event of conflict. The Navy would have to protect them against Soviet submarines and aircraft. Yet the decision as to what resources would be devoted to this NATO mission would be made, not by someone with overall responsibility for European defense, but by someone who balanced this need against the need to project forces elsewhere. The Navy's decision on this issue might or might not be congruent with the Army's decision on its needs for reinforcement.

Another major difficulty of the service restructuring solution is that the political problems involved in attempting to induce any of the services to surrender long held responsibilities, even though secondary ones, are enormous. The agreement worked out at Key West is in many respects arbitrary. To reopen it, however, would be to shake up a hornet's nest of fears, animosities, and service lobbying that would effectively preclude serious consideration of other defense issues for some period of time.

A second way that has been proposed to relate strategic purpose to defense organization has been to enhance the role of the unified and specified commands and of the chairman of the JCS as their spokesman. This proposal has received fairly widespread support. The CINCs, after all, are the officials who are responsible for using the military forces to achieve U.S. strategic purposes. Very modest steps to enhance their role in program determination and resource allocation have been taken under both Carter and Reagan, and the CINCs now appear semi-annually before the Defense Resources Board to present their needs.

Enhancement of the role of the CINCs undoubtedly would be useful. At the same time, however, it is not clear that such a move would satisfactorily close the gap between strategic purpose and defense organization. Many of the unified and specified commands are little more than service creatures and service fronts. Strengthening them will not create a strategic counterpoise to service interests. In addition, two or more commands contribute to each of the three major U.S. strategic purposes and hence no single CINC can represent the total needs of any such purpose. The physical location of the CINCs outside of—often at great distance from—Washington also makes it difficult for them to play a sustained role in the never-ending program determination and resource allocation process. Presumably the chairman of the JCS might, as many suggest, attempt to articulate their needs in Washington. As we have noted, the CINCs do share an interest in readiness which often puts them at odds with the services on such issues as maintenance, spare parts, joint exercises, and other issues. On major resource allocation issues, however, the divisions among the CINCs will be as deep as those among the services. It is not clear how the chairman can represent the views of the CINCs when those views can and must conflict with each other.

UNDER SECRETARIES FOR STRATEGIC MISSIONS

Service restructuring is thus probably impossible. An enhancement of the role of the CINCs would be only partially effective. A third, more promising, approach would be *to create at the highest level in the defense department offices concerned with each major strategic mission.* Such offices could be headed by under secretaries of defense, who would replace and assume the functions now associated with the under secretary of defense for policy. Each such under secretary would have the responsibility to ensure that the United States has military forces constituted, organized, trained, equipped, and deployed to carry out the mission for which he is responsible. Each under secretary would thus supervise, direct, and coordinate all those activities in the defense department primarily related to his strategic purpose. These would include both force development and operational planning. He would be the principal civilian advisor to the secretary of defense for everything connected with his mission, including budget allocations.

Each under secretary should have general supervisory responsibility for the unified and specified commands relevant to his mission. He would also be their spokesman in the process of force development and resource allocation. It would be up to him to review the CINCs' statements of their requirements and make recommendations concerning their needs to the secretary of defense. Once he received guidance from the secretary as to the resources that would be available to support his mission, it would then be up to the under secretary to determine the most effective allocation of those resources among the various forces, programs, and weapons. Given limited resources, each under secretary would have an interest in producing the combination of forces and programs that would most effectively and most efficiently meet the needs of his mission. The services and other defense department agencies would, correspondingly, have interests in demonstrating that their programs would meet those needs more effectively and efficiently than those of the other services. Unproductive interservice rivalry over ownership of programs and functions would be replaced by a more productive rivalry to develop the best programs and weapons to meet the key strategic needs of the nation.

The responsibilities of individual under secretaries might be defined in a variety of ways. The under secretary for strategic deterrence would presumably have authority over all strategic offensive and defensive forces and capabilities. He would also be responsible for offensive, defensive, and intelligence missions in space. He would have supervisory but not command authority over the strategic air command (SAC), the aerospace defense command, and Navy SLBM forces, and he would be the spokesman for their requirements in the process of force development and resource allocation. He would be the defense department's person on strategic arms limitation negotiations.

The under secretary for North Atlantic and European defense would be generally responsible for everything connected with NATO, including U.S. conventional forces allocated to that purpose, theater nuclear forces, and the naval forces designed to secure control of the North Atlantic. He would exercise supervisory authority over, and be the spokesman for the requirements of, the European and Atlantic commands. He would also be in charge of mobilization planning, since that process is driven by the requirements of a general war in Europe. He would be responsible for developing the defense department position for negotiations on nuclear weapons and conventional forces in Europe. He would share responsibility for antisubmarine warfare with the under secretary for strategic deterrence.

The under secretary for regional defense and force projection would generally be responsible for planning and preparations for military contingencies in East Asia, the Middle East and Persian Gulf, Latin America, and other Third World areas. He would have supervisory authority over, and be the spokesman for, the requirements of the Pacific, Central (Indian Ocean–Persian Gulf), Southern (Latin America), and readiness commands. He would coordinate military assistance programs for the countries in these areas. He would also have general responsibility for counterinsurgency and special operations. He would share responsibility for mobility capabilities with the under secretary for NATO affairs.

The undersecretaries would clearly compete with each other for resources to perform their missions. Unlike current interservice competition, however, where only service interests are at stake, this competition would involve critical issues of priority among central strategic missions. The differences among them would have to be resolved by the secretary of defense in meeting with them, the deputy secretary, and the chairman of the Joint Chiefs of Staff. That six man group would, in effect, be the top policy-making body in the Pentagon.

One of the most frequently voiced criticisms of the office of the secretary of defense has been that its officials tend to get involved in administrative detail, which should properly be left to the services or other agencies, and attempt to "micromanage" the department. This tendency is in large part a result of the gap that exists in the department between strategic purpose and organizational structure. As one expert on governmental organization has observed, "*The failure to group related programs in major purpose agencies inevitably produces a shift of power to the policy and managerial offices grouped around the President.*"[5] This is equally true within the Defense department, and the absence of "major purpose agencies" within the department has promoted the involvement of the office of the secretary of defense in administration and management. Creation of major purpose agencies related to strategic missions would encourage the decentralization of authority and would tend to focus attention on the major strategic issues–which would be at stake among the under secretaries—instead of on administrative details.

Movement in this direction would threaten neither the existence nor the roles and missions of the services. It would encourage the services to compete with each other in a more constructive fashion and would reward those services that came up with the most effective and least expensive programs to achieve strategic missions. The services would continue to do all that they do today, but their activities would be directed to a different mix of goals than they currently are.

In some measure, the creation of the three mission offices and under secretaries recommended here would follow naturally from developments already under way in the department. During the early years of the Carter Administration, the secretary of defense had an advisor for NATO affairs. In the Reagan Administration, the assistant secretary for international security affairs has generally been responsible for matters concerning the Third World, while the assistant secretary for international security policy has handled NATO matters, strategic forces, and arms control negotiations. Neither of these officials, however, has had the statutory authority or the defined responsibilities to carry out the crucial duties in force development which the proposed under secretaries would discharge. In the defense department, assistant secretaries simply do not have the status and clout required for this task. Responsible as they should be for achieving the defense department's major strategic purposes, these officials need to be under secretaries and second only to the secretary and his deputy in their authority and position with the department. In fact and in perception, they need to be mission "czars."

COMBAT COMMAND

The need for unity of command was the dominant theme of the Defense Reorganization Act of 1958. Combat forces, President Eisenhower argued, must be "organized into unified commands . . . singly led and prepared to fight as one, regardless of service." The act attempted to accomplish this end through a radical break with the past. Before 1958, "unified" commands had existed, but, with the notable exception of Eisenhower's command in Europe, these commands were largely identified with individual services, even when forces from several services were assigned to them. After World War II, a service department served as the "executive agent" for each unified command, linking it to the Joint Chiefs of Staff and the secretary of defense. The 1958 act seemed to change this pattern drastically. Unified or specified commands would be directly under the command of the president and the secretary of defense; they would, at least in theory, have no direct ties with particular services; and the services would have no responsibility for the conduct of military operations.

The unification of command over land, air, and sea elements was achieved, however, only by accepting two other critical distinctions in military organization. The services were to be the *providers* of military forces; that is, they were to recruit, train, equip, and generally prepare military forces for combat. These forces would then be turned over to the unified and specified commands who would be the *users* of military force. They would plan for and actually direct the use of those forces in combat. There would be a balanced pattern of departmental organization, with a clear separation between an administrative hierarchy and a military command hierarchy. Under the 1958 act, the Army, Navy, Air Force, and Marine Corps thus would not fight wars; the unified and specified commands would fight wars. By removing the services in theory from military operations, the United States adopted an organizational pattern which, among major powers, it shares only with the Federal Republic of Germany (a very special case, because all its combat forces are under the operational command of NATO). The United States is thus almost alone in attempting to exclude its military services entirely from the conduct of military operations and relegate them entirely to supporting roles.

To the distinction between provider and user, the 1958 act also added another and more troublesome distinction, that between operational command and administrative command. Conceivably, once a military service had organized and equipped a military unit (ship, division, air wing) it could have turned full authority for that unit over to the unified command to which it was assigned—the unit only returning to service control when, for one reason or another, it was felt necessary fundamentally to reconstitute, retrain, or re-equip it. Short of this, however, it would be under the full command, in all dimensions, of the unified commander. The 1958 act, however, did not establish this system. Instead, it provided that the CINC would have "full operational command of the forces assigned to him while the services would be "responsible for the administration" of those forces. The services have control over discipline, personnel, training, and logistics. The act thus provided for unified command of land, sea, and air forces at the expense of a divided command over the individual land, sea, and air components. Each subordinate component commander in a unified command is responsible to the CINC of his command on operational matters and to the chief of his service for everything else, which, in peacetime, is almost everything of importance.

The division decreed in the act between operational and administrative command in effect undermines the division of responsibilities between provider and user that was designed to ensure unity of command. The power of the CINCs over their service components remains highly constrained and limited. In 1970 the Blue Ribbon Defense Panel argued that the intent of the earlier reforms had been vitiated: "Despite the establishment of the unified command concept in the Defense Reorganization Act of 1958, as requested by President Eisenhower, the relationship and relative authority between the Unified Commander and the component commander, and between the component commander and his Military Department, remain substantially unchanged." Eight years later another official study made a similar comment. The CINCs "have limited power to influence the capability of the forces assigned to them. . . . The CINCs' forces are trained and equipped by their parent Services, who control the flow of men, money, and materiel to the CINC's components. The Services (and the components) thus have the major influence on both the structure and the readiness of the forces for which the CINC is responsible." As a result, the CINCs have to negotiate with their component commanders. Their only real power is the power of persuasion; they have only limited influence over what goes on in their service components.[6] The component commanders clearly exercise preponderant control over the combat forces assigned to unified commands. Unified commands, in short, are not truly unified.

The unified commands are also not truly unified in yet another sense. The 1958 act ended the system whereby a service department served as "executive agent" for each unified command. It could not and did not, however, end the identification of particular commands with particular services. The three specified commands—strategic air command, aerospace defense command, and military airlift command—are composed entirely of Air Force units and are commanded by Air Force officers. The Pacific and Atlantic commands are always commanded by naval officers. The European, Southern, and readiness commands have (with one brief exception) been under Army command. The central command, which developed out of the rapid deployment joint task force (commanded by a Marine), is now commanded by an Army officer.

At least some of the designated unified commands are more unified in theory than in practice. The Atlantic command has no Army of Air Force components regularly assigned to it. Except for three ships in the Persian Gulf, no Navy or Marine Corps units are regularly assigned to the readiness command or to the central command. Army units do exist in the Pacific command, most notably in Korea, but those are part of a subunified command headed by an Army general. The Southern command includes modest

Army and only minuscule Air Force and Navy forces. This leaves the European command, with substantial forces from all service departments, as the only truly comprehensive unified command. Apart from the European command, almost no naval forces are under the command of Army or Air Force officers, and only in the Pacific command are significant Army and Air Force units under a naval CINC—and that is mitigated through the device of the subunified command. Despite Eisenhower's intentions and the 1958 act, in most cases the operational chain of command, as well as the administrative one, remains a service chain of command. To the extent a unified command is unified, it is not a command, because of the limited control of the CINC over components from other services. To the extent that a unified command is a command, it is not unified, because its forces come exclusively or overwhelmingly from a single service.

Such is the system in peacetime. The situation in war or crisis, when military forces have to be deployed and used, is not substantially different, except that, invariably, ad hoc arrangements have to be devised. In developing such command arrangements for military operations, the service members of the Joint Chiefs of Staff are driven by two urges. First, each chief wants his service to have a significant role in the operation. Second, each chief is under pressure to minimize the extent to which forces from his service are under the command of someone from another service. The efforts to harmonize these two principles can often lead to complex, uncertain, and fragmented command relationships. The Vietnam War, for instance, occurred within the geographical area assigned to the Navy-headed Pacific command. Once significant Army forces were deployed to Vietnam, however, a subunified command, MACV, headed by an Army general, was created. In due course, Marine units were also assigned to Vietnam, and what was in effect a separate sub-subunified command was created for them in the northern provinces of South Vietnam. MACV, however, did not command the carrier task forces in the South China Sea or the B-52 bombers operating from Guam, both of which played significant roles in the air war. As a result, Vietnam was, as General Jones observes:

> perhaps our worst example of confused objectives and unclear responsibilities both in Washington and in the field. Each service, instead of integrating efforts with the others, considered Vietnam its own war and sought to carve out a large mission for itself. For example, each fought its own air war, agreeing only to limited measures for a coordinated effort. . . . Lack of integration persisted right through the 1975 evacuation of Saigon—when responsibility was split between two separate commands, one on land and one at sea; each of these set a different "H-hour," which caused confusion and delays.[7]

Comparable patterns have existed in smaller operations. Grenada is a relatively small island; but during the invasion, command over ground forces was divided between Marine and Army officers. In the Iran rescue mission, as the official Pentagon study concluded, command and control were "excellent at the upper echelons, but became more tenuous and fragile at intermediate levels." Within the joint task force that had been created for this operation, command relationships "were not clearly emphasized in some cases and were susceptible to misunderstandings under pressure." Among other things, during preparation for the mission it was unclear as to whether a Marine or Air Force officer was in charge of training the helicopter units that were to undertake the rescue.[8]

The existing unified and specified commands are organized in terms of both mission and geographical areas. The mission commands, however, as is the case most notably with SAC, do not necessarily include all the major forces that are dedicated to that mission, while the geographical commands, on the other hand, do have full responsibility for their entire geographical area. It is difficult to see the logic that divides command of U.S. strategic retaliatory forces among four separate commands (strategic air, Atlantic, Pacific, European) and yet established a single command for all U.S. forces from the Golden Gate to the Persian Gulf. Geographically defined commands, oriented toward a particular area, service, or mission, may not be well suited to plan for and carry out operations that are at the margin of their responsibilities. Thirteen years before the invasion of Grenada, the Blue Ribbon Defense Panel argued that the Atlantic Command "tends to be oriented toward a general war maritime role as distinguished from a perhaps more probable contingency involving land operations in its geographical area of responsibility." Nor is it surprising that the Long Commission on the terrorist bombing of the Marines at Beirut airport should conclude that there was "a lack of systematic and aggressive chain of command attention" to the Marines' antiterrorist security measures by European command headquarters.[9] The current structure of unified and specified commands thus often tends to unify things that should not be unified and to divide things that should be under a single command.

The deficiencies in the command of combat forces will not be corrected by any single panacea. A wide variety of individual corrective actions is desirable. First, however, it is necessary to ask: What purposes is unity of command meant to serve? There are really two: cooperation and fungibility. Cooperation is served when all military forces assigned to a particular mission are under a single command. Fungibility is served when all military forces of a particular type are under a single command. The needs of cooperation and fungibility often conflict with each other, as well as with other important values in military operations. In a complex modern military establishment, as a result, absolute unity of command is virtually impossible to achieve. Unifying military forces along one dimension will create disunities along another. Some form of divided command will exist in almost all circumstances; the problem is to identify that form of division that is least injurious to the accomplishment of the mission at hand.

MISSION COMMANDS, NOT AREA COMMANDS

The 1958 act was based on the absolute distinction between the provider-administrative role of the services and the user–operational role of the combat commands. This has, however, been a distinction impossible to maintain in practice. Much of the time, this effort at divorce is unnecessary and dysfunctional. Where there are operational missions that should be carried out with forces from a single service, no reason exists not to assign responsibility for that mission to the service. The assumption underlying the 1958 act — that all operational forces should be removed from the services — needs to be re-examined, particularly since in the specified commands and many "unified" commands they have never in fact been divorced. Conceivably, the United States might do well to follow a pattern comparable to that of the Soviets, in which in some cases the services are responsible for operational missions and in other cases they are not.

In keeping with this general approach, unified and specified commands should normally be organized in terms of mission, not area, and the scope of a command should be extended to all forces directly relevant to its mission. The strategic air command, for instance, should be converted into a strategic retaliatory command incorporating the ballistic missile submarines that are now assigned to three other commands. In keeping with the recommendations of various groups, the military airlift command might also be changed into a logistics command including sealift and related activities as well as airlift. Both of these commands would thus become unified rather than specified, commands and should be commanded by Navy admirals as well as by Air Force generals. The Atlantic command, on the other hand, should be converted into a purely naval Atlantic sea control command, with that as its only mission. Responsibility for force projection and amphibious operations in countries bordering the Atlantic, on the other hand, should be transferred to the readiness or Southern commands. There is also little logic in the writ of the European command extending over all of Africa and a good part of the Middle East. The European command should be directed to the defense of Europe. Given the importance of the area, a separate Eastern Mediterranean–Levantine command would clearly seem to be called for. In general, the scope of geographical commands should be limited to areas within which one mission is overwhelmingly dominant.

In some circumstances, services can serve strategic needs more directly. In other circumstances, however, the needs of cooperation will undoubtedly require the assignment of substantial forces from two or more services to a unifed command which can and should be divorced from the services. In such commands, the position of CINC should, like the chairmanship of the Joint Chiefs of Staff, normally be rotated among the participating services. The circumstances that require the creation of a unified command also require that such a command not be the preserve of any particular service. In addition, the CINCs of those commands should have greatly enhanced authority over the forces assigned to them. It is difficult to see what is gained by the services' retaining jurisdiction over such matters as administration, discipline, unit training, and logistics. The unified commander has the responsibility to ensure that the forces under his command are ready to fight and to fight successfully. He should be given the authority commensurate with that responsibility, including the authority to assign officers as he sees fit and to relieve them from command when he deems that necessary.

In some cases, thus, the artificial distinction between operational command and administrative command can be broken down by giving operational as well as administrative command to the services. In other cases, as in Europe, for instance, it can and should be broken down by giving administrative as well as operational command to the CINCs. In all cases, the central need is to recognize that no particular form of unity of command is universally relevant and that the choice in particular circumstances should reflect the mission to be accomplished and the nature of the forces required for that mission.

SUBORDINATING THE SERVICE VIEWPOINT

Militarism has been defined as that "doctrine or system" that, among other things, exalts "an institutional structure—the military establishment" and "accords primacy in state and society to the armed forces."[10] In somewhat parallel fashion, servicism is the doctrine or system that exalts the individual military service and accords it primacy in the military establishment. The individual military services are and will remain indispensible elements in that establishment. Service interests, service needs, and service power, however, have dominated U.S. defense structure, warping and frustrating efforts to establish rational systems of strategic planning, force development, and combat command. The result is, inevitably, an undesirable weakening of the collective military contribution in these areas. In the United States, the military view, as Clausewitz recommended, is kept subordinate to the political view. The service view should, in a similar manner, be kept subordinate to the military view.

The evils of servicism cannot be remedied, however, by any single organizational reform. A variety of measures is needed. The principal organizational proposals suggested in this essay involve three different approaches: in strategic planning, strengthen the authority of the chairman of the Joint Chiefs of Staff; in force development, create mission undersecretaries to represent the basic strategic purposes; and in combat command, orient commands to missions rather than geography, assigning responsibility for some to the services and enhancing the command authority of the CINCs of the others. Changes along these lines clearly will not solve all the organizational problems of the U.S. defense establishment.

Together, however, they will reinforce each other in elevating military needs over service interests, and in bringing defense organization more into line with strategic purpose. In its current incarnation, the U.S. defense establishment dates from World War II. It is middle aged and it shows many of the characteristics of middle age. Like any large bureaucratic structure, it has tended to become top-heavy, overweight, sluggish, and loaded down with activities, offices, installations, and personnel, which may once have been vital to its functioning, but no longer are. So long as there is no shortage of resources for defense, such excrescences can be tolerated. Real constraints on defense will, however, almost inevitably be the dominant theme of the second half of the 1980s. To ensure that priority goes to what is needed for the wars the United States is most likely to fight, or most needs to deter, requires an effective and coherent military voice in the formulation of national strategy, the allocation of resources to forces, programs, and weapons so as rationally to serve strategic purposes, and unified command structures for combat forces relevant to the missions they are to perform. If service needs and service perspectives continue to prevail over national needs and national perspectives, the United States will face grave difficulties meeting future challenges to its vital interests.

NOTES

1. Korb, Lawrence J., *The Joint Chiefs of Staff: The First Twenty-Five Years* (Bloomington: Indiana University Press, 1976), p. 24.
2. Nitze, Paul H., quoted in Piller, Geoffrey, "DOD's Office of International Security Affairs: The Brief Ascendency of an Advisory System," *Political Science Quarterly* 98 (Spring 1983): 65; Blue Ribbon Defense Panel, *Report to the President and the Secretary of Defense on the Department of Defense 1 July 1970* (Washington, D.C.: Government Printing Office, 1970), pp. 126-8: General Lewis Allen, Jr., quoted in *Armed Forces Journal International* 119 (June 1982): 64.
3. Meyer, Edward C., "The JCS—How Much Reform Is Needed?" *Armed Forces Journal International* 119 (April 1982): 86.
4. Byron, John L., "Reorganization of the U.S. Armed Forces," *U.S. Naval Institute Proceedings* 109 (Jan. 1983): 68-75; Halperin, Morton H. and Halperin, David, "The Key West Key." *Foreign Policy* 53 (Winter 1983-84): 114-30.
5. Dean, Alan L., "General Propositions of Organizational Design," in Peter Szanton, ed, *Federal Reorganization: What Have We Learned?* (Chatham, NJ: Chatham House, 1981), p. 138.
6. Blue Ribbon Defense Panel, *Report*, p. 50; Steadman, Richard C., *Report to the Secretary of Defense on the National Military Command Structure* (Washington, D.C.: July 1978), p. 16; see also Cushman, John H., *Command and Control of Theater Forces: Adequacy* (Cambridge: Harvard University, Center for Information Policy Research, Program on Information Resources

Policy, 1983), pp. 3–58. Here and elsewhere I have drawn heavily on General Cushman's penetrating analysis of the history and problems of the unified commands.

7. Jones, David C., "What's Wrong with Our Defense Establishment," *New York Times Magazine* (November 7, 1982): 70.

8. Special Operations Review Group, "Report on the Iranian Rescue Mission," in *Aviation Week & Space Technology* 113 (September 15, 1980): 63–70.

9. Blue Ribbon Defense Panel, *Report*, p. 48: *Report of DOD Commission on Beirut International Airport Terrorist Act*, October 23, 1983 (20 December 1983), p. 55.

10. Radway, Laurence I., "Militarism," in *International Encyclopedia of the Social Sciences* (New York: Macmillan and Free Press, 1968), vol. 10, p. 300.

Chapter 12

The Office of the Secretary of Defense

James Schlesinger

I have chosen to provide some ruminations on the office of the secretary of defense and on how the defense organization looks from the standpoint of that office. As many people know, that office evokes strong passions in some quarters. So I ask you to put aside preconceptions, and be guided by those words from Isaiah which are, perhaps, too painfully familiar to many from the Johnson years: "Come now let us reason together."

My initial observation bears on the nature of American democracy. In the United States, power is more broadly diffused than it is in any other major military nation. That dispersion of power markedly affects the American military establishment. In all nations, to be sure, there inevitably is tension between the military establishment and the political authority. In the United States, however, that tension occurs at many points, and, thereby, is ultimately diluted. Indeed such tensions are forged into a principle: the separation of powers.

In the United States power is widely dispersed, and all of these powers may come back to influence the operation of the Pentagon. There is, first of all, the White House. I refer here not to the commander in chief, but, rather, to the political operatives in the White House. There is the Congress, a steadily growing influence in the last fifteen years, whose overall role now transcends the historic functions of its duly appointed committees. There are the courts, which not only supervise the system of military justice, but are now concerned with such things as the relations between the sexes and the admissions policies of the service academies. In the United States, power is spread across the landscape. The system of checks and balances, fundamental as it may be to the American democracy, markedly detracts, not only from unity of command (save in periods of dire national emergency), but even from the possibility of coherent and consistent policy formation.

The political style of the Republic strongly influences the military establishment, perhaps most notably the Joint Chiefs of Staff (JCS) system. The JCS markedly reflects the dispersion of powers. Indeed, its present character reflects the resistance of the military services to the degree of unification desired by the executive branch. At the time of the 1947 National Security Act, the services (or at least one of the services) turned to the Congress for support in resisting encroachment on its own authority, and, thereby, in preserving the dispersion of power.

As many people will recall, the nominal reason cited in Congress for avoiding the establishment of a general staff was that we did not want to repeat the errors perpetually associated with the general staff of the *Wehrmacht*. But that, of course, was only the nominal reason. The real reason lies in the proclivity of the American Republic to disperse power, and in the prior history of the military establishment, divided as it had been into two separate departments. The Navy was reluctant to join in a fully unified military establishment. It opposed that course of action vigorously and effectively.

The difficulties in a split military establishment had been repeatedly manifested during World War II. Prior to World War II, the absence of unity had not been a serious issue. The niche of each of the services had then been more clearly defined. If the Navy could protect the Army to the point that it could deploy in Europe, as in World War I, the Army could carry on from there. It was only in World War II that the United States, by necessity, had been obliged to embark upon *joint* operations. That, of course, brought the issue of unity to the fore. In addition, the issue of joint operations has become ever more important as the United States has acquired *continuing* and world-wide responsibilities in the postwar period (particularly as America's gross military advantages have steadily declined). However inadequate the outcome, the quest for unification was intended to deal with this emerging postwar problem.

I recall the story of the Baptist farmer who was asked whether he believed in infant baptism. His response was immediate: "Believe in it—why I've seen it with my own eyes!" I use that story to underscore the inadequacy of the existing structure, for I have seen the defects of the JCS system with my own eyes. The built-in checks and balances have served gravely to handicap the performance of the JCS system. That system stands as a monument to the incompleteness of unification. It is also, therefore, a monument to the denial of the principle of unity of command. I have always found it both remarkable and ironical that many of those who attend the war colleges and who have been indoctrinated in the principle of unity of command will come back from those colleges and proceed to defend the existing JCS system.

If we are to achieve effective unity of command for the nation's forces, further reform of the JCS system is mandatory. I should emphasize, however, that while much of the criticism of the system is quite valid, there is no criticism intended of those many able men who have served within the system. All — or almost all — have been good men attempting to do an effective job under conditions of severe limitations.

RELATIONS WITH THE JCS

It is not my intention to spend a great deal of time on the JCS system and its defects. Nonetheless, understanding the limitations of the JCS system is a prerequisite to understanding the key role that is now played by the secretary of defense. The intermittent strengthening of that office is, in part, a reflection of failure to achieve complete unification. The role of the secretary of defense consequently goes beyond those activities that would normally fall to a minister of defense. The office becomes the focal point of the *collective* DOD effort — including some military functions. With the exception of the chairman of the JCS and his personal staff (of three), the secretary becomes not only the symbol of unification, but its principal patron. He, along with the chairman, becomes the source of unity and effectiveness in joint operations.

In brief, the secretary of defense and his office, the OSD, have become the focus of the DOD. The irony is that those who have sought to protect the services have, no doubt inadvertently, contributed enormously to the growing role of the office of secretary of defense. The jealously guarded perogatives of the individual services have led to the very great civilian eminence in military matters that the uniformed military certainly did not desire.

The upshot is that the secretary of defense regularly ignores the advice that comes up through the JCS system. David Jones has referred to such recommendations as the "pablum" that comes up from below. Indeed, one of the most remarkable contrasts in the Pentagon is the different behavior of the service chiefs in their corporate capacity, on the one hand, and in their individual or service capacity, on the other. In their service roles, the chiefs are normally forced to be responsible because of the budget limitations that they must straightforwardly deal with. Much sage advice can be obtained from service heads in their individual roles. It is only when they all come together in their corporate capacity that the breeding ground for irresponsibility is created.

No one should conclude that the organizational problems of the department of defense are confined to the JCS system. Any examination of the DOD's organizational chart reveals numerous anomalies that militate against efficient decisionmaking. The organization chart includes incongruous appendages, that would never appear on a corporate chart. These, too, reflect the checks and balances of the American system. Furthermore, every once in a while, Congress throws in an additional assistant secretary to satisfy some constituency group or to deal, purportedly through legislation, with some substantive problem. All in all, it forces one to recall Samuel Johnson's comment about the dog walking on its hind legs: it is not that he does it well, it is remarkable that he does it at all.

The incongruities that exist in the organizational structure are, however, considerably eased by the subformal and informal systems that actually permit the Pentagon to work. These subformal systems must be continually borne in mind, whenever one considers the necessity for reform. For such systems mean, first, that reform may not be as much required, as one would infer from the formal system, and, second, one must take care in any reform that one does not do damage to these useful subformal systems.

There are many, many systems of communications that truly reflect the reality of organizational politics and are operationally indispensable. Nonetheless, they are not included on the organization chart, indeed, they may be legislatively excluded. For example, the Air Force chief of staff is concerned with the creation and support of the forces, but is explicitly excluded from the chain of command. Nonetheless, if the U.S. organizes an airlift to Israel, that explanation does not reveal the underlying realities. In theory, orders go down through the chairman to the military airlift command (MAC). In practice, anyone who might believe that the chief of the staff of the Air Force is not indispensable to the entire process is under a misapprehension. In 1973, for example, the then chief of staff, George Brown, was critically involved in the organization of the airlift, even though he was nominally excluded from the chain of command that went from the chairman to the commander of MAC. When one looks at the DOD's organization chart, one may be astonished or appalled, but one is still missing something. It is very important to reflect on these subformal and informal systems that mitigate the deficiencies that one can see in the formal organization structure.

RESPONSIBILITIES VERSUS POWERS

The overall responsibility of the secretary of defense is to relate U.S. policy objectives, as established through the National Security Council (NSC) system, to the development, the sustaining, and the deployment of forces. That overall responsibility is broken down into specific tasks that are assigned to the secretary — tasks that I shall now outline. One should recognize, however, that there are no sharp lines — that all these tasks, to some extent, overlap. Broadly speaking, these tasks are divided into the categories of organizational, operational, and other responsibilities.

Foremost in the operational category is the development and articulation of strategy and the associated deployment of forces. In this connection, the secretary of defense, acting on behalf of the president, tends, along with the chairman, to be the principal advocate of force readiness. The services are far more uneven in their support for readiness. Whenever budget money is generous, the services can be enthusiastic about readiness. Yet, if the pursuit of readiness is going to interfere with procurement programs, readiness is likely to suffer in the service's budget submissions. Those in Washington, furthest from the deployed forces in the field, tend to be more partial to procurement. It is the secretary of defense who must weigh in to protect readiness money.

As part of his operational responsibilities, the secretary is primarily responsible for political and military affairs. In this role he becomes a major guardian of alliance relations. Those relations have become increasingly important as the gross military advantages of the United States have declined. In the fifties or the sixties, when the United States could hold the Soviet Union at bay simply by threatening to retaliate with its own nuclear forces, alliance relations could be kept low key. However, the defense of the free world now depends upon some minimal degree of consensus between the United States and its principal allies. The preservation of an effective conventional and overall deterrent for Western Europe depends on the health of those relations. In alliance relations, quite frequently the secretary of defense must play a larger role than does the secretary of state. One final point regarding the political–military responsibilities of the secretary (to which I will later return) is that the secretary of defense must establish the political framework — the context within which military operations are either prospectively or actually carried out.

Let me now turn from the operational to the organizational tasks. While several of the secretarial tasks can be described as critical, in terms of visibility and impact, budget formulation is second to none in importance. The budget is where it all comes together. It is the presumption (perhaps *hope* would be a better word) that the budget will reflect and carry forward the strategy that has been adopted. This requires unremitting effort and attention. Regrettably, the reality is frequently different from the expectation.

Broadly speaking, in allocating available resources, we are looking at tradeoffs amongst three factors: force structure, readiness, and modernization. When budgets are rising, the question of allocation should not be too painful. When, however, budgets are shrinking, the problem of allocation becomes increasingly painful. Indeed, this can occur even with rising budgets, when aspirations are rising even more rapidly. The temptation will always be to skimp on readiness; it remains the secretary's responsibility to resist that temptation. More generally, the problem for the department is that modernization can readily encroach upon the resources required to maintain the force structure or, above all, to maintain the forces in an ade-

quate readiness posture. One may surmise that the DOD will face this problem in the next two years, as the mortgages for extensive modernization
begin to fall due. It seems likely now that both force structure and force
readiness will suffer.

Beyond the problem of budget formulation, the secretary is responsible
for overall administration and coordination of the DOD. This includes
some obligation for keeping the DOD a relatively harmonious whole. That,
however, is easier said than done, for it cuts against the grain of some of his
other responsibilities. Hard decisions tend to detract from harmony, particularly when there is overall budgetary pressure. Nobody in the department of defense, especially the Navy and the Air Force, would wish a repetition of the explosion of 1949. As a consequence, many possible decisions,
which would seem logically sound, will, nonetheless, be avoided, simply for
the purpose of maintaining peace within the family. Bob McNamara was,
perhaps, the most notable example of a secretary prepared primarily to
follow his own logic, even at the cost of the internal harmony of the department. As a consequence, he may have pressed his luck too far. Nonetheless,
it was McNamara himself who observed: "One can only slay so many
dragons each day."

In the organizational area the secretary has a responsibility for personnel.
This includes approval of proposed candidates for three or four stars. It
also includes selection of prospective chiefs and major commanders, and
the forwarding of such recommendations to the White House. In different
administrations, the role of the secretary with respect to such promotions
may vary considerably.

Finally, it should be noted that operational and organizational responsibilities are supposed to be tied together by the secretary through the issuance of the policy guidance. Once again, this may be more hope than
reality: it is not certain that this occurs.

The secretary has *other* responsibilities. In a democracy, public relations
is vastly important. Much of the secretary's time is devoted to gathering
support for the department's activities. The secretary has overall responsibility for congressional relations. With the decline of the public authority
of the services and the chiefs over the years, the responsibility for congressional relations has become increasingly heavy. Congressional oversight has
become increasingly detailed. Consequently, congressional relations now
include the selling of the defense budget (call it proselytizing, if you wish),
the overseas deployment of various forces, the lobbying for specific
weapons systems that have become controversial, or the sale of weapons
systems to those allies who may not enjoy universal support on Capitol Hill.
This was clearly the case in regard to the sale of the AWACS to the Saudis.
Frequently, in such matters, the department will require White House or
even presidential support.

The secretary is also responsible for both White House relations and executive branch relations. This includes maintaining support across the river, down through both the White House and the OMB, for the activities and financing of the department.

These matters are simply the broader and weightier responsibilities of the secretary. In addition, he is obliged to pay attention to all sorts of details. These include such diverse matters as the number of positive indications in urinalysis for the forces deployed in Europe, striptease dancers on the foredeck of nuclear submarines in Hampton Roads, the reception of black colonels in Latin America and how their services handled such reactions, or homosexuality among commanding officers on U.S. Navy ships (a recent issue). These issues are specific and apparently less a responsibility. Nonetheless, such issues are the ones that can be most painful in public relations. It is the little things that kill you.

Let me offer two comments, now that I have arrayed this long list of the secretary's responsibilities. First, although the responsibilities are very imposing, they are not matched by the powers of the office. Those powers are not awe inspiring. To some extent it is like the office of the president. The office provides the secretary simply with a *license to persuade* outside parties. Even within the building, quite frequently, it is only a license to persuade. The powers of the office, not particularly awesome in themselves, have become even less suited to the fulfillment of the department's mission, as America's gross advantages in international competition have declined. When all one had to do was to threaten massive retaliation, persuasion was relatively easy — most clearly with one's prospective opponent, but also with one's allies and even within the country. It is both ironical and worrisome that, as America's gross advantages have declined, checks and balances have steadily increased. For example, congressional oversight (or meddling) is not likely to recede.

The upshot is that the overall system that sustains the department of defense has been deteriorating. I am not here talking about budget support. I am speaking of the overall political system that sustains the department. In the past, the powers of the secretary of defense may have been adequate in relation to his responsibilities. The question at the present time is whether or not they continue to be adequate.

My second comment regarding a secretary's responsibilities is somewhat more diffuse. One ought not generalize about the very different men who have served as secretary. They have had their own, and rather different, preferences, and they have had rather different skills as well. Some were generally talented; some had specific talents; some had no talents at all. In the latter case, the Pentagon system must effectively compensate for the defects of the secretary.

More generally, the system should take advantage of the secretary's strengths and build around his weaknesses. For example, Melvin Laird was extraordinarily good at congressional relations. He was one of their own. Indeed, he could be sufficiently good on the Hill to build backfires against orders from the White House or from the national security advisor. In my opinion, Harold Brown was simply superb in those things for which he had an affinity: research and development; evaluation of technology and its role; procurement; weapon systems analysis; and budget formation (aside from the fact that Jimmy Carter gave him insufficient funds). Harold loved to attend to these specific and detailed responsibilities. In simple truth, with the resources that he was given, Harold Brown was probably without peer. However, on other matters, such as deployments, alliance relations, and so on, he did not have a similar feel.

Robert McNamara was extremely good in the overall construction of the department. Even those who decry McNamara must still, even today, pay tribute to the PPB system. McNamara believed in and allowed logic to drive policy, to an extent that was admirable in a sense, but not entirely suited to this world. This was most clearly indicated in our relations with our European allies, when he generated long and, to some extent, unnecessary controversy over nuclear deterrence and alliance strategy. During the Vietnam years, some wag observed that McNamara was a great secretary of defense and a poor secretary of war. Perhaps there was some truth in that observation, but it points to a more general proposition: the inevitable variability of talent even in the most exceptional men. Perhaps the final point to be recognized is that the list of secretarial responsibilities is so imposing that no single individual can totally fulfill them all.

SALIENT ELEMENTS OF THE OFFICE

I turn now from a simple outline of the responsibilities to a deeper exploration of what I shall call the salient elements of the office. Of such elements, the first is *fixing strategy*. Especially important is the role of the secretary in determining doctrine and strategy for the use of nuclear weapons. That role reflects an environment in which the uniformed military have not been particularly perceptive regarding the radical changes wrought by nuclear weapons, not only in military calculations, but, more importantly, in the political environment. That environment explains the necessity of arms control negotiations or, if not arms control negotiations, at least the appearance of arms control negotiations. Nuclear weapons have raised political control from the level of desirability to the level of necessity. Consequently, the secretary is obliged to establish nuclear strategy. Since the late fifties, all secretaries have done so. Prior to that it was Secretary Dulles who articulated strategy, in "massive retaliation" and, later, in the more selective employment of nuclear weapons "at times and in places of our own choosing." (The early years of the Eisenhower Administration until Secretary Gates were not the high point for the office of secretary of defense. This reflected Eisenhower's own role and experience and the fact that he served, to a large extent, as his own secretary of defense.)

One way or another, any serious changes in nuclear doctrine — as opposed to a continuation of the existing routine — will have to come from the secretary of defense. It was McNamara who, after some flirtation with damage limiting, introduced mutual assured destruction (MAD). I myself moved sharply away from mutual assured destruction and emphasized selective strikes and city avoidance. In large degree this reflected my years at RAND. I had found mutual assured destruction politically and intellectually defective, particularly in its impact on alliance responsibilities, and dubious in terms of its morality.

Let me provide several cautionary notes. Perhaps I could start with a reminiscence regarding General Abrams, who, while sitting in my office one day, observed:

> The secretary of defense is up there on the bridge, enjoying the splendid view of the horizon and his authority to give orders. So he's signaling, "hard rudder left, hard rudder right" — and he thinks he's making some dramatic changes. What he forgets is that there are a lot of people down in the engine room who are simply getting seasick.

Some secretaries are simply not very good at the task of fixing strategy. When they are obliged to perform that role, the results can be unfortunate. I know of no cure for this problem, other than to leave existing doctrine in place. The major source of the difficulty is a lack of professionalism or a desire to placate domestic opinion — regrettably, if these defects are understood by others, at the cost of the effectiveness of deterrence. The least negative cost of such activities is strategic doctrine that is both unconvincing and amusing.

As part of the process of maintaining deterrence, the United States will elaborate a declaratory posture, normally enunciated by the secretary of defense. At present, this implies nuclear response in the event that the conventional forces of the Warsaw Pact overwhelm NATO, even as we back away from the notion of mutually assured destruction. But some cautions are in order here. There are three, quite separate elements: the declaratory posture, the war plans, and the capabilities of the weapons systems. These three elements do not have to coincide. Indeed, there may be considerable inconsistency among them. For example, when Bob McNamara was talking about mutual assured destruction, one should recall that the overwhelming majority of our weapons was directed against Soviet military targets, not against urban centers. The war plans diverged quite markedly from our declaratory posture. Similar gaps may occur with regard to the capabilities of the weapons systems. There has been a great deal of talk about counterforce over the years, for example. This may be reflected both in our declaratory posture and in our targeting doctrine (war plans). Nonetheless, the weapons in the inventory may not be able to destroy the targets. Thus, even when a strategy is publicly enunciated by the secretary, one should be cautious about whether that strategy can, indeed, be implemented. Declaratory posture is intended to affect the attitudes of both potential foes and allies. Although it may make a public splash, it is not necessarily implementable. One should always bear in mind that simple admonition in Clausewitz's *On War*: "In strategy then, everything is simple, but not, on that account, easy."

My final cautionary note involves the tendency, for reasons of domestic politics, to indulge in what is needless and counterproductive rhetoric regarding overall strategy. We have had too much of that in recent years. Too much effort has, for example, been invested in a fanciful debate over whether or not the one-and-a half war strategy (following the two-and-a-half war strategy) has been unduly constraining. The argument goes that we should not be so constrained, but prepared to fight *anywhere*. One might even agree with this underlying aspiration. Nonetheless, the reality at the present time is that we are not prepared to fight more than one war. Indeed, there is serious doubt whether we could fight even that one war on a non-nuclear basis. The very units that are committed to NATO reinforcement are also committed to the Middle East. When one is faced with such real world problems, it seems almost escapist fantasy to indulge in rhetorical extravagancies about whether our doctrine should limit us to one-and-a-half wars. (Incidentally, the move from the two-and-a-half war doctrine to the one-and-a-half war doctrine during the Nixon Administration simply registered the fact that China was no longer to be regarded as a prospective enemy.)

The second salient responsibility of the secretary is to establish the *political framework* within which the military must operate. This is, of course, closely related to the issue of strategy. National policy cannot be based on military considerations alone. For example, the strategy of arms control — to say nothing of detente — was not fully embraced even by the relatively enlightened military establishment of the 1970s. How much harder would it have been for, say, General LeMay to accept the political constraints embodied in the pursuit of arms control. The mutual acceptance of such limitations was simply too foreign to the Air Force thinking of the fifties and sixties. Nonetheless, it is simply a fact of life that the military, either in choosing weapons or in making war plans, must operate within the context of a political framework set from outside. It is only the national command authority, the president, and the secretary of defense, who can establish that political framework.

In the wake of Grenada, there has been a lot of chatter — in *Wall Street*

Journal editorials, for example—that finally we have taken responsibility for making decisions away from weak-kneed civilians and have given it back to the military men who can decide upon and carry out the right military actions. There is an eager belief in the efficacy of "letting military commanders do their own thing." Indeed, Secretary Weinberger has said quite recently: "I would not dream of overruling a military commander." Whether or not he dreams about doing such a thing is immaterial, so long as he actually would do it when required.

Much of this is just some more misreading of the so-called lessons of Vietnam. Let me underscore a few things about the need for a suitable political framework. The indispensible first point is that there is no reponsible and serious alternative to the careful creation of a political framework for the military. In matters of arms control this is, of course, axiomatic. It has also been implicit in all arrangements regarding nuclear release authority since the passage of the Atomic Energy Act. Such a political framework would apply to any use of nuclear weapons in time of war. This has been quite explicit, at least since the establishment of the various Single Integrated Operational Plan (SIOP) options for the president. Since the priority of political decision is so obvious in the case of nuclear weapons, I pass on to other episodes that exemplify the need for an effective political framework to provide for nonnuclear military forces.

It is not too long since we in this country had the opportunity to observe and react to a Soviet experience in allowing the military to determine their own rules of engagement. I refer, of course, to the shooting down of the KAL jetliner. Within the Soviet system of air defense, that outcome was quite logical and almost inevitable. Nonetheless, the Soviet Union has paid an enormously high political price for letting their military commanders do their own thing.

In this context, however, it is most important to consider our own reactions to the Soviets' allowing rules of engagement to be established on the basis of military considerations. I emphasize the KAL jetliner story because, here in the United States, the very people who have been most enthusiastic about getting rid of the civilian overlay and the political framework and letting military commanders do their own thing have been the most critical of the Soviet Union for its inflexibility and brutality in this incident.

At the time that Vietnam fell in 1975, I am sure that some will recall how strong was the disposition among our military to re-engage one way or another in South Vietnam. Many had invested a substantial part of their lives in attempting to maintain the independence of South Vietnam and they felt, quite strongly: "We can't let those bastards get away with *this*." The only problems with re-engagement, however, were that, first, it was against the law and, second, speaking politically in the light of prior experience, the United States had no reason—at least in my judgment—to get on that tar baby once again. In that troubled period much of my own efforts were devoted to heading off the instinctive response of our people who wanted to help and had forgotten the clear dictates of the law. I cite this experience, once again, because it indicates so clearly that the political framework has to be set and maintained by the civilian leaders at the Pentagon.

In the Mayaguez incident, after the American captives had been released by the Cambodians, it was necessary to give a direct order to the Commander in Chief, Pacific Command (CINPAC) to abandon his goal of overrunning Cambodian defenses on Koh-Ta. Whenever U.S. forces are engaged, the instinctive reaction is not to seek the political objective, but, rather, a military victory. Indeed, the inculcated reaction is to destroy one's opponents' military forces. It was quite clear to me at the time that the purpose of the engagement of U.S. military forces was simply to extract our people from Cambodia, and to provide a lesson for the Cambodians and others. But that political objective was lost sight of by one of our military leaders as the engagement wore on. It is not my intention, retrospectively, to chide him for an oversight. Rather, it is my intention to point out that even in these lesser contests, it is indispensible that the political framework be established by civilian leaders.

I close on this point by observing that the Grenada incident should not be taken, as some in the press have implied, as an indication of the ease and appropriateness of turning such matters over to the military. It is not a clear example which reverses the fundamental truths that I have outlined regarding the need for a political framework. Grenada was a case in which there was very little military opposition. In that case, the problem of dealing with one's allies was simply to cope with their reactions, not all of which can be said to be uniformly supportive. The simplicity and ease of the Grenada operation meant that the political constraints could be minimal. It does not vitiate the need for establishing coherence in a military operation through political guidelines. One should not conclude from the Grenadian example, that we could go back to a world that never existed, indeed, a world that exists only as the inverse of what was supposed to have happened in Vietnam.

Let me turn to my third salient element: how the secretary of defense influences the *military setting*. In this connection, I reiterate that the secretary of defense, backed up by the chairman and by the CINCs, must be the patron of readiness. When the services are driven to choose, they will, too frequently, choose either to maintain force structure or to achieve modernization over readiness. Thus, the secretary of defense will be obliged to insist on such "novel" principles as the need to "keep your powder dry" or, alternatively, to "get there fustest with the mostest." Such principles are, of course, not a novelty to field commanders; but in the quest for resources within the service bureaucracy, they can readily be shunted aside.

In a crisis, the secretary of defense should insist that the military professionals be responsible for setting military plans. There should be a rebuttable presumption in favor of the professionals, and they should be overruled *only* when there are clear political requirements to the contrary. The military should be responsible for the design and execution of the plan for dealing with the crisis. A wise secretary will keep that enormous host of aspiring field marshals — the logisticians, budgeteers, systems analysts, engineers, scientists, and the like, all those who want to have the fun of becoming a field marshal — well to the background in such a crisis.

The crisis distinctly sharpens the advice that comes up from the JCS. It is not the usual — what does one say? — "pablum". The circumstances focus the mind and thereby mitigate the deficiencies of the JCS system to which I referred earlier. In a crisis, the services, to a large extent, abandon the intramural sports that normally take place inside the Pentagon. Nevertheless, the response in a crisis could still be substantially improved through the reform of the JCS by further reducing service logrolling.

One should realize, of course, that debilitating logrolling can also come from the outside — from civilians. Too much shaving of the military plans for political reasons quite frequently results in disaster. The Bay of Pigs is but one relatively recent example of this point. In order to make Ambassador Stevenson happy, essential air strikes were cancelled. This may have spared the ambassador further bouts with his conscience, but the simple consequence was that any chance for the success of the Bay of Pigs operation was lost.

I would have thought that such an episode would remain a clear reminder to the political authorities that they should be extremely careful about cancelling air strikes. Nonetheless, all that was forgotten during the Mayaguez episode. After the removal of the American captives from the island, the only leverage the United States had was the threat to inflict punishment on Cambodia if the regime failed to return the captives. Nonetheless, for some mysterious reason, during the twenty minutes in which the secretary of defense was driven from the Pentagon to the White House for dinner, the White House cancelled the air strikes directed against Cambodia. After my arrival at the White House, I succeeded in getting the second and later strikes restored. Of course, the initial strike could not be belatedly restored. To put it mildly, the officers in the NMCC had been bemused by the sudden alternation of the plans by the White House. Only the restoration of the air strikes permitted the Mayaguez rescue operation to be successful.

William Y. Smith has told us that the military are the most reluctant to use force. I remind him that his initial statement, rapidly corrected, that the military were the least reluctant to use force, which I called a Freudian slip, was essentially correct. To be sure, the military are quite reluctant to have *recourse to force.* They are distinctly reluctant, for example, to put fourteen hundred Marines into Beirut, for they recognize that such a lodgment puts both the United States and the handful of Marines into a position in which, as the Soviets would say, the correlation of forces is adverse to us. Nonetheless, when the United States does decide to have recourse to force, the military are then most willing to use that force. Quite correctly, they are not inclined to shave the use of force for political purposes—particularly for domestic political purposes.

PROBLEMS IN BUDGET MAKING

Let me turn now to those salient responsibilities of the secretary of defense that fall outside of the operational area. It has always seemed to me that one of the most significant roles of the secretary is to establish incentives to which the services respond. Sometimes these incentives are established unwittingly, even haphazardly. Far better is it explicitly to face the issue of incentives, so that they can be consciously considered and consciously designed. Such decisions go far beyond the daily routine.

When McNamara introduced the PPB system within the Pentagon, he proceeded to use that system for a purpose not inherent in it. He determined precisely the force structure for the services. Yet, when he prescribed force structure, he created an overwhelming incentive for the services to drive up per-unit costs. Their goal, no doubt, was to get as much capability as one could into each force unit. Yet, by driving up per-unit costs, it moved us further along the road, later caricatured, of a military establishment ultimately consisting of one aircraft, one ship, and one tank. When the Army was told that it had sixteen divisions, it had an incentive to add support units to the divisions, to increase personnel and equipment. The budgetary incentives precluded the Navy from saying that it could get one-and-a-half cheaper carriers for the price of one large carrier, or the Air Force from saying that it could, through economizing on tactical air wings, get two additional ones for the same budget total. The services feared that if they designed cheaper capabilities they would simply lose resources.

In my years at the bureau of the budget, I had pondered those pernicious effects on service incentives, and had advocated that resources, rather than force structure, be frozen. So, when I became secretary of defense, I attempted to cure the problem as I saw it. The services were informed, somewhat to their disbelief, that we were not going to determine force structure. It was the service responsibility, and opportunity, to extract as much as possible out of the prescribed resources. If the service could increase force structure, it would be protected. The secretary of defense, under those circumstances, had a direct obligation to protect service resources from the "enemy"; that is, from the office of management and budget, the Congress, and, perhaps, even from the systems analysis office.

In the services there was considerable skepticism. The Army comptroller assured General Abrams that he should not trust any commitment that I made; intentionally or not, it was just a device to cut the Army budget. General Abrams decided to accept the bureaucratic risk. I indicated that we freeze personnel at the 785,000 level. If he could field additional combat units from obsolete, redundant, or marginal support activities, he would have my steady support and protection. The arrangements with General Abrams, sometimes described in the Army as the "golden handshake," became the basis for moving from thirteen to sixteen divisions.

Similar opportunities were created for the Air Force and the Navy, notably those involving the lightweight fighter competition. George Brown, who had become a devotee of the F-15 while at systems command, never saw much attraction in cost–quantity tradeoffs with the F-16. His successor as Air Force chief of staff, General David Jones, did some shrewd bargaining along the lines of the "golden handshake." He said, in effect: "The price, sir, is four additional tactical airwings," It was the introduction of the F-16—at roughly half the cost of the F-15—that permitted the expansion to twenty-six wings. However, we were not equivalently successful with the Navy. The Navy took the F-18 (successor to the YF-17), which was intended to be a low-cost fighter like the F-16, and ran the cost above that of the F-14, seemingly chasing the costs of the B-1. Indeed, since the departure of Admiral Zumwalt, the Navy has had little apparent interest in the high-low mix.

I, myself, believe it critical to proffer appropriate incentives to the services that are maintained over time. Failure of the services to accept the logic of cost–quantity tradeoffs should not be rewarded. That is, no doubt, a splendid principal, but it requires consistency over successive administrations, and it also requires the agreement of Congress. The services may be prepared to wait. In the long run, the Navy did not suffer much for its failures regarding the lightweight fighter and other cost-effective tradeoffs, even though it had to wait several administrations. The Army has had one notable experience that was similar. In 1974, the Army was instructed to acquire a low altitude air defense system, cheaply, from overseas. The Army chose the Roland. This decision went down rather badly with the managers of the Army procurement system, something like the introduction of a foreign organ into the host body. The usual antibodies were produced, ultimately leading to the rejection of the foreign system. The Army Americanized the system; it wasted an immense amount of money; and, finally, under a new secretary of defense, it got rid of the Roland in 1981. Although I do not wish to go into a system of rewards and punishments, I do not believe that the Army should be rewarded for what was essentially a parochial action.

I earlier touched upon the responsibility of the secretary of defense as the patron of "jointness" in the military establishment, along with the chairman and the CINCs, however feeble their powers may be in dealing with the component commands. In supporting "jointness," it is essential to establish the appropriate incentives regarding personnel. Say, for example, that twenty percent of those in a particular grade are promoted, then a slightly higher percentage of those in joint staff duty should be included. The effect would be to establish a powerful incentive within the system so that the services, whatever their reluctance, cannot fail to send their better people into joint staff positions. One must, of course, recognize that if service resistance is really entrenched, it cannot be overcome. Incentives may be helpful, but against entrenched resistance such incentives become mere gimmickry. If resistance is entrenched, it may be necessary to consider changing the chiefs of each of the services.

One final thought: I have long felt that one could encourage better integration of the services under a CINC by combining the intelligence activities of all three services under the one CINC. I once ran such an experiment under CINPAC, though I have not checked how well it worked in retrospect. Nonetheless, the effect of such actions is not only to provide better intelligence, in my judgment, but also to give the CINC much greater leverage in dealing with component commands.

Now let me turn to budget formulation, for it remains a preeminent responsibility of the secretary. There is a fundamental problem in budget making and it is getting worse. Of the discretionary resources of the U.S. Government, some ninety percent now goes to the department of defense. As everything other than entitlements payments, interest payments, and defense outlays diminish, that figure tends to rise. Given the distressing inflexibility of that number, and the nature of our decisionmaking processes, the support for Pentagon programs becomes inherently unstable. If one seeks to get the budget total down, there is now only one major source of discretionary spending: defense. That is the heart of the problem. The defense comptroller may decry the "midnight raids" of the Office of Management and Budget. For lack of alternatives, however, the OMB is driven to those midnight raids. Similarly, if Congress wishes to protect or increase social spending, there is only one serious source of funding.

Members of Congress increasingly learn more of the defects of Pentagon decisionmaking. Themselves past masters at tactical maneuvering, they understand full well the anomalous character of many of the outcomes in the Pentagon. Members of Congress have learned a good deal about the vested interests within the department. They are familiar with the various establishments — the research and development establishment, the health establishment, the nuclear establishment, etc. — even before they get into the parochial interests of the individual services. They may have heard Secretary of the Navy Lehman brag that he has now so arranged it that it will cost the United States Government more to cancel the new carriers than to actually construct them. Given all this knowledge, Congress has become increasingly wary. Congress also knows that all the tradeoffs in the budget request have been made on the basis of an overall number we recognize to be invalid. Congress recognizes, as well, the cobbling together of service programs. Such cobbling is unsustainable in the long run, simply because the mortgages resulting from the many modernization programs are so high that they would unduly squeeze the readiness and force structure components of the budget.

If one wishes significantly to improve the performance of congressional budget review, one must, at minimum, provide the Congress with serious and well-constructed material at the outset. I concede that the present system works quite poorly. That, too, is a reflection of checks and balances. There are too many field marshals on Capitol Hill and in the press, as well as in the Pentagon. The net result is the creation of side payments for almost everybody and a serious diminution in the defense capabilities in relation to what we spend. In recent years, Congress has drastically reordered the submissions of the DOD. Two years ago, in the research and development account, Congress reordered $4.8 billion out of a total of $13.6 billion; in the aircraft and missile account $9.4 out of $94 billion, and so on. How can one run a rational program on this basis? I do not know; but I do know that the initial step in the cure must be the reestablishment of congressional trust. I can state that only as a principle. I do not know how to execute it.

Finally, let me say a few words about the deficiencies of the weapons acquisition process as it influences the effectiveness of spending. The procurement system cries out for substantial, even radical, reform. The system has been undergoing steady deterioration since the 1950s. The upshot of this is that the U.S. Government now expends enormous resources, in both time and money, in buying paper from the weapons vendors, who are, themselves, uneasy about the process. Yet, so long as the U. S. Government is prepared to spend money to buy paper, the vendors will be prepared to provide that paper.

The requirements process does not permit efficient weapons acquisition. A major source of the problem is the Request for Proposals (RFPs) and the responses that they generate. By the time one gets through the RFP process, much of the damage is done, and the service is, in all probability, locked into costs that are outrageously high. I say outrageously high with some care. Let me point to one specific example: Northrup's development of the F-5 for the international market. Northrup asserted that it preferred not to sell to the Air Force, for if it had had to develop and produce the F-5 under Air Force procurement regulations, the cost per unit would have been twice as high as otherwise. Anyone familiar with, among other things, the 375 manuals, will find such assertions compelling. The 375 manuals prevent, at immense cost, the repetition of past developmental errors, by substantially augmenting the cost of future developments. Yet, something akin to the 375 manuals, with all their costs, is made virtually inevitable by the system of congressional oversight.

If we are significantly to improve the weapons acquisition process, we require a substantial reform of the procurement system. That is a high priority for this nation. But, in addition, the services must increasingly accept the logic of cost–quantity trade offs. They must be prepared to forget nice but unnecessary capabilities (particularly at the edge of the state of the art) that add only marginally to performance, and excessively to cost. To keep the services aware of cost–quantity tradeoffs, however, it is necessary to establish a firm and productive system of incentives, as I discussed earlier. Many of the defects of the system were developed not by the Congress, but in response to attitudes and actions taken by Congress. As our budget problems grow, the procurement process increasingly cries out for reform.

SOME SUGGESTIONS FOR REFORMS

It seems appropriate to me to close on some areas that seem ripe for reform. I am only a qualified believer in reform. Machinery alone cannot do the task. Yet, improved machinery can substantially ease the task and channel energies into more productive areas. In matters such as weapons aquisition, the machinery makes it almost impossible to do the task well, save in special cases of good luck.

A topical—and priority—area for reform is the structure of the Joint Chiefs of Staff. On this subject I have made my views known in congressional testimony. In brief, however, I believe that it is better to change by evolution, rather than by more radical surgery. Therefore, I support the type of reforms suggested by David Jones, giving the chairman greater authority and increasing his control over the joint staff. I very strongly favor the creation of a deputy to the chairman, most importantly to provide continuity in crisis. I do not accept General Smith's judgment that the problem within the Pentagon is the budget, not the organization —that is, that the OSD cuts without adequate military input. I believe that the chiefs have been plagued by declining authority for a long time. Unless there is change, I do not see how their authority can be rebuilt. Some have objected to the strengthening of the chairman's role because it would dilute the authority of the secretary of defense. This seems to me to be quite small minded and defensive. A stronger chairman can help get all sorts of things done. The secretary of defense has more than enough to do; a stronger chairman would enable him to see that more gets done.

A second area for reform is the internal budgetary process within the Pentagon. The *process itself dominates all thinking*. Following the routine in developing the budget now requires so much time and energy that, unless one has exceptional individuals in mind, the routine precludes adequate attention to longer-range strategic problems. Happily, this area for reform is the easiest to accomplish. As a start, one should consider combining the programming process and the budgeting process into a simultaneous consideration of these matters.

A third, and very popular area for reform is the office of the secretary of defense itself. Criticism of the OSD is fashionable with those who do not wish to face up to more serious problems, particularly to the incompleteness of the unification process. The OSD should not be scapegoated because it has frequently been forced to take on responsibilities that are not effectively discharged elsewhere in the system. Much of the service oriented criticism comes from the members of the armed services committees. It has abated somewhat in the last fifteen years. Some of those criticisms amount to the philosophy of decentralization, best summarized by one officer who said, "decentralize down to my level; centralize below my level." I would agree that there have been too many cases of micromanagement of the services by the OSD. Such micromanagement should be eliminated, but that scarcely justifies the more general criticism of the OSD.

Measures can be taken for the organizational strengthening of the OSD. I would urge that the senior staff increasingly be made professional with long-term commitments. (These are very easy things for nonpoliticians to urge.) The effect would be to take away many of the senior jobs at the Pentagon from the political brokers who use defense as just another political reward system. Loyalty, rather than political ties, should be made the basis of their careers. Appointments should be for terms of ten to fifteen years. In effect, this would move us closer to the British system.

This would permit us to cut senior civilian appointments across the broad, avoiding considerable duplication and permitting greater efficiency. The OSD and the service secretariats could thus be used as an example of a new drive for great efficiency. But such action would require a self-denying ordinance on the part of Congress, and of other elements in the executive branch. Congress would have to limit its inclination to establish new assistant secretaries of defense to deal either with pressing constituency groups or new and noteworthy problems. The White House power brokers would no longer be able to use defense as a system of political plums and rewards, and the president would have to sacrifice what Lyndon Johnson so elegantly defined as "jobs for slobs."

The final area that dramatically calls out for reform is procurement. We must increase the flexibility in the procurement system and go back towards the system of the early fifties. We must eliminate the rigidities that are now introduced through the lengthy Request for Proposal (RFP) process. We must reduce the amount of money and time invested in the vast production of paper that remains unread. Indeed, we must unleash the creativity of the defense industry, rather than attempting to channel it in predetermined ways at great cost and loss of prospective effectiveness. If we are to have radical reform, however, the cooperation, indeed, the sponsorship, of Congress is indispensable. There will be no serious reform of the procurement system until Congress alters the present system of second-guessing that is embodied in congressional review.

This is a brief agenda for reform. Nonetheless, it is a demanding one. Action is demanded of us; not more talk. The U.S. position in the world has eroded over the last fifteen years. It continues to erode. As our overall military advantages have declined vis-a-vis the Russians, we would be wise to compensate for that decline through more efficient creation and utilization of our forces. That requires reform. Time is getting short if we are to preserve the postwar structure of international politics.

It was Bismarck who reportedly said that "God takes care of fools, drunkards, and the United States of America." Let us impose less of the responsibility for our international position on God and more on ourselves.

Chapter 13

The JCS – Views of Participants

Chairman's Special Study Group*

THE VIEWS OF THE PROFESSIONALS

Historical Perspectives

The difficulties encountered in forging several military services into a coherent joint force without threatening their traditions and independence were recognized by professionals long ago, and rather succinctly. In a 1942 letter to Winston Churchill, Sir Frederick Maurice, who had been Director of Military Operations in Britain in 1918, said the following.

> . . . The one defect in the present [British] system, as I view it from outside, is the Joint Planning Committee. My experience is that the members of this committee are, *ex officio*, too much occupied with the affairs of their own Services to give their minds to joint planning, and that when they meet they are disposed rather to find difficulties in, and objections to, proposals for action than to initiate such proposals . . .[1]

And from Vannevar Bush in 1949:

> . . . We are confronted immediately by an apparent paradox. In recent times, we have done military planning of actual campaigns in time of war exceedingly well, and we have done military planning of broad nature in time of peace exceedingly badly. Yet both have been done largely by the same individuals, and so it will pay to look for reasons . . .

> . . . How have we determined such vital questions as the fraction of our effort to be placed in strategic air facilities, or whether an outsize aircraft carrier is now worth its great cost? By careful judgement in which expert opinions are balanced, supplemented, and vitalized by coolheaded public discussion? No. Rather, by arguments of these highly technical matters in public, in the press, in

---

*This is excerpted from Report for the Chairman, Joint Chief of Staff by the Chairman's Special Study Group, April, 1982 (often referred to as the Brehm Report).

magazine articles, some of them vitriolic and most of them superficial. By statements of high-ranking generals and admirals attacking one another's reasoning, and at times almost one another's veracity. By presidential and Congressional commissions paralleling almost entirely the organization for planning purposes established by law. By the action of committees of Congress, based on superficial examination of the facts and analyses, attempting to pick out from the chaos something that corresponds to reason. By the personality and appeal of enthusiasts for this or that, wherever placed. This is not planning; it is a grab bag. It will lead us to waste our substance. It will lead to strife between services of a nature that can destroy public confidence. It will render us vulnerable in a hostile world. It has already done so to an intolerable degree . . .[2]

And, finally, from William Frye writing about George Marshall in 1947:

. . . Conceived as an advisory group to the constitutional Commander in Chief, the gravest defect of the Joint Chiefs of Staff was . . . that it was unable to reach a decision except by unanimous consent . . .

Now the instruments of warfare had so altered the factors of time and space that the barriers of land and sea had lost meaning . . . Land, sea, or air, each required the services of the two others. Combined operations were the inescapable need. In this war now reaching a triumphant conclusion, the failures had been scored by separate services, the victories by a team.

Single command in a theater of operations had been accepted by all services as a minimum necessity. Yet how could theater command be truly effective unless it had at its disposal forces educated and trained in combined operations? Joint planning, not debate, would produce a team. Single authority over single purpose, not compromise of separate interest and jealoulsy guarded prerogative, was the only hope of achieving the soundest possible military establishment at a minimum cost . . .

Marshall looked at the organization of which he was a member: the Joint Chiefs of Staff — Marshall, Leahy, King, Arnold. Their achievements had been great; but there had been failures, too, and the weakness of the group was that, despite himself, each member had been caught by the fears and ambitions of service prestige and made an advocate of special, instead of national, interest. When that happened, there was no one short of the President to render a decision on what was, after all, a purely military problem. . . .

The national security is a single problem, and it cannot be provided for on a piecemeal basis, was his rational summation, . . .[3]

These men, in the 1940s, saw a different world — surely one less dangerous than we see today. Yet, even then, they feared that ways might not be found to enhance the joint perspective of the service for the common good. They were people experienced in managing war, from the top down. They were also remarkable prophets, as is demonstrated further in the paragraphs below, relating the views of senior military personnel now holding joint positions.

The Chairman of the Joint Chiefs of Staff

By law, the chairman is one among equals within the Joint Chiefs of Staff. Yet, he differs from his colleagues in important ways.

On the one hand, as the senior military officer he is the regular military link to the secretary of defense, the president, and the National Security Council. He is the only military witness who testifies frequently before the Congress on a defense-wide basis. As the one member of the JCS with no service responsibilities, the chairman is in the best position to treat interservice issues strictly on their merits and thus to advise on the resolution of interservice differences, a principal reason for having the JCS in the first place.

On the other hand, his potential effectiveness is, by law and by practice, curtailed. As one of five equals, he cannot speak authoritatively for the other members of the JCS as a corporate body unless they all agree or he states the positions of the individual service chiefs; he is not the "chairman of the board." Unlike the service chiefs, he manages few resources, and resources are an important source of influence. With regard to personnel, he controls no promotions and few assignments, so has little sway over the officers assigned to the joint staff and other joint organizations, including the unified commands.

The chairman is the only senior executive in the defense organization who does not have a "deputy." This imposes a heavy burden on the chairman. It also threatens continuity and often breaks it when he must be absent. Thus he tends to be inhibited from planning field trips that would be beneficial in forging stronger links between the JCS and the CINCs, and in giving greater emphasis to joint operational preparedness.

The unique activities in which the chairman is involved place unique requirements on the staff that supports him. One requirement is for timeliness. As things are now, he often cannot afford to wait for the whole mechanism of the joint staff system to function. Its procedures, though thorough, are not sufficiently responsive. A second requirement is for security. The chairman deals routinely with very sensitive issues. Many of these not only involve complex military factors, but become inextricably interwoven with political factors. They often touch on matters so sensitive that the chairman will not risk revealing them to a group as large as the joint staff, particularly with its routine involvement of the service staffs in its preparation of joint positions. Thus, on sensitive, urgent issues, the chairman is often forced to set up ad hoc arrangements to obtain the kind of staff support he needs.

THE VIEWS OF THE INCUMBENT CHAIRMAN

The current chairman[4] has been a member of the Joint Chiefs of Staff for over seven and one-half years, four as Air Force chief of staff. He notes that his view of the role and importance of joint activities has changed significantly since he became chairman. The following are his observations about the characteristics and shortcomings of the current JCS organization.

1. In the twenty years since the chairman attended the National War College, little has changed regarding joint activities. The chairman has

served with about a dozen different service chiefs. All have experienced dissatisfaction with the joint system. Most would like to see it changed.

2. Few service chiefs (the present chairman included) had much joint experience prior to being promoted to chief (other than perhaps National War College attendance). Few have brought a full appreciation for joint activities to their roles as members of the JCS.

3. The emphasis on service competition and independence, intended originally to restrict the power of the military within the government, has had the unintended effect of reducing the ability of the government to forge the services into effective joint forces.

4. The services have few joint operations in which all four services are significantly involved on a day-to-day basis in peacetime. The major command headquarters are mainly uniservice, or involve at most two services. And the combinations, when they exist, usually pair either the Army and Air Force together, or the Navy and Marine Corps. Of all the commands, the new rapid deployment joint task force (RDJTF) has the most direct involvement with the forces of all four services in peacetime, and would thus be best prepared to achieve joint effectiveness in wartime.

5. The statutory provisions that limit the tours and hence the experience of officers assigned to the joint staff are anachronistic. Staff officers assigned to joint positions generally are not prepared for joint duty, either through education or experience. Moreover, the allegiance of an officer assigned to a joint position is generally to his parent service; the service provides his basic environment, compensation, career development, and promotion opportunities. New personnel management procedures are needed that broaden the preparation of officers for joint duty, and reward them for effective work.

6. The elaborate staff procedures used by the JCS organization cause joint staff officers to act primarily as referees, working within committees of service staff representatives, rather than as independent staff officers developing joint positions. Thus, for most officers, joint duty is seen as undesirable, both because it has a reputation for being nonproductive and because it is not perceived as career enhancing. A way must be found to reduce service staff control over joint papers, while still allowing for service staff input to the preparation of joint papers.

7. The service chief, by tradition, depends on his own staff to prepare him for JCS meetings rather the joint staff. Naturally, his staff tends to take a service view of issues, and a service chief must back his service staff most of the time or he will risk losing their support. Thus, when a chief comes to a JCS meeting he may be "locked in" to a position before the meeting starts.

8. The service chief has a major job just managing his own service, and the job is growing in complexity. He has little time to address joint ac-

tivities even though he is supposed to give them priority. Sometimes the issues are complex and subject to almost daily development. Thus, the service chief often has little incentive and even some difficulty in being prepared to discuss such topics.

9. The service chief has the additional burden of being called on to perform as acting chairman, a custom that is growing increasingly impractical and that works against continuity in the chairman's position. This is important in many areas, but surely the most critical involves the role of the chairman as an advisor to the secretary and the president in the emergency use of strategic nuclear forces, now a highly technical subject.

10. There is not enough emphasis in the government on the "output" side of the defense program (e.g., readiness). In particular, there is too little emphasis on joint activities, which are primarily output oriented. The department of defense traditionally organizes around inputs, not outputs; its priorities are driven by such issues as procurement decisions, manpower levels and policies, budget deadlines, congressional hearings, and other program oriented activities. Thus, the DOD has tended not to deal effectively with "output" issues, such as readiness, integrated force capabilities, and crisis management preparations. The latter are all primary JCS issues—difficult under the best of circumstances, and certainly not resolved effectively when not given equal time in the defense management process.

11. The current chairman, with the perspective of having been a component commander under a unified command, a service chief, and chairman of the Joint Chiefs of Staff, believes that the position of chairman must be strengthened to allow the chairman to resolve more of the issues and to represent the joint military interest more effectively. Also, the service chiefs should be released from having to deal with joint issues of lesser significance, to give them more time to manage their services. Moreover, the CINCs should be brought into the deliberative process at the Pentagon to represent the joint point of view. These steps need not reduce the prestige or influence of the services, but must be taken to increase the sense of "jointness" within the defense establishment. The chairman believes these things to be essential now, and certainly in the years ahead. Requirements today are very different compared with those of twenty or thirty years ago. Change should not be forced upon the JCS organization in time of crisis, but should be introduced deliberately, as much as possible by the JCS themselves.

The Service Chiefs

The dual burden that a service chief bears—one as the military head of his own service, and the other as a member of the Joint Chiefs of Staff—is a heavy one. President Eisenhower's views on the subject were clear in his message to Congress of April 3, 1958.

> I have long been aware that the Joint Chiefs' [dual] burdens are so heavy that they find it very difficult to spend adequate time on their duties as members of the Joint Chiefs of Staff. . . . The problem is not new but has not yielded to past efforts to solve it. We need to solve it now, especially in view of the new strategic planning and operational burdens I have previously mentioned.
>
> I therefore propose that present law be changed to make it clear that each chief of a military service may delegate major portions of his service responsibilities to his vice chief. Once this change is made, the Secretary of Defense will require the chiefs to use their power of delegation to enable them to make their Joint Chiefs of Staff duties their principal duties.

That proposal was included in the Department of Defense Reorganization Act of 1958. However, twenty-four years later, the problem that President Eisenhower tried to rectify persists. While the service chiefs clearly have the power to delegate the running of their services to their vice chiefs, they have been reluctant to do so, and have not been required to do so. The current ASD (MRA&L), Dr. Lawrence J. Korb, suggests why in his book, *The Joint Chiefs of Staff*:

> The problem of the service chief is that he cannot divest himself of his service duties. The real problem is he does not want to. The man who spends nearly forty years as a follower in his service sees his appointment to the JCS as the opportunity to remake his service in his own image. He does not view it as an opportunity to serve as a principal military adviser to the President and the Secretary of Defense.

It should be expected that the service chiefs would have mixed feelings about the time they spend on joint matters. Their joint advice is not in demand. Their main interest and their constituencies lie with their services. They cannot deal with many major joint issues to their satisfaction because they cannot reach agreement without compromising their service positions or waffling their advice. Many of the joint issues they deal with they consider unnecessarily time consuming. And being a service chief is in itself a full-time job.

For example, the chiefs must travel extensively to meet their own service leadership obligations (and they rarely have time to visit the installations and activities of another service). Their travel schedules make it hard for the JCS to maintain continuity as a working group. Thus, only one-quarter of the time were all five principals present and 40% of the time two or more were gone.

Each chief does try to attend all of the more important JCS meetings, and will adjust his travel schedule accordingly. But nonetheless, the requirements of the two jobs inevitably compete for the time and attention of each man who bears the dual responsibility. The result is a lack of continuity in the JCS meetings.

Table 13.1 JCS Meeting Attendance (Principals)*

NUMBER ABSENT	PERCENT OF THE TIME
None	24%
One or more	76%
Two or more	40%
Three or more	14%

*Five Years, 1976-81 467 meetings (about 2 per week)

The vice chiefs attend JCS meetings in the chiefs' absences, but they have even greater difficulty being current on the issues than the chiefs themselves, since internal service management is their primary focus and they are present at JCS meetings less frequently than the chiefs.

What the current system demands of the chiefs is often unrealistic. They have one job that requires them to be effective advocates for their own service; they have another that requires them to subordinate service interests to broader considerations; and they are faced with issues where the two positions may well be antithetical. It is very difficult for a chief to argue in favor of something while wearing one of his "hats," and against it while wearing the other. Yet that is what the current system often asks of the service chiefs.

The Views of the Incumbent Service Chiefs

Persuasive reasons for change are supported by the views of the four incumbent service chiefs. Though they sometimes see the problems in different ways, their consensus is that the JCS organization fails in several of its basic institutional tasks. The chiefs agree that, though joint advice is vital, their joint deliberations are often inconsequential in affecting defense policy and programs. Indeed, what influence they have depends more on individual personal relationships than on joint institutional relationships.

The current chiefs also note that their responsibilities as the military heads of their services are extremely demanding and destined to be more so. Thus they see their joint activities as an unwelcome intrusion when the results are not productive.

Most disturbing to them of all is that joint advice has been too seldom sought and too seldom heeded in timely fashion by defense secretaries and presidents, the very executives the JCS organization was devised to support. They note that this is not a recent phenomenon, and indeed that individual management styles and personalities alter the situation only marginally. One must infer that the fault lies not with any particular group of military and civilian executives, but rather with the implementation of the JCS concept itself. Indeed, others who have evaluated the JCS organization over the years reached the same basic conclusion. The fact that the JCS organization has suffered constant criticism by both practitioners and observers supports that conclusion.[5]

Among the specific comments of the service chiefs are the following, paraphrased and without attribution:

(1) The JCS cannot carry out their statutory responsibilities. It is wrong to say that there is nothing wrong with the JCS organization. The basic organizational concept is flawed.

(2) Even when the JCS agree on an issue, their joint advice frequently has no impact.

(3) Of the major responsibilities of a service chief, the joint responsibility is by far the most frustrating. It seems to have little payoff. Uneven attendance by the principals at JCS meetings is clear evidence of the difficulty of having a service chief wear two hats.

(4) The DOD focus is on programs, almost to the exclusion of systematic examinations of how resources should or would be used, an obvious concern of the JCS and the CINCs. The result is a lack of effective planning, or, more precisely, a major mismatch between plans and resources. The JCS and the CINCs have very little corporate impact on shaping the defense program.

(5) The service chief has much more to do than he used to, and the future will place even greater demands on his time. Training and quality assurance in the services are getting more and more difficult. (Some countries use their service chiefs mainly as inspectors general.) It may be that it no longer makes sense for the service chiefs to split their responsibilities. Perhaps their joint roles should be reduced to being members of the board, available to comment on DOD tentative plans.

(6) The JCS staffing process is flawed. It seeks the lowest common denominator. To avoid 'split' papers for the secretary, the process constantly seeks agreement in resolving issues, even though that may be accomplished only by watering down the issues and by blunting the sharp edges of the chiefs' views.

(7) Such critical joint responsibilities as the overall direction of command, control, and communications are poorly handled and poorly supported by the services. Other programs that are obviously joint or national programs (e.g., rapid deployment and prepositioning) are not managed as such.

(8) The joint staff is not an initiator. It only reacts.

(9) Organizational changes within the joint staff to improve responsiveness and effectiveness are needed, with particular emphasis on improved war planning.

(10) Procedural changes within the joint process are needed to encourage prompt, objective, and joint consideration and resolution of issues. Single service views are emphasized too long in the present process.

(11) The J-3 should be more involved in the plan review process to ensure a more balanced approach between operations, plans, and policy, and to ensure that the operations people have a more intimate knowledge of the plans that must be implemented in times of crisis or war.

(12) The quality of the personnel in the joint staff, and in joint assignments in general, should be better assured. Joint education and joint assignments following school should be emphasized; personnel policy should be established and enforced. The chairman should have greater control over joint assignments, tour length, qualifications, and career incentives for joint duty.

(13) The current policy on joint or international experience as a prerequisite for selection for promotion to general officer is appropriate. However, the secretary of defense should strengthen the emphasis, among all of the services, on the importance of officer development through assignment to joint or international duty at the major through colonel level. We must develop leaders well-schooled in joint matters who possess a broad multiservice and international perspective.

(14) The chairman should have greater authority within the JCS. It may be appropriate to provide the chairman more decision authority to rule in favor of a position that has support of a majority of the chiefs. An increase in authority for the chairman should increase the efficiency of the process. Adequate channels for appeal would remain for the service chiefs.

(15) The chairman requires a small but effective staff to deal in resource matters and specifically in the PPBS process. The chairman should present his own views derived from the joint process in which the service chiefs participate. The chairman's views should emphasize joint war fighting capabilities and cross-service issues with significant operational impact.

(16) When considering improvements to the JCS it is important to consider the role of the service chiefs and their staffs. It is clear that the process is highly interactive and must be so. Service responsibilities for organizing, training and equipping forces, and related resource allocations are best executed in the context of planned joint operations and needed joint capabilities. This context is brought to the service staff most effectively through the effort of the service chief who is clearly dedicated and responsible for actions in both the joint and service arenas. The role of the service chief in the JCS needs greater emphasis, both to assure better performance as a member of the JCS and to assure better performance as a service chief with clear perspective of joint warfare.

These remarks do not in every instance represent a unanimity of views of the service chiefs. But the service chiefs are together on these points: They are frustrated by the lack of JCS impact on national policy, regret nonproductive time spent in the joint arena, and see the need for significant improvements in the interest of national security.

The Commanders in Chief. A major deficiency in the existing joint process is the lack of an effective mechanism through which the CINCs of the unified commands can participate in the DOD programming and resource allocation processes, contribute to the development of joint military advice concerning military strategy and other operational matters, and interact more thoroughly with the joint staff.

Today, the CINCs are at best only superficially involved in many things critical to their commands. They play almost no role in the programming and budgeting process (though they recently were invited by the secretary to participate occasionally in meetings of the Defense Resources Board) and have little influence in the JCS force allocation process. In addition, they are not strongly supported by either the services or the joint staff. They have practically nothing to say about the officers assigned to them; just as the joint staff has difficulty getting officers qualified in joint duty, so too do the CINCs. And while there are strong linkages between the service component commands and their parent service headquarters, similar bonds do not exist between the unified command headquarters and the joint staff.

The Views of the Incumbent CINCs

As a result, the CINCs, too, have expressed concern about the effectiveness of the JCS organization. Their perspective is somewhat different from that of the chairman and the service chiefs, but many points are the same. The following is a composite (though not necessarily a consensus) of the views of four of the incumbent CINCs (two of whom are former directors of the joint staff):

(1) The unified command headquarters need better qualified and better trained people. Some of this should come in the form of better focused education at the senior service colleges (not just the National Defense University) and at the Command and General Staff schools. The promotion system within the services should be disciplined to give positive value to joint duty.

(2) Return assignments to the joint staff are essential. The Armed Forces Staff College (AFSC) is the best joint educational experience, because it catches officers at the right point in their careers (Grade 0-3/0-4). Service in a unified command headquarters is not necessarily good preparation for service on the joint staff, though it is better than no previous headquarters staff experience at all.

(3) Attitudes regarding the desirability of joint duty are very different among the several services.

(4) The joint decisionmaking process takes far too long, primarily because its complex apparatus keeps seeking consensus.

(5) The joint staff spends too much time on day-to-day "crises"; it should also work harder on long-range planning, and should have greater interaction with CINCs in this critical area.

(6) There needs to be more emphasis on war planning in the joint staff. Moreover, the process used to develop military operation plans takes too long.

(7) The CINCs have difficulty getting strategic guidance covering specific politico–military issues.

(8) The CINCs sometimes get fuzzy guidance from the joint chiefs of staff. The CINCs recognize that JCS guidance must be based on OSD guidance that may itself tend to lack certain specifics; but it is virtually impossible for a military commmander to deal with a military mission that depends on guidance objectives such as "deter," or "dissuade."

(9) Crisis management capabilities within the Pentagon have traditionally been poor. One reason is that faith and trust are not mutual among the principals involved, and have seldom been in the past. The political leadership hasn't always taken the implementers into their confidence at the time they are considering options and making plans.

(10) The service chiefs should be relieved of the need to try to deal jointly with resource allocation under constrained resource circumstances.

(11) The influence of the joint community on the resource allocation process should be greater, and particularly of the CINCs, who are in a unique position to establish theater priorities. They should have a major input, particularly on such things as the sustainability of forces.

(12) There should be major functional contact between the joint staff and

the CINCs on promising technical innovations, such as cruise missile technology and all of its possible applications.

As noted, not all the CINCs necessarily would agree with all of these statements. One, with experience on the joint staff, believes that the procedure used to develop joint staff papers for the JCS is sound, primarily because it is thorough, and because it works. But that same individual is deeply concerned about the ability of the joint staff to support crisis management.

The Joint Staff. The principals within the joint staff are charged with making the basic staff mechanisms function. They perhaps are in the best position to see weaknesses attributable to organizational and procedural arrangements. These are the paraphrased views of several of them:

(1) The joint staff is a "derivative" staff. It is not original and it does not innovate. It answers questions, but doesn't ask them. It needs a better opportunity to be innovative and to interact with the JCS.

(2) The joint staff does not prepare the chairman well, nor does it prepare the chiefs. The chiefs get most of their preparation on joint issues from their own service staffs, which hardly grants them a joint orientation.

(3) The chairman often gets the "file drawer" treatment, in which a joint staff action officer, when given the task of preparing a briefing paper, simply compiles and tabs previous papers in a notebook and adds a bland summary sheet listing the tabs. The typical action officer, with limited staff experience in general and very limited joint experience in particular, is not equipped to do much else.

(4) There is little integration of briefing material for the chairman. This problem is exacerbated when issues arise that involve more than one functional directorate, and these cases are more the rule than the exception. Thus, the pressure is on the chairman's special staff group, or the chairman himself, to perform the integration and digestion of the material.

(5) It is difficult for the joint staff to examine options, a problem further complicated by any special sensitivity associated with the issue, since the staffing apparatus ties in the service staffs as well. It may be that a partial answer would be to provide a small special staff group to the director of the joint staff that could help integrate and digest material, and analyze options on issues of high sensitivity.

(6) Under current circumstances, it is frequently necessary for the chairman to insist on ad hoc arrangements, in an attempt to 'tailor' the joint staff to the problem and to limit access. If used too frequently, however, that option undermines the staff and its organization. Thus, the staff organization, procedures, and personnel preparation should be changed to permit it to be more responsive to the chairman's needs for high-quality support by the joint staff itself, with the ability to limit the numbers of officers involved when necessary.

(7) It takes far too long to get projects moving, such as the formation of the steering group to study the military operation planning system.

(8) More horsepower within the joint staff is needed in the PPBS and program objectives memoranda (POM) review area to help the chairman carry out responsibilities in the defense resources board decision process.

(9) On the policy side, what is needed most is more time—not calendar time, but fewer diversions. The people on the joint staff are good in the policy area.

(10) As it is now, each service chief "owns" the joint staff simply because his or her operations deputy has veto power on staff actions. Joint papers are derivative of service papers, not independent efforts.

(11) The quality of joint staff officers is not really a problem. A way must be found to capitalize on their strengths, and on the inherent importance of joint activity.

(12) The policy specialists on the joint staff constitute a substantial amount of capability, but, as of now, they are commentators, not generators.

(13) A service chief can seldom reverse himself on a position he has taken as chief of a service. However, he should have an interest, as a military man, in laying out the alternatives, rather than defaulting on this task to the OSD staff.

(14) The chairman is expected by Congress to lay out his views. He should have the best staff support possible.

(15) The mission of the U.S. Armed Forces is changing. We must have the capability to meet the Soviets anywhere (including in space). The joint system must be changed to give us the capability to do the necessary innovative studies and planning.

(16) The joint staff needs a stronger focal point for pulling together (and anticipating) crisis actions.

(17) Lack of Washington experience and the short terms of assignment for officers on the joint staff are really a problem. A three-year term is needed for flag-level officers.

(18) Officers tend to risk their careers on the joint staff if they move out too smartly. Yet, new and innovative moves are needed, in military planning and in command and control, to name two examples.

(19) Improvements to the planning system and the creation of the joint deployment agency are not fundamental changes in themselves. We must look beyond such steps.

(20) The service staffs have different perceptions of joint problems, which makes progress difficult given their strength in controlling joint actions.

(21) A better procedure is needed to provide continuity in the position of acting chairman. During one recent three-day period when the chairman was out of town, the responsibility for acting chairman changed hands seven times.

Summary

The views presented above are not the casual comments of executives complaining about life in the bureaucracy. They reflect the honest, deep-seated concerns of the military leadership itself about the viability of the most important joint military organization in the free world. Their overwhelming consensus is that changes are needed, and needed now.

JOINT DUTY – PERSONNEL
MANAGEMENT AND PROCEDURES

Preparation and Tenure of Officers

All professional military assignments have special requirements for prior training and experience. Submarine skippers, F-15 pilots, and infantry battalion commanders all require – and are given – careful preparation.

The same should be true for officers serving in joint assignments, such as the joint staff or the unified command headquarters. Aside from understanding how such staffs function, they face the immense problem of learning how the DOD and their sister services function. Few officers are expert in the several branches of their own service, let alone the other services. But officers serving on joint staffs should at least have a broad working knowledge of all the armed forces. Few do. Most assigned to joint duties have little formal preparation, and few stay long enough to acquire expertise on the job:

1. Of those officers now serving in the organization of the joint chiefs of staffs (OJCS),[6] only 2% had any previous joint staff experience and only 36% had prior service staff experience. Many have been assigned directly from the field.

2. Only 13% have attended the five-month resident course at the Armed Forces Staff College, the school specifically designed to train young officers for joint duty.

3. Of the colonels and Navy captains now assigned to the joint staff, about two-thirds have been to one of the five senior colleges—the three service war colleges and the NWC and ICAF in the NDU; but less than one-quarter have been to one of the two joint schools—NWC and ICAF—that are specifically provided for joint education.

4. The average tour length of officers in the OJCS—the most complex and important military staff in the defense establishment—is less than thirty months. This means that at any given time, the average experience level on the staff is no more than fifteen months, and there is virtually no corporate memory.

5. The leadership positions in the joint staff are filled by general and flag officers. Their normal tour is twenty-four months, less than that of their staff officers. Thus, the average level of experience on the joint staff for generals and admirals is about one year. For those who served during the past five years, less than 60% had served previously in a joint assignment, even though DOD policy states that a joint duty assignment is a prerequisite to promotion to flag rank. Moreover, many of the positions counted as "joint" are really not, and are simply not comparable in scope (as regards joint matters) to positions in the joint staff and unified command headquarters.[7]

The Armed Forces Staff College prepares officers at the 0–3 and 0–4 levels for joint duty. However, there is no assurance that most AFSC graduates will ever be assigned to joint duties. The same is true of the more senior National War College and the Industrial College of the Armed Forces, which are aimed at preparing officers at the 0–5 and junior 0–6 levels. NWC and ICAF are now revising their programs and curricula to prepare graduates better for joint duty. However, unless service officer assignment policies are changed, their revised curricula will be of little help in improving the background of the officers actually assigned.to joint duty. The investment in NDU is substantial. The total annual cost of operating the three schools under NDU, including the compensation of the military faculty and students, is estimated to exceed $30 million.

In summary, joint officers are asked to analyze major national issues such as arms control, develop national security objectives, oversee the development of joint military plans; and complete other major tasks that require a depth of knowledge of the other services, of defense strategy, and of the overall defense program that they simply have not had the opportunity to acquire. The combination of lack of staff experience, lack of practical knowledge of joint activities, and lack of formal preparation through the joint school system, all coupled with short tours, makes it very difficult for joint staff officers, no matter how capable (and many are very capable), to deal effectively with these major staff responsibilities. The result is that the chairman lacks the support he needs to carry out his responsibilities, and the secretary of defense is not provided the kind of military staff support he needs, has a right to expect, and could be provided if the services gave greater weight to joint duty positions in their management of officer personnel.

The Desirability of Joint Duty

Joint assignments are seldom sought by officers. A joint position removes them from the environment for which they have been trained, in which they have established relationships and reputations, and in which they seek advancement. It places them instead in a wholly new environment involving unfamiliar procedures and issues for which most of them have little or no formal training. Their fitness reports (which affect their careers and prospects for advancement) are often entrusted to officers of other services with little in common by way of professional background.

Adding to these concerns is the perception that much of the work on the joint staff is unproductive, and that too much effort is wasted on tedious negotiation of issues until they have been debased and reduced to the "lowest common level of assent."[8]

The general perception among officers is that a joint assignment is one to be avoided. In fact, within one service it is flatly believed to be the "kiss of death" as far as a continued military career is concerned. In contrast, service assignments are widely perceived as offering much greater possibilities for concrete accomplishments and career enhancement. As a result, many fine officers opt for service assignments rather than risk a joint duty assignment. Yet joint positions have the potential for making major contributions to the defense effort, and to offer challenging work to the finest officers. Indeed, the number of joint positions available and the relatively rich grade structure are impressive. With only 3% of the total number of officers in the four services (see Table 13.2), joint positions account for 13% of the general and flag officers, and 6% of the grades of 0–5 (lieutenant colonel and commander) and 0–6 (colonel and Navy captain).

At a minimum, the joint positions above the subtotal line—some 4,600 positions including 146 general/flag officer billets—could be specially managed as a group, to see that officers are assigned who have the proper experience, education, and motivation (i.e., rewards) to bring joint duty to the stature and effectiveness it deserves.

It is interesting that the office of the secretary of defense (OSD) itself has two-thirds as many officers (including generals and admirals) as the OJCS, so that the number of officers on the secretary's combined staff is 1,120, or nearly *three times* the official officer strength ceiling authorized for the joint staff. One can only speculate, but the fact that over the years the various secretaries have seen fit to create over 400 officer positions (including 19 of flag rank) within the "civilian" staff, suggests that somehow the joint staff is missing out on the opportunity to play a far more meaningful role in advising the secretary than it now does.

Table 13.2. Officer Positions In Joint-Duty and Other "Non-Service" Activities*

ACTIVITY	GRADE					
	0–3	0–4	0–5	0–6	GEN/FLAG	TOTAL
OSD	19	68	176	156	19	438
OJCS	2	70	368	211	31	682
JDA	5	26	30	9	4	74
Unified Commands	236	730	850	291	47	2,154
NATO Commands	162	405	478	209	45	1,299
Subtotal "Joint"	424	1,299	1,902	876	146	4,647
Percent of Total Grade	<1%	3%	6%	6%	13%	3%
Defense Agencies	545	986	882	380	35	2,828
Other Activities**	159	440	501	347	29	1,476
Total	1,128	2,725	3,285	1,603	210	8,951
Percent of Total Grade	1%	5%	10%	11%	19%	5%
Army						(3,317)
Navy/USMC						(2,400)
Air Force						(3,234)

*As of 28 September 1981. Excludes officers assigned to the service staffs whose principal or part-time responsibilities are in support of their service chiefs in joint activities. It is estimated by the services that at least 675 officers are so involved, including several of flag rank.
**Aerospace Defense Command; National Defense University; Armed Forces Staff College; Joint Strategic Target Planning Staff; Joint Electronic Warfare Center; Joint Strategic Connectivity Staff; Electromagnetic Compatibility Analysis Center; Inter-American Defense Board; Defense Attache System; Security Assistance Activities (MAAGS, MILGPs, etc).

Joint Staff Procedures

There are three characteristics of current joint staff procedures that tend to inhibit the utility of joint staff activities in the eyes of the secretary and his civilian assistants. First, JCS papers for the secretary of defense rarely cover the full range of possible alternative resolutions to the issue in question. The JCS traditionally has tried instead to resolve such issues through their internal deliberative process, and to avoid split recommendations even if that results in a bland and sterile presentation of their views. A service chief may hesitate to lend his name to a document that includes an alternative with which he takes issue, even if it is not recommended. Some of the chiefs also believe that split positions diminish the strength of their joint recommendations. (Some of the chiefs also believe that the opposite is true.) However, there are few defense issues with only one possible resolution, and any secretary of defense will be quite aware that alternatives do exist. If he does not find them in JCS papers, he will turn to his civilian staff to find them and to determine whether they are preferable to the one recommended by the JCS. But, no matter how useful this civilian advice, it cannot substitute for a competent military evaluation of the alternatives.

A second characteristic is that joint staff action officers, rather than drafting JCS papers themselves, often accept drafts authored by the services. This practice tends to subvert the joint process. If a service can frame the issues and the arguments in the initial draft, the terms of the subsequent deliberations may well be cast in a context most favorable to that service's position, and the other services may find themselves at a disadvantage. Joint staff action officers then tend to be "brokers" rather than initiators, and the process is aimed more at "damage limiting" for the services than at developing a paper reflecting true joint interest. Another result is that, for those papers involving issues of concern to the CINCs, the CINCs do not have adequate representation.

A third characteristic—one much debated—is the highly-stylized, multiple-level "flimsy/buff/green/red-stripe" staffing process. As noted earlier, it is possible, and indeed likely, for a JCS paper to go through four levels of staffing, each with multiple iterations of drafting, commenting, and revising. This admittedly thorough but prolonged process of trying to reach some mutually satisfactory compromise among the services tends not to sharpen and hone the issues, but rather to bury them. The more iterations this process involves, the longer the process takes, and the less substantive the paper becomes. The objective becomes one of agreement, at the expense of content.

Thus, rather than producing a paper with joint orientation that sets forth clearly defined alternatives and analyzes them for their pros and cons, joint staff procedures tend to filter out jointness and to "protect" service positions. Many issues are analyzed not by one staff but five—the joint staff and the four service staffs. Not only is there redundancy in the process, but it tends to be sterile, a fact known widely throughout the services and the joint staff—one of the major reasons that many competent officers are not attracted to joint duty. The approach is thorough, but often at the expense of content—and time.

The tight interlocking of the joint staff and the service staffs is traditional. Without doubt, when established decades ago, the procedure was intended to "protect" the services by assuring their individual control over joint staff activities. It serves the purpose well of keeping at least a certain group of officers on each service staff sensitive to joint issues. But whether the national interest is served by perpetuating these checks and balances designed in a different era is questionable. It is easier to conclude that by restricting the independence of the joint staff as is now done, a principal source of military advice is lost, or at least attenuated. The vacuum is either filled by civilians, or not filled at all.

NOTES

1. Churchill, Winston S., *The Hinge of Fate* (Boston: Houghton-Mifflin, 1950).
2. Bush, Vannevar, *Modern Arms and Free Men* (New York: Simon & Schuster, 1949).
3. Frye, William, *Marshall, Citizen Soldier* (Indianapolis: Bobbs-Merrill, 1947).
4. At the time of the report from which this chapter is excerpted, the incumbent chairperson was General David C. Jones.
5. Some might argue that there really is no need for joint military advice from the JCS. At the very least, that argument fails because the president and the secretary must avail themselves of a wide variety of diverse counsel as they lead the national security program and command its forces. Joint military advice is unique and absolutely critical to assure balance in the spectrum of views they obtain.
6. The OJCS comprises the statutory joint staff that is specifically limited by law to 400 officers, and a group of other staff elements established over the years to meet additional staff requirements. Both are under the direction of the director of the joint staff.
7. The senior civilian positions in DOD fare little better in regard to tenure. Among approximately thirty presidential appointee positions in OSD and the military departments requiring Senate confirmation (assistant secretaries and above), the average term of service for the 205 executives who have held those positions since 1960 has been only thirty-two months (a figure that allows for promotions and other reassignments that did not break continuity). Moreover, extended vacancies have occured in these positions 146 times with an average duration of five months.
8. Steadman, Richard C., *Report to the Secretary of Defense on the National Military Command Structure* (Washington, D.C.: Department of Defense, 1978).

Chapter 14

The U.S. Military Chain of Command – Present and Future

William Y. Smith

Increasing concern about U.S. military performance – from civilians and soldiers alike – has raised questions about U.S. military organization, about its hindering U.S. military professionals' ability to advise, to plan, and to conduct military operations in peace and war. Because the military chain of command is central to the effective accomplishment of their responsibilities by the U.S. military, two questions arise. How well does the military chain of command work today? What improvements, if any, should be made?

Analysis and judgment on these questions are affected by several considerations. First is one's attitude toward organizations and organizational solutions to substantive problems. When confronted with a difficult problem, we Americans are often tempted to reorganize without directly confronting the basic issues involved and facing up to their complexity. There are dangers in this approach, for, as President Wilson remarked in 1918 when Senator Chamberlain proposed creating a war cabinet to help the president conduct the war;[1] "The faith some people put in machinery is childlike and touching, but the machinery does not do the task. . . ." Others, however, believe that organizational structure does matter. Certainly, experienced people agree that a sound organization enables capable people to accomplish more, while a bad one can hamper even the most competent. The way to improve then, must be to deal with both substantive and organizational deficiencies.

That U.S. military professionals firmly believe in civilian control of the military is a second factor of importance when discussing the chain of command. But they also believe they should be heard on matters directly affecting them. As military people have often reminded civilians dealing with military policy, "The U.S. military do not mind being overruled – we are used to that. What we do dislike is to be ignored." Therefore, any change in the chain of command must not be so focused on streamlining that it ignores the need for broadly based input and for as broad a consensus as possible in the decisionmaking process.

THE U.S. MILITARY COMMAND SYSTEM TODAY

The U.S. military chain of command, extending from the president as commander in chief to the individual soldier, sailor, airman, and marine, is subject to the same checks and balances that characterize other aspects of the American form of government. Under the Constitution, the president is commander in chief of the armed forces, but only the Congress can declare war, and only the Congress can raise and support the Army and provide and maintain the Navy. Further, the War Powers Act attempts to limit the commander in chief's powers. In the department of defense the checks and balances find expression in civilian control of the military and in the complementary yet often competing functions of the operational chain of command down through the Joint Chiefs of Staff and the administrative chain down through the military departments.[2] In simplified terms, the operational chain is concerned with the deployment and employment of U.S. military forces, and the administrative chain is concerned with the establishment and the provisioning of those forces. Checks and balances help assure that government and governing in the United States remain limited in nature, but they also entail limits on efficiency and effectiveness. This has to be borne is mind when considering how the United States conducts its defense activities.

The military chain of command must basically perform three functions. It must execute orders from above and issue guidance and orders to subordinates; particularly, it is responsible for making and issuing the combat decisions necessary for the conduct of battle in time of war. This is what usually comes to mind when people think about the chain of command, but it is not the only thing the chain of command does. It must also pass advice and recommendations up the chain. Every young military officer is—or should be—taught the precept that any issue sent forward for resolution should include a recommended course of action. "Completed staff work," it is called. Finally, the military chain of command must allocate resources. At the lowest levels of command this may mean deciding how to use best the existing, in-place resources on a particular day. At the highest levels it includes not only that decision, but also the current allocation of resources to produce the desired type of military capabilities in the future. Although the three functions are separate and distinct ones, their interaction with one another is so complete that it is often difficult, in practice, to determine precisely where one ends and another begins. Still, it is important to understand their distinctness, and it is in determining how satisfactorily it carries out these three functions that the military chain of command can most productively be evaluated.

Executing Orders and Providing Guidance

All key military decisions are made by the president, or authorized by him to be made by others. The secretary of defense is, by law, his "principal assistant . . . in all matters relating to the Department of Defense" and as such as "direction, authority and control" over the department. That places him squarely in the military chain of command, and he exercises his authority most extensively. In the words of former Secretary of Defense Harold Brown:

> . . . the Secretary of Defense approves, or returns for modification, requests from the Joint Chiefs of Staff for authority to move military units—even a single aircraft or ship. He also approves plans drawn up by the Joint Strategic Target Planning Staff in Omaha for the use of U.S. strategic forces in case of a nuclear war.[3]

The operational military chain runs from the secretary of defense to the unified and specified commanders who, under the National Security Act of 1947 as amended, are "responsible to the President and the Secretary of Defense for such military missions as may be assigned to them by the Secretary of Defense with the approval of the President."

It is important to note here that the operational military chain of command runs between operational commanders, who have been assigned a mission, tasks, and responsibilities and who have the authority, without reference to higher headquarters, to make decisions and issue orders on all routine matters that fall within the scope of their mission. Nonroutine matters may necessitate consultation with higher headquarters. The Joint Chiefs of Staff, a committee, are not commanders. The legislation just cited implicitly recognizes this by making the field commanders responsible to the secretary and the president. The Chiefs' role in the chain is one of advising. A DOD directive, which states that the chain of command will run from the secretary "through" the Joint Chiefs of Staff to the unified and specified commands, assures that the chiefs will normally have an opportunity to advise (unless the secretary decides otherwise), but not to command.

The unified and specified commands receive their missions, tasks, and responsibilities by means of the unified command plan developed by the Joint Chiefs of Staff for approval by the president. This document is the principal authority for the operational command responsibilities and command relationships in the U.S. defense establishment. Pursuant to legislative direction, it sets forth the current U.S. unified and specified command structure and, as noted, the specific responsibilities of each major operational commander. Reviewed annually, it is modified as circumstances warrant. Each unified commander, with the exception of the readiness command, has responsibility for a geographical area; each specified commander has major responsibilities in a designated functional area, such as airlift or strategic air forces. (See the chapter Appendix for a brief description of the unified and specified command structure). To help him fulfill his responsibilities, each commander in chief (CINC) has a supporting staff composed in the case of a unified command of personnel from each of the services assigning combatant forces to the command; a specified command staff normally has personnel from only one service. Subject to instructions and guidance from the secretary of defense and Joint Chiefs of Staff, the CINC and his staff concern themselves with the planning for and actual employment of U.S. military forces in furtherance of the military objectives and policies of the United States.

As directed by the secretary of defense or as authorized by his mission, the unified commander issues guidance and orders to his service component commanders. These component commands are composed of personnel and units from a single military department, and it is here that in the field the operational chain of command links with the administrative chain of command that runs from the secretary of defense to the military departments. The specified commander does not face this same situation, in that he is at once responsible for both JCS operational matters and departmental administrative matters. Therefore, the remainder of this paper will focus principally on the role of the unified commander.

The unified commander has scant control and limited influence over the day-to-day activities of his component commands. That responsibility rests with the military departments. The Reorganization Act of 1958 removed the departments from the operational chain of command but charged them with responsibility to organize, train, equip, and administer service forces so that they become combatant forces to be assigned to a unified or specified command. The broad, service oriented charter of the military departments means that U.S. present and future military capabilities are developed predominantly on a unilateral service basis. The bulk of the operational doctrine for its forces is, likewise, decided by each individual service. Similarly, the nature and extent of the training necessary to make service forces combatant, that is, the readiness of the forces, is a service responsibility.

Readiness of assigned forces falls, as well, within the interest and the responsibility of the unified commander; he is the officer charged with the operational employment of the forces. The implications of this split responsibility can be seen in the training of personnel and units, a key factor in achieving the requisite high state of readiness. No clear separation exists between the type of training personnel and units perform to prepare them for assignment to a unified or specified command and the training they receive after such assignment. In fact, much of the training done by units assigned to a unified command is, in fact, service training as, for example, when an Army unit receives a new tank, or when an Air Force fighter wing receives a new aircraft. To be prepared to defend U.S. interests, however, the separate services must be melded together into an integrated fighting team. This is accomplished by joint exercises conducted under the auspices of the Joint Chiefs of Staff, and carried out by the unified commander. In joint exercises units of each service, which have largely been trained according to single service operational doctrine and procedures, are afforded the opportunity to train with units of other services under a scenario consistent with the units' missions. These joint exercises are very important to the unified commander because they permit the testing of joint procedures and doctrine; they help forge a combat-ready team, and they provide a basis for enhancing future effectiveness.

Given the importance of these maneuvers, the CINC inevitably wants a large number of them — more than the services believe they can afford — so questions frequently arise as to which joint exercises have priority among themselves, and which joint exercises have priority over individual service training that the military departments consider essential. In recent years, this competition has been exacerbated by the objective of regularly exercising U.S. forces assigned to contingency missions in Southwest Asia. Such could only be done at the expense of other exercise, primarily joint ones. Thus, for a variety of reasons, the CINC has historically not achieved what he believes is a satisfactory level of joint training. He has had to rely heavily on service training for the readiness of his units, but, as noted, he has had little or no influence or control over that training.

It is during potential or actual crises that the operational chain of command is placed under its greatest stress. In such circumstances, the key decisions are made by civilian authorities in Washington — the president and the secretary of defense. The forces to be committed, their mission, their plans are all determined at the highest levels and passed down the chain of command.

In crises, the means of communication become very important to assure the rapid transmission of orders, and a premium is placed on having constant, secure, reliable contact with the field unit. These improved communications bring with them the possibility not only for direct contact within the various echelons of command, but also around them. Almost without fail, at some point during a contingency operation, the temptation arises or the actuality occurs for the authorities in Washington to deal directly with the on-scene commander, bypassing the intermediate command levels.

One example of this frequent occurrence happened during the tree cutting incident in Korea in 1976. One high-level defense official wanted to deal directly with the first lieutenant on the scene to develop a proposed course of action. Only after some discussion was it made evident that the lieutenant did not control all the necessary resources to make an authoritative recommendation. If he responded to the incident with his small unit and the affair ended there, that was one thing. But should the North Koreans escalate their response in a way which required a reaction from other U.S. and Korean forces, not under the control of the lieutenatnt, then the situation would be far different; and the U.S. commander in Korea had to plan for that. After explanation, the defense official agreed that the use of the chain of command was the proper course.

Short-circuiting the chain of command, as was proposed in the example just given, can only lead to unnecessary confusion at a time when the requirement is to minimize it. It weakens the authority of the intermediate commanders, the need for whom becomes evident when events multiply in number and increase in complexity so that some devolution of authority becomes absolutely necessary.

It is far preferable to shorten the chain of command than to bypass it. It can be shortened by establishing a task force commander controlled directly from Washington, and this is sometimes done, though seldom if the operation is to take place in an area assigned to a unified commander. In that case the area CINC rightly gets the assignment. Even having a task force commander will not preclude bypassing the established command lines, however, if Washington wants to deal directly with the man on the cutting edge of U.S. military action. It is an old, but often forgotten, military axiom that issuing an order is but 10 percent of getting the job done. The other 90 percent is seeing to it that the order is carried out. That is where each echelon of the operational chain of command justifies its existence and why it should not be bypassed.

A condition different from bypassing the chain of command occurs when one wants to pass judgment after the fact. The Pearl Harbor investigation after World War II is probably the most famous such example, but there have been others, such as after the 1980 raid into Iran, and the one following the terrorist attack on the Marine headquarters in Beirut. In each case, it was decided to explore the matter in depth outside the operational chain of command, which normally would have investigated it. This approach is but another example of the checks and balances in action.

Providing Advice and Making Recommendations

At each level in the operational chain of command, the commander is often given the opportunity to recommend how he would carry out his assigned mission. In some cases it goes even further; he is given the opportunity to offer suggestions on how his mission should be worded. The objective in such cases is to assure that he understands precisely what he is tasked to accomplish. He knows what is feasible given his resources, and he should be able to make sound recommendations on how best to do the job. Therefore, it makes sense that he be involved in the "what" and "how" of his mission. This principle applies not only to operational orders, but also to resource allocation.

Up to the component command level, the advice and recommendations, even for matters of direct concern to the unified commander, go through military department channels. At that point, the matter formally enters into the unified command structure. Frequently it continues informally in service channels as well, because the component commander will either consult with or inform his peers in his military department about the recommendations he is forwarding to the unified commander. In some cases this approach is used to lend additional weight in Washington to the component's view, when the matter reaches that level; so it can either be in furtherance of, or in opposition to, the unified commander's recommendation, depending on how closely the CINC follows his subordinate's advice. Normally — although there are exceptions — he will follow it rather closely, recognizing that the component commander should be the best source of advice about the capabilities of his assigned forces. So, most often, the component commander's thinking via the military department will reinforce the CINC's recommendation to the Joint Chiefs of Staff. Additionally, in selected issues, the CINC will himself deal directly with a service chief or his staff, as well as with the joint chiefs. This can occur when a service is planning a major shift in organization or deployments and wants the CINC's views before making a final decision, or when some other service move is to occur that may have its chances of success increased if it enjoys CINC support. The reverse also happens: The CINC may have ideas, for example, on measures to raise his readiness that require service endorsement. It is a two-way street of assistance and support.

A number of ways exist to keep the unified commander and his subordinate component commanders on the same wavelength. In the European command, monthly meetings are held to discuss common problems. In addition, in recent years, the unified commander has established a framework of cooperation between his major headquarters that keeps all parties informed of issues affecting them, and that solicits advice from subordinates regularly. These arrangements do not preclude differences of opinion, but they do establish an environment in which problems can be settled more objectively.

The CINC of a unified command makes his formal recommendations to the Joint Chiefs of Staff or, in some cases, as specified by the secretary of defense, directly to the secretary. On direct, immediate, operational matters involving the deployment or employment of U.S. forces, the development of CINC recommendations seldom involves serious rivalry in his integrated staff; such recommendations predominantly concern the use of existing forces, thus substantially limiting the viable alternatives. The 1982 deployment of Marines in Beirut is an example. Given their location in the Mediterranean, plus the fact that they could maintain a logistics base offshore (to make clear that their stay ashore was to be a limited one), they were the logical and accepted choice for the mission. On force structure recommendations, and on other longer-term planning recommendations, the possibility for CINC staff disagreements increase as the alternatives for the type of forces to be employed increase in number.

With respect to the acceptance in Washington of his recommendations, a CINC can help assure their success if he has something of quality to offer. He can best make certain of this if he has his staff think and plan ahead in a unified framework, and then he can feed his ideas and plans to Washington, both formally and informally, through sevice, as well as joint channels. His ideas receive serious consideration for two reasons. One is that, since he has been assigned an area of responsibility, his staff should be more on top of how to relate U.S. military resources to an issue there than are the people in Washington, who have to deal with a much broader range of problems and, hence, at the outset of a contingency, most likely know less about that specific situation. Secondly, as noted earlier, as a general view, senior military officers listen carefully to the commander charged with the mission. Therefore, Washington, and particularly the joint chiefs, pay close attention to advice from the unified and specified commanders in resolving the many, often-conflicting, views presented. They do not always agree with the CINCs, to be certain, but they always listen carefully and accept CINC advice in the large majority of the cases.

In Washington, the joint staff[4] is the keystone of staff support for developing advice and recommendations for the Joint Chiefs of Staff to forward to the secretary of defense and the president. As such, it has important relationships not only with the unified and specified commands, but also with the military departments, with other appropriate agencies of the U.S. government, and with foreign military organizations.

The joint staff is divided into major subdivisions called "directorates," each of which has a defined functional responsibility. The precise number of directorates changes over time. At present there are five of them. Four basically conform to the standard staff elements of the traditional Army staff—personnel, operations, logistics, and plans and policy. These four directorates are called J-1 through J-5, the "J" standing for "joint." In addition, a directorate command, control and communications systems was established a few years ago. It does not have a J symbol, but is called C^3S. Each directorate is headed by a three-star flag or general officer, and above them stands the director of the joint staff, also a three-star officer, who is charged with the direction and supervision of the joint staff on behalf of the chairman and other members of the joint chiefs.

Historically, the director of the joint staff, the director of operations (J-3), and the director of plans and policy (J-5) have been the most important and influential jobs on the joint staff. Because of this, JCS policy provides that at any one time they should come from different services. Thus, if the director of the joint staff is, say, an Army officer, the director of operations and the director of plans and policy must come from the Navy or Marines and the Air Force, one from each service. The positions normally rotate among the services once every two years. An elaborate personnel bookkeeping system has been developed to assure and monitor this rotation. While the "horseblanket," as the personnel bookkeeping system is called, need not be religiously adhered to for senior officers, for the most part it is. The same also holds true for lower joint staff positions, each of which is designated to be filled by one of the services with an officer of a specified skill and rank. This arrangement is designed to help assure service balance and expertise in the joint staff.

Special mention should be made of the handling of intelligence in the joint staff. The joint staff has no J–2, or director of intelligence. Instead, the joint chiefs rely on the defense intelligence agency (DIA) for intelligence support. The director of the defense intelligence agency is responsible to the joint chiefs for the intelligence support they require. He similarly is responsible directly to the secretary of defense. The defense intelligence agency has established an assistant director, whose sole responsibility is to assure the needed intelligence support for the joint chiefs and the joint staff. He receives the requests for intelligence from the joint chiefs, coordinates in developing the DIA response, and forwards it to the director of the joint staff. He also is responsible for presenting the intelligence briefing each morning to the chairman of the joint chiefs.

As can be imagined, on occasion the dual responsibilities of the director of the DIA and his staff can produce a dilemma when the joint chiefs interpret the available information one way, and personnel in the office of the secretary of defense interpret it another way, with the DIA commissioned to represent both viewpoints throughout the intelligence community. It can satisfy that need by presenting both views, as well as its own independent judgment if appropriate; but this is not always easily done. That potential dilemma notwithstanding, most observers nonetheless agree that the DIA arrangement has worked adequately to date.

As noted, the J–3 and J–5 have historically been the most significant elements of the joint staff. The J–3 works primarily with the unified and specified commands on day-to-day operational and contingency planning matters. The J–5 looks more outward and to the future and is, therefore, heavily involved with the unified and specified commanders in the development of the defense guidance and its supporting programs and budget; the objective being to have CINC priorities and concerns clearly known and understood by the Joint Chiefs of Staff and the secretary of defense. Additionally, the J–5 works closely with the office of the secretary of defense and other government agencies on such matters as interagency political-military planning.

The effectiveness and influence of a particular element of the joint staff varies over time, and depends both on the individuals in key positions and on the needs of the time. With the growing interest in strategic mobility, for example, and in the logistic aspects of military planning and operations, J–4 has risen in stature and influence. The same holds for C^3S, which, until a few years ago, was a subordinate element of the J–3.

In discharging its advisory responsibilities, the joint staff is heavily dependent on information from other sources. It turns to the military departments for data on service forces, to the CINCs on operational matters, and to other agencies of government for information in their areas of expertise.

In operational matters, the joint staff plays a most singular role. As mentioned, it links the CINCs in the field with the authorities in Washington. In particular the operations directorate of the joint staff maintains both formal and informal contact with the CINC staff, literally twenty-four hours a day. This communication can be of great value in avoiding misunderstanding, in floating ideas and concepts in both directions, and in building mutual confidence. In broader political–military matters, the joint staff, and, especially, the J–5, works with other agencies on a wide range of issues—from arms control proposals and negotiations to emerging or continuing crises. It is here perhaps most evident why joint staff personnel need to be broad-gauged individuals, able to understand points of view beyond their own, and able to represent positions clearly and effectively.

To be certain, in its various dealings, the joint staff is not a free agent. It must represent the views of the joint chiefs. To this end, the chiefs have given the directors of the major staff elements of the joint staff the authority to issue instructions in the name of the joint chiefs to joint staff action officers for use in interagency fora, and to unified command headquarters on matters under JCS purview, as long as the instructions are in accord with approved JCS plans, policies and procedures. When circumstances call for position changes, the joint staff plays a dual educational role. It must keep the military departments abreast of the thinking of all parties involved, and, at the same time, convey to other elements of the government those aspects of the issue that trouble the joint chiefs and the services.

In carrying out its functions, the joint staff has to participate in developing formal, written views of the Joint Chiefs of Staff on a large number of subjects. Annually some 2,000 to 3,000 papers express the formal advice of the Joint Chiefs of Staff. In practice, the joint chiefs themselves see and discuss only a very small minority of issues—probably about 5 to 6 percent. The others are decided by the institution of the joint chiefs, in which a three-star deputy in each service plays a dominant role. These are the operations deputies, and they speak as the chiefs when they agree on a paper: not *for* the chiefs, but *as* the chiefs. Thus, it happens that the chiefs are said to hold views and to have provided advice on matters that they personally have not seen, and this can weaken their credibility.

That the process of developing formal JSC advice is, in essence, a process of negotiation has been roundly criticized by some because of service dominance in the process. This dominance comes about because once a joint staff officer has produced a preliminary draft of the proposed JCS view — normally in informal consultation with his service counterparts and, thus, with substantial service input — his draft is formally circulated to the services for comment, and a negotiating process begins. The paper at this juncture becomes a paper of the system, no longer in or under the control of the joint staff. That staff continues to have a central administrative role, but nothing more. Service agreement on an issue may be reached at the one- or two-star officer level on a matter considered routine, and will be signed off at that level as the formal view of the chiefs. Alternatively, the issue may be moved to the operations deputies or, in a few instances, to the chiefs themselves for discussion and resolution. In this process, each service briefs its principal before the meeting to insure that the service viewpoint is well presented and defended. The director of the joint staff may present the joint view as seen by the joint staff, but that view cannot prevail unless the services accept it. Without outside pressures, it can take considerable time to resolve controversial issues or to find a way to move them aside under this process. On the other hand, when time and circumstance demand, the joint system can respond with considerable speed.

It has been observed that this approach most often leads to a lowest common denominator point of view, of limited value to higher authority. If the aim of the common denominator is to obfuscate or avoid an issue — and that does happen — then the advice is of little value. But many of the positions taken by the joint chiefs are matters of judgment involving decisions that the services must, in part or in full, carry out, and here broad military agreement can be most beneficial. Successful implementation is more likely if the recipients of instructions have been a part of the decisionmaking process (even if their views have not completely prevailed), and if they are aware of some of the major implications of what they are told to do.

The joint staff is managed by the chairman on behalf of all the chiefs. Indeed, it is the chairman who is the focal point for the U.S. military participation in national security decisionmaking. He presently carries out this responsibility as the first among equals of the Joint Chiefs of Staff. Officially, he is the spokesman for the joint chiefs, and, informally, he is a personal military advisor to the secretary of defense. As noted earlier, he cannot issue orders to the field commands; the secretary does that.

As a member of the joint chiefs, the chairman is one of the statutory military advisors to the president, the NSC, and the secretary of defense. At meetings of the NSC it is he who normally represents the joint chiefs. He also represents the U.S. military in various international military fora, for example, the NATO military committee in chiefs of staff session, and the various other meetings between the department of defense and the major U.S. allies. Both directly and through the joint staff, he keeps in close touch with the unified and specified commands and is the principal link the field commands use to have their advice heard on critical matters under the purview of the joint chiefs.

In carrying out his responsibilities, the chairman relies heavily on the three-star assistant to the chairman and on the director of the joint staff. In general terms, in the past, the assistant to the chairman has been known as the "outside" man, and it is he who primarily deals with the other agencies of the executive branch in interdepartmental affairs. The director is the "inside" man, and he deals with those matters that reach down into the military departments. He thus has the lead in developing the JCS positions on various subjects. It is essential that the director and the assistant to the chairman work closely together in mutually supportive roles if the chairman is to be effective over the broad range of issues with which he must deal. The "outside" man, "inside" man roles are not airtight, and, in any event, it is the joint staff that supports both the director and the assistant to the chairman in their support of the chairman.

The chairman also has in his office a number of special assistants, the most important of whom are members of the chairman's staff group. They monitor for the chairman assigned regions of the world and critical ongoing functional issues, advising the assistant to the chairman and the chairman on developments that require attention. Among their other duties they monitor the development of JSC positions and advise the chairman of any problems that appear on the horizon. The director of the joint staff takes the lead in making known to the services and joint staff, either directly or inferentially, the chairman's thinking on an issue of personal interest so that they can be taken into account as the JCS paper is developed. The chairman's views carry great weight in such matters, but there are exceptions — and they may occur on significant problems. That the director and joint staff are instruments not only of the chairman but also of the body of the Joint Chiefs of Staff is well understood; the chairman manages it for the joint chiefs, but the staff must remain responsive to the needs of the collective body. Reference is made, again, to the negotiating nature of the JCS process and the workings of the joint staff. Still, the joint staff is the primary means the chairman has to get his ideas expressed, to have the necessary planning done. He can and does use other sources for advice, and in recent years has turned to outside consultants, usually retired military officers and former OSD officials to help with specific problems.

As first among equals, it is often incumbent on the chairman to take the lead in having the joint chiefs respond to a request for advice from the president, secretary of defense, or National Security Council — respond in a manner that is conscious of the predominant forces at work in the minds of senior administration officials, that is militarily sound and relevant, and that is timely. He also has to take the lead in having the chiefs consider important matters before they become pressing issues; that is, it is he who must get the chiefs to think ahead on emerging critical matters.

The chairman — and the other chiefs, for that matter — have avenues to provide advice other than through the joint chiefs' mechanism. The chairman, if he disagrees with the other chiefs and feels strongly on an issue, may forward to the secretary of defense a separate chairman's memorandum laying out his thoughts. Or he may choose to use that mechanism to forward his views on a subject not formally considered by the chiefs. He may or may not consult on his personal memoranda, but usually he does at least inform the other chiefs of his intentions, if for no other reason than that he can be certain that they will hear about it, probably sooner than later. Most chairmen have used separate memoranda only sparingly, either in the interest of maintaining good working relationships with the other chiefs or because they believed their views were adequately represented in the formal JCS position on the matter.

In an informal sense, the chairman has greater opportunity to express his views. The success he has in this regard depends to a large degree on the confidence he commands from the secretary of defense. He usually meets regularly and privately with the secretary to discuss issues of importance to them both. It is an ideal forum for a free exchange of ideas. Of course, if the chairman has accepted a corporate position with the other members of the joint chiefs on an issue, he will be careful not to stray too far from it, no matter what his personal beliefs, although he may and frequently does, explain to the secretary the factors that carried the greatest weight in the JCS recommendation, conveying some of the conflicting views that had to be reconciled. He may also explain why he agreed with the other chiefs, while personally preferring another view. These give and take sessions can be of great value to both the secretary and the chairman.

In operational matters, the chairman has the authority to offer advice to the secretary of defense in the name of the chiefs, when time does not permit formal consultation, and to issue the orders that flow from the secretary's decision. He will inform the chiefs of his actions later. His ability to act independently of the other chiefs in operational matters thus is considerable, particularly in evolving situations. Under such circumstances, the joint staff works closely with the appropriate service staffs and that of the appropriate unified commander to keep the chairman abreast of, and, if possible, ahead of, events. But it is in the chairman that the military leadership resides; he has to work closely with the secretary of defense and other appropriate officials across the government. As a crisis continues, the joint chiefs, as a formal body, take on larger repsonsibilities, and the military advice becomes more institutional, since time usually permits. But the chairman continues to play the major role, and the more he enjoys the confidence of the other chiefs, the more latitude he has to speak for them. If they are confident that their interests will be protected and that they will be brought in on those decisions that especially affect them, they will trust the chairman without a formal JSC view or consultation.

From this it can be seen there are large demands on the chairman's time and energies. In addition, the chairman has many representative functions, both of a domestic and international nature, and he does a goodly amount of traveling. Invariably, a problem arises as to how to handle his duties in his absence. The practice has been to appoint an acting chairman from among the other chiefs. On occasion, this has been done by assigning, on a rotational basis, one or the other chiefs present in Washington, with no real thought of continuity. That is one reason the assistant to the chairman rather than the acting chairman in the past has represented the chairman in a large number of meetings the chairman might personally attend were he in town.

Some meetings, however, require the presence of one of the chiefs, which means that the acting chairman must be prepared. The present practice is that the duty of acting chairman rotates among the chiefs on a quarterly basis. The most stringent rules for the acting chairman were those set forth by Secretary Rumsfeld in the mid-1970s. To assure that he had an informed acting chairman with whom he could work, he directed that the acting chairman be designated for one year at a time. Admiral James Holloway, then the chief of naval operations, filled that function. The arrangement worked some hardships on General George Brown, the chairman at the time, and on Admiral Holloway, in terms of coordinating their schedules, but it guaranteed that the acting chairman met the requirements of the then secretary of defense.

It is through the secretary of defense that civilian control of the U.S. military is routinely effectuated. As noted earlier, the secretary may, if he wishes, control military operations down to the movement of a single aircraft or ship, and all operational military orders from Washington are issued in his name. He is the only civilian in the department authoritatively in the military chain of command, unless the deputy secretary is acting for him in his absence. The other elements of the secretary's large office are advisors and assistants — advisors and assistants heavily relied on, but not formally in the military chain of command, although they, at times, in effect, assume that role when speaking for the secretary.

As the senior Pentagon official in the military chain of command, the secretary has the right to overrule his advisors, and on occasion he does. In operational matters he relies heavily on the judgments of the chairman and, as appropriate, the other members of the joint chiefs and the CINCs. Any overruling in that area normally stems from political factors that have to be integrated into the equation. On political–military matters under development in interdepartmental fora, the situation is somewhat different. An effort is always made to achieve a DOD position with which the various elements of the department can agree, because both the secretary of defense and the joint chiefs are heard individually and separately in matters that have military implications. Again, the process in reaching a DOD position is a negotiated one, and in most cases a view can be found that adequately represents the major views of both the secretary and the joint chiefs. When it cannot, the two agree to disagree, and do so at the meeting. This can be a delicate matter. No one wants the military to appear muzzled. On the other hand, the military do not want to appear to be going around their superiors, or taking their case to the public.

Allocating Resources

It can be argued that matters relating to the allocation of resources fall variously within the execution of orders and the forwarding of advice. There is some merit to that view, but the allocation of resources — present and future — is so important to the military chain of command that it warrants separate treatment.

It is through the allocation of resources that civilian control of the U.S. military is made manifest. After World War II, when the military organizations of the nation were being restructured, it was recognized that one primary way to preserve civilian control was to rest the purse strings securely in the hands of civilians. The military would be afforded full opportunity to recommend; the civilians would render the decisions. This civilian control of the purse strings was enhanced by certain legal measures. In the legislation dealing with the organization of the military departments, the position of comptroller of the departments — the office most directly concerned with the expenditure of funds — was structured in a manner different from other elements of the service staffs. All major service staff elements, with the exception of the comptroller, must report to the senior military officer on the staff — the chief of staff, the chief of naval operations, the commandant. The comptroller, however, must report directly to the civilian secretary of the military department or to one of his designated civilian assistants.[5] If the secretary agrees, the comptroller may also concurrently report to the service chief — but it is legally the secretary's choice as to whether this is done. Further, if the comptroller or his deputy is a military officer, the other must be a civilian. In day-to-day activities, the comptroller's reporting channel does not loom as significant, but on occasion it is important and, further, it is at all times a reminder of civilian control, with the secretary of defense at the pinnacle within the defense department.

Resource allocation begins through the medium of the well-known planning, programming, and budgeting system (PPBS). Advisors to the secretary of defense have an opportunity to be heard at a number of stages in the development of a defense-wide five-year program of effort. The three most significant points in this cycle are when

1. The policy guidance is issued.
2. The programing decisions are made.
3. The budget allocations are made.

Recent improvements have made available the opportunity for all elements of the defense department to be heard on these matters. The establishment of a Defense Resources Board (DRB) and its current method of operation have made it possible for the operational chain of command to be heard more fully than has been the case in the past, an important step in balancing inputs from the military departments. This means that the chairman has an even more critical role to play. Given his staff resources, however, the chairman carries the greatest weight in policy discussions, where detailed information is less essential. When he chooses to speak on specific, detailed issues he has to rely almost solely on data provided by the service concerned. That data flows to him easily when he supports a service position; when he opposes it, it can be difficult to assemble the necessary basic data from an uncooperative service. He has to turn to the services for data because the joint staff has no comprehensive staff element to deal with the complex, detailed programing and budget issues across the board. Partly because of this, the chairman has in practice generally entered into budget discussions on a selective basis, either on programs about which he had prior knowledge and well-developed views, or on matters concerning which a service chief or CINC has persuaded him that help is badly needed and is justified. At present, the chairman does not have the ability to satisfy those observers who believe that he should have a larger voice in the allocation of resources. These critics argue that since he is the single officer who speaks from an overall joint military viewpoint, the senior U.S. military officer should fashion complete and prioritized recommendations on future U.S. military capabilities.[6]

The service chiefs participate in the allocation of resources in both their roles — as members of the joint chiefs and as head of their service. It is here that the conflict of interest between their two responsibilities is seen as most obvious. As members of the joint chiefs, the service chiefs each year forward to the secretary a joint strategic planning document that outlines the military objectives, policies, strategy, plans, and forces the chiefs believe most suited to implementing the policy guidance promulgated by the secretary of defense. On the basis of this framework, they later assess how well the service proposed programs meet the secretary's guidance. The question that inevitably arises is how can a service chief fail to endorse as a member of the joint chiefs programs that he forwarded to the secretary as a chief of service. The answer is that most of the time he does endorse his service proposals. Advice from the JCS on resource allocation is thus considered as of limited utility, as the rule of unanimity applies here, as well as in other matters before the joint chiefs. Efforts by the chiefs to be "joint" are far overshadowed by their overall support for service programs.

Of the major improvements which have recently strengthened the weight of the operational chain of command in PPBS matters, one of the most significant is that of having the unified and specified commanders comment on the policy guidance that the secretary proposes to issue and on the programs that the services propose to carry out that guidance. In the European command, to give added weight to the CINC's recommendations, they were based on a series of priorities worked out in conjunction with the component commanders. The objective was to generate priorities that commanded the support of the components and then have them work those priorities through service administrative channels while the CINC worked them simultaneously through the operational channel.

As late as the 1960s, the prevailing wisdom, hammered home regularly, was that the unified and specified commanders were to concern themselves almost solely with how to use best their assigned forces. They were not to identify forces or capabilities believed necessary to fulfill their mission, nor forces they believed required in the future. Those responsibilities rested firmly in the hands of the military departments. Over the years that formulation proved to be too simplistic, and today the responsibilities of the field commanders are interpreted much more broadly. While it is still true that the unified and specified commanders focus primarily on short-term operational matters, their horizons are now considerably broader. Thus, in the priorities established in the European command, emphasis was placed primarily on operational shortfalls in adequate working and living conditions, in training, in readiness, and in sustainability; but they also reached out to the future to identify particularly critical shortfalls in current capabilities. One specific concern of high interest was the inadequate capability to attack the follow-on forces of the Warsaw Pact, forces that had to be attacked if the NATO allies were to be successful in defending allied territory.

The ability of the CINCs to influence policy has been greater than their ability to influence specific programs in the final stages of the programming–budgeting cycle. In other words, the CINCs have had more clout in determining the broad guidance establishing the basic strategy, guidelines for force employment, and the priorities for future action than they have in seeing that the approved guidance is faithfully carried out in the service budgets. One reason for this is that as decision time approaches, the specific elements of a proposed program—under constant discussion between the military departments and OSD—often change rapidly, and the CINCs learn that they have been asked to advise on an alternative no longer under active consideration.

In truth, the military departments—the administrative chain of command—play the dominant role in the allocation of resources outside of a specific operational necessity. That dominance comes from the legislation setting forth the responsibilities of the military departments—to organize, train, equip, administer. That is a large order which contains many broad implications that find expression in a myriad of different ways. Unless the law is changed, a large service participation in these matters is assured.

TOWARD THE FUTURE

The preceding review of how the military chain performs its three functions has been presented in some detail in order to show, among other things, that it is an evolving system, one that *does* undergo change over time. Therefore, arguments for or against changing the organization of the Joint Chiefs of Staff and the military chain of command miss the point when they talk as if the question were one of the status quo versus change. More accurately, the issue is one of the rate and direction of change. Few objections, if any, have been raised to one of the most promising changes made in recent years, that of increasing the part that the CINCs play in the chain of command.

Similarly, the question is not whether the present system works. It does. Far from perfectly, by any measure, but not disastrously, either. A lot depends—and will depend—on the personalities involved, the mood of the times, and compatibility in terms of outlook and objectives of the various agencies and elements of government. Next, while under the present arrangements the services and service chiefs are very major participants in their service roles, the joint chiefs do attempt to be "joint," although not always with complete success, as, for example, in their analysis of service program submissions to the secretary and in their recommendations for a future force structure that is constrained in fiscal realities. Finally, it must be noted, as one considers change, that the current organization does provide the secretary of defense and the president with the collective military views of their senior military advisors. While this can lead to recommendations from the chiefs that are not as "crisp" as some would like, it does mean that the collective military view is presented by those statutorily charged with the responsibility. If the recommendations may sometimes not be focused enough for the secretary's specific purposes, at a minimum it provides him the limits of agreement among his military advisors, and that is important for him to know. In this context, as noted earlier, the importance of some large measure of consensus on proposed courses of action greatly assists in implementation of the decision. United States experience in Southeast Asia made that need manifest for sustained military actions. The building of that support should begin with those charged with carrying out the decision.

Positive evolution notwithstanding, a number of trenchant criticisms—shown in the earlier discussion to have some merit—have been lodged against the military chain of command. Essentially, these fall into five major categories.

1. The lines of command are both diffused and confused.
2. The CINCs are not sufficiently consulted or represented in the chain of command.
3. The services play too dominant a role in the current organization.
4. The service chiefs face an "insuperable" conflict of interest when they are both a service chief and a member of the Joint Chiefs of Staff.
5. The joint staff is neither joint nor properly manned.

The lines of command are said to be confused both in Washington and in the field. In Washington the confusion comes because the role of the joint chiefs in the chain is not clear. As noted earlier, the law says the operational chain of command runs from the president and the secretary of defense to the unified and specified commanders. A DOD directive adds, however, that the line will run "through the Joint Chiefs of Staff." Confusion arises here on two counts. First, although, on inspection, it is evident that the chiefs are advisors, it is still not entirely clear what "through" means. What is their role in providing advice to the secretary and president before the decision is made? Moreover, are the chiefs merely a channel of communication and nothing more? Or, as the order passes through them, do they have the right to make additions, elaborations, changes? The second source of confusion in Washington is that to pass an order through a committee—in this case the joint chiefs—is not normal military procedure. Orders go from commander to commander, and to have a committee interposed along the way raises questions about who is in charge at that level.

The criticism of confusion in the field stems from the fact that the unified commander does not have sufficient control over his service component commanders to carry out his mission effectively. Since the components are primarily dependent on and subordinate to their military departments, the CINC of the unified command cannot ensure that his assigned forces have the proper training or that they are maintained at the requisite level of readiness.

The second charge leveled against the current organization—that the CINCs are not sufficiently consulted or represented in the chain of command—was also shown to have merit. One aspect of this is that the CINCs still do not have enough to say about the readiness of their assigned forces, about their joint training, about their ability to sustain themselves in combat, or about the future capabilities of their forces. Most importantly, the CINCs are said not to have enough voice in the overall policies or priorities that guide the development and employment of their armed forces.

The third major criticism is that the services are too dominant in the present organization, with the result that it is difficult to produce a joint view that rises above particular service interests. The cause of this problem lies largely in legislation that stipulates that if the chiefs cannot agree on an issue they report it to the secretary and the president. The result has been the emergence of what has been called by some the "principle of unanimity," that is, pressure is always on the chiefs to reach agreement. Under this construct, service desires must be taken fully into account — which gives them great weight in developing JCS advice. Parochialism can easily thrive in such an environment, as can efforts to avoid unpleasant issues by raising the level of generalization of the advice going forward.

With respect to the conflict of interest issue, critics argue that it is asking too much of an individual to propose as the primary guardian of his service an idea or program and then later judge his recommendation differently in his "joint" hat. Consequently, a service chief's position as a member of the joint chiefs is most often no more than a repeat of his earlier recommendation. Given the principle of unanimity, the advice of the JCS thus becomes no more than the sum of individual service proposals — which is not helpful to the secretary. To remedy this situation, some critics have proposed that service chiefs not be members of the joint chiefs.

The final major complaint against current procedures and organization, that the joint staff is neither joint nor composed of the proper personnel, is regularly heard. Ambassador Komer, in his testimony before the White subcommittee, succinctly stated the major shortcomings.[7] The joint staff is little more than a secretariat for reconciling service views, with emphasis on finding agreement. Next, joint staff personnel remain beholden to their own service for their future assignments and promotions; they, therefore, in the main, retain their services biases, hampering the emergence of a truly joint position. Thus, too often, a common denominator view is developed by the joint staff, a view often of limited value to the secretary. Another frequently repeated criticism is that the joint staff does not have the best people assigned from the services. Individually, in my experience, the personnel on the joint staff have been competent, motivated, dedicated people who have done a much better job than they have received credit for. Still the problem persists, as Secretary Harold Brown has underscored,[8] that the services normally send the joint staff good people but seldom those they consider their very best, particularly at the 0–5,0–6 level. Evidence supporting this comment is the relative dearth of promotions given joint staff personnel in the annual promotion cycles. Further, the argument goes, if the joint staff is merely there to reconcile service views, it does not require the best people. Like it or not, the image of the joint staff is not a good one, and that, in itself, impedes its work.

The present system works, albeit imperfectly, and is evolving positively; but it has not proved satisfactory to key decision makers. It still falls short of its potential in significant areas, particularly in addressing difficult issues and alternatives at the higher levels and in conducting military operations optimally in the field. That is the conclusion one draws from the comments just presented, and one that many officers who have had key responsibilities in the organization also have concluded. General David Jones and General E. C. Meyer are two examples. General George S. Brown was not fully satisfied with the functioning of the joint chiefs and planned to propose some changes at the conclusion of his term as chairman in 1978. In the fall of 1977 he asked several of us to give him our views on needed changes so that he could assess them in terms of his own. He intended to consult with the other chiefs during the spring of 1978 on organizational reform. Unfortunately, his battle with cancer began early in the year and he did not have the opportunity to follow through on his plan.

What then, can be done to encourage needed and essential further forward progress in improving U.S. military structure and performance? What steps can be accomplished with substantial consensus? Too abrupt a departure from current practice, no matter how sound it may seem, will generate opposition of a determined nature that may frustrate more modest, very worthwhile and consequential advances. With this in mind, it would seem that if two simple criteria were satisfied, the probability of success for necessary evolution would increase. These are:

1. The lines and responsibility in the chain of command must be made clear to eliminate any confusion or uncertainty.
2. The advice rendered by the senior military advisors to the president, the National Security Council, and the secretary of defense must address the difficult issues while taking into account the capabilities of the military departments woven into a fabric of unified military thought and activity.

The proposals which are outlined in the following paragraphs have been designed to be consistent with the criteria just given.

Unified and Specified Commanders

Unified and specified commanders should participate more actively in those matters that directly affect their capability to carry out their assigned missions. To that end:

1. *The CINCs should have a stronger voice in improving the readiness of*

their assigned forces. Many of the primary concerns of the CINCs are not glamorous and, consequently, are the first to be cut when budgets become tight. As the primary unified military spokesman for operations and maintenance funding to keep things functioning, for programs to increase the ability of assigned forces to sustain themselves in combat, for funds for training, and for funds to ensure that the U.S. military personnel have adequate working and living conditions, the CINCs must be heard. Otherwise, the deterrent capability of those forces will not be optimized. The opportunity for the CINC to make his priorities known in the development of the annual defense guidance must be continued, permitting the CINC to comment on the draft guidance in writing and to present his major concerns to the secretary and the DRB before the guidance is approved. Equally, if not more important, if the CINC's recommendations are accepted by the secretary, the OSD staff and the Joint Chiefs of Staff must develop procedures to ascertain that the military departments are following that guidance. This last, particularly, needs additional emphasis. It is recognized that the CINCs will not have a comprehensive global perspective given their assigned responsibilities, so their recommendations will not always be followed. They do, however, warrant a hearing, so that the Washington authorities can evaluate them and place them in an overall perspective of U.S. policy and strategy.

2. *The CINCs should have a larger voice in the determination of the future capabilities of their assigned or earmarked forces.* In so doing, however, they should not be in competition with the staffs of the military departments. The CINCs do not have, and do not need, a large research and development staff element. Rather, the CINCs should identify the most pressing specific shortcomings in the capabilities of their forces and ask that such capabilities be provided. They need not identify the particular weapon system required; that is the function of the military departments. An example of what is proposed here is found in the European command's recent emphasis on selected capabilities needed to attack the follow-on forces of the Warsaw Pact, in line with SACEUR's plan for the defense of NATO territory. The European command sought improved capabilities from the United States to seek out and identify targets, to pass critical target information rapidly to the NATO forces, and to attack what might be fleeting, mobile targets. The capabilities required were sought in generic terms, not in terms of particular systems or programs. When the services propose an answer to the CINC's requirements, the unified commander concerned should have the opportunity to comment on how well it meets his objectives, but the procurement and programming should be left to the military departments. Related to this, the CINC's voice in security assistance matters also needs to be enhanced. He will have to count on the forces of allies in his planning, so he should have a stronger voice in their overall military

capabilities to the extent that U.S. security assistance programs influence them.

3. *The CINCs should have more influence and control over their component commands.* In consultation with the component commanders, the CINC should establish overall priorities for his command, and the component commanders should then follow them in their deliberations with their respective military department. In this way, the component commanders and their staff would become an extension of the CINC that reaches into the military departments, as well as an extension of the service into the unified command. Next, the CINC should have a larger voice in the training of the forces assigned to his component commands. The CINC needs a better overview of and participation in training of component forces that directly affect the CINC's ability to fulfill his mission. The CINC needs to know that the training is responsive to those shortcomings he believes most limiting. The CINC needs to be able to reorient that training if necessary. To defend, at higher levels of authority, his requirements for improving the readiness of his forces, he needs more frequent reports and recommendations from his components on their unfulfilled training requirements. This is being done somewhat today, but the demands of deterrence require that the process be made more comprehensive. Related to the preceding, since the JCS exercise program is central to the CINC's ability to train his forces, JCS exercises should receive a higher priority in the available funding. A balance between service-oriented exercises and joint exercises is justified; however, the balance is not yet correct.

4. *More attention should be paid to the contingency plans that the CINCs develop in response to the taskings from the Joint Chiefs of Staff.* These plans rightly focus on potential emergencies that might require the deployment and/or the employment of U.S. military forces — forces either assigned to the CINC involved or made available from other sources. Such planning provides a detailed look at the concept of operations the CINC plans to use, and the forces he would require to carry out the tasking — forces that may exceed those assigned him or made available to him for the particular contingency. Taken on a global basis, these plans provide valuable insight into force requirements in the event that one or more contingencies should develop simultaneously or near simultaneously. In this way they can help sort out priorities for the use of existing forces and for the establishment of future forces. Key to this objective is the guidance from the secretary of defense to the joint chiefs. Clear guidance is required to make certain that the joint chiefs have tasked the unified commanders to plan for and emphasize those contingencies that the administration sees most probable, or most consequential, should they occur.

5. *In dealing with emergencies, uncertainty and confusion in the chain of command should be minimized by relying principally on the unified com-*

mander concerned for advice and execution of decisions involving his responsibilities. Implementation of the other measures proposed would go a long way toward assuring that the CINC would be a focal point in such situations, because the CINC would be playing an increasingly important role in DOD across the board. He would have to be provided the staff requisite to fill his enlarged role, that is, the expertise to plan for and see to the execution of his mission under the new conditions. But the linchpin of greater success in this area would be improved use of the chain of command. As noted, officials in Washington sometimes think they can deal with a far distant situation from the nation's capital, dealing directly with the on-scene commander. This practice is, however, a recipe for disaster over the long run. The CINC, his staff, and subordinate commanders have lived with the problems—real and potential—in their area, and they have a data base and understanding that they can bring to the issues, which does not exist in Washington. The preferred approach is to have within the framework of guidance and decisions originating in Washington the on-scene commander make those decisions that are within the scope of his mission, forwarding up the chain of command those that exceed his authority along with his recommendations. If not amenable to decisionmaking below him, the CINC will decide on the course of action to take or recommend to Washington. If the chain of command is faithfully used in this manner, recommendations can be forwarded and decided on rapidly.

The Joint Staff

A strong, confident, motivated joint staff is essential to the success of the Joint Chiefs of Staff.

1. *Personnel who are serving with, or have served with, the joint staff and unified command staffs should receive more than a proportionate share of the promotions at each level and, on leaving the joint duty, should be assigned to key billets in their service.* Promotions and assignments are the best indicators of the front runners in the services, and, if personnel assigned or formerly assigned to a joint staff get the fastest promotions and the best jobs, the services will send more of their best people to joint duty, and the personnel so assigned will carry with them the proper image of success and potential. The personnel assigned must be broad-gauged, able to work long and hard with people of diverse backgrounds and viewpoints, and prepared to live with frustrations. Meeting these criteria, they would merit a proportionately higher number of promotions. Thus, this proposal would stipulate that if, say, the selection rate for promotion of eligible majors in a service was decided on as 25 percent one year, the selection rate for personnel in joint assignments would be 30 percent. The skills required for joint duty are also essential to carrying out the responsibilities of a flag or general officer

and are also necessary to work successfully with allies in international situations.

2. *Joint duty should be a prerequisite for promotion to flag or general officer rank in all but a few specialized billets.* In the mid-1970s a DOD directive was issued which specified that officers promoted to general or flag rank must have served a joint duty tour or be assigned one on promotion. This was a step in the right direction, but in implementation the criteria that qualified assignments as "joint duty" were very broad and included a number of virtually service-only assignments. The directive needs to be strengthened to state that general and flag rank personnel will have had joint experience and understand how to operate in an integrated service environment. There may be a few exceptions in specialized technical areas, but only a very few, since practically all experts worthy of consideration for promotion to the highest ranks should have served in a joint billet during some point in their career.

3. *The joint staff should work principally for the chairman of the joint chiefs.* Under the overall guidance and direction of the chairman, joint staff action officers should develop papers for consideration by the joint chiefs. They should consult with and take into account, as appropriate, service views, but they should not be bound by them in the recommendations contained in their final paper. Service positions that are not accepted would be fairly presented under discussion of the various alternatives considered. Moreover, any service chief could have a paper discussed by the joint chiefs themselves and, if not satisfied at the conclusion of that, could carry his dissent to the secretary. It is this assurance of having a service view presented in any paper and forwarded to the secretary if so desired that leads to the proposal being worded that the joint staff work "principally" but not solely for the chairman. It should be noted here that having the joint staff develop JCS papers would not alter the basic sources of ideas currently going into those papers. The press of time and the need for thorough understanding of the issues and options would necessitate that the joint staff officer seek service input. What would change is that there would be no formal negotiation over word choices and no delay in a response to a difficult question. Since on most issues the chairman would not have a strong personal view as guidance, the joint staff would formulate the proposed position — a "percolate up" staff system. An approach along the lines described should improve JCS advice in several ways. It should enhance the timeliness of the advice, since there would not be inordinate negotiation over phraseology. For the same reason, it should make the resultant advice more "crisp." It would, further, make it more comprehensive, in that a discussion of alternatives would almost certainly be included on contentious issues. It probably would not, however, lead to a great increase in the number of split recommendations from the chiefs. First of all, no one in the military — at any level —

relishes the thought of sending a disagreement on to higher authority, for this normally results in what they consider to be a less militarily qualified group rendering military advice. At a lower level of importance, other considerations will facilitate development of a broadly supported military view. Joint staff members have to go back to their respective services, and they will have to work well with their counterparts from the other services if they are to succeed in the joint arena.

4. *The size of the joint staff should be increased to the level appropriate to the assigned tasks.* The current artificial and arbitrary legal definition of the joint staff should be modified so as to include all personnel in the organization of the Joint Chiefs of Staff supporting the joint chiefs. The existing situation leads only to confusion, misunderstanding, and misrepresentation to the extent that people believe that only 400 personnel assist the joint chiefs in fulfilling their responsibilities. In addition to including the some 1,400 personnel currently assigned, the joint staff would have to be enlarged to include a small number of personnel (probably less than twenty-five) to handle the increased selective involvement of the chairman in programming-budgetary matters proposed under the following recommendations dealing with the chairman.

The Chairman, Joint Chiefs of Staff

1. *The chairman, JCS, should have more authority with respect to operational matters.* At the present time, the chairman provides advice in the name of the joint chiefs on operational matters "if time to consult does not exist." That authority should be broadened to permit him to act in operational matters concerning the deployment and employment of U.S. military forces at all times. In so doing, he should consult with the other chiefs when feasible, he always should be fully aware of the views of the services, and he should make known to his civilian superiors any dissenting views. Giving the chairman such authority does not pose large problems, since in most short-fused operational matters the options for military action are normally very circumscribed by the disposition and capabilities of the in-being forces. Also, in the conduct of most operation, the differences are not usually among the military, but between the military and one or more of the other agencies of the government. The chairman should have no great difficulty in speaking authoritatively "for the military." In this connection, to help assure that he is well-acquainted with the view of the CINCs, as well as those of the other joint chiefs, the chairman should further strengthen his ties with the CINCs, consulting with them frequently, formally and informally, to gain better understanding of their viewpoint and either support them or inform them why he cannot.

2. *The chairman should selectively involve himself more in budgeting*

and programming matters. The chairman should take personal initiatives and/or lend support to others in those critical matters which he believes are receiving insufficient attention. He should support the CINCs when he agrees with their priorities; he should support the services under similar conditions; and he should push for specific actions in other areas that he considers inadequately funded. By focusing on selected issues, the chairman would not develop a detailed prioritized list of programs for each of the services, as some have recommended. It is doubtful that he could do so in any meaningful way, even if he were provided a large supporting staff. It is difficult, if not impossible, for a service chief to develop and hold within his grasp the details of the oft changing priorities for his own service. To ask the chairman to do so for four services is unrealistic. It could only work to the disadvantage of his overall effectiveness. Even by restricting himself to priority shortcomings, the chairman would need a staff somewhat larger than it now is; but it would not have to be a major staff element of the magnitude found in the services or OSD.

3. *The chairman should have more authority in personnel matters.* The chairman should have a controlling voice in personnel assigned to the joint staff, and he should have a voice in their follow-on assignments. This would contribute to highly qualified service personnel being selected for joint duty. It could also institute a good flow of professionals between the services and joint duty, an approach more desirable than creating an elite group of personnel serving only, or mainly, joint tours. If the joint staff is to represent the capabilities of the various services in interagency fora, and if the joint staff is to have the ability to recommend action in fast-moving situations, its personnel must have recent, first-hand knowledge of how the forces of the respective services operate. Only by returning to his service for additional experience can one keep up to date. Another authority the chairman should have is the right to pass judgment on all three- or four-star promotions to operational assignments, as well as on selected key assignments below those grades. This would formalize the informal voice the chairman now has in senior promotions, and it is an important change. It would send the proper signal concerning the importance of joint duty.

4. *The chairman should be made the principal military advisor to the National Security Council.* Currently, the chairman expresses before the NSC the views of the joint chiefs, adding his personal views as he believes necessary or is asked for. This practice should be reversed, with the chairman noting any dissent from his view. This conforms more with reality today, in that the chairman normally is the only chief to attend NSC meetings. Further, having the chairman designated the principal advisor would give a better focus to the military voice. The participation of the services in the formulation of the chairman's views would remain.

5. *The chairman should not become a member of the National Security*

Council. Both the Joint Chiefs of Staff and the recent House of Representatives bill would make the chairman a member of the NSC, instead of being an advisor.[9] To do so, however, would seem to be misguided. The function of the joint chiefs — and that of the chairman as well — is to render impartial, objective military advice to their civilian superiors. Those civilian superiors change as administrations change, and these successions bring with them differences in outlook and basic philosophy. Each administration has a point of view to which it wants to give expression and which can very basically affect national security matters as, for example, in the emphasis given to defense budgets. As a member of the NSC, the chairman would tend to be perceived as a member of the administration's political team, because he would be sitting with the other statutory members: the vice president and the presidentially appointed secretaries of state and defense. It is inadvisable for him to be so perceived, either at home or abroad. Furthermore, it is not inconceivable that the selection of a chairman under such conditions could become politicized, as each administration would want to make certain that it had a chairman fully compatible with and supportive of its outlook and objectives. This would gravely endanger our apolitical military tradition. Reinforcing the need to avoid such a danger is that, being an advisor, in fact, gives the chairman ample opportunity to discharge his statutory responsibilities. While he does not "vote" now, he would not "vote" as a member — there is no voting. The president hears the views of those present — of the statutory members, of the statutory advisors, of the other presidential advisors invited to the meeting by the president — and makes his decision. The chairman, as an advisor, has the opportunity to be heard. This meets the necessary objectives. Like the director of the Central Intelligence Agency, the chairman should remain an advisor in his area of expertise — an advisor influential to the extent that his views are sound and persuasively presented.

6. *The chairman should not be placed in the military chain of command as a commander.* Related to the discussion of the chairman as an advisor, another proposal that has found support from both military and civilian quarters is to alter existing legislation so as to place the chairman in the chain of command. As noted earlier, pursuant to a DOD directive, today the CINCs report to the secretary of defense "through" the Joint Chiefs of Staff, and the secretary uses the reverse channel to issue orders. In fact, under this arrangement, the chiefs are advisors and a means of communication. The bill passed by the House would have the channel go through the chairman instead of the Joint Chiefs of Staff. Such a change would enhance the image of the chairman, a worthwhile objective. To give the chairman such authority would not, however, place him in the chain of command, in the sense that the term is normally used by military professionals. Commanders are in the chain of command; advisors or staff of the commanders

are not. Commanders are given a mission, responsibilities, and authorities. Since the House bill stipulates[10] that orders would be issued by the president and the secretary of defense, it clearly is the intent to raise the chairman's prestige as an advisor. There is logic behind that intent, for if the aim were to place the chairman in the chain of command as a commander, in the sense just described, it would entail giving him decisionmaking authority, and the question is then raised, of what kind. Would the secretary forgo his authority to issue orders, to decide on such matters as military movements, leaving those solely to the chairman? Would the CINCs report only to the chairman, without the right or necessity to go to the secretary? The approach proposed of retaining the chairman as an advisor avoids those questions while giving him enhanced stature and importance, and facilitating more efficient use of the chain of command. There should be no confusion, however. The chairman should remain an advisor and not a commander. Since an important objective in any change in the JCS organization is to eliminate confusion, rather than referring to the chairman as being in the chain of command, it would be preferable to label him the principal military advisor to the secretary on military operations matters, also responsible for facilitating the transmittal of orders, communications, and advice between the president and the secretary of defense, and the unified and specified commanders.

The Joint Chiefs of Staff

1. *The service chiefs should remain members of the Joint Chiefs of Staff.* The service chiefs bring to the deliberations of the joint chiefs a perspective concerning the present and future capabilities of their services that is mandatory to sound decisions and action over the long run. They will also inevitably influence the implementation of any decision involving unified military operations. They will be much better prepared to do so if they have participated in making the decision and know the political, as well as the military, ramifications of actions proposed or undertaken. In operational matters, the service chiefs would basically act as advisors to the chairman, with the right to dissent on any item about which they felt strongly. In other matters that came before them, acting with the chairman they would continue, as now, to speak as the joint chiefs unless there were dissents. The papers considered, however, would have been developed by the joint staff in consultation with the services as previously described. In the event of dissent, it would be the chairman's view that would go forward to the secretary, with service differences being added to the chairman's position.

A service chief would have to deal with any conflict of interest between his two responsibilities at two levels. Initially, prior to sending recommendations forward, he should, as primary leader of a service, see that unified warfare is appropriately considered in the formulation of service positions; his membership on the joint chiefs should facilitate this. Second, if and when significant new factors or judgments were introduced in JCS delibera- tions, the service chief should accept some modification to his single service objective. This would not be all that unique a situation. The secretary of defense, for example, has to place defense department needs in the larger context of his responsibilities as a cabinet officer, and often must accept less funding than he thinks justified. No one sees that as unmanageable. Service chiefs should be selected who fully understand their responsibilities in this regard.

2. *The Joint Chiefs of Staff should consider only the critical aspects of issues relating to broad policy guidance, strategy, contingency planning, and force structure matters.* Central to what is proposed here is a sound working definition of what is "critical." That judgment would be made on a case-by-case basis, basically by the chairman in publishing the agenda for JCS meetings, which he has the authority for. Presently, however, too many administrative matters are handled personally by the chiefs. Under the proposed changes, the chiefs would concentrate more on difficult, sub- stantive issues. Still, any service chief could have placed on the agenda any item which he felt strongly about. A modification along these lines would have several significant advantages. First of all, it would help the chiefs focus more assiduously on the key aspects of their joint responsibilities. In so doing, it would strengthen their commitment to their JCS responsibilities by having them devote their time and talents to the major determinants of U.S. military power, present and future, rather than to administrative details. It also has the advantage that the chiefs should have to meet much less frequently during normal times, more like three or four times a month, as opposed to the current three or four times a week. The more routine mat- ters would be handled for the chiefs by the director of the joint staff. Based on papers developed by the joint staff, the director would sign on behalf of the joint chiefs or the chairman, as appropriate, all matters that had not been personally considered by the principals. The director signing for the principals would signify that the institution of the joint chiefs had con- sidered the paper, but that they themselves had not found it necessary to devote time to it. The director would thus sign *for* the chiefs, not *as* the chiefs, as is presently done.

Operating along the lines described earlier of having the joint staff develop the papers considered, the joint chiefs would be acting as an ad- visory body or council; an advisory body with clout, because of the service responsibilities of its members. In the event of differences, the recommen- dation forwarded would tell the secretary of dissents from the views of the chairman. Additionally, any service chief who wished could present his case personally to the secretary and the president. Some proponents of reorganization have proposed establishment of an advisory council distinct from the service chiefs. Experience has shown, however, that an advisory council within the joint system that does not do more than advise sees its influence diminish over time. In the early years of the Joint Chiefs of Staff, a joint strategic survey committee was established, charged with advising the chiefs on broad strategy matters, to be staffed by the best and the brightest young flag- and general-rank officers. The committee, with no control over resources, had substantial influence for a time. Then its impact eroded and it was disbanded. There is no reason to believe that the fate of a similar modern-day advisory board would fare any better.

3. *One of the service chiefs should be acting chairman in the absence of the chairman, holding that assignment for one year.* Without a vice chairman, the only way to ensure continuity in substituting for the chairman in his absence is to have an acting chairman who keeps up on issues, knowing that he may have to step in for the chairman on fairly short notice. This continuity is impossible to achieve if the duty of acting chairman is rotated too frequently.

A year's duration for a service chief to serve as acting chairman seems appropriate. It would allow each service chief to serve in the role during his tenure in office. Preferably his turn would come in the third or fourth year of his assignment. He thus would be thoroughly familiar with the JCS arena, and would have had an extra incentive to steep himself in joint matters, in order to be able to perform credibly when the time arrived to be acting chairman. This is an added attraction of the proposal.

The appointment of a four-star vice chairman has considerable support. It is argued that the chairman is the only senior DOD official who does not have a deputy and that one is badly needed. The vice chairman's functions are variously described as providing a more effective substitute for the chairman in the latter's absence than a service chief acting as chairman, thus allowing the chairman more opportunity to visit the field; as an alternate to attend certain meetings in the Washington area; as a troubleshooter to analyze and make recommendations on long-standing unresolved matters, (e.g., doctrinal issues, or short-fused problems); and, as an across-the-board deputy who would help in many different administrative and managerial tasks. Were the chairman to be given increased authority and responsibility, proponents argue, a vice chairman would be even more essential.

There is much to be said in support of a vice chairman, but there also are several caution flags to be raised. First, the vice chairman should come from a service other than that of the chairman. While the chairman would presumably have a say in his selection, that would not necessarily ensure that the vice chairman would have any personal loyalty to the chairman or necessarily share his point of view. Next, were a vice chairman to be a layer between the service chiefs and the chairman, or between the director of the joint staff and the chairman, he would isolate the chairman and, at the same time, isolate the service chiefs from the mainstream of decisionmaking, rendering their advice less pertinent. Moreover, if he added another staff layer, he could hinder the timeliness and responsiveness of the advice of the joint chiefs.

Next, the role of the vice chairman when the chairman is present for duty, would seem to be limited. Presumably he would attend most meetings with the chairman to keep fully informed so that he could step in during the chairman's absence. If he attended such sessions only to ensure continuity, it would not enhance his authority nor image as the second-ranking military officer. If he participated, and differed with the chairman, he might under-cut the chairman's authority. As a matter of fact, if a strong vice chairman, disagreeing with the chairman, were found by the secretary to offer the "better" advice, a counterproductive competition between the chairman and his deputy might result. If the vice chairman were to manage the joint staff, what would then be the function of the director of the joint staff? And would or should a chairman relinquish this most important function? If the vice chairman traveled for the chairman to consult more with the unified and specified commanders, he would lose the continuity sought in establish-ing the position, and, at the same time, could place a buffer between the chairman and the CINCs. Finally, if a vice chairman became a special project officer for the chairman to delve into "too hard" issues that demanded at-tention (e.g., doctrinal issues), he would be handling issues more properly in the hands of the director of the joint staffs, since the latter is in charge of the joint staff resources, that the vice chairman would require for support. In short, the basic question is how the vice chairman spends his time day-to-day. He is too senior to perform the functions provided by the assistant to the chairman; the assistant's job would, therefore, remain necessary. The assistant to the chairman is selected by the chairman, can easily be fired by the chairman, and is usually of the same service as the chairman. He is known throughout the executive branch as the "chairman's man," the in-dividual who reflects the chairman's views, the person who can get to the chairman formally or informally, quickly for answers, the officer who can represent the chairman and the joint chiefs at the subcabinet-level meetings of his peers; meetings at which policy initiatives are frequently generated or correlated. He is the man who can deal across the various agencies as ap-propriate and necessary in the furtherance of the objectives sought by the chairman and the joint chiefs. In view of the give and take, and the essen-tial, often blunt and direct exchanges required in such endeavors, to assign such functions to the second-ranking U.S. military officer with the right to speak authoritatively for the chiefs would give any discussions in which he was involved an air of formality and authoritativeness that would largely negate their valuable purpose. Thus, it does not seem that a four-star general or flag officer is needed as a vice chairman. In the case of the organization of the Joint Chiefs of Staff, it seems better to go with an acting chairman serving for a period of one year, a three-star assistant to the chairman closely attuned to the chairman's views, and a director of the joint staff responsible directly to the chairman.

Observations

The proposals advanced in this paper would help improve the performance of the Joint Chiefs of Staff in a manner consistent with the evolution of their organization to date, would meet the fundamental criteria for change set forth earlier, and would improve the performance of the military chain of command in the following ways. They would strengthen the issuance of guidance and orders, as well as military decisionmaking in peace and war by providing the chairman, Joint Chiefs of Staff, and the unified and specified commanders more authority in carrying out their responsibilities. The proposals offered would facilitate the forwarding of advice and recommendations up the chain of command by providing the field commanders increased opportunity to influence a broad range of decisions made in Washington. They would sharpen JCS advice to the secretary of defense and the president by replacing the "principle of unanimity" with advice developed by the joint staff in cooperation with military department staffs, but containing the basic views of the chairman along with any appropriate dissent from one or more service chiefs. Finally, the steps recommended would provide the chairman and the joint chiefs, separately and jointly, with the ability to provide more, and more detailed, advice on selected resource matters, so as to help establish priorities for military programs in the furtherance of approved defense policies.

While giving the chairman increased responsibilities, these proposals maintain the checks and balances within the military system by having the service chiefs continue as members of the joint chiefs, with the right to dissent on matters about which they feel strongly, and with direct access to the secretary of defense and the president. It is important to retain such checks and balances in the military organization. Maintaining them, for one thing, puts aside the need to consider the benefits and limits of a single military chief. The greatest drawback to a single military chief is not, however, that without countervailing forces a "man on horseback" would arise. Rather, it is the danger of the politization of the office of the chairman mentioned earlier. The temptation would be for him to be seen as too much the spokesman of an administration in power, rather than of the professional military. Just as membership for the chairman on the National Security Council carries with it potential partisan political implications, so does the idea of a single military chief. The temptation to dismiss the existing chairman and appoint its own man would be great for an incoming administration, and the time-honored system of impartial, objective military advice would be threatened. Under present practice, a chairman has been allowed to complete his appointed term, but, even so, in recent years, questions have been raised as new political leaders have publicly wondered whether the incumbent chairman could be a harmonious part of the new administration's team. Also important, it would be relatively easier to overrule a single military voice than to deal with the concerns of the different services. A strengthened chairman, but one who still, by law, must see that all service viewpoints are fairly represented and considered by his civilian superiors, seems far preferable.

The basic objective of any proposals for modifying the existing military organization of the country is to improve the caliber of military advice that the nation's leaders receive. What is good, sound, military advice? To some officials it, unfortunately, means hearing the advice that the advised wants to hear. Disagreement with a military course of action proposed by an administration or some elements of Congress has frequently been called "bad" advice. Was it good or bad advice when the joint chiefs did not favor the withdrawal of U.S. troops from Korea in 1977? What about when they supported the Panama Canal Treaty? What of the JCS finding the SALT II treaty a "modest but useful step" if the United States continued to modernize our military forces? What of the fact that the U.S. military have historically been among the most reluctant to propose direct employment of U.S. military force in hostilities, or that they have been the most anxious to employ military force in substantial strength once the decision to enter hostilities is made?[11] The simple answer is that what is sound advice to one person may be unsound to another. That means that the joint chiefs ought to address the difficult issues and say what they think, taking into account their individual views, so as to reach, if possible, a collective, responsible military view that they can all support and endorse. The alternative is not an attractive one. Once, early in 1961, President Kennedy asked for advice from the Pentagon on a course of action to be followed in Laos. He asked the secretary of defense, the service secretaries, and each of the joint chiefs, including the Marine Corps commandant. He received in response nine different proposed courses of action. That could not have been very helpful to him, and must have been a big headache to his national security advisor. It should also have been a concern to the Pentagon that a decision would be reached without meaningful military participation.

Two final observations deserve mention. First, as President Wilson noted, "the machinery does not do the task," it merely facilitates furtherance of the substantive ideas of the people who make up the machinery. This suggests that for any reorganization to be successful, it must be founded on a comprehensive understanding and fairly wide acceptance of the preferred ideas for dealing with the issues that prompted discussion of reorganization in the first place; understanding of the ideas so that the proposed new organization can be structured and judged cogently; and fairly wide acceptance, because if that does not exist the effectiveness of any organization — old or new — will be hampered. More specifically, assuming it is realistic to expect that a national policy and strategy backed up by a military strategy can be developed, how do we want that task accomplished? What precise role do the civilian authorities want to retain to themselves, and give to the military? How much freedom and independence in both formulating and implementing the strategy do they want the military to be allowed? To my knowledge, there is not yet wide agreement on these points. Similarly, it is recognized that the United States needs to improve its ability to procure major weapons; that we need improvement in decisions on what to procure, how to procure, and how to support major weapons from cradle to grave — but no clear understanding on how to do that task. Once a preferred complex of ideas for accomplishing these undertakings is agreed upon, then the respective organizational frameworks can be altered so that they can better contribute to successful implementation of the ideas. Short of wide and fundamental agreement on new approaches to dealing with defense matters, it seems preferable for now, when considering the military operational chain of command, to focus on the improvements suggested in this chapter: strengthen and clarify the role of the chairman and the unified and specified commanders; improve the joint staff; and have the service chiefs as members of the joint chiefs focus on the difficult substantive issues.

The final observation flows from the preceding one. Improvements in the military chain of command alone will not make certain that the national security mechanism will function without major flaws. Nor will reorganization of the joint chiefs to make them more effective assure that military advice will be properly integrated into national security decisionmaking. To help assure that, other elements in the mechanism also need review. The office of the secretary of defense cries for attention and improvement. The current interdepartmental arrangements likewise merit close scrutiny. And the U.S. Congress should look critically at its own participation in these matters. Realignment of the joint chiefs and the military chain of command would be but a small beginning. It should be only one of a number of efforts in this field.

NOTES

1. Daniels, Josephus, *The Wilson Era* (Chapel Hill: Univ. of North Carolina Press, 1944), II, p. 503.
2. In his book, *Reappraising Defense Organization* (National Defense Univ. Press, 1983), Archie D. Barrett refers to these two separate chains as the "employing arm" and the "maintaining arm."

3. Brown, Harold, *Thinking About National Security, Defense and Foreign Policy in a Dangerous World* (Boulder, Colorado: Westview Press, 1982), p. 204.
4. What is referred to here is not solely the 400 individuals who are by law the "joint staff," nor the some 5,000 officers cited by the 1982 chairman's special study group report as being involved in joint activities. Rather, it is the 1400 or so personnel identified in the 1978 *Report to the Secretary on the National Military Command Structure* as assigned to the organization of the Joint Chiefs of Staff. That organization includes personnel in the office of the chairman as well as those who operate under the supervision of the director of the joint staff. Over the years, the designation of a particular billet as part of the "joint staff" authorized by Congress, or as part of the large administrative body supporting the joint chiefs, has become increasingly discretionary as staff needs increased while the legal ceiling on the joint staff remained fixed. Basically, the concept is that those individuals who contribute directly to the advice the joint chiefs render to their superiors are the ones who are legally members of the joint staff. The remainder are considered administrative personnel. The dividing lines, however, are vague. The personnel in the national military command center, the command and control hub of the joint chiefs, are not considered part of the joint staff. Nor are some other individuals in other aspects of command, control, and communications functions. Yet both groups are integral to the functioning of the joint chiefs. It is for these reasons that the term "joint staff" must be used in the larger context.
5. U.S. Code 10, Sections 3014, 5061, 8014.
6. See, for example, the views of former secretary of Defense Harold Brown, in Brown, op. cit., p. 210, where he discusses a chief of military staff.
7. U.S. Congress, House, investigations subcommittee, committee on the armed services, *Hearings, Reorganization Proposals for the Joint Chiefs of Staff*, 97th Congress, p. 252.
8. Ibid., p. 112.
9. H.R. 3718, 98th Cong., 1st Sess.
10. Ibid.
11. Betts, Richard K., *Soldiers, Statesmen and Cold War Crises* (Cambridge: Harvard Univ. Press, 1978).

APPENDIX
U.S. UNIFIED AND SPECIFIED COMMANDS

The department of defense reorganization act of 1958 authorized a structure of unified and specified military combatant commands reporting to the president and the secretary of defense. These commands were to be responsible for the performance of military missions assigned them, and would be provided military forces from the military departments. Forces so assigned were to be under the "full operational command" of the unified or specified commander. The Joint Chiefs of Staff in their official *Dictionary of Military and Associated Terms* (JCS Publication #1) have defined operational command as "those functions of command involving the composition of subordinate forces, the assignment of tasks, the designation of objectives and the authoritative direction necessary to accomplish the mission." Significantly, the JSC definition further states "operational command should be exercised through the commanders of subordinate forces. . . . It does not include such matters as administration, discipline, internal organization, and unit training except when a subordinate commander requests assistance." Those responsibilities reside with the military departments.

A unified command is officially defined by the Joint Chiefs of Staff as

A command with a broad continuing mission under a single commander and composed of significant assigned components of two or more Services, and which is established and so designated by the President, through the Secretary of Defense, with the advice and assistance of the Joint Chiefs of Staff, or, when so authorized by the Joint Chiefs of Staff, by a commander of an existing unified command established by the President.

A specified command is

A command which has a broad continuing mission and which is so established by the President through the Secretary of Defense with the advice and assistance of the Joint Chiefs of Staff. It normally is composed of forces from but one Service.

Presently, there are three U.S. specified commands: the aerospace command, the military airlift command, and the strategic air command. All are headquartered in the United States with staffs almost solely from the U.S. Air Force. The aerospace command focuses on air defense matters, and the strategic air command on strategic nuclear and, to a lesser extent, non-nuclear strategic air operations.

Six U.S. unified commands exist today, five of which have geographical responsibilities: the European command, the Atlantic command, the Pacific command, the Southern command, and the central command. The Southern command has responsibilities in Latin and South America, the Central command in southwest Asia and the Horn of Africa. The remaining geographical areas are fairly clear from the names of the commands. One unified command, the readiness command, has no designated geographical area of responsibility but, instead, has functional responsibilities of developing joint doctrine, training of joint forces, and planning for the deployment of U.S.-based military forces to their designated overseas commander as directed by the secretary of defense in times of tension, emergency, or war.

Under the unified military commander are service component commands, with forces only from one military department. The size and nature of the component commands vary widely. The components of the European command, for example, have sizable headquarters staffs and a number of directly subordinate major units. These component commanders identify unified command operational tasks solely and completely with their European command and related NATO responsibilities. This is in contrast with the component commands of the readiness command and the central command, the components of which may, and most often do, have responsibilities to other than just those two unified commands, depending upon the differing missions and tasks assigned them and their subordinate units by the Joint Chiefs of Staff. For instance, the Army forces command and the Air Force's tactical air command are component commanders of the readiness command. Their duties and responsibilities far exceed that one commitment, however, and they have forces either earmarked or scheduled for assignment to various other unified commands under selected contingencies. The attention and focus of their commanders is consequently more diversified than that of the component commanders in Europe.

Thus, as can be seen, the U.S. unified and specified commanders cannot function efficiently and effectively in peace or war without strong, enduring, consistent support from the military departments — which is not always assured, because of competing demands for limited resources and conflicting priorities.

Chapter 15

Commands on Smith's Proposals

David C. Jones, Edward C. Meyer III,
and Thor Hanson

Thor Hanson

In addressing the U.S. military chain of command, General Smith states that the present system works ". . . not perfectly, by any measure, but not disastrously either." I would submit that it works so far from perfectly that more than just the "tweaking" that General Smith proposes is necessary. The organization should be constituted to do two things very well.

- Provide truly objective military advice to the president and the secretary of defense, particularly in the allocation of scarce resources.
- Plan operations in peace and execute them in war.

To perform these functions most effectively, I would propose a significant change—the creation of a chief of the military staff, charged by law to be the principal military advisor to the secretary of defense and the president and to have oversight of the unified commanders.

One of the biggest shortcomings of the present JCS organization is the failure of the Joint Chiefs of Staff, year in and year out to give, as a corporate body, useful advice on the setting of priorities when the service budget requests exceed the dollars available, as is usually the case. The chiefs do not collectively address the tough tradeoffs. Rather, they abdicate this responsibility to the secretary of defense and the program analysis staff.

It is easy to explain both why this has happened and will continue to happen as long as the individual service chiefs are asked, as a committee, to face that issue. A service chief who has spent months putting together his own program objective memorandum (POM) finds it difficult to trade away his service's priorities to another's. It has historically been impossible for an individual chief to overcome the institutional pressure brought on him by the need to represent his own service.

The chairman, the one member of the JCS without a foot in a service camp, is the only member institutionally able to give an objective view. Unfortunately, he does not have staff sufficient to perform this role. As a result, the judgments he takes to the secretary of defense and to the Defense Resources Board (DRB) must often be based on gut feeling alone, and defended without analytical materials.

The chief of the military staff that I propose would have his own staff, essentially the present joint staff (but unlimited by law to the present 400 members) and bolstered with an analytical programming capability. One possibility would be to transfer the present Program Analysis and Evaluation (PAE) staff of the secretary of defense to the chief of the military staff and then task that senior military officer with the responsibility for making the tough intra- and interservice tradeoff recommendations to the secretary of defense. Another route would be to give the chief of the military staff his own programming capability, with the secretary of defense retaining his.

In formulating recommendations, another essential input for the chief of the military staff would be those of the commander in chiefs (CINCs) of the unified and specified commands. General Smith argues that the CINCs should have a stronger voice in this process. Examination of their personal views for thirty minutes at a Defense Resources Board meeting is not enough. The place for detailed and constructive input by the CINCs to the PPBS system is logically at the stage when the chief of the military staff considers how to integrate the service POMS.

It is also at this senior military level that strategic planning and thinking must be done. The Joint Chiefs of Staff, four of whom have the responsibility of running the services, do not have the time to do (and certainly have not been doing) strategic thinking. Nor has the joint staff, which spends most of its time collating and synthesizing service positions on a myriad of issues, few of which involve strategy. The military staff of my proposed chief would also be the vehicle for reviewing, analyzing and balancing the contingency plans developed by the CINCs. As General Smith states in his chapter, more attention should be paid to these plans. Review at this level is necessary to determine if there are sufficient forces and lift capabilities to execute the plans of two or more area commanders simultaneously. This kind of analysis is the best way to highlight and make specific the existence and true magnitude of any strategy–force mismatch.

Should the chief of the military staff be, by law, in the command chain? I do not think this is crucial. As the chiefs are now in the chain by a secretary of defense directive so, too, could be the chief of the military staff. The orders of the secretary of defense should be issued through him, and he should be the principal military advisor to the secretary. That is the key point: that he, with the support of his staff, and with the advice of the unified commanders, should be the one to recommend both strategies and the allocation of resources. Such recommendations are not best made by a committee and especially not in wartime.

It is possible that were the chief of the military staff in the command chain by law, the temptation might be stronger for a president (or even an assistant to the president) to try to pass over the secretary of defense directly to the chief. Although I think that a bit farfetched, the CINCs must understand that the secretary of defense is the boss, that *he* issues the orders, even if through the chief of the military staff.

As General Smith has argued and as most studies of the defense department have shown, present practice does not award personnel assigned to the joint staff with the fastest promotions and the best assignments once they leave the joint arena. As a consequence, the joint system does not attract the best qualified officers from any of the services, especially those in the middle grades. General Smith recommends more than a proportionate share of promotions for people serving or those who have served with the joint staff and the unified command staffs. This is a needed incentive, but by itself it is not enough. What is required is a viable *career pattern* for officers in the joint arena. To become at home with, and expert at, thinking in joint terms, one must have recurrent tours of joint duty. Officers with that specialty should periodically return to their parent services for operational tours in order to keep current with service doctrine and practice. Their staff jobs, however, should all be joint, either with the military staff in Washington or with one of the CINCs. The key to making a joint duty career attractive, however, lies in the following two proposals.

1. That the commanders of the unified commands be chosen only from officers with this joint career speciality.
2. That the chief of the military staff be chosen only from the ranks of the CINCs.

Enforcing these two practices would motivate top officers to a joint career. In that the individual services would want their officers to have a chance to be the Chief of the Military Staff, these two practices would ensure the nomination of top officers for joint assignments.

Should the chief of military staff be a member of the National Security Council? No. He should be an *advisor* to the NSC, not a member, in the same sense that the director of central intelligence should be an advisor to, and not a member of, the cabinet. Advisors should not be members of policy-making groups.

I wish to address one other issue, that of whether a proposal for a chief of the military staff is too radical to be accepted at this time in the United States. It really should not be. After all, the position does exist, in somewhat varying form, in Canada, the United Kingdom, the Federal Republic of Germany, France, and the Soviet Union. Unfortunately, however, the strong service lobbies in the United States might well prevent the proposal from receiving congressional approval. If that be the case, I would opt for General Jones's proposal to make the present chairman the principal advisor to the national command authority and to give him oversight of the unified commanders. As General Jones also proposed, I would strongly advocate having the joint staff report to the chairman, *not* to the chiefs, and assign the chairman a four-star deputy. I would make the director of the joint staff the four-star deputy and assign him a three-star assistant to carry out the day-to-day details of directing the staff. To ensure that joint staff and unified command duty become sought after under the Jones proposal, I would include in it the same career pattern incentive I have previously outlined: that the CINCs and the chairman himself be appointed only from the ranks of those with a joint career specialty.

In my opinion, either a chief of the military staff or the Jones proposal is essential in order to provide objective military advice to the national command authority and to develop the best capability for planning and executing operations in peace and in war. I would prefer a chief of the military staff.

Edward C. Meyer

The chapter by General Smith is an excellent compilation of the strengths and weaknesses of the current system. Two of his remedies to what ails the current system should receive universal support: first, a stronger role for the chairman of the Joint Chiefs of Staff; and second, a stronger role for the commanders of the unified and specified commands. I believe, however, that Smith has based his evolutionary approach to improving the existing chain of command on a false premise, which he states thus: "The present system works, albeit imperfectly, and is evolving positively." The recent events in Lebanon, as analyzed by military professionals in the Long report, are simply the most current evidence that cast serious doubts on whether the system, as presently constituted, can ever be made to work.

There are three goals against which any organizational change should be assessed. First and foremost, civilian leaders must receive the best military advice possible and in a timely fashion. Second, whatever organization is in place in peacetime has to work well in war and in crises short of war. Periods of tension or war are not the times for confusion caused by the transition to different organizations or by the development of ad hoc entities. Third, the commanders of unified and specified commands must be given sufficient guidance and resources to do meaningful planning, must be required to do such planning, and must be intimately involved in short-term issues relating to the capabilities and readiness of the forces assigned to their commands.

All proposals for changes in the current JCS organization should be evaluated against these three criteria. If the changes contribute to improvements in the ability of the military to carry out these tasks, then they should be seriously considered for adoption. It is against these three criteria that I would like to evaluate the current JCS organization, the proposals made by General David Jones, and those proposed by General Smith.

THE ROLE OF THE CINC

General Smith outlined the problems the unified commander encounters in providing military advice. On the basis of my own experience, I believe these are the reasons why contingency war fighting plans developed by the CINCs have been inadequate.

1. The guidance from the JCS to the CINCs has, in most cases, been imprecise. Until very recently, the JCS has not focused on contingency planning, nor has there been a clear, overall, strategic perspective into which the individual commanders' plans could be fitted.
2. The JCS has believed that commanders in the field do not understand the political ramifications of military actions, as well as those military officials in Washington who must deal with the interagency crowd on a day-to-day basis. The result of this JCS view is that plans have been developed in Washington without the initial involvement of the commanders in the field who will be called upon to implement them.
3. For nearly twenty years, the planning element of the military was permitted to atrophy because of the emphasis placed on programming and budgeting. This state of affairs became frighteningly visible as the fledgling rapid deployment force took its first tentative steps.
4. There are many disparate, uncoordinated, planning elements throughout the department of defense. The under secretary for policy, each of the services, and the joint staff all have planning staffs. Much of the work they do is duplicative. Much is not only not orchestrated, but is even cacophonic. The nation does not need four separate service strategies. Nor does it need a civilian-developed military strategy and a military-developed strategy. With the paucity of experienced planners that exists today, we cannot afford to waste these unique talents in uncoordinated planning efforts.
5. There has been little linkage in the past between contingency plans developed by the CINCs, on the one hand, and force development plans developed by the service and the office of the secretary of defense, on the other. The low caliber of the plans has been one reason why they have not been used to assist in force development. This lack of linkage has created a situation in which the views of the field commander have only a modest impact on the force development plans of the services. The question of who the services are developing the forces for must be addressed.

Perhaps all these shortcomings were acceptable when the United States had a preponderance of military force over the Soviet Union. But clearly today this is not so. We need better planning because our military edge has waned. On his first day as chairman of the Joint Chiefs of Staff, General John Vessey directed the service chiefs and the unified and specified commanders to achieve this goal. A year and a half later, there was modest improvement in the planning system. But as the report by the Long commission made clear, inherent weaknesses remain. We must correct them if we are to ensure that "the best military advice possible" is made available to the president and the secretary of defense.

Because I believe in the critical importance of developing broad strategic alternatives, I endorse a strengthened role of the joint staff by the means proposed by Generals Jones and Smith. The development of joint staff officers who have a service-wide perspective is essential to better contingency planning. This, however, is the easy part. The tough part is how to ensure that the most senior and capable military officers focus on the broad strategic issues and develop the strategic options we require.

THE NATIONAL MILITARY COUNCIL

To fruitfully engage these senior officers, I have proposed a reorganization that separates the service chiefs from strategic planning and that gives that task to a national military advisory council.[1] The purpose of the council is to end the conflicting roles that the service chiefs now have. The clear separation between military authorities responsible for running their services and those responsible for providing advice on joint matters should significantly improve the objectivity, timeliness, and utility of joint military advice. Removal of the services from formal involvement in the relation of the chairman with the CINCs, moreover, would permit the CINCs to become more active and influential participants in the development of overall defense policy and in joint unique service programs. The CINCs would provide the council with their views on affordable and feasible military actions for the short-term, and on the measures necessary to improve existing force capabilities for the medium-term. Coupled with an improved joint staff, the CINCs' input would enhance the quality of the formulation of military strategy. This would be in sharp contrast to the current system, one that condemns the CINCs to a purely reactive mode, one in which they must try simply to implement policy already established. This proposal strengthens the role of the chairman and the CINCs, but it also lays the groundwork for a meaningful career progression for the officers who choose to specialize in the joint arena.

In contrast to some past proposals, under this one, the services would be intimately involved with the council in the development of strategic alternatives and would, thereby, help a strengthened joint staff to provide the individual land, sea, or air perspectives that are essential for truly joint planning and analysis. Periodically throughout the process, the services, represented by the service secretaries and service chiefs, would meet with the national military council as a collective board of directors to comment on the council's position on key issues. In addition, the service secretaries and chiefs would remain members of the Defense Resources Board, the one arena where major disagreements with the proposals of the chairman and the council can be brought before the secretary of defense. Such a structure should give the president and the secretary of defense the information requisite for making fundamental decisions on the significant alternatives that have not been settled at the service and joint arena levels. It should also provide a clearer rationale for the presentation of the defense budget to Congress.

The question asked most often of this proposal is what will the service chiefs do if they are not members of the Joint Chiefs of Staff. I have already indicated that they will be active members of a group evaluating proposals developed by the chairman with the help of the council and the CINCs. They will also be members of the Defense Resources Board and, hence, will be able to present service related views. Most importantly, they will be able to focus on what they are currently charged by law with doing: organizing, staffing, equipping, and training the forces with which the unified and specified commanders will fight. Guidelines that come to the services from the secretary of defense will be more precise than they are today and will be based on the joint needs defined by the chairman and the CINCs. Thus, the service chiefs will be able to focus their energies on the *execution* of their programs and budgets, the area that has received less than adequate attention in the past. If a service chief can focus on the present and future of air, land, or sea warfare, his service's ability to innovate should be enhanced and should ensure that the best technology and tactics will be developed. This in turn would give the CINCs options that are not now available.

POSSIBLE OBJECTIONS

The major objections to the proposals just outlined have been these:

1. The planner (chairman and council) is separated from the implementor (service chief); hence the service chief will not be required to think jointly.
2. The talents of the service chiefs are wasted.
3. A similar system to the council was disbanded because it did not prove useful.
4. A four-star assistant to the chairman is all that is needed.
5. Civilian control of the military could be usurped.

I will deal with each objection in turn. It is true that the service chief would no longer be formally involved in joint issues. But I have pointed out that he would be better able to influence decisions that he felt were wrong for his service and that he would have input in joint decisions. More to the point, his ability to focus more of his efforts on internal service matters would improve significantly the quality of his service's forces. That, in turn, would enable the services to improve their joint operations for combined warfare. The service chief must remember that it is not he who will command the forces in war. The CINCs will do that. Removing the service chiefs from the JCS would make that point crystal clear.

The second argument most often made against my proposal is that the talents of the service chiefs, especially with regard to broad policy issues, are wasted if they are not members of the JCS. Because members of the council could be ex-service chiefs and ex-CINCs, however, the broad skills of selected chiefs would not be lost. Also, the constant interaction between the chairman of the JCS and the council would ensure that the service chiefs' expertise are weighed appropriately. Also, their presence on the Defense Resources Board, together with their constitutional right of access to the president on issues they consider critical, should ensure that where they feel strongly about policy issues, their views will be heard.

Third, in General Smith's paper, he indicates that a setup similar to the national military advisory council was abolished because it was not considered useful. During World War II a joint strategic survey committee was established to draw up joint directives for prosecuting the war. Both Admiral King and General Marshall have written of its vital role in winning the war. Clearly, in the last major war in which we could claim outright victory, a need existed for a committee to address strategic issues. But this survey committee was abolished in the early fifties after the institution of the joint staff system. At that time, the directors of the joint staff for policy and for operations were in competition with the joint strategic survey committee. The three stars on the joint staff outranked the two stars on the committee, and the committee was dissolved. Since then, planning, policy, and operational matters have been handled for the JCS solely by the joint staff directors. Those who believe that broad strategic options are essential for the future and who are dissatisfied with the way such planning is done today would do well to review history, particularly the pivotal role that the joint strategic survey committee played in World War II. I argue that we need such an element — in the form of the national military advisory council — even more today than we did in the last major war we fought and won.

The fourth objection — that all we need do to improve the functioning of the JCS is to appoint a vice chairman — is more difficult to deal with. In his initial reorganization plan, General Jones proposed that there be a four-star vice chairman of the Joint Chiefs of Staff and that he represent the chairman in his absence at National Security Council and other interagency meetings. Unfortunately, General Jones did not spell out the specific relationship that would exist between the vice chairman and the service chiefs. Regardless of the stated roles of the vice chairman and the service chiefs, the latters' role would be significantly degraded. The vice chairman would be the spokesman in the absence of the chairman and would build up his own power base within the agencies of government. If this is the only change in JCS operations, it is my contention that it would diminish the role of the service chiefs within the JCS and, consequently, that the service chiefs would find less and less reason to attend JCS meetings, instead sending their vice chiefs. Thus, the de facto, as opposed to de jure, decoupling of the service chiefs from the JCS would take place. Therefore, I believe the introduction of a vice chairman would cloud the chain of command issue, rather than clarify it. Nothing would be done to bring about better joint planning.

The final argument made by opponents of change has to do with fears of German General Staffs, soldiers on horseback, and usurpation of civilian control by the military. The history of our nation has imbued in our military a deep sense of responsibility to obey civilian leadership. Countless examples of this subordinate attitude are available throughout our history. It does a disservice to our military leaders to argue that their desire to provide better military advice would lead to a change in our historic civil–military relationship. I realize that such an assertion bears scrutiny, but history, tradition, and historical loyalty to the nation lead me to conclude that this argument is nothing more than a canard.

The following chart (see Table 15.1) outlines the institutional roles under three options: today's system; General Jones's proposal, and a single hat for the service chiefs (the national military council).

In summary, I believe that General Smith has correctly identified the problem, but provides a solution that will fail to yield the best possible military advice in peace, war, or crises. The need for better strategic and regional planning requires full-time advisors on broad strategic alternatives and related policy issues. The movement from these plans and policies to the specific instructions to the military departments will ensure that coherent forces are designed for specific, agreed upon, combined missions. The beauty of thinking in peacetime about how we would have to organize our forces in war is that it provides us with a clear set of guidelines that direct us towards the proper relations among the chairman, joint staff, Joint Chiefs of Staff, unified and specified commanders, and service chiefs. It will also help to sort out the manner in which the relationships among the Joint Chiefs of Staff and the service departments, on the one hand, and the office of the secretary of defense, on the other, can best be organized.

David C. Jones

I view the military chain of command issue as much more serious than does William Smith. Many of you have heard me say that one of the concerns I expressed back in 1981 was that, because of underpricing, we needed the Reagan defense budget to fund the Carter defense program; but what we were likely to get was the Carter defense budget to fund the Reagan de-

Table 15.1. Institutional Roles under Three Options

	TODAY'S SYSTEM	GENERAL JONES' PROPOSAL	(SINGLE HAT FOR SERVICE CHIEFS)
CJCS	Is the first among equals. Influence rests on role as JCS spokesman.	Enjoys an enhanced role. Staffed to present independent views more capably.	Is supported fully to fill role as trusted advisor to secretary of defense, president, and Congress. Plays a major part in shaping the internal DOD debate and policy, and program initiatives.
Service Chiefs	Have major responsibilities in both joint and service arenas.	Will lose influence to vice chairperson. Will no longer have override authority on joint issues. Remain dual hatted.	Are able to focus more clearly on near- and long-term service improvements. Board of directors role.
CINCs	Possess little influence on programs.	Gain a strengthened voice in matching resources to operational plans.	Present needs in a continuous dialogue to the council, which is now much more capable of initiating change. Exercise considerable influence on near-term programs and budgets.
	—	—	Gives credible, uninhibited cross-service advice to CJCS and civilian decision makers.

fense programs. That has now happened. For even with the large Reagan increases, the budget is inadequate to fund the approved programs, and still the hard tradeoffs are not being made. No one is happy with how our defense programs are handled, but each tends to put the blame on others. The Pentagon blames the Congress. The Congress blames the Pentagon. The services blame the OSD and vice versa. Strengthening the joint system can have a substantial impact, although a complete solution will require actions by the OSD and the Congress.

PROBLEMS WITH THE CHAIN OF COMMAND

There are those who say that organizational arrangements are unimportant, that people make the difference. Smith alluded to this with his quote from Woodrow Wilson. Certainly people make a difference, but the current system has prevented even the best individuals from making major contributions. I submit that no military leader has had much impact on defense programs since the days of Admiral Rickover and General LeMay back in the fifties. These two were able to do so only when operating in narrow areas. LeMay's contribution came when he was head of the strategic air command (SAC), not while he was Air Force chief of staff; Rickover's came when he was concentrating on the Polaris program. Both had much less influence later in their careers. I have seen hundreds of senior officers and several dozen service chiefs come and go, each of whom had little long-term impact. Some were very competent, but the system tightly constrained them. Edward Meyer, when he was chief of staff of the Army, did a par-ticularly good job in beginning to turn the Army around in fundamental areas, but it takes a long time to make major changes.

One of the things that has struck me is that, compared to other nations, ours is the only one where the defense leadership — military and civilian — is tied up in the budget process year around. It dominates almost everything we do. It dominates the services and the joint system. People have very little time to do anything else, whether it be providing oversight on how we spend our money or on insuring readiness. I do not believe, moreover, that we in the military advise the civilian leadership well, even on the budget. That in-cludes the joint system, which tends to be an "echo plus" to whatever the services recommend. That is, the joint system usually recommends that the secretary give the services what they want, but states that they need even more money than they have asked for. The best advice from the services to the secretary comes when the secretary asks an individual chief for his views. That is the case because his views are his own candid judgment, not a reflection of a joint paper that has been compromised by accommodating the interests of each service.

Ironically, the weakest part of the work done by the military is in the area of strategy, common doctrine, war planning, and war gaming. With regard to war gaming, 95 percent of our capability rests in the services. There is lit-tle done in the joint system, whether in Washington or at the unifed com-mands. Studies, Analysis, and Gaming Agency (SAGA) does an analysis of the Single Integrated Operation Plan (SIOP) and holds a few seminars, but does not do any analysis of conventional war planning. General Smith made a good point when he stated that the CINCs should be given more respon-sibility for planning. They would, however, require the resources to do it well. When I was the air component commander in Europe, I discovered that my staff's knowledge of many systems and their capabilities was limited. We had good information on the nature of a direct Russian attack, but a rather poor capability to plan for an unusual contingency within a theater that ranged from the Scandinavian countries through Iran. I am not saying that we need go to highly centralized planning, but we must recognize there are severe planning limitations in the field that need to be remedied. We should not become complacent because we were successful in Grenada.

The planning there was done in only forty-eight hours, but we had two advantages: Grenada was close, and the small force on the island was easily overwhelmed. The unified staffs in the field today, unfortunately, do not fully understand the capabilities and limitations of each of the individual services. As a consequence, truly joint and combined-arms planning is seriously deficient.

James Schlesinger has remarked that a CINC is like a husband who knows his wife is committing adultery and, yet, has to accept it. This is what our component commanders in the unified commands do to their CINCs. As an ex-component commander in Europe, I knew that it was the chief of staff of the Air Force, not Commander in Chief, Europe (CINCEUR), who had the greatest say over my forces because he was the one who controlled my money and people.

POSSIBLE SOLUTIONS

As to what we should do, let me make several suggestions. First, should the chairman of the JCS be made a member of the National Security Council? I do not believe it would make much of a difference. My experience with four different presidents is that they listen to whomever they want, regardless of whether an individual is or is not on the NSC. Many times the most significant part of an NSC discussion would occur in the Oval Office after the conclusion of the formal NSC meeting. Recall that in the Cuban missile crisis, President Kennedy did not even use the NSC, but, rather, had a group of close advisors work with him. If a president wants to listen to the chairman of the Joint Chiefs of Staff, he will whether or not the chairman is formally on the NSC.

The same line of reasoning holds true for putting the chairman in the chain of command. I do not believe it would make a difference. My preference would be to put the chairman in the chain, but I would not expend much political capital to do so. Even if the chairman were in the chain, the president and the secretary of defense still constitute the national command authority. The chairman could take no more of an initiative than the CINC, who is already in the chain. General Bernard Rogers, as CINCEUR is in the chain of command, but he is tightly restrained in what he can do, except in the one contingency of protecting his troops in a surprise attack. He cannot, for example, redeploy his troops to the Middle East without prior approval of the secretary of defense. Putting the chairman in the chain of command may have some psychological impact, but it would not solve the fundamental problem that we face with the chain of command as it is constituted today.

Perhaps the most critical problem we face in the joint arena is how the officers of the joint staff operate. Members of the staff are beholden to their services because it is the services that control promotions and assignments. The services are able to keep better track of what their officers do on the joint staff than on what those who are assigned to the OSD do. All joint staff action meetings include representatives from the services. If, in these meetings, a joint officer does not toe the line of his service, the word quickly gets back to his service superiors.

With regard to joint service and promotions, we must find some way to give sufficient weight to time spent in the joint system, but not go to the extreme of promoting from a joint position an officer for whom little use would be found once he returned to the service for assignment. Moreover, if too much authority is exercised by those outside of a service on an individual's promotion, that is usually the last one he will get. Years ago, in an attempt to make joint assignments more attractive, the secretary of defense made it mandatory that promotion to 0–7 require that an officer have a tour of joint duty. Unfortunately, the definition of what constituted joint duty was left to the services. When I asked for the list of assignments that qualified for joint duty, I found some strange logic indeed. For example, the executive officer to the secretary of the Navy was on the list. So, too, was the instructor pilot on the aircraft flown by me, and the chief of staff of the Air Force. In another attempt to gain some influence over promotions, one secretary of defense changed the system from having only one name submitted to him for promotion to 0–9 or 0–10 to having two names submitted. Some of the chiefs worried about the waning of their influence until they found a way to beat the system: submit two names; the one the service wanted to promote and a second that no one would promote.

With regard to the issue of having a deputy chairman, I would advocate such a position. I would not, however, necessarily make him the number two ranking officer. A deputy is needed to provide continuity when a chairman is out of town and to help in resolving some of the long-standing JCS problems that continue to be shoved under the rug and that are beyond the capability of one man (the chairman) to handle. Most of those who have been directors of the joint staff would confirm that, whenever possible, the tough issues are set aside when the chairman is absent because it is virtually impossible for a service chief to step out of his service hat when he had to become acting chairman in the chairman's absence. A deptuy chairman could give invaluable help in raising and resolving some of the long-term problems that continue to be ignored. General Smith said that the assistant to the chairman should be the outside officer and the director of the joint staff the inside one. The chairman needs help in the outside arena, but in a different manner than that mentioned by Smith. Because of the press of work in Washington, the area that tends to get the chairman's lowest priority is working with the CINCs to ensure that everything is done to enhance readiness. This is the area where I believe the deputy should work.

With regard to the CINCs' involvement in major budget issues, they do appear before the Defense Resources Board for about thirty minutes twice a year and are pleased to have the opportunity. They are like galley slaves who have been let free on the deck. The result is that they do not have much influence but appreciate having been invited to Washington to talk to someone about the budget. Soon they will realize how truly limited their influence remains.

We should keep the service chiefs as a part of the joint system. We need, however, to modify the system so that the services do not dominate it. Their dominance will continue so long as the requirement remains that the services and their chiefs be involved in every paper or action, no matter how unimportant. The compromises that are inevitably made have prevented the development of common strategy, common doctrine, and a common approach to war fighting. I would, therefore, have the joint staff work for the chairman. In preparing positions, the chairman would seek the advice of the service chiefs, the CINCs, and others, and then make his recommendations to the secretary of defense or to the president, as appropriate. I would not require that the position of each service chief be attached. That would slow down the process by keeping the services haggling over secondary issues. My judgment is that the services would do as the Marine commandant did when the law was changed to allow Marine involvement in any issue of direct interest to the Marine Corps. He said that, from then on, anything in the joint arena was to be of direct interest to the Marine Corps.

It is better that service comments not be included in every case, but, rather, that provision be made for a service chief who feels strongly enough on a joint issue to forward his views to the secretary or the president. At NSC meetings, the chairman could register a service disagreement for the service chief. Today the services address each of the 3,000 issues that come to the joint system. What I advocate would mean that service chiefs choose from these 3,000 only a few that are so contentious and important as to require special treatment.

As you well know, the British made a significant change in their system just before the Falkland Islands conflict. I recently spoke to the chief of the British defense staff and found his observations interesting. At the time of the change, he was chief of the Army and had been in opposition to the proposed change. He now says the system is working well and that, despite occasional griping from a few staff officers, the chiefs like it because they are not spending so much time on minor issues and, therefore, are able to give more attention to the important ones. Their changes were almost identical to the ones I have recommended for the United States.

NOTES

1. See my article in *Armed Forces Journal International* (April 1982).

Chapter 16

Rewriting the Key West Accord*

Morton H. Halperin and David Halperin

In summer 1983 the world's biggest orphan finally found a home. The MX was assigned to existing Minuteman silos by the Scowcroft commission. Yet no one has explained how this basing mode solves the problem that justified a new missile: insuring the survivability of the third leg of America's strategic triad. New missiles in existing silos are as vulnerable as old missiles.

Earlier, a basing mode had been proposed for the MX that many experts believed would be relatively inexpensive, extremely effective, sufficiently distinct from existing submarine and bomber based forces to preserve the triad concept, and best of all, highly survivable. Proponents of this mode convincingly refuted all criticisms of their proposal. Yet their plan—to base the MX on small submarines operating off U.S. coasts—was never taken seriously by defense officials. Given the inadequacy of the Scowcroft proposal, one has to ask why.

The answer lies in a series of agreements made in the years following World War II to divide military functions among the armed services. The first and most important of these agreements was negotiated among the military services and then Secretary of Defense James Forrestal in 1948 at Key West, Florida. But while Key West and the subsequent agreements have clarified service responsiblities and missions, they have contributed to some of the most glaring failures and shortcomings of American military policy in the postwar era.

Vietnam, for example, has been called the "helicopter war." The U.S. Army relied on its helicopters to provide close air support for its ground troops, but these aircraft proved to be expensive, and extremely vulnerable

---

*This essay is a revised and expanded version of an article, "The Key West Key," *Foreign Policy* No. 53, Winter 1983–84. Material copyrighted by the Carnegie Endowment for International Peace. Reprinted with permission.

to attack by even the lightest of enemy arms. According to one source, approximately 10,000 helicopters crashed or were shot down in the war.[1] The Army was losing about one-third of its Vietnam-based helicopter force every year. Yet despite this dismal record, the Army continues to rely on its helicopters for close support for all contingencies, including the defense of Western Europe. Aircraft that could be knocked out by Vietcong automatic rifles would not last long against Soviet tanks and fighter planes. Although some Army officers have defended the helicopter program, many outside experts and other Army officials argue that small, slow flying airplanes are essential for carrying out the close support mission.

The United States also lacks sufficient airlift capability to carry ground troops into combat zones. The Vietnam war showed that helicopters are as inferior to small planes for tactical airlift as they are in providing close air support. Yet, thanks to Key West, the United States continues to rely in large part on helicopters to carry troops into battle.

Strategic air- and sealift capability needed to transport troops long distances have been considered inadequate since 1961, when both President John Kennedy and Secretary of Defense Robert McNamara called for rapid improvements. Executive-branch officials insist that the United States has vital interests in the Persian Gulf and other regions far from bases where American troops are stationed. Yet the Key West agreements have prevented the military from gaining the strategic lift capacity those officials have asserted that the United States needs.

America's most glaring military failure in recent years was the 1980 attempt to rescue the American hostages held in Iran. After the disastrous mission, Americans asked many questions about U.S. military readiness. But few asked why the helicopters used to fly 600 miles over desert were U.S. Navy helicopters equipped for mine-sweeping and why their pilots were Navy and Marine Corps fliers when Air Force pilots had more experience flying over land and more training for that kind of mission. Why did the United States not have helicopters built and equipped to fly off aircraft carriers and over land with pilots trained to fly them on such missions? And why are both still lacking? Again, Key West is the key.

COMPROMISE AT KEY WEST

An examination of the agreements and their sometimes disastrous consequences suggests that the Key West approach was fundamentally flawed. If the United States is to continue to defend its interests effectively without wasting vast sums of money, serious revisions of the responsibilities and missions of the armed forces will be needed.

In 1945 the two branches of the armed forces — the Army, then containing the Army Air Corps, which became the Air Force, and the Navy — began a battle over unification: The Army favored it, but the Navy, fearing that it would be swallowed up into the Army structure, resisted.[2] In 1947 Congress passed the National Security Act, which restructured the military. It established the department of defense headed by a secretary of defense, separated the Air Force from the Army, and gave legal status to the Joint Chiefs of Staff. The act, however, failed to decide which of the warring military factions should be given authority to do what. In the most important dispute, the Navy urged that each service be given all the forces that would be needed to carry out its missions independently. The Army and Air Force argued that such a move would create unnecessary duplication of forces and that the Army, Air Force, and Navy should work together as a team.

Unable to resolve their differences, the joint chiefs turned to Forrestal, who summoned them to the Key West Naval Base in March 1948. The document they produced, *Functions of the Armed Forces and the Joint Chiefs of Staff*, was approved by President Harry Truman.

The Key West agreement represented a compromise of sorts. The Navy gained many of its goals: retention of the Navy-based Marine Corps; the authority to provide close air support for Marine land operations; and the authority to carry out those air operations, including ground launched missions, which are required for sea battles. The Army and the Air Force, convinced that the services should avoid excessive duplication, were willing to give the Navy control over almost all sea operations. And the Army and Air Force agreed to cooperate with each other as a team on joint missions. Specifically, this meant that the Air Force pledged to provide the Army with airlift and close air support.[3] But this bargain would soon hurt both the Army and U.S. security.

The military that emerged from Key West consisted of three separate services, each given a set of primary responsibilities and each pledged to carry out certain functions to assist in the primary missions of the other services. But while Key West set up the basic structure of responsibilities and missions, interservice disputes did not end. Since each service had its own programs and doctrines to protect, none of the three wanted to waste valuable budget money and resources on programs designed to aid its Pentagon rivals. Under the Key West structure, there was very little incentive to do so.

The big problem was the Air Force, which proved to be a thankless child as it turned on the Army from which it was spawned and made it clear that Key West left the senior service at its mercy. In the 1956 memorandum for members of the armed forces policy council and again in the 1957 Department of Defense Directive No. 5160.22, the Pentagon denied the Army any fixed-wing aircraft heavier than 5,000 pounds and expressly prevented the Army from providing its own close air support and strategic or tactical airlift. Strictly speaking, the Army could employ its own airlift only within the combat zone.[4]

The agreements have crippled combat air support and strategic air- and sealift, and a review of the Iran rescue mission and MX basing reveals that Key West has affected these controversies as well.

As journalist Gregg Easterbrook showed in the September 1981 *Washington Monthly*, defense planners overwhelmingly believe that small airplanes are far superior to helicopters for close support as well as tactical airlift.[5] Key West assigned these functions to the Air Force, but the Air Force, far more interested in its primary responsibilities, has generally neglected these programs. And when the Army has tried to take matters into its own hands, it has found its hands tied by the 5,000-pound limit on airplanes. Thus the Army has had to rely almost exclusively on expensive and, many believe, ineffective, helicopters.

Helicopters not only often cost more than airplanes, they also consume about three times as much fuel per mission. Helicopters also cannot maneuver or accelerate as quickly as airplanes. Because they are so clumsy in the air and because they must be made of relatively light material to keep fuel costs down, helicopters are extremely vulnerable to enemy fire — thus the losses in Vietnam.

Why the Air Force has ignored its airlift and close support missions seems clear. The Air Force's primary responsibility is long-range bombing, and in the postwar period this has meant, above all, strategic delivery of nuclear weapons. Therefore, the Air Force has been in the business of acquiring and flying large, fast aircraft designed for bombing raids. Although some of these planes can perform tactical airlift and close support, they are far from optimal for these missions. But if they can get away with it, Air Force planners have reasoned, why shouldn't they spend the bulk of their money on aircraft designed for Air Force missions? Why should money for programs to help the Army come out of the Air Force budget?

Lacking the incentive under Key West to carry out close support or build the necessary craft, the Air Force has a shameful record in the field. Close support requires small planes "with short, stubby wings for maximum maneuverability at low altitudes," as Easterbrook explains. Until the early 1970s, the Air Force did not field a single close support aircraft. At the same time, the Air Force has jealously guarded against Army attempts to provide its own adequate close support. During the 1950s the Army attempted to acquire a close-support plane by asking that an Italian model, the G-91, be assigned to NATO. The Air Force blocked the move.

Thus the Army launched its own large-scale air program, one dominated — due to the Key West rules — by helicopters.[6] The Army effort peaked in the late 1960s, when the Army tried to build the Cheyenne, a large antitank helicopter priced at $8 million. This time the Air Force feared that the Army, with its new weapon, might be able to acquire officially the close-support function. While the Air Force still had no interest in providing close support, it wanted to protect its bureaucratic territory. Thus it developed the

Fairchild A-10, which Easterbrook notes, "many aircraft observers believe is one of the best planes ever built." Priced at $3 million, the A-10 could do a far better job than the Cheyenne at less than one-half the cost. The Cheyenne was canceled. But having headed off the Army, the Air Force saw no further use for the A-10 and attempted to cut the plane from its budget. Congress has insisted that the A-10s be built. But Air Force reluctance has sent the Army back to the drawing board, once again in the no-win realm of the helicopter.

Townsend Hoopes, under secretary of the Air Force in the Johnson administration, notes in his book, *The Limits of Intervention*, that the Air Force—using its large planes—did, indeed, provide some close support for the Army in Vietnam. He makes it clear, though, that, as in the case of the A-10, protecting turf was the main motive: "If the Air Force did not provide close air support in a ratio satisfactory to the Army, that would strengthen the Army's argument for developing its own means of close support. Already, through the development of helicopter gunships of increasing power, speed, and sophistication, the Army had pressed against that boundary."

The Air Force has been no more reliable in providing planes suited for tactical airlift. Needed here are small, propeller powered transport planes that can land and take off from short, improvised runways. But Air Force indifference during the Vietnam war forced the Army to use clumsy, inefficient, and vulnerable UH-1 "Huey" helicopters.

However, the Air Force did jump into action when the Army, through an exemption in the Key West agreement, employed a handful of its own propeller-driven airplanes. In 1966, the Air Force demanded that the Army give up these planes and "all claims for . . . future fixed wing aircraft designed for tactical airlift." The planes were turned over to the Air Force, which put many of them in reserve. Thus, because of the Key West structure, the tactical lift shortage remains serious.

MEETING MOBILITY REQUIREMENTS

"[A]n adequate airlift/sealift is essential to our global strategy," McNamara told the House Armed Services Committee in 1966. His statement is just as true nineteen years later. If Washington is serious about its pledges to defend U.S. interests in the Persian Gulf and elsewhere, the Pentagon must be able to move large numbers of troops quickly to troubled regions. Yet Defense officials continue to warn that U.S. strategic lift capabilities are inadequate. Key West is at work again. As in the case of close support, it is the Army that suffers, here at the hands of both the Air Force and the Navy, which simply lack the necessary incentives to perform these vital supporting functions.

Key West assigned the Air Force the strategic airlift task. The 1956 memorandum that set the 5,000-pound limit on Army airplanes also stated that the Air Force "presently provides adequate airborne lift in the light of currently approved strategic concepts." But remember that the key strategic concept of the day was massive retaliation. A military operating under that doctrine would have little need for sizable airlift capacity. In the event of a major war, the bomb would beat them to the action. Yet one voice was raised in dissent during the Eisenhower administration. Army Chief of Staff Maxwell Taylor insisted that his troops had not been provided with suffcient airlift.

Taylor's influence rose during the Kennedy administration, whose strategy of flexible response required significant lift capacity. In his annual defense posture statement to Congress in 1962, McNamara asserted that U.S. airlift capability fell far short of U.S. needs, criticized the Air Force for failing to provide adequate airlift for the Army, and pledged that the administration was moving to remedy the situation.

Kennedy and McNamara put strong enough pressure on the Air Force to double airlift capacity by 1966 with the procurement of the C-5A transport plane. According to McNamara's successors, however, the United States has failed to maintain an adequate strategic airlift capacity. Donald Rumsfeld, President Gerald Ford's defense secretary, complained to Congress in 1976 of inadequacies in the program. Harold Brown, President Jimmy Carter's Pentagon chief, told Congress in 1980 he doubted that the United States had sufficient lift capability to defend its interests in Western Europe and the Persian Gulf. The current secretary, Caspar Weinberger, in 1982 pointed to "the need for additional airlift to meet our near-term and future mobility requirements." Although the Air Force agreed to a program to increase airlift capacity contained in the massive Reagan defense budget, Weinberger stated that the effort "does not satisfy entirely our future airlift requirements." In addition, an editorial published several years ago in the *Armed Forces Journal* noted that "virtually every Pentagon planner agrees that the nation is critically short of airlift." Again, nothing in the Key West structure compels the Air Force to meet its responsibilities, to divert money from nuclear missile and jet aircraft programs in order to fly Army troops all over the globe.

Key West gave the Navy responsibility for nearly all sea oriented operations, including sealift for the Army troops. But the Navy's prime concern is control of the seas. Not surprisingly, Navy budget requests have not been dominated by demands for ships designed for transporting Army units. Why, reason the admirals, should Navy money be donated to the Army?

Official statements suggest that the sealift shortage has been just as serious as the airlift shortage. President Richard Nixon's first defense secretary, Melvin Laird, said in 1971, "We face serious sealift problems in executing the rapid deployment concept required under our national strategy in the early stages of a contingency." Rumsfeld gave Congress a similar message in 1976. He suggested that the United States increase the readiness of its National Defense Reserve Fleet, a collection of largely World War II-vintage ships that Laird had previously told Congress were obsolete and would be phased out by 1976. One supposes that Rumsfeld, faced with a Navy that would not spend its money on sealift programs, had nowhere else to turn. Brown's skepticism about the effectiveness of U.S. lift programs extended to sealift, and Weinberger testified that "currently available sealift resources . . . could not meet the immediate deployment requirements for the initial combat forces and their support."

In recent years, defense secretaries have stated that in the absence of sufficient strategic lift capacity, the United States should rely on American commercial vehicles and on prepositioning troops and equipment. But some analysts argue that neither is an adequate substitute for a military lift program. It takes time to commandeer commercial planes and ships, and such vehicles may often prove inefficient for or incapable of transporting heavy military hardware. (Under a proposed defense program, however, commercial airlines would receive fuel subsidies for building planes capable of transporting military equipment.) Increased reliance on prepositioning these, analysts say, would force the United States to spread even further, and thinner, its troops and equipment around the world. Such a trend is neither desirable nor, in a number of key areas, including the Persian Gulf, possible. We do not take a position on this issue, but simply point out that Key West prevents the service that relies on strategic lift, the Army, from making decisions about how to meet lift requirements.

THE IRANIAN RESCUE MISSION

Key West also affected the most recent U.S. military action in the Persian Gulf, the disastrous hostage rescue mission in Iran. The agreement's structure leaves the United States unprepared to deal with contingencies that require the use of ground forces deployed from aircraft carriers.

Under the mission's plan, eight helicopters were to lift off from the aircraft carrier *Nimitz*, stationed in the Arabian Sea, and fly 600 miles north over the Iranian desert, to a spot that planners named Desert One. There, the helicopters were to rendezvous with six transport planes that had taken off from Egypt carrying 90 Army commandos, and refuel. If six of the eight helicopters were able to continue the mission, they were to pick up the commandos and head for a point in the mountains outside Tehran. But only six of the eight had arrived at Desert One, and one had a broken hydraulic pump. The mission was aborted. Key West had insured that the United States would not have helicopter crews designed and trained to fly the mission.

Lifting off from a ship gave the helicopters the shortest safe flight path to their destination. But since Key West gave the Navy control of almost all sea operations, the helicopters had to be craft in the Navy inventory and had to fly off a Navy ship. However, since Key West also limited the Marines to amphibious operations and restricted the Navy to surface and undersea activity, it had no helicopters designed, or crews trained, specifically to fly over land.

The helicopter chosen was the Navy's RH-53D Sea Stallion, a craft equipped to sweep mines and designed to fly over water. The selection was explained by both Brown and an August 1980 report on the mission prepared by a panel of three active and three retired military officers chaired by retired Admiral James Holloway. According to Brown, the RH-53D was selected "based on its range, payload, and the fact that its familiarity as a fleet aircraft would help conceal its true reason for its presence in Iran's nearby waters." Similarly, the Holloway report says: "Primary criteria for selection included range, payload, and ability to be positioned rapidly; i.e., airliftable. Other major considerations were suitability of candidate helicopters to carrier operations and OPSEC [operations security—preserving the mission's secrecy]."

The transfer of an Army or Air Force helicopter, one designed for ground missions, might indeed have been detected and exposed the mission. And the RH-53D could fly over land. But thanks to Key West, which gave the Navy all the ships, and the Army and Air Force all the land missions, none of the carrier-based helicopter pilots had experience with ground rescue missions, and none of the Army and Air Force pilots had experience flying off aircraft carriers. The planners chose Navy and Marine pilots who knew the RH-53D and aircraft-carrier operations despite, according to the Holloway report, the availability of more than 100 Air Force pilots who had flown comparable Air Force helicopters and who were "more experienced in the mission profiles envisioned for the rescue operation." The Holloway panel argued that it is generally easier to learn to use a new aircraft than to learn a new mission. But its report agreed that bringing large numbers of Air Force pilots onto the *Nimitz* would have threatened the mission's secrecy. Because of the Key West boundaries, then, the presence on ships of the best qualified fliers would tip off enemy intelligence that business was not as usual. Thus, it seems that the United States did not send its best pilots on this crucial mission. Also, said the commander of the Army rescue unit, maintenance of the helicopters prior to their takeoff was carried out by a carrier crew that was unaware of their special purpose; he suggested that this situation could have affected the performance of the helicopters.[7]

No one can say whether, if the United States had crews that had long trained for such missions on ideal helicopters, the rescue attempt might have succeeded, or even that six helicopters in good working order might have arrived at Desert One. The argument is that if the United States wishes to perform missions such as this one, it should have crews trained to fly off aircraft carriers to missions on the ground. Pentagon planners should not have had to choose a mine-sweeper helicopter and between pilots who knew the equipment and pilots who knew the mission. But that is the sort of dangerous choice that the Key West agreements force U.S. military leaders to make.

The Iran episode also reveals how the Key West division of roles and missions makes planning in a contingency a difficult and often irrational process. Helicopters and their pilots represent only one facet of what was wrong with the mission: the United States did not possess a ready force capable of carrying it out, and thus had to rely on ad hoc planning and separate units and individuals who, in some cases, had never trained together or even met until the day of the mission. A few years prior to the rescue attempt, the Army had created a counterterrorist unit, but that outfit had not organic transport or support; nor was it permanently connected to any transport or support units or to an operational chain of command. Thus, the planners had to assemble the remaining forces ad hoc, and, as the Army rescue commander suspected, each service and even groups within services wanted "a piece of the action."[8] Thus, the Army counterterrorist "Delta" unit was joined not only by Marine and Navy pilots, but also by an Army Special Forces unit trained in West Germany, an Army Ranger unit, and an Air Force unit that provided the transport airplanes that landed at the Desert rendezvous point. Both the Holloway commission and the Delta commander, in critiquing the mission, stressed the problems caused by the ad hoc planning.

The rescue attempt is a stark example of a basic problem: the functions and forces required for some extremely important missions are split between services by the Key West rules. When the military is ordered to combat, the problem forces units that have not trained together or coordinated procurements to suit each other's needs to suddenly combine and go into action. Instead of inserting coherent permanent units, the United States deploys improvised coalitions of forces who must, on the spot, learn to work with strangers. Mission planning degenerates into bargaining among generals and admirals, each seeking a sizable piece of the action for his service. The 1983 invasion of Grenada—though it ultimately achieved its aims—once again revealed these problems.[9]

A SEA-BASED MX

We now return to the problem discussed at the beginning of this chapter: The Key West structure insured that the worthy idea of basing the MX on small submarines off U.S. shores was never taken seriously, even when the decision makers had virtually nowhere else to turn.

The submarine basing idea took shape at a summer 1978 conference of scientists and defense department advisors, who sought alternatives to the Minuteman intercontinental ballistic missile force. They sent the Pentagon a secret paper discussing the possibility of putting the MX to sea.[10] By 1979, two leading physicists and defense specialists, Richard Garwin of IBM and Sidney Drell of the Stanford University Linear Accelerator Center, had refined a proposal for a sea-based MX, which they called SUM (shallow underwater mobile). Drell recommended to the House Armed Services Committee in February 1979 that the missiles be placed in small submarines operating on the continental shelf in the Atlantic and in somewhat deeper Pacific waters. He said that shallow water basing would give the MX an excellent chance of surviving an enemy nuclear attack. The missiles would be guided, he said, by a combination of satellites and on shore transmitters; the arrangement would produce "very high accuracy for the missiles" and assure reliable communications with U.S. command centers—two principal advantages of land based missiles.

Garwin and Drell also noted that the necessary technology was already available, and that the missiles could be deployed relatively quickly. SUM basing would be relatively inexpensive and deployments would be easy to count and verify. Nor would SUM have meant completely abandoning the strategic triad concept. Submarine basing might indeed signal a realization that the best way to protect land based missiles is to get them off land. But the small, coast-based missiles would be sufficiently distinct from the Navy's Trident nuclear submarines to constitute a genuine third leg of the triad. Further, the 1981 Office of Technology Assessment report, *MX Missile Basing*, argued that, even if the Soviet Union did make dramatic gains in antisubmarine warfare technology, differences in characteristics and deployment locations between the Tridents and MX submarines would make it difficult, perhaps impossible, for the Soviets to develop weapons that could attack both vessels. The Tridents would remain in distant waters, while the MX submarines would be deployed near the coasts. The MX submarines would probably be substantially smaller than the Tridents, would rely, unlike the Tridents, in part on missile guidance systems located on land, and could be diesel or electric powered, in contrast to the nuclear powered Tridents.

The neglect of SUM cannot be attributed to a superior alternative. The Minuteman silo basing now contemplated is simply the only politically viable land based alternative. Key West is largely responsible. The 1948 agreement gave the Navy a virtual monopoly on sea based forces, but the MX belongs to the Air Force. Thus, for the United States to put missiles at sea, the Air Force would have to surrender the program to the Navy. But the Air Force is not about to give up such a prestigious, high priced, high technology program especially at a time when so many influential authorities have labeled the Minuteman force useless. Giving the Navy a SUM based MX would mean admission by the Air Force of inferiority in the field of strategic weapons delivery. Yet the Navy has not lobbied to take the program for itself. The Navy already has more of its funds invested in strategic forces than it would like. Moreover, while each service will battle to protect its own territory, it will rarely launch unprovoked invasions of its rival's domains. Drell recognized this problem from the outset. As he told the House Armed Services Committee, "The principal obstacle to the [submarine] system at this time is that it has no institutional home or constituency."

Forced, therefore, to find a land-based alternative, the Carter administration decided to adopt the costly, land devouring, racetrack basing scheme. The Pentagon, prompted by Air Force and Navy opposition to SUM and by signs of outside interest in the proposal, at last found grounds on which to oppose it. In March 1980, William Perry, under secretary of defense for research and engineering, told Congress that the submarine scheme would be vulnerable to the Van Dorn effect: A Soviet attack on coastal waters would create rough seas, which could prevent the submarines from firing their missiles.

Garwin admitted that the Van Dorn effect might play a role if the vessels were based on the continental shelf. But the East Coast shelf extends only 50–200 miles off the coast, and the West Coast shelf is much shorter. He asserted that placing the submarines beyond the shelves on both coasts would negate the Van Dorn effect. Pentagon officials, when pressed, conceded Garwin's point.[11] The Pentagon also claimed that SUM would cost as much as the racetrack plan, but Garwin discovered that the Pentagon's figures incorrectly assumed that SUM bases and maintenance would cost as much as Trident's.[12]

In 1981, perhaps spurred by Weinberger's expression of interest in a sea-based MX, Drell and Garwin modified their proposal. They recommended basing SUM in somewhat deeper waters "within 600 miles of the continental U.S. and in the Gulf of Alaska" and renamed it "smallsub undersea mobile." That took care of the Van Dorn effect. In addition, Drell and Garwin were able to show that, even in deeper water, the submarines would survive the shock effects of a Soviet attack. They asserted that deploying 55 submarines, each carrying two MX missiles, would be the cheapest way to provide the United States with an invulnerable MX deterrent.

At about the same time, an Office of Technology Assessment panel, of which Drell was a member, released its study on MX basing. The panel began by considering all possible basing modes. Eventually, the panel narrowed the list of modes with reasonable prospects for feasibility and survivability to five: the Carter racetrack scheme, the racetrack supplemented by an antiballistic missile system, a launch under attack policy, basing on large airplanes, and basing on small submarines. Neither the dense pack plan nor the Scowcroft solution were among those chosen. While the panel did not make a recommendation, the submarine alternative came out looking very good. The Office of Technology Assessment panel called the submarine based MX "highly survivable" and said it "would not be significantly less capable than the land-based MX." It asserted that a submarine based MX would be compatible with arms control and verification requirements, would damage the environment less than land based systems, and would provide an invulnerable deterrent at least as soon as the other plans.

But the panel acknowledged the politics of the situation: "[C]hanging the relative weight of land- and sea-based forces would create institutional problems for both the Air Force and Navy. . . . The Navy has shown little interest in small submarine basing of MX, and the Air Force opposes [the basing mode]." These observations reveal why the submarine based MX was doomed. Subsequently, a defense department options paper prepared for President Ronald Reagan ignored the submarine plan, and the United States moved toward the MX mess it is in today.

REWRITING KEY WEST

Key West has caused many other problems, and one suspects that more will become obvious in the future. If the United States is serious about meeting its military objectives, it must replace the Key West structure. The basic principle that should guide any reform effort is that no branch of the military should have to rely on other branches in order to carry out its duties. No longer should the services be expected to divert money from programs they care about the most in order to provide support for rival services. No longer should senseless turf rules prevent the services from carrying out their primary functions.

A reorganization of the armed forces should clarify the duties of each branch and give each branch the right to acquire all the equipment needed to carry out these duties. Thus, the Air Force would be given the responsibility for strategic delivery of nuclear and conventional warheads from land, air, or sea. If the Air Force controlled all strategic nuclear weapons, even those launched from submarines, it would be far less likely to obstruct a sensible basing mode for a new missile. A permanent Air Force–Navy group could be set up to coordinate strategic submarine activities with Navy missions for control of the seas and to provide for logistical support by the Navy for the Air Force submarines.

A question that would remain is which service would control intermediate range and short range nuclear forces deployed in Europe and South Korea. U.S. nuclear policy might gain greater coherence if all nuclear forces were placed under Air Force control, but since short range forces are integrated into Army combat units and plans, such a shift seems improbable. The best way out of the dilemma is to recognize that Army forces could defend U.S. interests more effectively and safely if short and intermediate range nuclear weapons were eliminated by arms control agreements.

The Army, under the proposal we suggest, would retain responsibility for large scale ground combat, but would gain the right to provide its own tactical airlift and close air support. Thus the Army could end its dangerous and expensive exclusive reliance on helicopters and build the small airplanes that it — and the United States — really needs.

Coherence might be further enhanced if the Army was given control of two other battlefield air missions: control of the air and interdiction of enemy supply lines close to the combat area. The Air Force would retain control of the two missions that require heavy bombers: deep interdiction — disruption of enemy supply lines farther from the combat zone — and, as mentioned above, strategic bombing. There would need to be coordination of the air missions of the two services, but this would be easier than the current need to coordinate two air components conducting the same mission of close support. The Army would at last have control over strategic lift programs for its troops. The creation of any Army sealift program might be rather expensive and would require the launching of a major training program. But it ought to be the decision of the Army and the Congress — and not the uninterested Navy — as to whether the United States develops such a capability.

The Navy would be responsible for control of the seas and have the right to buy whatever it needed, including unlimited land based aircraft, to fulfill its duties. The Navy would thus gain even greater self-sufficiency than it had achieved under Key West. The Navy would probably want to continue to depend on the Air Force or the Army for strategic lift of the ground package needed to support its ASW efforts, but it would be free to develop its own capability if it chose to do so. The Navy would relinquish one function — strategic sealift — it had been reluctant to carry out and another — strategic nuclear attack from submarines — which it was initially reluctant to accept.

The Marines would be responsible for all limited applications of conventional force, including ground operations launched from carriers and counterterrorist missions. The Marines could compete with the Army for missions that fell in the gray area between brief and small applications of force and large scale sustained combat. But in a crisis, U.S. decision makers would be wise to choose between the two services instead of allowing interservice bargaining and ad hoc planning. Problems — which would not be insurmountable — could arise if the Marines found themselves in a conflict whose scope and duration grew unexpectedly large. However, as the failed U.S. mission in Lebanon suggested, the Key West structure does not provide a ready solution to this problem. In Lebanon, the United States deployed a Marine force ill-equipped to deal with the threats which developed after it was deployed: terrorist attacks and sustained artillery fire. An Army unit would have been better prepared to handle the artillery fire but would have been no better trained for terrorist threats. The fact is that the United States had no ready force for such missions. If the U.S. wishes to pursue "presence" missions in the future, it should train a Marine and an Army contingent to carry them out and let them compete for assignments when the need arises.[13]

The reorganization we propose would not eliminate the rivalries and mistrust that permeate interservice relationships, but the plan would go far toward preventing such hostilities from interfering with America's ability to meet likely military contingencies. The new structure would insure that the incentives of the individual services and the defense requirements of the United States coincided.

Such a plan might lead to some large scale duplication of military equipment, as the Army and Air Force argued at Key West. But it is not clear that purchases of equipment needed to best perform distinct missions constitute duplication. Further, the cost of programs such as strategic lift for the Army might be offset by savings from such moves as a shift from helicopters to small planes for close support and tactical lift. In any case, those who wish to argue that the United States cannot afford an increase in strategic lift must be prepared to argue that America should limit its global role. It is simply irresponsible to claim the former without accepting the latter as its necessary consequence.

The nature of America's global responsibilities is a separate question. It is clear, though, that whatever goals the United States wishes to achieve with its military forces can never be achieved effectively and efficiently under Key West.

Unfortunately, America's armed services are not known for their love of radical change, especially change that would make serious inroads on their individual territories. The Navy would not give up its Trident nuclear program without a fight. The Air Force would be no more amenable to allowing Army soldiers the right to provide their own support functions than it has been in the past. And even the Army, which has suffered so much under Key West, might opt to preserve the status quo and protect its role in such activities as counterterrorist operations.

But if the United States truly wishes to provide for its military needs at prices that will not destroy programs or further bloat the federal deficit, it must stop pouring countless dollars down the Key West drain. If American military policy makers want America to meet its security commitments, destroying the shaky Key West structure is the necessary, and urgent, place to start.

NOTES

1. Easterbrook, Gregg, "All Aboard Air Oblivion," *Washington Monthly*, September 1981, pp. 14–26.
2. The following discussion relies heavily on Schnabel, James F., *The History of the Joint Chiefs of Staff: The Joint Chiefs of Staff and National Policy, Volume I: 1945-47* (Wilmington, Delaware: Michael-Glazier, 1979), pp. 238–47.
3. *The Department of Defense: Documents on Establishment and Organization, 1944-1978*, edited by Alice C. Cole et al. (Washington, D.C. : Office of the Secretary of Defense, Historical Office, 1978), pp. 275–85.
4. Ibid., pp. 306–15. Directive 5160.22 was canceled in 1971 because, according to Defense, it had "served the purpose for which it was issued." Yet despite this official revocation, carried out at the insistence of the Army, the Air Force has remained successful at keeping the Army from violating the spirit of Key West. See Ibid., pp. 330–31.
5. Easterbrook, op. cit.
6. See Bergerson, Frederic, *The Army Gets An Air Force* (Baltimore: The Johns Hopkins Press, 1980).
7. Beckwith, Col. Charlie, USA (Ret.) and Knox, Donald, *Delta Force* (N.Y.: Harcourt Brace Jovanovich, 1983), p. 285.
8. Ibid., p. 225
9. Halperin, David, and Halperin, Morton H., "How the Military Hobbles Itself," *Washington Post,* Jan. 6, 1984, p. A19.
10. Keller, Bill, "Attack of the Atomic Tidal Wave," *Washington Monthly*, May 1980, pp. 53–8.
11. Marshall, Eliot, *MX on Land or Sea*, Science, April 11, 1980, p. 155.
12. Keller, op. cit.
13. "How the Military Hobbles Itself," Op. cit.; U.S. House of Representatives, 98th Congress, 1st Session, committee on armed services, *Adequacy of U.S. Marine Corps Security in Beirut* (Washington, D.C.: U.S. Government Printing Office, 1983), pp. 43–54.

Chapter 17

Resource Allocation in the Pentagon

Vincent Puritano

INTRODUCTION

Every federal agency puts together its own budget package for inclusion in the president's January budget submission to the Congress. Over the years, a wide variety of resource allocation processes have been instituted to develop and execute those budgets. The resource allocation process for the department of defense (DOD) can be divided into five distinct but overlapping phases, or steps. The first three steps are internal to DOD and primarily consist of the three phases in the revised and continually evolving planning, programming, and budgeting system, or PPBS. The fourth step involves combining the DOD budget with the overall federal budget, a process in which the office of management and budget (OMB) and various other executive branch individuals play key roles. This fourth step overlaps considerably with the third phase of the PPBS. In fact, the submission of the DOD portion of the president's budget is often seen as the conclusion of the PPBS process. From that point, however, the budget must still go through the fifth step, which consists of the several layers of ever expanding congressional review, authorization, and appropriation.

This five step resource allocation process is a lengthy and complex one. By the time DOD components actually begin to obligate and expend the appropriated funds that Congress has approved, almost two years will have passed since the DOD staff began their revisions of policy and strategy goals in the budget planning phase for that fiscal year. Further, for particularly long-term systems under development, such as aircraft carriers, a decade or more may pass before all appropriated funds have been expended.

I will initially discuss the first three steps of the process and the changes we have instituted in the PPBS over the last three years. I will then touch on the fourth and fifth steps, including the heavy impact of congressional reviews and actions. I want to focus mainly on opportunities I see for further improvement in all five steps, both internal and external. I will make the point that further improvements of the process within DOD may be almost irrelevant unless Congress also changes its way of doing business.

THE PLANNING, PROGRAMMING, AND BUDGETING SYSTEM

The PPBS has three phases. The planning phase attempts to set military and civilian goals and objectives and outlines the forces and resources needed to achieve those objectives. The programming phase develops and approves programs for reaching those objectives. In the budgeting phase, the inputs required for those approved programs are budgeted and priced as precisely as possible for the immediate budget year, then folded into the president's overall federal budget for submission to Congress. The planning and programming phases cover a five-year period, the five-year defense plan or FYDP. The budgeting phase concentrates in depth on the first year of that five-year period, since that is the period to be decided on by the Congress.

At the top of the resource allocation process is the Defense Resources Board (DRB), the primary resource decisionmaking body in DOD. Although it existed prior to the current administration, both its role and membership were expanded in 1981. I will mention the changes in membership and functions in a later section.

Often, all three phases are going on at the same time. For example, in December of 1983, as I write this, DOD is preparing and reviewing the budget for fiscal year (FY) 1985, developing the plans and guidance for the FY 1986–1990 defense program and beginning to execute the FY 1984 budget. Since Congress enacted the FY 1984 appropriations legislation on November 18, 1983, two and a half months into the fiscal year, DOD was constrained to operate during that time under the restrictions of a continuing resolution. Because we did not know what the final FY 1984 budget would be, DOD was also constrained in its ability to develop the FY 1985 budget and the FY 1986–1990 plans.

The Planning Phase

The first step in the DOD resource allocation process is the planning phase, whose product is the defense guidance. This document is prepared annually and covers a five-year period (for example, FY 1986 through FY 1990). The defense guidance, through the inputs of the Joint Chiefs of Staff (JCS), begins by defining the threat against which DOD programs are measured. It further states national defense policy, objectives, and strategy; provides resource and forces guidance to achieve those objectives; and establishes the fiscal guidelines for the upcoming programming phase. The planning phase begins, more than two years before the first fiscal year in which planned funds will be expended, with a review of the previous year's guidance. That review is led by the under secretary of defense for policy, with the participation of OSD, the services, JCS, and the commanders in chief of the unified and specified commands (the CINCs). This review reflects major changes in policy, strategy, and the global situation; the results of the just completed programming phase; and the actions to date of the Congress on the previously submitted budget.

The drafting of the defense guidance also takes into account the long-range plans of the JCS, the defense intelligence agency, and others. The review and revision process involves all major DOD components, including, in the last two years (for the first time) the input of the CINCs. The defense guidance, in its final form, including the final fiscal guidance, is reviewed and signed by the secretary in late January or early February.

The Programming Phase

In the programming phase, the services and defense agencies propose programs that are designed to meet the mid-range (five year) objectives of the defense guidance and to fit within the fiscal constraints of the projected DOD budgets. In May, these programs, in the form of program objective memoranda (POMs) are submitted to the secretary for the program review.

The program review, conducted by the OSD, JCS, and service staffs, and led by the comptroller and the program analysis and evaluation directorate (PAE), examines the POMs for compliance with the defense guidance and the fiscal guidelines. Attention is also directed to duplications, overlaps, and missed opportunities for economies and efficiencies. Key issues are developed by the OSD and JCS staffs to better integrate and consolidate the DOD-wide program across service lines and to gain a total overview of the defense program for the secretary of defense. The comptroller, acting as executive secretary of the DRB, consolidates these issues, which usually number over 200, into approximately 45 to 50. Teams are then selected, with representation from JCS, the services, and the OSD offices, to analyze each of the issues, presenting alternatives and arguments for and against each alternative. The issues are arrayed in eight issue books, separated by subjects. These include policy and risk assessment, nuclear forces, conventional forces, modernization and investment, readiness and other logistics, manpower, intelligence, and management initiatives.

The DRB then meets for two hours or more per day for two to three weeks in July to evaluate and debate these key issues. The DRB review is completed in August, and the deputy secretary, who chairs the DRB, confirms the decisions and agreed-upon changes through the program decision memoranda (PDMs).

The Budgeting Phase

The POMs as amended by the PDMs become the basis for the September 15 budget estimate submissions from all DOD elements to the DOD comptroller. This includes the three military departments and the defense agencies and other elements, a total of 22 budget submissions. The comptroller leads an examination of these budgets during September, October, and November for accuracy of pricing, producibility, feasibility, scheduling, and consistency with established policies and previous decisions. The budget review is significantly more detailed than the program review and concentrates primarily on the budget year to be presented to Congress. The review is a full, thorough, and in-depth examination of the service and defense agencies' budgets. It is not selective, nor is it restricted to just incremental changes; budgets for long-standing functions are also examined. Other OSD staffs and OMB participate in the comptroller-led joint budget review, with full OMB participation in budget hearings and coordination on program budget decisions (PBDs).

This review leads to a number of major decisions that have to be made by the secretary in late November and early December, depending on the results of the congressional review of the previous year's budget and on the target topline given by the president to DOD in the late fall. Again, the services and the OSD offices participate in this final budget decision phase.

At this point, the third step begins to overlap with the fourth step, the OMB/Executive branch integration of the federal budget. The DOD comptroller pulls together a "final" DOD budget, and the secretary and the director of OMB discuss any outstanding OSD–OMB budget issues. In early or mid-December, the secretary meets with the president for his final directions and budget decisions. Often, there are problems with this fourth step of the resource allocation process. Late decisions on the final government-wide economic assumptions by OMB, when incorporated into the almost completed DOD budget, usually cause last minute adjustments in hundreds of budget line items, charts, and tables.

After the president has approved the final DOD budget, and OMB has incorporated it into the national budget, the process then begins to move into the fifth stage, the congressional review process. In preparation, DOD provides exhibits and narrative to OMB for printing in the federal budget and for submission to the Congress in late January. In addition, DOD begins preparing congressional justification documents, testimony for the secretary and other DOD witnesses, and various supporting documents in support of the budget. Last year, for example, more than 21,000 pages of documents and exhibits were prepared for these congressional presentations.

The congressional budget process involves three distinct but somewhat overlapping phases. First, the budget committees set an overall ceiling for the defense budget as part of the first concurrent budget resolution, due by mid-May. Next, the armed services committees put together the Defense Authorization Act, which tells DOD what it is authorized to spend in the coming year. This is usually completed in mid- to late-summer. Finally, the appropriations committees enact the Defense Appropriation Act, usually in the fall, which appropriates the funds that theoretically will pay for what has been authorized.

That briefly describes the five major steps of the resource allocation process in the defense department. It seems like a rational, orderly process. The process is, however, not without its problems.

1981 – PROBLEMS WITH THE PROCESS

The present administration came into office pledged to revitalize U.S. military strength and to do it in the most economical and efficient way. Both Secretary Weinberger and Deputy Secretary Carlucci felt that, in a federal agency, the budget process is *the* management process. Therefore, to fulfill its pledges, the new defense administration felt it had to quickly assess DOD's resource allocation process and make the necessary changes. Only a few weeks into the current administration, I organized and conducted a thirty-day review of the DOD PPBS at the request of the secretary and deputy secretary. Utilizing a steering group that I chaired, with four working groups and with full participation of all OSD staffs, the services, and JCS, we quickly began analyzing the major PPBS problems and discussing alternative solutions. The focus of the review was to delve quickly into internal process problems, to analyze their characteristics, to array and display the issues, and to focus on options for improving PPBS in DOD.

We quickly identified a number of broad problems with the internal PPBS process. Many of the problems resulted from system-wide distortions that had been created by the twenty-year accretion of differing objectives and management styles. In the McNamara years, the emphasis was on programming; the Laird era stressed participatory management; the Carter Administration added zero-based budgeting (ZBB). All three of these left major and potentially conflicting characteristics embedded in the PPBS.

This combination of three disparate systems led to two major problems. The first of these was a confusion of the line and staff relationships between OSD and the services. This encouraged a continuation of OSD directive and overly specific guidance to the services, generated huge amounts of additional paperwork, and created strong adversarial relationships between OSD and the services. The second major problem resulted from ZBB. The ZBB system did not materially aid the secretary in managing the department, but it added significantly to the data and paperwork load.

The combination of systems also led to too many data structures, so that there was no longer a common data base for the PPBS. A variety of competing formats, structures, and data banks had evolved, at both the service and OSD levels, with resulting paperwork overloads, confusion, and continuous duplication of data requests from numerous sources.

Neglect of execution was also evident. The emphasis and rewards were focused on the front end justification of programs and the obtaining of appropriations. In addition, most of the time of managers at all levels of DOD was spent on shepherding their programs through the various PPBS cycles. Program execution functions were generally neglected, as were strategic planning functions, and only limited feedback to policy makers and programmers was built into the system. Discontinuities existed between the PPBS and the procedures for review approval of major weapon systems acquisition. This showed in the continual conflicts surrounding and disrupting acquisition programs, the confusion over program costs, and the resulting program quantity adjustments and subsequent cost growth.

Specific Problems with the Planning Phase

Without fiscal constraints, the joint strategic planning document (JSPD) contained higher force levels than could be accommodated within the fiscal guidance. This led to plans that were far out of line with available resources and were thus less relevant during the programming and budgeting phases. The consolidated guidance (as it was then called) attempted to provide a sequence of planning development from the JCS and the services to the secretary. However, this guidance was constructed on an ad hoc basis for each item of approved guidance, with minimal high-level dialogue in the process.

As a result, the planning phase often produced significant mismatches between stated U.S. policies and both the current capabilities of the forces to implement those policies and the longer-term planned capabilities.

Specific Problems with the Programming Phase

As a result of the planning problems, and to help alleviate them, there was an overabundance of program direction in the consolidated guidance and an inordinate amount of detailed data requested in the program preparation instructions. This led to excessively large program documents that, when compared to the detailed guidance, gave rise to a massive number of detailed issues to be resolved during the program review phase. Still more issues were then raised by the inability of the DOD fiscal projections to fund all the objectives stated in the guidance.

Most of the program review was necessarily focused on the upcoming budget year, rather than the full five-year program. This was a direct result of the multitude of detailed program issues, the ZBB review requirements, and the consequent work demands of the services and the OSD staff. Top DOD officials had little time for realistic thinking about outyear issues and their implications. Each of the hundreds of issue papers contained a set of staff alternatives to a service program and all had to be reviewed and discussed by the various staffs during the program review.

All of these issues had to be addressed by the Defense Resources Board. Although intended to be the secretary's corporate review board for DOD, before 1981 the DRB did not include any service representation in either a permanent or associate status. The services merely provided observers on call. The JCS played only a minimal role in the program review. After their review of the service program proposals, the JCS issued their joint program assessment memorandum (JPAM) of the military risk involved in the service programs. In part because of the timing of the JPAM and in part because the JCS did not play an active role in the OSD program review, JCS views were rarely incorporated into issue papers.

The net effect of these problems was that major decisions were often postponed until the final days of the cycle and a significant amount of program instability resulted.

Specific Problems with the Budgeting Phase

In the budget phase, the ZBB procedures had quadrupled the number of exhibits, listing, displays, and formats of data presentation. As a result, the staffs of OSD, JCS, and the services all complained of the inability to provide quality work in a timely manner.

Revisitation of decisions regularly occurred in the existing PPBS environment. Issues decided in the programming phase were often resurrected in the budgeting phase by all participants, OSD, OMB, and the services. (That is, those who had "lost" the original decision wanted to revisit that decision. The "winners" liked the original decision and fought off the revisits.)

Another major problem in budgeting was the inability of the system to produce a consistent set of categories to describe the activities within the budget. As a result, much time was spent in translation, and justification of congressional categories sometimes drove programmatic decisions. The need to explain costs in appropriation categories led to the creation of large budget justification documents, taking information from program formats and transcribing it into other displays. Contradictions or perceived discrepancies among the various displays also generated additional workload to prepare explanations.

The budget phase was also plagued by problems with the fourth part of the DOD resource allocation process. Just prior to the presentation of the president's budget to the Congress in January, DOD often experienced sudden late changes to the budget estimates and supporting programs, brought on by late OMB and presidential decisions on fiscal levels, programs, and/or a revised inflation forecast. These new data had to be quickly incorporated into a myriad of documents without disturbing balances painstakingly developed over a course of several months. The result was often a crash series of meetings, culminating in conflicting guidance and unbalanced resource allocation in some program areas. This reduced confidence in the system and caused a persistent ripple effect on reorientation of policy, on implementation of budget decisions, and on program justification to the Congress. However, those problems were beyond the scope of the PPBS assessment we were doing. Therefore, we restricted our recommendations to the first three steps in the process.

HOW IT'S WORKING NOW

After analyzing the problems and alternative solutions, the March 1981 steering group reached consensus on a number of recommendations for improvement. These recommendations were reviewed by the secretary and deputy secretary, the Joint Chiefs of Staff, the service secretaries, and the under and assistant secretaries of defense. In announcing their decisions, the secretary and deputy secretary went beyond merely changing the PPBS. They established a broad set of management principles and philosophy that set the base for major improvements in DOD. These principles included the statement of their management formula of centralized policymaking and decentralized operational responsibility and authority, including full participation in the system by the services.

The central OSD staffs were asked to concentrate on broad central policy guidance rather than the detailed program guidance of previous years. By emphasizing cross-service and cross-command analysis, OSD would better assist the secretary make the high priority decisions. OSD and the services were also asked to create a more participative environment in the PPBS, to develop more teamwork and better communications throughout the entire cycle.

The program review phase was improved by getting OSD to concentrate on broader policy guidance, literally cutting the paperwork required by fifty percent, and greatly reducing the number of minor issues raised to the DRB level for decision, by concentrating only on the major, high priority policy level issues. Over the last two years, an average of 250 issues have been raised in the program review, but these have been reduced to 40 or 50 major issues that finally reach the DRB for decision.

The budget phase was streamlined by completely eliminating the ZBB paperwork requirements. The concept of prioritizing programs at the margin was retained but without the massive ZBB paperwork load. DOD was able to do this quickly because its summer program review already served the primary purpose of ZBB.

The Defense Resources Board, chaired by the deputy secretary, was strengthened and given the authority as the major governing body of the DOD resource allocation process. In addition to the chairman of the Joint Chiefs of Staff, the heads of the OSD organizations, and the OMB's associate director for national security affairs, the DRB was expanded to include the service secretaries. The service chiefs became, in effect, defacto members of the DRB, and are invited to all meetings where major policy issues are discussed. As another innovation, the commanders in chief (CINCs) of the unified and specified commands are invited twice a year to participate in the initial DRB deliberations during the planning and programming phases. The current comptroller was named executive secretary of the DRB and was charged with keeping the process on track with the new PPBS guidelines. Further improvements were made in the staff work provided for each DRB meeting to assure full participation at the staff level by representatives of all members and a comprehensive arraying of points of view and alternatives. Attendance has been firmly restricted to the principals only.

The responsibilities of the DRB were expanded to include, in the planning phase, the review and approval of the policy and strategy guidance that would set the base for future program and budget decisions. The deputy secretary, with the advice of the DRB and with the assistance of the executive secretary, was given responsibility for the total management of the revised PPBS.

The problems which the changes were designed to attack are complex, and the effort to overcome them will need, in many cases, to be sustained and long-term. Nonetheless, there seems to be a consensus in OSD, in the services, and certainly with the service secretaries and the secretary of defense, that the changes instituted in the last three years have significantly improved the resource allocation process. The PPBS is now more capable of making appropriate decisions at the right time, of addressing the major issues rather than insignificant details, and of assuring that all participants are heard when they need to be.

In addition, the PPBS reforms have addressed many of the specific problems outlined above. Planning documents now consider fiscal projections when setting mid-term objectives for force and resource planning. The addition of affordability considerations, coupled with the enhanced role of the services, the JCS, and the secretary, help produce a better match of policies with both current forces and longer-term plans.

The program review phase benefits from the improvements in the planning process; the defense guidance provides a better match of plans and resources and a more appropriate level of detail for program guidance. This helps produce a better set of program proposals (POMs), fewer major issues for DRB resolution, and a greater ability to focus on more than just the budget year. The fifty percent reduction in paperwork required for the program review has also enhanced the DRB's ability to focus on the entire five-year program, and the increased participation of the services and JCS helps ensure better quality program decisions.

This, in turn, carries over into the budgeting phase. Better program review decisions result in fewer revisits. Reduced paperwork, including the elimination of ZBB, allows a more focused review of the service budget submissions.

THE CONGRESSIONAL INFLUENCE

I would like to turn now to a resource allocation and management problem that is more than equal to internal DOD problems in this area, but which is, unfortunately, far less amenable to analysis and solution. That is the ever-expanding and deepening role of the Congress in the detailed management of DOD's affairs. I believe this role is expanding to a level of detail which is beyond any legitimate oversight function, to the extent that Congress is becoming an integral part of the problems of instability facing defense planning and management in the years ahead. This is in addition to the planning and executing problems caused by congressional failure to enact appropriating legislation at the beginning of the fiscal year.

Unlike many other functions in the federal government, the national defense budget is very much dependent on the annual authorization and appropriation process; few defense activities are set by statute. Both the annual review process and the results (or delays in obtaining results) of that process can cause serious problems, and those problems have been worsening in the past few years.

The Budget and Impoundment Control Act of 1974 instituted reforms designed to ensure that Congress completed all appropriations before the beginning of the budget (fiscal) year. The fiscal year was actually changed to begin three months later to assure that this would happen. These reforms have not succeeded; in the most recent six years under the Act (and in nineteen of the last twenty-one years), DOD has begun the fiscal year under a continuing resolution authority (CRA). The FY 1984 DOD Appropriations Act was not enacted until seven weeks after the beginning of the fiscal year, and the FY 1983 act was over three months late. Late congressional decisions on a budget leave too much uncertainty and program instability during the ongoing review of the current year's budget, the planning for the following five-year defense program, and especially the ability of DOD to execute properly the enacted program, since schedules, quantities, dollar amounts, and plans must be redrawn throughout the department.

Some means must be found to resolve this problem. The obvious and most helpful solution is for the Congress to complete all DOD appropriations before the new fiscal year begins. This would reduce the uncertainty for both the budget year and the subsequent program and planning years. Failing that, another possibility would be for the Congress to allow the department of defense in the continuing resolution authority to continue to obligate, automatically, funds for activities such as new starts and new multiyear procurement proposals. Restrictions built into the CRA each year prevent DOD from such actions, with resulting program uncertainty and instability.

A third option would be for the Congress to seriously think about a biennial budget for defense. This could improve DOD's ability to manage and plan, as well as better realize economies of stability. While the two-year process would require some careful and detailed development in order to preclude unintended problems and side effects, I believe that, when done intelligently, it could result in benefits for both DOD and for the Congress. For instance, Congress could concentrate in the first year of the process on overall DOD strategy, defense policy, goals and objectives, and major programs and weapons systems. In the second year, Congress could conduct more specific oversight reviews on programs and project details.

However, even with such a biennial budgeting process and/or with timely appropriations acts each cycle, there would still be the problems and conflicts growing from the overlapping and expanding roles of the Congress. There can be no question of the congressional role in review and approval of defense budget requests. Yet, the constantly expanding number of congressional hearings each year, before more and more committees and subcommittees, has reached the point where a vast amount of the time and resources of our top management must be allocated to this single purpose. This expenditure of time and resources leaves far less to actually plan, manage, and execute the budgets and programs that Congress finally approves.

Let me lay out some facts. In 1983, 1,306 DOD witnesses provided 2,160 hours of testimony in hundreds of appearances before a total of 96 different committees and subcommittees. In addition, there were approximately 85,000 written inquiries and nearly 600,000 telephone calls during the year from the Congress. In 1983, DOD provided Congress with 21,753 pages of justification documents in support of the FY 1984 budget request, a threefold increase over 1970. This growth in testimony and in the provision of documents has not necessarily served to produce better results. The vast number of committees and subcommittees have led to overlapping jurisdictional problems and to the addition of legislative directions and restrictions for DOD. For example, the enactment of authorization provisions or limitations into appropriations bills, in direct violation of congressional rules, has grown considerably. In FY 1984, there were 107 such general provisions in the DOD Appropriations Act. There were an additional 68 general provisions in the DOD Authorization Act, and another 41 general provisions appeared in the authorization and appropriations acts that cover military construction, for a total of 216 general provisions directed to DOD. This compares with only 101 such provisions in FY 1978, an increase of over 100 percent in only six years. In addition, in FY 1984 legislation Congress also directed 661 specific actions (compared to 382 in FY 1978) and called for 422 reports (compared to 153 in FY 1978) for the department of defense.

Many general provisions protect specific interests. For instance, DOD is forbidden by one provision from converting heating plants from coal to oil at defense facilities in Europe and by another from using European coal in European defense heating plants when U.S. coal is available. Other provisions prohibit DOD from buying manual typewriters from Warsaw Pact nations or from buying aircraft ejection seats for the F-18 fighter from Britain. There are other provisions limiting procurement of food, of clothing, of specialty metals, of commercial transportation, of insignia, of multiyear contracts, of aircraft power cables, and of cats and dogs for medical purposes. There are still more provisions that cover retirement pay, personnel ceilings, transportation of dependents and of household goods, relations with small business, the operation of commissaries, tuition for off duty training, real property, legislative liaison, public affairs activities, medical care, child counseling, abortions, plastic surgery, leasing of aircraft or vehicles or vessels, transferring the operations of schools for dependents to the department of education, selling or leasing Fort De Russy in Hawaii, the interdiction of narcotics trafficking, and free mailing privileges for service personnel. There are numerous specific provisions directing actions on contracts, spare parts, competition, and so on. The department of defense has carefully reviewed all general provisions in the DOD acts and is now asking Congress for deletion of more than half. However, the sheer number and wide ranging subject matter in these provisions further indicate the kind of congressional role problem I mentioned above.

It is clear that Congress needs to find some way to eliminate or reduce duplications and redundancies in its review process, while continuing to ensure that they receive all the necessary information to conduct appropriate review and approval functions. Failure to address this problem will continue to unnecessarily and unproductively drain top management resources in DOD, to the detriment of the department and of the nation.

The major problem that the defense department continues to have with Congress, however, is the year-long congressional budget review process that concentrates more on programmatic and budgetary detail than on policy-level, strategic or mission oriented, goal-related analysis and review. Confusing and contradictory decisions are made, and conflicting signals are sent, as the defense budget request moves through the budget, armed services, and appropriations committees and subcommittees. The appropriations act is then usually late, and DOD spends weeks trying to put the fiscal pieces together, both to carry out the final congressional decisions and to plan the following year's budget request.

SOME IDEAS FOR FURTHER IMPROVEMENTS OF THE DOD RESOURCE ALLOCATION PROCESS

Since the purpose of this chapter is to review current defense organization and management and how to improve it, I propose the following for consideration.

Internal DOD

As mentioned above, I believe that the DOD resource allocation process is basically sound. It has been improved over the last few years and has shown that it is a flexible and dynamic system that can handle evolutionary changes. Rather than creating a new process, I believe that the basic system, with continuing improvements, based on realistic assessments, can be of continuing value for the years ahead.

There are at least four major defense internal processes that need continuous internal review and modifications. One is the further improvement of the phases of the PPBS. The planning phase, although improved, needs more work. In particular, more effort is needed in the establishment of long-range objectives and in the formulation of strategy. The possible combination of the programming and budgeting phases into one integrated cycle, preferably taking place in the autumn, could save time and effort that could then be applied to improved long-range planning, as well as to providing more attention to the budget execution and management phases. Studies and analyses should be performed to see if this often-recommended change is really feasible in such a large and complex organization, or whether (as I think) both phases actually serve a necessary and important function.

To consider such PPBS process changes, however, are not enough. They must coincide with necessary organizational changes to assure that whatever process changes are made, the institutional framework is created to execute those changes. For instance, if the last two phases of the PPBS are to be combined, then serious consideration should also be given to combining the office of program analysis and evaluation (PAE) with the comptroller's organization. The resulting organization should be given full responsibility to organize and manage the new resource allocation system for the secretary. Unless both process and organizational changes happen together, successful reform will not be possible. It will take time to make such fundamental changes, and the necessary preparatory work and planning must take place first. The PPBS bureaucracy in DOD is far reaching; not only do the processes and organizations permeate OSD, but variations of these processes and organizations also exist in the services, stretching throughout their worldwide field structures. All the services have a PPBS, a comptroller, and a program analysis and evaluation office. All of these would have to be changed together — and all would have to participate in the advance planning for these changes.

As a second area of possible change in DOD's internal processes, I recommend that the OSD and service programming and budgeting staffs launch major studies and analyses for possible biennial budgeting experiments within DOD. Consultations with OMB and congressional staffs should be included. Initial target areas for this experimental approach should be those where there is a minimum of disagreement or friction among the components of the legislative and executive branches. Possible pilot program areas could be designated for biennial budgeting, and subsequently a comprehensive review and evaluation could be done by the services involved, OSD, OMB, and congressional staffs.

The third area for continuing review and improvement is the weapons acquisition process. Although not discussed in this chapter, the author led a DOD task force in 1981 that produced the thirty-two point defense acquisition improvement program (also known as the "Carlucci Initiatives"), which attempted fundamental and long-term reform of the acquisition process (see "Getting Ourselves Together on Systems Acquisition", by Vincent Puritano, *Armed Forces Comptroller*, V. 27, No. 1, Winter 1982, pp. 8–14). Some of these reforms have achieved excellent results — multiyear procurement, realistic budgeting for inflation, expanded use of independent cost estimating, closer attention to economic production rates for major systems, and efforts to enhance and increase competition and dual-source production. For example, in fiscal years 1982–1984, DOD submitted to Congress thirty-six candidates for multiyear procurement, of which twenty-one have been approved, for an estimated net savings of $3.4 billion over the period FY 1982–1988. In addition, independent cost analyses will be performed on twenty-seven major weapons systems as part of the summer program review in 1984. Furthermore, the program review process for every major system now has an analysis of economic production rates built in. Continued review, reform, and high-level management attention is still needed in this important process, including attention to tying the weapons acquisition process to the PPBS.

The fourth area for further consideration is somewhat related to the third and is also not discussed elsewhere in this chapter. That is the need to conduct a major review of the weapons requirements planning process in the services. Here again, there have been improvements, but more are needed. Weapons requirements should conceptually flow from a full and complete analysis of national security objectives, the strategy required to achieve those objectives, and the threats to that strategy. This has not always been the case; the long-range aspect of weapons planning needs improving. I believe that too much attention is spent on the shorter-range current budget and annual congressional aspects. More time and effort is needed to look beyond the current year's battles for resources.

Congress

Frankly, I do not think that the major problems in resource allocation are within DOD alone. We can and should do better in long-range strategic planning, in requirements planning for weapons acquisition, and in the entire acquisition process. Even with the internal improvements I have suggested, serious defense resource allocation problems will remain with the Congress. I have already covered some aspects of these problems:

- the major expansion of both the staffs and the committee structure in terms of hearings and oversight of DOD, and the resulting expansion of paper, time, and human resources committed in DOD to respond to ever-increasing congressional demands;
- the uncoordinated and overlapping distribution of defense review and oversight responsibility among the many budget, authorizing, appropriation, intelligence, and oversight committees and subcommittees;
- the short-range (one year), line item by line item focus of the congressional review, rather than a focus on longer-range and mission-wide analyses;
- the distortions of defense programs that result from political pressure on the Congress (and on the defense department) by defense industry;
- the need for Congress to better evaluate the DOD budget in relation to foreign policy and military objectives and goals—in the macro sense, rather than focusing on line item changes.

There have been many suggestions for congressional improvements. Some, if implemented, could be of great value in improving the defense resource allocation process. A simple listing of the most important of these from my point of view are to

- have appropriations bills completed by the beginning of the fiscal year;
- consider rationalizing responsibilities and jurisdictions among the budget, authorizing, and appropriations committees in both the House and Senate;
- consider utilizing joint hearings, either within the House and Senate or

even between the two houses, particularly on the same subjects (e.g., military construction, retired pay, personnel compensation, etc.);
- consider reducing the number of defense subcommittees and/or the number of hearings;
- consider the scheduling of more detailed briefings rather than hearings;
- consider biennial budgeting or an extension of the multiyear funding concept, particularly in areas where there is agreement between the executive and legislative branches;
- consider making all three years of the congressional budget resolutions binding on the Congress. (In FY 1984, DOD presented a budget request to Congress that met the FY 1984 target figure set in the FY 1983 concurrent budget resolution. Congress subsequently reduced that figure, in the end, by $18 billion);
- consider a presidential line item veto, so that marginal programs can be excised by the president without the need to veto or jeopardize the entire bill.

CONCLUSION

Any single change listed above, or a combination, whether in DOD or in the Congress, could help improve the defense resource allocation process. The fact that there is room for improvement does not mean that the existing budget process has not served DOD well. It has been pragmatic and has provided the structured arena within which the appropriate policy and political debates must and do take place, within the defense department, within the executive branch, and between the executive branch and the Congress. There is room for the type of pragmatic improvement, such as those that have been done in the past, that face the current realities and problems while continuing and maintaining the fundamentally sound overall resource allocation process.

Chapter 18

A Critique of the PPB System

Philip Odeen

Assistant Secretary Puritano carefully outlined the department of defense's planning, programming, and budgeting system (PPBS). He pointed out the reforms made during Secretary Weinberger's period in office. Therefore, I need not describe the system or point out its virtues, which are numerous. Instead, I will discuss the shortcomings, most of which predate Mr. Puritano's arrival in the defense department and most of which still remain.

HISTORICAL CONTEXT

I was fortunate to be "present at the creation" of PPBS, having joined the OSD comptroller staff in 1960, shortly before President Kennedy's election and his selection of Robert McNamara as secretary of defense. I then worked fairly closely with Charles Hitch, the comptroller, who was the principal architect of PPBS.

Although McNamara and Hitch developed the system, there were pressures prior to 1961 to develop a system that would give key executive and congressional officials a better understanding of the range of issues they were facing. In particular, they were concerned about

- The long-term commitments that they were making to new, and qualitatively different, weapons systems (ICBMs, Polaris submarines and missiles, etc.) in the context of a one year budget. There was no systematic way to assess or control the outyear costs of these decisions.
- The appropriate balance of resources allocated among missions. Were we spending enough or too much on strategic forces? Mobility? Sea control? The existing system focused on types of costs, that is, on military pay, research, production, and operating costs, not on mission oriented programs.
- the divisive competition among the services for new missions as new weapons (for example, long-range tactical aircraft, ballistic missiles, and

helicopters) blurred the traditional delineation of roles and missions (armies walk, navies swim, and air forces fly).

As a result, multiyear resource plans were developed for major weapon systems in the late 1950s; and, at the request of the House Appropriations Committee, a pro-forma budget by mission and service was developed in 1959. Although these efforts were in the right direction, they were ad hoc and unsophisticated. Moreover, the defense department was not managed in these terms. It was, therefore, impossible to ensure that any decisions made with these new approaches would, in fact, be implemented by the services.

The PPBS developed by McNamara and Hitch was designed to do five things:

1. Lay out the multiyear impact of decisions made this year (no more "buy-ins").
2. Look at the defense program in mission or output terms, not in service or budget input terms. It was to focus on what we were trying to do, not on who would do it.
3. Provide a way to tie missions, strategies, forces, and budgets together. The hope was for integrated plans, programs, and funding.
4. Facilitate cross-service or comparative analyses where missions overlap, and output oriented analyses (cost–benefit) for service-unique missions.
5. Make resource decisions according to a rational sequence, looking first at broad plans, then multiyear programs, and finally at the one year budget details.

While these goals are twenty years old, they still provide a sound measuring stick for evaluating the PPB system in defense.

BROAD CONSIDERATIONS

First, let me evaluate the system in light of these criteria. Then I will note some more specific shortcoming in the present PPBS. But before looking at the weaknesses of the system, one point must be made clear. Despite the faults of PPBS and the number of observers who criticize the system, no one wishes to abolish it. It provides an essential framework for allocating the $300 billion in resources that DOD will have at its disposal in 1985. If we did not have PPBS, we would be forced to create something very much like it. Thus, the real question is how can we make PPBS more effective and less burdensome to the services and the OSD staff.

In my view, there are five areas where PPBS still fails to meet the broad goals set for it twenty years ago. First, the planning phase has never been well done or appropriately integrated with the programming and budgeting efforts. It is frequently said that the first *P* in PPBS is silent. The planning that has taken place has too frequently been a sterile exercise, one that has received little serious attention by senior officials. In many cases, the objectives laid out are so ambitious that they are well beyond reach of the funds available. In other cases, the goals were stated so broadly that they were virtually meaningless as a guide for making difficult choices among programs. And priorities have seldom been provided to give guidance when, as almost always happens, it is necessary to decide which goals will be slighted or which strategies not fully supported. Good planning, one that leads to clear goals and well-defined strategies, is the essential first step in sound management of the defense department. If it is to be effective, planning should do three things.

1. Lay out the primary security goals the department of defense must be able to accomplish with reasonable forces and capabilities.
2. Lay out broad but clear strategies to be used to achieve the goals.
3. Provide priorities so that the most important goals will be achieved if resources are not adequate to meet them all.

Second, the issue of allocations among programs is not really addressed. The services largely determine the broad allocations, with political or institutional factors dominating the choices. Plans and strategies are seldom major considerations. The secretary of defense also rarely looks at these basic allocation issues. Instead, he focuses on a flood of small, marginal changes that would not produce significant changes in the allocations of resources among the services or among missions.

Third, the mission breakouts should be improved. The present program structure has many flaws. Some major areas, such as logistic support, are not structured to facilitate analysis. In other cases, the combat mission breakouts are outmoded and reserve and guard forces are not adequately addressed. A joint GAO/DOD team recently reviewed PPBS and pointed out a number of improvements in this area that are worthy of consideration.

Fourth, the accounting systems have not been updated to permit the programs to be executed and managed in the same way the decisions are made, that is, by mission. The tie between the program and the budget is loose. As a result, it is often difficult to ensure that budgets effectively reflect the multiyear program decisions made by the secretary of defense. Once the budget is approved by the Congress, the accounting and reporting systems, which are cumbersome and outmoded, have great difficulty tracking the execution. There is thus considerable ambiguity over what is really done with the funds.

Finally, the multiyear aspect of PPBS has not been well developed. Although the financial plans cover five years, the focus continues to be on the upcoming budget year. Moreover, most weapons programs have implications — cost as well as force structure — that go well beyond five years. An extended planning annex (covering another ten years) was added to give the outyear effects visibility. Unfortunately, this annex has received little attention and has seldom been a consideration in major decisions. One reason for this short-term, one-year focus is the strong pattern of instability in decisions. A decision never seems to be final. Most major program decisions are revisited time and time again, an issue which is discussed in more detail below.

SPECIFIC CRITIQUES

Let me now turn to some more specific problems with PPBS. The first is the excessive complexity of the process. Indeed, it is so complex that process often dominates substance, thereby displacing thought and analysis. The program submissions (called program objective memoranda — POMs) are enormous, and the supporting data are provided in great detail. Armies of analysts and budgeteers are kept busy for months pulling together the POMs that lay out each service's five-year program. A number of steps to simplify the process have been suggested, such as

1. Reducing the number of elements in the program structure.
2. Reducing the data requirements for the outyears.
3. Using models to generate outyear cost and program data rather than attempting to calculate such soft and uncertain information with "precision."
4. Going to a biennial program review.

Some progress was made in 1981 by Deputy Secretary Carlucci in simplifying the process, but more effort is needed.

A second problem relates to the accuracy of the underlying data used in PPBS. Weapon cost data are soft and almost always understated. This is due in part to poor costing techniques and in part to the strong incentives for most participants to understate costs. As a result, the outyear program contains more "program" than can, in fact, be supported. This "over-programming" leads to severe budget cutting problems when the next budget year arrives. The resulting cutbacks in quantity buys and the stretchouts in programs are wasteful. Steps, such as providing "planning wedges," that is, money set aside to cover future cost growth and use of independent cost estimates, should be adopted. Moreover, accounting data need improvement both to provide a better basis for estimates and to permit managers to ensure that resources used to execute a program match the budget allocated for the program. As was noted earlier, inadequate accounting systems and differences between program and budget data make program execution and monitoring virtually impossible.

Third, the present system revisits decisions too many times. It seems that an issue is never truly settled as long as there is still time and opportunity to reverse it. Program decisions are made in the summer, raised again during the budget review in the fall, and often debated another time during the congressional review of the budget the next year. The losers seldom concede; instead, they take their battle to a new forum, if necessary going around the secretary to the press or to the Congress. In many cases, this cycle starts over again when the next program is submitted to the OSD. The constant revisiting of decisions is not only an enormous drain on everyone's time, but is very disfunctional for program execution. Program managers spend most of their time and energy fighting the resource allocation battles rather than managing their program. The frequent program changes that result raise costs and slow development of the system.

FINAL THOUGHTS

Let me add two final points that affect PPBS, but are not directly related to the system or process in existence today. The first is the idea of a two year budget, a proposal getting considerable attention in Washington at present. As noted earlier, the PPBS process is terribly time consuming and a biennial budget would provide real benefits. The pros and cons are too lengthy to recite here, but despite some drawbacks, I believe it would be a useful reform. As suggested earlier, a shift to a biennial program review is also worth consideration. If a two year budget were adopted, the two major phases of the PPBS process could be alternated, with program development one year and budget development the next. Both the executive branch and the Congress would be able to focus more time on the difficult defense resource allocation issues they face, as well as on program execution and oversight.

Second, despite all the plaudits given the Defense Resources Board (DRB) by Secretary Puritano and others, I feel a critical review of its structure and operation is in order. The idea of a board composed of senior defense officials to address major resource allocation issues was adopted initially by Harold Brown in 1979. The original DRB was strictly an OSD body, in a sense the secretary's management committee composed of his key staff plus the chairman of the Joint Chiefs of Staff. It met regularly during the program review and advised the secretary on key program decisions. By all reports, it provided a useful, if less than central, service.

Secretary Weinburger expanded its membership and scope, and at present it is clearly the major DOD decisionmaking body. The service secretaries and chiefs of staff were added, as well as certain OSD staff not included in Brown's DRB. Moreover, it was used more extensively, especially during the budget cycle. It has been widely praised for forcing key staff and line officials to become more familiar with the issues (they do not have staff at meetings to back them up) and for providing a means for all points of view to be expressed in a real "give and take" atmosphere. No longer is the secretary forced to make decisions based on antiseptic memos prepared by anonymous staff members, nor can OSD ignore the views of the services, because they are active participants in the DRB.

All this is well and good and clearly of merit. Yet, I feel there are some questions about the DRB that should be raised. Let me pose four.

1. Can a group that large (usually about twenty-five members) really discuss complex and technical issues effectively? Are the full range of questions asked? Can the issues be explored in adequate depth?
2. Are the evidence and arguments presented fully and fairly, or do the more articulate or persuasive participants tend to dominate? Can the more complex issues be handled adequately verbally, or are carefully structured memoranda needed?
3. Can the participants really become knowledgeable on such a range of difficult problems? Does the lack of real understanding serve as a bar to participation and if not, is the search for the best answer really furthered?
4. Should the secretary delegate decision authority to this group or should he play a more central role himself?

The DRB appears to be a permanent fixture in DOD. This is probably a positive development. Yet, its functioning deserves careful review. In particular, consideration should be given to cutting its size (or varying membership depending on the issue) and using ad hoc (and much smaller) groups to thrash out many of the questions now addressed by the full DRB.

These criticisms should not detract from the overall value of PPBS as a key defense management tool. As noted earlier, if we didn't have PPBS, we would probably be forced to invent one. Nonetheless, the PPBS is not operating as well as it could. Action should be taken now to revamp the system for what I suspect will be a difficult period ahead. DOD faces a slowdown in the real growth of its budget and mounting criticism of its management practices by the Congress and the press. Better planning, more rigorous programs and budgets, and effective financial controls over the execution of programs – all these will give the taxpayers more for their money, and rebuild their faith in the management of our national defense.

Chapter 19

How to Improve the Acquisition of Weapons

Jacques S. Gansler

Over the last few years, there has been a growing consensus on the need to strengthen America's national security posture. The immediate response has been to spend more money, especially for military equipment. However, an examination of the trends over the last thirty years indicates that although increased dollars are clearly necessary, these alone will not be sufficient. *Broad changes are required in the way defense does its business* — from the formulation of national security policy through the management of the increasing budgets — if the desired strengthening of our national security posture is to be achieved.

We find ourselves today in a situation in which our national security paradigm has broken down.[1] The reality of current conditions does not match our existing policies, theories, organizations, or even our resource management practices. Three factors have caused this mismatch: shifts in the international balance of power, rapid technological change, and changes in the operation of the federal government, especially in the Congress.

TRENDS CAUSING CHANGE

Over the past thirty years, there has been a dramatic shift in the international balance of power. The position of the U.S. as the dominant nuclear power and the nation whose military equipment is far superior to its potential adversaries has eroded. There is now general agreement on at least parity between the U.S. and the U.S.S.R. in the strategic nuclear area and superiority in many tactical areas by the Soviet forces. Thus, where our prior military strategy of reliance on nuclear deterrence was once believed sufficient to contain all forms of Soviet aggression, it is now recognized as inadequate. Moreover, the stalemated nuclear balance, together with certain tactical imbalances, almost encourages Soviet aggressive (nonnuclear) military action. In this environment, dramatic changes in our broad national security posture are required, from geopolitical, economic, and arms control considerations through new military strategies and methods of selecting equipment. Yet, the U.S. has essentially ignored this need. In fact, there has been a lessened emphasis on analyzing and establishing broad national security postures and new service roles and missions. Instead, we have been living largely with policies established in the late 1940s and early 1950s. To make matters worse, no effort has been made to establish appropriate organizations within the U.S. government that could develop a new, credible, and affordable national security posture—one based on coordinated service requirements. Correcting this organizational deficiency is an important step in establishing the necessary posture. If no central authority is given the power to integrate requirements and to oversee effectively the implementation of weapons choices, we will continue to be guided by an outdated, and therefore dangerously deficient, posture.[2]

The second major event of the past thirty years is the dramatic change in the way wars will be fought and equipment designed, both caused by rapid advances in technology. The potential of capabilities, such as real-time reconnaissance from space and pinpoint accuracy with long-range missiles, has resulted in a great overlap in the traditional roles and missions of the air, land, and sea services. And yet, little effort has been made to redefine these roles and missions to eliminate the duplication. This overlap has created corresponding redundancies in the weapon system requirements of each service and has thereby resulted in significant inefficiencies in weapon selection. Similarly, the enormous technological changes of the last thirty years have contributed to dramatic increases in weapons system complexity, cost, and development time. In the defense arena, new technological "opportunities" have been pushed to their maximum in achieving increased military performance. What has not been done is to take full advantage of the opportunities these new technologies can also offer to reduce cost and improve reliability. Each example of cost increases brings only new congressional cries for greater governmental regulation, instead of the broader institutional changes required to adjust to the evolving environment.

The third major change of the last three decades is the enhanced congressional role in the management of the Pentagon, a role that has occurred because Congress has become heavily involved in the details of the defense budget. Since the executive branch has failed to establish an overall, coherent, and affordable national security strategy, the Congress has attempted to step in and do it. However, rather than playing a significant role in establishing broad policy, congressional "policy" is rather the resultant product of six different and largely uncoordinated committees (appropriations, authorizations, and budgets in both the Senate and House) annually examining every budget line item and making large numbers of small revisions in each. Moreover, the decline of the congressional seniority system has resulted in a lack of stability in this decision process. Thus, the numerous changes often lack consistency from year to year. The response to this congressional short-term and microscopic emphasis has been an equivalent type of emphasis by the DOD. All of this leads to program and budget instabilities and inefficiencies and reinforces the lack of any coherent, long-term national security policy or resource management perspective.[3]

By failing to adjust for the geopolitical, military, technological, and fiscal changes that have taken place over the last three decades, we are in the position today of having our overall national security policy established through detailed annual (or semi-annual) review of each budget line item — by Congress, the office of management and budget, the office of the secretary of defense, and the services. This process is all based on budgets submitted separately by the three services, whose roles and missions do not match either the way we are likely to be fighting wars or the technological opportunities possible for new weapons system optimization. The need for broad changes clearly exists. Essentially, three approaches are required: first, a restructuring of the roles and missions of the services; second, broad changes in the way in which policy, planning, programming, and budgeting are implemented, especially with regard to the congressional budget process; and third, a significant change in the way weapons systems are acquired. These three broad changes are interrelated; all are necessary if the required cultural changes are to be implemented. Because the first two are covered elsewhere within this volume, this chapter will address them only as they relate to the weapons acquisiton process. The crucial point to note, however, is that the third will accomplish little without the first two. Buying the wrong weapons more efficiently makes little sense.

WEAPONS ACQUISITION TRENDS

In contrast to newspaper headlines and frequent congressional attacks, the department of defense is generally acknowledged to be one of the best managed and least political of all government agencies in the acquisition process. There is little question that the United States has been able to keep its military equipment at the forefront of the technological state-of-the-art. We have, in fact, deployed very good weapons systems, and the performance capability of these systems has been increasing at the rate of five to six percent each year.[4] Numerous studies have shown that defense cost overruns are generally lower than those of most other federal agencies.[5] A comparison of even some of the worst examples within DOD with most other government programs, for example, the Rayburn House Office Building, the Hart Senate Building, or the D.C. and San Francisco metro systems, make this case very clearly. There is little question, however, that there is much room for improvement. If we are to get the maximum military capability for the increased defense dollars, we need significant improvement in the weapons acquisition process.

There are five specific trends that must be reversed. First, and most critical, is the extremely high and rising cost of the individual systems. We are now at the point where the cost of an individual ship is measured in the billions of dollars, an individual plane in the hundreds of millions, and an individual tank in the millions. We find that each new generation has been costing significantly more than the prior one. In *constant* dollars and *constant* quantities, average equipment costs have been rising by six to seven percent per year.[6] Figure 19.1 shows examples of the trend for some typical defense equipment, adjusted for inflation and quantities produced.[7] Similar curves (some much steeper) could be drawn for each class of weapons system. Clearly, the performance of each individual weapons system has been significantly improving as unit costs have been growing; but, with budget constraints, the effect of this increased cost has been the procurement of fewer and fewer systems, even in recent years when procurement budgets have been increasing. For example, in the 1950s the U.S. bought around 3,000 fighter planes per year; in the 1960s this went down to 1,000 per year; and in the 1970s, down to 300 fighter planes per year. (Norm Augustine has pointed out that, in the year 2054, this trend would result in our building one fighter plane per year.[8]) Clearly, the increasing unit cost is taking its toll in reduced quantities of equipment. However, quantity is absolutely critical for military capability, especially when the Soviets have been improving their quality to levels comparable to our own and when they have production rates that are often overwhelmingly greater than ours. Unless changes are made in the way defense defines weapons requirements and in the way it acquires weapons, this trend of rising unit costs is likely to result both in a far greater cost for each of our future weapon systems and in the procurement of far too few systems to represent a credible deterrent or a viable warfighting capability.

The second, long-term adverse acquisition trend is the greater time being taken for new weapon system development and deployment.[9] As indicated by Figure 19.2, for the submarine based ballistic missile program, a typical weapon system development time has grown from five to seven years to twelve to fifteen. This has had two adverse effects. New equipment arrives in the field much later, and some of it is nearly obsolete at the time it arrives. (Electronics for new commercial components are frequently obsolete in six months, so it is not hard to see how such long defense development cycles can result in the deployment of outdated equipment.)

The third and most publicized trend is the "cost overrun" on individual programs. As shown in Figure 19.3, and reconfirmed by more recent

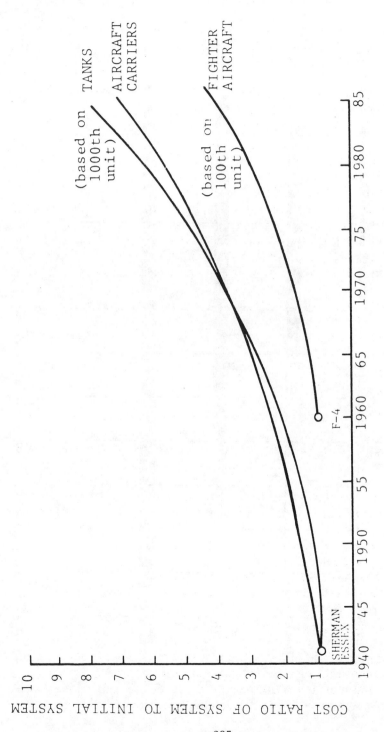

FIGURE 19.1. Growth in Unit Cost of Weapons Systems (adjusted for inflation and quantities)

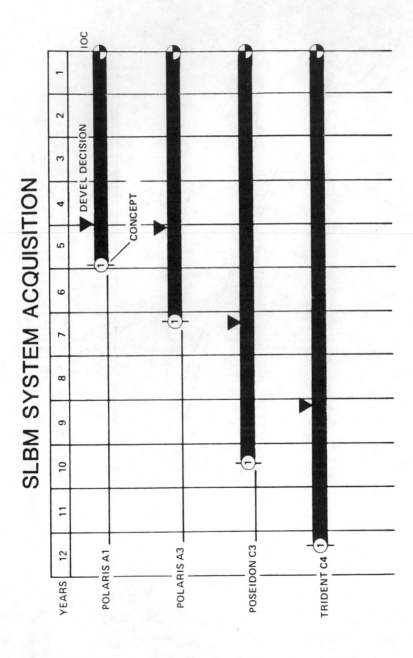

FIGURE 19.2. Schedule for Submarine-based Ballistic Missile Program

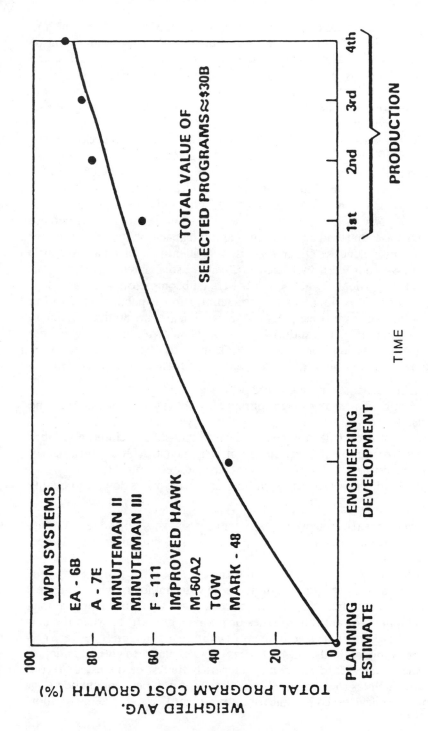

FIGURE 19.3. Cost Growth in Weapons Systems

studies[10], a typical weapons system program has approximately doubled in cost during its lifetime. (This, of course, is the average growth, and some of the more extreme cases—such as the Air Force's F-111 electronics, the Navy's DD963 ships, and the Army's Infantry Fighting Vehicle—are much larger.) The results of these cost increases have not only been bad press and adverse congressional hearings, but a further reduction in the numbers of weapons purchased.

The fourth major trend, particularly in the post-Viet Nam decade, is the growing inefficiency in, and lack of responsiveness of, the defense industrial base. A series of reports at the end of 1980 all indicated significant problems in the defense industrial base.[11] Typical of these was the House armed services committee report entitled, *The Ailing Defense Industrial Base, Unfit for Crisis*. These studies identified some sectors of the defense industrial base that had considerable excess capacity and concommitant economic inefficiencies. Other sectors were identified that had too little competition, again with inefficiencies. They also pointed out significant bottlenecks—particularly at the lower tiers (subcontractors and parts suppliers)—that resulted in a lack of production surge capability. (For example, it would take over three years for an existing aircraft production line to increase its output significantly.) These reports pointed out that the defense industry was suffering from many of the same problems as the overall U.S. industrial economy, only often more extremely. Areas noted included

- underinvestment in modernization of heavy industry;
- increasing reliance on foreign sources of supply for critical materials and parts;
- absence of economic conversion of large industrial facilities and labor forces from an older function to a newer one (structural adjustment);
- underinvestment in long-range research and development;
- lack of competitive forces to continuously drive prices down and quality up.

These trends are affecting weapons system costs adversely; and, equally significantly, they are reducing the responsiveness of "the arsenal of democracy."

The fifth adverse acquisition trend is the extreme difficulty in getting the services to accept the application of new technology, when the new technology would alter traditional service roles and missions (for example, the development of antiship missiles or pilotless aircraft) or when the new technology might entail the crossing of traditional boundaries between services (for example, the use of Air Force AWACS planes to give information about enemy aircraft to Army anti-aircraft batteries, or the use of reconnaissance satellites to supply real-time data to Army field commanders, or the ability to develop communications and identification systems to allow

Air Force, Army, and Navy pilots to talk to each other in a common combat environment). This reluctance to apply new technology to nontraditional equipment and missions contrasts strikingly with the services' enthusiasm (some say "requirement") to apply advanced technology to traditional equipment and missions, for example, a faster plane, a more heavily armored tank, or a bigger ship. Throughout the history of warfare, the nation that most rapidly applies nontraditional technological opportunities has obtained the most for its investment in military equipment and has achieved the decided military advantage. Such nontraditional technological opportunities often offer both quantitative and qualitative breakthroughs in military capability but require changes in service traditions; so they have historically been strongly resisted.[12]

Taken together, these five trends have meant that the U.S. has been buying fewer and fewer, very expensive, weapons systems. Furthermore, the concern is growing over whether the U.S. is buying the *right* systems. This is not a question of whether the ones being bought would be desirable to have, but whether they are the most effective for the money being spent. The heated debates now taking place over the desirability of spending twenty billion dollars to buy one hundred B-1 bombers, or the tens of billions of dollars of investment for a few fixed-site MX missiles, or the multibillion dollar investments in a few large ships – all reflect this growing concern.

CORRECTIVE ACTIONS

Literally hundreds of studies have been conducted on ways to improve the weapons acquisition process.[13] Each new administration has come in with a set of "initiatives" to correct the adverse trends. However, the overwhelming majority of these studies and initiatives have been at the "micro" level and within the existing organizations and practices. Few have addressed the broad structural and institutional changes that are necessary; almost none have addressed the needed changes in the weapon selection process. Instead, they have focused on the details of the acquisition implementation process after equipment requirements have been defined and after a weapon selection has already been made. Although many of these initiatives seem extremely desirable, including those pushed by former Deputy Secretaries Carlucci and Thayer, all could be implemented more effectively within a framework of broad structural changes in the way DOD business is done. Specifically, four significant changes are necessary to reverse the undesirable trends noted above. In priority order, they are

1. *Better selection:* A better definition of military requirements and an improved selection of weapons systems, both achieved through the establishment of a DOD long-range resource plan that is tied to national

security objectives, fiscally constrained, jointly arrived at, and with priorities clearly set.

2. *Greater stability:* Changes in the congressional and DOD budget process to achieve stability in DOD budgets and programs over a multiyear period.

3. *Lower unit costs:* Implementation of incentive techniques to lower costs on each program, and thereby to permit greater quantity buys.

4. *Strengthened industrial base:* Institutionalization of a mechanism to achieve greater industrial stability and responsiveness.

These four broad changes fit under the categories of "JCS reform," "budget reform," "procurement reform," and "defense industry revitalization." Taken together, as is clearly necessary, they would represent a dramatic change in the way the DOD acquires its weapons systems.

IMPROVED SELECTION

The first of these changes requires a shift in organizational responsibilities. Currently, each of the three services develops its own resource plans and requirements for new systems. Each then has complete autonomy in implementing these plans. (All with the approval of the office of the secretary of defense (OSD) and the Congress.) Although consistent with the stated decentralization objectives of the current administration, this practice, of each service going its own way, ignores the technological evolution that has caused service roles and missions to overlap heavily. For most future missions there need to be joint operations among the services, whether it be for combined air, land, and space operation for a battle in Central Europe, or for combined Marine, Army, Navy, Air Force, and space amphibious operations in the Persian Gulf or the Caribbean. But, in the future, even an at-sea operation by the Navy is likely to involve space and land based missiles or aircraft. Because the services will be fighting together, it is necessary to establish resource plans and weapon system requirements on a joint (multiservice) basis. Without such unified military planning and weapon selection, the U.S. will continue its less than optimum record in joint military operations. This has been a troubling area since World War II, and the problems in the Iranian rescue mission and the Granada incident revealed that they have not been corrected. (For example, in the latter case, the command center on the Navy carrier is reported not to have had communications equipment capable of talking directly to the Army troops on shore.)

Many of the proposals for "JCS reform" address the needed changes in the chain of command, but it is also necessary that these reforms include the development of unified resource plans. When such unified, long-range resource plans are established in the context of realistic five-to-fifteen-year fiscal constraints, tremendous advantages will accrue. Naturally, it must be recognized that the level of total defense dollars are likely to change in future years and that, therefore, there must be plans for possible changes in the level of weapons procurement. However, significant dollar changes of this type will not occur frequently and, if properly planned, will not affect each and every budget line item, as is currently the case. The objective would be to focus the weapon selection process on the five-to-fifteen year period, rather than as now on next year's budget. Such long-term, fiscally constrained resource plans would have the additional advantage of looking explicitly at the quantities of systems to be procured. If the total dollars for that weapon system were allocated on the basis of a long-range mission plan, then the quantity versus quality tradeoffs could be considered during the resource planning process.

If one wishes to make the office of the secretary of defense one of policy and oversight, responsibility for developing this long-range plan must reside with the Joint Chiefs of Staff. This is clearly not within their current responsibility, but it could be, if they had the proper staff and if there were the appropriate incentives to reduce the effects of service parochialism. In this concept, the chairman of the joint chiefs would submit a proposed long-range resource plan in his name to the secretary of defense, rather than, as is currently the case, each of the three services doing so. This unified resource plan would be based upon fiscal and policy guidelines provided by the defense secretary. It would be up to the services and the chiefs of the unified and specified commands, acting through the chairman, to establish the priorities, the new weapons system requirements, the quantities of systems to be procured, and the ties between these and the national security objectives.[14] Two key parts of the resource allocation question would be: the relative distribution of total dollars between mission areas; and, within the mission areas, among readiness, modernization, force structure, and sustainability. Tradeoffs on these critical issues would be made explicitly by the military.

This change would not require that the actual development and procurement of weapons systems be under the chairman of the joint chiefs. They could be fully decentralized, with implementation of the chairman and secretary of defense's decisions left to the services. This role, to develop, procure, train and support, is the legal domain of the services; they already have the manpower and capability for this job. Thus, the role of the service secretaries and the military departments could be more clearly defined. They could be held accountable for the management and budgets of those programs assigned to them by the chairman and the secretary of defense.

Notice that this change to a more unified decisionmaking procedure need not mean that all new weapon systems will be either multiservice or standardized. Rather, they would all be consistent with a plan developed jointly. It is fair to conclude, however, that more multiservice weapons systems would

undoubtedly result from this environment. Additionally, in order to overcome the incentive that exists for the services to favor their traditional
weapons systems and to ignore the nontraditional ones, OSD guidance
would be needed to encourage the development of nontraditional systems.
Similarly, the role of the defense advanced research projects agency (DARPA)
would continue to be to develop nontraditional technologies and weapon
systems. DARPA, like the military services, would have input in the
development of the unified, long-range resource plan. It is more likely that
these nontraditional systems would be recommended if they came from a set
of jointly developed requirements than if they came from sets of single service requirements.

This proposal—for the chairman of the JCS to submit a unified, long-
range resource plan—represents a dramatic change. Initially, it will be difficult to implement. But, it is critically important that it be started as soon
as possible. Weapons systems begun today will form the force structure for
the United States defense posture over the next twenty to thirty years.

ACHIEVEMENT OF STABILITY

Stability in DOD budgets and programs is probably the most important
single characteristic missing from the American defense acquisition process
today. Imagine a business—especially a very large buyer—changing all of
its purchasing commitments every year! Private companies could not and
do not operate this way. Multiyear purchasing agreements are the rule. As a
monopsony buyer, the U.S. government certainly cannot continue to
violate this rule if it has any interest in becoming efficient. Incredibly, the
United States is one of the few countries, if not the only country, in the
world with one-year defense budgets. Worse, members of Congress and
their staffs pore over every new budget submittal, making innumerable adjustments, stretchouts, redirections, and other "improvements." This
micromanagement is then mirrored by a similar set of extensive annual (or
semi-annual) line item revisions by the office of management and budget,
OSD, and the service staffs.

Rationalizing this process hinges on establishing a stable, multiyear
defense budget. Establishing a three-year budget, for example, does *not*
mean Congress would give up its flexibility to make annual adjustments in
the total level of defense expenditures, or even in major weapons systems. It
does mean that the focus of the congressional budget review would be
shifted from the one-year perspective to the longer term, and from the
detailed line item reviews to the broader issue of overall national security.
Clearly, if there are good reasons to increase rapidly resources allocated to
defense, then the levels of defense expenditure could change; and the three-
year plan could be adjusted accordingly. However, the Congress would

have constantly in view the longer-term implications of its revisions and, therefore, be far less likely to make the many small changes that do not reflect changing world conditions, but are simply an attempt to adjust to the interests of a large number of congressmen each year.

Implementation of this multiyear defense budget could be achieved by converting the two "out years" of the three-year concurrent budget resolution from "targets" to "budgets." The executive branch would be required to submit a three-year defense budget within these levels.[15] Currently, only the first year of the three is "binding" on the executive branch; so the others are ignored. To introduce some flexibility for future years' uncertainty, three other actions would be desirable.

1. Make authorizations for three years, but appropriations for only two (thus avoiding a possible constitutional question) because monies for the Army can be appropriated constitutionally for no more than two years at a time;
2. Provide the DOD with greater budget reprogramming authority (including between funding categories) — but only within mission areas; only on authorized programs (not on new starts); and only being permitted to go to Congress for reprogramming changes once each year;
3. Budget a small percentage of the outyears dollars for some "unknown items," to allow for some likely but as yet undefined expenditures so that these new items do not cause excessive disruptions.

If the Congress took this long-term perspective, it would encourage the executive branch, and particularly the defense department, to respond similarly. Currently, the defense department focuses almost all of its attention on next year's budget. It does so in response to the congressional lead. This practice encourages the services to devise ways to squeeze down and stretchout each of their programs to make them all fit within the amount allocated for next year, but with the hope of somehow "finding" the needed additional funds in future years. Besides the inefficiencies resulting from frequent disruptions, uncertainties, and changes, these stretchouts create absurdities, such as aircraft production rates of one every two months and fifteen year development periods for new weapons. When future budgets fall short of anticipated or hoped-for levels, defense planners have taken money from the readiness and sustainability accounts, with the hope of buying them "next year." But they are still left with the unpleasant choice of cancelling some programs or stretching them all further. The latter approach creates a vicious cycle. The additional inefficiencies that result from stretchouts lead to further cost increases, which in turn, encourage further stretchouts. For example, in the case of the production of the F-15 aircraft, the program was stretched out by three years and the cost of the inefficiencies attributable to the lower production rate was $2 billion. This is the equivalent of more than a full extra wing (actually 83 aircraft) of F-15s! It is estimated that savings of twenty percent could be achieved (after a few years time) by stabilizing the department of defense budget.[16]

The first initiative (to establish a unified, long-range resource plan), together with the second (to achieve budget and program stability), requires that total obligational authority for each weapon be estimated accurately by the OSD and the services for the outyears. One technique for achieving both realistic program estimates and greater program stability is a concept recently developed by the Air Force, which it calls "baselining." Under this technique, the performance, quantities, annual budgets, and total program costs are negotiated and "signed off" beforehand by all parties involved, from the operational users through the comptroller and program manager. The program is then put into all future fiscal plans at the dollar levels agreed to and is managed within these levels. (The $20.6 billion level for the B-1B is an early example of such a technique.) If technical changes or cost growth subsequently occur on the program, then other aspects must be cut or the service's management reserve utilized in order to adhere to the original budget. Congress must also stick to the original funding plan, or else agree to a revision in the program budget and thereby assume the responsibility for the resultant "overrun." With this procedure, Congress essentially agrees to later funding for the program's production at the time it releases money for full-scale development.[17] If there are problems, threat changes, or changes in national priorities, it can cancel the program at any time, as can the DOD; but there is less of a chance that programs will be inefficiently stretched out or changed on an annual basis.[18]

Initially, a consequence of accurate costing and long-range "affordability" analyses will be fewer programs started and perhaps some terminations. But over the long term, it will also result in far greater stability for existing programs, and hence more weapons for the dollars allocated.

TECHNIQUES FOR LOWERING UNIT COSTS

The third major initative is the application of techniques that will create incentives for the services and defense contractors to achieve lower unit equipment costs. In the civilian sector, under *normal market conditions*, costs tend to be driven down by such techniques as competition, productivity gains, and increased volume for lower prices. In the administered defense acquisition market, the trends over the last thirty years demonstrate that regulation cannot achieve comparable results. We must, therefore, find ways to introduce new techniques that can lower costs for future weapons systems. I recommend four specific actions.

1. Introduce price elasticity into defense procurements—wherein either the quantities bought or performance attained would be allowed to increase if prices were reduced.

2. Permit higher outyear profit margins (or reduce them) if actual unit costs are below (or above) these in the "baseline" plan.
3. Utilize some form of continuous competition on weapon systems in order to create market incentives.
4. Fully develop professional acquisition management career paths in all services and opportunities for promotion within these.

The first and fourth techniques are directed at the services; the second and third, at the defense industry.

The first technique permits the military to maximize a mission's effectiveness with the allocated program dollars. Currently, the size of the force structure is fixed; therefore, the services have an overriding incentive to obtain the maximum performance out of each individual piece of equipment, but none to make the quality/quantity tradeoffs. In many cases, only a little performance has to be sacrificed for a big increase in quantity. Squeezing the final five to ten percent of performance improvements out of new system designs usually adds twenty to fifty percent to their total cost. Thus, only slight reductions in performance can cut the price of a weapon system significantly. For most systems, a marginal reduction in the performance of each individual weapon would be overwhelmingly offset by the far greater military capability provided by the larger quantities of the system that could be bought.

If the services were allowed to buy larger amounts of an item when they drive the per unit prices on it down, they would have an incentive to make such trades. This incentive is achieved in the commercial market through price elasticity, when demand increases as prices are reduced. If long-term budget levels are accurately fixed and maintained for all programs, then the services should be given the flexibility to buy more systems (within the total program dollars planned and allocated) if the unit price of the system goes down. For example, if they had planned to buy 10,000 missiles for a billion dollars and now find that, due to lower prices, a billion dollars will allow them to buy 15,000 missiles, the services should be encouraged to do this, because it would improve our total military effectiveness. Currently, for almost all weapon systems, the authorized quantities of equipment have not been procured because the costs of each have increased dramatically. Even the presently authorized levels are frequently based on optimistic assumptions about such variables as battlefield "kill probability," equipment reliability, and continuous presence of command links. The greater amounts of equipment produced by this incentive could achieve higher confidence in a mission's success. On the other hand, for some weapons systems, such as strategic missiles, increased quantities may not yield an increase in mission effectiveness. For these cases, the services should be allowed to use the savings to improve performance or reliability.

Both these approaches have been tried successfully by the DOD in the past, but they have not been institutionalized. In the case of increased quantities for lower costs, Defense Secretary Schlesinger offered the Air Force an increased number of "wings" of aircraft if they would buy some of the lower cost F-16s instead of only the F-15s, an offer which they accepted. He also applied this cost-based incentive to the manpower area by promising the Army that for every "overhead" position (support job) they could eliminate, they could add combat personnel. In fact, the Army created two and a third new divisions this way. Finally, the Navy used the improved performance incentive on their sub launched strategic missile program by allowing savings to be plowed back into improved reliability. This Navy program has consistently been one of the DOD's best performers in terms of cost control and performance achievements.

Such rewards to the services for reducing the costs of their systems also encourages them to take the steps required to improve an individual weapons system's acquisition efficiency. These involve putting funds into management reserve to cover likely changes, giving the program manager the necessary flexibility to shift funds around as required, and utilizing commercial "design-to-cost" techniques that encourage new technology to be used to reduce costs as well as improve performance. Such rewards would also give a better measure of a program manager's accountability because he would now be responsible for both the quantity and quality of systems procured. The reward system today achieves the opposite result. A program manager and the producing company that underruns has the money taken away and given to someone else who overran.

The second technique addresses the industrial side of the equation. Currently, the government creates perverse incentives to industry by basing next year's unit production prices on the prior year's costs, and then adding a fee. Thus, the higher the past costs, the bigger the future fee. This process gives no incentive whatsoever for lowering costs. In fact, it creates the reverse incentive: the reward of a larger fee in the subsequent year for a higher cost in the previous one. What really matters to the government is the total price paid to their suppliers — the combination of cost, which is ninety percent of the price, and the ten percent (or less) of fee or profit to the firm. If the cost can be dramatically reduced below that projected, a firm should be rewarded with a significantly higher profit margin in the future years. (The inverse should occur if costs rise above the "baseline.") In this way, industry would have an incentive for driving down costs: profit margins would go up! At the same time, the government would still be way ahead, because the major share of its price, the cost of the equipment itself, would be going down far more rapidly than the increase in fee would be going up.

Notice that this technique (like the first) creates natural incentives to apply such cost-reducing approaches as "design-to-cost" and "value engineering." The result would be a splitting of the savings, with most of the gains going to the government, but a significant share going to the successful firm.

Continuous competition is the third of the cost-reducing techniques. On the average, program costs tend to double during the acquisition cycle. The most obvious explanation for this is the initial price "optimism" — real costs are underestimated. Not only do lower cost estimates make the program appear more attractive, but the government's winner-take-all bidding policy reinforces low bidding practices. There is fierce rivalry for the initial development contract award and only one company wins the contract. That firm then becomes the *sole* developer and producer of the new item for the next twenty years. The losers are effectively exiled from that specific market until the next major weapons system development comes along. By this process, the government creates a great incentive to "buy-in" by bidding low. The subsequent course of most programs, however, is that they experience substantial program changes. These changes mean that original contracts are voided, and the Pentagon is forced to renegotiate with a monopoly supplier. It should be obvious why program costs grow in such an environment.

The corrective action is to maintain continuous competition throughout the program's development *and* production phases. In this way, not only would the department of defense have alternate suppliers; but, by making clear to these suppliers that the share of the business they would receive will be a function of their performance and costs, the DOD would allow market operations to replace regulations in driving costs down and performance up. The critical distinction is between competition *for* an award and the *continuous* presense of competitive alternatives. When this technique (frequently referred to as "dual-sourcing") has been tried by the defense department, it has yielded an average net program cost savings of around thirty percent.[19]

This technique has been successfully used on a wide variety of defense products; from complex, low-volume systems, such as the guidance systems on the Minuteman and Polaris strategic missiles, to large production programs, such as tactical missiles, electronic subsystems, and bullets. In all cases where it was properly applied, the technique resulted in reduced costs and improved performance; and it frequently resulted in higher profit rates for the firms involved. Everyone gained. Why then is the techique not used more widely? The reason is clear: to set up a second producer takes a few more dollars up front. With the budget problems described above, the rationale is that "this year we can't afford the investment," even though the expected returns are likely to be quite high. For this technique to be implemented, the long-term budget perspective previously discussed must be used. The combination will result in significant payoff for the DOD.

The last technique to improve acquisition management deals with the conflict inherent in the military program manager's task. Each manager knows that what is best for his career is an operational or command assignment, and that the extensive experience required for running a complex, multibillion dollar program does not count for much for promotion. One frequently finds, particularly in the Army and Navy, an individual with little, or no, prior acquisition experience assigned to a high level program management job. A recent study found that at the level of major through colonel — and the Navy equivalents — the average number of years of acquisition experience for those currently in a program office was: Air Force, ten years; Navy, five years; and Army, two years.[20] This lack of sustained experience is a problem that must be addressed by the secretary of each service. Careers for officers or civilians who choose to specialize in weapons acquisition management must be made more attractive by promotions to higher ranks or by higher pay.[21] Both approaches have been used successfully by other countries.

The other required change is that competent program managers receive appropriate respect from the staff of the office of the secretary of defense and the Congress. Today, the program manager is typically assumed to be incompetent and is continuously attacked and insulted. Good managers deserve better; otherwise, the best will not seek or stay in these jobs.

These four techniques — greater quantities or improved performance if prices fall, larger profits if prices fall, continuous competition, better rewards for competent program management — when taken together, will change the basic nature of defense business from a system that attempts to control costs through detailed regulation to one that does so through competitive incentives.

REVITALIZATION OF THE DEFENSE INDUSTRY

The last of the four broad "cultural changes" required is to revitalize our industrial defense base. The United States is the only country in the world that does not treat its defense industry as a vital national resource. Our general assumption has been that the free market will create the required economic efficiency and strategic responsiveness. It is, however, simply not realistic to expect such a response in a market with only one buyer (the government) and usually only one or a few suppliers for any given product. In this unique market, the government needs to institutionalize an approach that consciously takes into account the health and responsiveness of the defense industry, and that, where appropriate, explicitly introduces industrial base considerations into both long-term Pentagon planning and specific program decisions.

Consider two examples in order to see how this supply side perspective would work. In the aircraft industry, there has been a dramatic reduction in the number of military planes built each year. The structure of the industry, however, has remained essentially the same, and so too has the number of plants. This has aggravated the cost problems described above. In order to pay for the manpower and overhead of these old, underutilized plants, it has been necessary to reduce the quantities of aircraft bought and to slip the schedules of the few programs currently in production. Worse yet, those firms whose plants are almost totally unused are required to "buy-in" on the next major contract in order to avoid going out of the business. We have too many plants with highly fluctuating workloads, and hence with the accompanying inefficiencies associated with instability, excess capacity, and a lack of capital investment.

The manpower loading data in Figure 19.4 (for Air Force Plant #4 in Fort Worth, Texas)[22] is typical of the labor instability found in most defense plants. Such rapid hiring and firing of skilled labor is grossly inefficient. Yet, it is repeated on each new plane, ship, or missile contract that is awarded.

Unfortunately, the existence of empty or underutilized defense plants does not ensure surge (or mobilization) responsiveness because of bottlenecks in other areas, usually at the lower tiers (the subcontractors and critical parts suppliers). The latter have been almost completely ignored by the department of defense and their prime contractors.

For corrective actions, in the aircraft industry case, the government should allow the competitive market to operate and permit a reduction in the number of plants to a few competitive, modernized facilities — capable of producing not only the current demand but also the increased level that the proposed acquisition changes would bring, as well as a surge capacity to even higher levels for crisis requirements.

By contrast, in the tracked-vehicle industry, there has been only one producer of tanks and one producer of armored personnel carriers for many, many years. Here, it is likely to be in the government's interest to create a viable, competitive market by requiring a second producer for each of these products.

Notice that the corrective steps for these two defense industry sectors are completely different. Action would reduce the number of firms in one case and create new producers in the other. This should be expected because each of the defense industry sectors is dramatically different. Therefore, a sector-by-sector analysis is required, at both the prime contractor level and the critical areas of the lower tiers.

There will be many who will argue that this call to inject an industrial strategy perspective into defense acquisition decisions does not enhance the role of the free enterprise system. What they fail to recognize is that the applicable economic theory under these nonideal conditions (of one buyer and only one or two suppliers) is "the theory of the second best."[23] For the defense sector, it is impossible to establish the necessary market conditions for free market operations. The federal government's dominant role in the defense sector is an impediment to the operation of a free market, one that cannot be removed. Similarly, the fact that the supply side has only a few

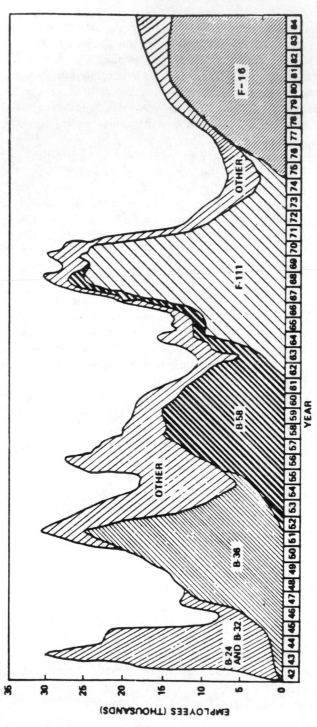

FIGURE 19.4. Employment History of Air Force Plant #4, Forth Worth, Texas

producers cannot be changed. This is dictated by economies of scale, high technology, low volume, large capital investments, and security restrictions. The minimum the government must do is have a set of policies that will produce economic efficiency, technological advance, and industrial responsiveness in each of the critical defense industry sectors.

Consider just six such policies that would improve the industry's performance. Note that, in each case, the corrective action for defense would directly and explicitly address a major problem of the overall U.S. economy.

1. *Achieve maximum economic gain from defense investments.* The government should encourage civilian and military production in the same plants. Currently, defense department policies and regulations discourage this combination. Joint production would reduce overhead costs, increase the transfer of technology from the military to the civilian sector, allow a more rapid surge of military production during a crisis, and reduce the impact of possible cutbacks in defense spending.

2. *Strengthen the domestic industrial infrastructure.* The defense department must become involved in maintaining research and development, production capability, and competition in the critical lower-tier sectors of the defense industry, such as in components and subsystems. In many areas, only a single supplier exists for a variety of parts that are critical for a large number of weapons. In such cases, the government should not designate the second firm; it should simply require that there be at least two suppliers for each critical item.

3. *Encourage major technological advance.* In traditional weapons systems, the defense department has been extremely successful in achieving technological advance. Provision must be made, however, for new, *nontraditional* technologies and systems—those that promise dramatic changes in the ways wars are fought, but threaten the established traditional organizations.

4. *Improve worldwide competitiveness.* The government should sponsor research and development on products that are both critical to defense and currently supplied only by foreign sources. This would create domestic production and an export capability for future generations of the equipment. Such a posture would be far better than establishing trade barriers on current military equipment, which would only lead to higher prices and have little long-term effect.

5. *Stimulate lower prices and improved quality.* We should create a second source for many products where the United States depends on a single domestic supplier. Such a move would allow continuous competition to drive down prices, drive up quality, stimulate innovation, encourage capital investment, and broaden our base for mobilization. In

areas with excess, old industrial capacity, the market should be allowed to reduce the number of firms down to a few that are modern and competitive.

6. *Implement an industrial strategy.* The Defense department must explicitly introduce industrial-base considerations into its major acquisition decisions. Issues, such as labor stability, plant utilization, and plant modernization can formally be considered in this way. Such an approach would replace the current situation of permitting a plant that is far less efficient than others to buy into a program.

These actions would revitalize the defense industry by restructuring the industrial base. Moreover, such actions would simultaneously strengthen the U.S. economy, and shift the defense industry from its current "ailing industry" status into a competitive, responsive, national resource.

CONCLUSION

Introduction of the suggested four major initiatives — *improved weapon selection* through jointly-established, long-range resource planning; *achievement of stability* in DOD budgets and programs; creation of *incentives for lowering costs*; and institutionalization of a mechanism for achieving *greater industrial stability and responsiveness* — would produce a dramatic change in the way defense does its business. After a few years, these policies would result in significantly increased quantities of weapons for the same levels of defense expenditures. These initiatives would also have the distinct advantage of convincing Congress and the public that the Pentagon had improved its ability to manage its resources.

Organizationally, for these initiatives to be implemented, three changes are required: a strengthening of the authority of the chairman of the joint chiefs and his staff by making them integrators of long-range resource plans — plans clearly tied to strategies; a strengthening of the role of the service secretaries as the responsible managers of the development, procurement, training, and support of the men and equipment for their services; and a marked shift in the role of the office of the secretary of defense from detailed line-item control of intra- and inter-service budget issues to a far broader focus on issues such as national security policy, long-range planning and resource distribution guidance, major research and development thrusts, and the health of the industrial base.

The proposed four broad acquisition initiatives can be implemented over the next few years because there is relatively wide recognition of the need for such significant change. It will not be easy. Nonetheless, it must be done because our national security posture requires it and the taxpayers deserve it.

NOTES

1. For an excellent discussion of the breakdown of paradigms and the difficulty of creation of new ones, see Kuhn, Thomas, *The Structure of Scientific Revolutions* (Chicago: The University of Chicago Press, 1962).

2. For a discussion of the broader national security strategy problems and corrective actions see *Understanding U.S. Strategy: A Reader*, Heyns, T. L., ed, (Washington, D.C.: National Defense Univ. Press, 1983), especially the two articles on reform of the Joint Chiefs of Staff by General David C. Jones, USAF (Ret.) p. 307, and by General Edward C. Meyer, USA (Ret.) p. 327.

3. For a detailed discussion of the defense budget problems and the needed corrective actions see Gansler, J. S., "Reforming the Defense Budget Process," *Public Interest Magazine*, Spring 1984.

4. Cherniavsky, E. A., and Timperlake, E. T., TR-3222-3, "Tacair Performance/Cost Analysis: Trends Over Time" (TASCFORM report on performance increases of 5-6 percent year), The Analytic Sciences Corporation (TASC), Sept. 18, 1981.

5. For example: "System Acquisition Performance of U.S. Government Agencies," Department of Defense Memorandum, Pyatt, OSD, April 14, 1976.

6. For a further, more detailed discussion of the rising cost trend in aircraft systems refer to: Cherniavsky, E. A., and Timperlake, E. T., op. cit.

7. Gansler, Jacques S., *The Defense Industry* (Cambridge: MIT Press, 1980), p. 16.

8. Augustine, Norman, "Augustine's Laws, " American Institute of Aeronautics and Astronautics, Inc. 1982.

9. For a detailed discussion of schedule stretchout, its effects and possible corrective actions, see "Affordable Acquisition Approach," Air Force Systems Command and The Analytic Sciences Corporation (TASC), Feb. 9, 1983. The data for Figure 19.2 comes from the Defense Science Board Summer Study of 1977.

10. The data in Figure 19.3 comes from a GAO study in 1972 (*Comptroller General of the United States, Acquisition of Major Weapon Systems DOD report B-163058, July 1972*). It was reconfirmed as slightly higher in a 1979 report ("Inaccuracy of DOD Weapons Acquisition Cost Estimates," House Committee on Government Operations, Nov. 16, 1979, Washington, D.C.) and again reconfirmed as slightly over 2 to 1 in 1981 by the "Affordable Acquisition Approach" study.

11. House Armed Services Committee, *Industrial Base Panel Report, The Ailing Defense Industrial Base: Unready for Crisis* (Chairman, Richard Ichord), Dec. 31, 1980; *Defense Science Board Task Force Report on Industrial Responsiveness* (Chairman, Robert Fuhrman), Nov. 21, 1980; The Air Force Systems Command statement on defense industrial base issues (General Alton Slay), Nov. 13, 1980; Gansler, Jacques S., *The Defense Industry*, op. cit.

12. For a more extensive discussion of the emphasis on and resistance to technology in traditional and nontraditional weapon systems refer to Gansler, Jacques S., "The U.S. Technology Base: Problems and Prospects" to be published in late 1984; and for an excellent historical perspective see: Morrison, Elting, *Men, Machines, and Modern Times* (Cambridge: MIT Press, 1966).

13. For example, the Weapons' Acquisition Library of The Analytic Sciences Corporation (TASC) has approximately 650 documents on this subject.

14. For a more detailed discussion of this concept of the JCS and the CINCs in the

resource allocation area refer to Barrett, Archie, *Reappraising Defense Organization* (National Defense University Press, 1983).

15. For an extensive discussion of this recommendation see Gansler, J. S., "Reforming the Defense Budget Process," *Public Interest Magazine*.

16. For a discussion of the effects of instability and the specific F-15 example see "Affordable Acquisition Approach."

17. Because almost all major weapon systems that enter full-scale development actually go into production (none have been cancelled by the services and only a handful by the president or the Congress, in the last thirty years) the decision to enter full-scale development is really a decision to produce the system—and it should be treated this way. (For a further discussion of this point see "Affordable Acquisition Approach".)

18. In order to encourage major modifications to existing weapon systems (rather than the development of totally new systems) these can be treated in the "baseline" concept as if it were a new start. Thus, for reporting to Congress and for program baselining, as an example, the F-4D aircraft and the F-4E aircraft, although modifications of the basic F-4 aircraft, would be treated as separate programs.

19. For a brief summary of some examples see Gansler, J. S., *Los Angeles Times*, "There's Precedent for Pentagon Thrift," p. 5, Part IV, Oct. 2, 1983; for more details see: "Dual Source Procurement: An Empirical Investigation," The Analytic Sciences Corporation (TASC), Aug. 12, 1983, which also includes a summary of a large number of prior studies.

20. A study currently underway for the joint logistics commanders looks at problems in managing multiservice programs.

21. The argument for civilians in these jobs is both for continuity and to allow the military officers to do the job they are trained for, that is, military command. The counter argument is that only the military understands what the equipment is for, and can make the necessary performance–cost tradeoffs.

22. This is an update of the data on page 52 of *The Defense Industry*.

23. In simple terms, this theory states that if some conditions for the traditional free market (the "first best") do not apply and cannot be created, then creating some additional free market conditions or moving more in the direction of free market conditions may actually result in reduced efficiency in the allocation of resources. For a more detailed discussion see Kipsey, R. G., and Lancaster, K., "The General Theory of the Second Best," *Review of Economic Studies*, Vol. 23, 1956–57, pp. 11–32.

Chapter 20

Congress and the Defense Budget: Enhancing Policy Oversight*

Robert J. Art

The purpose of this chapter is to determine how the Congress of the last decade has dealt with one policy area—the defense budget. In my subsequent analysis, I shall stress that powerful political forces have continued to push Congress into ever greater financial and programmatic oversight of defense spending at the expense of policy oversight.[1] Congress continues, that is, to look mostly at the details of defense spending, but rarely at the big picture.

Financial and programmatic oversight deal, respectively, with the efficiency with which funds are being spent and with how effectively particular programs are being managed. Policy oversight deals with the larger questions of whether particular programs are needed, how they serve the specific missions the Pentagon has delineated, and whether those missions and the strategies that they in turn serve are sensible. Both financial and programmatic oversight focus on the individual building blocks of the defense budget; policy oversight, on how all the blocks fit together. In my judgment, the congressional treatment of defense has suffered from so great a preoccupation with next year's budget that it has tended to crowd out consideration of the more basic questions and the longer-term perspective.

None of this should surprise us, however, because "money is policy" and annual budgeting is a powerful congressional tool for closely controlling executive action. Annual budgeting, when combined with the more activist, skeptical, aggressive, and better staffed Congress of the 1970s and

---

*This article also appeared in *Political Science Quarterly*, Summer 1985.

I should like to thank Barry M. Blechman, Demetrios Caraley, I. M. Destler, Richard Fenno, John Ford, Allen Schick, Warner R. Schilling, and Kenneth N. Waltz for comments on earlier drafts of this piece and Ruth Elvin for assistance in preparation of the tables.

1980s—the "new Congress, that is—has produced the world's most potent legislature. Both annual budgeting and the attributes of the new Congress are products of powerful political forces outside of the Congress.

If, however, the exercise of annual budgeting has tended to crowd out policy oversight, what can be done to restore it? In order to answer this question, in turn I shall look at how Congress deals with the defense budget and then prescribe a set of reforms that could offer some promise of restoring a better balance among the financial, programmatic, and policy oversight functions of Congress.

ATTRIBUTES OF THE "NEW" CONGRESS

There are three broad attributes of how Congress currently deals with the defense budget. First, in both the House and the Senate, the armed services and defense appropriations subcommittees overlap heavily in their functions, but remain fairly uncoordinated in their actions. The defense appropriations subcommittees are doing more legislating; the armed services committees are doing more "budgeteering." Both continue to operate autonomously. This raises the question of whether the original rationales of specialization of function and division of labor through separate authorizing and appropriating committees still makes sense for defense. Second, the financial and programmatic reviews of the annual budget by both committee actors have become voluminous and detailed. Well over sixty percent of Pentagon line item requests are changed by each chamber. This raises the question of whether "micromanagement" has set in, whether Congress is now trying to "micromanage" rather than oversee the Pentagon, when it is not institutionally equipped for management. Third, although Congress is now engaged in both financial and programmatic oversight, its conduct of more general policy oversight, according to the testimony of some significant congressional actors, remains tenuous, debatable, and highly dependent upon the initiatives of a few individuals. This raises the question of whether general defense policy oversight can be systematically built into the congressional budgetary process.

Redundancy among Committees

The redundancy between the armed services committees and the appropriations defense subcommittees came about largely because, in 1960, the armed services committees began to apply the technique of annual authorizations to the procurement part of the defense budget and because, once started on that road, they continued to expand its application to the other titles of the defense budget. Originally, annual authorizations had come about both because of the rivalry between armed services and appropriations for control over the defense budget and because of the desire of the former to exert a more direct influence over the defense department. Intercommittee rivalry and control over the Pentagon were the two political imperatives that drove the armed services committees into ever more detailed reviews of the annual budget and away from what had been their pattern from 1945–1960, namely, a rather general look at the nation's defense policies through annual posture hearings.[2] It has been through the use of annual authorizations that the armed services committees became heavily immersed in the details of the yearly budget, and thus began to experience the overlap in function with the defense subcommittees. Table 20.1 details the growth of annual authorizations since 1960.

The reasons why Congress extended annual authorizations to the operations and maintenance (O&M) and other procurement accounts in 1982 and 1983, respectively, tell us much about the current competition between armed services and the defense subcommittees and about why the former have become budgeteers. Traditionally, the defense subcommittees of the appropriations committees had carefully scrutinized the O&M account, while the armed services committees had largely ignored it. But a combination of

Table 20.1. Growth in the Scope of Annual Authorization of the Defense Budget

1959	Authorization required for the procurement of aircraft, missiles, and naval vessels.
1962	Authorization required for all research development, testing, or evaluation of aircraft, missiles, and naval vessels.
1963	Authorization required for all research, development, testing, or evaluation carried on by the Department of Defense.
1965	Authorization required for the procurement of tracked combat vehicles.
1967	Authorization required for personnel strengths of each of the Reserve components as a prior condition for the appropriation of funds for the pay and allowances for the Reserve components.
1969	Authorization required for the procurement of other weapons to, or for the use of, any armed force of the United States. (Essentially this covers heavy, medium, and light artillery; anti-aircraft artillery; rifles; machine guns; mortars; small arms weapons; and any crew-fired piece using fixed ammunition.)
1970	Authorization required for the procurement of torpedoes and related support equipment.
1970	Authorization required for the average annual active duty personnel strength (termed "end strengths") for each component of the Armed Forces.
1982	Authorization required for the Operations and Maintenance Account.
1983	Authorization required for Other Procurement (includes items such as trucks and electronic gear, that affect the readiness of the forces).

Sources: Derived from J. Ronald Fox, *Arming America: How the U.S. Buys Weapons* (Graduate School of Business Administration, Harvard University, 1974), p. 122; Interviews.

factors in the early 1980s pushed the House armed services committees to argue for extension of annual authorizations to this area, too. Its Senate counterpart went along, though reluctantly.

There were four factors at work. First, in the last few years, House armed services had become sensitized to the fact that the O&M and other procurement accounts involved items that affected both the readiness of the forces to go to war and their sustainability once in war. If the defense subcommittees continued to have a free hand in these accounts, then it would be they, not armed services, that would determine the state of readiness of the forces. Second was the calculation that "we might as well do this and finally extend our review to the entire budget." Third was the committee's calculation that, faced with large deficits and with the large investments in new weapons under the Reagan defense program, the House defense subcommittee, because it was under pressure to cut the president's defense request to help reduce the deficit, would naturally concentrate its cuts in an area over which it had an almost exclusive purview, namely, O&M. Unlike O&M, the other accounts were "protected" by armed services in the sense that specific items and dollar figures were authorized. Attacking the O&M account, where armed services had taken no action, was politically easier than attacking the other accounts where it had (although the latter was also done). Fourth, finally, was the fact that, unlike the other accounts, cuts in the O&M appropriations account produce a nearly equal cut in outlays. Monies that are legally obligated for spending (what is called budget authority or appropriations) are not necessarily spent during the year for which they have been appropriated. Outlays are the monies that are actually spent by the government in a given year. Personnel and O&M are the two defense accounts for which the gap between appropriations and outlays is the smallest. That is, for a given fiscal year, nearly all the O&M funds that are appropriated are actually spent. Because it is outlays, not appropriations, that determine the size of the deficit in any given fiscal year, Congress recently has scrutinized carefully those items that can produce large savings in outlays. Hence, cuts in O&M, compared to those in the other defense accounts, would yield the greatest savings for purposes of deficit reduction.[3]

Taken together, these factors—intense pressures to cut because of high deficits, the tried and true budget cutting technique of axing where you can easily ax, and the fear of House armed services that the O&M account, being unprotected, would bear more than its fair share of cuts—suggest the strategic reason for extension of annual authorization to the two remaining accounts: namely, "defensive protection by preemption." What explains the extension of annual authorizations to these two accounts also explains why the armed services committees have included more items for inclusion and review in each of the other defense accounts. What better way for the committees to try to protect the entire defense budget from appropriations' cuts than to justify in greater detail each of its parts? What better way for the armed services committees to protect readiness than to intrude into that area and attempt to create floors below which the defense subcommittees could not go?

A key staff member of House armed services, who helped push for annual authorizations of these two accounts, summarized the rationales well:

> In 1980–81, we deliberately went for annual authorization of O&M. Stennis [then chair of Senate Armed Services] said we have too much annual authorizations and not enough time for broad policy and did not favor the move. But we realized that when you come to the end of the year, O&M is the 'billpayer.' Appropriations has to cut to hit the budget outlay number and they do it with O&M. There are natural lobbyists for procurement and R&D, but no one was lobbying for readiness. Our theory was that since there was no constituency for readiness, we would create our own. Hence we set up the readiness subcommittee [of House armed services]. That tactic works in the House because a member has only one major committee, and he will develop the subcommittee he sits on as his constituency and speak for it. We decided later that we needed to authorize annually Other Procurement, which includes non-combat items like trucks and electronic gear. We realized that it was not just O&M that affected readiness, but a whole lot of other items that we were not dealing with.

Thus, in their quest for power vis-a-vis the defense subcommittees and in their search for control over the Pentagon, the two authorizing committees have become more akin to their defense subcommittee rivals. Competition for control has, in short, had a homogenizing effect. The armed services committees are acting more and more like an appropriations committee.

Detailed Scrutiny and Action

The current level of detailed scrutiny and action on the defense budget is a product of the larger political forces that produced the new Congress of the last fifteen years. Detailed congressional changes to the defense titles began in the early 1960s and have continued ever since. The advent of annual authorizations was probably the single most important factor in producing more detailed and voluminous reviews by both committee actors. The institution of annual authorization and its gradual expansion in scope clearly pushed the armed services committees into a closer scrutiny of the budget. And once they did so, the defense subcommittees were required to follow suit and take action on the larger number of line items on which the authorizing committees themselves had taken action. In the 1970s, both disillusionment with the "imperial presidency" and the antidefense mood of the country after Vietnam pushed Congress into ever more detailed scrutiny. In the 1970s, moreover, the single most important factor in enabling the Congress to engage in more detailed action on the defense budget was the expansion in the staff capability of the two defense committees. In the Senate and

House, respectively, the size of staff for the appropriations committees grew from twenty-three and thirty-five in 1947 to seventy-two and eighty-four in 1975. Comparable figures for the armed services committees are from ten and ten in 1947 to thirty and twenty-eight in 1975.[4] The growth in staff reflected the coming of age of a more assertive and active Congress.

There is quantitative evidence to support the judgment that the defense committees have engaged in increasingly detailed scrutiny of the budget. Tables 20.2 and 20.3 illustrate in one fashion the impact of more detailed annual reviews. With a few years of the 1960s for a benchmark, these two tables record by year the total number of pages in their reports on the authorizing and spending bills that armed services and appropriations recommended to their chambers. Although counting the pages of these reports may seem a trivial exercise, it is not, for each table measures the change over time in committee review activity; and both show a dramatic increase from the 1960s.

These reports have increased in size because there has been an increase in the number of titles included in the authorization and appropriations bills and because there has been an increase in the number of items reviewed in

Table 20.2 Number of Pages in
Appropriation Committees' Reports on DOD Budget

FISCAL YEAR	HOUSE	SENATE	TOTAL
1960	83	31	114
1961	74	47	126
1964	70	69	129
1965	51	52	103
1968	67	71	138
1969	68	56	124
1970	102	141	243
1971	119	221	340
1972	139	210	349
1973	256	204	460
1974	239	173	412
1975	171	207	378
1976	358	302	660
1977	226	277	503
1978	387	295	682
1979	446	217	663
1980	493	219	712
1981	398	227	625
1982	315	137	452
1983	259	157	416
1984	298	205	503

Sources: For fiscal years 1972–78, Robert L. Bledsoe, "Congress and the Defense Budget: Portent of Change?" Paper prepared for delivery at the annual meeting of the American Political Association, 1978 , Appendix B; for the other fiscal years, the House and Senate Appropriations Committees' Report on DOD Appropriations.

Table 20.3 Number of Pages in
Armed Services Committees Report on DOD Authorizations
(major reports only)

FISCAL YEAR	HOUSE	SENATE	TOTAL
1965	63	17	80
1969	91	31	122
1970	176	70	246
1971	95	121	216
1972	107	140	247
1973	115	177	292
1974	150	205	355
1975	132	190	322
1976	185	191	376
1977	169	204	373
1978	160	163	323
1979	163	158	321
1980	186	166	352
1981	171	242	413
1982	228	197	425
1983	233	222	455
1984	332	526	858

Source: Armed Services Committees Yearly Reports on the DOD Authorizations.

each title, especially for the procurement and the research and development titles.[5] The number of titles included in the two defense bills has increased from four in FY 1971, to seven in FY 1977, to ten in FY 1985. The increase in the number of items reviewed in the research and development and procurement accounts has increased dramatically:

FISCAL YEAR	PROCUREMENT	R&D
1975	85	74
1979	156	172
1983	204	159

As would be expected, because it reflects the great number of items reviewed, the largest number of pages in the authorization reports are devoted to the procurement and RDT&E accounts. Although the detail concerning each item considered has shown no increase over the years, clearly both the number of titles reviewed and the number of items per title considered have increased. It is in this fashion that the committees have increased the level of their detailed review.

There is other quantitative evidence that corroborates this picture. Robert Bledsoe has documented that, for the fiscal year 1976–1983 period, the two armed services and the two defense subcommittees together made over 10,000 changes in the dollar figures of the items contained in the eight budget requests submitted by the president to Congress, or, on the average, about 1,250 per year.[6] In a careful review of Congress's action on the fiscal year 1984 defense budget, *Armed Forces Journal International* found the following: of the 731 line items in the president's defense request to the armed services committees, the House made adjustments in 424 of them; the Senate, in 450. Of the 1,129 line items in the DOD request to the appropriations committees, the House made adjustments in 766; the Senate, in 710.[7] Finally, for each fiscal year, the comptroller's office of the Pentagon puts out a memorandum on "Actions on Recommendations in Congressional Committee Reports and Related Authorization and Appropriations Acts," in order to keep track of the actions required and recommended by the authorizing and appropriating committees and the actions taken by DOD to meet them. The memorandum for fiscal year 1984 ran to 942 pages and encompassed 624 items in the congressional reports that required special action. These items varied greatly in how many subitems each encapsulated and ranged from items like the MX missile, which had many subitems, to the Publications Management Center at Osan, Korea, which had few. The number 624 considerably understated the number of items Congress changed.[8]

The picture suggested, of armed services and of the four defense committee actors together devoting overwhelming proportions of their time and staff resources to annual budget review, is confirmed by the judgments of many congressional participants. The following is a selection of a few views:

[Senator Sam Nunn of senate armed services] The budget cycle drives the Congress, and the Congress drives the executive branch to such an obsession that we don't have time to think about strategy. We never had a strategy hearing since I've been in the Senate.[9]

[Senator William Roth, chairman of government operation committee] I can argue that it [the new budget process established by the Budget and Impoundment Act of 1974] is a failure, a failure because Congress has consistently failed to meet most of the deadlines, a failure because I think Congress has become mesmerized with the budget process to the detriment of other responsibilities and considerations. It spends so much time on budget matters that we really fail to adequately provide the kind of oversight that I think is necessary. We have failed to have the kind of debates that are essential on national issues such as foreign policy and defense.[10]

[A staff member of Senate armed services] From January through December, we are consumed by the annual budget. Many members of the Committee feel that the system is working so poorly that something has to be done. The issues are fought over and over and the level of detail is too great. Tower [then Chairman] said to the Committee in 1983: 'I want to see us get out of details.' We tried but we got back into the 'weeds'.

[A Member of the House armed services committee] We don't talk about strategy or tactics to my satisfaction in Armed Services. I think we should be involved in strategy. I don't want to micromanage. . . . we should be concerned with a proper overall defense policy and its match with our foreign policy. What the hell is seapower strategy? All they talk about [on the committee] are ships and where they are going to build them. There is too much line iteming and detail on Armed Services.

[A recently retired staff member of House armed services with many years of service on the committee] Things have gone too far, not in terms of getting into the knickers of the services, but in the sense that it [detailed review] consumes too much attention of representatives and senators. We don't do enough of the long term policy. But there is a natural constituency for concentration on weapons systems in the here and now. It is difficult for members to focus on the big issues because of the lack of time, because of the need to get reelected, and because of the fact that constituency service, not policy oversight, is what is necessary today to stay in office. How to get them to focus on policy, not programs, is the problem.[11]

Congress's treatment of the defense budget is not microscopic. The defense budget is simply too large and complex for that. Nor is any of the above to say that many items in the budget do not require close scrutiny. Many do because they are built on compromises that may make bureaucratic sense but little military sense. But control over programs does not necessarily mean control over policy. If the Pentagon policed its programs better, Congress would not have to scrutinize them so closely and would have more time for consideration of the broader policy issues.

Slighting of Policy Oversight

The third attribute of the "new" Congress's treatment of defense—the slighting of sustained and systematic policy oversight—is a more difficult matter to assess. It is easier to measure the amount and degree of financial and programmatic oversight because each involves items, whether they be dollars or discrete programs, that can be counted. General policy oversight is more qualitative and overarching in character. Whether it is now being done systematically, and whether it has gotten better or worse, cannot be determined simply by counting.[12] Inevitably, also, one's views about Congress's effectiveness in policy oversight hinge partly upon one's views about the adequacy of the executive's defense policies. Dissatisfaction with the latter usually brings calls for more of the former. Gauging congressional performance in policy oversight, then, is a highly subjective business.

Policy oversight differs from both the financial and programmatic varieties, although it can encompass elements of both. Fiscal or financial oversight means: Can we spend the money on this particular program efficiently? Program or programmatic oversight means: How well is this particular program being managed and how many of the systems do we need? General policy oversight means: What are our military requirements and commitments? What size, types, and mix of forces do we require to accomplish the missions that we have set and are these missions wise ones?

In theory, a nation first fixes its commitments and requirements; then it determines the size, shape, and mixture of the forces it needs and selects particular weapons to constitute those forces; and finally, it makes certain that the programs are being well managed. Matters never work out that neatly, but somehow all these steps should occur if resources on defense are to be spent intelligently. Obviously, in considering the financial and programmatic aspects of the defense budget, Congress inevitably does some general policy oversight. But the crucial point is how and when. At some point in its deliberations, the Congress must consider, apart from the financial and programmatic considerations, the broader policy contexts that inevitably constrain the financial and programmatic reviews.

To consider how many of a given weapon to buy and whether the program is being managed efficiently without considering first whether the weapon is needed and how it fits into the larger force structure is equivalent to managing the details without thinking about where they are taking you. In the defense realm, general policy oversight is most analogous to what in the Pentagon is called "force structure" or "force design issues." Force design issues are the links that connect national military commitments to the size and character of the nation's military forces.

In one fashion or another, most analysts who have previously studied the congressional defense role have argued that in force design issues and general policy oversight, Congress does not do well. Over the years, the continuity of their critique is remarkable:

> [1962] The major cause for Congress's lack of incentive [to play the role of coordinate budget maker] . . . would appear to lie not so much in the desire to avoid responsibility as in the expectation that there is little to be gained from trying to exercise it. The role of coordinate budget-maker can be justified Constitutionally, and it is feasible enough intellectually (provided the committees would limit themselves to a review of the high-policy choices involved), but politically the part is not very remunerative. Political conditions are normally such that Congress is little motivated and poorly set up to second-guess the President and make its own judgments stick.[13]

> [1977] The result of these past [until 1975] changes has been increasingly effective congressional oversight in virtually every aspect of defense policy save one: force design decisions. . . . In our view, these are the most critical decisions, because they drive the defense budget, dominate the design of weapon systems, and define the kinds of wars the armed forces will be able to fight. Congress at present simply does not have the institutional mechanisms to examine force design questions, with the result that oversight of overall defense policy is limited.[14]

> [1984] Members of [House] Armed Services do get into policy but only obliquely. For example, on the Lehman power projection or sea control issue. We made a decision in favor of the former by authorizing a 600-ship navy, but we did it this way: We justified a carrier by stating the policy behind it rather than the reverse. We did not debate which policy we needed and then determined the best weapons systems to achieve it. The members of the committee thus back

into policy. We debate policy when we attack or support specific weapon systems, but it should be the other way around. We should debate policy first and then determine which systems to procure. The hearings are program focused. If you say to the committee members, 'have a policy hearing first,' you will get the big Pentagon brass there; but the members' questions are either parochial or programmatic.[15]

Although I argued above that counting is not a reliable way to determine the frequency and effectiveness with which Congress engages in policy oversight, at least we can do a little to measure the frequency of it. The argument that follows, however, is merely suggestive, not definitive.

Robert Bledsoe has tried his hand at counting, and the results are interesting.[16] For the FY 1976–83 period, he counted, coded, and collated all the dollar changes that the four defense committees made in the procurement and R&D titles as they were listed and explained in each committee's report on the annual defense bill it voted out. (There were several thousand such changes). The three categories into which he grouped the changes were: management, fiscal, and policy. Here are the results of Bledsoe's heroic effort to code these (dollar) changes in line items into one of the three categories that he employed:

	POLICY	FISCAL	MANAGEMENT
House armed services	40%	43%	17%
Senate armed services	31%	53%	16%
House appropriations	25%	66%	9%
Senate appropriations	20%	75%	5%

According to Bledsoe's reckoning, fiscal oversight constituted the largest single category of changes for *all* four committees. The most policy oriented was House armed services; the most fiscally oriented, Senate appropriations. Neither of the armed services committees engaged in an overwhelming amount of policy oversight when measured by the rationales for making funding changes in the Pentagon's line item program requests.

According to the coding rules used to categorize each of the several thousand changes, Bledsoe's categories do not match up exactly to the three types of oversight that I have employed. The match between what he terms fiscal and what I term financial is nearly complete. His category of management is also subsumed in what I term financial. For his policy category, only about seven of the twelve coding statements signify what I would call policy oversight, that is, force design decisions. Therefore, only about sixty percent of the coding statements in his policy category are equivalent to my policy category; the remaining forty percent is roughly equivalent to what I have called programmatic changes. Therefore, if we combine his fiscal and management categories into one category (my financial oversight category) and split his policy category into two categories — sixty percent for general policy and forty percent for programmatic oversight — his findings would look like this:

	POLICY	PROGRAM	FINANCIAL
House armed services	24%	16%	60%
Senate armed services	19%	12%	69%
House appropriations	15%	10%	75%
Senate appropriations	12%	8%	80%

Obviously, this is an arbitrary but not wholly unreasonable manipulation of Bledsoe's data. It makes even stronger the finding he reached. Bledsoe concluded that the dollar line item changes made by all four committee in the procurement and R&D titles were dominated by what he called fiscal reasons. With my manipulation of his data, the financial (Bledsoe's fiscal) basis of the committees' actions looms even larger. There is a second conclusion that can be derived from Bledsoe's data. To the extent that the two armed services committees have concentrated their actions in the fiscal/ financial category, whether measured by his figures or mine, we have some tangible evidence that these committees have increasingly become budgeteers, and thereby, that the overlap between what they do and what the defense subcommittees do is great. We could draw a third conclusion and argue that the more financially based are the actions taken by the four committee actors, the more the Congress is trying to run the Pentagon and the greater the micromanagement in which it is engaging.

Obviously, Bledsoe's data, and particularly my manipulation of it, should be interpreted cautiously. What we are dealing with here are actions on specific programs in the authorizing and appropriating bill reports. The data obviously exclude the more general type of policy oversight that occurs in the other activities and hearings of the committees. Nevertheless, the results are suggestive in that they do measure the types of considerations that govern committee activity on line item programs.

None of this is to argue that the defense committee actors do no significant policy oversight at all. Notable examples in recent years are: Senator Sam Nunn's passage of legislation that required a review of the North Atlantic Treaty Organization's tactical nuclear stockpile, which paved the way later for significant changes in NATO's nuclear doctrine and forces; the Strategic Arms Limitation Talks hearings on the SALT II treaty; recent actions to control antisatellite weapons; recent hearings on Pentagon reorganization; and the recent study report by the House appropriations committee on the poor state of readiness of the military forces. Moreover, measured by the volume or number of hearings conducted per year, the armed services committees are among the most active overseers in the Congress today. They rank above every committee except agriculture and appropriations in the number of hearings held.[17] Policy oversight does occur. Some of it is quite important and has far reaching effects.

What we are dealing with here is not an either/or situation, but a question of the proper balance between policy oversight and budgeteering. No matter how large are the staffs of the armed services committees, it is impossible for them to do both equally well. If the members of those committees wanted to do more policy oversight and less budgeteering, they could. That they do not is a matter of their choice.

Why? The answer lies, not simply with the advent and continual growth of annual authorizations, not simply with committee rivalry within Congress, not simply with the assertiveness of the new Congress, but also with the political incentives of members today to conduct policy oversight. They are low. Policy oversight does not enhance a legislator's credit-taking posture; it does not garner him electoral votes; nor can it be tied directly to control over executive action. The impact of policy oversight is too general and diffuse, both on a legislator's career advancement and on those objectives he holds for public policy. As Seymour Scher perceptively put it over twenty years ago: "Congressmen tend to see opportunities for greater rewards in the things they value, more from involvement in legislative and constituent-service activity than from participation in oversight activity."[18]

Policy oversight requires disciplined analysis, hard work, perspective, time to reflect, and detachment from the agency one oversees. All of these are commodities in short supply in the harried and increasingly specialized Congress of today. Less attached to parties than they once were, today's members must rely more on their own efforts to gain attention and electoral advantage. They are constantly on the make for "the quick fix." They have to be shown, as Michael Malbin puts it, that "an issue will make them look good" before they will take it on.[19] The only thing worse than taking on an issue that will not make a legislator look good is taking on one that will make him look bad. Most issues of general policy oversight, however, involve longstanding and fairly intractable problems, ones in which the risk of looking bad is high. The penchant for the quick fix makes legislators conservative in their choice of how they spend their political resources. To tackle an intractable problem takes both political courage and a secure incumbency. If many members possess the former, most do not believe that they enjoy the latter, even if they do. They are constantly running hard both to discourage competitors for their seats from running against them and to beat those who choose, nevertheless, to do so.[20] Thus, the political incentives as they are structured on the Hill today put the bias on the short term, the specific, the details, the programs that can be grabbed, manipulated, changed, and sold. Such incentives do not encourage policy oversight.

In defense, the problem is even more acute. Nearly the entire budget is discretionary because it is annually authorized. That gives legislators lots of details and programs to fiddle with every year. The temptation is too great to resist. Taking credit for protecting, expanding, or starting a program is electorally more worthwhile than more diffuse policy oversight. It is intellectually easier to think about the specifics of a given program than it is to analyze the larger purposes into which the program fits. The latter involves questions of military contingency planning and force structure mixes for which there are no seemingly definitive answers. It is all rather open ended and slippery. This might appear exactly suitable for legislative consideration since views can be aired, no real decisions taken, no political resources expended, and no politically adverse effects suffered. Posturing on policy would appear to be politically advantageous and should be politically popular.

The problem with this, however, is that it gains a legislator little compared to the other things he can do. The type of action that, to use Warner Schilling's phrase, "creates a climate of opinion," is difficult to justify and take credit for because it does not have tangible, immediate, easy-to-point-to results. But that is precisely what policy oversight involves.[21] To modify John Maynard Keynes' famous dictum: "He who thinks only about the long term at the cost of neglecting the short term will in the medium term be (electorally) dead."

When he was chair of Senate Armed Services, one of Richard Russell's experiences in 1959–60 was central in his decision to push for annual authorizations: The failure of the committee to engage in effective policy oversight. Because the general hearings held by the Senate Armed Services Committee in the 1950s were not tied to specific legislative action or budgetary decisions, the senators on the committee did not take them seriously. There was an inverse relation between the amount of general policy discussion and the level of senatorial interest. The more was general policy discussed, the lower was senatorial attendance level. The armed services committees set out on the path of annual authorizations precisely because their members felt that such general policy reviews were ineffective and put them at a competitive disadvantage with the appropriations defense subcommittees, which actually controlled policy because they had the say over the details of spending. In short, annual authorizations were begun because policy oversight had failed. Or so was the view at the time.

The perceptions of members have remained the same today, if the views of staff from the armed services committees are correct, as I believe they are:

[House armed services] For the policy hearings, the members ask us: 'Do we have to do this?'; or, 'Why are we doing this?' Only when they have to do something [specific] will they come. Tower got their attention and attendance [on Senate armed services] when he focused on how the Pentagon is organized by getting them to realize that it might make a difference in what they [as committee members] did.

[Senate armed services] We tried to have major overviews and how that affected our force posture, but the Senators don't turn out. They are used to hearings for the bottom line, where hardware decisions are going to be made.[22]

Policy oversight, then, is difficult to obtain, not because legislators are not smart enough to do it, not because they do not have the time to do it, not because they do not have the staff to do it, but because they do not want to do it. If more policy oversight of defense is to occur, the political incentives to do it will have to be strengthened.

Enhancing Policy Oversight

What, then, can the Congress do to enhance its ability to deal with the larger issues embedded in the defense budget? How can it restore some balance among the financial, programmatic, and policy types of oversight? First, Congress must alter the structure of the Pentagon so that better results emerge from it. The better the quality of Pentagon proposals—the more coherent they are—the more effective and efficient Congress's oversight of them can be. Second, Congress, and particularly the armed services committees, can take specific steps to move away from budgeteering by diminishing somewhat the scope of annual authorizations. The less the focus on the details of the annual budget, the more resources will there be available for quality policy oversight. Third, Congress can institutionalize policy oversight by creating a body with a vested interest in it. Only if an element of the Congress has a political interest in asking the broad questions will they systematically and continually be asked.

Structural Change of The Pentagon. The most efficient place for Congress to begin, strangely enough, is not with itself but with the defense department. Congress must not try to do what it is institutionally not well-suited to do. We must distinguish between those measures that are organizationally necessary to initiate policy and those that are organizationally necessary to judge policy. The former is the task of the executive, the latter, of the Congress. The tasks of initiating and judging derive from the organizational differences between bureaucracies and legislatures. Congress's organizational structure is more nearly horizontal in nature; the executive branch's, more nearly hierarchical. Because it is a political institution where the actors are more nearly equal in power than are those in the more hierarchical executive branch, the Congress can never achieve the degree of centralized control that is requisite to develop, coordinate, and reconcile competing policy positions—all of which are necessary steps for policy initiation. What Congress is uniquely organizationally positioned to do is to judge. It does so by reacting to, and, hence, overseeing, executive proposals. Its decentralized structure ensures that multiple perspectives and points of view will flourish and be brought to bear upon anything that comes before it. Congress works best when it does what it is structurally most suited to do.

Congressman Les Aspin, a member of the House armed services committee, has aptly summarized the institutional nature of the Congress and why it is best suited for oversight, not initiation. His words are worth quoting at length:

> A second role that Congress performs [the first being a conduit for constituent views and the third acting as guardian of the processes of government] is as general overseer of government policies and resource allocation. In this role it acts not unlike a board of trustees. With very few exceptions, Congress is not the place where policy is initiated. Most Congressional committees or subcommittees have no over-all plan or policy which they would like to see implemented in the area of their concern. The Pay and Allowances Subcommittee of the House Armed Services Committee has, for example, no guiding policy about the structure of pay and allowances in the armed forces. They do not initiate legislation in this area, but simply modify, if necessary, and ultimately give their approval to what the Executive is proposing to do. In performing this role they have certain advantages. They have often had long years of experience, and they know what has been tried before. They have lines of communication open to various branches of the armed forces, which provide them with information that the Executive may not have; and they are very sensitive to the conflicting pressures that build up around any change in policy.
>
> There are, of course, exceptions to the rule. Some committees or subcommittees try to take the lead or initiate new policy. . . . But any effort to do so is hampered by divergences in the views of individual committee members and wariness about taking issues to the floor, where, without Administration support, they are likely to be defeated. Most committees wait for the Administration to send over its proposals, and then they consider them from what might be described as a board-of-trustees perspective; this can be very useful, but it does not constitute leadership. Even this board-of-trustees function could be vastly improved — investigative work and legislative supervision are both activities that Congressional committees could and should do better and more extensively.[23]

Even though Congress is best suited for oversight, its resources, even for this task, are limited. It must husband and use them efficiently. No matter how large its staffs become, Congress can never compete with the Pentagon in this respect. Of necessity it must be selective in its attempt to manage programs. Influencing policy by selective program management is a poorer way for Congress to operate than obtaining better Pentagon management on all programs. In a task as large and complex as the formulation of America's global defense posture, Congress can best influence policy by enabling and requiring the Pentagon to get things more nearly right before they come to Congress for consideration. Congress should take to heart the lesson it has applied to the task of federal budgeting in general: Congress does its task best when it gets the executive branch to do the bulk of the work for it. Structural reform of the Pentagon is, therefore, *the* fundamental step. Without a basic change in the way the major actors in the defense department do their business, procedural reforms in the way Congress does its business will improve matters only marginally.

Viewed in broad perspective, then, the three attributes of the new congressional role in defense—budgeteering by the armed services committees, attempts at detailed management of the budget by the four defense committee actors, and slighting of policy oversight by all committee actors—are pieces of the same whole. For they reflect the more general approach that Congress has taken to defense matters since the end of World War II. After the end of the war, Congress created a type of defense structure that inevitably drew it deeply into defense matters. That was done because that was what the Congress wanted.[24] Its subsequent modifications to that structure did little to retard its being drawn more deeply into military affairs. The advent of budgeteering and detailed management and the consequent slighting of policy oversight—all three were developments that naturally stemmed from the defense structure that the Congress had originally created and largely preserved intact.

Since 1945, the Congress has favored a decentralized, pluralistic, and competitive defense establishment, not a centrally run, highly hierarchical, and tightly controlled one. It has favored pluralism and competition there so as to be better informed about what is happening and so as to be better positioned to arbitrate among the competitors. A decentralized defense establishment is the type of structure that enhances Congress's own power over it. One more centralized would risk a diminuition of both Congress's access to the information necessary to make decisions and its power to arbitrate and decide. As Samuel P. Huntington once put it, "Congress's constant concern with the danger of the 'Prussian General Staff System' reflected not so much a fear of enhanced military power as a fear of enhanced executive power."[25]

A secretary of defense truly powerful in his bailiwick would likely curtail the role that Congress would play in the more daily and mundane affairs of the Pentagon. If the secretary had the power within the Pentagon to make the sensible tradeoffs needed, there would be greater confidence in Congress about the state of affairs there, greater confidence in the quality of the products that reach it for consideration, less reason for it to second-guess matters, and, hence, less need for it to attempt to manage defense affairs in such detail.[26] Similarly, if the nature and functioning of the Joint Chiefs of Staff were altered to produce better military advice for the secretary, his task—and that of the Congress—would be made easier. Just as the Congress can oversee and influence policy better if the Pentagon does better work, so, too, can the secretary of defense better oversee and influence military policy if the Joint Chiefs of Staff do better work.

Thus, the less confidence Congress has had in the Pentagon's management of its own affairs, the more deeply it has been drawn into them.[27] Congress's treatment of the defense budget suffers from too detailed a focus at the expense of the broader questions, but the same has applied to the secretary's position vis-a-vis the military services. The secretary has tried to do too much in military policy because the services have done too little. Lack of the proper defense structure has led to both congressional and secretarial micromanagement. Congress's sense of poor management in the Pentagon is due, then, mostly, though not wholly, to the structure it has created. The defense actors in the Pentagon are simply acting in ways that the structure in which they exist dictates. Congress's accurate sense of poor management stems from its creation of a framework "well-designed" to produce poor management. Congress has thus accepted poor management within the defense department as the price to be paid for its deep and detailed intervention in military affairs.

The specific details of the changes that Congress must make in Pentagon organization need not concern us. What is essential, however, is that two alterations of a general nature be made: first, the quality of military advice, of the chain of military command, and of service use of resources must be improved; and, second, the secretary must be given the authority necessary to engage in an across-the-Pentagon oversight that will improve the degree of coordination and integration of military affairs. Pentagon reform must begin with a strengthening of the only two integrating bodies that exist in the Pentagon today—the Joint Chiefs of Staff and the office of the secretary of defense.[28] Only by strengthening the two bodies that have a Pentagon-wide perspective can there be hope of reducing duplication of missions, redundancy among weapons, and neglect of what are nontraditional service, but urgently needed, missions. Only by strengthening these two agents will the hand of the commanders of the unified and specified commands who speak for readiness and sustainability be strengthened. Left to themselves, the separate service bureaucracies within the defense establishment will do what is in their best interests as they perceive them. Those are not necessarily what is in the best interest of the Pentagon as a whole. Only a strengthened secretary of defense and his military counterparts can perceive the collective interest and construct it from the separate ones.

Techniques for a Multiyear Perspective. In order to obtain a longer-term purview of the defense budget, Congress should take seriously a three year perspective in its budgeting so as to counteract the one-year-at-a-time focus of the present process. For example, if the Congress took more seriously the second- and third- year defense spending figures that are currently included in the budget resolutions required by the 1974 Budget and Impoundment Act, it could, in turn, require the executive to submit budget requests that conformed to the outyear outlay figures in the previous budget resolutions. Requiring the administration to submit requests that conform to the out-year figures, but not making the outyear figures have the force of law, could get around the constitutional provision that makes appropriations for the army beyond two years unconstitutional. Congress would, therefore, not make the outyear figures binding upon itself, but would require the administration to use them as the starting point for its budget formulation. The administration would have the flexibility to depart from those figures, but the onus should be on it to explain why there is the need to do so. If multiyear planning is to mean something, then steps must be taken to make the outyear figures a credible basis for planning within the Pentagon.

There are several things that the armed services committees could do if they truly wanted to do less budgeteering. They could move to multiyear authorizations of the defense budget to gain the time necessary for more leisurely consideration of general matters. Defense appropriations would still be done annually, and, as a consequence, the armed services committees would be giving up some of their close control over programs. The effects of the loss of power in a multiyear authorization and annual appropriation combination, however, could be lessened for the armed services committees if the reprogramming of defense funds were done on a more regular and systematic basis than is now the case.[29] The armed services committees could authorize the defense budget for a three year period, but be required, along with the defense appropriations subcommittees, to approve any Pentagon reprogramming of funds. If the defense department were required to come to the Congress on a predictable schedule for reprogramming actions, rather than haphazardly as is now the case, there would be orderly reviews of program changes. The armed services committees would retain control over the approval of new programs (research and development) and of production buys (procurement). They would give up fine tuning each program each year, but, through a regularized reprogramming process, they would be assured of being involved in any major program changes, such as cancellations or large alterations in production runs. They would, therefore, confine the bulk of their efforts on individual programs to initial approval and periodic review.

A variation of this approach has been suggested by John J. Hamre of the congressional budget office.[30] It calls for "milestone authorizations," a specific form of multiyear authorizations, in lieu of annual authorizations. Congress could establish its own "milestone review process," modeled after the Defense Systems Acquisition Review Council (DSARC) process of the Pentagon. At each phase in a weapons systems life cycle—research and development, full scale engineering and development, initial award of procurement funds, further production buys—the Congress would require full documentation from the Pentagon. At each point before another milestone decision is made, the armed services and appropriations committees would have to review, accept, modify, or cancel the Pentagon's proposed action. Congress would, therefore, review a given program intensively only during the critical decision points in its development.

This proposal would make sense, as Hamre argues, only in the framework of multiyear authorizations for both research and development and production. Its virtues are several: it retains for Congress the final say over any milestone decision; it forces the Pentagon to do the work by providing documentation in presentable form for congressional review; it pushes the committees out of detailed management; and it saves some always scarce committee time for other matters. In short, it substitutes selective review for annual management but without loss of significant control. It has the final advantage of tying congressional oversight to a specific procedure, something that always works well for an institution that is itself poorly run and buffeted by short-term political winds.

The armed services committees could also take up the suggestion of Senator Domenici and treat different aspects of the defense budget differently.[31] Research and development and procurement could be authorized on a multiyear basis; operations and maintenance, and personnel on an annual basis. Multiyear authorizations make a great deal of sense for programs in development, just as they do for those in production. Operations and maintenance involves items where the connection between budget authority and outlays is quite close. That is also the case for personnel. It makes sense that these two titles, which have a clear and significant affect on readiness, be annually authorized and protected from undue cutting by the appropriations committees.

These three devices have been presented merely for illustration. There is no dearth of ideas on how to get the armed services committees out of budgeteering and yet still enable them to retain a significant degree of control over the programmatic elements of the defense budget. The dilemma, however, is that the devices cannot substitute for the will to do so. And if the will is there, the exact devices best suited for a more selective, yet still influential programmatic control will quickly be found.

Institutionalizing Policy Oversight. Exactly the same problem exists for policy oversight. If the will is there, the means for doing it will quickly follow. If the will is not there, the devices will be ineffective. The problem, then, is how to create the incentives for doing policy oversight. Only one comes to mind, and here we can take a lesson from the House armed services committee. When it appeared that combat readiness was suffering because there was no constituency on the Hill to champion it, the committee created one by constituting a subcommittee on readiness. Why can the same not be done for policy oversight? A subcommittee whose province it is to oversee policy generally and which consists of members whose interests and energy run in that direction could create the agency necessary to begin systematically building policy oversight into the annual budgeting process. This type of subcommittee could combine a wide-ranging mandate with a group of self-styled policy entrepreneurs. That is, in fact, the way that Congress works best: It takes the individualistic and entrepreneurial nature of congressional initiative and matches that with the subcommittee structure of Congress. In short, it combines the personal and the institutional.

Over the long-term, the Senate armed services committee may be the best place to institutionalize such an agency, not only because the predilections of several of its younger members lean that way, but also because the Senate committee traditionally has taken the road of "high" policy.[32] Not every committee that deals with defense matters has to engage in policy oversight for such a task to be done. It is sufficient that one locale on the Hill does it. This is so due to the iron law of executive–legislative relations: Because the Congress reacts, the executive anticipates. If there is a clearly defined group within the Senate committee that will engage in more systematic oversight of general policy matters, the Pentagon will also be required to do so. What was the case for annual budgeteering can be the case for policy oversight. The overweening focus on the annual budget to the neglect of the longer-term occurred in the Pentagon to a large extent because it happened first in the Congress. The Pentagon had no choice but to focus only on the next fiscal year because Congress' actions required it to. In some fashion, the same should happen for policy oversight. If a Hill constituency performs this function, the Pentagon will be forced to do so out of self-defense.

This may seem a weak reed upon which to hang so momentous a task as policy oversight. Perhaps it is. But at least it is realistic. Members of Congress will do only what is in their political interests to do. The creation of a Hill constituency for policy oversight — by whatever means — is the only way that such a review will, in the long-run, be sustainable.

NOTES

1. My analysis of the congressional treatment of the defense budget from 1975 to 1984 relies primarily on over one hundred interviews that I conducted with congressional staff and to whom I promised confidentiality. To avoid numerous footnotes, I cite an interview source (by committee or personal staff) only when directly quoting someone. Thus, all assertions about the manner in which Congress deals with the defense budget are supported by at least three interviews. These were conducted with staff members of the defense subcommittees of the House and Senate appropriations committees, the House and Senate armed services committees, the House and Senate budget committees, personal staff of representatives and senators who handle foreign, defense, and budget issues, other selected staff, and relevant individuals from the congressional budget office. These interviews began in the summer of 1979 and were concluded in the

spring of 1984. They lasted anywhere from thirty to one hundred-twenty minutes and were open ended.

2. The best treatments of the advent of annual authorizations by the armed services committees are: Kolodziej, Edward A., *The Uncommon Defense and Congress, 1945–1963* (Columbus: Ohio State University Press, 1966), pp. 364–82; Dawson, Raymond H., "Innovation and Intervention in Defense Policy," in Peabody, Robert L., and Polsby, Nelson W., eds, *New Perspectives on the House of Representatives* (Chicago: Rand McNally, 1963), 273–304; Gordon, Bernard K., "The Military Budget: Congressional Phase," *Journal of Politics*, 23 (November 1961): 689–724; and Stephens, Herbert W., "The Role of the Legislative Committees in the Appropriations Process: A Study Focused on the Armed Services Committees," *Western Political Quarterly*, 24 (March 1971): 146–62.

3. Cuts in the personnel account are hard to effect. The armed services committees set both the rates of pay for various grades and the size of the forces. These two factors largely determine the appropriations for personnel.

4. See Fox, Jr., Harrison W., and Hammond, Susan Webb, *Congressional Staffs: The Invisible Force in American Lawmaking* (New York: The Free Press, 1977), p. 169.

5. The following data have been taken from the reports of the House armed services committees on its authorization bills for the fiscal year defense budget. I am indebted to Ruth Elvin for having found this material.

6. See Bledsoe, Robert, "Congressional Committees and the Defense Budget: By the Numbers," unpublished paper, Spring 1983, 3. (Prepared for the Roosevelt Center for the Study of Public Policy, Washington, D. C.)

7. See Kyle, Deborah M., "Congress 'Meddled' With Over Half of the DOD's FY 84 Budget Line Items," February, 1984, p. 24. My review of the documents on which this article was based, commonly called the "FADS," which are internal department of defense (DOD) documents that track the changes Congress makes in Pentagon spending requests, shows that Congress changed items that ranged in importance from the Trident submarine (a $1.5 billion item) to the "Naval Air Station Oceana Aircraft Parking Apron in Virginia (a $4 million item). See the DOD document, *Congressional Action on the FY 84 Authorization Request*, pp. 30 and 54.

8. See the table of contents of the FY 84 memorandum.

9. Quoted in the *National Journal*, 31 March 1984, p. 614.

10. Quoted in *Budget Reform Act of 1982*, Hearings before the Senate committee on governmental affairs, 97th Congress, 2nd Session, 19 August 1982, p. 1.

11. The last three quotes are taken from my interviews and must remain confidential.

12. See the discussion below for an attempt at such counting.

13. Schilling, Warner R., "The Politics of National Defense: Fiscal 50," in Schilling, Hammond, Paul Y., and Snyder, Glenn H., *Strategy, Politics, and Defense Budgets* (New York: Columbia University Press, 1962), p. 116.

14. Bearg, Nancy J., and Deagle, Jr., Edwin, A., "Congress and the Defense Budget," in Endicott, John E., and Stafford, Jr., Roy W., eds, *American Defense Policy*, 4th ed (Baltimore: Johns Hopkins Press, 1977), p. 337.

15. Interview with a former staff member of the House armed services committees.

16. See Bledsoe, Robert, "Congressional Committees and the Defense Budget," pp. 40–1 and the Appendix.

17. See Dodd, Lawrence C., and Scott, Richard L., *Congress and the Administrative State* (New York: John Wiley and Sons, 1979), p. 171.

18. Scher, "Conditions for Legislative Control," *Journal of Politics*, 25 (August

1963): 531. Scher's article remains the best single analysis of why oversight does not routinely occur and why, periodically, it does.

19. Malbin, Michael J., *Unelected Representives: Congressional Staff and the Future of Representative Government* (New York: Basic Books, 1980), pp. 35–6.

20. This is the message of Mayhew, David, *Congress: The Electoral Connection* (New Haven: Yale University Press, 1974). He argues that the safeness of an incumbent's seat is not a good measure of how hard he runs for reelection. The fact that his seat is safe can just as easily reflect how hard he runs while in office to discourage formidable competitors from taking him on, rather than being attributable to any other factors.

21. Schilling. "The Politics of National Defense," pp. 248–9.

22. These two quotes are drawn from my interviews.

23. Aspin, Les, "The Defense Budget and Foreign Policy: The Role of Congress," in Long, Franklin A., and Rathjens, George W., eds, *Arms, Defense Policy, and Arms Control* (New York: W. W. Norton, 1976), p. 168.

24. For a full discussion of Congress's role in postwar defense reorganization, see Caraley, Demetrios, *The Politics of Military Unification* (New York: Columbia University Press, 1962).

25. Huntington, Samuel P., *The Soldier and the State* (Cambridge: Harvard University Press, 1958), p. 423.

26. For an analysis of how little real power the secretary of defense has over the Pentagon, see the chapter in this volume by James Schlesinger.

27. Robert Pastor found that much the same pattern had occurred in foreign economic policy. The Congress delegated power to (or took it back from) the president in direct relation to the degree of trust (or distrust) it had in him. See Pastor, Robert, *Congress and the Politics of U. S. Foreign Economic Policy, 1929–1976* (Berkeley: University of California Press, 1980).

28. For a perceptive set of detailed suggestions for Pentagon reorganization, see the essay in this volume by Samuel P. Huntington.

29. I am indebted to former Secretary of Defense Melvin Laird for this suggestion, which was made when I presented several of my proposals for reform to the steering committee of the defense reorganization project, Georgetown Center for Strategic and International Studies, in February, 1984.

30. See John J. Hamre's unpublished paper, "Potential New Patterns of Congressional Review of Defense Budget Requests." Mr. Hamre is Deputy Assistant Director for National Security and International Affairs at the Congressional Budget Office.

31. See Peter V. Domenici's testimony before the Senate Budget Committee, 21 September 1982, in *Proposed Improvements in the Congressional Budget Act of 1974*, Hearings before the committee on the budget, U. S. Senate, 97th Congress, 2nd Session, 14, 16, 21, and 23 September 1982, 141.

32. At the time of this writing, the new chairman of the House armed services committee, Les Aspin, has just created such a general oversight agency, which he calls the policy panel. In doing so, he ran into opposition from the more traditional members of his committee (See *The New York Times*, 5 February 1985).

Index

About the Editors and Contributors

Robert J. Art, Herter Professor of International Relations and Chair, Department of Politics, Brandeis University

Harriet W. Critchley, Professor of Political Science and Director, Strategic Studies Program, University of Calgary

Vincent Davis, Director and Patterson Professor, Patterson School of Diplomacy and International Commerce, University of Kentucky

Jacques S. Gansler, Vice President, The Analytic Sciences Corporation

Morton H. Halperin, independent defense consultant (formerly Deputy Assistant Secretary of Defense/International Security Affairs and Staff Member, National Security Council)

David Halperin is a 1984 graduate of Yale University

Thor Hanson, VADM, USN, Ret., President, National MS Society (formerly Assistant to the Chairman of the Joint Chiefs of Staff)

Michael Hobkirk, formerly Permanent Assistant Secretary, United Kingdom Defense Ministry

Samuel P. Huntington, Director and Thomson Professor, Harvard Center for International Affairs

David C. Jones, GEN, USAF, Ret., BDM Corporation (formerly Chairman of the Joint Chiefs of Staff)

Catherine M. Kelleher, Professor of Public Affairs, University of Maryland

Robert W. Komer, Rand Corporation (formerly Under Secretary of Defense for Policy)

William J. Lynn, Fellow, Georgetown University Center for Strategic and International Studies, and Professional Staff, Institute for Defense Analysis

Edward C. Meyer, GEN, USA, Ret. (formerly Chief of Staff, U.S. Army)

Stephen M. Meyer III, Professor of Political Science, Massachusetts Institute of Technology

Philip A. Odeen, Regional Managing Partner, Coopers & Lybrand (formerly Director of Program Analysis, National Security Council, and Principal Deputy Assistant Secretary of Defense/Studies and Analysis)

Amos Perlmutter, Professor of International Politics, The American University

Vincent Puritano, Executive Vice President, Sears World Trade—Harbridge House Inc. (former Assistant Secretary of Defense, Comptroller)

James R. Schlesinger, Distinguished Senior Fellow, Georgetown University Center for Strategic and International Studies (formerly Secretary of Defense)

William Y. Smith, GEN, USAF, Ret., Woodrow Wilson International Center for Scholars (formerly Deputy Commander in Chief, United States European Command)

Edward L. Warner III, COL, USAF, Ret., Rand Corporation (formerly Special Assistant to the Chief of Staff, U.S. Air Force)

Aharon Yariv, MG, Israeli Army, Ret., Director, Center for Strategic Studies, Tel Aviv University (formerly Chief of Israeli Intelligence)